D0081467

LORD BYRON

The Complete Miscellaneous Prose

This volume collects together for the first time all Byron's miscellaneous prose writings, including his speeches in the House of Lords, short stories, reviews, critical articles, and Armenian translations, as well as such shorter pieces as memoranda, notes, reminiscences, and marginalia. Although some of this material has been published before—most notably in the appendices to Prothero's edition of the *Letters and Journals* (1898–1901)—a considerable proportion is here published for the first time. As well as bringing together all Byron's prose works, this edition presents them for the first time with full scholarly apparatus. The texts are reproduced from their original manuscripts wherever these are still extant; and the notes provide an introduction to each item, detailing the circumstances of its composition, its publication history, and its historical and literary background, as well as providing comprehensive annotation of individual points of obscurity, allusions, and other matters of content.

With the recent edition of the *Letters and Journals*, and the seven-volume *Complete Poetical Works* edited by Jerome J. McGann, Andrew Nicholson's editing of the *Miscellaneous Prose* brings to completion the much-needed modern and authoritative edition of Byron's entire *œuvre.*

The first page of the MS of 'Some Account of the Life and Writings of the late George Russell of A—— by Henry Ferguson', 1821.

(Reproduced, with permission, from the collection of John Murray Ltd.)

LORD BYRON

The Complete Miscellaneous Prose

EDITED BY

ANDREW NICHOLSON

CLARENDON PRESS · OXFORD

1991

Oxford University Press, Walton Street, Oxford OX2 6DP
Oxford New York Toronto
Delhi Bombay Calcutta Madras Karachi
Petaling Jaya Singapore Hong Kong Tokyo
Nairobi Dar es Salaam Cape Town
Melbourne Auckland
and associated companies in
Beirut Ibadan

Oxford is a trade mark of Oxford University Press

Published in the United States
by Oxford University Press, New York

British Library Cataloguing in Publication Data
(data available)

Library of Congress Cataloging in Publication Data
Byron, George Gordon Byron, Baron. 1788–1824.
[Selections, 1991]
The complete miscellaneous prose / Lord Byron; edited by Andrew Nicholson.
Includes bibliographical references.
I. Nicholson, Andrew, 1948– . II. Title. III. Title: Lord Byron.
PR4352.N53 1991
828'.708–dc20 91–75
ISBN 0–19–818543–X

Set by Joshua Associates Limited, Oxford
Printed and bound in
Great Britain by Biddles Ltd.,
Guildford and Kings Lynn

For
Leslie Marchand, Jerry McGann
and
Drummond Bone

'. . . *hoc opus, hic labor est.*'
Aeneid, vi

ACKNOWLEDGEMENTS

I owe my first and greatest debt of gratitude to Leslie Marchand and Jerry McGann, the two most distinguished Byron scholars and editors of this century, who have encouraged me throughout my work on this edition, and to whom it is dedicated in the first instance, as the only fitting expression of my sincere thanks to them for their many kindnesses, obligations and friendship. It is also dedicated to Drummond Bone, as a friend and scholar, my one-time pastor and master, and, as aye, 'the Ariosto of the North'. Whatever merit this work may have is entirely due to their inspiration; whatever its defects may be, they are mine alone.

I am particularly grateful to John Grey Murray for his most handsome and unsparing generosity to me throughout this venture, for allowing me complete and frequent access to the Murray archives, and for his kind permission to publish this material. Without his liberal co-operation this work could not have been accomplished.

I should also like to thank Virginia Murray for her remarkable patience and forbearance with my presence and persistent queries, and for her indefatigable energy in burrowing around in the Murray archives to trace stray manuscripts. I am also grateful to the Harold Hyam Wingate Foundation for a generous scholarship which enabled me to complete the work on this edition.

I am greatly indebted to the British Academy for an award that enabled me to carry out research in Europe and the United States, and to the Phoenix Trust for a grant towards research in this country.

For access to, and for permission to include material in this volume, I have to thank the following individuals and institutions: the Bodleian Library, Oxford; Biblioteca Classense, Ravenna; the British Library, London; the Brotherton Collection, University of Leeds; the Lord Byron; William Andrews Clark Memorial Library, University of California, Los Angeles; T. Cottrell Dormer, Rousham House, Oxford; Fales Library, New York University; the Records Office, House of Lords; Olin Library, Cornell University; Van Pelt Library, University of Pennsylvania; Harry Ransom Humanities Research Center, University of Texas; the Vaughan Library, Harrow School; Yale University Library (the Beinecke Rare Book and Manuscript Library).

I have met with considerable kindness during the course of my researches. In the United States, I should like to thank the following in particular: Mark Farrell, Curator of the Robert H. Taylor Collection, Princeton University; Cathy Henderson, Research Librarian at the Harry Ransom Humanities Research Center, University of Texas; Leslie Morris, Curator of Books and Manuscripts at the Rosenbach Foundation, Philadelphia; Laetitia Yeandle of the Folger Shakespeare Library, Washington, DC; and most especially, Georgianna Ziegler, Curator of Special Collections, Van Pelt Library, University of Pennsylvania. In this country, I wish to thank Pamela Wood, the Keeper responsible for Newstead, and the staffs of the Bodleian Library and the British Library who have been uniformly courteous and helpful beyond their call. I am also most grateful to London University Library for allowing me to use its resources.

A number of people have taken an interest in this project and have encouraged me in one way or another. In particular, I should like to mention the following: George Biddlecombe; T. A. Birrell; Connie Blackwell; Vincent Brome; John Clubbe; the late Richard Ellmann; David Erdman; Warwick Gould; Werner Huber; Dilwyn Knox; Corky McGuinness; Donald Reiman; Barbara Rosenbaum; Alison Thorne; Kathleen Tillotson; Deirdre Toomey; Tim Webb.

Finally, thanks of a very special kind go to my editors at Oxford University Press, Kim Scott Walwyn, Frances Whistler, and Harriet Barry, to my parents, John and Rosemary Nicholson, and to my dear Katy—all of whom have been an immense support and encouragement to me in a variety of ways. This work has been such a pleasure to undertake that I must thank Byron himself, for being such a wonderful companion over these years. He, together with Mahler, managed to pull me through those long stretches in A minor.

A.N.

Camden Town, London
22 January 1990

CONTENTS

ABBREVIATIONS AND SHORT TITLES

Listed below are the short titles and abbreviations of the manuscript sources, and of the works to which reference is most frequently made.

BAP	*Byron: A Portrait*, by Leslie A. Marchand (John Murray, 1971; Futura Publications, 1976 (pb); Cresset Library, 1987 (pb)).[1]
BLJ	*Byron's Letters and Journals*, ed. Leslie A. Marchand. 12 vols., 1973–82.
BL	The British Library at the British Museum (followed in parenthesis by the call mark or catalogue number).
Bodleian	The Bodleian Library, Oxford (followed in parenthesis by the name and number of the deposit).
Boswell's Life of Johnson	*Boswell's Life of Johnson*, ed. George Birkbeck Hill. Revised and Enlarged Edition by L. F. Powell. 6 vols., 1934–50.
Broughton Papers	The Broughton Papers (the journals and diaries of John Cam Hobhouse) at the British Library (followed by the call mark and folio number).
Byron's Bulldog	*Byron's Bulldog: The Letters of John Cam Hobhouse to Lord Byron*, ed. Peter W. Graham. 1984.
CHP	B's poem *Childe Harold's Pilgrimage.*
Coleridge	*The Works of Lord Byron: A New, Revised and Enlarged Edition, with illustrations. Poetry*, ed. Ernest Hartley Coleridge. 7 vols., 1898–1904.
CPW	*Lord Byron: The Complete Poetical Works*, ed. Jerome J. McGann. 5 vols., 1980–6.
DJ	B's poem *Don Juan.*
EBSR	B's poem *English Bards and Scotch Reviewers.*
Lady Blessington's Conversations	*Lady Blessington's Conversations of Lord Byron*, ed. Ernest J. Lovell, jr. 1969.
Lives of the English Poets	*Lives of the English Poets*, by Samuel Johnson, LL. D., ed. George Birkbeck Hill. 3 vols., 1905.
Marchand	*Byron: A Biography*, by Leslie A. Marchand. 3 vols., 1957.[1]

[1] Wherever possible, I cite both *BAP* and Marchand together, as the former is more available than the latter. The pagination in the hardback edition of *BAP* and in both its paperback editions is the same.

Medwin's Conversations	*Medwin's Conversations of Lord Byron*, ed. Ernest J. Lovell, jr., 1966.
Memoirs	*Memoirs, Journal, and Correspondence of Thomas Moore*, ed. Lord John Russell. 8 vols., 1853–6.
Moore	*Letters and Journals of Lord Byron: with Notices of His Life*, by Thomas Moore. 2 vols., 1830.
Murray	The archives of John Murray (Publishers) Ltd., London.
Prothero	*The Works of Lord Byron: A New, Revised and Enlarged Edition, with illustrations. Letters and Journals*, ed. Rowland E. Prothero. 6 vols., 1898–1901.
Recollections	*Recollections of a Long Life*, by Lord Broughton (John Cam Hobhouse). Edited by his daughter, Lady Dorchester. 6 vols., 1909–11.
Works	*The Works of Lord Byron with his Letters and Journals and his Life by Thomas Moore* [ed. John Wright]. 17 vols., 1832–3.

EDITORIAL INTRODUCTION

This volume collects together for the first time all Byron's miscellaneous prose writings. Some of this material has been published before, either during Byron's lifetime or thereafter, and a fair portion of it was collected in *Works* (1832, 1833), and again in Prothero (1898–1901). However, it seems always to have been regarded as the Cinderella of Byron's works. What was published by Prothero, for instance, appeared (in striking contrast to the letters he edited) with little or no annotation, no information as to the texts or their provenance, and small regard for their authority or place in the canon; and the work was, moreover, far from complete even as to what was then available to him. I do not say this to disparage Prothero, who was a fine editor, but merely to illustrate that the prose has never been treated with the serious editorial attention and rigour that the poetry and the letters and journals have enjoyed. I have sought to rectify this in the present edition, firmly believing that the prose is as important a part of Byron's output as are his other works, and that it should take its place beside them so that both they and our knowledge of him may be enriched. There is much new material here, and what has been previously published will be found to appear in a fresh, and I hope I can say truthfully, authoritative guise.

The volume runs chronologically; but I have assembled the more fragmentary pieces (notes, marginalia, memoranda, book inscriptions) in a section entitled 'Fragmentary Writings', which returns to 1801 and runs chronologically thereafter. This is not intended to suggest that these items are of relatively minor interest, but rather, if anything, that they differ in nature from the longer pieces.

At the end of the volume, in the Appendix, will be found the sale catalogues of Byron's libraries of 1816 and 1827. I appreciate that these have nothing to do with the prose as such, but I have included them for two reasons. First, they complement the 'Reading List' (1807) with which the volume opens, and thereby provide not a complete but certainly a fuller idea of the extent of Byron's reading. Secondly, I felt we all needed some consolation for the fact that the Review of Gell, for so long ascribed to Byron, was not written by him at all but by Francis Hodgson. I discuss briefly how this entered the canon in 'False

Ascriptions' below; but I know that it will come as a shock and a disappointment to many—as much as it did to me.

Throughout this work I have endeavoured to keep in mind the interests of the reader as much as those of Byron. I have tried to avoid imposing on the text in any way, and have sought merely to elucidate, clarify, and to provide helpful information in the notes. If these prove an encumbrance, then I must apologize, and trust the fault will be regarded as springing rather from the zeal of an admirer than from that of a meddling pedant. As Byron himself puts it, at the end of 'Observations upon Observations' (1821) below: 'Edite honestly—and even flatteringly—the reader will forgive the weakness in favour of mortality—& correct your adulation with a smile.' I should like to think that if I have erred, I have erred in this way.

Text and Notes

Wherever a manuscript is extant, this has been used as the copy text. If the particular item has also been published before, then all variants in the published text(s) (excepting letter case and punctuation), are given in the notes at the end of this volume. In the case only of 'Some Observations upon an Article in *Blackwood's Edinburgh Magazine*' (1820), for which both a partial galley proof and a corrected proof exist as well, all variants, additions and deletions in these are noted at the foot of the page. Again, in the case of both 'Some Observations' and the 'Letter to John Murray Esq$^{re.}$' (1821), Byron first sent Murray a completed MS, and then sent him instalments of additions and insertions, occasionally also asking him in a letter to add a phrase or a further example. In the text, I have indicated the latter by placing them within half-square brackets (⌜ ⌝); longer insertions are indicated by a line space at both ends of the insertion. All such additions, insertions, and interpolations are accompanied by an explanatory note at the end of the volume.

Where no manuscript is extant, the copy text is the first published version of the item.

Where a manuscript is the copy text, I have reproduced it exactly as Byron wrote it, not only to the letter, but—following his own splendid punctuation, or lack of it—to the dash. I hope this needs no apology, and that it captures and conveys some idea of the manner and style of his writing. He had the habit of using a series of dashes at the end of a sentence, frequently to fill up the space to the end of the line; this has sometimes resulted in ten or more dashes, but I have limited these to no more than five. He was also idiosyncratic in his opening and closing of quotation marks; I have preserved this, and drawn attention to it in some cases, but have not annotated every instance. His irregular use of 'it's' for 'its' has also been preserved, and not noted. All deletions are enclosed within angle brackets (⟨ ⟩), and, with the exception of one or two in the 'Fragmentary Writings' section, have been given at the foot of the page, where they appear thus, for example (p. 84):

cannot find] cannot ⟨conjecture⟩

This means that Byron first wrote 'cannot conjecture', then crossed out 'conjecture' and wrote 'find' in its stead. Again (p. 85):

conferring a] conferring ⟨upon⟩ ⟨some⟩

This means that he first wrote 'conferring upon', then crossed out 'upon' and substituted 'some', and then crossed out 'some' and replaced it with 'a'. Occasionally this appears in reverse, as at the beginning of a sentence, for example (p. 83):

Besides] ⟨Shall⟩ Besides

This means that he first began the sentence with 'Shall', then crossed it out and began again with 'Besides'. In some instances these deletions have been worthy of more comment. Where this is the case, a note is attached to the eventual substitute word in the text.

On several occasions, mostly in the 'Fragmentary Writings' section, there appear together on the same page of the text both Byron's comments *and* the passages to which those comments refer. In some cases, different type sizes have been used in order to distinguish between the two: normal text type for Byron's own words, and smaller type for the passages to which he refers. Although he has almost invariably written these comments as marginalia beside the passages to which they refer, they are printed here *beneath* their respective passages. Where there is more than one comment per passage, I have added numbers. In four instances some further refinements have been made. These are: 'Comments in Hobhouse's *Imitations*' (1811), 'Comments on Hunt's *Rimini*' (1815), 'Marginalia in D'Israeli's *The Literary Character*' (1818), and 'Marginalia in de Staël's *Corinne*' (1819). In these four cases Byron has marked the texts either by underscoring various words or phrases, or by drawing a vertical line in the margin down the length of the passage of the prose or verse in question. Passages marked in either of these ways are printed here in italics (reverting to roman type for words that are in italic in the original). Where he has both drawn a vertical line *and* underscored words in the same passage, the underscored words are printed in bold italic type. In 'A Note in Hobhouse's Diary' (1810), and 'Comments on Hunt's *Rimini*' (1815), Byron has also made a small addition to their texts; these are printed within back slashes (\ /). In 'Marginalia in D'Israeli's *The Literary Character*' (1818), and 'Marginalia in de Staël's *Corinne*' (1819), he has also deleted a word from their texts; these are printed within angle brackets (⟨ ⟩).

In the general note to each piece (at the end of the volume) will be found, under the title 'Text', firstly the location of the copy text, and then a brief history of its publication if it has been published before. For example, 'Reading List' (1807):

Text: MS Murray. First published (in part) in Moore i. 100–1, 95–8. Thereafter published (in part) in *Works* (1832), i. 146–8, 140–4.

This means that the copy text is the MS in the Murray archives, that it has been partially published before, first in Moore and then in *Works*, but that it was not collected in Prothero.

The Review of Wordsworth's *Poems* (1807):

Text: *Monthly Literary Recreations* xiii (July 1807), 65–6. Thereafter published in *Works* (1832), vi. 293–5, and Prothero i. 341–3.

This means that no MS is extant, that the copy text is the first publication of the review in *Monthly Literary Recreations*, that it was next published in *Works*, and that it was collected in Prothero. If there is any deviation from this practice, or any added complication, then the general note will explain why and will clarify the procedure. The general note also discusses the circumstances surrounding the composition of the piece, and provides a general, literary, or historical context for it, as well as any other information that may be pertinent.

All specific notes to the texts appear after the general note to each piece. In these, immediately after the number of the note, I have cited in italics the first and last few words of the passage in the text to which the note refers, before giving the note itself. I hope this facilitates identifying the full extent of the passage in question, which on occasions can be somewhat lengthy. Items written by Byron in Italian, or passages appearing on the page of the text in that language (for example, in 'Marginalia in de Staël's *Corinne*' (1819), 'Notes on Crawford's Deposition' (1822), and in 'Directives to Lega Zambelli'

(1824)), are translated in the notes. For every quotation, reference, and allusion made by Byron which I have been able to identify, I have given the source of my information, and in many cases have referred to such sources as would have been available to him, or that he himself was most likely to have consulted. Wherever appropriate, I have also referred to *BLJ* and *CPW*. Works cited in abbreviated form in the notes are given in full *either* in the Abbreviations list above *or* in the general note to the item under discussion.

FORGERIES, DUBIA, AND FALSE ASCRIPTIONS

Forgeries

The following is a list of books with inscriptions forged by Major Byron (alias De Gibler). All these books, with the exception of the last three listed here, were sold at Sotheby's at the auction of the library of the collector John Wilks, MP for Boston, Lincolnshire, on 17 May 1851, and they appear below with their respective lot numbers. Each of those items which I have been able to trace, and which I have seen, is followed by its present location. Those items which I have not been able to trace are given below as they appear in the sale catalogue at the BL (S-C.S. 336) within quotation marks. For an account of the thoroughly unscrupulous but intrepid Major Byron, see Theodore G. Ehrsam, *Major Byron: The Incredible Career of a Literary Forger* (1951), and in particular, pp. 82–8 which are especially relevant here.

Lot 1125. Ariosto, *Orlando Furioso*, 8 vols., 1818. Various critical observations on the flyleaves. Murray.

Lot 1126. 'Ariosto (Lod.) Rime and Satire, *Firenze*, 1822. "Byron, Genoa, 1823," with a note on fly leaf, respecting the portrait of Ariosto on the title.'

Lot 1127. *Les Œuvres de M. Boileau Despréaux*, 2 vols., Paris, 1740. Dated Venice 1819. Three pages of notes on the characters of Pope and Boileau. Rosenbach Foundation, Philadelphia.

Lot 1128. Lord Byron, *English Bards and Scotch Reviewers*, 1809. Dated Athens 1810. A short note on the Macri's house and 'two eyes opposite'. BL (Ashley 317).

Lot 1131. 'Catherine II., Vie de, 2 tom. *Par.* 1797. "Byron." On the fly leaves of vol. 2 is a copy of an unpublished letter of the Empress Catherine, preceded by some very interesting critical remarks by Lord Byron, comparing her character with that of Queen Elizabeth. The whole occupies five closely written pages.'

Lot 1132. 'Casti (Giamb.) Novelle Galanti, 2 tom. *Firenze*, 1812. "Byron, 1819." Between the stanzas of the "Protesta" of the author, is a

"Protest" of Lord Byron's, respecting him, thus ending, "Casti is the unlucky dog who has been libelled, as if he were the inventor of a mode of writing more coarse and licentious *than any* of his precursors. Is Richardson or Fielding more refined than Casti?"—*Byron.*'

Lot 1133. 'Catullus, Tibullus et Propertius, *morocco*, *Lond.* 1776. "Byron, Trin. Coll." Critical observations upon the merit of the Authors, and the English version thereof, occupy eleven pages of the fly leaves at the beginning and end of the volume'

Lot 1134. *Versi di Albo Crisso*, 2 tom, Londra, 1816. Dated Venice 1817. A brief note on the gift of the volumes. BL (C.28, f.15).

Lot 1136. 'Guarini (Cav.) Il Pastor Fido, *Par. Cazin*, 1785. "Byron, Venice, 1819," with note on fly leaf respecting the original MSS. of the author.'

Lot 1138. 'Lucretius de Rerum Naturâ, *Antw.* 1566. "Byron." "A woman of the darkest complexion is often found to be fairer than others by the candour of her manners," *see note on fly leaf.*' This was sold as lot 156 at the first session of the Sale of the library of John A. Spoor at Parke-Bernet Galleries on 26 April 1939. The inscription as a whole is of about ninety words and concerns the beauty and manners of the Greeks. A transcript is given in the catalogue, but sadly no facsimile. See *The Renowned Library of the late John A. Spoor*, Catalogue 110 (Parke-Bernet Galleries, 1939), pt. i, A–L, p. 62.

Lot 1139. *Martialis Epigrammata*, London, 1783. Dated Venice 1818. Four pages of notes in commendation of the epigrams. (Partial facsimile given in the Catalogue of the Sale of the Gordon A. Block library, at Sotheby Parke Bernet on 29 January 1974, Lot 47.)

Lot 1140. 'Ossian, Poems, translated by Macpherson, 2 vols. 1809. "Byron." . . . On the fly leaves of these volumes is a high encomium on the author. On the margin, also, of many of the pages are interesting observations illustrative of the poems.'

Lot 1141. *The Satires of Persius*, trans. William Drummond, London, 1797. Dated Cambridge 1808. A note in admiration of Persius. Murray.

Lot 1142. 'Petrarca, con l'Espositione di Gesualdo, *Venetia*, 1581. ["]Purloined from my lady's bower," *Ravenna*, *April* 9, 1820, "but received as a gift the next day." Byron, on the fly leaf, at the end is a note of two pages, wherein Lord Byron observes, "I have lately read his *letters*; all that he writes is pervaded by a strong and earnest humanity, which shows itself alike in vindication of the essential rights of man, and in sympathy with the various sentiments of the human heart."'

Lot 1143. 'Petrarque a Vaucluse, *Paris*, 1803. "Byron, Diodati, near Geneva, July 20, 1816." A biographical note respecting the author occupies the fly leaf.'

Lot 1144. *The Works of Peter Pindar*, 4 vols., 1809. Dated Newstead Abbey 1811. Introductory note to the spurious poem, 'To Mr. Phillips the Bookseller'. (See also *CPW* i. p. xlvi, no. 21.) The Harry Ransom Humanities Research Center, University of Texas.

Lot 1145. *C. Plinii Panegyricus, Lugduni Batavorum*, 1675. Dated Trinity College 1808. A short note on ill-health. The Roe-Byron Collection, Newstead.

Lot 1146. *Retour de la Fontaine de Vaucluse*, Avignon, 1805. Dated Diodati 1816. A brief note on the gift of the volume. BL (C.28. f.9).

Lot 1147, 'Rosa (Salvator) Satire, *Lond.* 1791. "Byron." "I have been compared in my time to all sorts of persons and things—the list beginning with Alcibiades, but ending with the Swiss Giantess or the Polish Dwarf, I forget which."—*Extract from note at end occupying three pages.*'

Lot 1149. 'Saint-Pierre, Etudes de la Nature, 2 tom. 1796. "Byron, Newstead Abbey, 1815." On the fly leaves are some interesting notes, including one on the Immortality of the Soul.'

Lot 1151. 'Shenstone (William) Works, 3 vols. 1777. "Byron, Trin. Coll., 1807." ... on the fly leaves of vol. 3 are three pages of critical remarks on the author's character, as given by Dr. Johnson, his biographer, *commencing*—"When a youth, I read Shenstone's Poems with eagerness and delight; their simplicity rendered them intelligible to my youthful capacity, and their beauty engaged my admiration;" *closing*, "As to Shenstone's Poems as a Poet, I agree with Johnson, that the *School Mistress* is the most pleasing of his productions, and I think it quite sufficient to entitle him to a conspicuous niche in the Pantheon of the British Muses. Could Johnson himself have written it half so well? Could Burns have done it better?"'

Lot 1152. Madame de Staël, *De l'Allemagne*, 3 vols., London, 1813. Undated. Three pages of comments on notes spuriously attributed to Lady Caroline Lamb. The Houghton Library, Harvard University.

Lot 1154. 'Tasso (T.) Jerusalem delivrée, 5 tom., *gilt leaves*, *Par.* 1785. Vols 1 and 5 contain some interesting remarks, and each volume bears the autograph "Byron."'

Lot 1155. Gilbert Wakefield (ed.), *P. Virgilii Maronis Opera*, 2 vols., London, 1796. Undated. Three pages of details of a soirée. The Robert H. Taylor Collection, Princeton University Library.

Lot 1156. 'Voltaire:—Le Genie de Voltaire par Palissot, *Par.* 1806. "Byron, Diodati, near Geneva, 1816." The fly leaves at the beginning and end contain some interesting anecdotes of Voltaire.'

M. Annei Lucani Civilis Belli, 1520. Dated Prevesa 1809. A comment on the flyleaf commending the work. The Vaughan Library, Harrow School.

Samuel Rogers, *The Pleasures of Memory*, 1801. Various notes on the text, and a spurious letter to Hanson dated 19 April 1823. (See also *BLJ* x. 225.) BL (Add. MS. 22119).

Owen Ruffhead, *The Life of Alexander Pope*, 1769. Dated Cambridge 1808. Various comments on Pope and on *The Rape of the Lock*. New York Public Library. As two of these comments have frequently been cited as if they were authentic *obiter dicta* by B, I give them here in order that the error may not be continued:

Of Pope's pithy conciseness of style Swift—no diffuse writer himself—has so emphatically said

"For Pope can in one couplet fix
More sense than I can do in six."

And having underlined the word 'mankind' (on p. 215 of the volume), De Gibler has written: 'A malignant race with Christianity in their mouths and Molochism in their hearts.'

Dubia

I am far from satisfied that the following four items ascribed to B are his. I have not seen their originals, nor is the present location of any of them forthcoming.

1. Autograph MS. About eighty words, 'containing instructions for speaking "*without being overheard in an assembly*".' (Lot 69 thus described in the Catalogue of the Sale of the Marsden J. Perry Library, Anderson Galleries, 11 March 1936, p. 41.)
2. Thomas Moore, *Epistles, Odes, and Other Poems*, 1806. Notes on the text quoting parallel passages in Burns, Pope, Johnson, and Gray.

(See Michelmore and Co., *Old Books, Autographs, and Manuscripts*, no. 21 (*c.*1930), pp. 30–1.) BL SC Michelmore 21.

3. Anna Seward, *Memoirs of the Life of Dr. Darwin*, 1804. Various undated marginal comments written in pencil. These were first published by the owner of the volume, Henry T. Wake, in *Notes and Queries*, 7th series, xii (July to Dec. 1891), 182–3. From this same source McGann prints the poem 'To These Fox Hunters in a Long Frost', and gives perfectly valid reasons for not doubting *its* authenticity (*CPW* i. 12, 357–8). However, Henry T. Wake was the Quaker bookseller of Fritchley, Derbyshire, who sold the copy of *EBSR* (with its forged inscription) to Sir Sydney Cockerell (see Lot 1128 under 'Forgeries' above). Cockerell wrote to Wise on 31 Dec. 1926 that he had bought it from Wake in Mar. 1901 (Unpublished autograph letter signed. BL. Ashley B.317, f.70). In the light of this I feel that Seward's volume is not above suspicion.

4. A comment on Coleridge's *Biographia Literaria*. Undated, and as follows: 'I was very much amused with Coleridge's Memoirs. There is a great deal of Bonhommie in that book, and he does not spare himself. Nothing, to me at least, is so entertaining as a work of this kind—as private biography.' This was first published by Leslie Marchand in *BAP*, p. 501, who there gives the following source: 'Quoted in "Lord Byron's Books—A Catalogue of Books, selected from the Library of the late Lord Byron (which were sold by Auction by Mr. Evans, on Friday, July 6, 1827,) and purchased by J. Brumby, Bookseller, 14, Mary-le-Bone St., Piccadilly, near Glasshouse Street, Golden Square."' Unfortunately, since that time, neither Leslie Marchand nor I have been able to trace (or retrace) the provenance of this. Brumby certainly bought B's autographed copy of Coleridge's *Biographia Literaria* (2 vols., 1817), at the sale of his library in 1827 (see 'Sale Catalogue' (1827), Lot 48, below); but it is not clear when, or even whether, Brumby himself drew up this catalogue, nor whether the note appears on a flyleaf of one of the volumes, or is tipped into one of them, or accompanies them at all.

False Ascriptions

The following four items have been erroneously ascribed to B; the first during his lifetime, the remaining three posthumously.

1. *The Vampyre: A Tale*, By the Right Honourable Lord Byron, 1819. This was the work of B's physician, Dr John William Polidori, who later admitted to being its author. For fuller details, see the general note on 'Augustus Darvell: A Fragment of a Ghost Story' (1816) below.

2. An article in the *Telegrafo Greco* (no. 5, 17 Apr. 1824), denying certain rumours about B, and about the reaction in Missolonghi, Greece, to the news of Sir Thomas Maitland's death. Although this alludes to B in the third person and certainly expresses his views, it was not written by him but most probably by Pietro Gamba, the editor of the *Telegrafo Greco*. (See, however, E. S. De Beer and Walter Seton, *Byroniana: The Archives of the London Greek Committee* (1926), pp. 5–6. See also 'The Present State of Greece' (1824) below.)

3. Two mock reviews of Rosa Matilda, entitled 'The New Epic', in the *Morning Chronicle*, 2 and 12 Sept. 1812. These were first ascribed to B, and vigorously argued as being his, by David V. Erdman in 'Byron's Mock Review of Rosa Matilda's Epic on the Prince Regent—A New Attribution' (*Keats–Shelley Journal*, xix (1970), 101–17). However, there is not the slightest evidence to suggest that these were written by him; and neither their style, idiom, and voice, nor the astronomical data and solar imagery they employ, are at all resonant of B.

4. A review of William Gell's *The Geography and Antiquities of Ithaca* (1807), and *The Itinerary of Greece* (1810), published in the *Monthly Review* (Enlarged Series), lxv (May–Aug. 1811), art. iv and art. v, pp. 371–85. This review first entered the canon in *Works* (1832), vi. 296–313, and was reprinted in Prothero i. 350–65. Moore wrote to Murray on 19 Apr. 1832: 'I write direct to say that the two books reviewed by Byron were, to the best of my recollection, Wordsworth's Poems and Sir W. Gell's Argolis (as I think the book was called)' (Wilfred S. Dowden (ed.), *The Letters of Thomas Moore*, 2 vols. (1964), ii. 744). On what authority Moore was relying is difficult to determine. There is not the slightest intimation elsewhere in B's works that he was the author of the review; and the only suggestion that he might have been so appears in the following passage from a letter from George Finlay to Colonel Leicester Stanhope of June 1824, which Stanhope printed in the second edition of his *Greece in 1823 and 1824* (1825), pp. 423–4:

> I was in the habit of praising Sir William Gell's Itineraries to Lord B. and he, on the other hand, took every opportunity of attacking his Argolis, though his attacks were chiefly directed against the drawings, and particularly the view of the bay. He told me he was the author of the article on Sir W. Gell's Argolis in the Monthly Review; and said he had written two other articles in this work, but I have forgotten them.

The review was written by Francis Hodgson with information supplied to him by B. Apart from circumstantial evidence to confirm this (such as the character of the review itself, and the time of its composition), there is a more conclusive testimony. The *Monthly Review* was founded in 1749 by Ralph Griffiths (1720–1803), who remained its publisher and proprietor until his death when his son, George Edward Griffiths (d. 1829), took over its management. The Griffiths' own copy of the *Monthly Review*, with each contributor's initials marked against his article, is in the Bodleian Library. Although Prothero knew this, he clearly did not consult that copy. Had he done so he would have found the review attributed to Hodgson on p. 385, and would also have seen Griffiths' comment beside B's review of Spencer's *Poems*, on p. 60 of the issue for Jan. 1812: 'Lord B-n. *1.st Art.*' (See also B. C. Nangle, *The Monthly Review, Second Series, 1790–1815* (1955), pp. 12–13, 127, 207, and Harold S. L. Wiener, *The Eastern Background of Byron's Turkish Tales* (unpublished doctoral dissertation, Yale University, 1938), pp. 254–6.)

CHRONOLOGY

Date	(Age)	
1788		22 Jan.: born at 16 Holles Street, Cavendish Square, London; the son of Captain Jack Byron and Catherine, *née* Gordon of Gight.
		29 Feb.: christened George Gordon Byron at Marylebone Parish Church.
1789	(1)	With mother at lodgings in Queen Street, Aberdeen.
1791	(3)	2. Aug.: his father dies in France. Mother takes flat at 64 Broad Street, Aberdeen.
1794	(6)	Enters Aberdeen Grammar School.
1798	(10)	21 May: the Fifth Lord Byron dies; B becomes Sixth Baron Byron of Rochdale.
		Aug: removes with mother to Newstead Abbey, Nottinghamshire (the ancestral estate).
1799	(11)	July: lives with John Hanson (his solicitor) in Earl's Court, Kensington.
		Sept.: enters Dr Glennie's School, Dulwich.
1801	(13)	Apr.: enters Harrow.
1803	(15)	21 July: his mother rents Burgage Manor, Southwell, Nottinghamshire.
1804	(16)	Mar: friendship with the Pigots begins.
1805	(17)	6 June: first Harrow Speech Day.
		4 July: second Harrow Speech Day.
		2 Aug.: plays in cricket match (Harrow vs. Eton).
		24 Oct.: takes up residence at Trinity College, Cambridge. Debts begin.
1806	(18)	July: at Southwell, preparing first volume of poetry.
		Sept.: involved with amateur theatricals at Southwell.
		Nov.: *Fugitive Pieces* privately printed.
1807		Jan.: *Poems on Various Occasions* privately printed.
	(19)	June: *Hours of Idleness* published.
		July: friendship with John Cam Hobhouse begins; writes 'Review of Wordsworth's *Poems*'.
		Nov.: draws up 'Reading List'.
		Dec.: leaves Cambridge.

1808 (20) Jan.: *Hours of Idleness* crushingly reviewed by Henry Brougham in the *Edinburgh Review*.

Mar.: *Poems Original and Translated* privately printed.

10 Nov.: Boatswain (B's dog) dies.

1809 (21) 22 Jan.: comes of age.

Mar.: *English Bards and Scotch Reviewers* published.

13 Mar.: takes seat in the House of Lords.

2 July: sails with Hobhouse from Falmouth on start of Grand Tour. (Over the next two years, visits Portugal, Spain, Gibraltar, Sardinia, Sicily, Malta, Albania, Greece, Turkey, and Asia Minor.)

31 Oct.: begins *Childe Harold* in Ioannina, Greece.

1810 (22) 3 May: swims the Hellespont.

17 July: Hobhouse returns to England.

1811 (23) Mar: writes *Hints from Horace* and *The Curse of Minerva* in Athens.

14 July: lands at Sheerness, and arrives in London at Reddish's Hotel, St James's Street.

1 Aug.: his mother dies.

19 Dec.: at Newstead with Francis Hodgson and William Harness; begins affair with Susan Vaughan, his Welsh maid.

1812 (24) Jan.: 'Review of Spencer's *Poems*'.

27 Feb.: Maiden speech in the House of Lords ('Frame Work Bill Speech').

10 Mar.: *Childe Harold* I and II published.

Apr.: liaison with Lady Caroline Lamb begins.

21 Apr.: second speech in the House of Lords ('Roman Catholic Claims Speech').

Oct.: liaison with Lady Oxford begins.

1813 1–17 Jan.: with Lady Oxford at Eywood, near Presteign; Lady Caroline Lamb forges letter in B's hand to procure portrait from Murray.

19 Jan.: takes lodgings at 4 Bennet Street, St James's, Piccadilly.

(25) Feb.: writes 'Review of Ireland's *Neglected Genius*'.

1 June: final speech in the House of Lords ('Presentation of Major Cartwright's Petition').

5 June: *The Giaour* published.

20 June: first meeting with Madame de Staël.

5 July: Caroline performs 'dagger Scene' at Lady Heathcote's ball.

July–Aug.: liaison with Augusta Leigh, his half-sister, begins.

Oct.: 'Platonic' affair with Lady Frances Webster.

Nov.: writes 'Bramblebear and Lady Penelope'.
2 Dec.: *The Bride of Abydos* published.

1814 (26) Jan.–Feb.: at Newstead with Augusta Leigh.
1 Feb.: *The Corsair* published (10,000 copies sold on day).
28 Mar.: takes apartment in the Albany, Piccadilly.
Apr.: Napoleon abdicates, and is sent to Elba; 'Ode to Napoleon Buonaparte' written.
Aug.: *Lara* published.
Aug.–Sept.: at Newstead with Augusta Leigh.
9 Sept.: proposes to Annabella Milbanke.
18 Sept.: receives Annabella's acceptance.

1815 2 Jan.: marries Annabella at Seaham, near Durham; 'treacle-moon' spent at Halnaby in Yorkshire.
(27) Feb.: writes 'Leake's *Researches in Greece*'.
26 Feb.: Napoleon escapes from Elba.
20 Mar.: Napoleon enters Paris.
28 Mar.: returns with Annabella to London; residence at 13 Piccadilly Terrace. Creditors become increasingly pressing.
7 Apr.: meeting with Walter Scott at Murray's.
May: *Hebrew Melodies* published; appointed to the Sub-Committee of Management of Drury Lane Theatre.
18 June: Napoleon defeated at Waterloo.
15 July: Napoleon surrenders to Captain Maitland on board the *Bellerophon*.
24–27 July: Napoleon in Torbay and Plymouth Sound.
29 July: writes 'A Letter on the State of French Affairs'.
8 Aug.: Napoleon sails for St Helena on board the *Northumberland*.
Nov.: bailiffs enter 13 Piccadilly Terrace.
10 Dec.: B's daughter, Augusta Ada, born.

1816 15 Jan.: Annabella leaves for Kirkby Mallory, Leicestershire, with Ada; B remains in London. They never meet again.
(28) 2 Feb.: receives Sir Ralph Milbanke's proposal for an amicable separation.
13 Feb.: *The Siege of Corinth* and *Parisina* published together.
Mar.: Claire Clairmont introduces herself to B.
14 Mar.: writes 'The Tale of Calil'.
5–6 Apr.: sale of library at auction.
21 Apr.: signs Deed of Separation.
25 Apr.: sails for Ostend, accompanied by Fletcher, Rushton, Berger, and Dr John Polidori.
1–6 May: at Brussels; begins *Childe Harold* III.

13 May: Shelley, Mary, and Claire arrive at Sécheron, near Geneva.

25 May: arrives at Sécheron.

27 May: meets Shelley for the first time.

10 June: moves into Villa Diodati; the Shelleys only a few hundred yards away at Montalègre.

17 June: writes 'Augustus Darvell: A Fragment of a Ghost Story'.

July–Aug.: frequent visits to Madame de Staël at Coppet.

26 Aug.: Hobhouse and Scrope Davies arrive.

28 Aug.: the Shelleys depart for England.

5 Oct.: leaves with Hobhouse for Italy.

10 Nov.: arrives in Venice.

18 Nov.: *Childe Harold* III published.

Nov.: begins studying Armenian.

1817 12 Jan.: B's natural daughter, Allegra, born in England to Claire Clairmont.

(29) Jan.–Feb.: writes 'Armenian Studies'.

17 Apr.: leaves Venice for visit to Rome.

29 Apr.: arrives in Rome.

28 May: returns to Venice.

16 June: *Manfred* published.

26 June: begins *Childe Harold* IV.

Oct.: *Beppo* written.

10 Dec.: receives news of sale of Newstead for £94,500 to Thomas Wildman.

Dec.: writes 'Donna Josepha: A Fragment of a Skit on the Separation'.

1818 8 Jan.: Hobhouse returns to England.

(30) Jan.–Feb.: carnival dissipations.

28 Feb.: *Beppo* published.

28 Apr.: *Childe Harold* IV published.

3 July: begins *Don Juan*.

1819 (31) Jan.: carnival dissipations.

2–3 Apr.: meets Teresa (née Gamba), Countess Guiccioli.

1 June: leaves Venice to visit the Guicciolis at Ravenna.

10 June: arrives in Ravenna.

18 June: begins *The Prophecy of Dante*.

28 June: 'Augustus Darvell: A Fragment of a Ghost Story' published as 'A Fragment' with *Mazeppa*, and 'Venice. An Ode'.

June–July: in love with Teresa.

15 July: *Don Juan* I and II published anonymously.

9 Aug.: follows the Guicciolis to Bologna.
16 Aug.: Peterloo massacre in Manchester.
22–3 Aug.: writes 'To the Editor of the *British Review*'.
12 Sept.: leaves Bologna with Teresa for Venice.
7–11 Oct.: visited by Moore in Venice; gives Moore the MS of his memoirs (written up to 1816 only).
24 Dec.: returns to Ravenna to join the Guicciolis.

1820 (32) Jan.: death of George III.
Feb.: moves into the Palazzo Guiccioli.
15 Mar.: writes 'Some Observations upon an Article in *Blackwood's Edinburgh Magazine*'.
Apr.: takes growing interest in Italian politics.
May: taken by Guiccioli 'quasi in the fact' with Teresa.
July: finishes *Marino Faliero*; uprising in Naples.
14 July: the Pope's Decree of Separation between Count Guiccioli and Teresa arrives; Teresa goes to her father's country estate at Filetto; B remains at the Palazzo Guiccioli; meets Count Pietro Gamba, Teresa's brother.
Aug.: initiated into the Carbonari by the Gambas.
19 Aug.: writes 'Italy, or *not* Corinna'.
Aug.–Nov.: trial and acquittal of Queen Caroline; B plans to take part in 'The Bowles Pope Controversy'.
9 Dec.: Commandant shot dead outside his apartment.

1821 4 Jan.: begins *Ravenna Journal.*
13 Jan.: begins *Sardanapalus.*
(33) 7 Feb.: writes 'Letter to John Murray Esqre.'
23 Feb.: Keats dies in Rome.
24 Feb.: planned uprising of Carbonari fails.
25 Mar.: writes 'Observations upon Observations'.
31 Mar.: 'Letter to John Murray Esqre.' published.
21 Apr.: *Marino Faliero* and *The Prophecy of Dante* published together.
5 May: Napoleon dies at St Helena.
12 June: begins *The Two Foscari.*
July: promises Teresa to discontinue *Don Juan*; the Gambas banished from the Romagna.
16 July: begins *Cain.*
4 Aug.: writes 'Some Recollections of my Acquaintance with Madame de Staël'.
15 Oct.: begins *Detached Thoughts.*
29 Oct.: leaves Ravenna to join Teresa, the Gambas, and the Shelleys at Pisa.
1 Nov.: arrives in Pisa; residence at the Casa Lanfranchi.

14 Nov.: Thomas Medwin arrives in Pisa.
1–2 Dec.: writes 'Some Account of the Life and Writings of the Late George Russell of A— By Henry Ferguson'.
19 Dec.: *Sardanapalus*, *The Two Foscari*, and *Cain* published together.

1822 15 Jan.: meets Trelawny.
(34) 28 Jan.: Lady Noel, his mother-in-law, dies; B takes name of Noel Byron.
Jan.–Feb.: resumes *Don Juan* (canto VI).
24 Mar.: 'Pisan Affray' with Sergeant-Major Masi.
20 Apr.: Allegra dies.
July: Leigh Hunt, and family, arrive, and are established in the Casa Lanfranchi.
8 July: Shelley and Williams drown in Bay of Spezia.
16 Aug.: cremation of Shelley on beach at Viareggio.
27 Sept.: leaves Pisa for Genoa.
Oct.: arrives in Genoa; residence at the Casa Saluzzo, Albaro.
15 Oct.: *The Vision of Judgment*, and 'Letter to the Editor of the *British Review*' published in the first number of the *Liberal.*
23 Nov.: *Werner* published.

1823 10 Jan.: finishes *The Age of Bronze.*
(35) Feb.: finishes *The Island.*
6 Feb.: writes 'An Italian Carnival'.
Apr.–June: sees much of the Blessingtons in Genoa.
May: elected member of the London Greek Committee.
24 July: sails from Leghorn for Greece on board the brig *Hercules*, with Pietro Gamba and Trelawny.
3 Aug.: lands at Argostoli, Cephalonia.
6 Sept.: Trelawny and Hamilton Browne leave for the Morea.
13 Nov.: signs agreement for loan of £4000 to the Greek government.
22 Nov.: Colonel Leicester Stanhope arrives from England.
29 Dec.: embarks for Missolonghi.

1824 4 Jan.: lands at Missolonghi to great welcome.
Jan.: takes 600 Suliotes into his pay and service.
14 Jan.: *Hellenica Chronica*, Greek newspaper, begun by Stanhope.
(36) 22 Jan.: writes the poem 'On This Day I Complete My Thirty-Sixth Year'.
23 Jan.: releases 28 Turkish prisoners to Patras and Prevesa.
25 Jan.: expedition against Lepanto projected.
5 Feb.: William Parry, fire-master, arrives from England.
15 Feb.: disbands Suliotes; has severe convulsive fit.

21 Feb.: Stanhope leaves for Athens; the first Greek loan signed by the Deputies—B named as one of the commissioners.

26 Feb.: writes 'The Present State of Greece'.

19 Apr., Easter Monday: dies of fever at 6 p.m.—dreadful thunderstorm, 'The great man is gone!'

READING LIST
(1807)

List of the different poets, Dramatic or otherwise, who have distinguished their respective languages by their productions.—

England[1]—	Milton, Dryden, Spenser, Pope Shakespeare, Massinger, Ben Johnson Beaumont & Fletcher. &c—
Scotland.—	Ossian or Macpherson,[2] Burns, Ramsay,[3] Walter Scott, Macneill[4] Home Author of Douglas.[5]—
Ireland—	Swift, a Hist[ory] in himself.
Wales———	Taliessin and the Bards.[6]
France———	Voltaire, Chaulieu,[7] Boileau, Moliere, Corneille, Racine, DeLille[8] esteemed the greatest of living Poets certainly the most successfull.—
Spain———	Lope de Vega,[9] Cervantes author of Galatea a Poem in 6 books but more renowned as the writer of Don Quixote.[10]
Portugal——	Camoens Author of the Lusiad, a dull poem, but prized by his countrymen as their only epic effort.[11]
Germany——	Klopstock, Wieland Goethe, Gesner,[12] Kleist, Lessing Schiller, Kotzebue
Italy	Tasso, Ariosto, Petrarch, Dante, Bembo, Metastasio.
Arabia,	Mahomet, whose Koran contains most sublime poetical passages far surpassing European Poetry
Persia—	Ferdausi,[13] author of the Shah Nameh the Persian Iliad, Sadi,[14] and Hafiz,[15] the immortal Hafiz the oriental Anacreon, the last is reverenced beyond any Bard of ancient or modern times by the

Persians, who resort to his tomb near Schiraz to celebrate his memory, a splendid copy of his works is chained to his Monument.—

Greece[16]— Homer, Hesiod, Anacreon, Sappho Alcæus, Apollonius Rhodius, Callimachus Menander, Aristophanes, Sophocles, Euripides, Æschylus, Pindar.

Latin Virgil, Lucan, Horace, Claudian, Statius, Ovid, Catullus, Tibullus, Propertius, Ennius Plautus, Terentius, Seneca

America, an epic Poet has already appeared in that Hemisphere, Barlow,[17] author of the Columbiad, but not to be compared with the work of more polished nations.—

Iceland, Denmark, Norway, were famous for their Skalds among these Lodbrog,[18] was one of the most distinguished, his death Song breathes ferocious sentiments, but a glorious and impassioned Strain of Poetry.—

Hindostan, is undistinguished by any great Bard at least the Sanscrit is so imperfectly known to Europeans, we know not what poetical Relics may exist.————

The Birman Empire, Here the natives are passionately fond of Poetry, but their Bards are unknown

China—————— I never heard of any Chinese Poet but the *Emperor Kien Long*, and his ode to *Tea*,[19] what a pity their Philosopher Confucius did not write Poetry with his precepts of morality.—

Africa———— In Africa, some of the native melodies are plaintive, & the words simple and affecting, but whether these[20] rude strains of nature, can be classed with Poetry, as the songs of the Bards, the Skalds of Europe &c. I know not—

This brief list of Poets, I have written down from memory, without any Book of Reference, consequently some errors may occur, but I think if

3 his Monument] his ⟨tomb⟩ 20 Europeans, we] Europeans, ⟨who⟩

any very trivial, the works of the European & some of the Asiatic, I have perused either in the original, or Translations, in my list of English, I have merely mentioned the greatest, to enumerate the minor poets would be useless, as well as tedious, perhaps Gray, Goldsmith, and Collins, or Thomson[21] might have been added as worthy of mention in a *Cosmopolite* account, but as for the others from Chaucer down to Churchill[22] they are "voces & præterea nihil"[23] sometimes spoken of, rarely read, & never with advantage.—Chaucer notwithstanding the praises bestowed on him, I think obscene, and contemptible,[24] he owes his celebrity, merely to his antiquity, which he does not deserve so well as Pierce Plowman, or Thomas of Ercildoune,[25] English living poets I have avoided mentioning, we have none who will not survive their productions. Taste is over with us, & another century, will sweep our Empire, our literature, & our name from all, but a place in the annals of mankind.[26]——————

Byron Nov.r 30.th *1807*

List of Historical Writers whose Works I have perused in different languages.

Hume,[27] Gibbon, Robertson,[28] Orme,[29] Voltaire,[30] Rollin,[31] Rapin,[32] Smollet,[33] Henry,[34] Knolles[35] Cantemir,[36] Paul Rycaut,[37] Vertot,[38] Livy, Tacitus, Eutropius, Arrian, Thucydides, Xenophon Herodotus, with several others whom I shall enumerate under their respective heads.

History of England——Hume, Rapin, Henry Smollet, Tindal,[39] Belsham,[40] Bisset[41] Adolphus,[42] Holinshed, Froissart's Chronicles belonging properly to France.——————

Scotland, Buchanan,[43] Hector Boethius,[44] both in the Latin,

Ireland, by, Gordon[45]

Rome,—— Hooke,[46] Decline and fall by Gibbon, Ancient History by Rollin, including an Account of the Carthaginians &c. &c. besides Livy, Tacitus, Eutropius, Cornelius Nepos,[47] Julius Caesar, Arrian Sallust,

15 from all] from ⟨every⟩ 30 Rome,——] Rome, ⟨by⟩ 32 besides Livy] besides ⟨Livy⟩ 34 Arrian Sallust,] Arrian ⟨&c.⟩

Greece,	Mitford's Greece,[48] Lelands Philip,[49] Plutarch, Potters Antiquities,[50] Xenophon Thucydides, Herodotus.
France———	Mezeray,[51] Voltaire.
Spain———	I Chiefly derived my Knowledge of old Spanish History from a Book called the Atlas, now obsolete, the modern history from the intrigues of Alberoni[52] down to the Prince of Peace[53] I learned from their connection[54] with European Politics.———
Portugal——	From Vertot, as also his account of the Siege of Rhodes, though the last is his own Invention, the real facts being totally different,[55]—so much for his Knights of Malta.—
Turkey,	I have read Knolles, Sir Paul Rycaut, and Prince Cantemir, besides a more modern History, anonymous, of the Ottoman History I know every event, from Tangralopix,[56] and afterwards Othman 1st[57] to the peace of Passarowitz, in 1718.[58]—the Battle of Crotzka in 1739[59] & the treaty between Russia & Turkey in 1790.[60]
Russia,	Tookes, Life of Catherine 2d[61] Voltaires Czar Peter.
Sweden,	Voltaires Charles 12th also Norberg's Charles 12th[62] in my opinion the best of the two, a Translation of Schiller's thirty years war contains[63] the exploits and Death of Gustavus Adolphus, besides Harte's Life of the same Prince,[64]——————I have somewhere read an account of Gustavus Vasa,[65] the Deliverer of Sweden, but do not remember the author's name.
Prussia,	I have seen at least twenty Lives of Frederick the 2d the only Prince worth recording in Prussian annals. Gillies,[66] His own works,[67] and Thiebault,[68] none very amusing, the last is paltry, but circumstantial.—

1 Greece, Mitford's] Greece, ⟨By⟩ Greece, Lelands] Greece, ⟨Lel⟩

Denmark, I know little of, of Norway I understand the natural History, but not the Chronological.—

Germany, I have read long Histories of the Houses of Swabia,[69] Wenceslaus[70] and at length Rudolph of Hapsburg & his *thick lipped* Austrian Descendants.[71]

Switzerland, Ah! William Tell and the Battle of Morgarten,[72] where Burgundy was slain.[73]—

Italy, Davila,[74] Guiccadini,[75] The Guelphs, & Gibellines,[76] the Battle of Pavia,[77] Massaniello, the Revolutions of Naples &c &c[78]

Hindostan—— Orme, & Cambridge.[79]

America,—— Robertson, Andrews American War.[80]

Africa—— merely from Travels as Mungo Parke,[81] Bruce.[82]

Biography—— Robertson's Charles 5th Caesar, Sallust, Catiline, & Jugurtha, Lives of Marlborough & Eugene,[83] Tekeli[84] Bonneval,[85] Buonaparte,[86] all the British Poets, both by Johnson & Anderson,[87] Rousseau's Confessions, Life of Cromwell,[88] British Plutarch,[89] British Nepos,[90] Campbell's lives of the Admirals,[91] Charles 12th Czar Peter, Catherine 2d, Henry Ld Kames,[92] Marmontel,[93] Teignmouth's Sir William Jones,[94] Life of Newton,[95] Belisaire,[96] with thousands not to be detailed.

Law, Blackstone,[97] Montesquieu.

Philosophy, Paley, Locke, Bacon, Hume, Berkeley, Drummond[98] Beattie,[99] and Bolingbroke,[100] Hobbes[101] I detest.—

Geography, Strabo, Cellarius,[102] Adams,[103] Pinkerton,[104] and Guthrie.[105]

Poetry,— all the British Classic's as before detailed, with

1 I understand] I ⟨under⟩ 8 Burgundy was slain.—] Burgundy ⟨fell.⟩ 13 Robertson, Andrews] Robertson, ⟨———⟩ 15 Sallust, Catiline] Sallust⟨'s⟩ 26 Philosophy, Paley] Philosophy, ⟨Newt⟩ Bacon, Hume] Bacon, ⟨&⟩

most of the living Poets Scott, Southey &c. some French in the original of which the Cid is my favourite,[106] a little Italian,[107] Greek & Latin without number, these last I shall give up in future, I have translated a good deal from Both languages, verse as well as prose.[108]——

Eloquence, Demosthenes, Cicero, Quintilian Sheridan,[109] Austin's Chironomia,[110] and Parliamentary Debates from the Revolution to the year 1742.——

Elocution, Enfield's Speaker.[111]—

Divinity, Blair,[112] Porteus,[113] Tillotson,[114] Hooker[115] all very tiresome,——
I abhor Religion,[116] though I reverence & love my God, without the blasphemous notions of Sectaries,[117] or a belief[118] in their absurd & damnable Heresies, mysteries, & thirty nine articles.[119] —

Miscellanies turn over[120]

Miscellanies,— Spectator,[121] Rambler,[122] World[123] &c &c novels by the thousand.———

All the Books here enumerated, I have taken down from memory, I recollect reading them, & can quote passages from any mentioned, I have of course omitted several, in my catalogue, but the greater part of the above I perused before the age of fifteen, but since I left Harrow[124] I have become idle, & conceited, from scribbling rhyme, & making love to Women—

B. Novr. 30th *1807*

I have also read (to my regret at present) above four thousand novels including the Works of Cervantes, Fielding, Smollett Richardson Mackenzie,[125] Sterne, Rabelais & Rousseau, &c &c—The Book in my opinion most useful to a man, who wishes to acquire the reputation of being well read, with the least trouble, is "Burton's Anatomy of

14—15 without the blasphemous notions of Sectaries,] without ⟨eating him in⟩ the blasphemous ⟨manner⟩ notions of ⟨Christians,⟩ Sectaries 25 rhyme, & making] rhyme, & ⟨tak⟩ 32 being well read, with] being ⟨a⟩ well read ⟨one⟩, ⟨at⟩ with

Melancholy"[126] the most amusing & instructive medley, of quotations & Classical anecdotes I ever perused.——But a superficial Reader must take care, or his intricacies will bewilder him, if however he has patience to go through his volumes, he will be more improved for literary conversation, than by the perusal of any twenty other works with which I am acquainted at least in the English Language.—

2 anecdotes I ever] anecdotes ⟨of ⟨from⟩ all languages,⟩ I ever

REVIEWS
(1807–1813)

Wordsworth's *Poems* (1807)

POEMS, By W. Wordsworth, 2 vols. pp. 328.

The volumes before us are by the author of Lyrical Ballads, a collection which has not undeservedly met with a considerable share of public applause.[1] The characteristics of Mr. W.'s muse are simple and flowing, though occasionally inharmonious verse, strong, and sometimes irresisitible appeals to the feelings, with unexceptionable sentiments. Though the present work may not equal his former efforts, many of the poems possess a native elegance, natural and unaffected, totally devoid of the tinsel embellishments and abstract hyperboles of several cotemporary sonneteers.[2] The last sonnet in the first volume, p. 152, is perhaps the best, without any novelty in the sentiments, which we hope are common to every Briton at the present crisis;[3] the force and expression is that of a genuine poet, feeling as he writes:[4]

"Another year! another deadly blow!
Another mighty empire overthrown!
And we are left, or shall be left, alone—
The last that dares to struggle with the foe.
'Tis well!—from this day forward we shall know
That in ourselves our safety must be sought,
That by our own right-hands it must be wrought;
That we must stand unprop'd, or be laid low.
O dastard! whom such foretaste doth not cheer!
We shall exult, if they who rule the land
Be men who hold its many blessings dear,
Wise, upright, valiant, not a venal band,
Who are to judge of danger which they fear,
And honor which they do not understand."[5]

The song at the Feast of Brougham Castle, the Seven Sisters, the Affliction of Margaret —— of —— possess all the beauties, and few of the defects of this writer; the following lines from the last are in his first style:

"Ah! little doth the young one dream
When full of play and childish cares,
What power hath e'en his wildest scream,
Heard by his mother unawares:
He knows it not, he cannot guess:
Years to a mother bring distress,
But do not make her love the less."[6]

The pieces least worthy of the author are those entitled "Moods of my own Mind,"[7] we certainly wish these "Moods" had been less frequent, or not permitted to occupy a place near works, which only make their deformity more obvious; when Mr. W. ceases to please, it is by "abandoning" his mind[8] to the most common-place ideas, at the same time clothing them in language not simple, but puerile: what will any reader or auditor, out of the nursery, say to such namby-pamby[9] as "Lines written at the foot of Brother's Bridge."

"The cock is crowing,
The stream is flowing,
The small birds twitter,
The lake doth glitter.
The green field sleeps in the sun;
The oldest and youngest,
Are at work with the strongest,
The cattle are grazing,
Their heads never raising,
There are forty feeding like one.
Like an army defeated,
The snow hath retreated,
And now doth fare ill,
On the top of the bare hill."[10]

"The plough-boy is whooping anon, anon," &c. &c. is in the same exquisite measure;[11] this appears to us neither more or less than an imitation of such minstrelsy as soothed our cries in the cradle, with the shrill ditty of

"Hey de diddle,
The cat and the fiddle:
The cow jump'd over the moon,
The little dog laugh'd to see such sport,
And the dish ran away with the spoon."[12]

On the whole, however, with the exception of the above, and other INNOCENT odes of the same cast, we think these volumes display a genius worthy of higher pursuits, and regret that Mr. W. confines his muse to such trifling subjects; we trust his motto will be in future, "Paulo majora canamus."[13] Many, with inferior abilities, have acquired a loftier seat on Parnassus, merely by attempting strains in which Mr. W. is more qualified to excel.[14]

Spencer's *Poems* (1812)

Poems by William Robert Spencer. 8vo. 10s. Boards. Cadell and Davies. 1811.

The author of this well-printed volume has more than once been introduced to our readers, and is known to rank among that class of poetical persons who have never been highly favoured by stern criticism. The "mob of gentlemen who write with ease"[1] has indeed of late years (like other mobs) become so importunate, as to threaten an alarming rivalry to the regular body of writers who are not fortunate enough to be either easy or genteel. Hence the jaundiced eye with which the real author regards the red Morocco binding of the presumptuous "*Littérateur*;" we say, *the binding*, for into the book itself he cannot condescend to look, at least not beyond the frontispiece.—Into Mr. Spencer's volume, however, he may dip farther, and will find sufficient to give him pleasure or pain, in proportion to his own candour. It consists chiefly of "*Vers de Société*,"[2] calculated to prove very delightful to a large circle of fashionable acquaintance, and pleasing to a limited number of vulgar purchasers. These last, indeed, may be rude enough to expect something more for their specie during the present scarcity of change, than lines to 'Young Poets and Poetesses,' 'Epitaphs upon Years,' Poems 'to my Grammatical Niece,' 'Epistle from Sister Dolly in Cascadia to Sister Tanny in Snowdonia,' &c.: but we doubt not that a long list of persons of quality, wit, and honour, "in town and country," who are here addressed, will be highly pleased with themselves and with the poet who has *shewn them off* in a very handsome volume: as will doubtless the 'Butterfly at the end of Winter,' provided that he is fortunate enough to survive the present inclemencies. We are, however, by no means convinced that the Bellman will relish Mr. S.'s usurpation of a 'Christmas Carol;' which looks so very like his own, that we advise him immediately to put in his claim, and it will be universally allowed.[3]

With the exception of these and similar productions, the volume contains poems eminently beautiful; some which have been already published, and others that are well worthy of present publication. Of 'Leonora,' with which it opens, we made our report many years ago: (in Vol. XX. N.S. p. 451.)[4] but our readers, perhaps, will not be sorry to see another short extract. We presume that they are well acquainted with the story, and therefore select one of the central passages:

'See, where fresh blood-gouts mat the green,
Yon wheel its reeking points advance;
There, by the moon's wan light half seen,
Grim ghosts of tombless murderers dance.
"Come, spectres of the guilty dead,
With us your goblin morris ply,
Come all in festive dance to tread,
Ere on the bridal couch we lie."

'Forward th' obedient phantoms push,
Their trackless footsteps rustle near,
In sound like autumn winds that rush
Through withering oak or beech-wood sere.
With lightning's force the courser flies,
Earth shakes his thund'ring hoofs beneath,
Dust, stones, and sparks, in whirlwind rise,
And horse and horseman heave for breath.

'Swift roll the moon-light scenes away,
Hills chasing hills successive fly;
E'en stars that pave th' eternal way,
Seem shooting to a backward sky.
"Fear'st thou, my love? the moon shines clear;
Hurrah! how swiftly speed the dead!
The dead does Leonora fear?
Oh God! oh leave, oh leave the dead!"'[5]

Such a specimen of "the Terrible" will place the merit of the poem in a proper point of view: but we do not think that some of the alterations in this copy of Leonora are altogether so judicious as Mr. S.'s well-known taste had led us to expect. 'Reviving Friendship' (p. 5.) is perhaps less expressive than "Relenting," as it once stood; and the phrase 'ten thousand *furlowed* heroes' (ibid.) throws a new light on the heroic character.[6] It is extremely proper that heroes should have 'furlows,' since school-boys have holidays, and lawyers have long vacations: but we very much question whether young gentlemen of the scholastic, legal, or heroic calling, would be flattered by any epithet derived from the relaxation of their respectable pursuits. We should feel some hesitation in telling an interesting youth, of any given battalion from Portugal, that he was a 'furlowed hero,' lest he should prove to us that his 'furlow' had by no means impaired his 'heroism.' The old epithet, "war-worn," was more adapted to heroism and to poetry; and, if we mistake not, it has very recently been superseded by an epithet which precludes "*otium cum dignitate*"[7] from the soldier, without imparting either ease or dignity to the verse. Why is "horse and horsemen *pant* for breath" changed to '*heave* for breath,' unless for the alliteration of the too tempting aspirate?[8] '*Heaving*' is appropriate enough to coals and to sighs, but panting *belongs* to successful lovers and spirited horses; and why should Mr. S.'s horse and horseman not have panted as heretofore?

The next poem in arrangement as well as in merit is the "Year of Sorrow;" to which we offered a tribute of praise in our 45th Vol. N.S. p. 288.[9]—We are sorry to observe that the compliment paid to Mr. Wedgewood by a "late traveller," (see note, p. 50.) viz. that "an Englishman in journeying from Calais to Ispahan may have his dinner served every day on *Wedgewood's ware*," is no longer a matter of fact.[10] It has lately been the good or evil fortune of one of our travelling department[11] to pass near to Calais, and to have journeyed through divers Paynim lands to no very remote distance from Ispahan; and neither in the palace of the Pacha nor in the caravansera of the traveller, nor in the hut of the peasant, was he so favoured as to masticate his pilaff from that fashionable service. Such is, in this and numerous other instances, the altered state of the continent and of Europe, since the annotation of the "late traveller;" and on the authority of a *later*, we must report that the ware has been all broken since the former passed that way. We wish that we could efficiently exhort Mr. Wedgewood to send out a fresh supply, on all the *turnpike roads* by the route of Bagdad, for the convenience of the "latest travellers."

Passing over the 'Chorus from Euripides,' which might as well have slept in quiet with the rest of the author's school-exercises,[12] we come to 'the Visionary,' which we gladly extract as a very elegant specimen of the lighter poems:[13]

'When midnight o'er the moonless skies
Her pall of transient death has spread,

When mortals sleep, when spectres rise,
And nought is wakeful but the dead!

'No bloodless shape my way pursues,
No sheeted ghost my couch annoys,
Visions more sad my fancy views;
Visions of long departed joys!

'The shade of youthful hope is there,
That linger'd long, and latest died;
Ambition all dissolved to air,
With phantom honours at her side.

'What empty shadows glimmer nigh!
They once were friendship, truth, and love!
Oh, die to thought, to mem'ry die,
Since lifeless to my heart ye prove!'

We cannot forbear adding the beautiful stanzas in pages 166, 167:

'To the Lady ANNE HAMILTON.

'Too late I staid, forgive the crime,
Unheeded flew the hours;
How noiseless falls the foot of Time,
That only treads on flow'rs!

'What eye with clear account remarks
The ebbing of his glass,
When all its sands are di'mond sparks,
That dazzle as they pass?

'Ah! who to sober measurement
Time's happy swiftness brings,
When birds of Paradise have lent
Their plumage for his wings?'

The far greater part of the volume, however, contains pieces which can be little gratifying to the public:—some are pretty; and all are besprinkled with 'gems,' and 'roses,' and 'birds,' and 'diamonds,' and such like cheap poetical adornments, as are always to be obtained at no great expence of thought or of metre.—It is happy for the author that these *bijoux* are presented to persons of high degree; Countesses, foreign and domestic; 'Maids of Honour to Louisa Landgravine of Hesse D'Armstadt;' Lady Blank, and Lady Asterisk, besides——, and ——, and others anonymous;[14] who are exactly the kind of people to be best pleased with these sparkling, shining, fashionable trifles. We will solace our readers with three stanzas of the soberest of these odes:

'Addressed to Lady SUSAN FINCASTLE, now Countess of Dunmore.

'What ails you, Fancy? your'e become
Colder than Truth, than Reason duller!
Your wings are worn, your chirping's dumb,
And ev'ry plume has lost its colour.

'You droop like geese, whose cacklings cease
When dire St. Michael they remember,
Or like some *bird* who just has heard
That Fin's preparing for September?

'Can you refuse your sweetest spell
When I for Susan's praise invoke you?
What, sulkier still? you pout and swell
As if that lovely name would choke you.'[15]

We are to suppose that 'Fin preparing for September' is the Lady with whose 'lovely name' Fancy runs some risk of being 'choked;' and, really, if *killing partridges* formed a part of her Ladyship's accomplishments, both 'Fancy' and Feeling were in danger of a quinsey.[16] Indeed, the whole of these stanzas are couched in that most exquisite irony, in which Mr. S. has more than once succeeded.—All the songs to 'persons of quality' seem to be written on that purest model, "the song by a person of quality;"[17] whose stanzas have not been fabricated in vain. This sedulous imitation extends even to the praise of things inanimate:

'When an Eden zephyr hovers
O'er a slumb'ring cherub's lyre,
Or when sighs of seraph lovers
Breathe upon th' unfinger'd wire.'[18]

If namby-pamby still leads to distinction, Mr. S., like Ambrose Phillips, will be "preferred for wit."[19]

'Heaven must hear—a bloom more tender
Seems to tint the wreath of May,
Lovelier beams the noon-day splendour,
Brighter dew-drops gem the spray!

'Is the breath of angels moving
O'er each flow'ret's heighten'd hue?
Are their smiles the day improving,
Have their tears enrich'd the dew?'

Here we have 'angels' tears,' and 'breath,' and 'smiles,' and 'Eden zephyrs,' 'sighs of seraph lovers,' and 'lyres of slumbering cherubs,' dancing away to 'the Pedal Harp!'—How strange it is that Thomson, in his stanzas on the Æolian lyre, (see the *Castle of Indolence*)[20] never dreamed of such things, but left all these prettinesses to the last of the Cruscanti![21]

One of the best pieces in the volume is an 'Epistle to T. Moore, Esq.,' which, though disfigured with 'Fiends on sulphur nurst,' and '*Hell's chillest Winter*,' ("poor Tom's a'-cold!")[22] and some other vagaries of the same sort, forms a pleasant specimen of poetical friendship.—We give the last ten lines:[23]

'The triflers think your varied powers
Made only for life's gala bow'rs,
To smooth Reflection's mentor-frown,
Or pillow joy on softer down.—
Fools!—yon blest orb not only glows
To chase the cloud, or paint the rose;
These are the pastimes of his might,
Earth's torpid bosom drinks his light;
Find there his wondrous pow'r's true measure,
Death turn'd to life, and dross to treasure!'

We have now arrived at Mr. Spencer's French and Italian poesy; the former of which is written sometimes in new and sometimes in old French, and, occasionally, in a kind of tongue neither old nor new. We offer a sample of the two former:[24]

'"QU'EST CE QUE C'EST QUE LE GENIE?"

'*Brillant est cet esprit privé de sentiment*;
Mais ce n'est qu'un soleil trop vif et trop constant,
Tendre est ce sentiment qu'aucun esprit n'anime,
Mais ce n'est qu'un jour doux, que trop de pluie abime!
Quand un brillant esprit de ses rares couleurs,
Orne du sentiment les aimables douleurs,
Un Phenomêne *en nait*, *le plus beau de la vie*!

C'est alors que les ris en se mêlant aux pleurs,
Font cet Iris de l'ame, *appellé le Genie*!'—

'*C'y gist un povre menestrel,*
Occis par maint ennuict cruel—
Ne plains pas trop sa destinée—
N'est icy que son corps mortel;
Son ame est toujours à Gillwell,
Et n'est ce pas là l'Elysée?'

We think that Mr. Spencer's Italian rhymes are better finished than his French; and indeed the facility of composing in that most poetical of all languages must be obvious: but, as a composer in Italian, he and all other Englishmen are much inferior to Mr. Mathias.[25]—It is very perceptible in many of Mr. S.'s smaller pieces that he has suffered his English versification to be vitiated with Italian *concetti*;[26] and we should have been better pleased with his compositions in a foreign language, had they not induced him to corrupt his mother-tongue. Still we would by no means utterly proscribe these excursions into other languages; though they remind us occasionally of that aspiring Frenchman who placed in his grounds the following inscription in honour of Shenstone and the Leasowes:[27]

"See this stone
For William Shenstone—
Who planted groves rural,
And wrote verse natural!"

The above lines were displayed by the worthy proprietor, in the pride of his heart, to all English travellers, as a tribute of respect for the resemblance of his paternal chateau to the Leasowes, and a striking coincidence between Shenstone's versification and his own.—We do not mean to insinuate that Mr. Spencer's French verses ('*C'y gist un povre menestrel*,' with an Urn inscribed W.R.S. at the top,) are *precisely* a return in kind for the quatrain above quoted: but we place it as a beacon to all young gentlemen of poetical propensities on the French Parnassus. Few would proceed better on the Gallic Pegasus, than the Anglo-troubadour on ours.

We now take our leave of Mr. Spencer, without being blind to his errors or insensible to his merits. As a poet, he may be placed rather below Mr. Moore and somewhat above Lord Strangford;[28] and if his volume meet with half their number of purchasers, he will have no reason to complain either of our judgment or of his own success.

Ireland's *Neglected Genius* (1813)

Neglected Genius: a Poem. Illustrating the untimely and unfortunate Fall of many British Poets; from the Period of Henry VIII. to the Æra of the unfortunate Chatterton. Containing Imitations of their different Styles, &c. &c. By W. H. Ireland, Author of the Fisher-Boy, Sailor-Boy, Cottage-Girl, &c. &c. &c. 8vo. pp. 175. 8s. Boards. Sherwood and Co. 1812.[1]

This volume, professing in a moderately long title-page to be 'illustrative of the untimely and unfortunate fate of *many* British Poets,' might with great propriety include the author among the number; for if his 'imitations of their different styles' resemble the originals, the consequent starvation of 'many British poets' is a doom which is calculated to excite pity rather than surprize. The book opens with a dedication to the present, and a Monody on the late Duke of Devonshire, (one of the neglected bards, we presume, on whom the author holds his inquest,) in which it were difficult to say whether the 'enlightened understanding' of the living or the 'intellect' of the deceased nobleman is more justly appreciated or more elegantly eulogized.[2] Lest the Monody should be mistaken for any thing but itself, of which there was little danger, it is dressed in marginal mourning, like a dying speech, or an American Gazette after a defeat. The following is a specimen:—the Poet is addressing the Duchess:[3]

> 'Chaste widow'd Mourner, still with tears bedew
>   That sacred Urn, which can imbue
> Thy worldly thoughts, thus kindling mem'ry's glow:
> Each retrospective virtue, fadeless beam,
>   Embalms thy *Truth* in heavenly dream,
> To soothe the bosom's agonizing woe.
>
> 'Yet soft—more poignantly to wake the soul,
>   And ev'ry pensive thought controul,
> Truth shall with energy his worth proclaim;
> Here I'll record his *philanthropic mind*,

Eager to bless all human kind,
Yet *modest shrinking* from the voice of *Fame*.

'As *Patriot* view him shun the courtly crew,
And dauntless ever keep in view
That bright palladium, England's dear renown.
The people's Freedom and the Monarch's good,
Purchas'd with Patriotic blood,
The surest safeguard of the state and crown.

'Or now behold his glowing soul extend,
To shine the polish'd social *friend*;
His country's *matchless Prince* his worth rever'd;
Gigantic Fox, true Freedom's darling child,
By kindred excellence beguil'd,
To lasting *amity* the temple rear'd.

'As *Critic* chaste, his judgment could explore
The beauties of poetic lore,
Or classic strains mellifluent infuse;
Yet glowing genius and expanded sense
Were crown'd with *innate diffidence*,
The sure attendant of a genuine muse.'

Page nine contains, forsooth, a very correct imitation of Milton:[4]

'To thee, gigantic genius, next I'll sound;
The clarion string, and fill fame's vasty round;
'Tis *Milton* beams upon the wond'ring sight,
Rob'd in the splendour of Apollo's light;
As when from ocean bursting on the view,
His orb dispenses ev'ry brilliant hue,
Crowns with resplendant gold th' horizon wide,
And cloathes with countless gems the buoyant tide;
While through the boundless realms of æther blaze,
On spotless azure, streamy saffron rays:—
So o'er the world of genius *Milton* shone,
Profound in science—as the bard—*alone*.'

We must not pass over the imitative specimen of 'Nahum Tate,' because in this the author approximates nearest to the style of his original:[5]

'Friend of great *Dryden*, though of humble fame,
The *Laureat Tate*, shall here record his name;

Whose sorrowing numbers breath'd a nation's pain,
When death from mortal to immortal reign
Translated royal *Anne*, our island's boast,
Victorious sov'reign, dread of Gallia's host;
Whose arms by land and sea with fame were crown'd,
Whose statesmen grave for wisdom were renown'd,
Whose reign with science dignifies the page;
Bright noon of genius—*great Augustan age*.
Such was thy Queen, and such th' illustrious time
That nurs'd thy muse, and tun'd thy soul to rhyme;
Yet wast thou fated sorrow's shaft to bear,
Augmenting still this catalogue of care;
The gripe of penury thy bosom knew,
A gloomy jail obscur'd bright freedom's view:
So life's gay visions faded to thy sight,
Thy brilliant hopes enscarf'd in sorrow's night.'

Where did Mr. Ireland learn that *hold fast* and *ballăst*,—*stir* and *hungĕr*,—*please* and *kidnĕys*,—*plain* and *capstāne*,—*expose* and *windōws*,—*forgot* and *pilōt*,—*sail on* and *Deucălon*! (Lempriere would have saved him a scourging at school by telling him that there was an I in the word) were legitimate Hudibrastic rhymes? see pages 116., &c.[6] Chatterton is a great favourite of this imitative gentleman; and Bristol, where he appears to have been held in no greater estimation than Mr. Ireland himself deserves, is much vituperated in some sad couplets, seemingly for this reason, "all for love, and a little for the bottle," as Bannister's song runs,[7]—"all for Chatterton, and a little for myself," thinks Mr. Ireland.[8]

The notes communicate, among other novelties, the new title of '*Sir* Horace' to the Honourable H. Walpole: surely a perusal of the life of the unfortunate boy, whose fate Mr. I. deplores, might have prevented this piece of ignorance, twice repeated in the same page;[9] and we wonder at the malicious fun of the printer's devil in permitting it to stand, for *he* certainly knew better.[10] We must be excused from a more detailed notice of Mr. Ireland for the present; and indeed we hope to hear no more of his lamentations, very sure that none but reviewers ever will peruse them: unless, perhaps, the unfortunate persons of quality whom he may henceforth single out as proper victims of future dedication. Though his dedications are enough to kill the living, his anticipated monodies, on the other hand, must add considerably to the natural dread of death in such of his patrons as may be liable to common sense or to chronic diseases.

SPEECHES
(1812–1813)

Frame Work Bill Speech: *Draft Notes* (1812)

1.

Subject not new to the country though to the house.—

2.

Detail superfluous.

3.

The day I left Notts outrages &c. 40 frames—*without detection or resistance.*

4

Distress the cause.

5

Military—Magistracy—Police—No real delinquent taken.—

6

Not idle though useless.

7.

Not the time to question. ye. injustice—Improvement in frames—1 man does the work of 4—Spider work injurious to the workmen—work not so well done

8.

Means of subsistence—Comfort destroyed—how—Method in Ms.[1]—

9.

Bankruptcy—fraud felony—Walsh,—pardoned[2]—but new capital punishments devised for the poor. Ms.—Spade—beg—means of employ.—

16 work of 4] work of ⟨1⟩

10

Masters of frames connive at their destruction—

11.

Conciliation—inquiry Sentence—Death warrants—

12

Military proved useless.—Major Sturgeon's campaign

13

Martial law—Sword—

14

County suffers—

15

Only 130 miles from London.—

16

Mob—&c.—people.

17

Readiness in favour of allies.—apathy at home

18.

Portuguese—Distress greater here than in Spain or Turkey

19.

Government—remedy.—something like Dr. Sangrados

20

Decimation—Martial law Sherwood forest.—capital punishments *already* too numerous.— / *Arnold*[3] Example—prevention—tranquillity

21.

Investigation previous temporizing.—

22.

Vote contra—why.—Injustice—irritation—Jury—B. Judge J.[4]—

Frame Work Bill Speech (1812)

Feb.^{ry} 28.th 1812. Spoken in the House of Lords F.^{y} 27.th 1812.

My Lords.—The subject now submitted to your Lordships for the first time though new to the house, is by no means new to the Country.—I believe it had occupied the serious thoughts of all descriptions of persons long before it's introduction to the notice of that legislature whose interference alone could be of real service.—As a person in some degree connected with the suffering county, though a stranger not only to this house in general, but to almost every individual whose attention I presume to solicit, I must claim some portion of your Lordships' indulgence, whilst I offer a few observations on a question in which I confess myself deeply interested.—To enter into any detail of these riots would be superfluous; the house is already aware that every outrage short of actual bloodshed has been perpetrated, & that the proprietors of the frames obnoxious to the rioters & all persons supposed to be connected with them have been liable to insult & violence.—During the short time I recently passed in Notts, not 12 hours elapsed without some fresh act of violence, & on the day I left the county, I was informed that 40 frames had been broken the preceding Evening as usual without resistance & without detection.[1]—Such was then[2] the state of that county & such I have reason to believe it to be at this moment.—But whilst these outrages must be admitted to exist to an alarming extent, it cannot be denied that they have arisen from circumstances of the most unparalelled distress.—The perseverance of these miserable men in their proceedings, tends to prove that nothing but absolute want could have driven a large & once honest & industrious body of the populace[3] into the commission of excesses so hazardous to themselves, their families, & the community.—At the time to which I allude, the town & county were burthened with large detachments of the military, the police was in motion, the magistrates assembled, &[4] all these movements civil & military had led to—Nothing.[5]—Not a single instance had occurred of the apprehension of any real delinquent actually taken in the fact, against whom there existed legal evidence sufficient for conviction.—But the police

4 it had occupied] it had ⟨already⟩ 16–17 not 12 hours] not ⟨a day⟩ 20 county & such] county & ⟨I have not heard⟩ 23 unparalelled] unparal⟨l⟩elled 25 once honest] once ⟨sober⟩

however useless were by no means idle, several notorious delinquents had been detected; men liable to conviction on the clearest evidence of the capital crime of poverty, men, who had been nefariously guilty of lawfully begetting several children, whom, thanks to the times! they were unable to maintain.———Considerable injury has been done to the proprietors of the improved frames.—These machines were to them an advantage inasmuch as they superseded the necessity of employing a number of workmen who were left in consequence to starve.—By the adoption of one species of frame in particular one man performed the work of many, & the superfluous labourers were thrown out of employment.[6]—Yet it is to be observed that the work thus executed was inferior in quality, not marketeable at home, & merely hurried over with a view to exportation.—It was called in the cant of the trade by the name of Spider work.[7] The rejected workmen in the blindness of their ignorance, instead of rejoicing at these improvements in arts so beneficial to mankind conceived themselves to be sacrificed to improvements in Mechanism.—In the foolishness of their hearts, they imagined that the well doing & maintenance[8] of the industrious poor was an object[9] of greater consequence than the enrichment of a few individuals by any improvement in the implements of trade which threw the workman out of employment & rendered the labourer unworthy of his hire.[10]—And it must be confessed that although the adoption of the enlarged machinery, in that state of our commerce which the County once boasted, might have been beneficial to the Master without being detrimental to the servant, yet in the present situation of our manufactures rotting in warehouses without a prospect of exportation,[11] with the demand for work & workmen equally diminished, frames of this construction[12] tend materially to aggravate the distress & discontents of the disappointed sufferers.—But the real cause of these distresses & consequent disturbances lies deeper.—When we are told that these men are leagued together not only for the destruction of their own comfort but their[13] very means of subsistence, can we forget that it is the bitter policy, the destructive warfare of the last eighteen years[14] which has destroyed their comfort, your comfort, all men's comfort; that policy which originating with "great statesmen now no more"[15] has survived the dead to become a

23 of the enlarged] of th⟨is⟩ 24 commerce which] commerce ⟨th⟩ 26 yet in the] yet in ⟨our⟩ manufactures] manufactures⟨,⟩ in warehouses] in ⟨our⟩ 28 diminished, frames] diminished, ⟨such⟩ construction tend] construction ⟨undoubtedly⟩ tend⟨ed⟩

curse on the living unto the third & fourth generation?[16]——These men never destroyed their looms till they were become useless, worse than useless, till they were become actual impediments to their exertions in obtaining their daily bread.[17]—Can you then wonder that in times like these when bankruptcy, convicted fraud, & imputed felony are found in a station not far beneath that of your Lordships,[18] the lowest though once most useful portion of the people should forget their duty in their distresses & become only less guilty than one of their representatives?—But while the exalted offender can find means to baffle the law, new capital punishments must be devised, new snares of death must be spread for the wretched mechanic who is famished into guilt.—These men were willing to dig, but the spade was in other hands, they were not ashamed to beg,[19] but there was none to relieve them, their own means of subsistence were cut off, all other employments preoccupied, & their excesses however to be deplored & condemned, can hardly be subject of surprise.—It has been stated, that the persons in the temporary possession of frames connive at their destruction,[20] if this be proved upon enquiry, it were necessary that such material accessaries to the crime should be principals in the punishment.——But I did hope that any measure proposed by his Majesty's goverment for your L^{ps} decision would have had conciliation for it's basis, or if that were hopeless, that some previous inquiry, some deliberation would have been deemed requisite, not that we should have been called at once without examination & without cause to pass sentences by wholesale, & sign deathwarrants blindfold.———

—But admitting that these men had no cause of complaint, that the grievances of them & their employers were alike groundless, that they deserved the worst; what inefficiency, what imbecility has been evinced in the method chosen to reduce them?—Why were the military called out to be made a mockery of? if they were to be called out at all.—As far as the difference of seasons would permit they have merely parodied the Summer campaign of Major Sturgeon & indeed the whole proceedings civil & military seem formed on[21] the model of those of the Mayor & Corporation of Garrat.—Such marchings & countermarchings! from Nottingham to Bulwell from Bulwell to Baseford from Baseford to Mansfield![22] & when at length the detachments arrived at their destination in all "the pride pomp &

1 generation?——These] generation?——⟨And can we wonder⟩ 6 station not] station ⟨only⟩ 11 be spread] be ⟨set⟩ 23 requisite, not] requisite, ⟨& that⟩ 24 should have] should ⟨not⟩ 29 the method] the ⟨means⟩

circumstance of glorious war"[23] they came just in time to witness the mischief which *had* been done, & ascertain the escape of the perpetrators, to collect the "spolia opima"[24] in the fragments of broken frames, & return to their quarters amidst the derision of old women & the hootings of children.—Now, though in a free country, it were to be wished that our military should never be too formidable, at least to ourselves, I cannot see the policy of placing them in situations where they can only be made ridiculous.[25]—As the Sword is the worst argument that can be used, so should it be the last, in this instance it has been the first, but providentially as yet only in the Scabbard.[26]—The present measure will indeed pluck it from the Sheath, yet had proper meetings been held in the earlier stages of these riots, had the grievances of these men & their masters, (for they also have their grievances) been fairly weighed & justly examined, I do think that means might have been devised to restore these workmen to their avocations & tranquillity to the County.—At present the county suffers from the double infliction of an idle military & a starving population.—In what state of apathy have we been plunged so long that now for the first time the house has been officially apprized of these disturbances? All this has been transacting within 130 miles of London and yet we "good easy men! have deemed full sure our greatness was a ripening"[27] & have sate down to enjoy our foreign triumphs in the midst of domestic calamity.—But all the cities you have taken, all the armies which have retreated before your leaders, are but paltry subjects of selfcongratulation, if your land divides against itself,[28] & your dragoons & executioners must be let loose against your fellow citizens.—You call these men a mob, desperate, dangerous & ignorant, & seem to think that the only way to quiet the "Bellua multorum capitum"[29] is to lop off a few of it's superfluous heads.—But even a mob may be better reduced to reason by a mixture of conciliation & firmness, than by additional irritation & redoubled penalties.—Are we aware of our obligations to a *Mob*?—It is the Mob, that labour in your fields & serve in your houses, that man your navy & recruit your army, that have enabled you to defy all the world, & can also defy you, when Neglect & Calamity have driven them to despair.—You may call the people a Mob, but do not forget, that a Mob too often speaks the sentiments of the People.—And here I must remark with what alacrity you are accustomed to fly to the succour of your distrest allies, leaving the

1 they came] they ⟨were⟩ 15–16 their avocations] their ⟨employ⟩ 26 against your] against ⟨f⟩ 32 It is the] It is ⟨a⟩

distressed of your own country to the care of Providence or—the parish.[30] When the Portuguese suffered under the retreat of the French every arm was stretched out, every hand was opened, from the rich man's largess to the widow's mite[31] all was bestowed to enable them to rebuild their villages & replenish their granaries.[32]—And at this moment, when thousands of misguided but most unfortunate fellow countrymen are struggling with the extremes of hardship & hunger, as your Charity began abroad, it should end at home.[33]—A much less sum, a tithe of the bounty bestowed on Portugal, even if these men, (which I cannot admit without inquiry) could not have been restored to their employments, would have rendered unnecessary the tender mercies of the bayonet & the gibbet.[34]—But doubtless our funds[35] have too many foreign claims to admit a prospect of domestic relief,—though never did such objects demand it.—I have traversed the seat of war in the peninsula, I have been in some of the most oppressed provinces of Turkey, but never under the most despotic of infidel governments, did I behold such squalid wretchedness as I have seen since my return in the very heart of a Christian country.—And what are your remedies?—After months of inaction, and months of action worse than inactivity, at length comes forth the grand specific, the never failing nostrum of all state physicians from the days of Draco[36] to the present time.—After feeling the pulse & shaking the head over the patient, prescribing the usual course of warm water & bleeding, the warm water of your mawkish police, & the lancets of your military, these convulsions must terminate in death the sure consummation of the prescriptions of all political Sangrados.[37]—Setting aside the palpable injustice & the certain inefficacy[38] of the bill; are there not capital punishments sufficient in your statutes? is there not blood enough upon your penal code?[39] that more must be poured forth to ascend to heaven & testify against you?[40]—How will you carry the bill into effect? can you commit a whole county to their own prisons? will you erect a gibbet in every field & hang up men like scarecrows? or will you proceed (as you must to bring this measure into effect) by decimation, place the country under martial law, depopulate & lay waste all around you, & restore Sherwood forest as an acceptable gift to the crown in it's former condition of a royal chace & an asylum for Outlaws?[41] Are these the remedies for a starving &

8 it should end] it should ⟨have⟩ 9 Portugal, even] Portugal, ⟨would⟩ 11 would have rendered] would have ⟨superseded⟩ 12 the tender mercies] the ⟨necessity⟩ 14 relief,—though] relief⟨.⟩—⟨Yet⟩ 35 & restore] & ⟨present⟩

desperate populace? Will the famished wretch who has braved your bayonets, be appalled by your gibbets? when death is a relief & the only relief it appears that you will afford him, will he be dragooned into tranquillity? will that which could not be effected by your Grenadiers, be accomplished by your "Jack Ketches?[42] If you proceed by the forms of law, where is your evidence? those who have refused to impeach their accomplices when transportation only was the punishment, will hardly be tempted to witness against them when death is the penalty.——With all due deference to the noble Lords opposite, I think a little investigation, some previous enquiry would induce even them to change their purpose.—That most favourite state measure, so marvellously efficacious in many & recent instances, *temporizing*, would not be without it's advantages in this.[43]——When a proposal is made to emancipate or relieve you hesitate, you deliberate for years you temporize & tamper with the minds of men, but a deathbill must be passed off hand, without a thought of the consequences.—Sure I am from what I have heard, & from what I have seen, that to pass the bill under all the existing circumstances, without enquiry, without deliberation, would only be to add injustice to irritation & barbarity to neglect.—The framers[44] of such a bill must be content to inherit the honours of that Athenian lawgiver whose edicts were said to be written not in ink but in blood.[45]—But suppose it past, suppose one of these men, as I have seen them, meagre with famine sullen with despair, careless of a life,—which your Lordships are perhaps about to value at something less than the price of a stocking frame,—suppose this man surrounded by those children for whom he is unable to procure bread at the hazard of his existence, about to be torn forever from a family which he lately supported in peaceful industry, & which it is not his fault that he can no longer so support, suppose this man,—& there are ten thousand such from whom you may select your victims, dragged into court to be tried for this new offence by this new law, still there are two things wanting to convict & condemn him—& these are in my opinion, twelve butchers for a Jury, & a Jefferies for a Judge.[46]—

1 the famished] the ⟨men⟩ 9 all due] all ⟨th⟩ 11 most favourite] most ⟨marvellous &⟩ 15 a deathbill] a ⟨bill for⟩ 16 consequences] consequen⟨ces⟩ 26–7 bread at] bread ⟨even⟩ 29 suppose this man] suppose ⟨one of them⟩ 31 into court] into ⟨your⟩ 32 him—&] him—⟨12 but⟩

Roman Catholic Claims Debate: *Draft Speech and Notes* (1812)

My Lords,

⟨In delivering my sentiments on the question before the house, I have to claim your indulgence not only as a stranger to this assembly in general, but almost to every individual whose attention I solicit.—Unconnected with party, I can neither claim the approbation of one part of the house, nor incur the animadversions of the other. I wish to say the little I have to offer without offence to either, & the sole object of my ambition is a patient hearing.——My voice & my vote must be for the Catholics.—⟩ The Catholic question has been so often, so fully & ably discussed, that it would be difficult to urge a new argument for or against it.—But with each succeeding discussion a difficulty has been removed, objections have been canvassed & conquered, & some of the warmest opponents to the petitioners have at length admitted the expediency of their relief.——But granting this, they present another obstacle, perhaps of no very formidable nature, & which whether so or not will one day prove as great an assistance to the Catholics, as it may now seem an argument against them, I mean, my Lords—*Time*—it is not the *time*, say they,—or it is an *improper* time, or there is *time* enough yet.——In this, I in some measure concur with the temporizers, inasmuch, as it is not the *time* I could have wished for the accomplishment of Catholic emancipation, that *time* is past my Lords, the Catholics should have been emancipated before, I should have had much more pleasure in seeing their proper proportion amongst my fellow peers than in discussing their petition.——"Non tempore tali &c" (quote)[1] But excepting the time which is past, it is the best of all times for doing an act of solemn justice & liberal policy, & simply because it is the time present.——It is one of the few opportunities that offer themselves of being at once generous & just.—The enemy is without, & distress within.[2]—It is too late to split upon doctrinal points, when you should unite in defence of other things than the thirty nine articles.[3]—In such an hour, when there should not be

4 individual whose] individual ⟨of⟩ 9 question has] question ⟨itself⟩ 11 against it] against ⟨them⟩ 12 objections have] objections ⟨&⟩ 13 the petitioners] the⟨ir⟩ 14 their relief] their ⟨measure⟩ they present] they ⟨have⟩ 16 an assistance] ⟨a friend⟩ 20 inasmuch, as] inasmuch, ⟨is⟩ 20–1 the accomplishment] the ⟨em⟩ 23 seeing their] seeing ⟨some of⟩

amongst us a cold heart, or an idle hand, must we dispute, not about the God we worship, for in that we are agreed, not about the King we obey, for to him we are loyal, but whether prayers are best made in Latin or English, & how far a crucifix is not an emblem of disaffection.—

We have heard much within & without doors of "Church & State"—with all my heart, we cannot hear them too often, hacknied as they have sometimes been, & watchwords to the meanest purposes; I am for Church & State, the State of Britain & the Church of Christ, but not the low Church, or the high Church, or the intolerant Church, or any church militant which excludes mankind not only from it's spiritual blessing, but all temporal blessings whatsoever.[4]—The Church in itself is possessed of due power, of ample revenues, long may it be the paramount the established church of these realms, but do not let it deprive us of the civil aid of men whose errors are unfortunate but not dangerous, nor exclude a most considerable, useful, & loyal portion of the population from the due participation of rights partly conceded & wholly deserved.—Let us cease then these petty cavils on frivolous points, these Lilliputian sophistries whether "our eggs are best broken at the broad or narrow end."[5]—On all great points Catholics & Protestants may "fear God honour the King" and serve both in perfect Good will.[6]—They have explicitly, openly, abjured with the sanction of the most learned in their universities all the temporal tenets which could alarm the most timid, in meekness have they borne their bondage, in lowliness have they prayed for relief, they have suffered for the sins of their fathers far beyond the period of divine denunciation "to the third & fourth generation"[7] & shall man presume to extend the period of punishment? if you still resist the supplications of Christians can you arrogate the name to yourselves? yes, but you have little to boast beyond your faith & are become the Pharisees of Christianity.[8]——

It was said within the walls of this house, I forget by whom, & am not very anxious to remember, that if the Catholics are to be

1 we dispute] we ⟨squabble⟩ 2 are agreed] are ⟨ag⟩ 3 whether prayers] whether ⟨men whose⟩ 10 Church, or[1]] Church, ⟨&⟩ 11 church militant] church ⟨in preference⟩ from it's] from ⟨the altar⟩ 14 the paramount] the ⟨first⟩ 15 civil aid] civil ⟨of⟩ 19 Lilliputian sophistries] Lilliputian ⟨argumentations⟩ 21 God honour] God ⟨&⟩ 22–3 openly, abjured] openly, ⟨dis⟩ 29 Christians can] Christians ⟨like yourselves⟩ ⟨&⟩ ⟨yet⟩ yourselves? yes] yourselves? ⟨no⟩ 30 have little] have ⟨forfeited one of your own claims to ⟨of⟩⟩ 32 It] ⟨A⟩

emancipated, why not the Jews?[9] to talk of emancipation in the words of Shylock,—

> "Would any of the tribe of Barrabas
> Might have it rather than a Catholic?[10]

is this fair to the Catholics or even to the Protestants? if there are eyes which cannot see the difference between a catholic Chapel & a Synagogue, those eyes are troubled with a "beam which must be plucked out, before they are capable of extracting the mote from their neighbours."[11]—It has been said that the Catholics, with the exception of the higher orders, are not interested in the question, that they are indifferent, & would be perfectly contented to remain as they are.[12]—This paradox is sufficiently contradicted by the present as by all the past petitions, you might as well say that the Negros did not wish to be emancipated, but this is an unfortunate comparison, for you have released them out of the "house of bondage"[13] I believe without any petition on their part, but many from their masters to a contrary purport.[14]——If the question were put to an Irish labourer, whether he desired emancipation, he would probably say that he did not understand you, but if you asked him the difference between himself & his Protestant neighbour, he would state a thousand little grievances the result of his situation which embittered the[15]

and have you then more consideration for a foreign potentate, than your own fellow subjects?[16]—who are confined in durance worse than than the prison of an Usurper,[17] inasmuch as the fetters of the mind are more galling than those of the body.——[18]

[Draft Notes[19]]

Disputes between Latin & Greek Churches during Siege of Constantinople.[20]

Ld. P.—Parliamentary &c.[21]

Paley. &c.[22]

4 Might have] ⟨Had had⟩ 5 is] ⟨if⟩ 11 remain as] remain⟨ed⟩ 20 a thousand] a⟨t⟩ 24 of an] of ⟨Valancy⟩

I.^h D^rum.r[23]
Maltese petition Sicilians &c.[24]
Mice—mountains.[25]

Protestants against all.

Dr. Johnson—&c.—Union—&c.—[26]

Roman Catholic Claims Speech: *Notes* (1812)

Notes

Question often discussed.

Difficulties removed.

Objections to the time—should have been done before.—Too late to cavil on doctrines

Church & State—great Ld. Peterborough

Lilliputian Sophistries.—Cc.[1] & Protestant can agree.—

Opponents divided into 2 classes.

Negros—Catholics contented how & why!—

Not allowed free exercise of Religion.—in the Army.—Bill for embodying Chaplains would have doubled the army.—Irish Ma. privilege. Duke of B's Adm.[2] granted as a favour although in 1793 established as a right.

Church cannot build Chapels but on leases of trust & sufferance these often betrayed—Instance at the town of Newton Barry 1806. Complaint in vain.—

Every pelting "petty" Officer—Schoolboy &c. laws for protection of worship useless.—

Trial by Jury—Sheriffs &c under Sheriffs.—Enniskillen Assizes case of Mc. Vournagh—Yeoman—acquittal—Justice Osborne.—Chaplains in

Jails law evaded in Co Fermanagh—Sus Cler presented—Je Fletcher—Gd.[3] Jury—

Such is law for the Catholic

Catholic endowments—Comers.[4] of Charitable donations.—

Maynooth College—Ld. C.[5] Bedford. Clergy.—

Protestant Charter Schools—41000.—Janizaries—Gypsies Case of Mr. Carthy's nieces at Coolgreny.—

Cathecism.——Paley—Tythes—Per Centage—Proctors

Orange lodges.

Those who assert the Cc are dissatisfied—like the Drummer who would not flog a friend to his satisfaction.—

Jews—Dr. Johnson—Fire in the deluge.—Antediluvians. "Caput Insanibile"—Protestants like Bayle.—Mice, Mountains.

Suppose the Irish did not wish we ought for our own sakes.—Value of Irish aid—Militia—Ld. Wellington. His brother—Difference between our foreign & domestic policy—

Union—

Ministers,—popularity Like the Wind——why—Midland Counties—Scotland—Ireland—City—Temple Bar Livery Bankrupts—Stockholders.—

Statues Walcheren—France——Catholics—Ln.[6] of Honour.—Well merited Consequence.

What they really are in public estimation.—

Roman Catholic Claims Speech (1812)

My lords; the question before the House has been so frequently, fully and ably discussed, and never perhaps more ably than on this night; that it would be difficult to adduce new arguments for or against

10 Those] ⟨Contented Catholics⟩ Those

it. But with each discussion, difficulties have been removed, objections have been canvassed and refuted, and some of the former opponents of Catholic Emancipation have at length conceded to the expediency of relieving the petitioners. In conceding thus much however, a new objection is started; it is not the time, say they, or it is an improper time, or there is time enough yet. In some degree I concur with those who say, it is not the time exactly; that time is past; better had it been for the country, that the Catholics possessed at this moment their proportion of our privileges, that their nobles held their due weight in our councils, than that we should be assembled to discuss their claims. It had indeed been better

> "Non tempore tali
> Cogere concilium cum muros obsidet hostis."[1]

The enemy is without, and distress within. It is too late to cavil on doctrinal points, when we must unite in defence of things more important than the mere ceremonies of religion.[2] It is indeed singular, that we are called together to deliberate, not on the God we adore, for in that we are agreed; not about the King we obey, for to him we are loyal; but how far a difference in the ceremonials of worship, how far believing not too little, but too much, (the worst that can be imputed to the Catholics,) how far too much devotion to their God, may incapacitate our fellow-subjects from effectually serving their King.

Much has been said, within and without doors, of Church and State,[3] and although those venerable words have been too often prostituted to the most despicable of party purposes, we cannot hear them too often; all, I presume, are the advocates of Church and State, the Church of Christ, and the state of Great Britain; but not a state of exclusion and of despotism, not an intolerant Church, not a Church militant,[4] which renders itself liable to the very objection urged against the Romish communion, and in a greater degree, for the Catholic merely withholds its spiritual benediction, (and even that is doubtful,) but our Church, or rather our churchmen, not only refuse to the Catholic their spiritual grace, but all temporal blessings whatsoever. It was an observation of the great lord Peterborough, made within these walls, or within the walls where the Lords then assembled, that he was for a "Parliamentary king and a parliamentary constitution, but not a parliamentary God and a parliamentary religion."[5] The interval of a century has not weakened the force of the remark. It is indeed time that we should leave off these petty cavils on frivolous points, these Lilliputian sophistries, whether our "eggs are best broken at the broad or narrow end."[6]

The opponents of the Catholics may be divided into two classes; those who assert that the Catholics have too much already, and those who allege that the lower orders, at least, have nothing more to require. We are told by the former, that the Catholics never will be contented: by the latter, that they are already too happy.[7] The last paradox is sufficiently refuted by the present as by all past Petitions; it might as well be said, that the negroes did not desire to be emancipated, but this is an unfortunate comparison, for you have already delivered them out of the house of bondage[8] without any Petition on their part, but many from their task-masters to a contrary effect;[9] and for myself, when I consider this, I pity the Catholic peasantry for not having the good fortune to be born black. But the Catholics are contented, or at least ought to be, as we are told; I shall therefore proceed to touch on a few of those circumstances which so marvellously contribute to their exceeding contentment. They are not allowed the free exercise of their religion in the regular army; the Catholic soldier cannot absent himself from the service of the Protestant clergyman, and unless he is quartered in Ireland or in Spain, where can he find eligible opportunities of attending his own?[10] The permission of Catholic chaplains to the Irish militia regiments was conceded as a special favour, and not till after years of remonstrance, although an Act, passed in 1793, established it as a right.[11] But are the Catholics properly protected in Ireland? Can the Church purchase a rood of land whereon to erect a chapel? No! all the places of worship are built on leases of trust or sufferance from the laity, easily broken and often betrayed.[12] The moment any irregular wish, any casual caprice of the benevolent landlord meets with opposition, the doors are barred against the congregation. This has happened continually, but in no instance more glaringly, than at the town of Newton Barry in the county of Wexford. The Catholics enjoying no regular chapel, as a temporary expedient, hired two barns; which being thrown into one, served for public worship. At this time, there was quartered opposite to the spot, an officer whose mind appears to have been deeply imbued with those prejudices which the Protestant Petitions now on the table, prove to have been fortunately eradicated from the more rational portion of the people;[13] and when the Catholics were assembled on the Sabbath as usual, in peace and goodwill towards men,[14] for the worship of their God and yours, they found the chapel door closed, and were told that if they did not immediately retire, (and they were told this by a Yeoman officer and a magistrate,) the Riot Act should be read, and the assembly dispersed at the point of the bayonet! This was complained of to the middle man of government, the Secretary at the Castle in 1806, and the answer was, (in lieu of redress,) that he would cause a letter to be written to the colonel, to prevent, if possible, the recurrence of similar disturbances.[15] Upon this fact no very great stress need be laid; but it tends to prove that while the Catholic Church has not power to purchase land for its chapels to stand upon, the laws for its protection are of no avail. In the mean time, the Catholics are at the mercy of every "pelting petty officer," who may choose to play his "fantastic tricks before high heaven,"[16] to insult his God, and injure his fellow creatures.

Every school-boy, any foot-boy, (such have held commissions in our service) any foot-boy who can exchange his shoulder-knot for an epaulet, may perform all this and more against the Catholic, by virtue of that very authority delegated to him by his sovereign, for the express purpose of defending his fellow subjects to the last drop of his blood, without discrimination or distinction between Catholic and Protestant.

Have the Irish Catholics the full benefit of trial by jury? They have not; they never can have until they are permitted to share the privilege of serving as sheriffs and under-sheriffs.[17] Of this a striking example occurred at the last Enniskillen assizes.—A yeoman was arraigned for the murder of a Catholic named Macvournagh; three respectable uncontradicted witnesses deposed that they saw the prisoner load, take aim, fire at, and kill the said Macvournagh. This was properly commented on by the judge; but to the astonishment of the bar, and indignation of the court, the Protestant jury acquitted the accused. So glaring was the partiality, that Mr. Justice Osborne felt it his duty to bind over the acquitted, but not absolved assassin in large recognizances; thus for a time taking away his licence to kill Catholics.[18]

Are the very laws passed in their favour observed? They are rendered nugatory in trivial as in serious cases. By a late act, Catholic chaplains are permitted in jails,[19] but in Fermanagh county the grand jury lately persisted in presenting a suspended clergyman for the office, thereby evading the statute, notwithstanding the most pressing remonstrances of a most respectable magistrate named Fletcher to the contrary.[20] Such is law, such is justice, for the happy, free, contented Catholic!

It has been asked in another place, why do not the rich Catholics endow foundations for the education of the priesthood?[21] Why do you not permit them to do so? Why are all such bequests subject to the interference, the vexatious, arbitrary, peculating interference of the Orange commissioners for charitable donations?[22]

As to Maynooth college, in no instance except at the time of its foundation, when a noble lord, (Camden) at the head of the Irish administration, did appear to interest himself in its advancement; and during the government of a noble duke, (Bedford) who, like his ancestors, has ever been the friend of freedom and mankind, and who has not so far adopted the selfish policy of the day as to exclude the Catholics from the number of his fellow-creatures; with these exceptions, in no instance has that institution been properly encouraged.[23] There was indeed a time when the Catholic clergy were conciliated, while the Union was pending, that Union which could not be carried without them, while their assistance was requisite in procuring addresses from the Catholic counties; then they were cajoled and caressed, feared and flattered, and given to understand that "the Union would do every thing;" but the moment it was passed, they were driven back with contempt into their former obscurity.[24]

In the conduct pursued towards Maynooth college, every thing is done to irritate and perplex—every thing is done to efface the slightest impression of gratitude from the Catholic mind; the very hay made upon the lawn, the fat and tallow of the beef and mutton allowed must be paid for and accounted upon oath.[25] It is true, this economy in miniature cannot sufficiently be commended, particularly at a time when only the insect defaulters of the Treasury, your Hunts and your Chinnerys,[26] when only those "gilded bugs"[27] can escape the microscopic eye of ministers. But when you come forward session after session, as your paltry pittance is wrung from you with wrangling and reluctance, to boast of your liberality, well might the Catholic exclaim in the words of Prior—

"To John I owe some obligation,
But John unluckily thinks fit
To publish it to all the nation,
So John and I are more than quit."[28]

Some persons have compared the Catholics to the beggar in Gil Blas:[29] Who made them beggars? Who are enriched with the spoils of their ancestors? And cannot you relieve the beggar when your fathers have made him such? If you are disposed to relieve him at all, cannot you do it without flinging your farthings in his face?—As a contrast, however, to this beggarly benevolence, let us look at the Protestant Charter Schools; to them you have lately granted 41,000*l.*:[30] thus are they supported, and how are they recruited? Montesquieu observes on the English constitution, that the model may be found in Tacitus, where the historian describes the policy of the Germans, and adds—"this beautiful system was taken from the woods;"[31] so in speaking of the charter schools it may be observed, that this beautiful system was taken from the gypsies. These schools are recruited in the same manner as the janissaries at the time of their enrolment under Amurath,[32] and the gypsies of the present day with stolen children, with children decoyed and kidnapped from their Catholic connections by their rich and powerful Protestant neighbours: this is notorious, and one instance may suffice to shew in what manner.—The sister of a Mr. Carthy, (a Catholic gentleman of very considerable property,) died, leaving two girls, who were immediately marked out as proselytes, and conveyed to the charter school of Coolgreny; their uncle, on being apprized of the fact, which took place during his absence, applied for the restitution of his nieces, offering to settle an independence on these his relations; his request was refused, and not till after five years struggle, and the interference of very high authority, could this Catholic gentleman obtain back his nearest of kindred from a charity charter school.[33] In this manner are proselytes obtained, and mingled with the offspring of such Protestants as may avail themselves of the institution. And how are they taught? A catechism is put into their hands, consisting of, I believe, 45 pages, in which are three questions relative to the Protestant religion; one of these queries is, "where was the Protestant religion before Luther?" Answer, "in the Gospel." The remaining forty-four pages and a half, regard the damnable idolatry of Papists![34]

Allow me to ask our spiritual pastors and masters, is this training up a child in the way which he should go?—is this the religion of the Gospel before the time of Luther? that religion which preaches "Peace on earth and glory to God?"[35] Is it bringing up infants to be men or devils? Better would it be to send them any where than teach them such doctrines; better send them to those islands in the South Seas, where they might more humanely learn to become cannibals; it would be less disgusting that they were brought up to devour the dead, than persecute the living. Schools do you call them? call them rather dunghills, where the viper of intolerance deposits her young, that when their teeth are cut and their poison is mature, they may issue forth, filthy and venomous, to sting the Catholic. But are these the doctrines of the Church of England, or of Churchmen? No, the most enlightened Churchmen are of a different opinion. What says Paley? "I perceive no reason why men of different religious persuasions should not sit upon the same bench, deliberate in the same council, or fight in the same ranks, as well as men of various religious opinions, upon any controverted topic of natural history, philosophy, or ethics!"[36] It may be answered, that Paley was not strictly orthodox; I know nothing of his orthodoxy, but who will deny that he was an ornament to the Church, to human nature, to Christianity?

I shall not dwell upon the grievance of tythes, so severely felt by the peasantry, but it may be proper to observe, that there is an addition to the burthen, a per centage to the gatherer, whose interest it thus becomes to rate them as highly as possible, and we know that in many large livings in Ireland, the only resident Protestants are the tythe proctor and his family.[37]

Amongst many causes of irritation, too numerous for recapitulation, there is one in the militia not to be passed over, I mean the existence of Orange lodges amongst the privates;[38] can the officers deny this? and if such lodges do exist, do they, can they tend to promote harmony amongst the men, who are thus individually separated in society, although mingled in the ranks? And is this general system of persecution to be permitted, or is it to be believed that with such a system the Catholics can or ought to be contented? If they are, they belie human nature; they are then, indeed, unworthy to be any thing but the slaves you have made them. The facts stated are from most respectable authority, or I should not have dared in this place, or any place, to hazard this avowal. If exaggerated, there are plenty as willing, as I believe them to be unable, to disprove them. Should it be objected that I never was in Ireland, I beg leave to observe, that it is as easy to know something of Ireland without having been there, as it appears with some to have been born, bred, and cherished there, and yet remain ignorant of its best interests.

But there are, who assert that the Catholics have already been too much indulged; see (cry they) what has been done, we have given them one entire college, we allow them food and raiment, the full enjoyment of the elements, and leave to fight for us as long as they have limbs and lives to offer, and yet they are never to be satisfied! Generous and just declaimers![39] to this, and to this only, amount the whole of your arguments, when stripped of their sophistry. Those personages remind me of a story of a certain drummer, who being called upon in the course of duty to administer punishment to a friend tied to the halberts, was requested to flog high, he did—to flog low, he did—to flog in the middle, he did—high, low, down the middle, and up again, but all in vain, the patient continued his complaints with the most provoking pertinacity, until the drummer, exhausted and angry, flung down his scourge, exclaiming, "the devil burn you, there's no pleasing you, flog where one will!"[40] Thus it is, you have flogged the Catholic high, low, here, there, and every where, and then you wonder he is not pleased. It is true, that time, experience, and that weariness which attends even the exercise of barbarity, have taught you to flog a little more gently, but still you continue to lay on the lash, and will so continue, till perhaps the rod may be wrested from your hands and applied to the backs of yourselves and your posterity.[41]

It was said by somebody in a former debate, (I forget by whom, and am not very anxious to remember) if the Catholics are emancipated, why not the Jews?[42] If this sentiment was dictated by compassion for the Jews, it might deserve attention, but as a sneer against the Catholic, what is it but the language of Shylock transferred from his daughter's marriage to Catholic emancipation—

> "Would any of the tribe of Barrabbas
> Should have it rather than a Christian."[43]

I presume a Catholic is a Christian, even in the opinion of him whose taste only can be called in question for his preference of the Jews.

It is a remark often quoted of Dr. Johnson, (whom I take to be almost as good authority as the gentle apostle of intolerance, Dr. Duigenan)[44] that he who could entertain serious apprehensions of danger to the Church in these times, would have "cried fire in the deluge."[45] This is more than a metaphor, for a remnant of these antediluvians appear actually to have come down to us, with fire in their mouths and water in their brains, to disturb and perplex mankind with their whimsical outcries. And as it is an infallible symptom of that distressing malady with which I conceive them to be afflicted, (so any doctor will inform you lordships) for the unhappy invalids to perceive a flame perpetually flashing before their eyes, particularly when their eyes are shut, (as those of the persons to whom I allude have long been) it is impossible to convince these poor creatures, that the fire against which they are perpetually warning us and themselves, is nothing but an Ignis fatuus of their own drivelling imaginations. "What rhubarb, senna, or what purgative drug can scour that fancy thence?"[46]—it is impossible, they are given over, theirs is the true

"Caput insanabile tribus Anticyrus."[47]

These are your true Protestants. Like Bayle, who protested against all sects whatsoever,[48] so do they protest against Catholic Petitions, Protestant Petitions, all redress, all that reason, humanity, policy, justice, and common-sense, can urge against the delusions of their absurd delirium. These are the persons who reverse the fable of the mountain that brought forth a mouse, they are the mice who conceive themselves in labour with mountains.[49]

To return to the Catholics. Suppose the Irish were actually contented under their disabilities, suppose them capable of such a bull[50] as not to desire deliverance, ought we not to wish it for ourselves? Have we nothing to gain by their emancipation? What resources have been wasted? what talents have been lost by the selfish system of exclusion? You already know the value of Irish aid; at this moment the defence of England is entrusted to the Irish militia;[51] at this moment, while the starving people are rising in the fierceness of despair, the Irish are faithful to their trust. But till equal energy is imparted throughout by the extension of freedom, you cannot enjoy the full benefit of the strength which you are glad to interpose between you and destruction. Ireland has done much, but will do more. At this moment, the only triumph obtained through long years of continental disaster has been achieved by an Irish general;[52] it is true he is not a Catholic, had he been so, we should have been deprived of his exertions, but I presume no one will assert that his religion would have impaired his talents or diminished his patriotism, though in that case he must have conquered in the ranks, for he never could have commanded an army.[53]

But he is fighting the battles of the Catholics abroad, his noble brother has this night advocated their cause, with an eloquence which I shall not depreciate by the humble tribute of my panegyric,[54] whilst a third of his kindred, as unlike as unequal, has been combating against his Catholic brethren in Dublin, with circular letters, edicts, proclamations, arrests and dispersions—all the vexatious implements of petty warfare that could be wielded by the mercenary guerillas of government, clad in the rusty armour of their obsolete statutes.[55] Your lordships will, doubtless, divide new honours between the Saviour of

Portugal, and the Disperser of Delegates.[56] It is singular, indeed, to observe the difference between our foreign and domestic policy; if Catholic Spain, faithful Portugal, or the no less Catholic and faithful king of the one Sicily (of which, by the bye, you have lately deprived him)[57] stand in need of succour, away goes a fleet and an army, an ambassador and a subsidy, sometimes to fight pretty hardly, generally to negociate very badly, and always to pay very dearly for our Popish allies.[58] But let four millions of fellow subjects pray for relief, who fight and pay and labour in your behalf, they must be treated as aliens, and although their "father's house has many mansions"[59] there is no resting place for them. Allow me to ask, are you not fighting for the emancipation of Ferdinand 7, who certainly is a fool, and consequently, in all probability, a bigot;[60] and have you more regard for a foreign sovereign than your own fellow subjects, who are not fools, for they know your interest better than you know your own; who are not bigots, for they return you good for evil, but who are in worse durance than the prison of an usurper,[61] inasmuch as the fetters of the mind are more galling than those of the body.[62]

Upon the consequences of your not acceding to the claims of the Petitioners, I shall not expatiate, you know them, you will feel them, and your children's children when you are passed away. Adieu to that Union so called as "Lucus a non lucendo,"[63] an Union from never uniting, which in its first operation gave a death-blow to the independence of Ireland, and in its last may be the cause of her eternal separation from this country. If it must be called an Union, it is the union of the shark with his prey, the spoiler swallows up his victim, and thus they become one and indivisible. Thus has Great Britain swallowed up the parliament, the constitution, the independence of Ireland, and refuses to disgorge even a single privilege, although for the relief of her swollen and distempered body politic.

And now, my lords, before I sit down, will his Majesty's ministers permit me to say a few words, not on their merits, for that would be superfluous, but on the degree of estimation in which they are held by the people of these realms. The esteem in which they are held has been boasted of in a triumphant tone on a late occasion within these walls, and a comparison instituted between their conduct, and that of noble lords on this side of the House.[64]

What portion of popularity may have fallen to the share of my noble friends (if such I may presume to call them) I shall not pretend to ascertain; but that of his Majesty's ministers it were vain to deny. It is, to be sure, a little like the wind, "no one knows whence it cometh or whither it goeth,"[65] but they feel it, they enjoy it, they boast of it. Indeed, modest and unostentatious as they are, to what part of the kingdom, even the most remote, can they flee to avoid the triumph which pursues them. If they plunge into the midland counties, there will they be greeted by the manufacturers, with spurned petitions in their hands, and those halters round their necks recently voted in their behalf, imploring blessings on the heads of those who so simply, yet ingeniously, contrived to remove them from their miseries in this to a better world. If they journey on to Scotland, from Glasgow to Johnny Groat's, every where will they receive similar marks of approbation?[66] If they take a trip from Portpatrick to Donaghadee, there will they rush at once into the embraces of four Catholic millions, to whom their vote of this night is about to endear them for ever. When they return to the metropolis, if they can pass under Temple Bar without unpleasant sensations at the sight of the greedy niches over that ominous gateway,[67] they cannot escape the acclamations of the livery, and the more tremulous, but not less sincere, applause, the blessings "not loud but deep"[68] of bankrupt merchants and doubting stock-holders.[69] If they look to the army, what wreaths, not of laurel, but of night-shade, are preparing for the heroes of Walcheren.[70] It is true there are few living deponents left to testify to their merits on that occasion; but a 'cloud of witnesses'[71] are gone above from that gallant army which they so generously and piously dispatched, to recruit the "noble army of martyrs."[72]

What if in the course of this triumphal career, (in which they will gather as many pebbles as Caligula's army did on a similar triumph, the prototype of their own)[73] they do not perceive any of those memorials which a grateful people erect in honour of their benefactors; what although not even a sign-post will condescend to depose the Saracen's head[74] in favour of the likeness of the conquerors of Walcheren, they will not want a picture who can always have a caricature; or regret the omission of a statue who will so often see themselves exalted in effigy. But their popularity is not limited to the narrow bounds of an island; there are other countries where their measures, and above all, their conduct to the Catholics must render them preeminently popular. If they are beloved here, in France they must be adored. There is no measure more repugnant to the designs and feelings of Buonaparte than Catholic Emancipation;[75] no line of conduct more propitious to his projects than that which has been pursued, is pursuing, and, I fear, will be pursued, towards Ireland.[76] What is England without Ireland, and what is Ireland without the Catholics? It is on the basis of your tyranny Napoleon hopes to build his own. So grateful must oppression of the Catholics be to his mind, that doubtless (as he has lately permitted some renewal of intercourse) the next cartel will convey to this country cargoes of seve-china,[77] and blue ribbands (things in great request, and of equal value at this moment) blue ribbands of the Legion of Honour for Dr. Duigenan and his ministerial disciples.[78] Such is that well-earned popularity, the result of those extraordinary expeditions, so expensive to ourselves and so useless to our allies; of those singular enquiries, so exculpatory to the accused and so dissatisfactory to the people; of those paradoxical victories, so honourable, as we are told, to the British name, and so destructive to the best interests of the British nation: above all, such is the reward of the conduct pursued by ministers towards the Catholics.

I have to apologise to the House, who will, I trust, pardon one, not often in the habit of intruding upon their indulgence, for so long attempting to engage their attention. My most decided opinion is, as my vote will be, in favour of the motion.

Presentation of Major Cartwright's Petition (1813)

My lords, the Petition which I now hold for the purpose of presenting to the House, is one which I humbly conceive requires the particular attention of your lordships, inasmuch as, though signed but by a single individual, it contains statements which (if not disproved) demand most serious investigation. The grievance of which the petitioner complains, is neither selfish nor imaginary. It is not his own only, for it has been, and is still felt by numbers. No one without these walls, nor indeed within, but may to-morrow be made liable to the same insult and obstruction, in the discharge of an imperious duty for the restoration of the true constitution of these realms, by petitioning for reform in parliament. The petitioner, my lords, is a man whose long life has been spent in one unceasing struggle for the liberty of the subject, against that undue influence which has increased, is increasing, and ought to be diminished;[1] and whatever difference of opinion may exist as to his political tenets, few will be found to question the integrity of his intentions. Even now oppressed with years, and not exempt from the infirmities attendant on his age, but still unimpaired in talent and unshaken in spirit—"*frangas non flectes*"[2]—he has received many a wound in the combat against corruption; and the new grievance, the fresh insult of which he complains, may inflict another scar, but no dishonour. The Petition is signed by John Cartwright, and it was in behalf of the people and parliament, in the lawful pursuit of that reform in the representation, which is the best service to be rendered both to parliament and to people, that he encountered the wanton outrage which forms the subject matter of his Petition to your lordships. It is couched in firm, yet respectful language—in the language of a man, not regardless of what is due to himself, but at the same time, I trust, equally mindful of the deference to be paid to this House. The petitioner states, amongst other matter of equal, if not greater importance, to all who are British in their feelings, as well as blood and birth, that on the 21st January, 1813, at Huddersfield, himself and six other persons, who, on hearing of his arrival, had waited on him merely as a testimony of respect, were seized by a military and civil force, and kept in close custody for several hours, subjected to gross and abusive insinuation from the commanding officer, relative to the character of the petitioner; that he (the petitioner) was finally carried before a magistrate and not released till an examination of his papers proved that there was not only no just, but not even statutable charge against him; and that, notwithstanding the promise and order from the presiding magistrates of a copy of the warrant against your petitioner, it was afterwards withheld on divers pretexts, and has never until this hour been granted.[3] The names and condition of the parties will be found in the Petition. To the other topics touched upon in the Petition, I shall not now advert, from a wish not to encroach upon the time of the House; but I do most sincerely call the attention of your lordships to its general contents—it is in the cause of the parliament and people that the rights of this venerable freeman have been violated, and it is, in my opinion, the highest mark of respect that could be paid to the House, that to your justice, rather than by appeal to any inferior court, he now commits himself.[4] Whatever may be the fate of his remonstrance, it is some satisfaction to me, though mixed with regret for the occasion, that I have this opportunity of publicly stating the obstruction to which the subject is liable, in the prosecution of the most lawful and imperious of his duties, the obtaining by Petition reform in parliament. I have shortly stated his complaint; the petitioner has more fully expressed it. Your lordships will, I hope, adopt some measure fully[5] to protect and redress him, and not him alone, but the whole body of the people insulted and aggrieved in his person, by the interposition of an abused civil, and unlawful military force between them and their right of petition to their own representatives.[6] [. . .]

Lord *Byron* replied, that he had, from motives of duty, presented this petition to their lordships' consideration.[7] The noble earl had contended, that it was not a petition, but a speech; and that, as it contained no prayer, it should not be received.[8] What was the necessity of a prayer? If that word were to be used in its proper sense, their lordships could not expect that any man should pray to others. He had only to say, that the Petition, though in some parts expressed strongly perhaps, did not contain any improper mode of address, but was couched in respectful language towards their lordships; he should therefore trust their lordships would allow the Petition to be received.

WRITINGS
(1813–1816)

Bramblebear and Lady Penelope: A Chapter of a Novel
(1813)

LETTERS.

— J —, 180–.

— Darrell to G.Y.

(*The first part of this letter is lost.*)[1]

***** So much for your present pursuits. I will now resume the subject of my last. How I wish you were upon the spot; your taste for the ridiculous would be fully gratified; and if you felt inclined for more serious amusement, there is no 'lack of argument.'[2] Within this last week our guests have been doubled in number, some of them my old acquaintance. Our host you already know—absurd as ever, but rather duller, and I should conceive troublesome to such of his very good friends as find his house more agreeable than its owner. I confine myself to observation, and do not find him at all in the way, though Veramore and Asply are of a different opinion. The former, in particular, imparts to me many pathetic complaints on the want of opportunities (nothing else being wanting to the success of the said Veramore,) created by the fractious and but ill-concealed jealousy of poor Bramblebear, whose Penelope seems to have as many suitors as her namesake, and for aught I can see to the contrary, with as much prospect of carrying their point. In the mean time, I look on and laugh, or rather, I should laugh were you present to share in it: Sackcloth and sorrow are excellent wear for Soliloquy;[3] but for a laugh there should be two, but not many more, except at the first night of a modern tragedy.

1 LETTERS.] LETTER I. 2 — J — , 180–.] Not in *Sir F.D.* 3 — Darrell to G.Y.] *Sir Francis Darrell to the Hon. Lewis Vernon.* Bramblebear Hall. 4 (*The first part of this letter is lost.*)] Not in *Sir F.D.* 8 this] the 11 conceive troublesome] conceive very troublesome 13–14 way, though Veramore] way. Veramore 16 wanting] wanted 20 their] the 22 but] and

You are very much mistaken in the design you impute to myself; I have *none* here or elsewhere. I am sick of old intrigues, and too indolent to engage in new ones. Besides, I am, that is, I used to be, apt to find my heart gone at the very time when you fastidious gentlemen begin to recover yours. I agree with you that the world, as well as yourself, are of a different opinion. I shall never be at the trouble to undeceive either; my follies have seldom been of my own seeking. 'Rebellion came in my way and I found it.'[4] This may appear as coxcombical a speech as Veramore could make, yet *you* partly know its truth. You talk to me too of 'my character,' and yet it is one which you and fifty others have been struggling these seven years to obtain for yourselves. I wish you had it, you would make so much *better*, that is *worse*, use of it; relieve me, and gratify an ambition which is unworthy of a man of sense. It has always appeared to me extraordinary that you should value women so highly and yet love them so little. The height of your gratification ceases with its accomplishment; you bow—and you sigh—and you worship—and abandon. For my part I regard them as a very beautiful but inferior animal. I think them as much out of their place at our tables as they would be in our senates. The whole present system, with regard to that sex, is a remnant of the chivalrous barbarism of our ancestors; I look upon them as grown up children, but, like a foolish mamma, am always the slave of some *only* one. With a contempt for the race, I am ever attached to the individual, in spite of *myself*. You know, that though not rude, I am inattentive; any thing but a 'beau garçon.'[5] I would not hand a woman out of her carriage, but I would leap into a river after her. However, I grant you that, as they must walk oftener out of chariots than into the Thames, you gentlemen Servitors, Cortejos, and Cicisbei,[6] have a better chance of being agreeable and useful; *you* might, very probably, do both; but, as you can't swim, and I can, I recommend you to invite me to your first water-party.

Bramblebear's Lady Penelope puzzles me. She is very beautiful, but not one of my beauties. You know I admire a different complexion, but the figure is perfect. She is accomplished, if her mother and music-master may be believed; amiable, if a soft voice and a sweet smile could make her so; young, even by the register of her baptism; pious

2–5 I am sick . . . recover yours.] Omitted in *Sir F.D.* 7 either] it 11 these seven years] for years 22 am always the slave of some *only* one.] I pet some *only* one. 23 attached to] pleased with 32 She is very beautiful] She is beautiful and chaste, and doting on her husband, according to Bramblebear's observation; equally loving, *not* of her husband, though rather less pious, and *t'other* thing, according to Veramore's; and, if mine hath any discernment, she detests the one, despises the other, and loves—herself. That she dislikes Bramblebear is evident; poor soul, I can't blame her; she has found him out to be mighty weak, and *little*-tempered; she has also discovered that she married too early to know what she liked, and that there are many likeable people who would have been less discordant and more creditable partners. Still she conducts herself well, and in point of good-humour, to admiration.—A good deal of religion, (*not* enthusiasm, for that leads the contrary way[7]), a prying husband who never leaves her, and, as I think, a very temperate pulse, will keep her out of scrapes. I am glad of it, first, because, though Bramblebear is bad, I don't think Veramore much better; and next, because Bramblebear is ridiculous enough already, and it would only be *thrown* away upon him to make him more so; thirdly, it would be a pity, because no body *would pity* him; and, fourthly, (as Scrub says)[8] he would then become a melancholy and sentimental harlequin,[9] instead of a merry, fretful, pantaloon, and I like the pantomime better as it is now cast.

More in my next.

Yours, truly,
— Darrell.

Leake's *Researches in Greece* (1815)

Without possessing Major L's skill in diplomacy and artillery—without aspiring to the composition of a Polyglott Grammar—and but too happy to circumscribe our sins against the moods & tenses to fewer tongues—and dialects than our author—it may still have been our fortune to have traversed no inconsiderable portion of the provinces where he accumulated his compilation.—There—without having carried out with us a larger share of the ancient—or acquired upon the

1 doting] doating 3 *t'other* thing] *t'other thing* 3–4 if mine hath any discernment] according to mine 17 *would pity*] would *pity* 23 — Darrell.] F. Darrell. 24 in diplomacy] in ⟨the nearly connected⟩ 26 to circumscribe] to ⟨confine⟩ to fewer] to ⟨one language only⟩ 28 portion] portion⟨s⟩ 30 us a] us ⟨more⟩

spot much more of the modern languages than has enabled us to prove that the Major knows nothing of the one—and rather worse than nothing of the other or *just enough to blunder withal*—it was with peculiar gratification that we seized such opportunities as are offered to the traveller—of observing countries and nations where intercourse with our own shores is still partial & limited.——

At a time when the Russian Alexander so celebrated for magnanimity and waltzing may be meditating in the bounty of his heart the same deliverance of Greece and Constantinople which he has already accorded to France—Saxony and Poland[1]—every country which probability renders liable to Muscovite liberation becomes an object of some interest in the eye of Great Britain where government will doubtless have something to do with the matter when time and taxes permit.[2]—The obstacles to the accomplishment of such a plan are not apparently very great to the Conquerors of Napoleon——unless the difficulties of enlisting an invading army—and the united spirit of patriotism—religion—and the most decided nationality should enable the Mussulmans—as it did the Spaniards to oppose an obstinate and protracted resistance to their proposed expulsion.[3]——Austria in particular since the days of Eugene has had reason to repent her aggressions on the Turkish side—and even that greatest of her Generals experienced a temporary check on the side of Bosnia from her warlike & bigotted population—although the fields of Peterwaradin & Belgrade confirmed his final triumph.[4]—But the war of 1737–8–9—was a contest of uniform disgrace and discomfiture—and in 1788—the desolation of the Bannat—& the defeat on the heights of Caransebes taught the Emperor Joseph and the finest army ever sent by Austria into the field—that "the battle is not always to the strong"[5] nor even to the skilful & the unjust.[6]————

Were a new Kuperli to arise amongst them—or an enterprising Renegade such as Bonneval[7]—much might be done—less perhaps by attempting totally to reform their warfare to the model of European tactics—than by partial amendment and sounder direction of their

1–2 prove that] prove ⟨perhaps⟩ 2 knows nothing] knows ⟨rather⟩ and rather] and ⟨j⟩ 5 of observing] of ⟨[*illegible?*] His own int⟩ ⟨observing⟩ 6 still partial] still ⟨so⟩ 7 the Russian] the ⟨magnanimous⟩ 9 deliverance of] deliverance ⟨f⟩ 10 to France] to ⟨Sax⟩ 12 eye] eye⟨s⟩ Britain where] Britain ⟨which⟩ 22 Bosnia from] Bosnia ⟨—thou⟩ 24 Belgrade confirmed] Belgrade ⟨have effaced⟩ 26 the desolation] the ⟨rou⟩ 30 Kuperli] K⟨i⟩uperli 31 Bonneval—much] Bonneval—⟨or⟩ 32 to reform] to ⟨adapt⟩ 33 and sounder] and ⟨directing⟩

own peculiar mode of attack:—all the materials for the first of armies might be found in Turkey—numbers courage—strength—temperance—long suffering—and individual skill in the use of weapons—every Mussulman is born a soldier—their present military establishment is at least equal in "*material*" to what the Portuguese possessed before the invasion of Junot[8]—and a similar cause—a contest for existence—might produce similar effects—repulse to the enemy—& renovation to the people.——

These are however unprofitable & probably not popular speculations—but should the moment arrive that strikes the Crescent from the minarets of Constantinople—the command of the isles & of the waters may rouse a more Gigantic and not less stubborn competitor for naval supremacy—in the Meditteranean[9]—than America has marshalled but too successfully against our baffled flag in the Atlantic.[10]———

A Letter on the State of French Affairs (1815)

July 29th 1815.

Sir/

From the list of the Proscribed which is published in the French official paper—it should seem that the twice expelled Louis the desired is firmly fixed in his desirable situation.—It is well—"shed blood enough old Renault"[1]—Paris is filled with foreign troops—the army is or is to be disbanded—Bonaparte a helpless exile—and last not least Lord Castlereagh British Minister.[2]—All these are powerful sanctions to the measures about to be adopted in France—and whatever be the result not a life about to be shortened will be sacrificed in vain.—But let us look to the actual position of the person assisted by the allies & the newspapers to be sovereign of France.[3]——It were superfluous to allude to the personal character of the present repre-

1 attack:—all] attack ⟨to the⟩ 1–2 armies might] armies ⟨may⟩ 3 long suffering] long ⟨courage⟩ 6 Junot—and] Junot—⟨and⟩ 10 the moment] the ⟨tim⟩ moment arrive] moment ⟨come⟩ 11 the command] the ⟨dominion⟩ of the isles] of ⟨the seas⟩ 13 supremacy—in] supremacy—⟨than⟩ 19–20 desired is] desired ⟨has be⟩ 20 is firmly] is ⟨restored to⟩ 23 Castlereagh British] Castlereagh ⟨our foreign⟩ 23–4 powerful sanctions] powerful ⟨motives for⟩ 26 person assisted] person ⟨who aided and⟩

sentative of the Bourbons. Strict in devotion—skilful in cooking—kind to his favourites—a good & probably a mild man but—a martyr to the Gout—the allies & his new subjects—between the disorders of his person & his government his few remaining years will be probably embittered by his physicians & his own & foreign ministers.——He is understood to have selected for his premier—a remarkable & judiciously chosen individual.[4]—This man—the renegade from all religions—the betrayer of every trust—the traitor to every government—the Arch Apostle of all apostasy—Ex-bishop—Ex-royalist Ex-citizen—ex-republican—Ex-minister—Ex-prince—whose name every honest lip quivers to pronounce—the very thought of whom is a pollution from which the imagination struggles to escape—this living record of all that public Treason private Treachery and moral Infamy can accumulate in the person of one degraded being—is the organ of the regenerated government of France.—

The Tale of Calil (1816)

March 14th 1816.

Demir Bash was born in the city of Samarcand in the 800th year of the Hegira:[1] his father and mother quarrelled before his birth and never agreed after it; the cause of difference was whether their son (the Stars had foretold it would be a son) should be called Demir *Bash* or Demir *T*ash—the father somehow carried this point and it was the only domestic one he ever did carry—and the boy was called Demir *B*ash by all the citizens of Samarcand and by his father ever after—though Sudabah his mother and her particular friends could never be brought to denominate him otherwise than Demir *T*ash.——Upon her death-bed many years afterwards—she sent for this only son on whom she doated with the fondest affection—her afflicted husband Calil stood with a mute and overwhelming air of sorrow at her left hand her Son in tears upon her right—there was a sick Nurse in the chamber in the act of shaking a mixture prescribed by one of two physicians who

1 in devotion] in ⟨his⟩ 7 the renegade] the ⟨Apostate of⟩ 8 traitor to] traitor ⟨of⟩ 11 pronounce—the] pronounce—⟨whose⟩ 12 living record] living ⟨monument⟩ of all] of ⟨of⟩ 13 Infamy can] Infamy ⟨of all kinds⟩ 23 the citizens] the ⟨d⟩ 24 friends could] friends ⟨would⟩

were discussing in an ante-room whether the disease sprang from a redundance of Bile—or a total want of it[2]—the only point in which they coincided—was—that the patient was in no danger:—Sudabah however could but just articulate—she beckoned with a faint smile to her son to approach—"Farewell—said she—I am going to heaven my dear Demir *T*ash" the last word—of these her last words—she uttered with as much emphasis as her strength permitted—and turning to her husband with a look of triumph and pious resignation—she repeated the word "*T*ash" and quietly expired.——She was deeply lamented and had an expensive funeral—with a pretty monument which was kept in good repair—till Calil married again which he did at last—though inconsolable for many weeks:——this might seem a work of Supererogation as the Law allows to every true Mussulman *four* wives—but during the lifetime of Sudabah—Calil had found it as well to dispense with the other three—and even after her demise he never availed himself of the full benefit of the Statute.————

The city of Samarcand was at this period under the dominion of Timour Lenc—or—Timour the Lame—who had conquered all of Asia—and as much of Europe as he found time to overrun: the greatest part of his life having been passed in this laudable pursuit—he had but rarely leisure to sojourn long in his good city of Samarcand—and when he did pay it a visit—the whole of the inhabitants trembled for their pockets—which he and his ministers had contracted a habit of emptying:—he also cut off heads—but with this practice his subjects found little or no fault—provided that decapitation and confiscation did not go together.—If the Sultan decollated the father of a family—his majesty was responsible to Mahomet for the sin—and the Son might find another—or at least a father in law—(or four as allowed by the law) but it was extremely difficult to acquire another estate when the first had been confiscated.——For these reasons those who had lost relatives and properties were greatly disaffected—those who were deprived of their relations only were resigned and loyal—but the most outrageous and treasonable of subjects were such persons as had been permitted to retain and maintain large families—but had been stripped of their patrimonies by repeated exactions.—However—the whole people exclaimed—when Timour was too far off to hear them—

1 were discussing] were ⟨disputing⟩ disease sprang] disease ⟨arose⟩ 5 she—I] she—⟨my d⟩ 14 had found] had ⟨ha⟩ 19 to overrun] to ⟨overcome:⟩ 25–6 confiscation did] confiscation ⟨were⟩ 31 were greatly] were ⟨much⟩ 33 and treasonable] and ⟨traitorous⟩

against the payment of money—and perpetually swore that they had no more money to pay:—they inveighed against war—they dispatched deputies to Timour—who had just taken Delhi—to congratulate him on his victories—and implore a release from certain imposts—the collection of which they averred to be impossible.—Timour accepted their compliments with an admirable grace—his reply was most gracious—he said "that his greatest Glory—except the especial protection of Mahomet—was the approbation of the Citizens of Samarcand—that his sole object in fighting—was to conquer for them—that the legion raised by that faithful metropolis had covered itself and the field of battle with immortal honour more particularly the eleven thousand who had fallen in the arms of Victory—which were capacious enough to receive them all—that their names would be everlasting—and the Gazette of that day got by heart by all posterity—that he only required a few thousand recruits and five hundred thousand Tomans[3] of gold to finish the contest—which he trusted would be forthwith furnished—that in the mean time half the number of the deputies should remain in pledge—and the remainder return to Samarcand with three standards and a Heron's tail[4] taken from the head of the dead Mogul General—to be placed in the Mosque of Samarcand between the bridle of Balaam's ass and the sacred curtains brought from the shrine of Mecca.[5]———

Such were the politics of Samarcand at the birth of Demir Bash——the whole city went out to meet the standards—all the citizens were delighted with the Heron's tail—to be sure the account of killed—had put some three and thirty thousand persons into mourning—but all agreed that Glory was—Glory—especially the taylors.—A day of festivity was appointed and kept—public thanksgivings were thanked—songs were sung—wine—(for they were not rigid Mahometans) was drunk——the Mosques were illuminated with circles of lamps as during the Bairam[6]—the women danced & talked without ceasing—the men stalked about in their holiday garments the whole city rang with mirth and Music to the very suburbs—the rich made feasts for their equals—and plentiful tables (for that day only) were

13 were capacious enough] were ⟨so⟩ capacious⟨ly opened⟩ 14 everlasting] everlasting⟨ly⟩ 18 remain in pledge] remain ⟨as⟩ pledge⟨s⟩ 19 a Heron's] a ⟨Peacock's⟩ 19–20 the head] the ⟨turban⟩ 20 the Mosque] the ⟨b⟩ 21 Samarcand between] Samarcand ⟨near to⟩ 21–2 curtains brought] curtains ⟨of⟩ 24 standards–all] standards–⟨the⟩ 25 the account] the ⟨list⟩ 26 but all] but ⟨then⟩ 27 taylors.] taylors ⟨—and—weapon-manufacturers.⟩ 28 public thanksgivings] public ⟨pray⟩ 31 Bairam—the] Bairam—⟨the⟩

furnished for the poor—all was unvaried festivity——the day was delightful—the night was sublime—and the next morning all Samarcand awoke with the headache.——————

The next day at six by the Mahometan reckoning—but twelve by all Christian clocks—(for they differ as much in their mode of apportioning Time as Eternity)—the next day at noon—as Calil looking like Saffron from the excess of yesterday walked forth to the Bazar—where he met many of his acquaintance in a like condition—he heard the voice of the Crier from the Minaret—but the state of his stomach not permitting him to perform the requisite prostrations of a devout Mussulman he determined to postpone his prayers till the evening.——But he soon found that the words of the Crier regarded temporal concerns only and joining the crowd which accumulated in the open space around the Mosque his ears were regaled with the following proposition.—"In the name of Timour the lame—whose form is perfection—whose word is wisdom—whose deeds are mercy—the brother of the Sun and Moon—cousin to the planets—and a distant connection of the remotest stars—the king of the world to whom nothing can be refused—and if it is refused is taken nevertheless—You his faithful subjects and honoured citizens of Samarcand are hereby summoned to decide by lot to the amount of eleven thousand volunteers for the invincible army of the most indulgent of Sovereigns—and to provide further with all speed the sum of five hundred thousand tomans for his royal accommodation in such equitable divisions of payment—as may become the first of cities—to the most generous of monarchs.—And in virtue of this being done all further imposts—taxes—duties—customs &c &c shall be remitted—saving only one small and optional tax—which none need pay—who prefer dispensing with the article on which it is laid—viz—a tax on Respiration—and those who do not choose to respire—shall be exempt from all demands.[7]———

It would be difficult to describe the emotions of the hearers at this brilliant harangue—to which the peroration and promised remissions by no means reconciled any body:—they first stared—then looked on the ground—then whispered—then murmured—the poor would not serve—but every one suggested the expediency of serving to his next neighbour—the rich complimented each other with the precedence in

2 was sublime] was ⟨happiness⟩ 5–6 apportioning Time] apportioning ⟨Time⟩ 12 Crier regarded] Crier ⟨concerned⟩ 19 is taken] is ⟨ne⟩ 28 and optional] and ⟨indispensable⟩ 30 not choose] not ⟨wish⟩

furnishing the contribution—no one seemed disposed to be magnificent—or warlike—at length the murmurs became like the rush of waters—and louder & louder—till a furious tumult ensued—blows were struck—stones were thrown—guards were called for—the men ran home for their sabres—the women screamed—and the children roared—all the streets were in an uproar—the fact was—that the city of Samarcand was not yet sober.—A party of the younger inhabitants of the Bazar—headed by an Armenian breeches-maker who had become bankrupt by furnishing Tamerlane's body guard with trousers upon credit—broke open the door of the minaret and ascending to the gallery at the summit—threw down the Crier—who cried out more lustily than ever—but was less listened to:—he fell amongst a party of Parthian Guards just arrived to disperse the mob—dismounting the officer who led them—& breaking two ribs—and the small bone of his right ancle in the concussion—besides receiving several contusions which the surgeon said required many embrocations & long attendance.—Every body was by this time too fully employed to mind him—& his was not the only surgical case already fit for investigation.——The Parthians flew upon the crowd—and the citizens belaboured the Parthians—a great many turbans and some heads amongst them flew about——the clamour and the mob increased every moment—and as all the citizens were armed—the disturbance might have been very fatal had they divided into equal parties—but their whole fury was bent against the unlucky soldiery—who were only doing their duty—and after a severe conflict were obliged to withdraw which they did at full speed—leaving the market place to the victors—with all the wounded—dead—dismounted—and missing—as trophies:—and then the conquerors began to ask why they had been fighting?———This was a question which nobody seemed at leisure to answer—but all agreed that as they had begun—it was as well to go on—and on this principle before Sunset—all Samarcand was in open rebellion.————

Calil in the beginning of the fray had been contented to remain a spectator—but example being very contagious—the fumes of yesterday's festival being also condensed into that kind of headache—which

1 contribution—no] contribution—⟨and⟩ 1–2 be magnificent] be ⟨ostentatious⟩ 2 rush] rush⟨ing⟩ 3 and louder] and ⟨at⟩ 10 the door] the ⟨turret-⟩ 12 but was] but ⟨in vain:⟩ 18 case already] case ⟨already⟩ 18–19 The Parthians] The ⟨G⟩ 23 they divided] they ⟨known which⟩ 29 seemed at] seemed ⟨disposed to or able⟩ 30 and on] and ⟨bef⟩ 34 very contagious] very ⟨tempting⟩

renders a man of spirit rather fractious—more particularly when the peccant part[8] is admonished by the flat side of a sabre—which a Parthian thought proper to apply by way of plaister to Calil's skull as he stood gazing at the commencement of the riot:—all these reasons induced Calil without reasoning at all—to betake himself to what he afterwards called Self-defence—that was to lay about him and every one within reach of his weapons in the most offensive manner—so—that before the victory was decided—he had done enough to forfeit fifty heads and twice as many estates—if Tamerlane's government should ever govern again.——All the Citizens were of the same opinion—they therefore shut the gates—examined their fortifications—chose a council—elected the Armenian breeches-Maker—whose name was Dumouss—General in chief—and then began to look about for an army.———This was not the easiest thing in the world to find—at least an army to oppose Tamerlane's—for the brilliant youth of the city had been drafted off to those cursed campaigns—which at last seemed likely to end at home——and those who remained though sufficiently numerous to beat the guards in garrison (who were few—as Samarcand had been esteemed the most loyal of all possible cities) and cut a respectable figure in a popular tumult—yet they had neither inclination nor ability to muster force for the open field—& still less to stand a regular siege.——They therefore determined to throw themselves on the protection of the Sophi of Persia[9]—and selected Calil as their ambassador.———

Calil—who had not yet recovered from his headache—which had been considerably increased by the application before mentioned— & several additional bumps in the course of the conflict—was at home rubbing his sinciput with a balsam (Opodeldoc had not yet been compounded & exported[10]) and cursing his stars—together with all tax-gatherers—potentates—guards—sabres—and venders of wine whatsoever—while Subadah his wife stood by him asking questions—when he received his credentials.————

He took them without much parley—peeped at Demir-bash who was sprawling on a Sopha & patted his cheek—gave Subadah a short domestic charge—and calling for his slaves—mounted a dromedary which set off carrying him and the fate of Samarcand in a letter to the

1 spirit rather] spirit ⟨somewhat⟩ 4 stood gazing] stood ⟨gaping⟩ 13 then began] then ⟨only thing that⟩ 19 Samarcand had] Samarcand ⟨was⟩ 28 Opodeldoc had] Opodeldoc ⟨was⟩ 35–6 dromedary which] dromedary ⟨&⟩

Sophi—written in very good Arabic, by the Clerk of the Cauzee (or Cadi as it is metamorphosed in European orthography[11]) and looked upon as an exquisite specimen of diplomatic supplication.—

Before Calil had got an hour's ride from the city gate—he began to commune with himself on the nature of his charge—& it's probable consequences——he could calculate with no great probability on the Sophi's succour—or it's efficacy if granted—He knew that Tamerlane neither wanted the power nor the will on the smallest pretext to make a mummy of the Sophi—and a pyramid of the numskulls of Samarcand with his own in particular as a pinnacle to the edifice[12]—he considered all this with the deepest attention for three minutes—and in the end—like a true patriot changed his politics and his road at the same moment—and instead of the way to Isfahan pursued the route to Delhi.[13]——

His retinue seemed a little surprized—but the affair was his—not theirs—and it became them to follow the ambassador's dromedary.—The ambassador's dromedary having travelled that road before—appeared to give it the preference—and this was an additional inducement to Calil—who thought that Mahomet had inspired the animal with this predilection in favourable coincidence with his own.—It never occurred to him that a dromedary could have any notions of his own—or that Mahomet had other things to think of than the politics of Samarcand.——

In a reasonable number of weeks they reached Tamerlane's encampment round the city of Delhi—and were luckily the first bearers of the intelligence of the revolt—for nobody had heard anything of the fugitive remains of the Parthian garrison.—Tamerlane was at this time solacing himself in his Haram:—he had the legal number of wives—and was an attentive husband—but on his expeditions these were left at home—and the Tartar Sovereign was permitted the indulgencies of chaste Concubinage—during the warlike season of the year.—————

But on the day after Calil's arrival—& before the ambassador could be presented—his Majesty was seized with a fit of the Gout—which enflamed his toes and his temper to that degree—that Calil began to wish that he had pursued the route prescribed by his instructions—a

1 the Clerk] the ⟨Cadi's⟩ 9 a mummy] a ⟨mumm⟩ 10 as a] as ⟨the⟩ 12 true patriot] true ⟨politician⟩ politics and] politics ⟨at⟩ 13 the route] the ⟨road⟩ 16 follow the] follow ⟨their⟩ 22 of than] of ⟨but⟩ 23 of Samarcand] of ⟨his⟩ 30 was permitted] was ⟨confined to⟩

consideration which came a little of the latest—But there was no avoiding the audience—for Timour was a man of business—and though indisposed—would postpone nothing—so between two long double rows of white and black eunuchs—ranged like the pieces of a game at drafts;—clothed in a long Caftan of state—and led through the avenues of the royal pavilion—Calil with many palpitations and prostrations made his obeisance in the sublime presence.—When Tamerlane instead of the expected men & money heard nothing but rebellion of subjects & expulsion of troops—he became furious—and swore by the pigeon that picked the pease from the ear of Mahomet—and by the hump of the holy Camel—that he would sow with salt the ground where Samarcand stood—and make a supper for the crows of all the inhabitants.————

This was his first ebullition—but by & bye he thought of contenting himself by what he called decimating the citizens—that was—according to the royal mode of calculation—punishing nine out of ten with corporal infliction—and the tenth man by mulct[14]— from this he made however an amnesty in favour of Calil—(who had made ashes of his Arabic credentials to the Sophy—) whom he firmly believed to be the most loyal & only faithful subject of his native city.——

Tamerlane was not a man of many words—before Samarcand had a notion of Calil's having had a reply from the Sophi—the inhabitants awaking one morning found that the town had become the head quarters of Timour and that his army had the honour of forming a guard for their immaculate ambassador the faithful Calil.—

Augustus Darvell: A Fragment of a Ghost Story (1816)

June 17th 1816.—

In the year 17–– having for some time determined on a journey through countries not hitherto much frequented by travellers I set out accompanied by a friend whom I shall designate by the name of Augustus Darvell.——He was a few years my elder—and a man of

11 would sow] would ⟨not leave⟩ 12 the crows] the ⟨s⟩ 15 by what] by ⟨deci⟩ 18 amnesty in] amnesty ⟨excepting⟩ made ashes] made ⟨fire⟩ 24 Timour] Timour⟨'s⟩ of forming] of ⟨contain⟩ 27 June 17th] June 1⟨6⟩ 28 year 17––] year 1⟨8–⟩

considerable fortune—and antient family—advantages which an extensive capacity prevented him alike from undervaluing or overrating.—Some peculiar circumstances in his private history had rendered him to me an object of attention of interest and even of regard, which neither the reserve of his manners—nor occasional indications of an inquietude at times nearly approaching to alienation of mind—could extinguish.———

I was yet young in life which I had begun early but my intimacy with him was of a recent date—we had been educated at the same schools & university, but his progress through these had preceded mine—and he had been deeply initiated into what is called the World—while I was yet in my noviciate.——While thus engaged I had heard[1] much both of his past & present life—and although in these accounts there were many and irreconcileable contradictions I could still gather from the whole that he was a being of no common order—and one who whatever pains he might take to avoid remark—would still be remarkable.—I had cultivated his acquaintance subsequently—and endeavoured to obtain his friendship—but this last appeared to be unattainable—whatever affections he might have possessed seemed now—some to have been extinguished—and others to be concentred: ——that his feelings were acute I had sufficient opportunities of observing—for altough he could controul he could not altogether disguise them—still he had a power of giving to one passion the appearance of another—in such a manner—that it was difficult to define the nature of what was working within him:—and the expressions of his features would vary so rapidly though slightly that it was useless to trace them to their sources:—it was evident that he was a prey to some cureless disquiet—but whether it arose from ambition—love—remorse—grief—from one or all of these—or merely from a morbid temperament akin to disease—I could not discover,—there were circumstances alledged which might have justified the application to each of these causes—but as I have before said—these were so contradictory and contradicted—that none could be fixed upon with accuracy—where there is Mystery—it is generally supposed that there must also be Evil—I know not how this may be—but in him there certainly was the one—though I could not ascertain the extent of the

2–3 from undervaluing or overrating.—] from ⟨overvaluing or contemning.——⟩ 4 attention of] attention ⟨and⟩ 11 been deeply] been ⟨ushered into⟩ 12 yet in] yet ⟨preparing for my initiation.—⟩ 23 a power] a ⟨power⟩ 26 rapidly though] rapidly ⟨thou⟩ 33–4 with accuracy] with ⟨any⟩

other—and felt loth—as far as regarded himself—to believe in it's existence.—My advances were received with sufficient coldness—but I was young—& not easily discouraged—and at length succeeded in obtaining to a certain degree that common place intercourse and moderate confidence of common & every day concerns—created & cemented by similarity of pursuit—and frequency of meeting—which is called intimacy or friendship—according to the ideas of him who uses those words to express them.———

Darvell had already travelled extensively—and to him I had applied for information with regard to the conduct of my intended journey:—it was my secret wish that he might be prevailed on to accompany me—it was also a probable hope—founded upon the shadowy restlessness which I had observed in him—& to which—the animation which he appeared to feel on such subjects—and his apparent indifference to all by which he was more immediately surrounded—gave fresh strength:—this wish I first hinted—& then expressed,—his answer though I had partly expected it—gave me all the pleasure of surprize—he consented—and after the requisite arrangements[2]—we commenced our voyages.—After journeying through various countries of the South of Europe—our attention was turned towards the East—according to our original destination—and it was in my progress through those regions that the incident occurred upon which will turn what I may have to relate.—————

The Constitution of Darvell—which must from his appearance have been in early life more than usually robust—had been for some time gradually giving way; without the intervention of any apparent disease;—he had neither cough nor hectic—yet he became daily more enfeebled—his habits were temperate—and he neither declined nor complained of fatigue—yet he was evidently wasting away:—he became more & more silent—and sleepless—and at length so seriously altered that my alarm grew proportionate to what I conceived to be his danger.———

We had determined on our arrival at Smyrna on an excursion to the ruins of Ephesus and Sardis—from which I endeavoured to dissuade him in his present state of indisposition—but in vain:—there appeared to be an oppression on his mind and a solemnity in his manner—which ill corresponded with his eagerness to proceed on what I regarded as a mere party of pleasure—little suited to a valetudinarian;

12 hope—founded] hope—⟨gr⟩ 21 in my] in ⟨our early⟩ 31 that my] that ⟨I⟩ alarm grew] alarm ⟨became⟩ 35 of indisposition] of ⟨h⟩

but I opposed him no longer—and in a few days we set off together accompanied only by a Serrugee and a single Janizary.[3]——We had passed halfway towards the remains of Ephesus—leaving behind us the more fertile environs of Smyrna—and were entering upon that wild & tenantless track through the marshes and defiles which lead to the few huts yet lingering over the broken columns of Diana:—the roofless walls of expelled Christianity—and the still more recent but complete desolation of abandoned Mosques——when the sudden and rapid illness of my companion obliged us to halt at a Turkish Cimetary—the turbaned tombstones of which were the sole indication that human Life had ever been a sojourner in this wilderness.——The only Caravansera[4] we had seen was left some hours behind us—not a vestige of a town or even cottage was within sight or hope—and this "City of the Dead"[5] appeared to be the sole refuge for my unfortunate friend—who seemed on the verge of becoming the last of it's inhabitants.———

In this situation I looked round for a place where he might most conveniently repose:—contrary to the usual aspect of Mahometan burial-grounds—the cypresses were in this few in number and these thinly scattered over it's extent—the tombstones were mostly fallen & worn with age:—upon one of the most considerable of these and beneath one of the most spreading trees—Darvell supported himself in a half-reclining posture—with great difficulty—he asked for Water:—I had some doubts of our being able to find any—and prepared to go in search of it with hesitating despondency—but he desired me to remain—and turning to Suleiman our Janizary—who stood by us smoking with great tranquillity—he said—"Suleiman Verbana Su" (ie bring some water)[6] and went on describing the spot where it was to be found with great minuteness—at a small well for Camels a few hundred yards to the right—the Janizary obeyed.—I said to Darvell—"How did you know this?—he replied—from our situation you must perceive that this place was once inhabited—& could not have been so without springs—I have also been here before———

"You have been here before—how came you never to mention this to me—& what could you be doing in a place where no one would remain a moment longer than they could help it?

To this question he returned[7] no answer.—In the mean time

6 lingering over] lingering ⟨up⟩ ⟨ami⟩ 8 of abandoned] of ⟨mos⟩ 13 a town] a ⟨habitation was to be seen⟩ sight or] sight ⟨or near it⟩ 15 becoming the] becoming ⟨it's⟩ ⟨its⟩ 21 with age] with ⟨y⟩ 33 without springs] without ⟨wells⟩

Suleiman returned with the water—leaving the Serrugee and the horses at the fountain.—The quenching of his thirst had the appearance of reviving him for a moment—and I conceived hopes of his being able to proceed or at least to return—and I urged the attempt.—He was silent—and appeared to be collecting his spirits for an effort to speak.—He began.———————

"This is the end of my journey—and of my life—I came here to die—but I have to request to make[8]—a command—for such my last words must be—you will observe it?

"Most certainly—but have better hopes—

"I have no hopes—nor wishes—but this—conceal my death from every human being—

"I hope there will be no occasion—that you will recover—and—

"Peace—it must be so—promise this—

"I do—

"Swear it by all that"—he here dictated an Oath of great Solemnity—

"There is no occasion for this—I will observe your request—& to doubt me is—

"It cannot be helped—you must swear—

I took the oath——it appeared to relieve him—he removed a seal ring from his finger on which were some Arabic characters—and presented it to me—he proceeded—

"On the ninth day of the Month at Noon precisely—(what month you please but this must be the day) you must fling this ring into the Salt Springs which run into the bay of Eleusis—the day after at the same hour you must repair to the ruins of the temple of Ceres—and wait one hour

"Why?—

"You will see

"The *9th* day of the month[9]—you say—

"The Ninth.—

As I observed that the present was the 9th day of the month[10] his countenance changed—and he paused—as he sate evidently becoming more feeble—a Stork with a Snake in her beak perched upon a tombstone near us—and without devouring her prey appeared to be steadfastly regarding us[11]—I know not what impelled me to drive it away—but the attempt was useless—she made a few circles in the air &

16 of great] of ⟨Solem⟩ 33 that the] that ⟨it was⟩

returned exactly to the same spot.—Darvel pointed to it—and smiled—he spoke—I know not whether to himself or to me—but the words were only "Tis well"

"What is well?—what do you mean?—

"No matter—you must bury me here—this evening—and exactly where that bird is now perched—you know the rest of my injunctions—

He then proceeded to give me several directions as to the manner in which his death might be best concealed—After these were finished he exclaimed "you perceive that bird"

"Certainly.—

"And the Serpent writhing in her beak.——

"Doubtless—there is nothing uncommon in it—it is her natural prey.—But it is odd that She does not devour it.—

He smiled in a ghastly manner—& said faintly "it is not yet time" as he spoke the Stork flew away—my eyes followed it for a moment—it could hardly be longer than *ten* might be counted I felt Darvell's weight as it were increase upon my shoulder—and turning to look upon his face perceived that he was dead.——————

I was shocked with the sudden certainty which could not be mistaken—his countenance in a few minutes became nearly black—I should have attributed so rapid a change to poison—had I not been aware that he had no opportunity of receiving it unperceived—the day was declining—the body was rapidly altering—and nothing remained but to fulfil his request—with the aid of Suleiman's ataghan[12] & my own sabre—we scooped a shallow grave upon the spot which Darvell had indicated—the earth easily gave way having already received some preceding[13] Mahometan tenant—we dug as deeply as the time permitted us—and throwing the dry earth upon all that remained of the singular being so lately departed—we cut a few sods of greener turf from the less withered soil around us—and laid them upon his sepulchre.———

Between astonishment & grief I was tearless—

1–2 and smiled] and ⟨said—⟩ 3 "Tis well"] "Tis ⟨well⟩ 5 "No matter—you] "⟨Never mind—⟩ 6 bird is] bird ⟨h⟩ 15 time" as] time" ⟨and⟩ 16 the Stork] the ⟨bird⟩ 17 than *ten*] than ⟨you⟩ 18 upon my] upon ⟨the⟩ 20 which could] which ⟨it⟩ 24 was declining] was ⟨advancing⟩ 26 sabre—we] sabre—⟨I⟩

ARMENIAN STUDIES
(1816–1817)

The Armenian Alphabet (1816)

⟨aip⟩ ayp—*a* sounded as in Latin 1
pien. pronounced quickly.— 2
kum K. 3
ta⟨r⟩ —the *a* as in Latin— 4
yetch 5
za —a as in Latin.— 6
a —*a*—sounded as in *English* 7
yet — 8
tow 9
j. as in French.— 10.
ini. —pronounced as the first two syllables in "Initial."—
leun—
Cha —aspirate as X Greek. the *a* as in English.
dza. —*a* as in ⟨English.⟩ Latin.—
Ghien.—
⟨ho.⟩ hwo.—
tza.
ghad.—
j or g.—
mien.—
he
nu.
sha.
wo.
Cha
ba.
Che
r.r.—
Sa.
viev.—
diun.

re Hajg, il nome del primo Eroe Arm.
tzo. Aram, il secondo.
huin haj. Armeno.
piur. hajK, Armeni.[1]
⟨ke.⟩ K. ke,
O.
Fa.—or. Pha.—

The Armenian Language: A Note (1817)

Veram shabuk in his reign.—in the 4th Century.—Mesrob, or Mashtotz a learned Armenian invented the Armenian Alphabet:[1]—consisting of 36 letters—before that period the nation used the Syriac. Persian—or

2 1

Greek character.[2]—Mesrob invented the characters from Ayp to to K.—in the 12th Cent^{ry}—the two remaining characters O. & F. (O—Ֆ) were introduced.[3]—No M.S. exists of a date previous to the 4th Cent^{ry}—& the invention of their Alphabet—the reason of this being the sudden disuse & neglect of the foreign alphabet hitherto adopted—and in different subsequent periods—many M.S.S. were purposely destroyed by apostates from their religion.——as also by the Christians themselves who wished to destroy all records pertaining to Paganism.[4]——But the Armenians had a literature & a language—rich & cultivated before this period.——The translation of the Scriptures was made at this time—by Mesrob—the Patriarch Isaac—& others.—the two being the principals. The Armenians call themselves the Haijk nation from the first king of their country so called—an Armenian would say "I am *Haay*"—that is—an Armenian.[5]—

The Armenians in their poetry have a power from the wealth of their language—of composing poems of many hundred lines—all ending with different words—but the same rhyme—this may be monotonous—but shews great copiousness[6]—

The Armenian Grammar: Two Comments (1817)

[1.] This Grammar is for the use of the *Armenians* to acquire English & not for our Nation.—

[2.] The power of speech is a faculty peculiar to man, and was bestowed on him by his beneficent Creator for the greatest and most excellent uses; but alas! how often do we pervert it to the worst of purposes?

Orinag—Example

[The above in written Armenian]

this sentence is the *above English* in Armenian Characters that is in the *written* character the *printed* character is as below / B^{n}

[the above in printed Armenian]

Preface to the Armenian Grammar (1817)

2 January 1817[1]

The English reader will probably be surprised to find my name associated with a work of the present description, and inclined to give me more credit for my attainments as a linguist than they deserve.

As I would not willingly be guilty of a deception, I will state, as shortly as I can, my own share in the compilation, with the motives which led to it.[2] On my arrival at Venice in the year 1816, I found my mind in a state which required study, and study of a nature which should leave little scope for the imagination, and furnish some difficulty in the pursuit.[3]

At this period I was much struck—in common, I believe, with every other traveller—with the society of the Convent of St. Lazarus, which appears to unite all the advantages of the monastic institution, without any of its vices.[4]

The neatness, the comfort, the gentleness, the unaffected devotion, the accomplishments, and the virues of the brethren of the order, are well fitted to strike the man of the world with the conviction that 'there is another and a better'[5] even in this life.

These men are the priesthood of an oppressed and a noble nation, which has partaken of the proscription and bondage of the Jews and of the Greeks, without the sullenness of the former or the servility of the latter. This people has attained riches without usury, and all the honours that can be awarded to slavery without intrigue. But they have long occupied, nevertheless, a part of 'the House of Bondage,' who has lately multiplied her many mansions.[6] It would be difficult, perhaps, to find the annals of a nation less stained with crimes than those of the Armenians, whose virtues have been those of peace, and their vices those of compulsion. But whatever may have been their destiny—and it has been bitter—whatever it may be in future, their country must ever be one of the most interesting on the globe; and perhaps their language only requires to be more studied to become more attractive.

If the Scriptures are righly understood, it was in Armenia that Paradise was placed[7]—Armenia, which has paid as dearly as the descendants of Adam for that fleeting participation of its soil in the happiness of him who was created from its dust. It was in Armenia that the flood first abated, and the dove alighted.[8] But with the disappearance of Paradise itself may be dated almost the unhappiness of the country, for though long a powerful kingdom, it was scarcely ever an independent one, and the satraps of Persia and the pachas of Turkey have alike desolated the region where God created man in his own image.[9]

Translations from the Armenian: *Two Extracts* (1817)

From: *Corenensis in his Armenian History*.[1]

Arsaces the great King of the Persians and Parthians is said with the Parthians to have revolted from the Macedonians,[2] to have reigned over all Assyria and the East; and having slain the King Antiochus at Nineveh[3] to have reduced the world under his dominion.

He appointed his brother Valarsaces[4] King of Armenia, rightly deeming that his dominions would thus become more secure and consolidated; he bestowed upon him the royal city of Nisibin,[5] and assigned the limits of his territory, one part from the west of Syria, and Palestine and Asia and all the inland places and Thitalia[6] from the Pontic sea to the spot where Caucasus ends in the western Ocean, and

Atropatane,[7] and "whatever else thy prudence or valour may acquire. For to the brave, he says, their arms are boundaries, what they win, they wear".

He, when he had completely tranquillized his kingdom, and established his power, desired to know, who and what sort of men had reigned before him over Armenia, and whether they were valiant or indolent.

Having chosen therefore a Syrian, Maribas (or Marabas) of Catina,[8] a learned man, and very skilful in Chaldaic and Greek literature, he sent him to his brother Arsaces, with proper presents, to entreat him to permit the inspection of the royal Archives; and furnished him with letters of which the following is a specimen.

"To Arsaces King of Earth and Sea, whose form and image are like those of our Gods, but his fortune and fate above all Monarchs, and the greatness of his mind such as is the heaven above the earth; Valarsaces his younger brother and fellow-Soldier, appointed by him King of Armenia, sends Health and Victory in all things.

Since I received thy commands to cultivate valour and wisdom, I have never neglected this thine admonition; but have administered in all things with diligent care, to the extent of my capacity and power.

Being delegated by thee to this kingdom, I have resolved to enquire what order of men ruled over Armenia before me, and what was the origin of these Satrapies around me.[9] For neither indeed appears any regularity of things here whence it may be seen, what was the worship in the temples, or what was first or last done in this region, nor are there any certain laws, but all is confused and barbarous.

For which reason I pray thee, my Lord, that to this man, who will abide in the presence of thy Majesty the ingress of the royal Library may be permitted that he may acquire the knowledge of such things as thy brother and son desires, and return to us with the truth. And the pleasure which is to arise from the fulfilment of our wishes, we well know will be a joy to thee also. Farewell, oh thou illustrious dweller among the Gods!"

When Arsaces the great had received these letters from Maribas of Catina, with the greatest alacrity he permitted him to search the royal Archives of Nineveh, rejoicing that his brother to whom he had committed the government of half his kingdom, was endued with such a disposition.

When Maribas therefore inspected the Manuscripts, he found a certain book, in the greek character, of which this is said to have been the title.

"This Volume was translated from the chaldaic language into greek, by order of Alexander, and contains the authentic history of the Antients and our Ancestors, who are said to commence with Zeruanus, Titan, and Apetosthes;[10] in this book each of these three celebrated men and their posterity are registered in order each in his proper place for many years".

From this volume Maribas of Catina conveyed to king Valarsaces then in the city of Nisibin the history of our Nation faithfully compiled and written in syriac and greek.

When . . . Valarsaces had received this Manuscript . . . esteeming it amongst his chief treasures,[11] he directed the volume to be diligently preserved, and ordered a portion of it's contents to be engraven on a column.

Which narrative, we having verified the series of our facts, are now about to repeat at thy command, and to trace back our early government to the Chaldean Sardanapalus,[12] and even beyond.

From: *Lampronensis in his Synodical oration.*[13]

It was beautiful then to behold Christ as a bridegroom nobly adorned for the nuptial chamber, who spake with a soft voice to his most pure beloved:[14] "Enlarge the place of thy tent, and of thy porch; spare not, plant it, lengthen thy cords, and strengthen thy stakes; for thou shalt break forth on the right hand and on the left, and thy seed shall inherit the Gentiles, and thou shalt renew the ruined cities of the Idolaters. Fear not, though till now by means of these I have covered thee with confusion. For I swear, that I shall never repent to make my abode of pleasure with thee who art my repose for ever and ever".[15]

Then the first Enemy, in ambush for his prey, perceiving that his snares were discovered, and that the worship of God flourished throughout the world, observing that those who had been deceived were redeemed, and that the inheritors of Paradise returned to their country, that the celestial holiness poured forth it's glory, that the instrument of hatred being broken, the fruits of charity began to multiply themselves, and the hope of all no longer turned to the earth, ascended to the heavenly abodes, forth from the cave of his malice he issued like the lion roaring in his anger, and roamed about with open and insatiate jaws, to devour the Church recovered by Christ.[16]

Translations from the Armenian: *Two Epistles* (1817)

The Epistle of the Corinthians to St. Paul the Apostle.[a]

1 STEPHEN,[b][1] and the elders with him, Dabnus, Eubulus, Theophilus, and Xinon, to Paul, our father and evangelist, and faithful master in Jesus Christ, health.[c][2]

2 Two men have come to Corinth, Simon by name, and Cleobus,[d][3] who vehemently disturb the faith of some with deceitful and corrupt words;

3 Of which words thou shouldst inform thyself:

4 For neither have we heard such words from thee, nor from the other apostles:

5 But we know only that what we have heard from thee and from them, that we have kept firmly.

6 But in this chiefly has our Lord had compassion, that, whilst thou art yet with us in the flesh, we are again about to hear from thee.[4]

7 Therefore do thou write to us, or come thyself amongst us quickly.

8 We believe in the Lord, that, as it was revealed to Theonas, he hath delivered thee from the hands of the unrighteous.[e]

9 But these are the sinful words of these impure men, for thus do they say and teach:

10 That it behoves not to admit the Prophets.[f]

11 Neither do they affirm the omnipotence of God:

a Some MSS. have the title thus: *Epistle of Stephen the Elder to Paul the Apostle*, *from the Corinthians.*

b In the MSS., the marginal verses published by the Whistons are wanting.

c In some MSS. we find, *The elders Numenus*, *Eubulus*, *Theophilus*, *and Nomeson*, *to Paul their brother*, *health*!

d Others read, *There came certain men*, . . . *and Clobeus*, *who vehemently shake.*

e Some MSS. have, *We believe in the Lord*, *that his presence was made manifest*; *and by this hath the Lord delivered us from the hands of the unrighteous.*

f Others read, *To read the Prophets.*

1 *Apostle.*] *Apostle.* (*Found in the Armenian Bible as an Apocryphal writing.*) *subtitle in Aucher* 5 Cleobus] Clebus *Aucher* 12 them, that we] them, we *Aucher* 25 published by] published first by *Aucher* 28 Others read,] Some M.S.S. read. *Aucher*

12 Neither do they affirm the resurrection of the flesh:

13 Neither do they affirm that man was altogether created by God:

14 Neither do they affirm that Jesus Christ was born in the flesh from the Virgin Mary:

15 Neither do they affirm that the world was the work of God, but of some one of the angels.

16 Therefore do thou make haste[g] to come amongst us.

17 That this city of the Corinthians may remain without scandal.

18 And that the folly of these men may be made manifest by an open refutation. Fare thee well.[h]

The deacons Thereptus and Tichus[i5] received and conveyed this Epistle to the city of the Philippians.[j6]

When Paul received the Epistle, although he was then in chains on account of Stratonice,[k] the wife of Apofolanus,[l7] yet, as it were forgetting his bonds, he mourned over these words, and said weeping:[8] "It were better for me to be dead, and with the Lord.[9] For while I am in this body, and hear the wretched words of such false doctrine, behold, grief rises upon grief,[10] and my trouble adds a weight to my chains; when I behold this calamity, and progress of the machinations of Satan, who searcheth to do wrong."

And thus with deep affliction Paul composed his reply to the Epistle.[m11]

g Some MSS. have, *Therefore, brother, do thou make haste.*

h Others read, *Fare thee well in the Lord.*

i Some MSS. have, *The deacons Therepus and Techus.*

j The Whistons have, *To the city of Phœnicia*: but in all the MSS. we find, *To the city of the Philippians.*

k Others read, *On account of Onotice.*

l The Whistons have, *Of Apollophanus*: but in all the MSS. we read, *Apofolanus.*

m In the text of this Epistle there are some other variations in the words, but the sense is the same.

11 The deacons] 19. The Deacons *Aucher* conveyed this] conveyed the *Aucher* 14 Stratonice] Statonice *Aucher* 29 The Whistons . . . *Apofolanus.*] Some M.S.S. have. *of Apollophanus. Aucher*

Epistle of Paul to the Corinthians.[a]

1 Paul, in bonds for Jesus Christ,[12] disturbed by so many errors,[b] to his Corinthian brethren, health.[13]

2 I nothing marvel that the preachers of evil have made this progress.[14]

3 For because the Lord Jesus is about to fulfil his coming,[15] verily on this account do certain men pervert and despise his words.

4 But I, verily, from the beginning, have taught you that only which I myself received from the former apostles,[16] who always remained with the Lord Jesus Christ.

5 And I now say unto you that the Lord Jesus Christ was born of the Virgin Mary, who was of the seed of David,

6 According to the annunciation of the Holy Ghost, sent to her by our Father from heaven;[17]

7 That Jesus might be introduced into the world,[c][18] and deliver our flesh by his flesh, and that he might raise us up from the dead;

8 As in this also he himself became the example:

9 That it might be made manifest that man was created by the Father,

10 He has not remained in perdition unsought;[d]

11 But he is sought for, that he might be revived by adoption.[19]

12 For God, who is the Lord of all, the Father of our Lord Jesus Christ, who made heaven and earth, sent, firstly, the Prophets to the Jews:

13 That he would absolve them from their sins, and bring them to his judgment.

a Some MSS. have, *Paul's Epistle from prison, for the instruction of the Corinthians.*

b Others read, *Disturbed by various compunctions.*

c Some MSS. have, *That Jesus might comfort the world.*

d Others read, *He has not remained indifferent.*

1 *Corinthians.*] *Corinthians.* (*Found in the Armenian Bible as an Apocryphal writing.*) *subtitle in Aucher* 23 firstly] first *Aucher* 26 judgment] justice *Aucher* 27 Some MSS. have,] Some M.S.S. have this title. *Aucher* *instruction*] *lesson Aucher* 28 Others read,] Some M.S.S. read. *Aucher* 29 Some MSS. have,] Others read. *Aucher* 30 Others . . . *indifferent.*] In some M.S.S. are find. *is not remained indifferent. Aucher*

14 Because he wished to save, firstly, the house of Israel, he bestowed and poured forth his Spirit upon the Prophets;

15 That they should for a long time preach the worship of God, and the nativity of Christ.

16 But he who was the prince of evil, when he wished to make himself God, laid his hand upon them,

17 And bound all men in sin.[e]

18 Because the judgment of the world was approaching.

19 But Almighty God, when he willed to justify, was unwilling to abandon his creature;

20 But when he saw his affliction, he had compassion upon him:

21 And at the end of a time he sent the Holy Ghost into the Virgin foretold by the Prophets.

22 Who, believing readily,[f][20] was made worthy to conceive, and bring forth our Lord Jesus Christ.

23 That from this perishable body, in which the evil spirit was glorified, he should be cast out, and it should be made manifest

24 That he was not God: For Jesus Christ, in his flesh, had recalled and saved this perishable flesh, and drawn it into eternal life by faith.[21]

25 Because in his body he would prepare a pure temple of justice for all ages;

26 In whom we also, when we believe, are saved.

27 Therefore know ye that these men are not the children of justice, but the children of wrath;[22]

28 Who turn away from themselves the compassion of God;

29 Who say that neither the heavens nor the earth were altogether works made by the hand of the Father of all things.[g]

e Some MSS. have, *Laid his hand, and them and all body bound in sin.*

f Others read, *Believing with a pure heart.*

g Some MSS. have, *Of God the Father of all things.*

1 firstly] first *Aucher* 12 a time] the time *Aucher* 17 he should be cast out, and it should be made manifest] he should be reproved, and manifested, *Aucher* 21 he would] he should *Aucher* 30 Others read,] Some M.S.S. have. *Aucher* 31 Some MSS. have,] Others read. *Aucher*

30 But these cursed men[h] have the doctrine of the serpent.

31 But do ye, by the power of God, withdraw yourselves far from these, and expel from amongst you the doctrine of the wicked.

32 Because you are not the children of rebellion,[i][23] but the sons of the beloved church.

33 And on this account the time of the resurrection is preached to all men.

34 Therefore they who affirm that there is no resurrection of the flesh, they indeed shall not be raised up to eternal life;

35 But to judgment and condemnation shall the unbeliever arise in the flesh:

36 For to that body which denies the resurrection of the body, shall be denied the resurrection: because such are found to refuse the resurrection.

37 But you also, Corinthians! have known, from the seeds of wheat, and from other seeds,

38 That one grain falls[j][24] dry into the earth, and within it first dies,

39 And afterwards rises again, by the will of the Lord, endued with the same body:

40 Neither indeed does it arise with the same simple body, but manifold, and filled with blessing.[25]

41 But we produce the example not only from seeds, but from the honourable bodies of men.[k]

42 Ye also have known Jonas, the son of Amittai.[l][26]

43 Because he delayed to preach to the Ninevites, he was swallowed up in the belly of a fish for three days and three nights:

h Others read, *They curse themselves in this thing.*
i Others read, *Children of the disobedient.*
j Some MSS. have, *That one grain falls not dry into the earth.*
k Others read, *But we have not only produced from seeds, but from the honourable body of man.*
l Others read, *The son of Ematthius.*

20 arise with the] arise the *Aucher* 22 we produce] we must produce *Aucher* seeds] seed *Aucher* 27 Others read,] In some M.S.S. are find. *Aucher* 28 Others read,] Some M.S.S. read. *Aucher* *of the disobedient.*] *of disobedient. Aucher* 29 Some MSS. have,] In some M.S.S. are find, *Aucher* 30 Others read,] Some M.S.S. have. *Aucher* *have not only*] *have only Aucher* *man*] *men Aucher*

44 And after three days God heard his supplication, and brought him out from the deep abyss;

45 Neither was any part of his body corrupted; neither was his eye-brow bent down.[m][27]

46 And how much more for you, oh men of little faith![28]

47 If you believe in our Lord Jesus Christ, will he raise you up, even as he himself hath arisen.

48 If the bones of Elisha the prophet, falling upon the dead, revived the dead,[29]

49 By how much more shall ye, who are supported by the flesh and the blood and the Spirit of Christ, arise again on that day with a perfect body?

50 Elias the Prophet, embracing the widow's son, raised him from the dead:[30]

51 By how much more shall Jesus Christ revive you, on that day, with a perfect body, even as he himself hath arisen?

52 But if ye receive other things vainly,[n]

53 Henceforth no one shall cause me to travail; for I bear on my body these fetters,[o][31]

54 To obtain Christ; and I suffer with patience these afflictions to become worthy of the resurrection of the dead.

55 And do each of you, having received the law from the hands of the blessed Prophets and the holy gospel,[p] firmly maintain it;

56 To the end that you may be rewarded in the resurrection of the dead, and the possession of the life eternal.

57 But if any of ye, not believing, shall trespass, he shall be judged with the misdoers, and punished with those who have false belief.

58 Because such are the generations of vipers,[32] and the children of dragons and basilisks.[33]

m Others add, *Nor did a hair of his body fall therefrom.*

n Some MSS. have, *Ye shall not receive other things in vain.*

o Others finish here thus, *Henceforth no one can trouble me farther, for I bear in my body the sufferings of Christ. The grace of our Lord Jesus Christ be with your spirit, my brethren. Amen.*

p Some MSS. have, *Of the holy evangelist.*

19 fetters,] bonds, *Aucher* 27 those] these *Aucher* 30 Others add,] Some M.S.S. join. *Aucher* 31 Some MSS. have,] Others read. *Aucher* 32 Others finish] Others finished *Aucher* 34 Some MSS. have,] Others read. *Aucher*

59 Drive far from amongst ye, and fly from such, with the aid of our Lord Jesus Christ.

60 And the peace and grace of the beloved Son be upon you.[q][34] Amen.

q Others add, *Our Lord be with ye all. Amen.*

Done into English by me, January–February, 1817, at the Convent of San Lazaro, with the aid and exposition of the Armenian text by the Father Paschal Aucher, Armenian Friar.

BYRON.

Venice, April 10th, 1817.

I had also the Latin text,[35] but it is in many places very corrupt, and with great omissions.[36]

3 be upon you] be with you *Aucher* 5 Others add,] Others join. *Aucher* *with*] *upon Aucher*

WRITINGS
(1817–1820)

Donna Josepha: A Fragment of a Skit on the Separation
(1817)

A few hours afterwards we were very good friends, and a few days after she set out for Arragon, with my son, on a visit to her father and mother. I did not accompany her immediately, having been in Arragon before, but was to join the family in their Moorish chateau within a few weeks.

During her journey I received a very affectionate letter from Donna Josepha, apprizing me of the welfare of herself and my son. On her arrival at the chateau, I received another still more affectionate, pressing me, in very fond, and rather foolish, terms, to join her immediately. As I was preparing to set out from Seville, I received a third—this was from her father, Don Jose di Cardozo, who requested me, in the politest manner, to dissolve my marriage. I answered him with equal politeness, that I would do no such thing. A fourth letter arrived—it was from Donna Josepha, in which she informed me that her father's letter was written by her particular desire. I requested the reason by return of post—she replied, by express, that as reason had nothing to do with the matter, it was unnecessary to give any—but that she was an injured and excellent woman. I then inquired why she had written to me the two preceding affectionate letters, requesting me to come to Arragon. She answered, that was because she believed me out of my senses—that, being unfit to take care of myself, I had only to set out on this journey alone, and making my way without difficulty to Don Jose di Cardozo's, I should there have found the tenderest of wives and—a strait waistcoat.

I had nothing to reply to this piece of affection but a reiteration of my request for some lights upon the subject. I was answered that they would only be related to the Inquisition. In the mean time, our domestic discrepancy had become a public topic of discussion; and the world, which always decides justly, not only in Arragon but in

Andalusia, determined that I was not only to blame, but that all Spain could produce nobody so blamable. My case was supposed to comprise all the crimes which could, and several which could not, be committed, and little less than an auto-da-fé was anticipated as the result. But let no man say that we are abandoned by our friends in adversity—it was just the reverse. Mine thronged around me to condemn, advise, and console me with their disapprobation.—They told me all that was, would, or could be said on the subject. They shook their heads—they exhorted me—deplored me, with tears in their eyes, and—went to dinner.

To the Editor of the *British Review* (1819)

To the Editor of the British Review.

My Dear Roberts—

As a believer in the Church of England—to say nothing of the State—I have been an occasional reader—and great admirer—though not a subscriber to your Review.[1] But I do not know that any article[2] of it's contents ever gave me much surprise till the eleventh of your late 27th number made it's appearance.[3]—You have there most manfully[4] refuted a calumnious accusation of bribery and corruption—the credence of which in the public mind might not only have damaged your reputation as a Clergyman[5] and an Editor, but what would have been still worse—have injured the circulation of your Journal—which I regret to hear is not so extensive as the "purity (as you well observe) of it's &c. &c." and the present taste for propriety would induce us to expect.[6]———The charge itself is of a solemn nature—and although in verse is couched in terms of such circumstantial gravity as to induce a belief little short of that generally accorded to the thirty nine articles to which you so generously[7] subscribed—on taking your degrees.[8]—It is a charge the most revolting to the heart of man from it's frequent occurrence;—to the mind of a Statesman[9] from it's occasional truth—and to the Soul of an Editor from it's moral impossibility.—You are

14 have been] have ⟨always⟩ 16 me much] me ⟨so⟩ much surprise] much ⟨pleasure ⟨with some⟩ ⟨which has⟩ as⟩ surprise till] surprise ⟨till⟩ 23 for propriety] for ⟨morality⟩ 28–9 frequent occurrence] frequent ⟨man from it's⟩ 30 it's moral] it's ⟨utter⟩

charged then in the last line of one octave stanza and the whole eight lines of the next—viz—209th & 210th of the first canto of that "pestilent poem" Don Juan—with receiving—and still more foolishly acknowledging the receipt of certain monies to eulogize the unknown author, who by this account must be known to you if to nobody else.—An impeachment of this nature so seriously made there is but one way of refuting—and it is my firm persuasion—that whether you did or did not (and *I* believe that you did not) receive the said monies of which I wish that he had specified the sum, you are quite right in denying all knowledge of the transaction.—If charges of this nefarious description—are to go forth sanctioned by all the solemnity of circumstance—and guaranteed by the veracity of verse (as Counsellor Phillips would say)[10]—what is to become of readers hitherto implicitly confident in the not less veracious prose of our critical journals? what is to become of the reviews? and if the reviews fail—what is to become of the Editors?—It is common cause and you have done well to sound the alarm—I myself in my humble sphere will be one of your echoes.——In the words of the tragedian Liston "I love a row"[11]—and you seem justly determined to make one.——————

It is barely possible—certainly improbable that the writer might have been in jest—but this only aggravates his crime.—A joke the proverb says "breaks no bones"[12] but it may break a bookseller, or it may be the cause of bones being broken.—The jest is but a bad one at the best for the author—and might have been a still worse one for you—if your copious contradiction did not certify to all whom it may concern your own indignant innocence and the immaculate purity of the British review.——I do not doubt your word—my dear Roberts—yet I cannot help wishing that in a case of such vital importance—it had assumed the more substantial shape of an Affidavit sworn before the Lord Mayor[13] Atkins—who readily receives any deposition, and doubtless would have brought it in some way as evidence of the designs of the reformers to set fire to London—at the same time that he himself meditates the same good office towards the river Thames.[14]——————

I am sure, my dear Fellow[15]—that you will take these observations of mine in good part—they are written in a spirit of friendship not less pure than your own editorial integrity—I have always admired you—and not knowing any shape which friendship and admiration can

8 monies of] monies ⟨(⟩ 9 had specified] had ⟨named⟩ sum,] sum⟨)⟩
13 implicitly confident] implicitly ⟨relying upon⟩ 23 broken.—The] broken ⟨which⟩
36 editorial integrity] editorial ⟨conduct⟩ 37 and not] and ⟨do⟩

assume more agreeable and useful than that of good advice—I shall continue my lucubrations mixed with here & there a monitory hint as to what I conceive to be the line you should pursue in case you should ever again be assailed with bribes,—or accused of taking them.———

By the way—you don't say much about the poem except that it is "flagitious" this is a pity—you should have cut it up—because to say the truth in not doing so—you somewhat assist any notions which the malignant might entertain on the score of the anonymous asseveration which has made you so angry.———

You say no bookseller "was willing to take upon himself the publication though most of them disgrace themselves by selling it"—now my dear friend—though we all know that those fellows will do any thing for money—methinks the disgrace is more with the purchasers—and some such doubtless there are for there can be no very extensive selling (as you will perceive by that of the British Review) without buying.—You then add "what can the Critic say?"—I am sure I don't know, at present he says very little and that not much to the purpose.—Then comes "for praise as far as regards the *poetry many* passages might be exhibited; for condemnation as far as regards the morality all:"—now—my dear good Roberts—I feel for you—& for your reputation—my heart bleeds for both—and I do ask you whether or not such language does not come positively under the description of "the puff collusive" for which see Sheridan's farce of "the Critic" (by the way a little more facetious than your own farce under the same title)—towards the close of scene second—Act the first.[16]—————

The poem is it seems sold as the work of Lord Byron—but you feel yourself "at liberty to suppose it not Lord B's composition" why did you ever suppose that it was?———I approve of your indignation—I applaud it—I feel as angry as you can—but perhaps your virtuous wrath carries you a little too far when you say that "No misdemeanour, not even that of sending into the world obscene and blasphemous poetry the product of studious lewdness and laboured impiety appears to you in so detestable a light as the acceptance of a present by the Editor of a review as the condition of praising an author"—the devil it don't?[17]—think a little.—This is being critical overmuch.—In point of Gentile benevolence or Christian Charity it were surely less criminal to praise for a bribe—than to abuse a fellow creature for nothing—and

4 assailed with] assailed ⟨from⟩ 15 selling (as] selling (⟨except perhaps of⟩ 23 see Sheridan's] see ⟨the farce⟩ 24 title)—] title) ⟨scene⟩ ⟨scene⟩ 32 impiety appears] impiety ⟨can⟩ 36 Christian Charity] Christian ⟨it⟩

as to the assertion of the comparative innocence of blasphemy and obscenity confronted with an Editor's "acceptance of a present" I shall merely observe that as an Editor you say very well—but as a Christian divine[18] I would not recommend you to transpose[19] this sentence into a sermon.[20]———

And yet you say "the miserable man (for miserable he is as having a soul of which he cannot get rid)"—but here I must pause again—and enquire what is the meaning of this parenthesis?———We have heard of people of "little Soul" or "of no Soul at all"—but never till now of "the misery of having a soul of which we cannot get rid" a misery under which you are possibly no great sufferer having got rid apparently of some of the intellectual part of your own when you penned this pretty piece of eloquence.—But to continue.—You call upon Lord Byron always supposing him *not* the author, to disclaim "with all gentlemanly haste &c. &c."—I am told that Lord B. is in a foreign country some thousand miles off it may be so that it will be difficult for him to hurry to your wishes.—In the mean time perhaps you yourself have set an example of more haste than gentility—but "the more haste the worse speed."[21]——————

Let us now look at the charge itself, my dear Roberts, which appears to me to be in some degree not quite explicitly worded.—

"I bribed my *Grandmother's* review, the British."—

I recollect hearing soon after the publication this subject discussed at the tea-table of Mr. S. the poet[22]—who expressed himself—I remember—a good deal surprized that you had never reviewed his epic poem of "Saul"[23] nor any of his six tragedies of which in one instance the bad taste of the pit—and in all the rest the barbarous repugnance of the principal actors prevented the performance.[24]—Mrs. & the Miss's S—being in a corner of the room perusing the proof sheets of Mr. S's poems in Italy or *on* Italy—as he says[25]—(I wish by the bye Mrs. S. would make the tea a little stronger) the male part of the Conversazione were at liberty to make some[26] observations on the poem—and passage in question—and there was a difference of opinion.——Some thought the allusion was to the "British Critic."[27]—Other that by the

1 the assertion] the ⟨comparison of⟩ 6 as having] as ⟨not⟩ 7 soul of] soul ⟨he⟩ 8 what is] what ⟨all⟩ 9 of "little] of ⟨no soul or of⟩ 10 misery of] misery ⟨of⟩ 10–11 misery under] misery ⟨by the⟩ 12 some of] some ⟨part⟩ 16 it will] it ⟨may⟩ 20 Let us] ⟨It is⟩ Let us Roberts, which] Roberts, ⟨"⟩ 24 the tea-table] the ⟨teat⟩ 25 reviewed his] reviewed ⟨the⟩ 26 tragedies of] tragedies ⟨for⟩

expression "my Grandmother's review" it was intimated that "my Grandmother" was not the reader of the review but actually the writer—thereby insinuating, my dear Roberts, that you were an old woman—because, as people often say—"Jeffrey's Review"—Gifford's review" in lieu of Edinburgh & Quarterly—so "my Grandmother's review" and Roberts's—might be also synonimous.[28]——Now whatever colour this insinuation might derive from the circumstance of your wearing a gown—as well as from your time of life—your general style and various passages of your writings—I will take upon myself to exculpate you from all suspicion of the kind—and assert without calling M.rs Roberts in testimony—that if ever you should be chosen Pope—you will pass through all the previous ceremonies with as much credit as any Pontiff since the parturition of Joan.[29]——It is very unfair to judge of Sex from writings—particularly from those of the British review.—We are all liable to be deceived—and it is an indisputable fact that many of the best articles in your journal which were attributed to a veteran female,—were actually written by you yourself—and yet to this day there are people who could never find out the difference.[30]—But let us return to the more immediate question.—————

I agree with you that it is impossible Lord B. should be the author not only because as a British peer and a British poet—it would be impracticable for him to have recourse to such facetious fiction—but for some other reasons which you have omitted to state.—In the first place his Lordship has no Grandmother.—Now the author—and we may believe him in this—doth expressly state that the "British" is his "Grandmother's review," and if—as I think I have distinctly proved—this was not a mere figurative allusion to your supposed intellectual age and sex—my dear friend—it follows—whether you be She or no that there is such an elderly Lady still extant. And I can the more readily credit this—having a sexagenary Aunt of my own who perused you constantly—till unfortunately falling asleep over the leading article of your last number her spectacles fell off and were broken against the fender—after a faithful service of fifteen years,—and she has never been able to fit her eyes since,—so that I have been forced to

1 was intimated] was ⟨intended to be insinuated⟩ 4 as people] as ⟨the⟩ 8 life—your] life—⟨and various passages of your⟩ 10 and assert] and ⟨loudly⟩ assert without] assert ⟨that⟩ 13 very unfair] very ⟨f⟩ 17 a veteran] a ⟨female⟩ 31 who perused] who ⟨read⟩

read you aloud to her—and this is in fact the way in which I became acquainted with the subject of my present letter—and thus determined to become your correspondent.[31]

In the next place place Lord B's destiny seems in some sort like that of Hercules of old who became the author of all unappropriated prodigies.[32]—L.d B. has been supposed the author of "the Vampire" of a "Pilgrimage to Jerusalem"—"to the dead Sea" of "Death upon the pale horse" of Odes to "La Valette" to "Saint Helena" to the Land of the Gaul—and to a sucking Child.[33]——Now—he turned out to have written none of these things—besides you say he knows in what a spirit of &c. you criticise—are you sure he knows all this? that he has read you like my poor dear Aunt? they tell me he is a queer sort of a man—and I would not be too sure if I were you either of what he has read or of what he has written.———I thought his style had been the serious and terrible.—As to his sending you money—this is the first time that ever I heard of his paying his reviewers in *that coin*, I thought it was rather in *their own*—to judge from some of his earlier productions. Besides though he may not be profuse in his expenditure—I should conjecture that his reviewer's bill is not so long as his tailor's.—

Shall I give you what I think a prudent opinion.—I don't mean to insinuate—God forbid—but if by any accident—there should have been such a correspondence between you and the unknown author whoever he may be—send him back his money,—I dare say he will be very happy to have it again—it can't be much considering the value of the article—and the circulation of the Journal; and you are too modest to rate your praise beyond it's real worth,—don't be angry—I know you wont—at this appraisement of your powers of eulogy—for on the other hand—my dear fellow[34]—depend upon it your Abuse is worth, not it's own weight that's a feather; but *your* weight in gold. So don't spare it—if he has bargained for *that*—give it handsomely—and depend upon your doing him a friendly office.———

But I only speak in case of possibility—for as I said before—I cannot believe in the first instance that you would receive a bribe to praise any person whatever, and still less can I believe that your praise could ever

2–3 determined to] determined ⟨me⟩ 9 a sucking] a ⟨suckin⟩ 10 written none] written ⟨of⟩ 17 Besides] ⟨Shall⟩ Besides 18 he may] he ⟨is rather⟩ 19 his reviewer's] his ⟨tailor's bill may be larger than his reviewer's—⟩ 23 money,] money ⟨again⟩ 26 worth,—don't] worth,—⟨there is no doubt that⟩ 27 at this] at ⟨my⟩ 28–9 worth, not] worth, ⟨it's⟩

produce such an offer.—You are a good creature—my dear Roberts—and a clever fellow—else I could almost suspect that you had fallen into the very trap set for you in verse by this anonymous Wag, who will certainly be but too happy to see you saving him the trouble of making you ridiculous.—The fact is that the Solemnity of your eleventh article does make you look a little more absurd than you ever yet looked in all probability, and at the same time does no good—for if any body believed before in the octave stanzas they will believe still—and you will find it not less difficult to prove your negative than the learned Partridge found it to demonstrate his not being dead—to the satisfaction of the readers of Almanacks.[35]—— What the motives of this writer may have been for—(as you magnificently translate his quizzing you)—"stating with the particularity which belongs to fact the forgery of a groundless fiction" (do pray my dear R.—talk a little less "in King Cambyses' vein"[36]) I cannot pretend to say;—perhaps to laugh at you—but that is no reason for your benevolently making all the world laugh also.—I approve of your being angry—I tell you I am angry too—but you should not have shown it so outrageously. Your solemn "*if* somebody personating the Editor of the &c. &c. has received from L.d B. or from any other person" reminds me of Charley Incledon's usual exordium when people came in to the tavern to hear him sing without paying their share of the reckoning "If a Maun—or *ony* maun—or *ony other* maun"—&c. &c.—you have both the same redundant eloquence.[37] But why should you think any body would personate you?—nobody would dream of such a prank who ever read your compositions—and perhaps not many who have heard your conversation.——But I have been inoculated with a little of your prolixity.—The fact is, my dear Roberts, that somebody has tried to make a fool of you—and what he did not succeed in doing, you have done for him & for yourself.—— ———

With regard to the poem itself—or the author whom I cannot find out—(can you?)—I have nothing to say—my business is with you.—I am sure that you will upon second thoughts be really obliged to me for the intention of this letter—however far short my expressions may

7 ever yet] ever ⟨were before⟩ 9 to prove] to ⟨establish⟩ 10 Partridge found] Partridge ⟨did⟩ 13 translate his] translate ⟨it⟩ the particularity] the ⟨solemnity⟩ 15 little less] little ⟨like men of⟩ ⟨less⟩ 20 L.d B.] L.d ⟨or⟩ 23 a Maun] a ⟨Man⟩ *ony* maun] *ony* ⟨ma⟩ 27–8 have been] have ⟨caught⟩ 32 cannot find] cannot ⟨conjecture⟩

have fallen of the sincere good will—admiration—and thorough esteem with which I am ever—my dear Roberts—

most truly yours—
Wortley Clutterbuck.[38]

Sept.r 4.th 1819.[39]
Little Pidlington.

P.S. My letter is too long to revise—and the post is going.—I forget whether or not I asked you the meaning of your last words, though not dying speech and confession let us hope,[40]— "the forgery of a groundless fiction." now as all forgery is fiction—and all fiction a kind of forgery—is not this tautological? The Sentence would have ended more strongly with "forgery" only—it hath an awful bank of England sound;—and would have ended like an indictment besides sparing you several words and conferring a[41] meaning upon the remainder.—But this is mere verbal criticism.—Good bye—once more y^rs truly

W.C.

P.S. 2nd.—Is it true that the Saints make up the losses of the review?—It is very handsome in them to be at so great an expence—Pray pardon my taking up so much of your time from the bar, and from your clients, who I hear are about the same number with the readers of your journal. *Twice* more yours,

W.C.[42]

Italy, or *not* Corinna (1820)

Ravenna. August 19.th 1820.

Italy, or *not* Corinna:—a travelling Romance by an "Ecrivain en poste".[1]

In the year 181– not very long after the peace of Lord Castlereagh's which only resembled that of the Deity, in its passing "all

3 most] ⟨Y⟩ most 10 now as] now ⟨though⟩ all forgery] all ⟨fic⟩ 11 this tautological] this ⟨aski⟩ 14 conferring a] conferring ⟨upon⟩ ⟨some⟩ 26 after the] after ⟨that⟩

understanding"[2]—among the 100000 travellers who broke loose from Great Britain in all directions—there were two whose movements we mean to follow, and some others who will be found to follow those movements.—They were young men between twenty and thirty years of age—their names were Amundeville and Clutterbuck,[3]—which are still recorded in the various Inn-books of their route with considerable variations of orthography according to the accomplishments of the waiter who took them down for the police, they are also carved on some of the window frames, and written in the Album of Arqua[4] immediately under those of Mr. Solemnboy the poet Mrs. Solemnboy and the six Miss Solemnboys—who much about the same period began to travel—the young ladies for improvement, the old lady—for company, and Mr. Solemboy himself at the age of Sixty for the acquisition of languages—being addicted to translation.—The two single Gentlemen above mentioned posted in their light barouche,[5] with no great luggage—and a patience acquired on the great English North road of nine miles an hour, which however became more worthy of comparison with that of Job,[6] by the probationary exercise of several days Journey on German roads with German postillions, in their way to a more genial climate.———Mr. Solemnboy and family had more soberly contracted with a Vetturino[7] for the sum of twelve louis to convey them to Paris—finding them in food and the French language on the way—in consequence of which agreement they had ample leisure afforded for the digestion of the one and the acquisition of the other.—On their arrival at the grand metropolis of the civilized World, which at this period was civilizing the Bashkirs who had travelled all the way from the Chinese wall to see it[8]—they wondered, and were delighted—and Mr. Solemnboy published an Ode to the uppermost Emperor of the day[9]—which Mr. Galignani who appropriates most English works by republication has not yet pirated,[10]—though it has now been several years printed.—After a short stay in Paris, they accompanied their Vetturino to Switzerland and Italy in the same ratio as before and in the same vehicle—which though large—was neither speedy nor convenient.—It admitted the rain, but excluded the light, and was only airy during a high wind, or a snow storm.—However by dint of being obliged to get out on going up a hill, and of being thrown

12 the young] the ⟨Mi⟩ 14 translation.] translation ⟨and⟩ 16 a patience acquired] a patience ⟨proportioned to⟩ ⟨learned⟩ 22–3 language on] language ⟨by⟩ 24 afforded for] afforded ⟨by⟩ ⟨them⟩ 32–3 ratio as] ratio ⟨of⟩ 33 before and] before ⟨of⟩ 35 airy during] airy ⟨in⟩

out in going down one they contrived to see so much of the Country as to acquire a tolerable notion of landscape, and their letters dated G— were full of past and present description with very little assistance from Coxe's Guide-book.[11]——————

1 contrived to] contrived ⟨to⟩ 2 notion of landscape] notion of ⟨the⟩ 3 present description] present ⟨raptures⟩ 4 from Coxe's] from ⟨the⟩

SOME OBSERVATIONS UPON AN ARTICLE IN *BLACKWOOD'S EDINBURGH MAGAZINE* (1820)

Dedication

Dedication.—

To

—— Israeli Esqre.[1]

The amiable and ingenious Author of "the Calamities" and "Quarrels of Authors," this additional Quarrel and Calamity, is inscribed by one of the Number.————

[scrawl]

Motto.—

"Why how now Hecate? you look angrily.
Macbeth.[2]

Some Observations upon an Article in Blackwood's Edinburgh Magazine— No – August 1819.

March 15th 1820.

"The Life of a writer"—has been said, by Pope I believe—to be "*a warfare upon earth*"[1] as far as my own experience has gone I have nothing to say against the proposition—and like the rest having once plunged into this state of hostility—must, however reluctantly, carry it on.——An article has appeared in a periodical work—entitled "Remarks on Don Juan" which has been so full of this spirit on the part of the writer—as to require some observations on mine.—————

1 *Dedication.*—] *omitted in Proof* 3 —— Israeli Esqre.] J. D'Israeli, Esq. *in Proof* 5 this additional] this ⟨a⟩ by one] by ⟨his one⟩ 6 the Number] the ⟨Nu⟩ 8 Motto.—] *omitted in Proof* 20 been so] been ⟨very⟩

In the first place—I am not aware by what right—the Writer assumes this work which is anonymous to be my production.—He will answer that there is internal evidence—that is to say—that there are passages which appear to be written in my name or in my manner—but might not this have been done on purpose by another? He will say—why not then deny it?—To this I could answer that of all the things attributed to me within the last five years——Pilgrimages to Jerusalem—Deaths upon pale horses—Odes to the land of the Gaul—Adieus to England Songs to Madame La Valette—Odes to St Helena;—Vampires and what not—of which—God knows—I never composed nor read a syllable—beyond their titles in advertisements, I never thought it worth while to disavow any, except *one* which came linked with an account of my "residence in the Isle of Mitylene" where I never resided—and appeared to be carrying the amusement of those persons—who think my name can be of any use to them—a little too far.[2]—————

I should hardly therefore, if I did not take the trouble to disavow these things published in my name—& yet not mine, go out of my way—to deny an anonymous work; which might appear an act of Supererogation.—With regard to Don Juan—I neither deny nor admit it to be mine—every body may form their own opinion,—but if there be any—who now—or in the progress of that poem—if it is to be continued—feel or should feel themselves so aggrieved as to require a more explicit answer privately—and personally—they shall have it.—————

I have never shrunk from the responsibility of what I have written, and have more than once incurred obloquy by neglecting to disavow what was attributed to my pen without foundation.—————

The Greater part however of the "Remarks on Don Juan" contain but little on the work itself, which receives an extraordinary portion of praise as a composition.———With the exception of some quotations—and a few incidental remarks the rest of the article is neither more nor less than a personal attack upon the imputed author.———It is not the first in the same publication—for I recollect to have read some time ago—similar remarks upon "Beppo" (said to have been written by a

2 work which] work ⟨to be m⟩ 11 syllable—beyond] syllable—⟨except⟩ 12 never] have not *B's correction in GP* 15 use to] use ⟨of⟩ 19 to deny] to ⟨disa⟩ work; which] work; ⟨p⟩ 21 it to] it ⟨as⟩ opinion,—but] opinion,—⟨and⟩ 27 have more] have ⟨often⟩ to disavow] to ⟨contradict⟩ 33 the imputed] the ⟨supposed⟩

celebrated Northern Preacher) in which the conclusion drawn was that "Childe Harold—Byron—and the Count in Beppo were one and the same person"[3]—thereby making me turn out to be, as Mrs Malaprop says—"*like Cerberus three Gentlemen at once*."[4]——That article was signed "Presbyter Anglicanus" which I presume being interpreted means Scotch Presbyterian.———I must here observe, and it is at once ludicrous and vexatious to be compelled so frequently to repeat the same thing—that my case as an Author is peculiarly hard in being everlastingly taken or mistaken for my own Protagonist.——It is unjust and particular.———I never heard that my friend Moore was set down for a fire-worshipper on account of his Guebre[5]——that Scott was identified with Roderick Dhu or with Balfour of Burleigh;[6]—or that notwithstanding all the Magicians in Thalaba—any body has ever taken Mr Southey for a Conjuror.[7]———Whereas I have had some difficulty in extricating me even from Manfred—who as Mr Southey slily observes in one of his articles in the Quarterly—"Met the devil on the Jungfrau—and bullied him"[8]—and I answer Mr Southey—who has apparently in his political life not been so successful against the great Enemy,—that in this Manfred exactly followed the sacred precept—"Resist the Devil and he will flee from you."[9]——————I shall have more to say on the subject of this person—not the devil but Mr[10] Southey—before I conclude—but for the present I must return to the article in the Edinburgh Magazine.——————

In the course of this article amidst some most extraordinary observations there occur the following words—"It appears in short—as if this miserable man having exhausted *every species* of sensual Gratification, having drained the cup of Sin even to it's bitterest dregs—were resolved to show us that he is no longer a human being even in his frailties—but a cool unconcerned fiend laughing with a detestable glee over the whole of the better and worse elements of which human life is composed."—In another place there appears "the lurking place of his selfish and polluted exile."——"By my troth these be bitter words!"[11]—

1 celebrated Northern] celebrated ⟨Scottish⟩ 10 that my] that ⟨Mo⟩ 11 worshipper on] worshipper ⟨although⟩ his Guebre] his ⟨Hafed⟩ 13 Magicians in] Magicians ⟨of⟩ 14, 15, 17 Mr Southey] Mr * * *B's correction in Proof* 15 in extricating] in ⟨separating myself⟩ Manfred—who] Manfred—⟨in the public of⟩ 17 him"—and] him"—⟨to which⟩ 18 successful against] successful ⟨with⟩ 19 this Manfred] this ⟨he⟩ 21 person—not] person—⟨I mean⟩ but Mr] but ⟨this⟩ Mr] his humble servant Mr *B's correction in Proof* 23 article in] article ⟨in the⟩ 30 and worse] and ⟨the⟩ 31 composed."—] composed" ⟨&c with⟩ appears "the] appears ⟨these words⟩ 31–2 his selfish] his ⟨self⟩

With regard to the first sentence—I shall content myself with observing that it appears to have been composed for Sardanapalus, Tiberius—The Regent Duke of Orleans—or Louis 15th[12]—and that I have copied it with as much indifference as I would a passage from Suetonius—or from any of the private Memoirs of the Regency—conceiving it to be amply refuted by the terms in which it is expressed, and utterly[13] inapplicable to any private Individual.[14]——On the words "lurking place and "selfish and polluted exile" I have something more to say.—How far the capital city of a Government which survived the vicissitudes of thirteen hundred years, and might still have existed but for the treachery of Buonaparte and the iniquity of his imitators,—a City which was the Emporium of Europe when London and Edinburgh were dens of barbarians—may be termed a "lurking place" I leave to those who have seen—or heard of Venice to decide.[15]——— How far my exile may have been "polluted"—it is not for me to say—because the word is a wide one—and with some of it's branches may chance to overshadow the actions of most men; but that it has been "*selfish*" I deny.——If to the extent of my means—and my power—and my information of their calamities—to have assisted many miserable beings, reduced by the decay of the place of their birth, and their consequent loss of Substance;—if to have never rejected an application which appeared founded on truth—if to have expended in this manner sums far out of proportion to my fortune—there and elsewhere,—be selfish then have I been selfish.——To have done such things I do not deem much—but it is hard indeed to be compelled to recapitulate them in my own defence—by such accusations as that before me—like a pannel[16] before a Jury calling testimonies to his Character—or a soldier recording his services to obtain his discharge.—If the person who has made this[17] charge of "selfishness" wishes to inform himself further on the subject—he may acquire not what he would wish to find—but what will silence—and shame him—by applying to the Consul General of our Nation resident in the place—who will be in the case either to confirm or deny what I have asserted.[18]—————

I neither make—nor have ever made pretensions to Sanctity of demeanor—nor regularity of Conduct;—but my means have not

5 or from] or ⟨the⟩ 7–8 words "lurking] words ⟨self⟩ 9 of a] of ⟨g⟩ 13 were dens] were ⟨the⟩ 20 beings, reduced] beings, ⟨in⟩ reduced] to poverty *B's addition in GP* 24 selfish.——To] selfish.——⟨if⟩ ⟨To have⟩ 27–8 a soldier] a ⟨disbanded⟩ 28 soldier recording] soldier ⟨p⟩ 31 silence—] silence ⟨him⟩ by applying] by ⟨asking⟩ 35 regularity of] regularity ⟨in⟩ but my] but ⟨there⟩

been expended principally on my own gratification—neither now nor heretofore—neither in England nor out of it—and it waits[19] but a word from me,—if I thought that word decent or necessary, to call forth the most willing witnesses—at once witnesses and proofs—in England itself—to show that there are those who have derived not the mere temporary relief of a wretched boon, but the means which led them to immediate happiness and ultimate independence—by my want of that very "*Selfishness*" as grossly as falsely now imputed to my conduct.[20]— ————

Had I been a selfish man—had I been a grasping man—had I been in the worldly sense of the word—even a *prudent* man—I should not be where I now am,—I should not have taken the step which was the first that led to the events which have sunk a Gulph[21] between me and mine; but in this respect the truth will one day be made known—in the mean time as Durandarte[22] says in the Cave of Montesinos "Patience and shuffle the Cards."[23]——————

I bitterly feel the ostentation of this statement, the first of the kind I have ever made,—I feel the degradation of being compelled to make it; but I also feel it's *truth*, and I trust to feel it on my death-bed—should it be my lot to die there.—————I am not less sensible of the Egotism of all this—but Alas! who have made me thus egoistical[24] in my own defence?—if not they who by perversely persisting in referring fiction to truth—and tracing poetry to life—and regarding characters of imagination as creatures of existence—have made me personally responsible for almost every poetical delineation which my Fancy and a particular bias of thought may have tended to produce.——————

The writer continues—"Those who are acquainted, *as who is not*? with the *main* incidents of the private life of Ld B.—&c." assuredly whoever may be acquainted with these "main incidents" the writer of "the remarks on Don Juan" is not, or he would use a very different language. —That which I believe he alludes to as a "main incident" happened to be a very subordinate one—and the natural and almost inevitable consequence of events and circumstances long prior to the period at which it occurred. It is the last drop which makes the Cup run over,—

1 been expended] been ⟨all⟩ 3 forth the] forth ⟨such⟩ 5 itself—to] itself—⟨of⟩ 6 wretched boon] wretched ⟨dole⟩ the means] the ⟨nec⟩ 13 led to] led ⟨the way⟩ to the] to ⟨my⟩ have sunk] have ⟨built a barrier⟩ ⟨raised⟩ 15 as Durandarte] as ⟨Montesinos says—or⟩ 18 make it] make ⟨it⟩ 23 tracing poetry] tracing ⟨poetical⟩ 24 imagination as] imagination ⟨for⟩ 25 my Fancy] my *deleted by B in Proof* 30 very different] very ⟨di⟩ different language] different ⟨tone⟩

and mine was already full.[25]———But to return to this man's charge—he accuses Ld. B. of "an elaborate satire on the character and manners of his wife."—From what parts of Don Juan the writer has inferred this, he himself best knows,—as far as I recollect of the female characters in that production—there is but one who is depicted in ridiculous colours,—or that could be interpreted as a Satire upon any body.[26]—But here—my poetical sins are again visited upon me[27]—supposing that the poem be mine.—If I depict a Corsair—a Misanthrope—a Libertine—a Chief of insurgents—or an Infidel—he is set down to the Author—and if in a poem by no means ascertained to be my production—there appears a disagreeable, casuistical, and by no means respectable female pedant—it is set down for my wife.——Is there any resemblance? if there be it is in those who make it;—I can see none.——In my writings I have rarely described any character under a fictitious name—those of whom I have spoken—have had their own—in many cases a stronger satire in itself than any which could be appended to it.——But of real circumstances I have availed myself plentifully both in the serious and in the ludicrous—they are to poetry—what landscape is[28] to the painter—but my *figures* are not portraits.——It may even have happened that I have seized on some events that have occurred under my own observation, or in my own family,—as I would paint a view from my grounds did it harmonize with my picture, but I never would introduce the likenesses of it's living members—unless their features could be made as favourable to themselves as to the effect—which in the above instance would be extremely difficult.—————

My learned brother proceeds to observe that "it is in vain for Ld. B. to attempt in any way to justify his own behaviour in that affair—and now that he has so *openly* and *audaciously* invited enquiry and reproach—we do not see any good reason why he should not be plainly told so by the voice of his countrymen."—How far the "openness" of an anonymous poem—and the "audacity" of an imaginary character which the writer supposes to be meant for Lady B. may be deemed to

2 accuses Ld.] accuses ⟨me⟩ 3 has inferred] has ⟨deduced⟩ 4 this, he] this ⟨conclusion⟩ knows,—as] knows,—⟨b⟩ 5 one who] one ⟨that⟩ depicted in] depicted ⟨as⟩ 11 appears a] appears ⟨to⟩ 11–12 means respectable] means ⟨very moral⟩ 12 it] She *B's correction in GP* 14 my writings] my ⟨?main⟩ have rarely] have ⟨never⟩ 15 have spoken] have ⟨satirized⟩ ⟨named⟩ have had] have ⟨been put under their⟩ 18 are to] are ⟨the lan⟩ 20 on some] on ⟨such⟩ 21 that have] that ⟨may⟩ 22 my grounds] my ⟨own⟩ 23 never would] never ⟨introduced nor⟩ of it's] of ⟨such⟩ 27 that "it] that ⟨now⟩

merit this formidable denunciation from their "most sweet voices"[29] I neither know nor care, but when he tells me that I cannot "in any way *justify* my own behaviour in that affair" I acquiesce—because no man can "*justify*" himself until he knows of what he is accused,—and I have never had—and, God knows, My whole desire has ever been to obtain it—any specific charge in a tangible shape submitted to me—by the adversary—nor by others—unless the atrocities of public rumour, and the mysterious silence of the Lady's legal advisers may be deemed such.—But is not the Writer content with what has been already said and done?—But is not the Writer content with what has been already said and done? Has not "the general voice of his Countrymen" long ago pronounced upon the subject—sentence without trial—and condemnation without a charge?——Have I not been exiled by Ostracism, except that the shells which proscribed me were anonymous?[30]—Is the writer ignorant of the public opinion—and the public conduct upon that occasion?—If he is—I am not—the Public will forget both long before I shall cease to remember either.————

The Man who is exiled by a faction has the consolation of thinking that he is a Martyr, he is upheld by hope and by[31] the dignity of his cause real or imaginary,—he who withdraws from the pressure of debt may indulge in the thought that time and prudence will retrieve his circumstances—he who is condemned by the law has a term to his banishment—or a dream of it's abbreviation—or it may be the knowledge or the belief of some injustice of the law or of it's administration in his own particular;—but he who is outlawed by general opinion without the intervention of hostile politics,—illegal judgement,—or embarrassed circumstances,—whether he be innocent or guilty must undergo all the bitterness of Exile without hope—without pride—without alleviation.[32]———

This case was mine.—Upon what grounds the Public founded their opinion—I am not aware—but it was general—and it was decisive.—Of me or of mine—they knew little except that I had written what is called poetry—was a nobleman—had married, become a father—and

1 denunciation from] denunciation ⟨of⟩ 3 that affair"] that ⟨behaviour⟩ 6 in a] in ⟨any⟩ 6–7 the adversary] the ⟨parties⟩ 7 others—unless] others—⟨except⟩ the atrocities] the ⟨violence⟩ of public] of ⟨popular⟩ 14 which proscribed] which ⟨sentenced⟩ 19 Martyr, he] Martyr ⟨to a good cause—that⟩ 20 he who] he ⟨is⟩ the pressure] the ⟨oppression⟩ 21 may indulge] may ⟨ha⟩ 23 a dream] a ⟨hope⟩ be the] be ⟨a⟩ 26 of hostile] of ⟨polit⟩ politics,—illegal] politics,—⟨law⟩ ⟨adverse⟩ 32 knew little] knew ⟨nothing⟩

been involved[33] in differences with my wife and her relatives,—no one knew why, because the persons complaining refused to *state* their grievance.[34]——————

The fashionable world was divided into parties, mine consisting of a very small minority—the reasonable world was naturally on the stronger side—which happened to be the lady's as was most proper and polite—the press was active and scurrilous—& such was the rage of the day that the unfortunate publication of two copies of verses rather complimentary than otherwise to the subjects of both—were tortured into a species of crime or constructive petty treason.[35]———I was accused of every monstrous vice by public rumour,—and private rancour; my name which had been a knightly or a noble one since My fathers helped to conquer the kingdom for William the Norman, was tainted.—I felt that, If what was whispered and muttered and murmured was true—I was unfit for England,—if false—England was unfit for me.—————I withdrew—But this was not enough.—In other countries—in Switzerland—in the shadow of the Alps—and by the blue depth of the Lakes I was pursued and breathed upon by the same blight.———I crossed the Mountains—but it was the same—so I went little farther,[36] and settled myself by the waves of the Adriatic,—like the Stag at bay who betakes him to the waters.[37]——————

If I may judge by the statements of the few friends who gathered round me—the outcry of the period to which I allude was beyond all precedent, all parallell, even in those cases where political motives have sharpened slander—and doubled enmity.—I was advised not to go to the theatres lest I should be hissed,—nor to my duty in parliament lest I should be insulted by the way—even on the day of my departure my most intimate friend told me afterwards that he was under apprehensions of violence—from the people who might be assembled at the door of the Carriage.[38]—However I was not deterred by these counsels from seeing Kean in his best characters;[39] nor from voting according to my principles,[40] and with regard to the third and

1 relatives,—no] relatives.—⟨Upon these grounds or the like⟩ 4 The] ⟨With⟩ The 5 reasonable world] reasonable ⟨party⟩ 8 of two] of ⟨some lines⟩ 9 to] to one of *B's addition in GP* to the] to ⟨the⟩ ⟨both⟩ 9 of both] *deleted by B in GP* 9–10 were tortured] were ⟨construed⟩ 11 monstrous vice] monstrous ⟨crime⟩ 12 which had] which ⟨for⟩ since My] since ⟨the⟩ 13 fathers helped] fathers ⟨had⟩ 14 whispered and] whispered ⟨and⟩ 17 shadow] shadow⟨s⟩ 20 myself by] myself ⟨in⟩ ⟨amidst⟩ the waves] the ⟨waters⟩ 21 the waters.] the ⟨pool.———⟩ 25 and doubled] and ⟨cried on the hounds⟩ doubled enmity] doubled ⟨en⟩ 26 theatres lest] theatres ⟨for⟩ hissed,—nor] hissed,—⟨and⟩ 27 even on] even ⟨at⟩ 29 the people] the ⟨persons⟩ 32 principles, and] principles, ⟨nor from⟩

last apprehensions of my friends—I could not share in them—not being made acquainted with their extent till some time after I had crossed the Channel.————Even if I had been so—I am not of a nature to be much affected by men's anger—though I may feel hurt by their aversion, against all individual outrage I could protect or redress myself—and against that of a crowd I should probably have been enabled to defend myself with the assistance of others as has been done on similar occasions.—————

I retired from the country perceiving that I was the object of general obloquy; I did not indeed imagine Like Jean Jacques Rousseau that all mankind was in a conspiracy against me—though I had perhaps as good grounds for such a chimera as ever he had,[41]—but I perceived that I had to a great extent become personally obnoxious in England—perhaps through my own fault—but the fact was indisputable;—for the public in general would hardly have been so much excited against a more popular character—without at least an accusation or a charge of some kind actually expressed or substantiated——for I can hardly conceive that the common & every day occurrence of a separation between man and wife could in itself produce so great a ferment.——I shall say nothing of the usual complaints of "being prejudged"[42] "condemned unheard" "unfairness"—"partiality" and so forth—the usual changes rung by parties who have had—or are to have a trial—but I was a little surprized—to find myself condemned without being favoured with the act of accusation—and to perceive in the absence of this portentous charge or charges—whatever it or they were to be—that every possible or impossible crime was rumoured to supply it's place—and taken for granted.———This could only occur in the case of a person very much disliked—and I knew no remedy—having already used to their extent whatever little powers I might possess of pleasing in society.—I had no party in fashion—though I was afterwards told that there was one—but it was not of my formation—nor did I then know of it's existence—none in literature—and in politics I had voted with the whigs—with precisely that importance which a

5 their aversion] their ⟨dislike⟩ I could] I ⟨can⟩ protect or] protect ⟨and⟩ 10 imagine Like] imagine ⟨th⟩ all] *deleted by B in GP* 10–11 all mankind] all ⟨Europe⟩ 13 personally obnoxious] personally ⟨odious⟩ 14 for] *deleted by B in Proof* 16 least an] least ⟨a cause⟩ 18 common &] common ⟨event⟩ 20 usual] common *B's correction in GP* 24 to perceive] to ⟨find⟩ the absence] the ⟨dearth⟩ 25 it or] it ⟨was,⟩ 28 disliked—and] disliked—⟨an⟩ ⟨truth which⟩ 31–2 nor did] nor ⟨di⟩ 33 voted with] voted ⟨with⟩

whig vote possesses in these Tory days, and with such personal acquaintance with the leaders in both houses as the society in which I lived—sanctioned—but without claim or expectation of anything like friendship from any one except a few young men of my own age and standing, and a few others more advanced in life—which last it had been my fortune to serve in circumstances of difficulty.[43]———This was in fact to stand alone—and I recollect some time after Madame de Stael said to me in Switzerland——"You should not have warred with the World—it will not do—it is too strong always for any individual—I myself once tried it in early life—but it will not do."[44]——I perfectly acquiesce in the truth of this remark,—but the World had done me the honour to begin the war; and assuredly if peace is only to be obtained by courting and paying tribute to it; I am not qualified to obtain it's countenance.———I thought in the Words of Campbell—

"Then wed thee to an exiled lot
And if the World hath loved thee not
It's absence may be borne.——[45]

I recollect however that having been much hurt by Romilly's conduct, (he having a general retainer for me had acted as adviser to the adversary—alledging[46] on being reminded of his retainer that he had forgotten it as his Clerk had so many) I observed that some of those who were now eagerly laying the axe to my roof-tree[47]—might see their own shaken, and feel a portion of what they had inflicted.—His fell and crushed him.[48]——————

I have heard of, and believe that there are human beings so constituted as to be insensible to injuries,——but I believe that the best mode to avoid taking vengeance—is to go[49] out of the way of the temptation.———I hope that I may never have the opportunity—for I am not quite sure that I could resist it, having derived from my mother something of the "perfervidum ingenium Scotorum."[50]—I have not sought—and shall not seek—it, and perhaps it may never come in my path.———I do not in this allude to the party, who might be right or

1 days, and] days, ⟨"⟩ with such] with ⟨little⟩ 2 leaders in] leaders ⟨of⟩ 5 life—which] life—⟨whom⟩ 6 in circumstances] in ⟨their⟩ 8 me in] me ⟨aft⟩ 9 World—it] World—⟨no—⟩ do—it] do—⟨they are⟩ 10 I myself] I ⟨have⟩ 14 thought in] thought ⟨of⟩ 19 he having] he ha⟨d⟩ me had] me ⟨and⟩ ⟨nevertheless⟩ 21 that some] that ⟨tho⟩ 22 now eagerly] now ⟨acting with such eagerness to⟩ 23 they had] they ⟨wished to⟩ 26–7 best mode] best ⟨way to⟩ 27 mode to] mode ⟨of⟩ is to] is ⟨not to h⟩ 27–8 of the temptation] the *deleted by B in Proof* 32 party, who] party, ⟨who⟩

wrong;—but to many who made her cause the pretext of their own bitterness.——She indeed must have long avenged me in her own feelings—for whatever her reasons may have been—(and She never adduced them to me at least) She probably neither contemplated nor conceived to what she became the means of conducting the father of her child, and the husband of her choice.———————

So much for "the General voice of his countrymen" I will now speak of some in particular.———————

In the beginning of the year 1817,—an article appeared in the Quarterly Review—written I believe by Walter Scott—doing great honour to him—and no disgrace to me—though both poetically and personally more than sufficiently favourable to the work & the author of whom it treated.[51]——It was written at a time, when a selfish man would not, and a timid one dared not have said a word in favour of either—it was written by one to whom temporary public opinion had elevated me to the rank of a rival—a proud distinction and unmerited, but which has not prevented me from feeling as a friend—nor him from more than corresponding to that sentiment.———The article in question was written upon the third Canto of Childe Harold—and after many observations which it would as ill become me to repeat as to forget, concluded with "a hope that I might yet return to England."[52]———How this expression was received in England itself—I am not acquainted but it gave great offence at Rome to the respectable ten or twenty thousand English travellers then and there assembled.—I did not visit Rome till some time after, so that I had no opportunity of knowing the fact, but I was informed long afterwards that the greatest indignation had been manifested in the enlightened Anglo-circle of that year, which happened to comprize within it—amidst a considerable leaven of Welbeck Street, and Devonshire Place broken loose upon their travels, several really well born—and well-bred families, who did not the less participate in the feeling of the hour.[53]———"*Why* should he return to England?" was the general exclamation—

1 cause the] cause ⟨a me⟩ 2 She indeed] She ⟨ha⟩ 10 Walter Scott] It was also written when another poetical friend having formerly ventured a line of praise in his M.S. *afraid* to publish—and ashamed to cancel—*waited* for a year or two, and at last ventured ⟨t⟩ ⟨with⟩ to print not without considerable apprehension that the 3 or 4 lines of compliment to me might not ruin his whole work. *B's additional note in GP* 12 sufficiently favourable] sufficiently ⟨favour⟩ 15 one to] one ⟨wh⟩ whom temporary] whom ⟨the⟩ 18 from more] from ⟨amply⟩ 25 after, so] after, ⟨but⟩ 26 informed long] informed ⟨subsequently⟩ 28–9 considerable leaven] considerable ⟨leaven⟩

I answer—*Why*?.———It is a question I have occasionally asked myself and I never yet could give it a satisfactory reply.—I had then no thoughts of returning—and if I have any now—they are of business, and not of pleasure.—Amidst the ties that have been dashed to pieces,[54] there are links yet entire though the chain itself be broken.—There are duties, and connections, which may one day require my presence—and I am a father.——I have still some friends whom I wish to meet again, and, it may be, an Enemy.[55]——————These things and those minuter details of business which Time accumulates during absence—in every man's affairs and property—may & probably will recall me to England—but I shall return with the same feelings with which I left it,—in respect to itself—though altered with regard to individuals, as I have been more or less informed of their conduct since my departure—for it was only a considerable time after my departure[56] that I was made acquainted with the real facts and full extent of some of their proceedings and language.——My friends—like other friends—from conciliatory motives witheld from me much that they could—and some things which they *should* have unfolded——however that which is deferred is not lost,[57]—but it has been no fault of mine that it has been deferred at all.————

I have alluded to what is said to have passed at Rome—merely to show that the Sentiment which I have described was not confined to the English in England—and as forming part of my answer to the reproach cast upon what has been called my "selfish exile" and my "voluntary exile."[58]——"Voluntary" it has been—for who would dwell among a people entertaining strong hostility against him?—how far it has been "selfish" has been already explained.

I have now arrived at a passage describing me as having vented my "spleen against the lofty minded and virtuous men" men "whose virtues few indeed can equal"—meaning I humbly presume the notorious triumvirate known by the name of "Lake Poets" in their aggregate capacity, and by those of Southey—Wordsworth—and Coleridge when taken singly.———I wish to say a word or two upon

2 yet could] yet ⟨gi⟩ 5 entire though] entire ⟨that bind me as firmly as a heavier chain.—⟩ 8 Enemy.] Enemy ⟨,——when I meet the latter⟩ 9 minuter details] minuter ⟨details⟩ 12 with regard] with ⟨respect⟩ 14 after my departure] after it *B's correction in Proof* 17 me much] me ⟨all⟩ 18 *should*] *emphasis omitted in Proof and restored by B* 21 have alluded] have ⟨referred⟩ passed at] passed ⟨in⟩ 25 would dwell] would ⟨live⟩ 26 entertaining strong] entertaining ⟨the opinions manifested⟩ 31 triumvirate known] triumvirate ⟨of⟩ 32 by those] by ⟨that⟩ 33 Coleridge when] Coleridge ⟨in their⟩

the virtues of one of those persons—public and private—for reasons which will soon appear.——————

When I left England in April 1816,—ill in mind—in body, and in circumstances—I took up my residence at Cologny by the lake of Geneva.[59]——The sole companion of my journey was a young Physician—who had to make his way in the world, and having seen little of it—was naturally and laudably desirous of seeing more Society—than suited either my present habits or my past experience.——I therefore presented him to those Gentlemen of Geneva for whom I had letters of introduction—and having thus seen him in a situation to make his own way,—retired for my own part entirely from society—with the exception of that of one English family living at about a quarter of a mile's distance from Diodati,—and with the further exception of some occasional intercourse with Coppet—at the wish of Madame de Stael.[60]——————The English family to which I allude consisted of two ladies, a Gentleman—and his son—a boy of a year old.——————

One of "*these lofty minded and virtuous men*" in the words of the Edinburgh Magazine—made I understand about this time or soon after a tour in Switzerland.—On his return to England, he circulated—and for anything I know—invented a report—that the Gentleman to whom I have alluded—and myself were living in promiscuous intercourse with two Sisters "having formed a league of Incest" (I quote the words as they were stated to me)[61]—and indulged himself in the natural comments upon such a conjunction—which are said to have been repeated publicly with great complacency by *another* of that poetical fraternity,—of whom I shall say only that even had the Story been true—*he* should not have repeated it as far as it regarded myself,—except in Sorrow.[62]—The tale itself requires but a word in answer—the ladies were *not* Sisters—nor in any degree connected—except by the second marriage of their respective parents—a widower with a widow—both being the offspring of former marriages—neither of them were in 1816.—nineteen years old.[63]——"Promiscuous intercourse" could hardly have disgusted the great patron of Pantisoc-

1 persons—public] persons—⟨at⟩ 5 Geneva.——The] Geneva.——⟨I had no⟩ 7 laudably desirous] laudably ⟨to see⟩ 8–9 therefore presented] therefore ⟨introduced⟩ 9 to those] to ⟨such⟩ 11 part entirely] part ⟨to⟩ 12 that of] *deleted by B in Proof* 14 the wish] the ⟨particul⟩ 15–16 of two] of ⟨three⟩ of a] of ⟨three⟩ 23–4 the natural] the ⟨usual⟩ 24 which are] which ⟨were⟩ 26 say only] say ⟨nothing⟩ 29 degree connected] degree ⟨rl⟩ ⟨related⟩ 30 parents—a] parents—⟨both⟩ 31 both being] both ⟨these⟩ marriages—neither] marriages—⟨and⟩ 32 them were] them ⟨at⟩

racy—(does Mr Southey remember such a scheme?) but there was none.[64]——————

How far this Man—who as author of Wat Tyler—has been proclaimed by the Lord Chancellor guilty of a treasonable and blasphemous libel,—and denounced in the House of Commons by the upright and able Member for Norwich—as a "rancorous renegado" be fit for sitting as a Judge upon others—let others judge.———He has said that for this expression—"he brands W. Smith on the forehead—as a Calumniator," and that "the mark will outlast his Epitaph."[65]—How long Wm Smith's epitaph will last—and in what words it will be written—I know not—but William Smith's words form the Epitaph itself of Robert Southey.———He has written Wat. Tyler and taken the office of Poet Laureate—he has in the life of Henry Kirke White denominated reviewing "the ungentle Craft" and has become a reviewer,[66]—he was one of the projectors of a scheme called "Pantisocracy" for having all things including Women in common (query common women?) and he sets up as a moralist—he denounced the battle of Blenheim—and he praised the battle of Waterloo,[67] he loved Mary Wollstonecraft and he tried to blast the character of her daughter—(one of the young females mentioned[68]) he wrote treason and serves the king, he was the Butt of the Antijacobin, and he is the prop of the Quarterly Review[69]—licking the hands that smote him—eating the bread of his enemies, and internally writhing beneath his own contempt,—he would fain conceal under anonymous bluster, and a vain endeavour to obtain the esteem of others after having forever lost his own, his leprous leprous sense of his own degredation.——

What is there in such a man to "*envy*"?—who ever envied the envious?———Is it his birth—his name—his fame—or his virtues that I am to "envy?"———I was born of the Aristocracy which he abhorred, and am sprung by my Mother from the kings who preceded those whom he has hired himself to sing;[70]—it cannot then be his birth;—as a poet, I have for the past eight years had nothing to apprehend from a

3 as author] as ⟨the⟩ 4 Chancellor guilty] Chancellor ⟨as⟩ 6 and able] and ⟨wise⟩ 10 and in] and ⟨of⟩ 11 words form] words ⟨are⟩ the Epitaph] the ⟨actual⟩ 12 itself of] itself ⟨of Mr Southey.⟩ Southey.———] Southey⟨,—Poet Laureate.⟩ 14 reviewing "the] reviewing ⟨as⟩ 16–17 query common] query ⟨whether⟩ 21 the Butt] the ⟨theme of⟩ ⟨Scorn⟩ the Antijacobin] the ⟨Antij⟩ 21–2 the prop] the ⟨pride⟩ 24 contempt,—he] contempt,—⟨which⟩ conceal under] conceal ⟨beneath⟩ 26 own, his] own⟨.——————⟩ his leprous] his ⟨hideous⟩ 29 the Aristocracy] the ⟨A⟩ 30 who preceded] who ⟨prec⟩ 31 it cannot] it ⟨is not⟩ his birth] his ⟨station⟩ 32 the past] the ⟨last⟩

competition—and for the future "that life to come in every poet's creed"[71] it is open to all.——I will only remind Mr. Southey in the words of a Critic—who if still living would have annihilated Southey's literary existence now and hereafter—as the sworn foe of Charlatans and impostors from Macpherson downwards—that "those dreams were Settle's once and Ogilby's"[72]—and for my own part—I assure him—that whenever he and his sect are remembered—I shall be "proud to be forgot."[73]—That he is not content with his success as a poet may be reasonably believed—he has been the Nine-pin of reviews, the Edinburgh knocked him down—and the Quarterly set him up—the Government found him useful—in the periodical line, and made a point of recommending his works to purchasers[74]—so that he is occasionally bought—(I mean his books as well as the author) and may be found on the shelf,—if not upon the table,—of most of the gentlemen employed in the different offices.——————With regard to his private virtues—I know nothing;—of his principles—I have heard enough.———As far as having been to the best of my power—benevolent to others, I do not fear the comparison—and for the errors of the passions was Mr. S. *always* so tranquil and stainless? Did he *never* covet his neighbour's wife?—did he never calumniate his neighbour's wife's daughter?—the offspring of her he coveted?[75]——So much for the Apostle of Pantisocracy.——

Of the "lofty minded virtuous" Wordsworth—one anecdote will suffice to speak his sincerity.——In a conversation with Mr. Rogers—upon poetry—he concluded with "after all I would not give five shillings for all that Southey has ever written."[76]—Perhaps this calculation might rather show his esteem for five shillings than his low estimate of Mr. Southey, but considering that when he was in his need and Southey had a shilling—Wordsworth is said to have had generally sixpence out of it—it has an awkward sound in the way of valuation. This anecdote was told me by Moore—who had it from Rogers—who

1 the future] the ⟨futh⟩ 3 who if] who ⟨had he still ⟨existed⟩ lived⟩ 4 existence now] existence ⟨h⟩ hereafter—as] hereafter—⟨sw⟩ 6 for my] for ⟨my⟩ 9 the Nine-pin] the ⟨puppet⟩ 10 Edinburgh knocked] Edinburgh ⟨wrote⟩ Quarterly set] Quarterly ⟨wrote⟩ 13 as the] as ⟨himself⟩ the author] the ⟨aut⟩ 18 I do] I ⟨ha⟩ and for] and ⟨with th⟩ 20 never calumniate] never ⟨bear⟩ 21 coveted?——So] coveted?——⟨But I have done with him for the present.——————⟩ 24 suffice to] suffice ⟨for⟩ Mr. Rogers] *deleted by B in Proof; a dash substituted by B.* 27 shillings than] shillings ⟨rather⟩ his low] his ⟨contempt⟩ 31–p. 103 2 Moore ... genealogy] persons—who if quoted by name would ⟨show⟩ prove that it's genealogy is poetical as well as true.—*B's correction in Proof*

had it from Wordsworth himself—so that it has a most poetical genealogy.[77]——I give my authority—for this; and am ready to adduce it for Mr. Southey's circulation of the falsehood before mentioned.[78]—————

Of Coleridge I shall say nothing—*why*—he may divine.[79]———

I have said more of these people than I intended in this place—being somewhat stirred by the remarks which induced me to commence upon the topic.———I see nothing in these men as poets, or as individuals—little in their talents and less in their characters to prevent honest men from expressing for them considerable contempt—in prose or rhyme—as it may happen.——Mr. Southey has the Quarterly for his field of rejoinder—and Mr. Wordsworth his postscripts to "Lyrical ballads"—where the two great instances of the Sublime are taken from himself and Milton.——"Over her own sweet voice the Stockdove broods"[80] that is to say—She has the pleasure of listening to herself, in common with Mr. W. upon most of his public appearances.—"What Divinity doth hedge"[81] these persons—that we should respect them—is it Apollo?—Are they not of those who called Dryden's Ode "a drunken song"[82] who have discovered that Gray's elegy is full of faults (See Coleridge's life—vol. 1st. Note—for Wordsworth's kindness in pointing this out to him)[83] and have published what is allowed to be the very worst prose that ever was written to prove that Pope was no poet and that William Wordsworth is.[84]—In other points are they respectable—or respected? is it on the open avowal of apostacy—on the patronage of Government—that their claim is founded?—Who is there who esteems these[85] parricides of their own Principles?——They are in fact well aware that the reward of their change has been anything but honour.———The times have preserved a respect for political consistency, and even the[86] Changeable honour the unchanged.——Look at Moore—it will be long ere Southey meets with such a triumph in London as Moore met with in

2 I give] I can *B's addition in Proof* and am] and ⟨for⟩ to adduce] to ⟨give⟩ 3 it for] it also *B's addition in Proof* 7–8 to commence] to ⟨re⟩ 9 individuals—little] individuals—⟨too⟩ ⟨nothing⟩ 10 prevent honest] prevent ⟨me⟩ them considerable] them ⟨the⟩ 11 or rhyme] or ⟨verse⟩ 16 to herself] to ⟨her⟩ ⟨her⟩ Mr. W. upon] Mr. W. ⟨himself⟩ 23 poet and] poet ⟨.———⟩ is.—In] is.—⟨The only thing proved in Wordsworth's ⟨two⟩ postscript—is that⟩ 24 other points] other ⟨res⟩ it on] it ⟨by⟩ the open] the ⟨p⟩ 25 apostacy—on] apostacy—⟨by⟩ the patronage] the ⟨pay⟩ 27 They are] ⟨Are t⟩hey ⟨not⟩ aware that] aware ⟨of⟩ the reward] the ⟨sole⟩ 28 their change] their ⟨Virtue's⟩ 29 consistency, and] consistency, ⟨and which⟩ 31 a triumph] a ⟨reception⟩

Dublin—even if the Government should subscribe for it & set the money down to Secret Service.[87]————It was not less to the Man than to the poet, to the tempted but unshaken patriot—to the poor but[88] incorruptible fellow Citizen that the warm hearted[89] Irish paid the proudest of tributes.——Mr. Southey may applaud himself to the World—but he has his own heartiest contempt, and the fury with which he foams against all who stand in the phalanx which he forsook is as William Smith described it—the "rancour of the renegado"—the bad language of the prostitute who stands at the corner of the Street—and showers her Slang upon all—except those who may have bestowed upon her her "little Shilling."—————

Hence his quarterly overflowings political and literary—in what he has himself termed "the ungentle Craft," and his especial wrath against Mr. Leigh Hunt—notwithstanding that Hunt has done more for Wordsworth's reputation as a poet (such as it is)—than all the Lakers could in their interchange of Self-praises for the last twenty five years.[90]————

And here I wish to say a few words on the present State of English Poetry.——That this is the Age of the Decline of English Poetry will be doubted by few who have calmly considered the Subject.—That there are men of Genius among the present Poets—makes little against the fact—because it has been well said that "next to him who forms the taste of his Country—the greatest Genius is he who corrupts it."[91]—No one has ever denied Genius to Marini who corrupted not merely the taste of Italy—but that of all Europe for nearly a Century.[92]—————

The great cause of the present deplorable state of English Poetry is to be attributed—to that absurd and systematic depreciation of Pope, in which for the last few years there has been a king of Epidemical concurrence.——Men of the most opposite opinions have united upon this topic.—Warton and Churchill began it,[93] having borrowed the hint probably from the heroes[94] of the Dunciad—and their own internal conviction that their proper reputation must[95] be as nothing

1 should] shall *in Proof, deleted by B* set the] set ⟨it⟩ 2 Service.—] Service ⟨secrecy.⟩ 3 poor] not opulent *B's correction in Proof* 4 warm] vain- *in Proof*] warm- *B's correction in Proof* 7 who stand] who ⟨have⟩ 11 have bestowed] have ⟨purchased her⟩ 12 Hence] ⟨This interval⟩ Hence 14 Hunt—notwithstanding] Hunt—⟨who⟩ 18 present State] present ⟨State⟩ 24 Marini] Marino *in Proof*] Marini *B's correction in Proof* 28 that absurd] that ⟨atrocious and⟩ 29 years there] years ⟨it⟩ 32 heroes] hero *in Proof*] heroes *B's correction in Proof* 33 their proper] their ⟨own⟩ must] can *in Proof; uncorrected by B*

till the most perfect and harmonious of poets—he who having no fault—has had REASON made his reproach—was reduced to what they conceived to be his level—but even *they* dared not degrade him below Dryden.[96]———Goldsmith and Rogers and Campbell his most successful disciples, and Hayley who however feeble has one poem "that will not be willingly let die"[97] (the Triumphs of Temper) kept up the reputation of that pure and perfect Style, and Crabbe—the first of living Poets—has almost equalled the Master.[98]——Then came Darwin who was put down by a single poem in the Antijacobin,[99] and the Cruscans—from Merry to Jerningham—who were annihilated—(if *Nothing* can be said to be annihilated) by Gifford—the last of the wholesome English Satirists.[100]——————

At the same time Mr. Southey was favouring the Public with Wat. Tyler. and Joan of Arc to the great glory of the Drama and Epos.—I beg pardon—Wat Tyler—with Peter Bell was still in M.S.S.[101]—and it was not till after Mr. Southey had received his Malmsey Butt, and Mr. Wordsworth became qualified to gauge it, that the great revolutionary tragedy came before the public and the Court of Chancery.[102]——— Wordsworth was peddling his Lyrical Ballads—and brooding a preface to be succeeded in due course of years by a postscript,[103] both couched in such prose as must give peculiar delight to those who have read the prefaces of Pope and Dryden—both[104] scarcely less celebrated for the beauty of their prose than for the charms of their verse.—Wordsworth is the reverse of Moliere's Gentleman "who had been talking prose all his life without knowing it"[105] for he thinks that he has been all his life writing both prose and verse, and neither of what he conceives to be such can be properly said to be either one or the other.*[106]———Mr. Coleridge—the future Vates,—poet & Seer of

* Goldsmith has anticipated the definition of the Lake poetry—as far as such things can be defined—"Gentlemen—the present piece is not one of your *common epic poems*, which come from the press like paper kites in Summer; there are none of your Turnuses or Didos in it;[107] *it is an heroical description of Nature.*—I only beg you'll endeavour to make your

1 he who] he ⟨to⟩ who⟨m⟩ 3 his level] his ⟨proper⟩ level—but] level—⟨viz—⟩ 4 Goldsmith] ⟨Hayley⟩ Goldsmith 5 feeble has] feeble ⟨elsewhere,⟩ 6 Temper) kept] Temper) ⟨have⟩ 7 the first] the ⟨only li⟩ 10 Merry to] Merry ⟨and down⟩ 11–12 the wholesome] the ⟨gr⟩ 14 and Epos] and ⟨Epic.——⟩ 15 Bell was] Bell ⟨were⟩ in M.S.S.] in ⟨the Pr⟩ 16 his Malmsey] his ⟨Butt⟩ 17 that the] that ⟨those two⟩ 19 and brooding] and ⟨writing the⟩ 20 in due] in ⟨the⟩ 22 Dryden—both] Dryden—⟨scarcely inferior⟩ both] *deleted by B in Proof* 23 the charms] the ⟨harmony⟩ 24 Wordsworth] ⟨Assuredly⟩ Wordsworth is the] is ⟨not⟩ 27 be properly] be ⟨truly⟩ 31 are none] are ⟨none of⟩

the Morning Post, (an honour also claimed by Mr. Fitzgerald of the "Rejected Addresses") who ultimately prophesied the downfall of Buonaparte[108] to which he himself mainly contributed by giving him the nickname of "*the Corsican*," was then employed in predicating[109] the damnation of Mr. Pitt, and the desolation of England in the two very best copies of verses he ever wrote—to wit—the infernal[110] eclogue of "Fire, Famine, and Slaughter" and the "Ode to the departing Year."[111]————

These three personages Southey—Wordsworth, and Coleridge had all of them a very natural antipathy to Pope, and I respect them for it—as the only original feeling or principle—which they have contrived to preserve.—But they have been joined in it by those who have joined them in nothing else,—By the Edinburgh Reviewers, by the whole heterogeneous Mass of living English Poets[112]——excepting Crabbe, Rogers, Gifford and Campbell—who both by precept and practice—have proved their adherence; and by me,—who have shamefully deviated in practice—but have ever loved and honoured Pope's Poetry with my whole soul, and hope to do so till my dying day.———I would rather see all I have ever written lining the same trunk in which I actually read the eleventh book of a modern Epic poem at Malta in 1811—(I opened it to take out a change after the paroxysm of a tertian—in the absence of my Servant, and found it lined with the name of the Maker—Eyre Cockspur Street,—and with the epic poetry alluded too[113]) than sacrifice what I firmly believe in as the Christianity of English Poetry—the Poetry of Pope.——————

But the Edinburgh Reviewers, and the Lakers—and Hunt and his school,[114] and every body else with their School, and even Moore—

Souls in unison with mine, *and hear with the same enthusiasm with which I have written.*[115]—Would not this have made a proper proem to the Excursion—and the poet, and his pedlar?[116]—it would have answered perfectly for that purpose had it not been unfortunately written in good English.[117]—————

1 Fitzgerald of] Fitzgerald ⟨immortalized in⟩ 2 Addresses") who] Addresses") ⟨of the Morning Post,⟩ ultimately prophesied] ultimately ⟨predicated⟩ 3 contributed by] contributed ⟨in a principal⟩ 4 predicating] predicting *in Proof*] predicating *B's correction in Proof* 6 the infernal] *deleted and then restored by B in Proof* 10 Pope, and] Pope, ⟨one⟩ 12 have been] have ⟨j⟩ 14 Poets——excepting] Poets——⟨ab⟩ 15 Rogers, Gifford] Rogers, ⟨and⟩ 19 written lining] written ⟨upon⟩ 20 read the] read ⟨a modern⟩ 21 change after] change ⟨during⟩ 22 Servant, and] Servant, ⟨an⟩ 26–7 his school] his ⟨sh⟩ 29 this have] this ⟨had⟩ and the] and ⟨its⟩ 30 pedlar?—it] pedlar?—⟨only that it is written in good⟩ been] *deleted by B in Proof* 30–1 unfortunately written] unfortunately been written *B's addition in Proof*

without a School[118]—and dilettanti lecturers at Institutions[119]—and elderly Gentlemen who translate and imitate,[120]—and young ladies who listen and repeat—Baronets who draw indifferent frontispieces for bad poets,[121] and noblemen who let them dine with them—in the Country,[122] the small body of the wits and the great body of the Blues[123]—have latterly united in a depreciation of which their fathers would have been as much ashamed as their Children will be.—In the mean time what have we got instead? The lake School, which begun[124] with an Epic poem "written in Six weeks" (So Joan of Arc proclaimed herself) and finished with a ballad—composed in twenty years—as "Peter Bell's" creator takes care to inform the few who will enquire.[125]——What have we got instead? a deluge of flimsy and unintelligible romances imitated from Scott and myself who have both made the best of our very bad materials, and erroneous System.[126]——What have we got instead?—Madoc which is neither an Epic nor anything else; Thalaba, Kehama, Gebir and such Gibberish, written in all metres and in no language.[127]———Hunt who had powers to have made "the Story of Rimini" as perfect as a fable of Dryden—has thought fit to sacrifice his Genius and his taste, to some unintelligible notions of Wordsworth—which I defy him to explain.[128]———Moore has—but why continue?—all with the exception of Crabbe and Rogers and Campbell who may be considered as having taken their Station—will by the blessing of God survive their own reputation—without attaining any very extraordinary period of longevity.—Of course there must be a still further exception in favour of those who having never obtained any reputation at all, unless it be among provincial literati, and their own families, have none to lose;—and of Moore who as the Burns of Ireland, possesses a fame which cannot be lost.[129]—

The greater part of the poets mentioned however have been able to gather together a few followers.——A paper of the Connoisseur says that "It is observed by the French that a Cat, a Priest, and an old woman are sufficient to constitute a religious sect in England."[130]——The same number of animals—with some difference in kind will

1 School—and] School—⟨have joined more or less in this miserable outcry.—And for⟩ 1–2 and elderly] and ⟨absurd⟩ 3 repeat—Baronets] repeat—⟨the small⟩ 4 and noblemen] and ⟨lords⟩ 6 in a] in ⟨a⟩ ⟨the⟩ ⟨depreciation of a Genius who⟩ ⟨wh⟩ 14 very] *deleted by B in Proof* 16–17 Gibberish, written] Gibberish⟨.————⟩ 17 who had] who ⟨might have ma⟩ 28 who as] who ⟨is⟩ Ireland,] Ireland⟨.———⟩ 28–9 possesses a fame which cannot be lost.] *possesses a fame which cannot be lost. in Proof; uncorrected by B* (*see also note*) 31 Connoisseur says] Connoisseur ⟨observes⟩ 32 the French] the ⟨French⟩ 34 animals—with] animals—⟨but⟩

suffice for a poetical One.—If we take Sir George Beaumont[131] instead of the Priest, and Mr Wordsworth for the old Woman we shall nearly complete the quota required—but I fear that Mr Southey will but indifferently represent the CAT, having shown himself but too distinctly to be of a species to which that nobler creature is peculiarly hostile.[132]——Nevertheless I will not go so far as Wordsworth in his postscript, who pretends that *no* great poet ever had immediate fame, which being interpreted, means that William Wordsworth is not quite so much read by his cotemporaries as might be desirable.[133]—This assertion is as false as it is foolish.—Homer's Glory depended upon his present popularity;—he recited, and without the strongest impression of the moment, who would have gotten the Iliad by heart, and given it to tradition?———Ennius—Terence—Plautus—Lucretius—Horace—Virgil;—Æschylus, Sophocles—Euripides——Sappho, Anacreon—Theocritus—all the great poets of Antiquity were the delight of their cotemporaries.——The very existence of a poet previous to the invention of printing depended upon his present popularity—and how often has it impaired his future fame? Hardly—ever; history informs us that the best have come down to us.—The reason is evident, the most popular found the greatest number of transcribers for their M.S.S. and that the taste of their cotemporaries was corrupt can hardly be avouched by the moderns, the mightiest of whom have but barely approached them.———Dante, Petrarch Ariosto, And Tasso were all the darlings of the cotemporary reader.——Dante's poem was celebrated long before his death, and after it[134] States negociated for his ashes, and disputed for the sites of the composition of the Divina Commedia.[135]——Petrarch was crowned in the Capitol.[136]——Ariosto was permitted to pass free by the public Robber who had read the Orlando Furioso.[137]—I would not recommend Mr Wordsworth to try the same experiment with his Smugglers.[138]——Tasso—notwithstanding the criticisms of the Cruscanti—would have been crowned in the Capitol but for his death.[139]——

It is easy to prove the immediate popularity of the chief Poets of the

1 George Beaumont] *B deletes* -eorge *and* -eaumont *in Proof* Beaumont instead] Beaumont ⟨for⟩ 5 of a] of ⟨that Genus⟩ 10 Glory depended] Glory ⟨dep⟩ 11 without the] without ⟨pleasing⟩ 12 gotten the] gotten ⟨him⟩ given it] given ⟨him⟩ 20 of transcribers] of ⟨copyists,⟩ 21 was corrupt] was ⟨less read⟩ 25 and after] and, not long *B's addition in Proof* States negociated] States ⟨battled⟩ 28 was permitted] was ⟨pak⟩ pass free] pass ⟨by a⟩ 29 I would] I ⟨wish the author of the⟩ 31 the Cruscanti] the ⟨Crusc⟩ 33 It] ⟨So much for the Poets of⟩ ⟨This may be proved⟩ It

only modern nation in Europe that has a poetical language.[140]———— In our own—Shakespeare—Spenser, Jonson[141]—Waller—Dryden Congreve—Pope—Young—Shenstone Thomson—Johnson, Goldsmith, Gray,—were all as popular in their lives as since. Gray's elegy pleased instantly, and eternally.—His Odes did not, nor yet do they please like his Elegy.[142]———Milton's politics kept him down,—but the epigram of Dryden, and the very Sale of his work in proportion to the less reading time of it's publication—prove him to have been honoured by his cotemporaries.[143]——I will venture to assert that the Sale of the Paradise lost was greater in the first four years after it's publication than that of "the Excursion" in the same number—with the difference of nearly a Century & a half between them of time, & of thousands in point of general readers notwithstanding Mr. Wordsworth's having pressed Milton into his Service as one of those not presently popular, to favour his own purpose of proving that our Grand-Children will read *him*—the said William Wordsworth.[144]—I would recommend him to begin first with our Grand-mothers.—But he need not be alarmed—he may yet live to see all he envies pass away—as Darwin and Seward, and Hoole, and Hole and Hoyle—have passed away—but their declension will not be his ascension;[145] he is essentially a bad writer, and all the failures of others can never strengthen him,—he may have a sect, but he will never have a public, and his "*audience*" will always be "*few*" without being "*fit*," except for Bedlam.[146]—————

It may be asked me[147]—why—having this opinion of the present state of Poetry in England, and having had it long—as my friends & others well know,—possessing too[148] as a writer the ear of the Public for the time being—I have not adopted a different plan in my own compositions, and endeavoured to correct rather than encourage the taste of the Day.—To this I would answer, that it is easier to perceive the wrong than to pursue the right, and that I have never contemplated the prospect "of filling (with Peter Bell see it's preface) permanently a

1 language.] language the Italian.— *B's addition in Proof* 2 Jonson] Johnson *in Proof; uncorrected by B* 4 popular in] popular ⟨as⟩ 6 please like] please ⟨as⟩ kept him] kept ⟨do⟩ 8 the less] the ⟨time—⟩ less reading] less ⟨literary acq⟩ 9 will venture] will ⟨b⟩ 12 of nearly] of ⟨more than⟩ 13 thousands in] thousands ⟨of readers⟩ 14 into his] into ⟨the⟩ 19 and Seward] and ⟨Hayley⟩ and Hole] and ⟨Hole⟩ 20 declension will] declension ⟨is not⟩ 21–2 never strengthen] never ⟨elevate⟩ 25 me] *deleted by B in Proof* 27 possessing too] possessing or having possessed *B's addition in Proof* writer the] writer ⟨having⟩ 30 I would] I ⟨answer⟩ to perceive] to ⟨see⟩ 32 filling (with] filling (⟨like⟩

station in the literature of the Country."[149]———Those who know me best—know this,—and that I have been considerably astonished at the temporary success of my works—having flattered no person and no party, and expressed opinions which are not those of the general reader.———Could I have anticipated the degree of attention which has been accorded, assuredly I would have studied more to deserve it.———But I lived[150] in far countries abroad, or in the agitating world at home which was not favourable to study or reflection, so that almost all I have written, has been mere Passion, passion it is true of different kinds—but always passion—for in me (if it be not an Irishism to say so) my *indifference* was a kind of Passion—the result of experience and not the philosophy of Nature.[151]——Writing grows a habit, like a Woman's gallantry; there are women who have had no intrigue, but few who have had but one only; so, there are millions of men who have never written a book, but few who have written only one.———And thus having written once, I wrote on; encouraged no doubt by the success of the moment, yet by no means anticipating it's duration, and I will venture to say, scarcely even wishing it.———But then I did other things besides write, which by no means contributed either to improve my writings or my prosperity.——————

I have thus expressed publicly upon the Poetry of the day the opinion I have long entertained and expressed of it to all who have asked it, and to some who would rather not have heard it.———As I told Moore not very long ago "we are all wrong except Rogers, Crabbe, and Campbell."[152]—Without being old in years, I am old in days, and do not feel the adequate Spirit within me to attempt a work which should show what was right[153] in Poetry, and must content myself with having denounced what is wrong. There are I trust younger Spirits rising up in England who escaping the Contagion which has swept away Poetry from our literature, will recall it to their Country, such as it once was & may still be.——————

In the mean time the best Sign of amendment will be repentance—and new and frequent Editions of Pope and Dryden.———

There will be found as comfortable Metaphysics and ten times more poetry in the "Essay on Man" than in the "Excursion."—If you

5 anticipated the] anticipated ⟨even⟩   7 I lived] I have *B's addition in Proof*   9 been mere] been ⟨of mere⟩   17 yet by] yet ⟨most truly no⟩   27 was] I think *B's substitution in Proof*   28 having denounced] having ⟨told them⟩   29 who escaping] who ⟨disclaiming⟩   34–5 times more] times ⟨the⟩   35 If] ⟨If you want Passion where will you find it⟩ If

search for Passion where is it to be found stronger than in the Epistle from Eloisa to Abelard?[154]—or in Palamon and Arcite?—do you wish for invention—imagination—Sublimity—Character? seek them in the Rape of the Lock, the fables of Dryden—the Ode on Saint Cecilia's day—& Absalom and Achitophel: you will discover in these two poets only *all* for which you must ransack innumerable metres, and—God only knows—how many *writers* of the day,—without finding a tittle of the same qualities, with the addition of wit—of which the latter have none.———I have not however forgotten Thomas Brown the younger, and the Fudge Family, nor Whistlecraft, but that is not Wit, it is Humour.[155]—————I will say nothing of the harmony of Pope and Dryden—in comparison—for there is not a living poet (except Rogers, Gifford, and Crabbe)[156] who can write a heroic[157] couplet.——The fact is that the exquisite beauty of their versification has withdrawn the proper[158] attention from their other excellencies,[159] as the vulgar eye will rest more upon the Splendour of the uniform than the quality of the troops.———It is this very harmony particularly in Pope—which has raised the vulgar and atrocious Cant against him,—because his versification is perfect—it is assumed that it is his only perfection,—because his truths are so clear—it is asserted that he has no invention, and because he is always intelligible, it is taken for granted—that he has no Genius.———We are sneeringly told that he is the "Poet of reason" as if this was a reason for his being no poet.[160]———Taking passage for passage I will undertake to cite more lines teeming with *imagination* from Pope than from any *two* living poets—be they who they may.——To take an instance at random—from a species of composition not very favourable to imagination—Satire; set down the character of Sporus—with all the wonderful play of fancy which is scattered over it—and place by it's side an equal number of verses

1 where is] where ⟨will⟩ 4 Dryden—the] Dryden—⟨and⟩ Ode on] Ode ⟨to⟩ 5 Achitophel: you] Achitophel: ⟨that is to say⟩ 6 only] *B inserts a comma in Proof* *all* for] *all* ⟨that⟩ ⟨there⟩ must ransack] must ⟨search⟩ ransack innumerable] ransack ⟨in vain⟩ 7 day,—without] day,—⟨before you can⟩ ⟨without finding a tittle of the same qualities?⟩ without finding] without ⟨discover⟩ 8 latter have] latter ⟨h⟩ ⟨are totally innocent.⟩ 10 and] nor *in Proof; uncorrected by B* Family, nor] Family, ⟨but that is not wit⟩ 13 and] Campbell and *B's substitution in Proof* a] an *B's correction in Proof* 14 the[1]] the⟨ir⟩ 15 proper] public *B's substitution in Proof* excellencies] excellences *in Proof*] excellencies *B's correction in Proof* 18 Cant against] Cant ⟨of⟩ him,—because] him,—⟨his⟩ 21 he is] he ⟨does not rave,⟩ intelligible, it] intelligible, ⟨that he has⟩ 22 no Genius] no ⟨Imagin⟩ 23 reason for] reason ⟨that⟩ 24 lines teeming] lines ⟨full of⟩ 26 at random] at ⟨hazard⟩ 27 imagination] imagin⟨g⟩ imagination—Satire] imagination—⟨set⟩ 29 by it's] by ⟨this⟩ of verses] of ⟨his⟩

from any two existing poets, of the same power and the same variety.—Where will you find them?[161]——————

I merely mention one instance of many in reply to the injustice done to the memory of him who harmonized our poetical language.———The attorneys' clerks, and other self educated Genii found it easier to distort themselves to the new Models—than to toil after the symmetry of him who had enchanted their fathers.———They were besides smitten by being told that the new School were to revive the language of Queen Elizabeth—the true English—as every body in the reign of Queen Anne, wrote no better than French, by a species of literary treason.[162]———Blank Verse—which unless in the Drama—no one except Milton ever wrote who could rhyme—became the order of the day, or else such rhyme as looked still blanker than the verse without it.———I am aware that Johnson has said—after some hesitation—that he could not "prevail upon himself to wish that Milton had been a rhymer"[163]—The Opinions of that truly Great Man—whom it is also the present fashion to decry[164]—will ever be received by me with that deference which Time will restore to him from all—but with all humility—I am not persuaded that the Paradise lost would not have been more nobly conveyed to Posterity, not perhaps in heroic couplets although even *they* could sustain the Subject—if well balanced, but in the Stanza of Spenser, or of Tasso, or in the terza rima of Dante—which the Powers of Milton could easily have grafted on our language.[165]——————The Seasons of Thomson would have been better in rhyme, although still inferior to his Castle of Indolence——— and Mr. Southey's Joan of Arc no worse—although it might then have taken up six months instead of weeks in the composition.[166]———I recommend also to the lovers of Lyrics the perusal of the present Laureate's Odes by the side of Dryden's on Saint Cecilia, but let him be sure to read *first* those of Mr. Southey.[167]——————

1–2 variety.—Where] variety⟨,—w⟩ 3 many in] many ⟨of⟩ 4 harmonized our] harmonized ⟨the⟩ 4–5 The attorneys'] The ⟨har⟩ 5 clerks, and] clerks, ⟨and other ⟨f⟩ students⟩ ⟨the⟩ Genii found] Genii ⟨of the⟩ ⟨that were spawned ⟨by⟩ about the ⟨R⟩ beginning of the French Revolution⟩ 5–6 to distort] to ⟨write after the manner of⟩ 7 enchanted their] enchanted ⟨our⟩ 7–8 besides smitten] besides ⟨particularly⟩ ⟨bitterly⟩ 11 which unless] which ⟨except⟩ 12 ever wrote] ever ⟨willingly⟩ 13 as looked] as ⟨might as well have⟩ ⟨was rather⟩ 16 Man—whom] Man—⟨which⟩ 17 to decry] to ⟨depreciate⟩ be received] be ⟨with⟩ ⟨by me⟩ 19 not persuaded] not ⟨at all⟩ 20–1 couplets although] couplets ⟨indeed—but in⟩ 21 well balanced] well ⟨wielded⟩ ⟨poised⟩ 22 Tasso, or] Tasso⟨.———⟩ 23 Milton could] Milton ⟨would⟩ 26 Southey's Joan] Southey's ⟨Madoc⟩ 27 weeks in] weeks ⟨for the⟩ 28 to the] to ⟨all⟩ of the] of ⟨that person's⟩

To the heaven-born Genii and inspired young Scriveners of the day[168]—much of this will appear paradox, it will appear so even to the higher order of our Critics; but it was a truism twenty years ago and it will be a re-acknowledged truth in ten more.———In the mean time I will conclude with two quotations both intended for some of my old Classical friends who have still enough of Cambridge about them—to think themselves honoured by having had John Dryden as a predecessor in their College—and to recollect that their earliest English poetical pleasures were drawn from the "little Nightingale" of Twickenham.[169]—————

The first is from the Notes to the poem of "the Friends" page[170] 181. 182—"It is only within the last twenty or thirty years that those notable discoveries in Criticism have been made,—which have taught our recent versifiers to undervalue this energetic, melodious, and moral poet; the Consequences of this want of due esteem for a Writer whom the Good sense of our predecessors had raised to his proper Station, have been NUMEROUS AND DEGRADING ENOUGH.—This is not the place to enter into the Subject, even as far as it *affects our poetical numbers alone*; and there is matter of more importance that requires present reflection.[171]—

The Second is from the volume of a young person†[172] learning to write poetry, & beginning by teaching the art.—Hear him—

"—But ye were dead
To things ye knew not of, were closely wed
To musty laws lined out with wretched rule

† Mr. Keats died at Rome about a year after this was written of a decline produced by his having burst a blood vessel on reading the article on his "Endymion" in the Quarterly Review.—I have read the article before and since—and although it is bitter——I do not think that a man should permit himself to be killed by it.—But a young man little dreams what he must inevitably encounter in the course of a life ambitious of public notice.—My indignation at Mr. Keats's depreciation of Pope—has hardly permitted me to do justice to his own Genius—which malgrè all the fantastic fopperies of his style—was undoubtedly of great promise.—His fragment of "Hyperion" seems actually inspired by the Titans and is as sublime as Æschylus.—He is a loss to our literature the more so—as he himself before his death is said to have been persuaded that he had not taken the right line, and was reforming his style upon the more Classical models of the language.

Novr. 12th. 1821.

2 day—much] day—⟨all⟩ so even] so ⟨to⟩ 6 who have] who ⟨are⟩ 11 page] pages *in Proof; unaltered by B* 19–20 reflection.—] reflection.—⟨"The friends⟩ 21 the volume] the ⟨poet⟩ 25 rule] rule⟨s⟩ 32 which malgrè] which ⟨through⟩ 33 by the] by ⟨one of⟩ 34 literature the] literature ⟨and⟩

And compass vile; so that ye taught a School††
Of Dolts to SMOOTH, *inlay*, and *clip*, and *fit*,
Till, like the certain wands of Jacob's wit,
Their verses tallied.—Easy was the task:
A thousand handicraftsmen wore the mask
Of Poesy.—Ill-fated impious race
That blasphemed the bright Lyrist to his face,
And did not know it, no, they went about
Holding a poor, *decrepid*, Standard out
Marked with most flimsy mottos, and in large
The name of *one* Boileau!—————

A little before the manner of Pope is termed

"a *Scism*†††
Nurtured by *foppery* and Barbarism—
Made great Apollo blush for this his land.[173]

I thought "*foppery*" was a consequence of *refinement*, but n'importe.———

Further on we have[174]

"The hearty grasp that sends a pleasant Sonnet—
Into the brain ere one can think upon it,
The Silence when some rhymes are coming out,
And when they're come the *very pleasant rout*;
The Message certain to be done tomorrow.—
'Tis perhaps as well that it should be to borrow
Some precious book from out it's snug retreat,
To cluster round it when we next shall meet.
Scarce can I scribble on &c. &c.

Now what does this mean?——————

Again—

"And with these airs come forms of elegance
Stooping their shoulders oer a *horse's prance*.

where did these "*forms of elegance*" learn to ride—with "*stooping shoulders*"? again—

"Thus I remember all the pleasant flow
Of words at opening a Portfolio.

†† It was at least a *Grammar* "School." B.
††† so spelt by the author———

2 *clip*] *chip in Proof; uncorrected by B* 9 *decrepid*] *decrepit in Proof; unaltered by B*
15 blush] blush⟨ed⟩ 25 snug retreat] snug ⟨ret⟩ 29 Again] ⟨Further on⟩ Again
32 where] ⟨I wonder⟩ where learn] learn⟨ed⟩ 35 by the] by ⟨the Mr. Keats.⟩

Again—

"yet I must not forget
Sleep, quiet with his poppy coronet:—
For what there may be worthy in these rhymes
I *partly owe* to *him*: &c.[175]

This obligation is likely to be mutual.*[176]——

* As a balance to these lines, and to the Sense and Sentiments of the new School, I will put down a passage or two from Pope's *earliest* poems—taken at random—

————"Envy her own snakes shall feel,
And Persecution mourn her broken wheel,
There Faction roar, Rebellion bite her chain,
And gasping Furies thirst for blood in vain.[177]

Ah! what avails his glossy varying dyes
His purple Crest, and scarlet-circled eyes
The vivid green his shining plumes unfold;
His painted wings, and breast that flames with gold.[178]—

Round broken Columns clasping Ivy twined,
Oer heaps of Ruin stalked the stately hind;
The Fox obscene to gaping tombs retires
And savage howlings fill the sacred quires.[179]—

[scrawl]

Hail Bards triumphant born in happier days[180]

Amphion there the loud creating lyre
Strikes, and behold a Sudden Thebes aspire.—
Cithæron's echos answer to his call
And half the Mountain rolls into a wall.[181]—

[scrawl]

So Zembla's rocks—the beauteous work of Frost
Rise white in air, and glitter oer the coast,
Pale Suns, unfelt, at distance roll away,
And on th'impassive ice the lightnings play;
Eternal Snows the growing mass supply,
Till the bright Mountains prop th'incumbent Sky,
As Atlas fixed each hoary pile appears
The gathered Winter of a thousand years.[182]——

[scrawl]

Thus when we view some well-proportioned dome,
The World's just wonder, and even thine O Rome!
No Single parts unequally surprise,
All comes united to the admiring eyes;
No monstrous height, or breadth, or length appear,
The Whole at once is bold, and regular.[183]—

7 new School] new ⟨Scholars—⟩ 12 Furies thirst] Furies ⟨thirst⟩ 41 No] ⟨No⟩ No appear,] appear⟨s⟩

It may appear harsh to accumulate passages of this kind from the work of a young man in the outset of his career.—But—if he will set out with assailing the Poet whom of all others a young aspirant ought to respect and honour & study;—if he will hold forth in such lines—his notions on poetry, and endeavour to recommend them by terming such men—as Pope—Dryden—Swift—Addison—Congreve—Young—Gay, Goldsmith, Johnson &c. &c.—"*a School of dolts*"—he must abide by the consequences of his unfortunate distortion of intellect.——— But like Milbourne he is "the fairest of Critics" by enabling us to compare his own compositions with those of Pope at the same age—and on a similar subject viz—Poetry.[184]———As Mr. K. does not want imagination nor industry—let those who have led him astray look to what they have done;—surely they must feel no little remorse in having so perverted the taste and feelings of this young man, and will be satisfied with one such victim to their Moloch of Absurdity.[185]—————

Pope little expected that the "Art of sinking in Poetry"[186] would become an object of serious Study—and supersede not only his own but all that Horace—Vida—Boileau—and Aristotle had left to Posterity, of precept,—and the greatest poets in all nations—of example.[187] ——

The above will suffice to show the notions, entertained by the new performers on the English Lyre, of him who made it most tuneable,—and the great improvements of their "variazioni."

The writer of this is a a tadpole of the lakes, a young disciple of the six or seven new Schools, in which he has learnt to write such lines and such sentiments as the above.———He says "Easy was the task" of

[scrawl]

A thousand similar passages crowd upon me, all composed by Pope before his *two and twentieth year*—and yet it is contended that he is no poet, and we are to be told so in such lines as I beg the reader to compare with these *youthful* verses of the "*No* poet."——Must we repeat the question of Johnson—"*If Pope is not a Poet where is Poetry to be found?*"[188]—Even in *descriptive* poetry—the *lowest* department of the Art, he will be found on a fair examination to surpass any living writer.

3 the Poet] the ⟨sole⟩ whom of] whom ⟨can be truly useful to⟩ 5 notions on] notions ⟨of⟩ by terming] by ⟨decrying⟩ 7 —Gay] —⟨and⟩ —"*a*] —⟨as⟩ 16 Pope little] Pope ⟨probably⟩ 18–19 Posterity, of] Posterity, ⟨had left⟩ 19 poets in] poets ⟨of⟩ 24 a a] a ⟨young disciple of ⟨Leigh Hunt⟩ Mr. Leigh Hunt, who at least knows better, and⟩ 29 is contended] is ⟨ask⟩ poet, and] poet⟨.——⟩ 31 *found?*" —Even] *found?*"—⟨In Mr. Wordsworth or in Mr. Keats—I must observe that⟩ 33 living writer.] living ⟨poet.⟩

imitating Pope, or it may be of equalling him—I presume; I recommend him to try—before he is so positive on the subject, and then compare what he will have *then* written, and what he has *now* written with the humblest and earliest compositions of Pope—produced in years still more youthful than those of Mr. K.—when he invented his new "Essay on Criticism" entitled "Sleep and Poetry" (an ominous title) from whence the above Canons are taken.——Pope's was written at nineteen and published at twenty two.[189]——————

Such are the triumphs of the new Schools, and such their Scholars. ——The disciples of Pope were Johnson, Goldsmith, Rogers, Campbell Crabbe, Gifford, Matthias, Hayley, and the Author of the Paradise of Coquettes; to whom may be added Richards, Heber, Wrangham, Bland, Hodgson, Merivale,[190] and others who have not had their full fame—because "the race is not always to the Swift, nor the Battle to the Strong'[191] and because there is a Fortune in Fame as in all other things. Now of *all* the new Schools—I say *all* for "like Legion they are many"[192]—has there appeared a single scholar who has not made his master ashamed of him? unless it be Sotheby who has imitated every body and not unfrequently surpassed his models.[193]———Scott found peculiar favour and imitation among the fair Sex, there was Miss Holford, and Miss Mitford, and Miss Francis,[194] but with the greatest respect be it spoken; none of his imitators did honour to the Original, except Hogg the Ettrick Shepherd[195] until the appearance of "the Bridal of Triermain," and "Harold the dauntless" which in the opinion of some equalled if not surpassed him, and lo! after three or four years they turned out to be the Master's own composition.[196] Have Southey, or Coleridge, or t'other fellow[197]—made a follower of renown?—Wilson never did well till he set up for himself in the "City of the Plague."[198]———Has Moore or any other living Writer of reputation, had a tolerable imitator, or rather disciple?——Now it is remarkable that almost all the followers of Pope whom I have named have produced beautiful and Standard works, and it was not the number of his *imitators* who finally hurt his fame, but the despair of

3 compare what] compare ⟨the⟩ 4 produced in] produced ⟨at an age⟩ 5 still more] still ⟨still⟩ than those] than ⟨that⟩ he invented] he ⟨produced⟩ 6 an ominous] an ⟨awkward⟩ 9 their Scholars] their ⟨disciples.⟩ 13 have not] have ⟨had⟩ 16 I say] I ⟨sa⟩ 17 —has] —⟨is⟩ 19 not unfrequently] occasionally *B's substitution in Proof* 22 of his] of ⟨these⟩ did honour] did much *B's addition in Proof* 23 Shepherd] Shepherd⟨'s⟩ 25–6 after three] after ⟨three⟩ 26–7 composition] compositions *in Proof; unaltered by B* 27 —made] —⟨left⟩ 29 Has] ⟨James Hogg is⟩ Has 32–3 the number] the ⟨frequency⟩ 33 his fame] his ⟨reputation⟩

imitation, and the *ease* of *not* imitating him sufficiently.——This, and the same reason which induced the Athenian burgher to vote for the Banishment of Aristides—"because he was tired of always hearing him called *the Just*"[199] have produced the temporary exile of Pope from the State of Literature.——But the term of his Ostracism—will expire, and the sooner the better, not for him, but for those who banished him, and for the coming Generation who

"Will blush to find their fathers were his foes."[200]—

I will now return to the writer of the Article which has drawn forth these remarks, whom I humbly[201] take to be John Wilson, a man of great powers and acquirements, well known to the public as the author of the "City of the Plague" "Isle of Palms," and other productions.[202]——I take the liberty of naming him by the same species of Courtesy which has induced him to designate me as the author of Don Juan.———Upon the score of the Lake Poets he may perhaps recall to mind that I merely express an opinion long ago entertained and specified in a letter to Mr. James Hogg, which he the said James Hogg, somewhat contrary to the Law of pens, showed to Mr. J. Wilson, in the year 1815, as he himself informed me in his answer, telling me by way of apology, that "he'de be d—d if he could help it."[203]—And I am not conscious of any thing like "envy" or "exacerbation" at this moment which induces me to think better or worse of S. W. and C.[204] as poets, than I do now, although I do know one or two things more which have added to my contempt for them as individuals.———And in return for Mr. Wilson's invective I shall content myself with asking one question, did he never compose, recite, or sing, any parody or parodies upon the Psalms, (of what nature this deponent saith not) in certain jovial meetings of the youth of Edinburgh?[205]——It is not that I think any great harm if he did—because it seems to me that all depends upon the intention of such a parody.—If it be meant to throw ridicule on the sacred original it is a Sin;—If it be intended to burlesque the profane subject or to inculcate a moral truth it is none.——If it were, the

1 the *ease*] the ⟨*easiness*⟩ 5 But the] But ⟨his Os⟩ Ostracism] Ostracism⟨s⟩ 5–6 and the] and ⟨these wretched⟩ ⟨the⟩ 6 who banished] who ⟨banishment⟩ 10 humbly] honestly *in Proof; uncorrected by B* Wilson, a] Wilson, ⟨auth⟩ 18 the year] the ⟨1⟩ 1815] 1814. *B's correction in Proof* 19 answer, telling] answer, ⟨and⟩ 20 "he'de] "he'd *in Proof; unaltered by B* 22 of S.] of ⟨them⟩ 25 question, did] question, ⟨which⟩ 27 not) in] not) ⟨to⟩ 30 of such] of ⟨the⟩ 31 to burlesque] to ⟨degrade⟩

Unbeliever's Creed,—the many political parodies of various parts of the Scripture and Liturgy—particularly a celebrated One of the Lord's prayer—and the beautiful moral Parable in favour of toleration by Franklin, which has often been taken for a real extract from Genesis, would all be sins of a damning nature.[206]———But I wish to know if Mr Wilson ever has done this, and *if* he *has—why he* should be so very very angry with similar portions of Don Juan?[207]—Did no "parody profane" appear in any of the earlier numbers of Blackwood's Magazine?[208]—— ———

I will now conclude this long answer to a short article repenting of having said so much in my own defence, and so little on the "crying left hand fallings off, and national defections"[209] of the poetry of the present day.———Having said this, I can hardly be expected to defend Don Juan, or any other "*living*" poetry, and shall not make the attempt.——And although I do not think that Mr J^no^ Wilson has in this instance treated me with candour or consideration, I trust that the tone I have used in speaking of him personally—will prove that I bear him as little malice as I really believe at the *bottom* of his *heart*, he bears towards me.——But the duties of an Editor like those of a tax-gatherer are paramount and peremptory.———I have done.[210]———

2 Scripture] Scriptures *in Proof; unaltered by B* particularly a] particularly ⟨one⟩ 3 Parable in] Parable ⟨of⟩ 6 Wilson ever] Wilson ⟨never⟩ this, and] this, ⟨nor if nothing of the kind was ever⟩ 6–7 very very angry] very angry *in Proof; uncorrected by B* 15 Mr J^no^ Wilson] Mr. John Wilson *in Proof; unaltered by B* 20 I have done.———] I have done. BYRON. *in Proof; unaltered by B*

THE BOWLES/POPE CONTROVERSY (1821)

Letter to John Murray Esqre. (1821)

Letter to John Murray Esqre.[1]—

"I'll play at *Bowls* with the Sun and Moon,"
Old Song.[2]

"My mither's auld, Stir, and She has rather forgotten hersel in speaking to my Leddy—that canna weel bide to be contradickit,—(as I ken naebody likes it if they could help themsels.)

Tales of my Landlord
Old Mortality—
page 169.[3] vol 2d[4]

Ravenna. February 7th *1821.*

Dear Sir /

In the different pamphlets which you have had the goodness to send me—on the Pope and Bowles Controversy—I perceive that my name is occasionally introduced by both parties. Mr Bowles refers more than once to what he is pleased to consider "a remarkable circumstance" not only in his letter to Mr Campbell—but in his reply to the Quarterly.[5]—The Quarterly also—and Mr Gilchrist have conferred on me the dangerous honour of a quotation[6]—and Mr B. indirectly makes a kind of appeal to me personally—by saying—"Lord B. *if he remembers* the circumstance will *witness*"—(*witness in Italics* an ominous character for a testimony at present.)[7]————

I shall not avail myself of a "non mi ricordo"[8] even after so long a residence—in Italy;—I *do* "remember the circumstance,"—and have no reluctance to relate it (since called upon so to do)—as correctly as the distance of time and the impression of intervening events will permit me. In the year 1812. more than three years after the publication

2 "I'll play at *Bowls* with the Sun and Moon," ⟨"And beat them with Eclipses."—⟩ 13 me—on] me—⟨I perceive⟩ 17 have conferred] have ⟨done⟩ 18 and Mr] and ⟨as⟩ 20 *Italics* an] *Italics*⟨)⟩ 22 ricordo" even] ricordo" ⟨though⟩ 24 do)] do ⟨so⟩

of "Eng. B. and S.R."[9]—I had the honour of meeting Mr. Bowles in the house of our venerable host of "Human Life" &c." the last Argonaut of Classic English poetry—and the Nestor of our inferior race of living poets.[10]——Mr. Bowles calls this "soon after" the publication—but to me three years appear a considerable segment of the immortality of a modern poem.————I recollect nothing of "the rest of the company going into another room"—nor though I well remember the topography of our Host's elegant and classically furnished mansion,—could I swear to the very room where the Conversation occurred—though the "taking *down* the poem" seems to fix it in the library.——Had it been "taken *up*" it would probably have been in the drawing-room.——I presume also that the "remarkable circumstance" took place *after* dinner—as I conceive that neither Mr. Bowles's politeness nor appetite would have allowed him to detain "the rest of the company" standing round their chairs in the "other room" while we were discussing "the Woods of Madeira" instead of circulating it's vintage. Of Mr. Bowles's "good humour" I have a full and not ungrateful recollection—as also of his gentlemanly manners and agreeable conversation.—I speak of the *whole*—and not of particulars—for whether he did or did not use the precise words printed in the pamphlet—I cannot say—nor could he—with accuracy.—Of "the tone of seriousness" I certainly recollect nothing—on the contrary I thought Mr. B. rather disposed to treat the subject lightly—for he said (I have no objection to be contradicted if incorrect) that some of his good-natured friends—had come to him and exclaimed "Eh! Bowles! how came you to make the Woods of Madeira &c. &c.?"——and that he had been at some pains—and pulling down of the poem to convince them that he had never made "the Woods" do any thing of the kind.——He was right—and *I was wrong*—and have been wrong—still up to this acknowledgement, for I ought to have looked twice before I wrote that which involved an inaccuracy capable of giving pain. The fact was—that although I had certainly before read "the Spirit of Discovery" I took the quotation from the review.[11]—But the mistake was mine—and not the *review's*—which quoted the passage correctly enough I believe.——I blundered—God knows how—into attributing the tremors of the lovers—to the "Woods of Madeira" by which they were surrounded.——And I hereby do fully and freely—declare and asseverate that the Woods did *not* tremble to a kiss—and that the Lovers did.———I quote from Memory—

2 &c." the] &c." ⟨then⟩ 2–3 of Classic] of ⟨the⟩ 3 of our] of ⟨the living poets.⟩
29 and have] and ⟨am⟩ 33 review.] review ⟨alluded to⟩

"—a kiss
Stole on the listening silence &c. &c.
They (the lovers) trembled—even as if the Power &c.

and if I had been aware that this declaration would have been in the smallest degree satisfactory to Mr. B.—I should not have waited nine years to make it,—notwithstanding that E.B. and S.R. had been suppressed some time previously to my meeting him at Mr. Rogers's.— —Our worthy host might indeed have told him as much—as it was at his representation that I suppressed it.——A new edition of that lampoon was preparing for the press—when Mr. Rgs. represented to me that—"I was *now* acquainted with many of the persons mentioned in it—& with some on terms of intimacy" and that he knew "one family in particular to whom it's suppression would give pleasure."[12]———I did not hesitate one moment—it was cancelled instantly—and it was no fault of mine that it has ever been republished.—When I left England in April 1816. with no very violent intentions of troubling that country again—and amidst scenes of various kinds to distract my attention—almost my last act—I believe—was to sign a power of Attorney—to yourself—to prevent or suppress any attempts (of which several had been made ⌜*in Ireland*⌝)[13] at a republication.——It is proper that I should state——that the persons with whom I was subsequently acquainted—whose names had occurred in that publication—were made my acquaintances at their own desire——or through the unsought intervention of others, I never to the best of my knowledge sought a personal introduction to any.——Some of them to this day—I know only by correspondence—& with one of those it was begun by myself——in consequence however of a polite verbal communication from a third person.[14]——I have dwelt for an instant on these circumstances because it has sometimes been made a subject of bitter reproach to me to have endeavoured to *suppress* that Satire.———I never shrunk—as those who know me—know—from any personal consequences which could be attached to it's publication.—Of it's subsequent suppression—as I possessed the copyright—I was the best Judge and the sole master.——The circumstances which occasioned the suppression I have now stated;—of the motives—each must judge according to his candour or malignity.—Mr. Bowles does me the

4 I had] I ⟨have⟩ 5 Mr. B.—I] Mr. B.—⟨it had⟩ 20) at]) ⟨towards⟩ It] ⟨It is⟩ It 21 that the] that ⟨of all those with⟩ 22 —whose] —⟨and⟩ had occurred] had ⟨et⟩ 24–5 knowledge sought] knowledge ⟨sought⟩ 34 The] ⟨Of⟩ The 35 motives—each] motives—⟨these⟩

honour to talk of "noble mind" and "generous magnanimity"——and all this—because "the circumstance would have been explained—had not the book been suppressed."[15]—I see no "nobility of mind" in an act of simple Justice,—and I hate the word "*Magnanimity*" because I have sometimes seen it applied to the grossest of impostors, by the greatest of fools;[16]—but I would have "explained the circumstance" notwithstanding "the Suppression of the book" if Mr. B. had expressed any desire that I should.—As the "Gallant Galbraith" says—to "Baillie Jarvie" "Well, the devil take the mistake—and all that occasioned it."[17]———I have had as great and greater mistakes made about me personally and poetically—once a month for these last ten years—and never cared very much about correcting one or the other—at least, after the first eight and forty hours had gone over them.[18]————

I must now however say a word or two about Pope—of whom you have my opinion more at large in the unpublished letter—*on*—or *to* (for I forget which) the Editor of B.E.M.[19]——and here I doubt that Mr. Bowles will not approve of my Sentiments.——Although I regret having published E.B. and S.R.—the part which I regret the least is that which regards Mr. B. with reference to Pope.——Whilst I was writing that publication—in 1807—and 1808.—Mr. Hobhouse was desirous that I should express our mutual opinion of Pope—and of Mr. B's edition of his works.——As I had completed my outline—and felt lazy—I requested—that *he* would do so.—He did it.—His fourteen lines on Bowles's Pope are in the first edition of E.B.—and are quite as severe and much more poetical than my own in the Second.—On reprinting the work—as I put my name to it—I omitted Mr. Hobhouse's lines—and replaced them with my own—by which the work gained less than Mr. Bowles.——I have stated this in the preface to the 2d. Edition.[20]——It is many years since I have read that poem——but the Quarterly Review—Mr. Octavius Gilchrist—and Mr. Bowles himself—have been so obliging as to refresh my memory and that of the public.——I am grieved to say that in reading over those lines—I repent of their having so far fallen short of what I meant to express upon the subject of B's Edition of Pope's works.——Mr. B. says—that "Ld B. *knows* he does *not* deserve this character"[21]—I know no such thing.—I have met Mr. B. occasionally—in the best Society in

6 would have] would ⟨not⟩ have "explained] have ⟨waited⟩ 15 letter—] letter ⟨to ⟨on⟩ the Editor⟩ 16 for I] for ⟨wh⟩ of B.] of ⟨the E.B.⟩ 23 His fourteen] His ⟨fourteen⟩ 34 of B's] of ⟨that⟩ 36 the best] the ⟨very⟩

London—he appeared to—me—an amiable—well informed—and extremely able man—I desire nothing better than to dine in company with such a mannered man every day in the week—but of "his character" I know nothing—personally—I can only speak to his manners—and these have my warmest approbation.———But I never judge from manners—for—I once had my pocket picked by the civilest gentleman I ever met with; and one of the mildest persons I ever saw was Ali Pacha.[22] Of Mr. B's "*character*"—I will not do him the *injustice* to judge from the Edition of Pope—if he prepared it heedlessly—nor the *Justice*—should it be otherwise, because I would neither become a literary executioner, nor a personal one.——Mr. Bowles the individual—and Mr. Bowles the Editor appear the two most opposite things imaginable.—

"And he himself one —— antithesis"[23]

I won't say "vile"—because it is harsh—nor "mistaken" because it has two syllables too many—but every one must fill up the blank as he pleases.[24]————

What I saw of Mr. B. encreased my surprise and regret that he should ever have lent his talents to such a task. If he had been a fool, there would have been some excuse for him—if he had been a needy or a bad man—his conduct would have been intelligible—but he is the opposite of all these—and thinking and feeling as I do of Pope—to me the whole thing is unaccountable.——However I must call things by their right names—I cannot call his edition of Pope a "candid" work—and I still think that there is an affectation of that quality not only in those volumes—but in the pamphlets lately published.—

"Why *yet* he doth *deny* his prisoners"[25]—

Mr. B. says that "he has seen passages in his letters to Martha Blount which were never published by me, and I *hope never will* be by others—which are so *gross* as to imply the *grossest* licentiousness."[26]———Is this fair play?—It may or it may not be that such passages exist—and that Pope—who was not a Monk—although a Catholic—may have occasionally sinned in word and deed with women—in his youth—but is this a sufficient ground for such a sweeping denunciation?———

7 met with] met⟨—and⟩ 9 if he] if ⟨it should prove anything otherwise⟩ it heedlessly] it ⟨thoughtlessly⟩ 10 would neither] would ⟨not⟩ 12 Editor appear] Editor ⟨are⟩ 21 man—his] man—⟨it⟩ 22 do of] do ⟨about⟩ 29 by me] by ⟨him⟩

Where is the unmarried Englishman—of a certain rank of life—who (provided he has not taken orders) has not to reproach himself between the ages of sixteen and thirty with far more licentiousness than has ever yet been traced to Pope?——Pope lived in the public eye from his youth upwards—he had all the dunces of his own time for his enemies—and I am sorry to say—some who have not the apology of dullness for detraction—since his death—and yet to what do all their accumulated hints and charges amount?—to an equivocal liaison with Martha Blount—which might arise as much from his infirmities as from his passions—to a hopeless flirtation with Lady Mary W. Montague—to a story of Cibber's and to two or three coarse passages in his works.*[27]—*Who* could come forth clearer from an invidious

* In my opinion[28] Pope has been more reproached for this couplet than is justifiable.—It is harsh—but partly true—for "*libelled by her Hate*" he was—& with regard to the supposed consequences of "*her Love*" he may be regarded as sufficiently punished in not having been permitted to make the experiment.[29]—He would probably have run the risk with considerable courage.——The *coarseness* of the line is not greater than that of two lines which are easily to be found in the great Moralist Johnson's "London":—the one detailing an accomplishment of a "fasting Frenchman" and the other on the "Monarch's air" of Balbus.[30]——I forbear to quote the lines of Johnson in all their extension—because as a young lady of Trumpington used to say of the Gownsmen—(when I was at College,)—and she was approached with too little respect—they are so "curst undiliket."[31]——

Lady Mary appears to have been at least as much to blame as Pope——some of her reflections and repartees are recorded—as sufficiently exasperating.[32]—Pope in the whole of that business is to be pitied.—When he speaks of his "miserable body"[33] let it be recollected that he was at least aware of his deformity—as indeed deformed persons have in general sufficient wit to be.[34]——It is also another unhappy dispensation of Nature—that deformed persons—and more particularly those of Pope's peculiar conformation—are born with very strong passions.—I believe that this is a physical fact,—the truth of which is easily ascertained.—Montaigne has in his universal speculations written a chapter upon it more curious than decent.[35]—So that these unhappy persons have to combat not only against the passions which they feel, but the repugnance they inspire.—Pope was unfortunate in this respect by being born in England;—there are climates where his Humpback would have made his (amatory) fortune.—At least I know one notorious instance of a hunch-back who is as fortunate as the "grand Chancelier" of de Grammont.[36]—To be sure—his climate and the morals of his country are both of them favourable to the

6 I am] I ⟨regret⟩ the apology] the ⟨excuse⟩ 7 for detraction] for ⟨his⟩ 10 to a] to ⟨an unaccepted passion for⟩ 12 *Who*] ⟨I wonder⟩ *Who* 13 In] ⟨It is⟩ In opinion Pope] opinion ⟨that⟩ —It] —⟨They are⟩ 14 he was] he ⟨has been⟩ 18 one detailing] one ⟨on the⟩ 19 accomplishment] accomplishment⟨s⟩ 19–20 of Balbus] of ⟨Balbus⟩ 22 so "curst] so ⟨"curst undilicate."—⟩ 24 —as] —⟨which were⟩ 26 indeed deformed] indeed ⟨all⟩ 27 general sufficient] general ⟨too much⟩ wit to] wit ⟨not⟩ 29 —the]—⟨it is easily as—⟩ ⟨but this⟩ 32 but the] but ⟨against⟩ repugnance they] repugnance ⟨which⟩ 35 as fortunate] as ⟨celebrate⟩ 36 and the] and ⟨his⟩ are both] are ⟨by⟩

inquest on a life of fifty six years?—Why are we to be officiously reminded of such passages in his letters—provided that they exist.——
—Is Mr. B. aware to what such rummaging among "letters" and "stories" might lead?—I have myself seen a collection of letters of another eminent—nay—pre-eminent deceased poet—so abominably gross—and elaborately coarse, that I do not believe that they could be parallelled in our language.—What is more strange is—that some of these are couched as *postscripts* to his serious and sentimental letters—to which are tacked either a piece of prose—or some verses—of the material portion of that passion of which Buffon says—that "the refined *Sentiment* is alike fictitious and pernicious."[37]——————

I think that I could show if necessary—that Lady Mary Wy. Montague was also greatly to blame in that quarrel[38]—*not* "for having rejected but for having encouraged him,"[39] but I would rather decline the task——though she should have remembered her own line "*he comes too near, that comes to be denied.*"[40] I admire her so much,—her beauty,—her talents,—that I should do this reluctantly.—I besides am so attached to the very name of "*Mary*" that—as Johnson once said—"if you called a dog *Hervey*—I should love him"[41]—so—if you were to call a female of the same species—"Mary" I should love it better than others (biped or quadruped) of the same sex with a different appellation.[42]——She was an extraordinary woman—she could translate *Epictetus*—and yet write a song worthy of Aristippus.[43]—The lines—

"And when the long hours of the Public are past
And we meet with Champaigne and a Chicken at last,
May every fond pleasure that moment endear!
Be banished afar both discretion and fear!
Forgetting or scorning the airs of the Crowd
He may cease to be formal, and I to be proud,
Till lost in the Joy, we confess that we live,
And he may be rude, and yet I may forgive.[44]

There—Mr. Bowles—what say you to such a Supper with such a woman? And her own description too?—Is not her "*Champagne and Chicken*" worth a forest or two?[45]—Is it not poetry? It appears to me that this Stanza contains the "*puree*" of the whole Philosophy of Epicurus.—I mean the *practical* philosophy of his School—not the precepts of the Master—for I have been too long at the University—not to know that the Philosopher was himself a moderate man.[46]——But after all—would not some of us have been as great fools as Pope? For my part—I wonder that with his quick feelings—her coquetry—and his disappointment—he did no more—instead of writing some lines—which are to be condemned—if false—and regretted if true.———

4 "stories" might] "stories" ⟨may⟩ 4–5 of another] of ⟨an⟩ 7 that some] that ⟨t⟩ 8 his serious] his ⟨more⟩ 10 "the refined] "the ⟨whole⟩ ⟨mere⟩ 12 was also] was ⟨most⟩ 16 so attached] so ⟨much⟩ 18 same species] same ⟨Mar⟩ 20 translate] translate⟨d⟩ 21 The lines] The ⟨two⟩ 22 Public are] Public ⟨of⟩ ⟨were⟩ 30 a Supper] a ⟨"Souper"⟩ 32 It] ⟨Is there not the whole⟩ It 36 For] ⟨Should we not have fallen in love—⟩ For her coquetry] her ⟨d⟩ 37 writing some] writing ⟨two⟩ 37–8 be condemned] be ⟨regretted⟩ 38 and regretted] and ⟨still more to be regretted ⟨deplored⟩ if true⟩ regretted if] regretted ⟨if⟩

most hyperbolic indecency.—He himself says that if "obscenity (using a much coarser word) be the Sin against the Holy Ghost—he must certainly not be saved."[47]—These letters are in existence—and have been seen by many besides myself,—but would his *Editor* have been "*candid*" in even alluding to them?——Nothing would have even provoked *me*, an indifferent spectator—to allude to them but this further attempt at the depreciation of Pope.———

What should we say to an Editor of Addison—who cited the following passage from Walpole's letters to George Montagu?—"Dr Young has published a new book &c.—Mr. Addison sent for the young Earl of Warwick, as he was dying, to show him in what peace a Christian could die—unluckily he died of *brandy*—nothing makes a Christian die in peace like being maudlin!—but don't say this in Gath where you are."——Suppose the Editor introduced it with this preface—"One circumstance is mentioned by Horace Walpole—which, if true, was indeed *flagitious*.—Walpole informs Montagu that Addison sent for the young Earl of Warwick when dying to show him in what peace a Christian could die—but unluckily he died drunk—&c. &c."[48]—Now—although there might occur on the subsequent or on the same page—a faint show of disbelief—seasoned with the expression of "the *same candour*"—(the *same* exactly as throughout the book)—I should say that this Editor was either foolish or false to his trust—such a story ought not to have been admitted except for one brief mark of crushing indignation—unless it were *completely proved*.—Why the words—"*if true*"?—that "*if*" is not a peacemaker.[49]————Why talk of "Cibber's testimony" to his licentiousness?—to what does this amount?—that Pope when very young was *once* decoyed by some Nobleman and the player to a house of Carnal recreation.[50]——Mr. Bowles was not always a Clergyman—& when he was a very young man was he never seduced into as much?—If I were in the humour for story-telling—and relating little anecdotes—I could tell a much better story of Mr. B than Cibber's—upon much better authority—viz—that of Mr. B. himself.—It was not related by *him* in my presence—but in that of a third person—whom Mr. B. names oftener than once in the course of his

1 if "obscenity] if ⟨"*indecency*⟩ "obscenity (using] "obscenity ⟨be⟩ 3 be saved] be ⟨lost⟩ 7 attempt at] attempt ⟨to⟩ 8 who cited] who ⟨introduced⟩ 9 Walpole's letters] Walpole's ⟨late⟩ letters to] letters ⟨from⟩ 20 disbelief] dis⟨praisal⟩ of "the] of ⟨"⟩ 23 admitted except] admitted ⟨expe⟩ one brief] one ⟨short⟩ 27 young was] young ⟨*once* accompanied⟩ and the] and ⟨that⟩ 28 a house] a ⟨brothel⟩ 29 man was] man ⟨did he never do⟩

replies.—This Gentleman related it to me as a humourous and witty anecdote—and so it was—whatever it's other characteristics might be.[51]—But should I, for a youthful frolic—brand Mr B. with "a libertine sort of love"—or with "licentiousness"?—is he the less now a pious or a good man—for not having always been a priest?—No such thing—I am willing to believe him—a good man—almost as good a man as Pope—but no better.—————

The truth is that in these days the grand "primum mobile" of England is *Cant*—Cant political—Cant poetical—Cant religious—Cant moral—but always *Cant*—multiplied through all the varieties of life.—It is the fashion—& while it lasts—will be too powerful for those who can only exist by taking the tone of the time.—I say *Cant*—because it is a thing of words—without the smallest influence upon human actions—the English being no wiser—no better—and much poorer—and more divided amongst themselves—as well as far less moral—than they were before the prevalence of this verbal decorum.——This hysterical horror of poor Pope's not very well ascertained—& never fully proved amours—(for even Cibber owns that he prevented the somewhat perilous adventure in which Pope was embarking) sounds very virtuous in a controversial pamphlet—but all men of the world who know what life is—or at least what is[52] was to them in their youth—must laugh at such a ludicrous foundation of the charge of "a libertine sort of love"—while the more serious will look upon those who bring forward such charges upon an isolated fact—as fanatics or hypocrites—perhaps both.—The two are sometimes compounded in a happy mixture.—————

Mr Octavius Gilchrist speaks—rather irreverently—of a "second tumbler of *hot* white-wine Negus."[53]—What does he mean?—Is there any harm in Negus?—or is it the worse for being "*hot*"—or does Mr B. drink negus?—I had a better opinion of him—I hoped that whatever wine he drank was neat——or at least that like the Ordinary in Jonathan Wild—"he preferred *punch* the rather as there was nothing against it in Scripture."[54]——I should be really sorry to believe that Mr B. was fond of Negus—it is such a "candid" liquor—so like a wishy-washy compromise between the passion for wine and the propriety

5 a priest] a ⟨strict disciplinarian⟩ 9 political—Cant] political—⟨Cant political⟩ 15 as well] as ⟨f⟩ 17 of poor] of ⟨P⟩ 18 never fully] never ⟨ascertained⟩ 19 adventure in] adventure ⟨upon⟩ 22 of "a] of ⟨profligacy⟩ 24 upon an] upon ⟨such grounds⟩ as fanatics] as ⟨zealots⟩ 25 compounded in] compounded ⟨a⟩ 35 the passion] the ⟨thirst for⟩

of water.—But different writers have divers tastes—Judge Blackstone composed his "Commentaries" (he was a poet too in his Youth) with a bottle of Port before him.—Addison's conversation was not good for much till he had taken a similar dose.[55]——Perhaps the prescription of these two great men was not inferior to the very different one of a soi-disant poet of this day—who after wandering amongst the hills—returns—goes to bed—and dictates his verses—being fed by a bystander with bread and butter, during the operation.[56]—

I now come to Mr. B's "invariable principles of poetry."—These Mr. B. and some of his correspondents pronounce "unanswerable"—and they are "unanswered" at least by Campbell—who seems to have been astounded by the title.[57]—The Sultan of the time being—offered to ally himself to a King of France—because "he hated the word League"[58]—which proves that the Pa*di*shaw (*not Pacha*)[59] understood French.——Mr. Campbell has no need of my alliance—nor shall I presume to offer it—but I do hate that word "*invariable*."——What is there of *human*—be it poetry—philosophy—wit, wisdom—science—power—glory—mind—matter—life—or death——which is "*invariable*"?—Of course I put things divine out of the question.—Of all arrogant baptisms of a book—this title to a pamphlet appears the most complacently conceited.—It is Mr. Campbell's part to answer the contents of this performance—and especially to vindicate his own "Ship" which Mr. B. most triumphantly proclaims to have struck to his very first fire.——

"Quoth he there was a *Ship*;
Now let me go—thou grey-haired loon
Or my Staff shall make thee skip.[60]

It is no affair of mine—but having once begun—(certainly not by my own wish but called upon by the frequent recurrence to my name in the pamphlets) I am like an Irishman in a "row" "any body's Customer."[61]——I shall therefore say a word or two on the "Ship."————

Mr. B. asserts that Campbell's "Ship of the Line" derives all it's poetry not from "*art*" but from "*Nature*."——"Take away the waves—the winds—the Sun &c. &c. &c. *one* will become a stripe of blue bunting—and the other a piece of coarse canvas on three tall poles."[62]———Very true—take away the "waves"—"the winds" and there will be no ship at

6 this day] this ⟨present⟩ 11 "unanswered" at] "unanswered" ⟨att⟩ 13 to a] to ⟨Henry⟩ word League] word ⟨*league*"—or "*Fronde*"⟩ 16 What] ⟨Now⟩ What of *human*] of ⟨any thing⟩ 27 begun—(certainly] begun—⟨and⟩ 34 of coarse] of ⟨canvas⟩ canvas on] canvas ⟨up⟩ Very] ⟨Tak⟩ Very

all—not only for poetical—but for any other purpose—& take away "the Sun" and we must read Mr. B's pamphlet by candle-light.—But the "poetry" of the "Ship" does *not* depend on the "waves &c."—on the contrary—the "Ship of the line" confers it's own poetry upon the waters—and heightens *theirs*.———I do not deny that the "waves and winds"—and above all "the Sun" are highly poetical—we know it to our cost by the many descriptions of them in verse—but if the waves bore only the foam upon their bosoms—if the winds wafted only the Sea-weed to the shore—if the Sun shone neither upon Pyramids—nor Fleets—nor Fortresses—would it's beams be equally poetical?—I think not—the poetry is at least reciprocal.——Take away "the Ship of the line" "swinging round" the "calm water"—and the calm water becomes a somewhat monotonous thing to look at particularly if not transparently *clear*—witness the thousands who pass by without looking on it at all.———What was it attracted the thousands to the launch?—they might have seen the poetical "calm water" at Wapping—or in the "London Dock," or in the Paddington canal or in a horsepond—or in a slop basin—or in—any other vase——They might have heard the poetical winds howling through the chinks of a pig-stye—or the Garret-window—they might have seen the Sun shining on a footman's livery—or on a brass warming pan—but could the "calm water"—or the "wind"—or the "Sun" make all—or any of these "poetical?"—I think not—Mr. B. admits "the Ship" to be poetical—but only from those accessories—now if they *confer* poetry so as to make one thing poetical—they would make other things poetical—the more so—as Mr. B. calls a "ship of the line" without them——that is to say—it's "masts and sails and streamers"—"blue bunting"—and "coarse canvas" and "tall poles."——So they are—and Porcelain is Clay—and Man is dust—and flesh is grass————and yet the two latter at least are the subjects of much poesy.[63]—————

Did Mr. B. ever gaze upon the Sea?——I presume that he has—at least upon a Sea-piece——did any painter ever paint the Sea *only* without the addition of a ship—boat—wreck—or some such adjunct?—Is the Sea itself—a more attractive—a more moral a more

3 &c."—on] &c."—⟨only⟩ 7 them in] them ⟨in⟩ 13–14 not transparently] not ⟨very⟩ 15 looking on] looking ⟨at⟩ 18 horsepond—] horsepond ⟨"⟩ a slop] a ⟨dish of tea⟩ 19 howling through] howling ⟨round⟩ the chinks] the ⟨parish weather-cock⟩ 21 on a[1]] on ⟨the⟩ brass warming] brass ⟨t⟩ 22 the "calm] the ⟨waves—or⟩ not—Mr.] not—⟨but⟩ 24 they *confer*] they ⟨make one⟩ 25 make other] make ⟨every⟩ 26 "ship of] "ship ⟨with⟩ 29 grass————] grass——⟨and of nothing—nothing can come⟩

poetical—object with or without a vessel—breaking it's vast but fatiguing monotony?—Is a Storm more poetical without a Ship?—or in the poem Of the Shipwreck[64]—is it the Storm or the Ship—which most interests?—both *much* undoubtedly—but without the vessel—what should we care for the tempest?—It would sink into mere descriptive poetry—which in itself was never esteemed a high order of that art.——I look upon myself as entitled to talk of naval matters at least to poets—with the exception of Walter Scott—Moore—and Southey—perhaps—who have been voyagers I have *swum* more miles—than all the rest of them together now living ever *sailed*—and have lived for months and months on Shipboard;—and during the whole period of my life abroad—have scarcely ever passed a month out of sight of the Ocean.—Besides being brought up from two years till ten on the brink of it.—I recollect—when anchored off Cape Sigeum in 1810—in an English frigate—a violent Squall coming on at Sunset—so violent as to make us imagine that the Ship would part cable—or drive from her anchorage.——Mr. H. and myself and some officers had been up the Dardanelles to Abydos and were just returned in time.——The aspect of a storm in the Archipelago is as poetical—as need be—the Sea being particularly short—dashing—and dangerous—and the navigation intricate and broken by the isles—and currents.——Cape Sigeum—the tumuli of the Troad——Lemnos—Tenedos—all added to the associations of the time.——But what seemed the most "*poetical*" of all—at the moment—were the numbers (about two hundred) of Greek and Turkish Craft—which were obliged to "cut and run" before the wind—from their unsafe anchorage—some for Tenedos—some for other isles—some for the Main—and some it may be for Eternity.——The Sight of these little scudding vessels darting over the foam in the twilight—now appearing—and now disappearing between the waves in the cloud of night—with their peculiarly *white* sails (the Levant sails not being of "*coarse canvas*" but of white cotton) skimming along—as quickly—but less safely than the Sea-Mew which hovered over them—their evident distress—their reduction to fluttering specks in the distance—their crowded succession—their *littleness* as contending with the Giant element—which

1 with or] with⟨out⟩ 7 myself as] myself ⟨up⟩ 8 poets—with] poets—⟨w⟩ 12 have scarcely] hav⟨ing⟩ passed a] passed ⟨two⟩ 17 cable—or] cable—⟨and she actually began to⟩ 19 The aspect] The ⟨St⟩ 21 and broken] and ⟨broken⟩ 27 Main—and] Main—⟨others⟩ and some] and ⟨all⟩ 30 the cloud] the ⟨shad⟩

made our stout 44.'s *teak* timbers (she was built in India) creak again,—their aspect—and their motion—all struck me as something far more "poetical" than the mere broad—brawling—shipless Sea & the sullen winds could possibly have been without them.[65]————

The Euxine is a noble Sea to look upon[66]—and the port of Constantinople the most beautiful of harbours—and yet I cannot but think that the twenty Sail of the line—some of one hundred and forty guns—rendered it more "poetical" by day in the Sun—and by night perhaps still more—for the Turks illuminate their vessels of war—in a manner the most picturesque——and yet all this is *artificial*. As for the Euxine—I stood upon the Symplegades—I stood by the broken altar still exposed to the winds upon one of them——I felt all the "*poetry*" of the situation, as I repeated the first lines of Medea—but would not that "poetry" have been heightened by the *Argo*?[67]—It was so even by the appearance of any merchant vessel arriving from Odessa.———But Mr. B. says "why bring your ship off the Stocks"?[68] for no reason that I know—except that ships are built to be launched.—The water &c. undoubtedly HEIGHTENS the poetical associations—but it does not *make* them; & the Ship amply repays the obligation; they aid each other—the water is more poetical with the Ship—the Ship less so without the water.—But even a Ship—laid up in dock—is a Grand and a poetical sight.—Even an old boat keel upwards wrecked upon the barren sand—is a "poetical" object—(and Wordsworth who made a poem about a Washing tub—& a blind boy may tell you so as well as I)[69] whilst a long extent of sand & unbroken water without the boat would be—as like dull prose as any pamphlet lately published.—————

"What makes the Poetry"[70] in the image of the "*Marble waste of Tadmor*" in[71] Grainger's "Ode to Solitude" so much admired by Johnson?[72]—is the "*marble*" or the "*Waste*" the *artificial* or the *natural* object?——the "waste" is like all other *wastes*;—but the "*Marble*" of Palmyra makes the poetry of the passage as of the place.[73]——————

1 our stout] our ⟨huge⟩ creak again] creak ⟨like⟩ 1–2 again,—their] again,—⟨like⟩ 2 their aspect] their ⟨flight⟩ 11 I stood by] I ⟨looked upon⟩ 16 "why bring] "why ⟨y⟩ 17 are built] are ⟨meant⟩ 18 associations—but] associations—⟨as the Ship does the like by those of the water—⟩ 21 a Grand] a ⟨grand⟩ 23 "poetical" object] "poetical" ⟨sight⟩ 25 I) whilst] I) ⟨and⟩ of sand] of ⟨barren⟩ 26 be—as] be ⟨much less so⟩ ⟨plain prose⟩ 28 Poetry" in] Poetry" ⟨of⟩ 30 the *artificial*] the ⟨obj⟩

The beautiful but barren Hymettus——the whole Coast of Attica—her hills & mountains——Pentelicus Anchesmus—Philopappus—&c. &c. are in themselves poetical—and would be so if the name of Athens—of Athenians—and her very ruins were swept from the earth.—But am I to be told that the "Nature" of Attica would be *more* poetical without the "Art" of the Acropolis? of the Temple of Theseus? & of the still all Greek and glorious monuments of her exquisitely artificial Genius?—Ask the traveller what strikes him as most poetical—the Parthenon—or the rock on which it stands?—The COLUMNS of Cape Colonna? or the Cape itself? The rocks at the foot of it? or the recollection that Falconer's *Ship* was bulged upon them?[74]——There are a thousand rocks and capes—far more picturesque than those of the Acropolis and Cape Sunium—in themselves,—what are they to a thousand Scenes in the wilder parts of Greece? of Asia Minor? Switzerland,—or even of Cintra in Portugal, or to many scenes of Italy—and the Sierras of Spain?—But it is the "*Art*"—the Columns—the temples—the wrecked vessel—which give them their antique and their modern poetry—and not the spots themselves.—Without them the *Spots* of earth would be unnoticed and unknown—buried like Babylon and Nineveh in indistinct confusion[75]—without poetry—as without existence—but to whatever spot of earth these ruins were transported if they were *capable* of transportation—like the Obelisk and the Sphinx—and the Memnon's head—*there* they would still exist in the perfection of their beauty—and in the pride of their poetry.——I opposed—and will ever oppose—the robbery of ruins—from Athens to instruct the English in Sculpture—(who are as capable of Sculpture—as the Egyptians are of skating)[76] but why did I do so?——the *ruins* are as poetical in Piccadilly as they were in the Parthenon—but the Parthenon and it's rock are less so without them.[77]——Such is the Poetry of Art.—

Mr. B. contends again that the Pyramids of Ægypt are poetical because of "the association with boundless deserts" and that a "Pyramid of the same dimensions" would not be sublime in "Lincoln's Inn fields"[78]—not *so* poetical certainly—but take away the "Pyramids" and what is the "*desert*"?—Take away Stone-henge from Salisbury plain—and it is nothing more than Hounslow heath or any other

5 would be] would ⟨be more⟩ 6 Acropolis? of] Acropolis? ⟨and⟩ 7 of her] of ⟨her ⟨art, and of her empire⟩ artists?⟩ 9 the Parthenon] the ⟨Acropolis⟩ ⟨temple of the⟩ 10 Cape itself] Cape ⟨Colon⟩ 11 was bulged] was ⟨bulged⟩ 15 of Cintra] of ⟨the⟩ 25 the robbery] the ⟨tran⟩ 26 the English] the ⟨Stupid⟩ 33 be sublime] be ⟨so in⟩

uninclosed down.———It appears to me that St Peter's—the Coliseum, the Pantheon—the Palatine the Apollo—the Laocoon—the Venus di Medicis,—the Hercules—the dying Gladiator—the Moses of Michel Agnolo[79]—and all the higher works of Canova[80]—(I have already spoken of those of antient Greece still extant in that Country—or transported to England) are as *poetical* as Mont Blanc or Mount Ætna—perhaps still more so—as they are direct manifestations of mind—& *presuppose* poetry in their very conception——and have moreover as being such a something of actual life which cannot belong to any part of inanimate nature—unless we adopt the System of Spinosa—that the World is the deity.[81]—There can be nothing more poetical in it's aspect than the City of Venice—does this depend upon the Sea or the canals?—

"The dirt and Sea-weed whence proud Venice rose"[82]

Is it the Canal which runs between the palace and the prison—or the "Bridge of Sighs" which connects them that render it poetical?—Is it the "Canal' Grande" or the Rialto which arches it,—the Churches which tower over it?—the palaces which line and the Gondolas which glide over the waters—that render this city more poetical than Rome itself?—Mr B. will say perhaps—that the Rialto is but marble—the palaces & Churches only stone—and the Gondolas a "coarse" black Cloth—thrown over some planks of carved wood—with a shining bit of fantastically formed iron at the prow—"*without*" the water.—And I tell him that without these—the Water would be nothing but a clay coloured ditch—and whoever says the contrary deserves to be at the bottom of that where Pope's heroes are embraced by the Mud Nymphs.[83]———There would be nothing to make the Canal of Venice more poetical than that of Paddington—were it not for the artificial adjuncts above mentioned—although it is a perfectly natural canal—formed by the Sea—and the innumerable islands which constitute the site of this extraordinary city.——————

The very Cloaca of Tarquin at Rome—are as poetical as Richmond

4 Michel Agnolo] Michel ⟨Angelo⟩ 10 of inanimate] of ⟨actual⟩ 17 which arches] which ⟨arches⟩ 18 line and] line ⟨it⟩ Gondolas which] Gondolas ⟨gl⟩ 23 the water] the ⟨*Canal.*⟩ 24 the Water] the ⟨Canal is⟩ 25 ditch—and] ditch—⟨which he ⟨would⟩ deserves to be at the bottom of for having talked so like a lubber of a "ship of the line."—I use the word "lubber" in the naval sense only—I mean a landsman insensible to all Sea matters.—⟩ 27–8 Venice more] Venice ⟨preferable to⟩ 29 adjuncts above] adjuncts ⟨I have⟩ 30 which constitute] which ⟨are⟩ 32 are as] are ⟨far more⟩ poetical as] poetical ⟨than⟩

Hill—many will think more so——take away Rome—and leave the Tyber and the seven Hills—in the Nature of Evander's time—let Mr. Bowles—or Mr. Wordsworth or Mr. Southey—or any of the other "Naturals" make a poem upon them—and then see which is most poetical—their production—or the commonest Guide-book which tells you the road from St. Peter's to the Coliseum—and informs you what you will see by the way.—The Ground interests in Virgil because it *will* be *Rome*—and not because it is Evander's rural domain.[84]—————

Mr. B. then proceeds to press Homer into his service in answer to a remark of Mr. Campbell's that "Homer was a great describer of works of art."—Mr. B. contends that all his great power even in this depends upon their connection with nature.———The "shield of Achilles derives it's poetical interest from the subjects described on it."[85]—And from what does the *Spear* of Achilles derive it's interest? and the helmet and the Mail worn by Patroclus—and the celestial armour—and the very brazen greaves of the well-booted Greeks?[86]—Is it solely from the legs and the back and the breast—& the human body which they enclose?—In that case—it would have been more poetical to have made them fight naked—and Gulley and Gregson as being nearer to a state of nature—are more poetical boxing in a pair of drawers—than Hector and Achilles in radiant armour and with heroic weapons.[87]————Instead of the clash of helmets—and the rushing of chariots—and the whizzing of spears—and the glancing of swords—and the cleaving of shields—and the piercing of breastplates—why not represent the Greeks & Trojans like two savage tribes—tugging & tearing—and kicking—and biting, and gnashing—foaming grinning and gouging in all the poetry of martial Nature—unincumbered with gross prosaic artificial arms—an equal superfluity to the natural warrior and his natural poet.——Is there anything unpoetical in Ulysses striking the horses of Rhesus with *his bow*—(having forgotten his thong) or would Mr. B. have had him kick them with his foot—or smack them with his hand—as being more unsophisticated?[88]—

In Gray's elegy is there an image more striking than his "shapeless Sculpture"?[89]—Of Sculpture in general it may be observed that it is

4 upon them] upon ⟨it⟩ 5–6 which tells] which ⟨Guides⟩ 6 you the] you ⟨from⟩ 16 the celestial] the ⟨cl⟩ 18 human body] human ⟨and⟩ 20 and Gulley] and ⟨Cribb and Gulley⟩ 23 of helmets] of ⟨armour⟩ 25–6 the Greeks] the⟨m⟩ 27 and gnashing] and ⟨gouging⟩ 29 artificial arms] artificial ⟨weapons⟩ equal superfluity] equal ⟨incumbrance⟩ and his] and ⟨the⟩ 32 or smack] or ⟨strike⟩

more poetical than Nature itself—inasmuch as it represents and bodies forth that ideal beauty & sublimity which is never to be found in actual Nature.—This at least is the general opinion.[90]——But always excepting the Venus di Medicis I differ from that opinion—at least as far as regards female beauty—for the head of Lady Charlemont (when I first saw her nine years ago—seemed to possess all that Sculpture could require for it's ideal.[91]——I recollect seeing something of the same kind in the head of an Albanian Girl who was actually employed in mending a road in the mountains,[92]—and in some Greek and one or two Italian faces.—But of *sublimity* I have neither[93] seen anything in human nature—at all to approach the expression of Sculpture either in the Apollo—the Moses—or other of the sterner works of ancient or modern art.———

Let us examine a little further this "Babble of green fields"[94] & of bare Nature in general as superior to artificial imagery for the poetical purposes of the fine Arts.—In Landscape painting the great Artist does not give you a literal copy of a country—but he invents & composes one.—Nature in her actual aspect does not furnish him with such existing scenes as he requires.—Even where he presents you with some famous city—or celebrated Scene from Mountain or other Nature—it must be taken from some particular point of view—& with such light & shade and distance &c. as serve not only to heighten it's beauties but to shadow it's deformities.——The poetry of Nature alone *exactly* as she appears is not sufficient to bear him out.—The very Sky of his painting is not the *portrait* of the Sky of Nature—it is a composition of different *skies* observed at different times—and not the whole copied from any *particular* day.—And *why*?—because Nature is not lavish of her beauties—they are widely scattered—and occasionally displayed—to be selected with care—and gathered with difficulty.———

Of Sculpture—I have already spoken[95]—it is the great scope of the Sculptor to heighten Nature into heroic beauty—i.e.—in plain English to surpass his model. When Canova forms a Statue—he takes a limb

3 least is] least ⟨I⟩ opinion.——But] opinion.——⟨I partly⟩ 5 beauty—for] beauty—⟨for⟩ ⟨but always excepting the Venus Medicis⟩ 12 or other] or ⟨any⟩ 14–15 of bare] of ⟨naked⟩ 15 as superior] as ⟨a high⟩ 16 Arts.—] Arts ⟨in general⟩ In Landscape] In ⟨Lads⟩ great Artist] great ⟨Landscape-⟩ 17 a literal] a ⟨real landscape⟩ 19–20 with some] with ⟨the⟩ 28 scattered—and] scattered—⟨and⟩ 29 displayed—to] displayed—⟨& difficultly⟩ 33 model.] model⟨s⟩

from one—a hand from another—a feature from a third—and a shape it may be from a fourth—probably at the same time improving upon all—as the Greek of old did in embodying his Venus.[96]———— Ask a portrait-painter—to describe his agonies in accommodating the faces with which Nature and his Sitters have crowded his painting-room to the principles of his Art.—With the exception of perhaps ten faces in as many millions there is not one which he can venture to give without shading much, and adding more.—Nature,—exactly, simply, barely, Nature,—will make no great Artist of any kind—and least of all a poet—the most artificial perhaps of all Artists is his very essence. With regard to natural imagery the poets are obliged to take some of their best illustrations from *art*.—You say that a "fountain is as clear—or clearer than *glass*"—to express it's beauty—

> "Oh fons Bandusiæ splendidior vitro"[97]—

In the speech of Mark Antony—the body of Cæsar is displayed—but so also is his *Mantle*—

> "You all do know this *Mantle* &c
>
> —————
>
> Look in this place ran Cassius' *dagger* through[98]

if the poet had said that Cassius had ran his *fist* through the rent of the Mantle—it would have had more of Mr Bowles's "Nature" to help it—but the artificial *dagger*—is more poetical than any natural *hand* without it.——In the sublime of sacred poetry—

> "Who is this that cometh from Edom? with *dyed garments* from Bozrah?[99]

would "the Comer" be poetical without his "*dyed garments*"? which strike and startle—the spectator—and identify the approaching object.———The mother of Sisera is represented listening for the "*wheels of his Chariot*."[100]——Solomon in his song compares the nose of his beloved to "a tower"—which to us appears an Eastern exaggeration.[101]—If he had said that her Stature was like that of a "tower's" it would have been as poetical as if he had compared her to a tree.—

4 describe his] describe ⟨the⟩ agonies in] agonies ⟨of⟩ 5–6 his painting-room] his ⟨canvas⟩ 8 give without] give ⟨as it exactly is.—⟩ 14 beauty—] beauty—⟨you do not say that⟩ 21 to help] to ⟨heighten⟩ 24 "Who] "⟨Who cometh⟩ 26 startle—the] startle—⟨and⟩ 27 The] ⟨And⟩ The 31 have been] have ⟨seemed⟩

"The virtuous Marcia *towers* above her sex—"[102]

is an instance of an artificial image to express a *moral* superiority.—— But Solomon it is probable did not compare his beloved's nose to a "tower" on account of it's length—but of it's symmetry—and making allowance for Eastern hyperbole—and the difficulty of finding a discreet image for a female Nose in Nature—it is perhaps as good a figure as any other.——————

Art is *not* inferior to Nature for poetical purposes.*[103]—What makes

* In the composition of this letter—I omitted to cite three very celebrated passages in three different languages ancient & modern—the whole of whose merit consists in artificial imagery.—The first is from Congreve—and Dr. Johnson pronounces this[104] opinion upon it.——"If I were required to select from the *whole mass of English* poetry the most poetical paragraph I know not what I could prefer to an exclamation in "the Mourning Bride:"

"No—all is hushed and still as death—'tis dreadful!
How reverend is the face of this tall pile
Whose ancient pillars rear their marble heads
To bear aloft it's arched and ponderous roof
By it's own weight made steadfast & immoveable
Looking tranquillity! it strikes an awe
And terror on my aching sight; the tombs
And monumental caves of death look cold
And shoot a chillness to my trembling heart
Give me thy hand—& let me hear thy voice
Nay—quickly speak to me—& let me hear
Thy voice—my own affrights me with it's echoes.

"He who reads those lines enjoys for a moment the powers of a poet; he feels what he remembers to have felt before, but he feels it with great increase of Sensibility; he recognizes a *familiar image*, but meets it again amplified & expanded, embellished with beauty—& enlarged with Majesty.—

Johnson's Lives &c.[105]

Here is the finest piece of poetry in our language so pronounced by the noblest critical mind which our Country has produced,—& the whole imagery of this quintessence of poetry is unborrowed from *external* nature.——I presume that no one can differ from Johnson that as description it is unequalled.—For a controversy upon the subject the reader is referred to Boswell's Johnson.—Garrick attempted a parallel with Shakespeare's Description of Dover Cliff—but Johnson stopped him (I quote from Memory not having the book) with "nay Sir—

half way down
Hangs one who gathers Samphire—dreadful trade!

I am speaking of a description in which nothing is introduced from life to break the effect.[106]———

2 an instance] an⟨other⟩ 3 is probable] is ⟨probably⟩ 9 the composition] the ⟨first publication⟩ 24 hear] hear ⟨thy⟩ 31 Here] ⟨Now⟩ Here the noblest] the ⟨first⟩ 33 poetry is] poetry ⟨has⟩ presume that] presume ⟨no one⟩ 35 attempted a] attempted ⟨to⟩ parallel with] parallel ⟨it⟩ with Shakespeare's] with ⟨the⟩ 36 from Memory] from ⟨Memory⟩

a regiment of soldiers a more noble object of view—than the same mass of Mob?—Their arms—their dresses—their banners—and the *art*—and artificial symmetry of their position and movements.—A Highlander's plaid—a Mussulman's turban and a Roman toga—are more poetical than the tattooed—or un-tattoo-ed buttocks of a New-Sandwich Savage, although they were described by William Wordsworth himself—like the "idiot in his glory."[107]———

I have seen as many Mountains as most men—and more fleets than the generality of landsmen—and to my mind—a large Convoy with a few sail of the line to conduct them—is as noble—and as poetical a prospect as all that inanimate nature can produce.—I prefer the "mast of some great Ammiral"[108] with all it's tackle—to the Scotch fir or the Alpine Tannen,—and think that *more* poetry *has been* made out of it.—In what does the infinite superiority of "Falconer's Shipwreck"—over all other Shipwrecks' consist?—In his admirable application of the terms of his Art—in a poet-Sailor's description of the Sailor's fate.—These *very terms* by his application—make the strength & reality of his poem—why?—because he was a poet—and in the hands of a poet *Art* will not be found less ornamental than Nature.——It is precisely in general Nature—& in stepping out of his element that Falconer fails—where he digresses to speak of Ancient Greece and "such branches of learning."[109]————

In Dyer's Grongar Hill upon which his fame rests—the very

The other two passages of a familiar & celebrated image—are first in Lucretius—

"Sed veluti pueris absinthia tetra medentes
Cum dare conantur, prius oras *pocula* circum
Contingunt dulci mellis flavoque liquore &c.[110]

and the second the same closely copied by Tasso—

"Cosi a l'egro fanciul porgiamo aspersi
Di soave licor gli orli del vaso, &c.[111]

A more familiar—& household image can hardly be conceived—than that of a nurse sweetening the rim of a cup of physic to coax a sickly brat into taking it,—& yet there are few passages in poetry more quoted and admired than the Italian lines.—

In Cowper—(whom Mr. B. thinks a poet) "the twanging horn oer yonder bridge"—and Toby "banging the door" are quite as effective as his laboured minutiæ of the Wood or the Shrubbery.[112]—————

1–2 same mass] same ⟨number⟩ 2 banners—and] banners—⟨above—⟩ 5 un-tattoo-ed buttocks] un-tattoo-ed ⟨faces ⟨limbs⟩ of the New-Sandwich Savages.⟩ 8 and more] and ⟨as many⟩ 10 few sail] few ⟨l⟩ 19 less ornamental] less ⟨poetical⟩ 20 Falconer fails] Falconer⟨'s⟩ 31 be conceived] be ⟨imagined⟩ 31–2 nurse sweetening] nurse ⟨sweete th⟩ 32 the rim] the ⟨rim⟩ to coax] to ⟨deceive⟩ 33 in poetry] in ⟨poel⟩ 35 are quite] are ⟨much better than⟩ minutiæ of] minutiæ ⟨of⟩

appearance of Nature herself is moralized into an artificial image.*[113]—

"Thus is Nature's *vesture* wrought
To instruct our wandering thought—
Thus She *dresses green and gay*
To disperse our cares away.—

And here also we have the telescope—the misuse of which from Milton has rendered Mr Bowles so triumphant over Mr Campbell.[114]—

"So we mistake the future's face
Eyed through Hope's deluding *Glass*.

By the way[115] a word en passant to Mr. Campbell—

"As yon Summits soft and fair
Clad in colours of the air
Which to those who journey near
Barren, brown, and rough appear
Still we tread the same coarse way—
The present's still a cloudy day.

Is it not this[116] the original of the far-famed

"Tis distance lends Enchantment to the view
And robes the Mountain in it's azure hue?[117]

To return once more to the Sea—let any one look on the long wall of Malamocco ⌜"*i Murazzi*"⌝[118]—which curbs the Adriatic—and pronounce between the Sea and it's master.—Surely that Roman work (I mean *Roman* in conception and performance) which says to the Ocean "thus far shalt thou come and no further"[119] and is obeyed, is not less sublime and poetical than the angry waves which vainly break beneath it.———

* ⌜Corneille's celebrated lines on Fortune—

"Et comme Elle a l'éclat du *Verre*
Elle en a la fragilité."

are a further instance of the noble use which may be made of artificial imagery, & quite equal to any taken from Nature.⌝

7 And here] And ⟨soon after⟩ telescope—the] telescope—⟨or rather microscope—⟩
12 to Mr.] to ⟨my friend⟩

Mr B. makes the chief part of a Ship's poesy depend upon the "*wind*"—then why is a Ship under sail more poetical than a Hog in a high wind?[120]—The Hog is all nature—the Ship is all art—"coarse canvas" "blue bunting" and "tall poles"—both are violently acted upon by the wind—tossed here and there to and fro—and yet nothing—but excess of hunger could make me look upon the pig as the more poetical of the two—and then only in the shape of a griskin.———— —

Will Mr Bowles tell us that the poetry of an Aqueduct consists in the *water* which it conveys?—Let him look on that of Justinian——on those of Rome—Constantinople—Lisbon—and Elvas—or even at the remains of that in Attica.——————

We are asked "what makes the venerable towers of Westminster Abbey more poetical as objects than the tower for the manufactory of patent shot, surrounded by the same scenery".[121]—I will answer—the *Architecture*. Turn Westminster Abbey or Saint Paul's into a Powder Magazine—their poetry as objects remains the same—the Parthenon was actually converted into one by the Turks during Morosini's Venetian siege—and part of it destroyed in consequence.[122]——Cromwell's dragoons stabled their steeds in Worcester Cathedral[123]——was it less poetical as an object than before?———Ask a foreigner on his approach to London—what strikes him as the most poetical of the towers before him—he will point out Saint Paul's and Westminster—Abbey—without perhaps knowing the names or associations of—either—and pass over the "tower for patent shot"—not that for anything he knows to the contrary—it might not be the Mausoleum of a Monarch, or a Waterloo Column—or a Trafalgar monument—but—because—it's Architecture is obviously inferior.[124]——————

To the question "whether the description of a game of cards be as poetical, supposing the execution of the Artists equal, as a description of a Walk in a forest?[125]——it may be answered—that the *materials* are certainly not equal—but that "the *Artist*" who has rendered the "game of cards poetical" is *by far* the *greater* of the two.———But all this "ordering" of poets is purely arbitrary on the part of Mr B.——there may or may not be in fact different "orders" of poetry—but the poet is always ranked according to his execution and not according to his branch of the art.[126]————

Tragedy—is one the highest[127] presumed orders——Hughes has

1 makes the] makes ⟨the⟩ the chief] the ⟨great⟩ 8 in the] in ⟨it's⟩ 20 Ask] ⟨Take⟩ Ask 23–4 of—either] of ⟨either⟩ 28 the description] the ⟨question⟩

written a tragedy—and a very successful one—Fenton—another and Pope none.[128]—Did any man however—will even Mr. B. himself—rank Hughes and Fenton as poets above *Pope*? Was even Addison (the author of Cato)—or Rowe (one of the higher order of dramatists as far as Success goes)—or Young—or even Otway—and Southerne ever raised for a moment to the same rank with Pope in the estimation of the reader or the Critic—before his death or since?[129]——If Mr. B. will contend for classifications of this kind—let him recollect that descriptive poetry has been ranked as among the lowest branches of the art—and description as a mere ornament—but which should never form "the subject" of a poem.[130]—The Italians—with the most poetical language—and the most fastidious taste in Europe—possess now five *great* poets—they say,—Dante—Petrarch—Ariosto—Tasso—and lastly—Alfieri*[131]——and whom do they esteem one of the highest of these—and some of them the very highest—Petrarch the *Sonneteer*—it is true that some of his Canzoni are *not less* esteemed—but *not* more;—who ever dreams of his Latin Africa?[132]———Were Petrarch to be ranked according to the "order" of his compositions—where would the best of Sonnets place him?—with Dante and the others?—No—but—as I have before said the poet who *executes* best—is the highest—

* Of these, there is one ranked with the others for his SONNETS, and *two* for compositions which belong to *no class* at all.[133] Where is Dante? His poem is not an *epic*; then what is it? He himself calls it a "divine comedy;" and why? This is more than all his thousand commentators have been able to explain.[134] Ariosto's is not an *epic* poem; and if poets are to be *classed* according to the *genus* of their poetry, where is he to be placed? Of these five, Tasso and Alfieri only come within Aristotle's arrangement, and Mr. Bowles's class-book. But the whole position is false. Poets are classed by the power of their performance, and not according to its rank in a gradus. In the contrary case the forgotten epic poets of all countries would rank above Petrarch, Dante, Ariosto, Burns, Gray, Dryden, and the highest names of various countries. Mr. Bowles's title of "*invariable* principles of poetry," is, perhaps, the most arrogant ever prefixed to a volume. So far are the principles of poetry from being "*invariable*," that they never were nor ever will be settled. These "principles" mean nothing more than the predilections of a particular age; and every age has its own, and a different from its predecessor. It is now Homer, and now Virgil; once Dryden, and since Walter Scott; now Corneille, and now Racine; now Crebillon, now Voltaire. The Homerists and Virgilians in France disputed for half a century.[135] Not fifty years ago the Italians neglected Dante—Bettinelli reproved Monti for reading "that barbarian;"[136] at present they adore him. Shakespeare and Milton have had their rise, and they will have their decline. Already they have more than once fluctuated, as must be the case with all the dramatists and poets of a living language. This does not depend upon their merits, but upon the ordinary vicissitudes of human opinions. Schlegel and Madame de Stael have endeavoured also to reduce poetry to *two* systems, classical and romantic.[137] The effect is only beginning.

8 recollect] recollect⟨ion⟩ 9 lowest branches] lowest ⟨orders⟩ 14 and whom] and ⟨of⟩

whatever his department—and will ever be so rated—in the World's esteem.——————

Had Gray written nothing but his Elegy—high as he stands—I am not sure that he would not stand higher——it is the Corner-stone of his Glory—without it his Odes would be insufficient for his fame.[138]———The depreciation of Pope is partly founded upon a false idea of the dignity of his order of poetry—to which he himself has partly contributed by the ingenuous[139] boast

> "That not in fancy's maze he wandered long
> But *stooped* to Truth and moralized his Song.[140]

He should have written "rose to truth."——In my mind the highest of all poetry is Ethical poetry—as the highest of all earthly objects must be moral truth.——Religion does not make a part of my subject—it is something beyond human powers and has failed in all human hands except Milton's and Dante's—and even Dante's powers are involved in his delineation of human passions—though in supernatural circumstances.——What made Socrates the greatest of men?—His moral truth.—His Ethics.——What proved Jesus Christ the Son of God—hardly less than his miracles?—his Moral precepts.———And if Ethics have made a philosopher the first of men—and have not been disdained as an adjunct to his Gospel by the Deity himself;—are we to be told that Ethical poetry—or Didactic poetry—or by whatever name you term it—whose object is to make men better and wiser—is not the *very first order* of poetry—and am[141] we to be told this too by one of the Priesthood?—It requires more mind—more wisdom—more power—than all the "Forests" that ever were "walked" for their "description" and all the Epics that ever were founded upon fields of battle.——The Georgics are indisputably—and I believe *undisputedly* even—a finer poem than the Æneid.——Virgil knew this—he did not order *them* to be burnt.[142]——————

> "The proper Study of Mankind is Man"[143]

It is the fashion of the day to lay great stress upon what they call "Imagination" and "Invention" the two commonest of qualities[144]—an Irish peasant with a little whisky in his head will imagine and invent

1 be so] be ⟨so⟩ 4 not stand] not ⟨still⟩ 5 Odes would] Odes ⟨alone⟩ 7 the dignity] the ⟨importance⟩ 8 ingenuous boast] ingenuous ⟨lines⟩ 12 is Ethical] is ⟨moral⟩ 16 in supernatural] in ⟨a⟩ 17 the greatest] the ⟨p⟩ 18–19 God—hardly] God—⟨no⟩ 19–20 Ethics have] Ethics ⟨are⟩ 24 am we] am ⟨I⟩

more than would furnish forth a modern poem.—If Lucretius had not been spoiled by the Epicurean system—we should have had a far superior poem to any now in Existence.—As mere poetry—it is the first of Latin poems.——What then has ruined it?—his ethics.[145]——Pope has not this defect—his moral is as pure—as his poetry is glorious.————

In speaking of artificial objects I have omitted to touch upon one—which I will now mention.——Cannon may be presumed to be as highly poetical as Art can make her objects.—Mr. B. will perhaps tell me that this is because they resemble that grand natural article of Sound in heaven, and Similie upon earth—Thunder.—I shall be told triumphantly that Milton has[146] made sad work with his artillery when he armed his devils therewithal.[147] He did so—and this artificial object must have had much of the Sublime to attract his attention for such a conflict.—He *has* made an absurd use of it—but the absurdity consists not in using *Cannon* against the Angels of God, but any *material* weapon.—The thunder of the clouds would have been as ridiculous and vain in the hands of the devils—as the "villainous salpetre"[148]——the Angels were as impervious to the one as to the other.—The thunderbolts become sublime in the hands of the Almighty not as such—but because *he* deigns to use them as a means of repelling the rebel Spirits——but no one can attribute their defeat to this grand piece of natural electricity—the Almighty willed—and they fell, his word would have been enough—and Milton is as absurd—&[149] (in fact *blasphemous*) in putting material lightnings into the hands of the Godhead—as in giving him hands at all.———The Artillery of the demons was but the first step of his mistake, the thunder the next—and it is a step lower. It would have been fit for Jove but not for Jehovah.[150]—The Subject altogether, was essentially unpoetical—he has made more of it than another could—but it is beyond him—and all men.—————

In a portion of his reply—Mr. B. asserts that Pope—"envied Phillips"—because he quizzed his Pastorals in the Guardian—in that most

1 furnish forth] furnish ⟨fil⟩ 2 spoiled by] spoiled ⟨his poem⟩ Epicurean system] Epicurean ⟨t⟩ 7 artificial objects] artificial ⟨images⟩ have omitted] have ⟨for⟩ 9 Art can] Art ⟨wishes⟩ 10 natural article] natural ⟨object⟩ 11–12 told triumphantly] told ⟨that⟩ 17 of the] of ⟨heaven⟩ 18 salpetre"——] salpetre" ⟨liquid fire that⟩ 19 as impervious] as ⟨impervious⟩ 19–20 The thunderbolts] The ⟨bolts⟩ 24 & (in] & ⟨for⟩ 29 was essentially] was ⟨not poe⟩ essentially unpoetical] essentially ⟨poetical⟩

admirable model of irony, his paper on the subject.[151]—If there was any thing enviable about Phillips—it could hardly be his Pastorals.——They were despicable—and Pope expressed his contempt.—If Mr Fitzgerald published a volume of Sonnets—or a "Spirit of Discovery"—or a "Missionary"—and Mr B. wrote in any periodical Journal—an ironical paper upon them—would this be "envy?"[152]—The Authors of the "Rejected Addresses" have ridiculed the sixteen or twenty "first living poets" of the day—but do they "envy" them?[153]—"Envy" writhes, it don't laugh.—The Authors of the R.A. may despise some——but they can hardly "envy" any of the persons whom they have parodied—and Pope could have no more envied Phillips than he did Welsted—or Theobalds—or Smedley—or any other given hero of the Dunciad.[154]———He could not have envied him even had he himself *not* been the greatest Poet of his Age.—Did Mr Ings "*envy*" Mr Phillips when he asked him "how came your Pyrrhus to drive Oxen and say "I am *goaded* on by Love."?—This question silenced poor Phillips—but it no more proceeded from "envy" than did Pope's ridicule.[155]—————

Did he envy Swift?—did he envy Bollingbroke?—did he envy did he envy Gay the unparallelled Success of his "Beggar's Opera"?[156] we may be answered that these were his friends;—true—but does *friendship* prevent *envy*?—Study the first woman you meet with—or the first scribbler,——let Mr B. himself (whom I acquit fully of such an odious quality) study some of his own poetical intimates; the most envious man I ever heard of is a poet and a high one[157]——besides it is an *universal* passion—Goldsmith envied not only the puppets for their dancing—and broke his shins in the attempt at rivalry—but was seriously angry because two pretty women received more attention than he did.[158]——*This is Envy*—but where does Pope show a sign of the passion?—In that case Dryden envied the hero of his Mac'Flecknoe.[159]—————

Mr B. compares when and where he can—Pope with Cowper (the same Cowper whom in his Edition of Pope he laughs at for his attachment to an old woman Mrs Unwin,—search—and you will find it—I

4 or a "Spirit] or ⟨an⟩ 6 paper upon] paper ⟨with⟩ 10 persons whom] persons ⟨of⟩ 15 to drive] to ⟨die⟩ 17 it no] it ⟨probably⟩ 21 these were] these ⟨are⟩ friends] ⟨"⟩friends⟨"⟩ 22–3 first scribbler] first ⟨poet⟩ 23 scribbler,——let] scribbler,——⟨the⟩ himself (whom] himself ⟨f⟩ 24 poetical intimates] poetical ⟨inmates⟩ 34 Unwin,—] Unwin,⟨)⟩

remember the passage though not the page)[160] in particular he requotes Cowper's Dutch delineation of a wood[161]—drawn up like a Seedsman's Catalogue*[162] with an affected imitation of Milton's style, as burlesque as the "Splendid Shilling.[163]——————

* I will submit to Mr Bowles's own judgement—a passage from another poem of Cowper's to be compared with the same writer's Sylvan Sampler.[164]—In the lines to Mary

"Thy *Needles* once a shining Store" &c
For my sake restless heretofore
Now rust disused and shine no more,—(My Mary)[165]

contain a simple household "*indoor*"—artificial and ordinary image;[166]—I refer Mr B. to the Stanza—and ask if these three lines about "*needles*" are not worth all the boasted twaddling about trees so triumphantly re-quoted;—and yet in *fact* what do they convey?—A homely collection of images and ideas—associated with the darning of Stockings, and the hemming of shirts—and the mending of breeches—but will any one deny that they are eminently poetical & pathetic as addressed by Cowper to his Nurse?———The trash of trees reminds me of a Saying of Sheridan's.—Soon after the "Rejected Address" Scene in 1812—I met Sheridan.—In the course of dinner—he said—"Ld B. did you know that amongst the writers of Addresses—was Whitbread himself? I answered by an enquiry of what sort of an Address he had made—"Of that replied Sheridan—I remember little except that there was a *Phœnix* in it."—A Phœnix!! well How did he describe it?—"*Like a Poulterer*" answered Sheridan—"it was—green & yellow—and red—and blue—he did not let us off for a single feather."[167]——And just such as this Poulterer's account of a Phœnix—is Cowper's a Stick-picker's detail of a wood,—with all it's petty minutiæ of this that and the other.——————

One more poetical instance of the power of Art—& even it's *superiority* over Nature—in poetry; and I have done.—The Bust of *Antinous*?—is there any thing in Nature like this marble excepting the Venus?——Can there be more *poetry* gathered into existence than in that wonderful creation of perfect beauty?—But the poetry of this bust is in no respect derived from Nature—nor from any association of moral exaltedness—for what is there in common with moral Nature and the Male Minion of Adrian?[168]—The very execution is *not natural* but *super*-natural—or rather—*super-artificial*—for Nature has never done so much?[169]——

Away then with this cant about Nature—and "invariable principles of poetry"—a great Artist will make a block of Stone as sublime as a mountain—and a good poet can imbue a pack of Cards with more poetry than inhabits the forests of America. It is the business and the proof of a poet to give the lie to the proverb—and sometimes to "*make a silken purse out of a Sow's ear*"—and to conclude with another homely proverb "a good workman will not find fault with his tools.[170]

1 page) in] page) ⟨in particular ⟨in a tiresome⟩ ⟨in a drawn out⟩⟩ 2 wood—drawn] wood—⟨an affect⟨ation⟩ ed⟩ ⟨like a "hortus siccus" or⟩ 3–4 style, as] style ⟨of verse⟩ 5 will submit] will ⟨refer⟩ 6 with the] with ⟨this Dutch poetical⟩ 10 contain] ⟨contain a Simple and even household "*indoor*" artificial⟩ contain —I] —⟨but⟩ 11 and ask] and ⟨demand of him⟩ not worth] not ⟨far⟩ 12 —and] —⟨which reminds me of a saying of Sheridan's.——Soon after the "Rejected Address Scene of 1812,⟩ they convey?] they ⟨contain?⟩ 15 pathetic as] pathetic ⟨so employed⟩ 20 there was] there ⟨l⟩ 22 let us] let ⟨us⟩ such as] such ⟨a⟩ 29 of moral] of ⟨Natural ideas⟩ for what] for ⟨the⟩ 30 and the] and ⟨with⟩ 33 this cant] this ⟨atr⟩ 34 can imbue] can ⟨turn⟩ 35 Cards with] Cards ⟨in to⟩

These two writers—for Cowper is no poet—come into comparison —in one great work—the translation of Homer.[171]——Now—with all the great—and manifest, and manifold—and reproved—and acknowledged—and uncontroverted faults of Pope's translation—and all the Scholarship—and pains—and time—and trouble—and blank verse of the other—who can ever read Cowper?—and who will ever lay down Pope—unless for the Original?——Pope's was "not Homer it was Spondanus"[172]—but Cowper[173] is not Homer either, it is not even Cowper.—As a Child I first read Pope's Homer with a rapture which no subsequent work could ever afford—& Children are not the worst Judges of their own language.—As a boy I read Homer in the original—as we have all done—some of us by force—and a few by favour—under which description I came[174] is nothing to the purpose—it is enough that I read him.—As a Man I have tried to read Cowper's version—and I found it impossible.—Has any human reader ever succeeded?———

And now that we have heard the Catholic reproached with Envy —duplicity—licentiousness—avarice—what was the Calvinist?—He attempted the most atrocious of crimes in the Christian Code—viz—Suicide—and why? because he was to be examined whether he was fit for an office which he seems to wish to have made a sinecure.[175]——His Connection with Mrs Unwin was pure enough for the old lady was devout and he was deranged—but why then is the infirm and then elderly Pope to be reproved for his connection with Martha Blount? Cowper was the Almoner of Mr Throgmorton—but Pope's charities were his own—and they were noble and extensive—far beyond his fortune's warrant.[176]—Pope was the tolerant yet steady adherent of the most bigoted of sects—and Cowper the most bigoted and despondent Sectary that ever anticipated damnation to himself or others.——Is this harsh?—I know it is—and I do not assert it as my opinion of Cowper—*personally* but to *show what might* be said—with just as great an appearance of truth—and candour—as all the odium which has been accumulated upon Pope—in similar speculations. Cowper was a Good man—and lived at a fortunate time for his works.——————

2 the translation] the ⟨gran⟩ 6 the other] the ⟨verse⟩ read Cowper] read ⟨him?—⟩ 9 read Pope's] read ⟨Pope's⟩ 10 subsequent work] subsequent ⟨reading⟩ 11 their own] their ⟨Judges⟩ 17 heard the] heard ⟨Pope⟩ 21 for an] for ⟨the⟩ 22 old lady] old ⟨woman⟩ 22–3 was devout] was ⟨religious⟩ 23 was deranged] was ⟨insane⟩ and then] and ⟨moral⟩ 27 fortune's warrant] fortune's ⟨p⟩ 28 bigoted and] bigoted ⟨of those whom⟩ 34 works.——————] works—⟨when all things began to⟩

Mr. B. apparently not relying entirely upon his own arguments—has in person or by proxy—brought forward the names of Southey and Moore.——Mr. Southey "agrees entirely with Mr. B. in his *invariable* principles of Poetry."[177]—The least that Mr. B. can do in return is to approve the "invariable principles of Mr. Southey."———I should have thought that the word "*invariable*" might have stuck in Southey's throat—like Macbeth's "Amen"[178]—I am sure it did in mine—and I am not the least consistent of the two—at least as a voter.—Moore (*Et tu Brute*!)[179] also approves and Mr. J. Scott.[180]—There is a letter also of two lines from a Gentleman in Asterisks—who it seems—is a Poet of "the highest rank"—who *can* this be?—not my friend Sir Walter surely——Campbell it can't be—Rogers it wont be;—

> "You have *hit the nail in* the head, and
> ++++ (Pope I presume) *on* the head also—
> I *remain* yrs affectionately
> (four *Asterisks*.)

And in Asterisks let him remain.[181]—Whoever this person may-be—he deserves for such a Judgement of Midas—that "the Nail" which Mr. B. has "hit *in* the head" should be driven through his own ears, I am sure that they are long enough.[182]——

The attempt of the poetical populace of the present day to obtain an Ostracism against Pope is as easily accounted for as the Athenian's Shell against Aristides—they are tired of hearing him always called "the Just."[183]——They are also fighting for Life—for if he maintains his station—they will reach their own—by falling.———They have raised a Mosque by the side of a Grecian temple of the purest Architecture—and more barbarous than the Barbarians from whose practice I have borrowed the figure—they are not contented with their own grotesque edifice—unless they destroy the prior and purely beautiful fabric which preceded and which shames them & theirs forever and ever.[184]——I shall be told that amongst these—I *have* been—(or it may be still *am*)—conspicuous;—true—and I am ashamed of it;—I *have* been amongst the builders of this Babel attended by a confusion of tongues[185]—but *never* amongst the envious destroyers of the classic temple of our Predecessor.——I have loved and honoured the fame

5 should have] should ⟨have⟩ 7 it did] it ⟨has⟩ 8 Moore (*Et*] Moore ⟨it seems⟩ 9 approves and] approves⟨.—There is a letter⟩ 12 surely—] surely⟨?⟩ 24 maintains his] maintains ⟨th⟩ 29 edifice—unless] edifice—⟨unless⟩ 34 of the] of ⟨that⟩

and name of that illustrious and unrivalled man—far more than my own paltry renown—and the trashy Jingle of the crowd of "Schools" and upstarts—who pretend to rival—or even surpass him.—Sooner than a single leaf should be torn from his laurel—it were better that all which these men—and that I as one of their set—have ever written, should

> "Line trunks—clothe spice—or fluttering in a row
> Befringe the rails of Bedlam—or Soho.——[186]

There are those who will believe this—and those who will not. You—Sir—know how far I am sincere—whether my opinion not only in the short work intended for publication——and in private letters—which can never be published—has or has not been the same.[187]——I look upon this as the declining age of English poetry—no regard for others—no selfish feeling—can prevent me from seeing this—and expressing the truth.—There can be no worse sign for the taste of the times than the depreciation of Pope.—It would be better to receive for proof Mr Cobbett's rough but strong attack upon Shakespeare and Milton[188]—than to allow this smooth and "candid" undermining of the reputation of the most *perfect* of our poets—and the purest of our Moralists.———

Of his power, in the *passions*—in description—in the mock heroic—I leave others to descant—I take him on his strong ground—as an *Ethical* poet—in the former none excel—in the mock heroic and the Ethical none equal him——and in my mind—the latter is the highest of all poetry, because it does that in *verse*—which the greatest of men have wished to accomplish in prose.—If the Essence of poetry must be a *Lie*——throw it to the dogs—or banish it from your republic—as Plato would have done[189]—he who can reconcile Poetry with truth and wisdom—is the only true "*Poet*" in it's real sense—"*the Maker*" "*the Creator*"—why must this mean the "liar"—the "feigner" the "tale teller"?[190] a man may make and create better things than these.—————

I shall not presume to say that Pope is as high a poet as Shakespeare

1 far more] far ⟨th⟩ 4–5 all which] all ⟨that⟩ 7 clothe] clo⟨a⟩the 10 opinion not] opinion ⟨in the a⟩ 11 in private] in ⟨letters⟩ 12 been the] been ⟨ab⟩ 14 others—no] others—⟨f⟩ 14–15 and expressing] and ⟨I record it⟩ 15 expressing the] expressing ⟨the feeling⟩ 16 to receive] to ⟨take for granted⟩ 17 proof] proof⟨s⟩ attack] attack⟨s⟩ 18 "candid" undermining] "candid" ⟨and⟩ 22 I take] I ⟨take⟩ 24 mind—the] mind—⟨it⟩ 26 the Essence] the ⟨Essential⟩ 28 reconcile Poetry] reconcile ⟨it⟩ 29 true "*Poet*"] true ⟨I thin⟩

and Milton—though his enemy Warton* places him immediately under them.[191]—I would no more say this—than I would assert in the Mosque (once Saint Sophia's)[192] that Socrates was a greater man than Mahomet.—But if I say that he is very near them—it is no more than has been asserted of Burns—who is supposed

"To rival all but Shakespeare's name below."[193]

I say nothing against this opinion.—But of what "*order*" according to the poetical Aristocracy are Burns's poems?——There are his "opus magnum" "Tam o' Shanter" a *tale*—the Cotter's Saturday Night—a descriptive Sketch—some others in the same style—the rest are songs.[194]———So much for the *rank* of his *productions*,—the rank of *Burns* is the very first of his Art.—————

Of Pope I have expressed my opinion elsewhere—as also of the effect which the present attempts at Poetry have had upon our literature.[195]—If any great national or natural Convulsion could or should overwhelm your Country in such sort as to sweep Great Britain from the kingdoms of the Earth—and leave only that—after all the most living of human things,—a *dead language*, to be studied and read and imitated by the wise of future and far generations—upon foreign shores,—if your literature should become the learning of Mankind, divested of party cabals—temporary fashions—and national pride and prejudice—an Englishman anxious that the Posterity of Strangers should know that there had been such a thing as a British Epic and Tragedy—might wish for the preservation of Shakespeare and Milton—but the surviving World would snatch Pope from the Wreck—and let the rest sink with the People.———He is the moral poet of all Civilization—and as such let us hope that he will one day be the

* If the opinions cited by Mr. Bowles, of Dr. Johnson *against* Pope, are to be taken as decisive authority, they will also hold good against Gray, Milton, Swift, Thomson, and Dryden: in that case what becomes of Gray's poetical, and Milton's moral character? even of Milton's *poetical* character, or indeed of *English* poetry in general? for Johnson strips many a leaf from every laurel.[196] Still Johnson's is the finest critical work extant, and can never be read without instruction and delight.[197]

4 them—it] them—⟨I say⟩ 7 I say] I ⟨do not⟩ nothing against] nothing ⟨upon⟩ 8 his "opus] his ⟨gr⟩ 12 is the] is ⟨in⟩ 13 elsewhere—as] elsewhere—⟨and⟩ 16 overwhelm your] overwhelm ⟨our⟩ such sort] such ⟨a manner—as to render your language a dead⟩ 18 of human] of ⟨all⟩ 19 the wise] the ⟨learned⟩ generations—upon] generations—⟨and⟩ 20 become the] become ⟨a⟩ 24 Tragedy—might] Tragedy—⟨would⟩ 25 the surviving] the ⟨rest of the⟩ 26–7 all Civilization] all ⟨civilized nations—and⟩

National poet of Mankind.—He is the only poet that never shocks—the only poet whose *faultlessness*—has been made his reproach.[198]——Cast your eye over his productions—consider their extent—and contemplate their variety.——Pastoral—Passion—Mock-heroic—Translation—Satire—Ethics——all excellent—and often perfect.—If his great charm be his *melody*—how comes it that foreigners adore him even in their diluted translations?——————

But I have made this letter too long—Give my compliments to Mr. Bowles———

yrs ever very truly
Byron.

Post Scriptum.—

Long as this letter has grown—I find it necessary to append a postscript—if possible, a short one. Mr. Bowles denies that he has accused Pope of "a sordid money getting passion" but he adds—"if I had ever done so—I should be glad to find any testimony that might show he was *not* so."[199]—This testimony he may find to his heart's content in Spence and elsewhere.—First—there is Martha Blount—who, Mr. B. charitably says—"Probably thought he did not save enough for her as legatee."[200]—whatever she *thought* upon this point—her words are in Pope's favour.—Then there is Alderman Barber—See Spence's anecdotes.—There is Pope's cold answer to Halifax—when he proposed a pension—his behaviour to Craggs and to Addison[201]—upon like occasions—and his own two line[202]

> "And, thanks to Homer, since I live and thrive
> Indebted to no Prince or peer alive.[203]—

Written when Princes would have been proud to pension and peers to promote him—and when the whole army of Dunces[204] were in array against him & would have been but too happy to deprive him of this boast of Independence.—But there is something a little more serious in Mr. Bowles's declaration that he "*would* have spoken" of his "noble generosity to the Outcast, Richard Savage and other instances of a compassionate and generous heart *had they occurred to his recollection when he wrote*.[205] What? is it come to this?—Does Mr. B. sit down to write a minute and laboured life and edition of a great poet?—does he anatomize his character moral and poetical?—does he present us with

1–2 shocks—the] shocks—⟨&⟩ 13 to append] to ⟨add⟩ 19 charitably says] charitably ⟨thinks⟩ 35–6 he anatomize] he ⟨argue upon⟩

his faults and with his foibles?—does he sneer at his feelings, and doubt of his sincerity?—does he unfold his vanity and duplicity? and then omit the good qualities which might in part have "covered this multitude of Sins"?[206]—and then plead that "*they did not occur to his recollection*?"—Is this the frame of Mind and of Memory with which the illustrious dead are to be approached?—If Mr. Bowles who must have had access to all the means of refreshing his memory—did not recollect these facts—he is unfit for his task—but if he *did* recollect and omit them—I know not what he is fit for—but I know what would be fit for him.——————

Is the plea of "not recollecting" such prominent facts to be admitted.—Mr. B. has been at a public School—and as I have been publicly educated also—I can sympathize with his predilection.—When we were in the third form even—had we pleaded on the Monday morning—that we had not brought up the Saturday's exercise because "we had forgotten it"—what would have been the reply?——— And is an excuse which would not be pardoned to a Schoolboy—to pass current in a matter which so nearly concerns the fame of the first poet of his age, if not of his country?—If Mr. B. so readily forgets the virtues of others—why complain so grievously that others have a better memory for his own faults? They are but the faults of an author—— while the virtues he omitted from his catalogue—are essential to the Justice due to a Man.——————

Mr. B. appears indeed to be susceptible—beyond the privilege of Authorship. There is a plaintive dedication to Mr. Gifford—in which *he* is made responsible for all the articles of the Quarterly.[207] Mr. Southey it seems "the most able & eloquent writer in that review" approved of Mr. Bowles' publication.[208]—Now it seems to me the more impartial that notwithstanding that the great writer of the Quarterly[209] entertains opinions opposite to the able Article on Spence—nevertheless that Essay was permitted to appear.—Is a review to be devoted to the opinions of any *one* man?—must it not vary according to circumstances—and according to the subjects to be criticised?—I fear that Writers must take the sweets and bitters of the public Journals as they occur—and an author of so long a standing as Mr. B.—might have

1 his feelings] his ⟨love⟩ 1–2 and doubt] and ⟨at his friendship?⟩ 4 —and] —⟨because⟩ 17 And is] And ⟨which⟩ 19–20 the virtues] the ⟨good qualities of⟩ 20 have a] have ⟨no⟩ 21 author] author⟨s⟩ 25 Authorship.] Authorship ⟨to⟩ 28 it seems] it ⟨appears⟩ 31 that Essay] that ⟨article⟩ 33 subjects to] subjects ⟨off⟩

become accustomed to such incidents—he might be angry but not astonished. I have been reviewed in the Quarterly almost as often as Mr. B. & have had as pleasant things said and some *as un*pleasant—as could well be pronounced.—In the review of "the Fall of Jerusalem" it is stated—that I have devoted "my powers &c. to the worst parts of Manicheism"—which being interpreted means that I worship the Devil.[210]——Now—I have neither written a reply—nor complained to Gifford.——I believe that I observed in a letter to you—that I thought "that the Critic might have praised Milman without finding it necessary to abuse me"—but did I not add at the same time or soon after—(apropos—of the Note in the book of travels) that I would not—if it were even in my power—have a single line cancelled on my account in that nor in any other publication.[211]—Of course I reserve to myself the privilege of response when necessary.———

Mr. B. seems in a whimsical state about the author of the article on Spence.—You know very well that I am not in your confidence—nor in that of the Conductors[212] of the Journal.—The moment I saw that article I was morally certain that I knew the author—"by his Style."[213]——You will tell me that I do *not know* him——that is all as it should be—keep the secret—so shall I—though no one has ever entrusted it to me.——He is not the person whom Mr. B. denounces.[214]

——————

Mr. B's extreme sensibility reminds me of a circumstance which occurred on board of a frigate in which I was a passenger and guest of the Captain's for a considerable time.——The Surgeon on board—a very gentlemanly young man—and remarkably able in his profession—wore a *Wig.*—Upon this ornament he was extremely tenacious.—As Naval jests are sometimes a little rough—his brother officers made occasional allusions to this delicate appendage to the Doctor's person.—One day a young Lieutenant in the course of a facetious discussion—said—"Suppose now, Doctor,—I should take off your *hat*"——"Sir—replied the Doctor—I shall talk no longer with you—you grow *Scurrilous*. He would not even admit so near an approach as to the *hat* which protected it.[215]——————In like Manner if any

5 &c. to] &c.⟨”⟩ 11 (apropos] (⟨that⟩ I would] I ⟨should⟩ 15 whimsical state] whimsical ⟨certainty⟩ article on] article ⟨of⟩ 18 —“by] —⟨I knew him⟩ 21 He] ⟨It⟩ He Mr. B. denounces] Mr. B. ⟨supposes⟩ ⟨designates⟩ 23 circumstance which] circumstance ⟨to⟩ 23–4 which occurred] which ⟨I was a witness⟩ 24 a passenger] a ⟨passenger⟩ 25 for a] for ⟨some mont⟩ 28 little rough] little ⟨pers⟩ 29 occasional] occasional⟨ly⟩ this delicate] this ⟨sensitive part of⟩ 34 the *hat*] the ⟨*hat*⟩

body approaches Mr. Bowles's laurels even in his outside capacity of an *Editor*—"they grow *scurrilous*."——————

You say that you are about to prepare an Edition of Pope—you cannot do better for your own credit as a publisher nor for the redemption of Pope from Mr. B. and of the public taste from rapid degeneracy.[216]——————

Addenda[217]

It is worthy of remark that after all this outcry about "*indoor* Nature" and "artificial images"[218] Pope was the principal inventor of that boast of the English;—*Modern Gardening*.—He divides this honour with Milton.—Hear Warton. "It hence appears that this *enchanting* art of modern Gardening, in which this kingdom claims a preference over every nation in Europe—chiefly owes *it's origin* & it's improvements to two great Poets, Milton and *Pope*.[219]——

Walpole (no friend to Pope) asserts that Pope formed *Kent's* taste—and that Kent was the artist to whom the English are chiefly indebted for diffusing "a taste in laying out grounds."———The design of the Prince of Wales's Garden—was copied from *Pope's* at Twickenham.—Warton applauds "his singular effort of art and taste in impressing so much variety and scenery on a spot of five acres."[220]—Pope was the *first* who ridiculed the "formal, French, Dutch—false and unnatural taste in Gardening" both in *prose* and verse (See for the former "the Guardian.")[221]———

"Pope has given not only some of our *first* but *best* rules and observations on *Architecture* and *Gardening*."[222]

See Warton's Essay Vol 2d. 237. &c. &c.

Now is it not a shame after this to hear our Lakers in "Kendal Green"[223] and our Bucolical Cockneys[224] crying out (the latter in a Wilderness of bricks and mortar)—about "Nature" and Pope's "artificial indoor habits."———Pope had seen all of Nature that *England* alone can supply.—He was bred in Windsor Forest—and amidst the beautiful scenery of Eton—he lived familiarly & frequently at the country seats of Bathurst—Cobham—Burlington—Peterborough—

1 body approaches] body ⟨approximates⟩ laurels even] laurels ⟨even⟩ 4 publisher nor] publisher ⟨or⟩ 8 It is] It ⟨may be⟩ remark that] remark ⟨to observe⟩ 12–13 over every] over ⟨all⟩ 20 on] ⟨up⟩on 28 Cockneys crying] Cockneys ⟨crrying⟩ 29 of bricks] of ⟨bricks and m⟩ ⟨Winds⟩ 29–30 "artificial indoor] "artificial ⟨tastes—⟩ 33 —Peterborough] —⟨Pet⟩

Digby—and Bolingbroke——amongst whose seats was to be numbered *Stow*.[225]—He made his own little "five acres" a model to Princes—and to the first of our Artists who imitated Nature—Warton thinks—"that the most engaging of *Kent's* works was also planned on the model of Pope's at least in the opening & retiring "shades of Venus's Vale."[226]————

It is true that Pope was infirm & deformed—but he could walk—& he could ride—(he rode to Oxford from London at a stretch) and he was famous for an exquisite eye.[227]—On a tree at L.d Bathurst's is carved "here Pope sang."[228] He composed beneath it.—Bolingbroke in one of his letters represents them both writing in the Hay field.[229] No Poet ever admired Nature more or used her better than Pope has done—as I will undertake to prove from his works—*prose* and *verse* if not anticipated in so easy and agreeable a labour. I remember a passage in Walpole somewhere—of a Gentleman who wished to give directions about some willows to a man who had long served Pope in his grounds—"I understand Sir—he replied—you would have them hang down—Sir—*somewhat poetical*."[230]—Now if nothing existed but this little anecdote—it would suffice to prove Pope's taste for *Nature* & the impression which he had made on a common-minded man.—But I have already quoted Warton & Walpole (*both* his enemies) and were it necessary I could amply quote Pope himself——for such tributes to *Nature*—as no Poet of the present day—has even approached.—His various Excellence is really wonderful;—Architecture—painting—*gardening* all are alike subject to his Genius.—Be it remembered—that English *Gardening* is the purposed perfectioning of niggard *Nature*——and that without it England is but a hedge and ditch, double post and rail, Hounslow heath, and Clapham Common sort of Country, since the principal forests have been felled.—It is in general far from a picturesque country.—The case is different with Scotland—Wales—and Ireland—and I except also the Lake Counties—and Derbyshire—together with Eton, Windsor, and my own dear Harrow on the Hill; and some spots near the Coast. In the present rank fertility of "great poets of the Age"—and "Schools of poetry" a word which like "Schools of Eloquence" and of "Philosophy" is never introduced till

1 amongst whose] amongst ⟨which⟩ seats was] seats ⟨are⟩ ⟨is⟩ 3 —Warton] —⟨"I am⟩ 8–9 he was] he ⟨had an⟩ 16 willows to] willows ⟨which⟩ 17 replied —] replied ⟨the man⟩ ⟨he⟩ 19 prove Pope's] prove ⟨his⟩ 20 impression which] impression ⟨it⟩ 25 are alike] are ⟨equally⟩ —Be] —⟨But⟩ 26 English *Gardening*] English ⟨Nat⟩ 29 —It] —⟨England is not in itself⟩ 33 spots near] spots ⟨on⟩

the decay of the art has increased with the number of it's Professors——in the present day then,—there have sprung up two Sects of Naturals—the Lakers—who whine about Nature because they live in Cumberland—and their *under-Sect*—(which some one has maliciously called the "Cockney School")—who are enthusiastical for the country because they live in London.——It is to be observed that the rustical founders are rather anxious to disclaim any connection with their metropolitan followers—whom—they ungraciously review—& call Cockneys—Atheists—foolish fellows—bad writers and other hard names not less ungrateful than unjust.[231]——I can understand the pretensions of the Aquatic gentlemen of Windermere to what Mr Braham terms "*entusymusy*"[232] for lakes and mountains and daffodils—and buttercups——but I should be glad to be apprized of the foundation of the London propensities of their imitative brethren to the same "high argument"?[233]—Southey—Wordsworth—& Coleridge—have rambled over half Europe—and seen Nature in most of her varieties—(although I think that they have occasionally not used her very well)—but what on Earth—of Earth—and Sea—and Nature—have the others seen?—Not a half nor a tenth part so much as Pope.——While they sneer at his Windsor forest—have they ever seen any thing of Windsor except it's *Brick*?[234]—The most rural of these Gentlemen is my friend Leigh Hunt—who lives at Hampstead.—I believe that I need not disclaim any personal or poetical hostility against that Gentleman.—A more amiable man in society—I know not—nor—(when he will allow his sense to prevail over his Sectarian principles)—a better writer.—When he was writing his "Rimini"—I was not the last to discover it's beauties long before it was published.—Even then I remonstrated against it's vulgarisms—which are the more extraordinary—because the Author is anything but a vulgar man.—Mr Hunt's answer—was that he wrote them upon principle—they made part of his "*System*—,"—I then said no more. When a man talks of his *System*—it is like a woman's talking of her *Virtue*———I let them talk on.—————Whether there are writers who could have written "Rimini"—as it might have been written I know not—but Mr Hunt is probably the

3 who whine] who ⟨rave⟩ 8–9 call Cockneys] call ⟨Cok⟩ 9 and other] and ⟨what not.⟩ 13 be apprized] be ⟨made aware⟩ 22 I believe] I ⟨beg leave to⟩ 23 disclaim any] disclaim ⟨all⟩ 25 prevail over] prevail ⟨or⟩ 28 it's vulgarisms] it's ⟨vulgarity⟩ 29 Mr Hunt's] Mr ⟨Hunt⟩ 32 —I] —⟨they are both pretending to something which ⟨they have⟩ is not in them——by way of delu[?ding] themselves as well as others.—⟩

only poet who would[235] have had the heart to spoil his own—Capo d'Opera.[236]——————

With the rest of his young people—I have no acquaintance except through some things of theirs—(which have been sent out without my desire) and I confess that till I had read them I was not aware of the full extent of human absurdity.——Like "Garrick's Ode to Shakespeare"—"*they defy Criticism.*"[237]———These are of the personages who decry Pope—one of them,—a Mr. John Ketch, has written some lines against him of which it were better to be the subject than the author.[238]—Mr. Hunt redeems himself by occasional beauties—but the rest of these poor creatures seem so far gone—that I would not "march through Coventry with them that's flat"[239] were I in Mr. Hunt's place.——To be sure he has "led his ragamuffins where they will be well peppered."[240]———But a System-maker must receive all sorts of proselytes.——When they have really seen life—when they have felt it—when they have travelled beyond the far-distant boundaries of the wilds of Middlesex—when they have overpassed the Alps of Highgate—and traced to it's sources the Nile of the New River[241]—then—& not till then—can it properly be permitted to them to despise Pope——who had if not *in Wales*—been *near* it—when he described so beautifully—the "*artificial*" works of the Benefactor of Nature—& Mankind—the "Man of Ross"—whose picture still suspended in the parlour of the Inn I have so often contemplated with reverence for his memory—and admiration of the poet—without whom—even his own still existing good works would[242] hardly have preserved his honest renown.[243]————

I would also observe to my friend Hunt that I shall be very glad to see him at *Ravenna*—not only for my sincere pleasure in his company and the advantage which a thousand miles or so of travel might produce to a "natural" poet—but also to point out one or two little things in "Rimini"—which he probably would not have placed in his opening to that poem—if he had ever *seen Ravenna*—unless indeed—it made "part of his System."[244]——————

I must also crave his indulgence for having spoken of his disciples—

4 through some] through ⟨their⟩ 8 Ketch, has] Ketch, [*about eight words heavily deleted and irrecoverable*] 11 that I] that ⟨surely if one⟩ 12 them that's] them ⟨were I their⟩ 20 had if] had ⟨at least been in⟩ —been] —⟨or⟩ 21 of Nature] of ⟨Man and⟩ 22 still suspended] still ⟨hangs his⟩ 23 Inn I] Inn ⟨of⟩ 28 for my] for ⟨the⟩ pleasure in] pleasure ⟨of⟩ 29–30 might produce] might ⟨be⟩ 34 disciples——] disciples—⟨to me⟩

—by no means an agreeable or self-sought subject.—If they had said nothing of *Pope*—they might have remained "alone with their glory,"[245] for aught I should said[246] or thought about them or their nonsense.—— But if they interfere with the "little Nightingale" of Twickenham,[247]— —they may find others who will bear it—*I* wont.——Neither time—nor distance—nor grief—nor age—can ever diminish my veneration for him—who is the great Moral poet—of all times—of all climes—of all feelings—and of all stages of existence.—The delight of my boyhood—the Study of my Manhood—perhaps—(if allowed to me to attain it) he may be the consolation of my Age.——His poetry is the Book of Life.—Without canting, and yet without neglecting, Religion, he has assembled all that a good and great man can gather together of moral wisdom cloathed in consummate beauty. Sir William Temple observes—

"That of all the numbers of mankind—that live within the compass of a thousand years for one man that is born capable of making a *great poet*, there may be a *thousand* born capable of making as great Generals and Ministers of State as any in Story.—————[248]

Here is a Statesman's opinion of Poetry—it is honourable to him & to the Art.——Such a "poet of a thousand years" was *Pope*.——A thousand years will roll away before such another can be hoped for in our literature.—But it can *want* them—he himself is a literature.———

One word upon his so brutally abused translation of Homer——"D.r Clarke whose critical exactness is well known—has *not been* able to point out out above three or four mistakes *in the sense* through the whole Iliad.—The real faults of the translation are of a different kind.[249]—So says Warton himself a Scholar—it appears by this then—that he avoided the chief fault of a translator.——As to it's other faults—they consist in his having made a beautiful English poem of a sublime Greek one.—It will always hold—Cowper—and all the rest of the Blank pretenders may do their best and their worst——they will never wrench Pope from the hands of a single reader of sense and feeling.——————

1 agreeable or] agreeable ⟨subject⟩ 5 find others] find ⟨those⟩ 11 —Without] —⟨without⟩ Without canting] Without ⟨becoming prim,—⟩ 12 and great] and ⟨wise⟩ 13 in consummate] in ⟨immortal⟩ 20 Such] ⟨This⟩ Such 22 can *want*] can ⟨want⟩ 23 brutally abused] brutally ⟨abused⟩ 25 or four] or ⟨three⟩ *sense* through] *sense* ⟨of⟩ 28 he avoided] he ⟨at least⟩ 31 their worst] their ⟨worst;⟩

The grand distinction of the Under forms of the New School of poets—is their *Vulgarity*.—By this I do not mean that they are *Coarse*—but "shabby-genteel"—as it is termed.[250]—A man may be *coarse* & yet not *vulgar*—and the reverse.——Burns is often coarse—but never *vulgar*.———Chatterton is never vulgar;—nor Wordsworth—nor the higher of the Lake School, though they treat of low life in all it's branches.—It is in their *finery* that the New-under School—are most vulgar;—and they may be known by this at once—as what we called at Harrow—"a Sunday Blood"[251] might be easily distinguished from a Gentleman—although his cloathes might be the better-cut—and his boots the best-blackened of the two—probably because he made the one—or cleaned the other with his own hands.——

In the present case I speak of writing,—*not* of persons.——Of the latter I know nothing—of the former I judge as it is found.—Of my friend Hunt—I have already said that he is anything but vulgar in his manners——and of his disciples therefore—I will not judge of their manners from their verses.——They may be honourable & *gentlemanly* men for what I know—but the latter quality is studiously excluded from their publications.—They remind me of Mr. Smith and the Miss Branghtons at the Hampstead Assembly in "Evelina."[252]——In these things (in private life at least)—I pretend to some small experience—because in the course of my youth—I have seen a little of all sorts of Society—from the Christian—Prince—and the Mussulman Sultan and Pacha—& the higher ranks of their countries,—down to the London boxer, "the *Flash and the Swell*"[253]—the Spanish Muleteer—the wandering Turkish Dervise——the Scotch Highlander—and the Albanian robber;—to say nothing of the curious varieties of Italian social life.——Far be it from me to presume that there ever was or can be such a thing as an *Aristocracy* of *Poets*—⌜I do not mean that they should write in the Style of the Song by a person of Quality—or *parle Euphuism*—⌝[254] but there *is* a Nobility of thought and of Style—open to all Stations—and derived partly from talent—& partly from education—which is to be found in Shakespeare—and Pope—and Burns—no less than in Dante and Alfieri—but which is no-where to be perceived in the Mockbirds & bards of Mr. Hunt little chorus.[255]—

7–8 most vulgar] most ⟨terribly⟩ 8 be known] be ⟨distinguished⟩ 10 the better-cut] the ⟨costliest⟩ ⟨best-cut⟩ 12 other with] other ⟨him⟩ 13 of writing] of ⟨poetry⟩ 19 and the] and ⟨young Branghtons⟩ 20 —In] —⟨Of⟩ 22 seen a] seen ⟨all⟩ 25 boxer, "the] boxer, ⟨and the⟩ ⟨and⟩ Muleteer—the] Muleteer—⟨and⟩ 29 of *Poets*] of ⟨Poetry—⟩ 35 be perceived] be ⟨found⟩ the Mockbirds] the ⟨Underlings⟩ of Mr.] of ⟨the⟩

—If I were asked to define what this Gentlemanliness is—I should say that it is only to be defined by *examples*,——of those who have it—& those who have it not.—In *Life*——I should say that most *military* men have it—& few *Naval*——that several men of rank have it—and few lawyers—that it is more frequent among authors than divines (when they are not pedants) that *fencing*-masters have more of it than dancing-masters—and Singers than players——and that (if it be not *an Irishism*[256] to say so) it is far more generally diffused among women than among men.—In poetry as well as writing in general—it will never *make* entirely a poet or a poem—but neither poet nor poem will ever be good for any thing without it.—It is the *Salt* of Society—and the Seasoning of composition.—*Vulgarity* is far worse than downright *Blackguardism*—for the latter comprehends wit—humour—and strong sense at times——while the former is a sad abortive attempt at all things—"signifying nothing."[257]—It does not depend upon low themes—or even low language—for—Fielding revels in both——but is he ever *vulgar*?—No—you see the man of education the gentleman and the Scholar sporting with his subject——it's Master—not it's Slave.—Your vulgar Writer is always most vulgar—the higher his subject—as the Man who showed the Menagerie at Pidcocks—was wont to say—"this (Gentlemen)—is the *Eagle* of the *Sun* from ArchAngel in Russia—the *otterer* it is—the "igherer—he flies."[258]——But to the proof—it is a thing to be felt—more than explained—let any man take up a volume of Mr Hunt's subordinate writers—read (if possible) a couple of pages—& pronounce for himself if they contain not the kind of writing—which may be likened to "Shabby-genteel" in actual life?[259]—When he has done this let him take up Pope——and when he has laid him down—take up the Cockneys again;—if he can.———

1 this Gentlemanliness] this ⟨is⟩ ⟨Gentle refinement is⟩ 2 —of] —⟨by⟩ ⟨of⟩ of those] of ⟨which⟩ 4 that several] that ⟨many⟩ 9 poetry as] poetry ⟨and⟩ it will] it ⟨is as little⟩ 15 not depend] not ⟨att⟩ 16 —or] —⟨and⟩ 17 education the] education ⟨of⟩ 18 —it's] —⟨&⟩ 20 showed the] showed ⟨the beast⟩ ⟨his⟩ 23 felt—more] felt—⟨& not⟩ 24 —read] —⟨and⟩ 26 which may] which ⟨bears the sa⟩ 27 and when] and ⟨I venture to prophesy that he⟩

Observations upon Observations (1821)

Observations upon Observations of the Revd. W. L. B. &c. &c. &c.[1]

Ravenna. March 25th. *1821.*

Dear Sir—

In the further "Observations" of Mr. B. in rejoinder to the charges brought against his Edition of Pope—it is to be regretted that he has lost his temper.——Whatever the language of his antagonists may have been—I fear that his replies have afforded more pleasure to them than to the Public.——That Mr. B. should not be pleased is natural—whether right or wrong;—but a temperate defence would have answered his purpose in the former case—and in the latter no defence however violent can tend to anything but his discomfiture. I have read over this third pamphlet which you have been so obliging as to send me—and shall venture a few observations in addition to those—upon the previous controversy.————

Mr. B. sets out with repeating his "*confirmed conviction*" that "what he said of the moral part of Pope's character was (generally speaking) true; and that the principles of *poetical Criticism* which he has laid down are *invariable* and *invulnerable* &c."—& that he is the *more* persuaded of this by the "*exaggerations* of his opponents."[2]—This is all very well—and highly natural & sincere. Nobody ever expected that either Mr. B.—or any other author would be convinced of human fallibility in their own persons.—But it is nothing to the purpose—for it is not what Mr. *B.* thinks—but what is to be thought of *Pope* that is the question.——It is what he has asserted or insinuated against a name which is the patrimony of Posterity—that is to be tried—& Mr. B. as a party can be no Judge.—The more *he* is persuaded—the better for himself if it give him any pleasure——but he can only persuade others by the proofs brought out in his defence.—

After these prefatory remarks of "conviction &c."—Mr. B. proceeds to Mr. Gilchrist.—whom he charges with "Slang" and "Slander"—besides

6–7 has lost] has ⟨so far⟩ 8 replies] repl⟨y⟩ replies have] replies ⟨hitherto⟩ 13 over this] over ⟨with sensible like attention⟩ 14 those—upon] those—⟨which I have already sent you⟩ 14–15 upon the] upon ⟨the former what I had previously said of⟩ 25 It is] It i⟨t⟩ 28 but he] but ⟨it⟩ 28–9 proofs brought] proofs ⟨he brings⟩ 29 his defence] his ⟨support⟩

a small subsidiary indictment of "Abuse, Ignorance—Malice"—and so forth.[3]———Mr. Gilchrist has indeed shown some anger—but it is an honest indignation—which rises up in defence of the illustrious dead.—It is a generous rage which interposes between our ashes and their disturbers.—There appears also to have been some slight personal provocation.—Mr. Gilchrist with a chivalrous disdain of the fury of an incensed poet put his name to a letter avowing the production of a former Essay in defence of Pope—and consequently of an attack upon Mr. Bowles.—Mr. B. appears to be angry with Mr. G. for four reasons—firstly—because he wrote an article in the L. Magazine—secondly—because he afterwards avowed it—3dly. because he *was* the author of a still more extended article in the Quarterly Review—and fourthly—because he was NOT the author of the said Quarterly article—and had the audacity to disavow it—for no earthly reason but because he had NOT written it.[4]————

Mr. B. declares that "he will not enter into a particular examination of the pamphlet which by a *mis-nomer* (in Italics) is called "Gilchrist's Answer to Bowles" when it should have been called "Gilchrist's Abuse of Bowles." on this error in the baptism of Mr. G's pamphlet it may be observed that an answer may be abusive and yet no less an answer, though indisputably a temperate one might be the better of the two;——but if *abuse* is to cancel all pretensions to *reply*—what becomes of Mr. B's answers to Gilchrist?———

Mr. B. continues "But as Mr. G. derides my *peculiar sensitiveness to criticism* before I show how *destitute of truth is this representation*—I will here explicitly declare the only grounds &c. &c. &c.——Mr. B's sensibility in denying his "sensitiveness to criticism" proves perhaps too much;——but if he has been so charged—& truly;—what then? there is no moral turpitude in such acuteness of feeling—it has been & may be combined with many good & great qualities——is Mr. B. a poet or is he not?—if he be—he must from his very essence be sensitive to criticism—& even if he be not—he need not be ashamed of the common repugnance to being attacked——all that is to be wished is that he had considered how disagreeable a thing it is before he assailed the greatest moral poet of any age—or in any language.————

1 subsidiary indictment] subsidiary ⟨attack⟩ 4 between our] between ⟨the⟩ ashes and] ashes ⟨of ou⟩ 7 to a] to ⟨his one⟩ letter avowing] letter ⟨and⟩ avowing] avow⟨ed⟩ 9–10 for four] for ⟨three⟩ 19 on] ⟨of⟩ on 20–1 answer, though] answer, ⟨and⟩ 28 & truly] & ⟨if it be true⟩ 29 such acuteness] such ⟨sense⟩ acuteness of] acuteness ⟨it⟩ 32 of the] of ⟨a dislike⟩ 34 he assailed] he ⟨meddled with⟩ assailed the] assailed ⟨our⟩

Pope himself "sleeps well"—nothing can touch him further"[5] but those who love the honour of their country—the perfection of her literature, the glory of her language—are not to be expected to permit an atom of his dust—to be stirred in his tomb—or a leaf to be stripped from the laurel which grows over it.——————

Mr. B. assigns several reasons why & when "an author is justified in appealing to every *upright* & *honourable* mind in the kingdom"——if Mr. B. limits the perusal of his defence to the "upright & honourable" only—I greatly fear that it will not be extensively circulated.—I should rather hope that some of the downright & dishonest will read and be converted or convicted.——But the whole of his reasoning is here superfluous—"*an author is justified in appealing &c.*" when & why he pleases——let him make out a tolerable case and few of his readers will quarrel with his motives.——

Mr. B. "will now plainly set before the literary public All the circumstances which have led to *his name* and Mr. G's being brought together &c.——Courtesy requires in speaking of others & ourselves that we should place the name of the former first—& not "*Ego* et Rex meus"[6]——Mr. B. should have written "Mr. Gilchrist's name and *his*."———This point he wishes "particularly to address to those *most respectable characters*, who have the direction and management of the Periodical Critical Press. That the press may be in some instances conducted by respectable characters is probable enough—but if they are so—there is no occasion to tell them of it;—& if they are not it is a base adulation;—in either case it looks like a kind of flattery—by which those gentry are not very likely to be softened,—since it would be difficult to find two passages in fifteen pages more at variance than Mr. B's prose at the beginning of this pamphlet and his verse at the end of it.—In page 4. he speaks of "those most respectable characters who have the direction &c. of the periodical press"—and in page 16. we find—

"Ye *dark inquisitors*, a monk-like band
Who oer some shrinking victim author stand,
A solemn, secret, and *vindictive brood*
Only terrific in your cowl and hood—

4 be stirred] be ⟨shaken in⟩ 5 which grows] which ⟨spreads⟩ 8 the perusal] the ⟨circulation⟩ 9 extensively circulated] extensively ⟨read⟩ 10 will read] will ⟨peruse and⟩ 11 But] ⟨but⟩ But 13 tolerable case] tolerable ⟨justification⟩ 16 and Mr.] and ⟨that⟩ 17 of others] of ⟨ourselves⟩ 26 —since] —⟨and⟩ it would] it ⟨is⟩ 29 who have] who ⟨&c. &c.—⟩

And so on—to "bloody law"—and "red scourges" with other similar phrases[7]—which may not be altogether agreeable to the above-mentioned "most respectable characters."—Mr. B. goes on—"I concluded my observations in the last Pamphleteer with feelings *not unkind* towards Mr. Gilchrist *or* (it should be *nor*) to the author of the Review of Spence be he whom he might."[8]—"I was in hopes, *as I have always been ready* to *admit any errors* I might have been led into, or prejudices[9] I might have entertained that even Mr. Gilchrist might be disposed to a more *amicable* mode of discussing what I had advanced in regard to Pope's moral character.—As Major Sturgeon observes "there never was a set of more *amicable* Officers—with the exception of a boxing-bout between Captain Shears and the Colonel."[10]

A page and a half—nay only a page before—Mr. B. re-affirms his conviction that "what he has said of Pope's moral character is (*generally speaking*) *true*" & that his "poetical principles are *invariable & invulnerable*"—he has also published three pamphlets aye, *four* of the same tenor——& yet with this decla*r*ation & these decla*m*ations staring him and his adversaries in the face—he speaks of his "readiness to admit errors—or to abandon "prejudices"!!!——His use of the word "amicable" reminds me of an[11] Irish Institution (which I have somewhere heard or read of) called the "*Friendly* Society" where the President always carried pistols in his pocket so that when one amicable gentleman knocked down another—the difference might be adjusted on the spot at the harmonious distance of twelve paces.[12]——

But Mr. B. "has since read a publication by him (Mr. G.) containing "such vulgar slander—affecting *private* life and character &c. &c."——— and Mr. Gilchrist has also had the advantage of reading a publication by Mr. Bowles—sufficiently imbued with personality—for—one of the first and principal topics of reproach is that he is a *Grocer*, that he has a "pipe in his mouth"—"ledger book" green canisters, dingy shop-boy—half a hogshead of brown treacle &c.—" nay—the same delicate raillery is upon the very title page.[13]——————When Controversy has once commenced upon this footing,—as Dr. Johnson said to Dr. Percy— "Sir —there is an end of politeness—we are to be as rude as we please—Sir —you said that I was *short-sighted*."[14]—As a Man's profession is generally no more in his own power than his person—both having been made out for him—it is hard that he should be reproached with

2 be altogether] be ⟨peculiarly⟩ 8 might be] might ⟨have been led⟩ 19 or to] or ⟨prejudices⟩ 28 —sufficiently] —⟨little⟩ 29 a *Grocer*] a ⟨Groc⟩ 33 —as] —⟨we may say⟩ 33 —"Sir] —⟨"nay⟩ 34 of politeness] of ⟨decorum⟩

either—& still more that an honest calling should be made a reproach.——If there is anything more honourable to Mr Gilchrist than another it is—that being engaged in commerce he has had the taste—and found the leisure to become so able a proficient in the higher literature of his own & other countries.——Mr Bowles who will be proud to own Glover, Chatterton, Burns and Bloomfield for his peers[15]—should hardly have quarrelled with Mr Gilchrist for his Critic.——Mr G's Station however which might conduct him to the highest civic honours—and to boundless wealth—has nothing to require apology,—but even if it had—such a reproach was not very gracious on the part of a clergyman—nor graceful on that of a gentleman.—The allusion to "*Christian* Criticism" is not particularly happy—especially where Mr G. is accused of having "*set the first example of this mode in Europe*."—What *Pagan* criticism may have been we know but little, the names of Zoilus and Aristarchus survive—and the works of Aristotle Longinus & Quintilian.[16]—But of "Christian Criticism"—we have already had some specimens in the works of Philelphus—Poggius—Scaliger—Milton—Salmasius—The Cruscanti (versus Tasso) The F. Academy (against the Cid—) & the antagonists of Voltaire & of Pope—to say nothing of some articles in most of the Reviews since their earliest institution in the person of their respectable and still prolific parent "the Monthly."[17] Why then is Mr Gilchrist to be singled out "as having set the first example"?—a sole page of Milton or Salmasius contains more abuse; *rank—rancorous—unleavened*—abuse—than all that can be raked forth from the whole works of many recent Critics:—there are some indeed who still keep up the good old custom—but fewer English than foreign.—It is a pity that Mr B. cannot witness some of the Italian controversies—or become the subject of one—he would then look upon Mr Gilchrist as a panegyrist.[18]—

In the long sentence quoted from the article in the L.M.—there is one coarse image—the justice of whose application I shall not pretend to determine.——"The pruriency with which his nose is laid to the ground"—is an expression which, whether founded or not, might as well have been omitted.[19]—But the "*anatomical minuteness*" appears to

4 and found] and ⟨has⟩ 6 own Glover] own ⟨Burns⟩ ⟨Glover⟩ Chatterton, Burns] Chatterton, ⟨Dr Johnson—⟩ 8 Mr G's] ⟨His⟩ Mr G's 9 nothing to] nothing ⟨in it⟩ 10 was not] was ⟨not⟩ 23 a sole] a ⟨single⟩ 24 abuse; *rank*] abuse; ⟨than⟩ 25 be raked] be ⟨singled out⟩ raked forth] raked ⟨out of⟩ 26 of many] of ⟨every⟩ 28 cannot witness] cannot ⟨see⟩

me justified even by Mr. B's own subsequent quotation.—To the point.—"*Many facts* tend to prove the peculiar susceptibility of his passions—nor can we implicitly believe, that the connexion between him and Martha Blount was of a nature so pure and innocent as his panegyrist Ruffhead would have us believe &c. &c. &c.————At *no time* could she have regarded *Pope personally* with attachment—&c.—But the most extraordinary circumstance in regard to his connexion with female Society was the strange mixture of *indecent* and even *profane* levity which his conduct and language often exhibited.—The cause of this particularity may be sought, perhaps, in his consciousness of physical defect,—which made him affect a character uncongenial, and a language opposite to the truth."[20]———If this is not "minute moral "anatomy"—I should be glad to know what is?—It is dissection in all it's branches.

I shall however hazard a remark or two upon this quotation.——To me it appears of no very great consequence whether Martha Blount was or was not Pope's Mistress—though I could have wished him a better.——She appears to have been a cold-hearted—interested—ignorant—disagreeable—woman upon whom the tenderness of Pope's heart in the desolation of his latter days was cast away, not knowing whither to turn as he drew towards his premature old age, childless and lonely—like the Needle which approaching within a certain distance of the Pole—becomes helpless & useless—& ceasing to tremble, rusts.[21]—She seems to have been so totally unworthy of tenderness that it is an additional proof of the kindness of Pope's heart to have been able to love such a being.—But we must love something.[22]—I agree with Mr. B. that *She* "could at no time have regarded *Pope personally* with attachment," because she was incapable of attachment.—But I deny that Pope could not be regarded with personal attachment by a worthier woman.——It is not probable indeed that a woman would have fallen in love with him as he walked along the Mall—or in a box at the Opera—nor from a balcony—nor in a ball-room—but in society he seems to have been as amiable as unassuming—and with the greatest disadvantages of figure—his head & face were remarkably handsome, especially his eyes.[23]—He was

11 a character] a ⟨language⟩ 14 branches.] branches⟨?⟩ 15 however hazard] however ⟨make bold to put a query or two upon the results⟩ 19 whom the] whom ⟨the whom⟩ 20 days was] days ⟨threw itself⟩ 21 turn as] turn ⟨itself⟩ 22 —like] —⟨like⟩ 23 —&] —⟨& rests in it's rust⟩ 26 But we] But ⟨we⟩ ⟨those who feel,⟩ 29 attachment.] attachment ⟨to any⟩ 32 the Opera] the ⟨theatre⟩ 34–5 head &] head ⟨was⟩ 35 handsome, especially] handsome, ⟨particularly⟩

adored by his friends—friends of the most opposite dispositions, ages and talents—by the old and wayward Wycherley—by the cynical Swift—the rough Atterbury—the gentle Spence—the stern Attorney-bishop Warburton—the virtuous Berkeley and the "cankered Bolingbroke."[24]—Bolingbroke wept over him like a child—and Spence's description of his last moments is at least as edifying as the more ostentatious account of the death-bed of Addison.[25]——The soldier Peterborough—and the poet Gay—the witty Congreve—and the laughing Rowe—the eccentric Cromwell—and the steady Bathurst, were all his intimates.[26]—The Man who could conciliate so many men of the most opposite description—not one of whom but was a remarkable or a celebrated character—might well have pretended to all the attachment which a reasonable man would desire of an amiable woman.—Pope in fact—wherever he got it—appears to have understood the Sex well.—Bolingbroke—"a Judge of the subject" says Warton—thought his "Epistle on the Characters of women" his "Masterpiece."[27]——And even with respect to the grosser passion—which takes occasionally the name of "*romantic*"—accordingly as the degree of sentiment elevates it above the definition of Love by Buffon[28]——it may be remarked that it does not always depend upon personal appearance, even in a woman.—Madame Cottin—was a plain woman—and might have been virtuous, it may be presumed, without much interruption.——Virtuous she was, and the consequences of this inveterate Virtue—were that two different admirers, (one an elderly Gentleman) killed themselves in despair.—(See Lady Morgan's "France.")[29] I would not however recommend this rigour to plain women in general in the hope of securing the glory of two suicides apiece.—I believe that there are few men who in the course of their observations on life may not have perceived that it is not the greatest female beauty who forms the longest & the strongest passions.—

But Apropos of Pope.—Voltaire tell us that the Marechal Luxembourg (who had precisely Pope's figure) was not only somewhat too amatory for a great man—but fortunate in his attachments.[30]——La

2 the cynical] the ⟨austere⟩ 4 the "cankered] the ⟨haughty⟩ 9 the eccentric] the ⟨rake⟩ 10 many men] many ⟨characters⟩ 11–12 remarkable or] remarkable ⟨and⟩ 13 an amiable] a ⟨good-hearted⟩ 19 it above] it ⟨from⟩ definition of] definition ⟨of⟩ 20 it does] it ⟨by no means⟩ depend] depend⟨s⟩ 22 it may] it ⟨might⟩ 23 without much] without ⟨diffi⟩ much interruption] much ⟨difficulty⟩ 24 different admirers] different ⟨gentlemen of ⟨different⟩ opposite ages⟩ 27 the hope] the ⟨notion⟩

Valiere the passion of Louis 14th had an unsightly defect.[31]—The Princess of Eboli—the Mistress of Philip the second of Spain—and Maguiron the Minion of Henry the third of France—had each of them lost an eye—and the famous Latin epigram was written upon them—which has I believe—been either translated or imitated by Goldsmith.[32]—

"Lumine Acon dextro, capta est Leonilla sinistro
Et potis est forma vincere uterque Deos;
Blande puer, lumen quod habes concede sorori,
Sic tu cæcus Amor, sic erit illa Venus.

Wilkes—with his ugliness—used to say that "he was but a quarter of an hour behind the handsomest man in England"—and this vaunt of his is said not to have been disproved by circumstances.[33]———Swift, when neither young—nor handsome—nor rich—nor even amiable—inspired the two most extraordinary passions upon record—Vanessa's & Stella's—

"Vanessa aged scarce a Score
Sighs for a gown of *forty four*.—

He requited them bitterly—for he seems to have broken the heart of the one—and worn out that of the other; and he had his reward—for he died a solitary idiot in the hands of servants.[34]——————

For my own part I am of the opinion of Pausanias—that Success in love depends upon Fortune.—

"They particularly reverence celestial Venus; into whose temple &c. &c. &c. I remember too to have seen a building in Ægira in which there is a Statue of Fortune holding a horn of Amalthea; and near her there is a winged Love.—The meaning of this is, that the Success of men in Love affairs depends more on the assistance of Fortune than the charms of Beauty.—I am persuaded, too, with Pindar (to whose opinion I subscribe in other particulars) that Fortune is one of the Fates, and that in a certain respect She is more powerful than her Sisters."—See Pausanias.—Achaics.—book 7th Chap. 26th page 246. "Taylor's Translation."———[35]

Grimm has a remark of the same kind on the different destinies of the younger Crebillon—and Rousseau.—The former writes a licentious novel—and a young English Girl of some fortune & family—(a

21 died a] died ⟨an⟩ of servants] of ⟨his⟩ 22 that Success] that ⟨Love⟩ ⟨the⟩ Success in] Success ⟨of⟩ 25 seen a] seen ⟨in⟩ 29 other particulars] other ⟨respects⟩

Miss Strafford) runs away—& crosses the Sea to marry him, while Rousseau the most tender and passionate of lovers is obliged to espouse his Chamber-maid.—If I recollect rightly—this remark was also repeated in the Edinburgh Review of Grimm's Correspondence, seven or eight years ago.[36]—

In regard "to the strange mixture of indecent and sometimes *profane* levity which his conduct and language *often* exhibited"—& which so much shocks Mr. Bowles—I object to the indefinite word "*often*" and in extenuation of the occasional occurrence of such language it is to be recollected that it was less the tone of *Pope*—than the tone of the *time*.—With the exception of the correspondence of Pope and his friends—not many private letters of the period have come down to us—but those, such as they are—a few scattered scraps from Farquhar and others—are more indecent and coarse than any thing in Pope's letters.[37]—The Comedies of Congreve—Vanbrugh—Farquhar Cibber &c. which naturally attempted to represent the manners & conversation of private life are decisive upon this point—as are also some of Steele's papers—and even Addison's.[38]———We all know what the Conversation of Sir R. Walpole for seventeen years the prime Minister of the country—was at his own table—and his excuse for his licentious language—viz. "that every body understood *that*—but few could talk rationally upon less common topics."[39]——The refinement of latter days—which is perhaps the consequence of Vice which wishes to mask & soften itself as much as of virtuous Civilization—had not yet made sufficient progress.—Even Johnson in his "London" has two or three passages—which cannot be read aloud, and Addison's "Drummer" some indelicate allusions.[40]———

The expression of Mr. B. "his consciousness of physical defect" is not very clear.—It may mean deformity or debility.—If it alludes to Pope's deformity it has been attempted to be shown that this was no insuperable objection to his being beloved.—If it alludes to debility, as a consequence of Pope's peculiar conformation—I believe that it is a physical & known fact that humped-backed persons are of strong and vigorous passions.—Several years ago—at Mr. Angelo's fencing rooms—when I was a boy and a pupil of him & of Mr. Jackson—who

2 lovers is] lovers ⟨was⟩ 2–3 to espouse] to ⟨marry⟩ 4 of Grimm's] of ⟨the same⟩ 12 —not] —⟨few⟩ 15 Farquhar Cibber] Farquhar ⟨&c.⟩ 24 mask &] mask ⟨it's⟩ much as] much ⟨as⟩ of virtuous] of ⟨civilizing Virtue⟩ 25 Even Johnson] Even ⟨the Satire of Juvenal imitated by⟩ 28 "his] "⟨the⟩ 30–1 no insuperable] no ⟨paramount⟩ 34 Several] ⟨Several⟩ Several 35 a boy] a ⟨pupil⟩

had the use of his rooms in Albany on the alternate days;—I recollect a gentleman named B–ll–gh–t remarkable for his strength—& the fineness of his figure. His skill was not inferior for he could stand up to the great Capt. Barclay himself—with the muffles on, a task neither easy nor agreeable to a pugilistic Aspirant.—As the bye-standers were one day admiring his athletic proportions—he remarked to us that he had five brothers as tall & strong as himself—and that *their father & mother were both crooked & of very small stature*.—I think he said—neither of them five feet high.[41]——It would not be difficult to adduce similar instances but I abstain—because the subject is hardly refined enough for this immaculate period, this Moral Millennium of expurgated editions in books, manners—and royal trials for divorce.[42]—————

This laudable delicacy—this crying-out elegance of the day, reminds me of a little circumstance which occurred when I was about eighteen years of age.—There was then—(& there may be still) a famous French "Entremetteuse" who assisted young gentlemen in their youthful pastimes.——We had been acquainted for some time—when something occurred in her line of business more than ordinary—and the refusal was offered to me—(and doubtless to many others) probably because I was in cash at the moment—having taken up a decent sum from the Jews,—& not having spent much above half of it.——The adventure on the tapis it seems required some caution and circumspection.—Whether my venerable friend doubted my politeness I cannot tell—but she sent me a letter couched in such English as a short residence of sixteen years in England had enabled her to acquire.—After several precepts and instructions the letter closed.—But there was a postscript.—It contained these words——"Remember Milor, that *delicaci ensure everi Succés*."[43]—The *Delicacy* of the day is exactly in all it's circumstances like that of this respectable foreigner——"It ensures every "*Succes*" & is not a whit more moral—than, & not half so honourable—*as*—the coarser candour of our less polished ancestors.——

To return to Mr. B.—"If what is here extracted can excite in the mind (I will not say of any "layman" of any "Christian" but) of any *human being*"—&c. &c. &c.————Is not Mr. Gilchrist a "human being"? Mr. B. asks "whether in *attributing* an article &c. &c. to this Critic he had

7 brothers as] brothers ⟨all⟩ 11 period, this] period, ⟨of⟩ this Moral] this ⟨Mu⟩ 13 the day] the ⟨times⟩ 20 was in] was ⟨always out⟩ 23 doubted my] doubted ⟨of⟩ 28 day is] day ⟨reminds⟩ 31 coarser candour] coarser ⟨character⟩

any reason for distinguishing him with that courtesy &c. &c. &c." but Mr B. was wrong in "attributing the article" to Mr Gilchrist at all—& would not have been right in calling him a dunce and a Grocer—if he had written it.[44]—————

Mr B. is here "peremptorily called upon to speak of a circumstance which gives him the greatest pain; the mention of a letter he received from the Editor of the London Magazine."[45]———Mr B. seems to have embroiled himself on all sides,—whether by editing—or replying, or attributing—or quoting—it has been an awkward affair for him.—————

Poor Scott is now no more.——In the exercise of his vocation he contrived at last to make himself the subject of a Coroner's inquest.—But he died like a brave man—and he lived an able one.—I knew him personally though slightly.—Although several years my Senior—we had been Schoolfellows together at the "Grammar Schule" (or as the Aberdonians pronounce it "*Squeel*") of New Aberdeen.[46]——He did not behave to me quite handsomely in his capacity of Editor a few years ago—but he was under no obligation to behave otherwise.—The moment was too tempting for many friends and for all enemies.—At a time—when all my relations (save one)[47] fell from me—like leaves from the tree in Autumn winds—and my few friends became still fewer—when the whole periodical press (I mean the daily & weekly—*not* the *literary* press) was let loose against me in every shape of reproach—with the two strange exceptions (from their usual opposition) of "the Courier" and "the Examiner"—the paper of which Scott had the direction was neither the last nor the least vituperative.[48] Two years ago I met him at Venice—when he was bowed in grief by the loss of his Son—and had known by experience the bitterness of a domestic privation.—He was then earnest with me to return to England—and on my telling him with a smile that he was once of a different opinion—he replied to me—"that he & others had been greatly misled—& that some pains & rather extraordinary means had been taken to excite them.—Scott is no more—but there are more than one living who were present at this dialogue.[49]———He was a man of very considerable talents—& of great acquirements.—He had made his way as a literary character with high success and in a few years.—Poor fellow—I recollect his joy—at some appointment which he had

8 have embroiled] have ⟨been⟩ by editing] by ⟨appealing⟩ 14 Although] ⟨Some⟩ Although 22 (I] (⟨f⟩ 33 to excite] to ⟨mislead⟩ are more] are ⟨those⟩

obtained—or was to obtain through Sir Jas Mackintosh—& which prevented the further extension (unless by a rapid run to Rome) of his travels in Italy.[50]—I little thought to what it would conduct him.—Peace be with him!—and may all such other faults as are inevitable to humanity—be as readily forgiven him—as the little injury which he had done to one—who respected his talents and regrets his loss.————

I pass over Mr B's page of explanation upon the correspondence between him & Mr S.[51]——it is of little importance in regard to Pope,—and contains merely a re-contradiction of a contradiction of Mr Gilchrist's.—We now come to a point—where Mr Gilchrist has certainly rather exaggerated matters—and of course Mr Bowles makes the most of it.—Capital letters like Kean's name "large upon the bills" are made use of six or seven times to express his sense of the outrage.[52]———The charge is indeed very boldly made—but like "Ranald of the Mist's" practical joke of putting the bread & cheese into a dead man's mouth—is as "Dugald Dalgetty" says—"somewhat too wild and—Sa*l*vage, besides wasting the good victuals."[53]——

Mr G. charges Mr B. with "suggesting" that Pope "attempted" to commit "a rape" upon Lady M. Wortley Montague.———There are two reasons why this could not be true.—The first is that like the chaste "Letitia's" prevention of the intended ravishment by "Fire-blood"—(in Jonathan Wild) it might have been impeded by a timely compliance.[54]——The second is—that however this might be—Pope was probably the less robust of the two, and (if the lines on Sappho were really intended for this Lady) the asserted consequences of her acquiescence in his wishes would have been a sufficient punishment.[55]——The passage which Mr B. quotes however insinuates nothing of the kind.——It merely charges her with encouragement, & him with wishing to profit by it.—A Slight attempt at seduction and no more.[56]—The phrase is—"a step beyond decorum." Any physical violence is so abhorrent to human Nature that it recoils in cold blood from the very idea.—But—the Seduction of a woman's mind as well as person—is not perhaps the least heinous Sin of the two in Morality. Dr

4 are inevitable] are ⟨incidental⟩ 5 as the] as ⟨I have long⟩ 17 a dead] a ⟨ded⟩ "Dugald Dalgetty"] "Dugald ⟨Dugald⟩ 18 Sa*l*vage, besides] Sa*l*vage,⟨"⟩ 25 the less] the ⟨least strong⟩ and (if] and ⟨as rape is⟩ ⟨might perhaps have found that he would have had enough upon his shoulders even had the Lady gratified his unlawful desires.⟩ 27 acquiescence in] acquiescence ⟨even⟩ 32 that it] that ⟨we⟩

Johnson commends a Gentleman—who having seduced a Girl—who said "I am afraid we have done wrong" replied "Yes we *have* done wrong"—"for I would not *pervert* her mind also."[57]—Othello would not "kill Desdemona's *Soul*"[58]—Mr. B. exculpates himself from Mr. G.'s charge—but it is by substituting another charge against Pope.—"A step beyond decorum" has a soft sound—but what does it express? In all these cases "Ce n'est que le premier pas qui coûte."[59]——Has not the Scripture something upon "the lusting after a woman" being no less criminal than the crime?[60]——"A Step beyond decorum" in short—any step beyond the instep—is a step from a precipice to the Lady who permits it.—For the Gentleman who makes it—it is also rather hazardous—if he don't succeed,—& still more so if he does.———

Mr. B. appeals to the "*Christian* reader!" upon this "*Gilchristian* Criticism."—Is not this play upon such words "a step beyond decorum" in a Clergyman? but I admit the temptation of a pun to be irresistible.[61]—

But "a hasty pamphlet was published in which *some personalities* respecting Mr. Gilchrist were suffered to appear."[62]—if Mr. B. will write "hasty pamphlets" why is he so surprized on receiving short answers?—The grand grievance to which he perpetually returns is a charge of "Hypochondriacism" asserted or insinuated in the Quarterly.[63]——I cannot conceive a man in perfect health being much affected by such a charge—because his complexion and conduct must amply refute it.—But were it true—to what does it amount?—to an impeachment of a liver complaint.—"I will tell it to the World"—exclaimed the learned Smelfungus——"You had better (said I—) tell it to your Physician."[64]—There is nothing dishonourable in such a disorder—which is more peculiarly the malady of Students.—It has been the complaint of the good and the wise—and the witty—and even of the Gay.——Regnard the author of the best French Comedy after Moliere—was atrabilarious—and Moliere himself saturnine.[65]—Dr. Johnson Gray—& Burns—were all more or less affected by it occasionally.—It was the prelude to the more awful malady of Collins—Cowper—Swift & Smart[66]—but it by no means follows that a partial affliction of this disorder—is to terminate like theirs.—But even were it so—

"Nor best—nor wisest are exempt from thee—
Folly—Folly's only free—

(Penrose.)[67]

1 Johnson commends] Johnson ⟨mentions⟩ 7 cases "Ce] cases ⟨C'est⟩ 14 words "a] words ⟨quite not⟩ 15 of a] of ⟨any⟩ 16 was published] was ⟨suffered to appear⟩ 24 —exclaimed] —⟨replied⟩

If this be the criterion of exemption—Mr. B.s last two pamphlets form a better certificate of Sanity than a Physician's.———Mendehlson and Bayle were at times so overcome with this depression—as to be obliged to recur to seeing puppet-shows—and "counting tiles upon the opposite houses," to divert themselves.[68]—Dr. Johnson at times "would have given a limb to recover his Spirits."[69]—Mr. B.—who is (strange to say—) fond of quoting Pope—may perhaps answer—

> "Go on, obliging Creatures, let me see
> All which disgraced my betters met in me."[70]—

But the charge—such as it is—neither disgraces them nor him.——It is easily disproved—if false, and even if proved true, has nothing in it to make a man so very indignant.——Mr. B. himself appears to be a little ashamed of his "hasty pamphlet" for he attempts to excuse it by the "great provocation"—that is to say—by Mr. B's supposing that Mr. G. was the writer of the article in the Quarterly—which he was *not*.—

"But in extenuation not only the *great* provocation should be remembered, but it ought to be said that orders were sent to the London Booksellers that the most direct personal passages should be *omitted entirely* &c.[71]——This is what the proverb calls "breaking a head and giving a plaister"[72] but in this instance the plaister was not spread in time, and Mr. Gilchrist don't seem at present disposed to regard Mr. Bowles's courtesies like the rust of the Spear of Achilles—which had such "skill in Surgery."[73]———

But "Mr. Gilchrist has *no right* to object—as the *reader* will see."——I am a reader—a "gentle reader" and I see nothing of the kind.—Were I in Mr. Gilchrist's place—I should object exceedingly to being abused, firstly—for what I *did* write—& secondly—for what I did *not* write,—merely—because it is Mr. B's will & pleasure to be as angry with me for having written in the L.M. as for not having written in the Q.R.[74]—

————

"Mr. G. has had AMPLE revenge for he has in his answer said so & so &c.—"[75] there is no great revenge in all this—and I presume that nobody either seeks or wishes it—*What* revenge?—Mr. B. calls names—and he is answered.—But Mr. G. and the Quarterly Reviewer

1 pamphlets form] pamphlets ⟨prove him perfectly Compos.⟩ 2 Sanity than] Sanity ⟨better⟩ Physician's.] Physician's ⟨bulletin.—⟩ 12 very indignant] very ⟨angry⟩ 21 to regard] to ⟨come⟩ 22–3 had such] had ⟨"⟩ 27 for what²] for⟨,⟩ 27–8 merely] —⟨and thirdly⟩ 28 angry with] angry ⟨not only⟩ 29 L.M. as] L.M. ⟨&⟩

are not poets nor pretenders to Poetry—therefore they can have no envy nor malice against Mr. B.—they have no acquaintance with Mr. B.—& can have no personal pique—they do not cross his path of life—nor he theirs—there is no political feud between them—what then can be the motive of their discussion of his deserts as an Editor?—veneration for the Genius of *Pope*—love for his memory—and regard for the Classic Glory of their Country.——Why would Mr. Bowles edite?—had he limited his honest endeavours to poetry—very little would have been said upon the subject—and nothing at all by his present Antagonists.————

Mr. B. calls the pamphlet a "Mud-cart"—and the writer a "Scavenger."[76]—Afterwards he asks "Shall he fling dirt and receive *Rose-water*?"—This metaphor by the way is taken from Marmontel's memoirs—who lamenting to Champfort the shedding of blood during the French Revolution was answered "Do you think that Revolutions are to be made with *Rose-Water*?"[77]————For my own part I presume that "Rose-water" would be infinitely more graceful in the hands of Mr. B. than the substance which he has substituted for that delicate liquid.—It would also more confound his Adversary—supposing him "a Scavenger."—I remember (& do you remember, Reader, that it was in my earliest youth "Consule Planco")[78] on the morning of the great battle (the second) between Gulley and Gregson;——*Cribb* who was matched against Horton for the second fight on the same memorable day—awaking me—(a lodger at the Inn in the next room—) by a loud remonstrance to the Waiter against the abomination of his towels—which had been laid in *Lavender*.—Cribb was a Coal-heaver—& was much more discomfited by this odoriferous effeminacy of fine linen—than by his Adversary Horton—whom he "finished in Style"—though with some reluctance—for I recollect that he said—he "disliked hurting him he looked so pretty" Horton being a very fine fresh-coloured young man.[79]———

To return to the "Rose-water"—that is,—to gentle means of rebuke——Does Mr. B. know how to revenge himself upon a Hackney Coachman when he has overcharged his fare?—In case he should not—I will tell him.—It is of little use to call him "a rascal a

3 cross his] cross ⟨hith⟩ 5 his deserts] his ⟨merit⟩ 6 —love] —⟨honour⟩ 7 the Classic] the ⟨Classic⟩ 18 substance which] substance ⟨with⟩ 24 —(a] —⟨who was⟩ 33 to revenge] to ⟨make a⟩ 34 Coachman when] Coachman ⟨really angry⟩ 35 "a rascal] "a ⟨"⟩

scoundrel—a thief—an impostor—a blackguard—a villain, a raga-muffin—a—what you please——all *that* he is used to—it is his Mother tongue and probably his Mother's.——But look him steadily and quietly in the face—and Say "upon my Word—I think you are the *Ugliest fellow* I ever saw in my life" and he will instantly roll forth the brazen thunders of the Charioteer Salmoneus,[80] as follows—"*Hugly*! what the H–ll are *You*?—YOU a *Gentleman*! My[81] —!—So much easier it is to *provoke*—and therefore to vindicate—(for Passion punishes him who *feels* it, more than those whom the Passionate would excruciate) by a few quiet words the aggressor—than by retorting violently.—— The "Coals of fire" of the Scripture—are *benefits*—but they are not the less "Coals of Fire."[82]——

I pass over a page of quotation & reprobation—"Sin up to my Song"—Oh let my little bark"—"Arcades Ambo" "Writer in the Quarterly Review & himself" "Indoor Arcadians[83] indeed" "Kings of Brentford" "One Nosegay" "Perennial Nosegay"—"Oh Juvenes" and the like.[83]—

Page 12. produces "*more Reasons*" (the task ought not to have been difficult for as yet there were none) "to show why Mr. B. attributed the Critique in the Quarterly to Octavius Gilchrist.—All these "reasons" consist in *surmises* of Mr. B. upon the presumed character of his opponent.—"He did not suppose there could exist a man in the kingdom so *impudent* &c. &c. except Octavius G. He did not think there was a Man in the kingdom who would *pretend ignorance* &c. &c. except Octavius G.—He did not conceive that one man in the kingdom would utter such *stupid* flippancy &c. &c. except—Octavius G. He did not think there was one man in the kingdom who—&c. &c. would so utterly show his ignorance *combined with conceit* &c. as Octavius G.——He did not believe that there was a Man in the kingdom—so perfect in Mr. G.'s "Old Lunes &c." He did not think the *mean mind* of any one in the kingdom &c."—and so on—always beginning with "any one in the Kingdom"—and ending with "Octavius Gilchrist," like the word in a Catch.[85]—I am not "in the Kingdom"—and have not been much in the Kingdom since I was one and twenty (about five years in the whole since I was of age) and have no desire to be in the Kingdom again—and I regret nothing more than having ever been "in the Kingdom"

5 instantly roll] instantly ⟨kindle⟩ 9 than those] than ⟨those⟩ 18 (the] (⟨this⟩ to have] to ⟨be⟩ 19 there were] there ⟨are⟩ 25 kingdom would] kingdom ⟨who⟩ 25–6 would utter] would ⟨p⟩ 31 one in] one ⟨of⟩ 33 been much] been ⟨not⟩ 36 ever been] ever ⟨"⟩

at all.——But though no longer "a man in the Kingdom" Let me hope that when I have ceased to exist—it may be said—as was answered by the Master of Clanronald's Henchman the day after the battle of Sheriff-Muir when he was found watching his Chief's body.———He was asked "who that was?" he replied—"it was a Man yesterday."[86]—— ———And in this capacity "in" or out of "the kingdom" I must own that I participate in many of the objections urged by Mr. Gilchrist.—I participate in his love of Pope—& in his not always understanding—and occasionally finding fault with the last Editor—of our last truly great poet.———

One of the reproaches against Mr. G. is that he is (it is sneeringly said) an F.*S.A.*[87]—If it will give Mr. B. any pleasure—I am not an F.S.A. but a Fellow of the Royal Society at his Service[88]—in case there should be anything in that association also which may point a paragraph.———

"There are some other reasons" "but "the author is now *not* unknown"[89]—Mr. B. has so totally exhausted himself upon Octavius G.—that he has not a word left for the real Quarterer of his Edition although now "deterré."[90]————

The following page refers to a mysterious charge of "duplicity" "in regard to the publication of Pope's letters."[91]—Till this charge is made—in proper form we have nothing to do with it; Mr. G. hints it—Mr. Bowles denies it—there it rests for the present.——Mr. B. professes his dislike to "Pope's *duplicity—not* to *Pope*"[92]—a distinction apparently without a difference—however I believe that I understand him.——We have a great dislike to Mr. B's Edition of Pope but *not* to Mr. Bowles—nevertheless, he takes up the subject as warmly as if it was personal.——With regard to the fact of "*Pope's* duplicity" it remains to be proved—like Mr. B's benevolence towards his Memory.—

In page 14. we have a large assertion that the "Eloisa alone is sufficient to convict him of *gross licentiousness*"[93]—thus—out it comes at last Mr. B. *does* accuse Pope of "*gross* licentiousness"—and grounds the charge upon a poem.—The *licentiousness* is a "grand peutêtre" according to the turn of the times being.—The "*grossness*" I deny.—On the contrary—I do believe that such a subject never was—nor ever

1 though no] though ⟨not⟩ longer "a] longer ⟨"one⟩ man in] man ⟨of⟩ Kingdom" Let] Kingdom" ⟨I⟩ 7 the objections] the ⟨charges brought against⟩ objections urged] objections ⟨of⟩ 12 am not] am ⟨an F.R.S.⟩ 17 real Quarterer] real ⟨Quarterly—Quarterer⟩ 18 although now] although ⟨discovered⟩ 26 nevertheless, he] nevertheless, ⟨if⟩ 26–7 was personal] was ⟨a⟩ 27 personal.] personal ⟨matter.⟩ 29 have a] have ⟨an⟩ 33 times being] times ⟨we live in.⟩

could be treated by any poet with so much delicacy mingled with at the same time with such true and intense passion.——Is the "Atys" of Catullus *licentious*?[94]—No—nor even *gross*.—And yet Catullus is often a coarse writer.——The Subject is nearly the same, except that Atys was the Suicide of his Manhood—and Abelard the victim.—The "licentiousness" of the Story was *not* Pope's—it was a fact.—All that it had of gross—he has softened, all that it had of indelicate he has purified—all that it had of passionate he has beautified—all that it had of holy—he has hallowed.—Mr Campbell had admirably marked this in a few words—(I quote from memory) in drawing the distinction between Pope and Dryden—& pointing out where Dryden was wanting.——— "I fear, says he, that had the subject of "Eloisa" fallen into his (Dryden's) hands—that he would have given us but a *coarse* draught of her passion."[95]—Never was the delicacy of Pope so much shown as in this poem—with the facts and the letters of "Eloisa" he has done what no other Mind—but that of the best and purest of poets could have accomplished with such materials.—Ovid—Sappho—(in the Ode called hers) all that we have of ancient—all that we have of modern poetry sinks into nothing compared with him in this production.—Let us hear no more of this trash about "licentiousness"—is not "Anacreon" taught in our Schools? translated—praised—and edited?—Are not his Odes the amatory praises of a boy?—Is not Sappho's Ode on a Girl?—Is not this sublime & (according to Longinus) fierce love for one of her own Sex?—And is not Phillips' translation of it in the mouths of all your women?[96]—And are the English Schools or the English women the more corrupt for all this?—When you have thrown the Ancients into the fire—it will be time to denounce the moderns. ——"Licentiousness!"—there is more real mischief and sapping licentiousness in a single French prose Novel,—in a Moravian Hymn—or a German Comedy[97]—than in all the actual poetry that ever was penned—or poured forth Since the rhapsodies of Orpheus.——The Sentimental Anatomy—of Rousseau & Made de S.—are far more formidable than any quantity of verse.——They are so—because they sap the principles—by *reasoning* upon the *passions*—whereas poetry is

1 with at] with ⟨th⟩ 9 in a] in ⟨two⟩ 15 has done] has ⟨dealt ⟨in a manner which⟩ so as⟩ 22 Odes the] Odes ⟨in⟩ 27 the moderns] the ⟨few⟩ 28 —— "Licentiousness!"] ——⟨But don't bank on it—they have neither the will nor the fame of⟩ and sapping] and ⟨serious⟩ 31 forth Since] forth ⟨in a transport—by past or present.⟩ 32 far more] far ⟨fo⟩ 34 —by] —⟨and⟩

in itself passion—and does not systematize.[98]—It assails—but does not argue—it may be wrong—but it does not assume pretensions to Optimism.———

Mr. B. now has the goodness "to point out the difference between a *traducer* and him who sincerely states—what he sincerely believes."[99]—He might have spared himself the trouble.——The One is a liar—who lies knowingly—the other (I speak of a Scandal-monger of course) lies charitably believing that he speaks truth—& very sorry to find himself in a falsehood;[100]—because he

> "Would rather that the Dean should die
> Than his prediction prove a lie."———[101]

After a definition of a "traducer"—which was quite superfluous (though it is agreeable to learn that Mr. B. so well understands the character[102]) we are assured—that "he feels equally indifferent—Mr. Gilchrist—for what your malice can invent or your impudence utter."—This is indubitable—for it rests not only on Mr. B's assurance—but on that of Sir Fretful Plagiary—and nearly in the same words.——"And I shall treat it with exactly the same calm indifference and philosophical contempt, and so your Servant."[103]—

"One thing has given Mr. B. concern"—it is "a passage which might seem to reflect on the patronage a young man has received."[104]—MIGHT seem!!——The passage alluded to—expresses that if Mr. G. be the reviewer of "a certain poet of Nature" his praise and blame are equally "contemptible."—Mr. B. who has a peculiarly ambiguous Style—where it suits him—comes off with a "*not* to the *poet* but the *critic*" &c.————In my humble opinion the passage referred to both. Had Mr. B. really meant fairly—he would have said so from the first—he would have been eagerly transparent.——"A Certain poet of Nature"—is not the style of commendation.—It is the very prologue to the most Scandalous paragraphs of the Newspapers—when

> "Willing to wound—& yet afraid to strike.[105]

"A certain high personage"—"a certain peeress" "a certain illustrious

1 It assails] It ⟨implores⟩ 2 assume pretensions] assume ⟨the⟩ pretensions to] pretensions ⟨of⟩ 4 out the] out ⟨to you⟩ 7 Scandal-monger of] Scandal-monger⟨)⟩ 8 to find] to ⟨discover⟩ 13 (though] (⟨but of which⟩ 13–14 the character] the ⟨γνῶθι σεαυτόν⟩ 14 that "he] that ⟨he himself⟩ 17 and nearly] and ⟨almost⟩ 22 ——] —⟨It did seem⟩ —expresses] —⟨states⟩ 24 Mr. B. who] Mr. B. ⟨with⟩ 27 meant fairly] meant ⟨this⟩ 29 —is] —⟨this⟩

foreigner" what do these words ever precede but defamation? Had he felt a spark of kindling kindness for John Clare—he would have named him.—There is a Sneer in the sentence as it stands.——How a favourable review of a deserving poet can "rather injure than promote his cause"—is difficult to comprehend.——The article denounced is able and amiable—and it *has* "served" the poet—as far as poetry can be served by judicious and honest criticism.—

With the next two paragraphs of Mr. B's pamphlet it is pleasing to concur.[106]—His mention of "Pennie" and his former patronage of "Shoel" do him honour,—I am not of those who may deny Mr. B. to be a benevolent man,——I merely assert that he is not a candid Editor.— ———

Mr. B. has been "a writer occasionally upwards of thirty years"—and never wrote one word in reply in his life "to Criticisms, merely—*as* Criticisms."—This is Mr. Lofty in Goldsmith's "Good-natured Man"—"And I vow by all that's honourable, my resentment has never done the men—as mere men—any manner of harm—that is—*as mere men.*"[107]————

"The letter to the Editor of the Newspaper" is owned—but "it was not on account of the Criticism."—It was because the criticism came down "in a frank *directed to Mrs. Bowles!!!*"[108]—(the Italics & three notes of admiration appended to Mrs Bowles are copied verbatim from the quotation) and Mr. Bowles was not displeased with the criticism—but with the frank and the address.—I agree with Mr. B. that the intention was to annoy him—but I fear that this was answered by his notice of the reception of the criticism.—An anonymous letter-writer—has but one means of knowing the effect of his attack.—In this he has the superiority over the viper.—He knows that his poison has taken effect,—when he hears the victim cry.—The Adder is *deaf*.—The best reply to an anonymous intimation is to take no notice directly nor indirectly.—I wish Mr. B. could see only one or two of the thousand which I have received in the course of a literary life which though begun early does not yet extend[109]—to a third part of his —existence as an author.—I speak of *literary* life—only——were I to add *personal*—I might double the amount of *anonymous* letters.—If he could but see the

1 foreigner" what] foreigner" ⟨to⟩ ever precede] ever ⟨prelude⟩ but defamation] but ⟨to⟩ 4 can "rather] can ⟨h⟩ 5 is difficult] is ⟨more than I am able to⟩ ⟨it is com⟩ article denounced] article ⟨is⟩ 10 Mr. B.] Mr. B⟨'s⟩ 11 not a] not ⟨an honest⟩ 25 but I] but ⟨that⟩ 31 see only] see ⟨the⟩ 33 extend—] extend ⟨yet⟩ —existence] —⟨literar⟩

violence—the threats—the absurdity of the whole thing—he would laugh—& so should I—& thus be both gainers. To keep up the farce; within the last month of this present writing (1821.) I have had my life threatened in the same way which menaced Mr. B's fame—excepting that the anonymous denunciation was addressed to the Cardinal Legate of R. instead of to "Mrs Bowles."—The Cardinal is I believe the elder lady of the two. I append the menace in all it's barbaric but literal Italian that Mr. B. may be convinced.[110] And as this is the only "Promise to pay"[111] which the Italians ever keep—so my person has been at least as much exposed to "a Shot in the Gloaming" from "John Heatherblutter" (See Waverley)[112] as ever Mr. B's Glory was from an Editor.—I am nevertheless on horse-back and lonely for some hours—(*one* of them twilight) in the Forest—daily——& this—because it was "my custom in the afternoon"[113] and that I believe if the tyrant cannot escape amidst his guards (should it be so written)—so the humbler individual would find precautions useless.

Mr. B. has here the humility to say that "he must succumb—for—with Ld. B. turned against him he has no chance"—a declaration of Self-denial not much in unison with his "promise"—five lines afterwards—that "for every 24 lines quoted by Mr. G. or his friend to greet him with as many from his unpublished poem of the "Gilchrisiad," but so much the better.[114]—Mr. B. has no reason to "succumb"—but—to Mr. Bowles.—As a poet the author of "the Missionary" may compete with the foremost of his Cotemporaries—let it be recollected—that all my previous opinions of Mr. Bowles's poetry were *written* long before the publication of his last and best poem—and that a poet's *last* poem should be his best is his highest praise.[115]—But however he may duely and honourably rank with his living rivals—there never was so complete a proof of the Superiority of Pope as in the lines with which Mr. B. closes his "*to be Concluded in Our Next*."[116]—

Mr. Bowles is avowedly the Champion and the Poet of Nature. Art and the Arts are dragged—some before—and others behind his

4 menaced Mr.] menaced ⟨his⟩ 6–7 the elder] the ⟨more⟩ 7 elder] elder⟨ly⟩ it's barbaric] it's ⟨barbarous⟩ 9 my person] my ⟨situation⟩ 10 been at] been ⟨somewhat more⟩ 11 from an] from ⟨a critical⟩ 12 am nevertheless] am ⟨also always⟩ for some] for ⟨two⟩ 13 daily——] daily—⟨and as practicably as need be,⟩ 14 afternoon" and] afternoon" ⟨& because I am a "fatalist" and a⟩ 15 (should] (⟨if⟩ so the] so ⟨with⟩ 16 useless.] useless. ⟨Death is the "necessary end" and the murderer earns his own damnation only by anticipating the stroke of the Deity which [remainder of line irrecoverable]⟩ 22 "succumb"—] "succumb" ⟨to any one⟩ 25 long before] long ⟨previously⟩ 30 closes his] closes ⟨the⟩

chariot.—Pope where he deals with Passion and with the Nature of the Naturals of the day—is allowed even by themselves to be sublime—but they complain that too soon

"He stooped to truth & moralized his song"[117]

and *there* even *they* allow him to be unrivalled.—He has succeeded—and—even surpassed them—when he chose—in their own *pretended* province—let us see what their Coryphæus effects in Pope's.[118]—But it is too pitiable—it is too melancholy to see Mr. B. "sinning" not "*up*" but "*down*"[119] as a poet to his lowest depth as an Editor.—By the way—Mr. B. is always quoting *Pope*—I grant that there is no poet—not Shakespeare himself—who can be so often quoted—with reference to Life——but his Editor is so like the Devil quoting Scripture—that I could wish Mr. B. in his proper place quoting in the pulpit.——And now for his lines.—But it is painful,—painful—to see such a Suicide—though at the Shrine of Pope.——I can't copy them all.[120]

"Shall the rank loathsome miscreant of the age
Sit—like a Nightmare, grinning oer a page"—

—————

"Whose pye-bald character so aptly suit
The two extremes of Bantam and of Brute—
Compound grotesque of Sullenness and Show
The Chattering Magpie, and the Croaking Crow.

—————

"Whose heart contends with thy Saturnian head—
A root of Hemlock, and a lump of lead;

—————

"Gilchrist proceed—&c. &c.

—————

"And thus stand forth spite of thy venomed foam
To give thee *bite for bite*, or lash thee limping home.

With regard to the last line the only one upon which I shall venture for fear of infection——I would advise Mr. Gilchrist to keep out of the way of such reciprocal morsure—unless he has more faith in the "Ormskirk Medicine"[121] than most people—or may wish to anticipate the

7 us see] us ⟨hear⟩ 12 but his] but ⟨it is so like⟩ ⟨Mr. B. is⟩ 27 last line] last ⟨couplet⟩ 30 or may] or ⟨would⟩ ⟨may⟩ to anticipate] to ⟨ensure⟩

pension of the recent German professor (I forget his name but it is advertised & full of consonants) who presented his Memoir of an infallible remedy for "the Hydrophobia" to the German Diet last month coupled with the philanthropic condition of a large annuity—provided that his Cure cured.[122]—Let him begin with the Editor of Pope—and double his demand.———

yrs ever,
B[123]

P.S.

Amongst the above-mentioned lines there occurs the following *applied* to *Pope*

"*The Assassin's vengeance, and the Coward's lie.*"[124]—

And Mr B. persists that he is a Well-wisher to Pope!!!—He has then edited an "Assassin"—and a "Coward" wittingly as well as lovingly.—In my former letter I have remarked upon the Editor's forgetfulness of Pope's benevolence.[125]——But where he mentions his faults it is "with sorrow"[126]—his tears drop—but they do not blot them out.—The "recording Angel" differs from the recording Clergyman.[127] A fulsome Editor is pardonable though tiresome like a panegyrical Son whose pious Sincerity would demi-deify his father.—But a detracting Editor is a parricide.—He sins against the nature of his office——& connection.—He murders the life to come of his victim.[128]——If his author is not worthy to be remembered—do not edite at all.—If he be—Edite honestly—and even flatteringly—the reader will forgive the weakness in favour of mortality—& correct your adulation with a smile.—But to sit down "Mingere in patrios cineres"[129]—as Mr B. has done—merits a reprobation so strong that I am as incapable of expressing, as of ceasing to feel it.—

B[130]

1 the recent] the ⟨late⟩ 2 his Memoir] his ⟨Memorial⟩ 3 infallible remedy] infallible ⟨Cure⟩ 4 of a] of ⟨a pension⟩ annuity—] annuity ⟨of a specified sum in thousands of Florins⟩ 5 with the] with ⟨Mr Bowles's Edition⟩ 13 Well-wisher to] Well-wisher ⟨of⟩ 22 his victim] his ⟨vit⟩ 26 down "Mingere] down ⟨to⟩ 27 strong that] strong ⟨and decided⟩ 28 feel it] feel ⟨what⟩

WRITINGS
(1821–1824)

Some Recollections of my Acquaintance with Madame de Staël (1821)

Some recollections of my acquaintance with Madame de Stael.

Ravenna. August 4th 1821.—

It has been intimated to me from Paris, that the Chevalier-Professor William Augustus Schlegel (I cannot add "*Von*" till I see his quarterings) meditates a fierce and thorough criticism of me and mine.——To this my reply shall be a simple and sincere narrative of my acquaintance with him and his late *Mistress*—I mean in the hospitable—not the *amatory* sense—in justification of her personal—whatever it may be—of her—literary taste.———

In the year 1813. I had the honour of being—amongst the earliest of my countrymen—presented to Me de Stael—on the very night of her arrival in London.—She arrived,—was dressed—and came "with her Glory"[1] to Lady Jersey's[2]—where in common with many others—I bowed—*not* the knee—but the head and heart—in homage to an extraordinary and able woman driven from her own country by the most extraordinary of men.[3]——They are both dead and buried—so we may speak without offence—she may then

"with noble Percy lie
till—"Embowelled we may see her by and bye."[4]—

Mr Schlegel of all men may excuse an application from Shakespeare——the idol of which he would fain be the high-priest.——

On the day after her arrival I dined in her company at Sir Humphrey Davy's[5]—being the least of one of "a legion of honour"[6] invited to greet her.—If I mistake not——and can Memory be treacherous to such men?—there were present—Sheridan—

1 *Madame de Stael.*] *Madame de Stael.* ⟨*Anticipation the 3d*[?]⟩ 6–7 narrative of my] narrative of ⟨of⟩ 7–8 in the hospitable] in the ⟨*House-keeping*⟩ 18–19 lie till] lie ⟨till⟩

Whitbread—Grattan—the Marquis of Lansdowne[7]—without counting our illustrious host,—the first experimental philosopher of his own (or perhaps any other *preceding* time) was there to receive the most celebrated of women—surrounded by the flower of our wits, the foremost of our remaining orators and Statesmen—and condescending even to invite the then youngest and and it may be still least of our living poets.[8]————

Of these guests, it would be melancholy to relate even in common life that three of the foremost are in the grave with her who met them—and with him who was the great cause of their meeting—(at least in England)—in the short space of seven years—or little better—& none of them aged;[9] but when we utter their names—it is something more—it is awful—it shows us how frail they *were*—in their very greatness—and we who remain—shrink as it were—into nothing.————

Of this "Symposium" graced by these now Immortals—I recollect less than ought to have been remembered,—but who can carry away the remembrance of his pleasures unimpaired and unmutilated?—the general impression remains—but the tints are faded.—Besides I was then too young—and too passionate to do full justice to those around me.—Time—Absence and death—mellow and sanctify all things.—I then saw around me but the men whom I heard daily in the Senate—and met nightly in the London Assemblies—I revered—I respected them—but I *saw* them—and neither Beauty nor Glory can stand this daily test.——I saw the woman of whom I had heard marvels—she justified what I had heard—but she was still a mortal—and made long speeches—nay the very day of this philosophical feast in her honour—she made *very* long speeches to those who had been accustomed to hear such only in the two Houses—she interrupted Whitbread—she declaimed to Lord L.[10]—She misunderstood Sheridan's jokes for assent—She harangued—she lectured—She preached English politics to the first of our English Whig politicians—the day after her arrival in England—and (if I am not much misinformed—) preached politics no less to our Tory politicians the day after.——The Sovereign himself—if I am not in error was not exempt from this flow of Eloquence—as Napoleon had been lectured on the destinies of France—the Prince Regent of England was asked "what he meant to do with America"?—

1 Grattan—the] Grattan—⟨the⟩ 2 the first experimental] the first ⟨scientific⟩ ⟨scientific⟩ ⟨practical⟩ 5 orators and Statesmen] orators and ⟨our⟩ 6 youngest and and] youngest and ⟨least⟩ 12 when we utter] when we ⟨speak⟩ 13 shows us how] shows us ⟨what⟩

At present *I* might—with all humility ask—"what America means to do with *him*?"[11]—In twenty or thirty years more—which he cannot—(and I in all human chances—shall not)—live to see this will be to his successor a serious question.—*Who* will be *his* successor?—The Dukes all of them half a century old cannot last forever—and who will be their successors? the little Princesses!—this is a "grand peutetre."[12] —In the mean time his Majesty—is crowned—and long may he reign!—his father was crowned at twenty and reigned sixty years;—*he* is crowned at sixty—and may reign twenty years—tis a long time—as reigns usually go.—But he is not a bad king—and he *was* a fine fellow,—it is a great pity that he did not come to his crown thirty years before—I cannot help thinking that if he had done so—all this outcry about morals—and wives—and frivolities—might have been prevented.[13]— —But "Hope delayed maketh the heart sick"[14] and it is to be feared that out of a *sick* heart there never came a sound body nor a temperate Soul.—Let it not be forgotten—that he was one of the most persecuted of princes—and the fruit of persecution has been in all ages the same.—I shall not presume to be so treasonable—as to say that he is bad—but *if* he were—with the provocation he has had—I should only wonder that he is not worse.———

But I prate about kings—and forget my Learned Mandarine—and his great Umbrella—Madame de Stael's petticoat.—

Some Account of the Life and Writings of the late George Russell of A— by Henry Ferguson (1821)

Some account of the Life and Writings of the late George Russell of A— by Henry Ferguson.

Dec. 1st (or 2d) 1821.

In the present age of innumerable authors—I know not how far one who never aspired to that title in his lifetime may be permitted to obtrude a name upon the public which as yet merely forms part of a brief and obscure epitaph.—Indeed such an attempt in it's behalf on the part of surviving friendship may give rise to suspicions (from

1 At present *I* might] At present *I* ⟨will⟩ 3 this will be] this will ⟨to see⟩ 21 my Learned Mandarine] my ⟨little professor⟩

the total ignorance of the World with the name of him who has lately left it—) that the subject of the following pages—has not *ceased* to exist; but—that he has never existed at all.——The poems of the celebrated Thomas Little—and the more facetious remains of Ensign Odoherty might sanction such a notion, while the relics of Henry Kirke White and other young men[1]

"Whose sleepless souls have perished ere their prime"[2]—

show that many Spirits pass early, and almost unknown, from the Earth—whose longer Life might have extorted the gratitude of Mankind—from which their blighted youth must now be content to implore a transient recollection.—Perhaps it is imprudent in surviving friends to attempt these things—but on such points it is difficult to reason.——The worst result of a dull book to the author—can be but oblivion—and when he himself is where "nothing can touch him further"[3]—those who loved him are apt to think, (or to dream—)[4] that his thoughts may claim something of the sympathy which even the ashes of a Stranger obtain from all men in their better moods of mind.——The costly monument—like the simple stone—the voluminous biography—as the brief notice—are all to be traced upon the whole to our better feelings.—Both—but especially the former, have been made subjects of contempt and reproach as oftentimes exhibiting falsehood for the sake of ostentation, or the exaggeration of a blind and selfish sorrow.—But surely that Ostentation—which labours for the dead—is the least harmless[5] of our vices——it cannot hurt them—it can injure no one but ourselves—& that but slightly,—whereas—a real however blind—regard for the departed—if not a virtue—at least may tend to virtue.—I know not—whether that indefinable veneration for that which was yesterday with us—and to-day is no longer by our side—does not induce a greater desire to do well—than the approbation—even though it should swell to applause—of the living.—Sure I am that the Grave of a dead friend, at any distance of time, has deeper eloquence—than the Orator or the preacher.—I have walked away from the Graves of Fox—Pitt—and Grattan[6]—(and I have heard and

1 the total] the ⟨inacquaintance⟩ ⟨ignorance of⟩ 2 not *ceased*] not ⟨only⟩ ⟨so much⟩ 2–3 exist; but] exist; ⟨as⟩ 4 and the] and ⟨of⟩ 10 blighted youth] blighted ⟨li⟩ now be] now ⟨to⟩ 12 attempt these] attempt ⟨it—⟩ ⟨such⟩ 14 is where] is ⟨"⟩ 18 monument—like] monument—⟨or⟩ 23 which labours] which ⟨is⟩ 29–30 approbation—even] approbation—⟨however⟩ 31 time, has] time, ⟨is a Sign⟩ 31–2 deeper eloquence] deeper ⟨homily⟩

admired them all) with a feeling—deeper than their words ever impressed—higher than their words *could* express——and—of course—I shall not attempt to give it utterance in mine.————

But I must return to my purpose—which is to give an outline of the life and writings of a dead friend—who—I think perhaps erroneously—deserved that part of what he has written should survive him.———

George Russell was born in the year 1791. in the town of A— —in Scotland—of a respectable family of some antiquity—but I have reason to believe in no respect related to their more illustrious namesakes of England.[7]—Being a second son he was intended for the Sea service—a destination which was afterwards changed—for family reasons.—My acquaintance with him began at the Grammar School—of A. where we both received our education.—As his Senior I was two classes above him—being in the third when he entered the first—then under the direction of Mr L.——My own family being intimate with his—he was naturally recommended to my notice as the Senior boy.——I mention these little particulars "en passant" to account for the commencement of the interest which I took in his welfare—and retain for his memory.—

His progress in his classical studies was fair—but not remarkable—he was like most other boys—idle when he could contrive to be so—without punishment;—and sometimes at the head of his class—and sometimes in the lowest *faction* of it—for in Scotland—or at least in this part of it—it was then the custom (as it may still be) to take places according to immediate merit—so that every lesson is a renewed contest—and a boy must have singular perseverance as well as powers to remain long in the same station.——The word "faction" may be only intelligible to a Southern reader in it's newspaper sense—viz—the appellation given to every part which is not your own,—but in our Scotch Schools it has a less invidious meaning—being simply the bench which contains a certain number of boys.—Every class may contain twenty, more or less—of these "factions." whereas a Nation can hardly sustain two in any comfort. Through all the varieties of these did George Russell wind his way—not without some application of the "*taws*" a word as well as instrument of no pleasing recollec-

1 feeling—deeper] feeling—⟨which⟩ ⟨higher⟩ 6 should survive] should ⟨him⟩ 25 *faction* of] *faction*⟨—⟩ 31 simply the] simply ⟨a⟩ 33 "factions." whereas] "factions."⟨——But⟩ 35–6 application of] application ⟨and⟩ 36 word as] word ⟨of⟩

tion.—Here I again doubt that I must recur to interpretation for the benefit of the "Southron"[8] although with more difficulty——than in the former instance.—The "taws" then is supposed to answer all the purposes of the English "Rod"—although very different—and I think—more formidable in it's appearance.—It is composed of leather of greater or less thickness according to the disposition of the pastor and master.—This long strap (for such it is) is divided at the end into several smaller straps or tails—of greater or less number according to the humour of the preceptor—already referred to.——The upper part contains a hole—through which is past the finger of the Exercitator[9]—that it may not slip during the operation.——By a timely and not infrequent application of this instrument to the hands and elsewhere—of our Scottish youth—may be fairly attributed that general superiority in the Latin tongue—over our Neighbours—which whether admitted or not—should never cease to be claimed, by all true lovers of Truth as well as of their Country.——Having had also the advantage of dividing my own education between Scotland and England—my opportunities of comparison between the two great instruments of discipline—have not been neglected, my personal experiences having led to a frequent acquaintance—and lively recollection of both.——I shall therefore say—that if I had to go to School again—my personal preference would be given to the Rod of the Saxon,—but if I had children to place there—I should remit them to the domain and dominion of the "Taws"—not only because it is my native land—and that the education is fifty times cheaper—but from a firm conviction that by that Instrument more Latin is administered in a less time.————

At a very early period of his life my deceased friend began to manifest a strong poetical propensity.[10]—I do not mean by this in the vulgar way of making verses—or indeed of reading them—for excepting Pope's Homer—and blind Harry's William Wallace—together with Chevy Chace—Gil Morice and some warlike Scottish Ballads[11]—he betrayed an utter detestation of all poesy whatsoever.—But nevertheless the observer of the human Mind might discover in his a natural poetical bias.——He had an aversion from learning his letters—a partiality for Gingerbread, for kicking shins when he was whipt—and

14 tongue—over] tongue—⟨which⟩ 19 discipline—have] discipline—⟨hath⟩ 24 domain] domain⟨s⟩ 25 land—and] land—⟨but⟩ 26 that by] that ⟨under⟩ administered in] administered ⟨than⟩ 33 he betrayed] he ⟨manifested⟩ 34 Mind might] Mind ⟨will⟩ 36 Gingerbread, for] Gingerbread, ⟨and⟩

for not telling the truth when it was inconvenient—which evinced a determined spirit—and a lively imagination.—After passing through the usual quantum of infantine woes and pleasures; having enjoyed his holidays, and toiled through his tasks—having fought a reasonable number of battles—and got the better of a considerable quantity of black eyes—he was sent to College which is done much earlier in Caledonia[12] than in the Southern Country.—Amidst his feats of youthful emprize I cannot recollect that he was addicted to robbing of Orchards[13]—but this circumstance may possibly be attributed rather to a Scarcity of the fruit than a want of the Propensity.—Indeed I had occasion to observe that in general the Organ of Covetiveness[14]—was considerably developed in my friend, although as far as my experience enabled me to decide—it seemed rather to be exhibited in his hands than his head.[15]—His very first indication of a strong poetical bias was displayed in the Abstraction of a "Gradus ad Parnassum"[16] belonging to myself—with the aid of which he composed his first copy of Nonsense Verses.——On my manifesting an inclination to reclaim my property—he knocked me down with it,—but as I was the Senior and the Stronger—this piece of superfluous valour on his part, was severely retaliated by a considerable beating.—But the Castigation was not attended by any permanent effect—for the very next week he conveyed—("the Wise *convey* it call")[17] and converted to his poetical purposes—a copy (mine also) of George Buchanan's Latin Psalms[18]—and having thus become master of the book—he conceived naturally that he was no less proprietor of the author—one of whose Psalms he shortly after showed up as a Version of his own.——Upon being charged with this—he denied the plagiarism—and made out with considerable plausibility a claim of simple coincidence—which left a very doubtful title of originality to George Buchanan.———

An Italian Carnival (1823)

Fy. 6th 1823.

In the year 18— a young Englishman had resided for some time in the Italian City of T.[1]——for the Geography of which the reader is

7 than in] than ⟨by her⟩ 11 that in] that ⟨upon other occasions⟩ 12 although as] although ⟨not⟩ 16 with the] with ⟨which⟩

referred to the Map—and for the description to the Guide Book.—It is possible that he may derive no great information from either of these sources—inasmuch as it is but little frequented by the second-hand Society of half-pay economists—no pay dandies—separated wives, unseparated *not* wives——the Starke—or Invalid—or Forsyth—or Eustace or Hobhouse travellers—as they are called according to their Manual[2]—neither had the great Irruption of Welbeck Street broke loose—as yet invaded it's venerable precincts.[3]—In short the middle ton—which is a very distinct thing from the *bon ton* which England possessed[4]—(and may perhaps still possess—) had neither disgusted the natives—nor dishonoured their Country—perhaps Rome and Naples can say the same—or Florence,——Ask them.—The Inhabitants from their slight and transient intercourse with strangers—had preserved more of the older Italian character and customs than is to be found in the usual marts for foreigners to which the principal cities of Italy are now degraded.—They are, or were, braver and perhaps more ferocious.——The city was rich and consequently preserved something both of the virtues and vices of independence.—The inhabitants felt it is true the common disgust of Italy as well as Europe at the Holy Alliance—and the Austrian despotism[5]—for—though nominally exempt from them they felt their influence in some measure—and indeed what Nation does not?—but as the pressure was less upon them than upon the provinces immediately trampled on by that atrocious power—their aversion might be rather less—still it was great—and it was open.——The nobility were in general well to pass in their properties—and some of them of very considerable wealth;—the Citizens also presented fewer of those wretched inequalities,—so obvious in general over the peninsula.———

The concluding festivals of the Carnival—that universal Harlequinade in Catholic Countries—but more especially in Italy—were now in their final orgasm of Buffoonery—intrigue—and universal amusement.—As their term approached—their joy—or at least their hilarity was redoubled.—All was Music—and Masque—and "Christian fools with varnished faces."[6]——Beneath these same "varnished faces"—chiefly confined to the females—there were many beautiful—and a "quantum sufficit"[7]—of some which acquired their beauty from the

9 *bon ton* which] *bon ton* ⟨of what⟩ 14 and customs] and ⟨cust⟩ 18 The inhabitants] The⟨y⟩ 21 them they] them ⟨it⟩ 27 Citizens also] Citizens ⟨in general⟩ 34 Beneath] ⟨Un⟩ Beneath

mystery of their vizor.—But grave and gay—old and young—handsome—and those who might be called so by Courtesy—were all abroad—laughing—flirting—tormenting—pleasant—and sometimes pleasing.—The Men, in general—with few exceptions—and those of the lower orders—were in their usual garb—and perhaps by this—added to the genuine spirit of the Scene—by appearing in their own characters—such as they were.——In England—I—that is We—(for the anonymous—like Sovereigns multiply their Egotism into the plural number) have seen many a splendid and dull Masquerade—dull—because they attempted to support Characters under a piece of paste-board without having even any of their own.—But the Italians pretend to nothing of the kind—at least at present—or when they do at some more solemn festival—I suspect—that it is none of the most agreeable.——A masque is merely a dress—or a disguise—but not an attempt at farce or Comedy.—Their parts are not studied.—On the contrary—what Somebody has said of Somebody—that "he (or She, I forget which) is never less alone than when alone[8]—it may be observed—that a woman, at least a Continental woman is never less a Masque than when a Masque—unless perhaps to her husband—or some truculent relation.—It is at this periodic Saturnalia[9] (—for one great distinction between England and Catholic Countries in this respect—is—that the Populace are the equal and perhaps the merriest partakers of the amusements—) that all ranks are jostled—and mingled—and delighted—and all this without fear—observance—or offence.—A Masque is privileged to a certain point—and that is decency—and there are—the multitude considered—few who transgress the rule.——There is—to a foreigner—a mixture of mystery and hilarity in this general burst from every day cares—that renders a Carnival peculiarly attractive.—There is a Masque—and recollect that it is a female one—at every turn—at every corner—in every threatre—in every street—in every hall—in every cottage, in every palace—Curiosity is always excited—some times Passion—and occasionally Pleasure.——If you do not always recognize you are generally recognized—(the men that is—who rarely masque) and the jest—or the hint—or the present of a flower with which you are greeted have a novelty even from a former acquaintance.——Life becomes for a

9 splendid and] splendid ⟨but⟩ 9–10 Masquerade—dull] Masquerade—⟨and⟩
10 support] support⟨ed⟩ 17–18 be observed] be ⟨so⟩ 22 the merriest] the ⟨most⟩
23 of the] of ⟨of⟩ 36 from a former] from a⟨n⟩

moment a drama without the fiction.——Perhaps, the Italians would but ill exchange their Carnival for a Parliament,—but they long for the latter[10]—and if England would barter with them—there might be no great loss to either—it would be Masquerade for Masquerade—with the people represented by themselves.[11]—

The Present State of Greece (1824)

Febry. 26th, 1824.

The present state of Greece is perhaps different from what has been represented both by friends and enemies. The foreigners in Greece have, with few exceptions, never been in the Country before, and of those exceptions still fewer have visited these regions before the revolution.[1] Those who have will be rather surprised that the disorganization is not still greater, although, in any other country, it would appear unbounded. The Greeks have been downright Slaves for five centuries, and there is no tyrant like a Slave. The Delegate of a Despot is still a bondsman, and men whose fathers' fathers, farther than they can reckon, were absolute vileins,[2] without property even of their own persons, still move as if they were in fetters, or, in many instances, may seem only to have exchanged the chains of the prisoner for the freedom of the jailor. This is a hard truth; but we fear that it *is* one. We are not here to flatter, but to aid, as far as in our power, to a better order of things, and, whether *of* the Greeks or *to* the Greeks, let the truth be spoken.

The number of pamphlets which have been published in Europe on the subject of the Greek contest has of course been sufficient. We have not been in the way of seeing many of these, and those we have seen were not much to the purpose. The narratives of travellers, military and civil, may not have been less numerous. Without entering into their merits or demerits, it is more essential to advert to the person, or rather to the circumstances which have produced them. *One* thing it is essential to remark, viz. that hitherto *no* stranger has succeeded in Greece, either in doing much for the natives, or for himself. French, Germans, Italians, English, Poles,—men of all nations, ages, and conditions,—military and naval, rich and poor, good and evil, speculative and practical,—merchants, officers, tars,[3] Generals, German

Barons and Bankers, English gentlemen and adventurers,—and surely some men of talent and good intention amongst them—have in the course of the last three years run the Gauntlet of Greece, and, of the Survivors of fever, famine, fatigue, and the sword, the greater part of those who have not gone back in disgust—remain in misery. Perhaps they would complain less of penury in a climate, where neither friends nor foes are embarrassed with wealth; but some of them, and not without justice, may remonstrate against neglect, for, on most occasions where opportunity has permitted, it has been allowed by the Greeks themselves that the strangers have done their duty.

FRAGMENTARY WRITINGS
(1801–1824)

Inscriptions in a Schoolbook (1801)

Byron, Harrow on the Hill, Middlesex, Alumnus Scholæ Lyonensis primus in anno Domini 1801, Ellison Duce.
Monitors, 1801.—Ellison, Royston, Hunxman, Rashleigh, Rokeby, Leigh.

Inscriptions in *Homeri Ilias* (1804)

[1.]

Drury's Pupils 1804,
Byron
Drury
Sinclair
Hoare
Boldero
Annesley
Calvert
Strong
Acland
Gordon
Drummond.

[2.]

Byrone. October 23^{d} 1804
Monday Dr Drury's *Museum*
Harrow on the Hill
Middlesex
England
Europe
the world
the universe.

Inscription in *Euripidis Hecuba* (1804)

Porson's Edition of Hecuba. the bequest of Byron
To the Monitors library prior to his leaving Harrow
Tuesday Decr 4th AD. 1804

Inscriptions in *Scriptores Græci* (1804–1811)

[1.] George Gordon Byron Wednesday June 26th A.D. 1805
3 quarters of an hour past 3 o clock in the afternoon
3^{d} School Calvert monitor, Tom Wildman on my left hand; and Long on my Right—
Harrow on the Hill Byron Byron

[2.] B. January. 9$^{th.}$ 1809
Newstead Notts
Of the 4 persons, whose names are here mentioned, one is dead, another in a distant climate, *all* separated, and not four years have elapsed since they sat together in school, and none are yet twenty one years of age.

[3.] "Eheu fugaces Posthume! Posthume!
"Labuntur Anni.—

[4.] Byron 1804. Byron 1804. Harrow Harrow on the Hill
Middlesex 1804

[5.] Returned to England from the East July 14th 1811.
absent two years & twelve days in Spain Portugal, Sardinia, Sicily, Malta, Albania, Greece, Asia Minor, Constantinople.
B^{n} 1811

[6.] Sublime Sublime Sublime
His Holiness Byron 1804
Pug Hoare no slight Mountebank

4 June] Ju⟨ly⟩ 17 Byron[1]] ⟨W$^{m.}$ Assheton⟩ ⟨Wm Assheton⟩ ⟨April 26th 1804⟩ Byron

Speakers July 1805

Franks
Wildman
Byron
Long
Bazett
East
Hoare
Drury

Now complete

[7.] Byron Byrone

Harrow Notebook (1805)

[Folio 2.]

Wolliams S Collins
Lord Byron.
Sunday Febry 17th 1805.

Byron Ex dono Georgii Sinclair
Sunday February 17th 1805
Harrow on the Hill

[Folio 4.]

Agesilaus. +
Wolsey.
+ Chatham.
Peterborough.
Roscius.
Scaurus.
Socrates.
Richard +
Barrymore
Lowen
Ge. Drummond.
+ Hamilton.
Curran.
Edgecumbe
Anacreon
Garrick
Adrian

Pitt
Fox
Grattan
Couthon +
Mirabeau
Cicero
+ Pope
Johnson.
Foster
Wilkes
⟨Burns⟩
⟨[?]⟩
[Folio 5.] Richman +
⟨Caesar⟩
Valiere +
Potemkin
Gibbon.

Belchers 2.
Parkyns +
North
Dunning.
Talleyrand +
Luxemburgh
Zanger
Olivarez
Flood
Tamerlane +
Topal Osman +
Robinson Cricketer.
Mason.
Kerr +
Carr +
Dalrymple.
Barre.
Æsop
Gasca
Gifford
Lewis
[Folio 6.] Cornelius Mussus.
Appius Claudius
Muleasses.
Milton,

Democritus,
Seneca
Horace
Wadislaus,
Epictetus
Alexander,
Augustus.
Homer
Blacklock
Melancthon
Galba
[Folio 7.] Boccharis,
Wolcott,
Scarron,
Tydeus,
Swift.
Lepaux—
Darwin
Burke.
Voiture.
Horace
Virgil.
Sterne
+ Walter Scott

[Folios 9–11.]

Homer.	—	Zoilus
Pope; Addison.	—	Dennis.
Dryden	—	Settle.
Cowper.	—	Reviews.
Hayley.— Strangford.— Moore		Jefferies.
Milton		Lauder Johnson
[Folio 12.] Gray Mason.		Lloyd Coleman Johnson.

Lyttleton	—	{Johnson. Smollet
Garrick		{Hill.
Shakespeare		{Voltaire.
Chatham		{Wilkes.
Mansfield		{Junius.
Johnson		{Symmons
[Folio 14.] Glover		{Epigram.
Sheridan		{Dibdin.
Shenstone		{Gray
Kemble		{Carlisle. Drury

[Folio 26.] Southwell.
Smith
Dr Barrow
Jno. Becher.
Mrs Burland
Pigot's.
Tos. Falkner.
Wylde K.
Hutchinson.
[Folio 27.] Watson.
Houson.
Bristoe.
S. Wright.
Nickinson.
Mr. Lucy K.
Pearson.
R. Lowe Sr. K
Calvert & Shee.
[Folio 34.] Delawarr
Clare
De Bathe
Claridge
Dorset
Gordon
Bradshaw
G.D.R.
J Wingfield

Tattersall
Long.
Pepper
Duff
Sinclair
Edleston.
Brett
Dawson
[Folio 36] Dr. Drury
Hanson
Pigot
Leacroft
Massingberd
Chaworth
Bankes
Carlisle
Pepper.
Sinclair
Hutchinson.
Faulkner
Ellis.
Murray
Brough
Eyre
Jn. Becher.
Wildman.

[Folio 37.]	Chatham	Tattersall
	Fox	Pigot
	Cicero	J^{n}. Becher.
	Mirabeau	Giles
	Demosthenes	Euston
	Carteret	Pollington
	Bolingbroke	Angelo
	Richelieu	Devon
	Garrick	Hobhouse
	Barry	DeBathe
[Folio 39.]	Murray	M. Bernard
	Price	Grimaldi
	Ferrall	Caroline.
	Long	Pearson
	Wilson Fr.	Wallace
	Crawford	Sir Busick H.
	Jackson	Bold Webster.
	Tavell	Chisholme.
	Bernard.	

[Folio 40.]

Dr Drury. 3
Butler. —
M. Drury.
Duchess of Dorset.
M^{r}. Montagu.
Sir T Acland.
Ed. M. P.ost. June. 1805.
Ed. B. P.ress. June. 1805.
Delawarr.
De bathe. S^{r}.
M. D. Wise
G. De. R.
Fisher——Harrogate. *Septr. 1806.*
Tattersall

[Folio 41.]

Wilmot.
H. Drummond.
⟨Bowater.⟩
M. Drury.
Butler.
Kent.

Incomparably
Open.

Monson.
Northwicke
Haybrooke
Bernard.
Lady Calthorpe.
Mr. Birch
Mrs. Adolphus.
Clare.

Saunders.
Emerson.
Pownall.
Hammersley.
H. X. U.
E⟨dlest⟩ Pigot.
Edleston.
John Becher
B. Maltby.
Rogerson
Kent.
Hobhouse
Vince.
Macnamara
Mansel Philips.
DeBathe.

[Folio 42.] Variety of Action

Long.
S. Webb.
Gordon.
⟨E. Pigot⟩
M. Chaworth.
Simmons.
N. Bernard.

[Folio 43.] Modulation of Voice
Oratorical Talents
Matter

Kemble 2.
Elliston
⟨Braham⟩
Betty
Grassini

[Folio 44.] Mary Duff. —
Fanny Parkyns. —
Susan Pepper.
Antoinetta Parker. —
Augusta Parker. —
Alice Hill
—— Ellis —
—— ⟨Thomson⟩
Mary Anne Chaworth.
Eliza Pigot —
Julia Leacroft. —
Jesse Abercrombie

[Folio 45.]

⟨Wm. Harness. 1803,⟩

⟨*K.*⟩ Dorset 1
1805
⟨K̟.⟩ Delawarr 2
1804.
⟨*K*⟩ Bradshaw 3.
1804
⟨Brock
1804⟩
⟨*K*⟩ J Wingfield 4
⟨*K*⟩ DeBathe 5
⟨*K*⟩ Claridge 6
1805
⟨*K*⟩ Gordon 7
⟨*K*⟩ Clare 8.
1805
Wm. Harness 1803.

[Folio 46.]

Duff.
Pepper
Morgan.
Stuart
Nicolson
Lowes
Curtis Reid.
Parkyns.
Paul
Reid Sr.
Ellis.
Osborne
Musters.

Tattersall
K Clare.
J G Brett
Peel Sr
Porter.
Peel Jn.
Ackers.
Hunter
Curzon
Long
Wildman
Pitt
Price
Brock
⟨Peel Sr⟩
T—Blackburne
Clinton
C Drummond
J Drummond
Sinclair.
Ellison
Dawson.

[Folio 48.]

K̟ Delawarr
K Dorset
K DeBathe Sr.
K Claridge Sr.
K J. Wingfield
R. Wingfield
K Bradshaw
K C—Gordon

[Folio 49.] *K.* Macnabb.
Wm Harness.

1805

[Folio 109.] Sinclair——7 New Norfolk Street Park Lane
twice

Delawarr——17 upper Grosvenor S^{t}

Clare——15 Savile Row
3

John Wingfield—12 Stratford Place
1 Oxford Street

Tattersall——Otterden Place
Chairing Maidstone
G^{2} Kent.

C—Drummond J^{r} Esqr Chairing Cross
2

[Folio 110.] Oh go not yet! even thus two Friends condemned
Embrace, and kiss, and take ten thousand leaves,
Loather a thousand times to part, than die
Yet now farewel, and fare well life! with thee!

Shakespeare.—
K. Henry 6th
Act 3^{d} Scene 2^{d}
Lines 736 & 740.

[Folio 111.] And wheresoeer we went like Juno's Swans,
Still we went coupled, and inseparable.

Shakespeare
As you like it
Act 1st Scene 3^{d}
Line 36 & 37.

Quod nec Jovis Ira, nec Ignis,
Nec poterit Ferrum, nec edax abolere vetustas

Inscriptions in *Catullus, Tibullus et Propertius* (1806)

Byron. Southwell Notts
Nov.r 1.st 1806.

Poems translated or paraphrased
"Ille mi par esse Deo videtur"
"Lugete oh Veneres, Cupidinesque"
"Surripui dum ludis &c &c
"Mellitos oculos tuos &c &c

Recipients of *Hours of Idleness* (1807)

J— Wingfield at Harry Drury's
Old DeBathe—at Mother Leith's
Old Gordon—Ditto.
L.d Clare—at Butler's.—

Byron
April 8.th 1807

Memo on Playbill (1810)

This farce was enacted off the Troad by some sailors of his M.y's Ship Salsette 44 guns (rated 36) while we lay at anchor in expectation of a firman to permit us to pass the Dardanelles in our way to Constantinople (to return with Adair.)—It was well done,—we were more than a month on board during which we visited the Troad, Tenedos &.cc April—May—*1810*.
May the 3.d I swam from Sestos to Abydos in one hour & ten minutes, Lieu.t Ekenhead of the Marines did it also at the same time. Byron

— 1810 —

16 were more] were ⟨nearly⟩

A Note in Hobhouse's Diary (1810)

Thursday May. 3^{d} 1810

This instant 3 m p 10 am—write this in the Dardanelles at anchor. Byron & Ekenhead gone to swim now swimming across the Hellespont—Ovid's Hero to Leander open before me. Mr Ekenhead performed this in one hour & 5 minutes setting off two miles above Europe castle & coming out a mile at least below Dardanelles, Ld B. in 1 `hour´ & 10 minutes. got under weigh & wind failing only drifted further below where anchored—

Constantinople

P.S. The whole distance E. & myself swum was more than 4 miles the current very strong and cold, some large fish near us when half across, we were not fatigued but a little chilled. did it with little difficulty.
May 26th 1810. Byron

Endorsement on a Letter from Suleyman Aga (1811)

Received from Suleyman Aga Waywode of Thebes this Letter ⟨March⟩ April 17th *1811* B.—Athens

Endorsement on a Copy of a Romaic Song (1811)

Greek Song copied out for
me in Athens April 19.th 1811
by *Δŏδŏ* Roque the daughter
of a French Merchant of that
City previous to my leaving
Greece.—

B—

Memorandum (1811)

[1.] July 2^{d} 1811. This day I have completed *two years* absence from England, which have been passed in Spain, Portugal, Malta, Albania, Greece, Ætolia, Asia Minor, Constantinople, Morea Attica, & some of the Cyclades. Aged 23 years and five months & some days.

B.—Volage Frigate.
Bay of Biscay.—

[2.] Arrived in England July 14th 1811 after an absence of two years & twelve days.—B.

Memo on a Letter Wrapper (1811)

My Mother's Letters.
Augst 4th *1811*

Comments in Hobhouse's *Imitations* (1811)

[1.] Preface too long,—M. said it was like Walsh. *B.*

[2.]
When you, my lord! the splendid feast prepare
For all the nobles of St. James's air,
Who but admires the liberal, just expense,
By wealth supported, and allow'd by sense?

Good

[3.] "Jones plays the fool in his peculiar sphere." i.e. The H--se of Com--ns, a sphere which seems to have been chosen by many for the same purpose.

Good

[4.]
If you who saw the course which ***B---y***[1] *ran*,
Would see what other rogues and spendthrifts can,
Attend.—When empty stewards aid refuse,
They run to *Britton*,[2] or some brother Jews;

[1]Who is he?
[2]Thomas, King Moore, Howard all much more Jewish, never heard of Britton.—

[5.] At last, when frighten'd *synagogues* suspect,

(Good)

[6.] *Not like the priest who calls the glutton sinner,*
Then swills and surfeits at his vestry dinner.

double rhymes bad.

[7.] Here eggs, but not from *Ireland**,[1] fresh and warm,

* "But not from Ireland." *Whence most of the eggs* consumed in London are brought.[2]

[1](Scotland)
[2]The Author may now eat them fresh at *Enniscorthy*.—

[8.] *At top a flounder, or at best a* ***jowl****;*
My second course a rabbit or a fowl.

a better *dish* & *rhyme* than *Soul* as it once stood

[9.] *Sir William Temple, the celebrated ambassador from the English court in the days of Charles II. to the Hague—a wise statesman, an uncorrupted patriot, and a learned man. He preserved his integrity intire in times of the most extreme corruption; and had the happiness of serving the last two monarchs of the Stuart race with fidelity, at the same time that he was the friend of William the Third. As an author he has the merit of being one of the first of English prose writers, who improved the stile of composition, and introduced an ease and purity of language before almost unknown.*

He had the merit of maintaining that *Beast* of impure ideas *Swift.*

[10.] *On festive days, just thrice a year* **perchance***,*
A well-fed buck might furnish out a **haunch***:*

Perchance! *Haunch*! Ah Hobhouse were not "*staunch*" "*launch*," "*cranch*" "*paunch*," all at hand?—

[11.] *Dragg'd from the bosom of the Atlantic* **main***,*
*To glad the peer and glut the alder***man***.*

Main! *Man*! Oh Byshe! Byshe! Byshe!

[12.] *If then the gay luxurious lords* **forsook**
Their wonted willow for too precious **oak***,*

sook! Oak! Oh Lauk.

[13.] *Let him partake such joys who joins the dance*
At Ca--sh' house, with Ca--sh nymphs from France:
Palace impure, where vice and F---r reign,
Whence common girls too modest much, abstain.

Keen but Gross

[14.] *I am to observe, that since the writing of this, something which I hope may be more lasting than either the cough or the cholic, namely, the good sense of the public, has kept master Betty from the London stage.*

Good

[15.] *Devils and ghosts! a start! a cry! a* ***groan****!*
And then to please the court, a windy **clown** *.

Bad rhyme worse ⟨i⟩ idea

* *"And then to please the court." &c. A certain pantomime, which always brought crowded houses, and was honoured by his Ma--y's and the Prin--sses*[1] *company more than once, introduced this ingenious attempt at practical humour. The active operator was loudly applauded, and the performance of his slight encored.*
N.B. "Windy." *The clown swallowed gunpowder, and underwent all the pangs and consequences of a well dissembled cholic.*[2]

[1]Catwife
[2]Sporco

[16.] Altogether very good, versification in general excellent.—B.

[17.] *Kn--t*[1] thinks his legs are no disgrace,
Then let him pardon *F---'s* face[2];

[1](poor Gally)
[2]*Farrel*, Dan's mouth like the Postoffice—*mem* once put in a letter by mistake & he swallowed it like a *Sandwich* B

[18.] *Condemn'd to rot in* ***Dorset*** *jails,*
Or hear his verse and bitter tales;

Bankes alluded to⟨o⟩ why?

[19.] Should W---*r*[1] *once like Fuller roar,*
Or wipe his boots upon your floor;
Or with a rude, untimely paw,
Seize on your **fav'rite lobster**[2] *claw;*

Must you, my lord! your commerce end,
And for a fish forsake a friend?

[1]Sir Godfrey
[2]I never will forgive him, he stole it at the Bedford.—B

[20.] Good—but I wish it was in heroic couplets.—

[21.] *Since prose alone, and that beyond the Tweed*[1] *,
To names like these, and Gifford dare succeed;

** The imitator here alludes to a certain Review, the best written critique on all the dull productions of the day.*[2]

[1]A puff for the E.R.
[2]Hobhouse you dog!

[22.] How great the courage, and perhaps how vain,
To venture satire in our George's reign!
To please the judging few be all my bent,
Their blame will punish, and their praise content:
This be my first, my last, my only aim,
And this the road I follow on to fame.
'Tis true, a verse like this can ne'er succeed,
Not ten will praise it, if ten thousand read.
Mine be this fate, my case however hard,
Not rank'd with Hafiz, and no fav'rite bard;
Still to creep on, and still indulge my lays,
Without the vulgar itch of vulgar praise:
Too proud to buy with verse my bed and board,
And wear, like Pratt, the livery of a lord.
Flow smoothly, Strangford; hobble on, Carlisle,
While courts applaud, a wretch* like me may smile.

Pulchre! Bene! Recte!

** My lord Carlisle is used, when speaking of plebeians, to denominate them poor* wretches, *unfortunate* wretches, *miserable* wretches, *&c. See his eighteen penny pamphlet, in which he draws a most pathetic picture of the crowd coming out of the playhouse, and tumbing one over the other down stone stair-cases, which he proposes should be made spiral to prevent this catastrophe.*

Bene

[23.] This & the first poem the best in the Book.—

[24.] An address to Miss Mortlock daughter to the Mayor of Cambridge by Hobhouse.—I always protested against *this* & the *preface. B.*

[25.] How came the author to personate a Lady? & such a strumpet as *Amoret*?—

[26.] Forget the fair one, and your fate delay;
If not avert, at least defer the day
When you beneath the female yoke shall bend,
And lose your *wit*, your *temper*, and your *friend*.

I have lost them all & shall wed accordingly B. *1811*

[27.] To give more charms than e'er had *Xeuxis*' five,

Zooks! these be harsh syllables!

[28.] When at your feet the *youth* of *Lisbon* lie,

pretty youth they are.—dingy Devils

Memo on a Billet-doux from Susan Vaughan (1812)

Pray dont forget me, as I shall never cease thinking of you my Dearest *And only Friend*

S.H.V.

This was written on the 11.th of January 1812.—on the 28.th I received ample proof that the Girl had forgotten *me* & *herself* too.—*B.* Heigh ho!

Note on Lady Caroline Lamb's Forgery (1813)

Once more my Dearest Friend let me assure you that I had no hand in the satire you mention so do not take affront about nothing but call where I desired—as to his refusing you the Picture—it is quite ridiculous—only name me or if you like it shew but this note & that will suffice—you know my reasons for wishing them not to allow *all* who call the same latitude explain what ever you think necessary to them & take which Picture you think most like but do not forget to return it the soonest you can—for reasons I explained.

My Dearest Friend take care of ⟨your [about ten more words heavily deleted by Lady Caroline]⟩

Byron

This letter was forged in my name by Caroline L. for the purpose of obtaining a picture from the hands of M^{r}. M.—

January 1813
Byron

Memo on Invitation Card (1813)

Lady Heathcote.
at home
Monday July 5th
A Small Waltzing Party
10 o Clock

This Card I keep as a curiosity—since it was at the Ball (to which it is an invitation) that L^{y}. Caroline L. performed y^{e}. dagger Scene—of indifferent memory.————1813.—

The Couplet Club (1814)

The Couplet Club

1 It is proposed and agreed to by the undersigned—that a club be formed to dine together every friday—

2 That the members of this club be the undersigned—

3. That the members of this club be the undersigned only.

4 That the dinner be formed to the exclusion of butcher's & other meat.

5 That it is not yet decided wherther or not eggs are to be accounted meat—

6 That it shall never be decided whether or not eggs are to be accounted meat, and that whatever decision may be determined upon eggs when eaten shall, upon pain of expulsion never be called meat.

13 The Couplet Club] ⟨*The Friday Club.*⟩ The Couplet Club 23–4 determined upon] determined ⟨egg⟩

7—That the dinner hour, except a previous arrangement of all the members of the club shall settle otherwise, be on each club day—six in the evening—

8—That sherries and port wines be excluded from the dinner & dessert—excepted always, if unanimously required, one glass of port wine subsequent to the cheese—

9—That a common concern, be the first and only toast—

10. That one memory be also drunk—always the same and only one—

11. That no excuse for non attendance except positive illness or actual absence from London be permitted to any member of this club—

12—That no more than one stranger be admitted to dine with the club on any single day and that if an equal division of voices propose two strangers—the choice shall be settled by drawing lots—it being understood that the first preference in the succeeding meeting be given to the person unsuccessfully proposed—

13. That it shall be a sufficient objection to any proposed stranger that he is disagreable to any one member of the club

14—That the club consist of only two and those the undersigned members, and that a proposal for a third member be considered as a virtual dissolution of the said club—

15 That any arrangements respecting viands or other matters not positively settled by the laws of the club, shall, at once, and without argument be decided by drawing lots—

16—That the two members do by their ensuing signatures bind themselves to the literal & punctual observance of all the laws of the said club—

Byron
John. Hobhouse—

Signed & delivered before us this present twelfth day of March. A.D. 1814

John Hobhouse
Biron

1 arrangement of] arrangement ⟨shall be⟩ 14 the choice] the ⟨str⟩ 15 in the] in ⟨every⟩ 16 the person] the ⟨uns⟩

Comments on Hunt's *Rimini* (1815)

[1.] . . . the swarming insects fry,
Opening with noisome din, *as you go by*.

prosaic

[2.] A moment's trouble find the knights to rein
Their horses in, which feeling turf again,
Thrill, & curvet, & long to be at large
To scour the space & give the winds a charge,
Or pulling tight the bridles, as they pass,
Dip their warm mouths into the freshening grass.
But soon in easy rank, from glade to glade,
Proceed they, coasting underneath the shade,
Some baring to the cool their placid brows,
Some looking upward through the glimmering boughs,
Or peering grave through inward-opening places,
And half prepared for glimpse of shadowy faces.

Very good indeed

[3.] [Various the trees and passing foliage here,—
Wild pear, and oak, and dusky juniper,
With briony between in trails of white,
And ivy, and the suckle's streaky light,
And moss, warm gleaming with a sudden mark,
Like flings of sunshine left upon the bark,
And still the pine, long-haired, and dark, and tall,
In lordly right, predominant o'er all.]

Very Very good

[4.] Sad is the strain, with which I cheer my long
And *caged* hours, & try my native tongue,
Now too while rains autumnal, as I sing,
Wash the dull bars, chilling my sicklied wing,[1]
And all the climate presses on my sense;
But thoughts it furnishes of things far hence,
And *leafy* dreams affords me, [and a fe]eling
Which I should else disdain, *tear-dipp'd* & healing;

[1]very excellent verse

[5.] *Enough of this. Yet how shall I disclose*
The weeping days that with the morning rose,
How bring the bitter disappointment in,—
The holy cheat, the virtue-binding sin,—
The shock, that told this lovely, trusting heart,
That she had given, beyond all power to part,
Her hope, belief, love, passion, to one brother,
Possession (oh the misery!) to another![1]
Some likeness was there 'twixt the two,—an air
At times, a **cheek**,[2] *a* **colour**[3] *of the hair,*
A tone, when speaking of indifferent things;
Nor, by the scale of common measurings,
Would you say more perhaps, than that the one
Was **somewhat stouter**, **t'other**[4] *finelier spun;*
That of the two, Giovanni was the graver,
Paulo the livelier, & the more in favour.[5]

[1]all good
[2]smile
[3]suppose you say "a *colour*⟨ing⟩ of the *cheek* or hair"—or in lieu of "cheek" "a smile"
[4]more robust the other
[5]very good too—as a whole—

[6.] Some tastes there were indeed, that would prefer
Giovanni's *countenance* as the martialler;

visage—or *aspect*

[7.] [Paulo] could put on
A glowing frown, as if an *angel* shone,

say a "*Spirit*" the common idea of Angelic is benignant—notwithstanding your authority from Tasso & Milton

[8.] A *nose of taste* was his,

Say—Grecian—Roman—what you will—but not "of taste"—

[9.] *It was a face in short, seem'd made to shew,*
How far the genuine flesh & blood could go;—
A morning glass of unaffected nature,—
Something, that baffled every pompous feature,—
The visage of a glorious human *creature.*

Excellent—particularly the first & last of the triplet—I would cut out the second not because bad but unequal to the other two.——

[10.] *The* **worst**[1] *of Prince Giovanni, as his bride*
Too quickly found, was an ill-temper'd pride.
Bold, handsome, **able if he** *chose*[2]ˋ,ˊ *to please,*
Punctual & right in common offices,
He lost the sight of conduct's only worth,
The scattering smiles on this uneasy earth,
And on the strength of virtues of small weight,
Claim'd tow'rds himself the exercise of great.
He kept no reckoning with his sweets & sours;—
He'd hold a sullen countenance for hours,
And then if pleas'd to chear himself a space,
Look for the immediate rapture in your face,
And wonder that a cloud could still be there,
How small soever, when his own was fair.
Yet such is conscience,—so design'd to keep
Stern, central watch, though all things else go sleep,
And so much knowledge of one's self there lies
Cored, after all, in our complacencies,
That no suspicion would have touch'd him more,
Than that of wanting on the generous score:[3]

[1]Colloquial—say "*sin*" of—
[2]"*formed* wheneer he chose" or "wished" or "willed" as "*chose* & *please* bring the s's's'—too nearly together
[3]The whole passage is ⟨however⟩ very fine & original—

[11.] *He would have whelm'd you with a weight of scorn,*
Been proud at eve, inflexible at morn,
In short, ill-tempered for a week to come,
And all to strike that desperate error dumb.
Taste had he, in a word, for high-turn'd merit,
But not the patience, or the genial spirit;
And so he made, 'twixt virtue & defect,
A sort of fierce demand on your respect,
Which, if assisted by his high degree
It gave him in some eyes a dignity,
And struck a meaner deference in the many,
Left him, at last, unloveable with any.

Capital—& true to Nature

[12.] *The frame for broidering, with a piece half done,*
And the white falcon, basking in the sun,
Who when he saw her, sidled on his stand,
And twin'd his neck against her *trembling*[1] **hand.**[2]

[1]fondling
[2]This passage is superlative—but why *trembling*? say "fondling" unless her ⟨fe⟩ fears are not from the bird but some other cause—if she feared ⟨him⟩ she would hardly play with him——

[13.] *She, who had been beguil'd,—she, who was made*
Within a gentle bosom to be laid,—
To bless & to be bless'd,—to be heart-bare
To one who found his better'd likeness there,—
To think for ever with him, like a bride,—
To haunt his eye, like **taste**[1] *personified,—*
To double his delight, to share his sorrow,
And like a morning beam, wake to him every morrow.[2]

[1]grace
[2]This is very fine

[14.] [Paulo] Began to bend down his admiring eyes
On all her touching looks & qualities,
Turning their shapely sweetness every way,
Till 'twas his food & habit day by day,
And she became companion of his thought;
Silence her gentleness before him brought,
Society her sense, reading her books,
Music her voice, every sweet thing her looks,[1]
Which sometimes seem'd, when he sat fix'd awhile,
To steal beneath his eyes with upward smile:
And did he stroll into some lonely place,
Under the trees, upon the thick soft grass,
How charming, would he think, to see her here!
How heighten'd then, & perfect would appear
The two divinest things this world has got,
A lovely woman in a rural spot!

[1]Beautiful—

[15.] . . . *Giovanni sometimes wore*
A knot his bride had work'd him, green & gold;—
For in all things with nature did she hold,
And while 'twas being work'd, her fancy was
Of sunbeams mingling with a tuft of grass.

This sounds like a concetto—but yet it is too good to part with.—

[16.] [Francesca from herself could ill but hide
What pleasure now was added to her side,—

How placidly, yet fast, the days succeeded
With one who thought & felt so much as she did,—
And how the chair he sat in, & the room,
Began to look, when he had failed to come.
But as she better knew the cause than he,
She seem'd to have the more necessity
For struggling hard, & rousing all her pride;
And so she did at first; she even tried]
To feel a sort of anger at his care;
But these extremes brought but a kind despair;
And then she only spoke more sweetly to him,
And found her failing eyes give looks that melted through him.

Superlative

[17.] *The other ground was flatter, & a scene*
Of colour'd brightness just refresh'd with green.
There was the pouting rose, both red & white,
The flamy heart's-ease, flush'd with purple light,
Blush-hiding strawberry, sunny-colour'd box,
Hyacinth, handsome with his clustering locks,
The ***lady lily****, looking gently down,*
Pure lavender, to lay in bridal gown,

all good—but "*lady lily*" is perfection in expression.—

[18.] [. . . Paulo turned, scarce knowing what he did,
Only he felt he could no more dissemble,
And kissed her, mouth to mouth, all in a tremble.
Sad were those hearts, and sweet was that long kiss;
Sacred be love from sight, whate'er it is.
The world was all forgot, the struggle o'er,
Desperate the joy.—That day they read no more.]

Dear Byron, Shall I keep this couplet?

why not? unless you can make it better—& this will not be done easily—
With the whole since my last pencil mark in the first pages—I have no fault to find—but many more beauties than there is time or place to express here.—

A Note in Boswell's *Life of Johnson* (1815)

JOHNSON. "... I value myself upon this, that there is nothing of the old man in my conversation. I am now sixty-eight, and I have no more of it than at twenty-eight." BOSWELL. "But, Sir, would you not wish to know old age? He who is never an old man, does not know the whole of human life; for old age is one of the divisions of it." JOHNSON. "Nay, Sir, what talk is this?" BOSWELL. "I mean, Sir, the Sphinx's description of it;—morning, noon, and night. I would know night, as well as morning and noon." JOHNSON. "What, Sir, would you know what it is to feel the evils of old age? Would you have the gout? Would you have decrepitude?"—Seeing him heated, I would not argue any farther.

Septr 30th 1815 I am now *not twenty eight* by some months & yet I feel decrepid both in head & heart.—I shall never be sixty eight ⟨—unless I go quite mad. B⟩

Endorsement on a Power of Attorney (1816)

Do not forget if the poem called "Hints from Horace" should ever be published to erase—expunge—and omit—any part or parts of it in the text or notes in which M^{r} J^{y} is mentioned—(whether I be dead or alive) the poem was written many years ago—some time before my return to England—and as a copy (I believe) has been kept back by Cawthorn—in which those lines are contained—I give this caution & make this request to you in the hope of your keeping better faith—if ever you publish it yourself which *he* never shall with my consent.———

Byron

14 omit—any] omit—⟨all⟩ 17 believe) has] believe) ⟨to have⟩ 18 lines are] lines ⟨were⟩

Detail of Domestics and Intended Itinerary (1816)

Servants.—

—Berger—a Swiss.—
⟨P⟩
William Fletcher—
⟨Robert Rushton⟩
Robert Rushton—

John William Polidore.—M.D.—

Swisserland—Flanders—Italy
—& (perhaps) France.———

Marginalia in D'Israeli's *The Literary Character* (1818)

[1.] *The defects of great men are the consolation of the dunces.*

[2.] . . . a copy which has accidentally fallen into my hands formerly belonged to the great poetical genius of our times; and the singular fact that it was twice read by him in two subsequent years, at Athens, in 1810 and 1811, instantly convinced me that the volume deserved my attention. . . . *the marginal notes of the noble writer convey no flattery—but amidst their pungency and sometimes their truth, the circumstance that a man of genius could, and did read, this slight effusion at two different periods of his life*, was a sufficient authority, at least for an author, to return it once more to the anvil.

I was wrong, but I was young and petulant, & probably wrote down any thing little thinking that those observations would be betrayed to the Author whose abilities I have always respected & whose works in general I have read oftener than perhaps those of any English Author whatever—except such as treat of Turkey.—
———

[3.] From the perusal of *Rycaut's* folio of Turkish history in childhood, the noble and impassioned bard of our times retained those indelible impressions, which gave life and motion to the "Giaour," the "Corsair," and "Alp." A voyage to the country produced the scenery. *Rycaut* only communicated the impulse to a mind susceptible of the poetical character; and without this Turkish history we should still have had our poet.

When a boy I never could bear to read any poetry whatever without disgust & reluctance.—

Knolles. Cantemir. De Tott. Lady Mary Wortley Mr. Hawkins's translation from Mignot's History of the Turks—the Arabian Nights all travels or histories or books upon the East I could meet with I had read as well as Rycaut before I was ten years old—I think the Arabian Nights first. After these I preferred the history of Naval Actions—Don Quixote—and Smollet's Novels particularly R. Random.—and I was passionate for ye Roman History.—
———

When I was in Turkey I was oftener tempted to turn Mussulman than poet, & have often regretted since that I did not.— 1818

[4.] The great poetical genius of our times has openly alienated himself from the land of his *brothers*;[1] he becomes immortal in the *language* of a *people* whom he would *contemn*; he accepts with ingratitude the fame he loves more than life, and he is only truly great on that *spot* of *earth*, whose genius, when he is no more, will contemplate ⟨on⟩ his shade in anger and in sorrow.

[1] *Cains*.
What was rumoured of me in that Language?—if true—I was unfit for England—if false—England was unfit for me.—"There is a World Elsewhere" I have never regretted for a moment that Country—but often that I ever returned to it at all. It is not my fault that I am obliged to write in English—if I understood my present language equally well I would write in it—but this will require ten years at least to form a Style, no tongue so easy to acquire a little of, or so difficult to master thoroughly as Italian.—

[5.] Vittorio Alfieri, and a brother-spirit in our own *noble poet*, were *rarely seen* amidst the *brilliant circle* in which they were born;[1] the workings of their imagination were perpetually emancipating them, and one *deep loneliness*[2] of feeling proudly insulated them, among the impassioned triflers of their rank.

[1]I fear this was not the case—I have been but too much in that circle, especially in 1812—13—14.
[2]true.

[6.] . . . when the heads of the town, unawares to Petrarch, conducted him to *the house where the poet was born, and informed him that the* **proprietor** *had* **often** *wished to make alterations, but that the towns-people had risen to insist that the house which was consecrated by the birth of Petrarch should be preserved unchanged; this was a triumph more affecting to Petrarch than his coronation at Rome.*

It would have pained me more that the proprietor should have "*often*" wished to make alterations than ⟨that⟩ it could give pleasure that the rest of Arezzo rose against his *right* (for *right* he had) the depreciation of the lowest of mankind is more painful than the applause of the highest is pleasing, the sting of a Scorpion is ⟨far⟩ more in torture than the possession of anything short of Venus could be in rapture.—

Anecdote of an Amatory Affair in Spain (1818–1820)

For some time I went on prosperously both as a linguist and a lover, till, at length, the lady took a fancy to a ring which I wore, and set her heart on my giving it to her, as a pledge of my sincerity. This, however, could not be;—any thing but the ring, I declared, was at her service, and much more than its value,—but the ring itself I had made a vow never to give away.[1] . . . Soon after this . . . I sailed for Malta, and there parted with both my heart and ring.

Four Memoranda from B's Memoirs (1818–1820)

[1. On Curran]

The riches of his Irish imagination were exhaustless. I have heard that man speak more poetry than I have ever seen written,—though I saw him seldom and but occasionally. I saw him presented to Madame de Staël at Mackintosh's;—it was the grand confluence between the Rhone and the Saone, and they were both so d—d ugly, that I could not help wondering how the best intellects of France and Ireland could have taken up respectively such residences. * * * *

[2. On Madame de Staël]
Her figure was not bad; her legs tolerable; her arms good. Altogether, I can conceive her having been a desirable woman, allowing a little imagination for her soul, and so forth. She would have made a great man.

[3. On the Duchess de Broglie]
Nothing was more pleasing than to see the developement of the domestic affections in a very young woman.

[4. On Madame de Staël]
Madame de Staël was a good woman at heart and the cleverest at bottom, but spoilt by a wish to be—she knew not what. In her own house she was amiable; in any other person's, you wished her gone, and in her own again.

Two Notes in Foscolo's *Jacopo Ortis* (1819)

[1.] *Cœlum, non animum mutant qui trans mare currunt.*

[2.] Most men bewail not having attained the object of their desires. I had oftener to deplore the obtaining mine, for I cannot love moderately, nor quiet my heart with mere fruition. The letters of this Italian Werther are very interesting, at least I think so, but my present feelings hardly render me a competent judge.

Marginalia in de Staël's *Corinne* (1819)

[1.] *Il mio talento non esiste più; m'incresce d'averlo perduto.*

Byron.

[2.] *Fa egli d'uopo il sottomettersi o il combatterlo? Ah! quali tempeste mai non avvengono nel profondo del core.*

Byron.

[3.] *Il talento dovrebb'essere una risorsa; quando il Domenichino fu rinchiuso in un convento, egli dipinse dei quadri superbi sulla muraglia della sua prigione, e lasciò dei capi d'opera in segno del suo soggiorno; ma egli soffriva per delle circostanze esteriori,* ***il male*** ⟨non⟩ ***era nell'anima; quando è là, niuna cosa è possibile; è disseccata la sorgente di tutto.***

Byron.

[4.] *Qualche volta mi esamino, come potrebbe farlo una persona diversa da me, ed ho pietà di me stessa. Io era* ***spiritosa, sincera, buona, generosa, sensibile,*** *perchè mai tutto ciò è egli riuscito cotanto male?*

B^{n}.

[5.] *E'propriamente un danno: io era nata per essere una persona distinta; morrò senza che si abbia alcuna idea di me, quantunque io sia celebre. Se fossi stata felice; se la febbre del core non mi avesse divorata, avrei dalla maggiore altezza contemplato l'umano destino, io vi avrei discoperto delle relazioni sconosciute tra la natura e il cielo; ma l'artiglio della sventura mi ha afferrata; come pensar liberamente, quando si fa sentire ogni volta che tentasi di respirare.*

B. B. B.

[6.] *vi è nella realtà della esistenza qualche cosa di arido che si sforza indarno a cangiare.*

[7.] *Quando mi rammento i miei fortunati successi, provo un sentimento d'irritazione. Perchè dirmi che io era vezzosa, se non dovevo essere amata?*

[8.] *Quanto mai gli uomini son felici, andando alla guerra, esponendo la loro vita ai pericoli, e dandosi in preda all'entusiasmo dell'onore e del rischio!*

No.—*No.*

[9.] *Qualche volta quando ascolto della musica, essa mi rammenta i talenti che possedevo; il canto, la danza, e la poesia; mi sento allor la smania di sbarazzarmi dalla infelicità,*

Oimè!

[10.] *Fermossi alfine il cor, che balzò tanto.*

[11.] I knew Madame de Stael well—better than She knew Italy;—but I little thought that one day I should think with her thoughts in the country where she has laid the scene of her most attractive production.—She is sometimes right and often wrong about Italy and England—but almost always true in delineating the heart, which is of but of one nation and of no country or rather of all.——

Byron. Bologna. August 23^{d} 1819

A Note on Apostasy (1821)

The world visits change of politics or change of religion with a more severe censure than a mere difference of opinion would appear to me to deserve. But there must be some reason for this feeling;—and I think it is that these departures from the earliest instilled ideas of our childhood, and from the line of conduct chosen by us when we first enter into public life, have been seen to have more mischievous results for society, and to prove more weakness of mind than other actions, in themselves, more immoral.

A Note on Sculpture (1821)

Sculpture the noblest of the arts because the noblest imitation of Man's own nature with a view to perfection—being a higher resemblance of man so approaching in it's ideal to God who distinctly made him in his *own* image—that the Jehovah of the Jews forbade the worship of Images—because he was "a jealous God"—that is jealous of man's embodied conceptions of deity.————

An Extract from a Journal (1821)

At Harrow I fought my way very fairly. I think I lost but one battle out of seven; and that was to H——;—and the rascal did not win it, but by the unfair treatment of his own boarding-house, where we boxed—I

14 approaching in] approaching ⟨to⟩ it's ideal] it's ⟨effect⟩ 15 his *own*] his ⟨age⟩
16 God"—that] God"—⟨and⟩

had not even a second. I never forgave him, and I should be sorry to meet him now, as I am sure we should quarrel. My most memorable combats were with Morgan, Rice, Rainsford, and Lord Jocelyn,—but we were always friendly afterwards. I was a most unpopular boy, but *led* latterly, and have retained many of my school friendships, and all my dislikes—except to Doctor Butler, whom I treated rebelliously, and have been sorry ever since. Doctor Drury, whom I plagued sufficiently too, was the best, the kindest (and yet strict, too) friend I ever had—and I look upon him still as a father.

P. Hunter, Curzon, Long, and Tatersall, were my principal friends. Clare, Dorset, Cs. Gordon, De Bath, Claridge, and Jno. Wingfield, were my juniors and favourites, whom I spoilt by indulgence. Of all human beings, I was, perhaps, at one time, the most attached to poor Wingfield, who died at Coimbra, 1811, before I returned to England.

Endorsement on a Letter from the Earl of Clare (1821–1822)

This and another letter were written, at Harrow, by my *then* and, I hope, *ever* beloved friend, Lord * *, when we were both schoolboys, and sent to my study in consequence of some childish misunderstanding,—the only one which ever arose between us. It was of short duration, and I retain this note solely for the purpose of submitting it to his perusal, that we may smile over the recollection of the insignificance of our first and last quarrel.

Byron.

Notes on Crawford's Deposition (1822)

Translated Copy of the deposition of Dr. Crawford, M.D.——The Original was sent to the Marquis Viviani Governor of Pisa—and the other English Copy to the English Minister Mr. Dawkins—now resident in Florence

23 of Dr.] of ⟨James⟩ 24 Original was] Original ⟨is at⟩ 25–6 resident in] resident ⟨at⟩

Lord Byron* aveva in mano una Canna. Il Dragone minacciava di trarre la Sciabola. Giunti sotto le nostre Finestre Lord Byron Stese** la Mano al Dragone, e gli domando il Nomo, e l'indirizzo Suo.[1]

Note * I mistook this Sergeant-Major for an *Officer* the whole time as he was well dressed & mounted——I was quite ignorant at the moment of what had occurred during the arrest at the Gates of the City.

Noel Byron.—

Note ** To give the hand (in some parts of the Continent) is a pledge either of hostility or otherwise according to circumstances.—The reader of this must judge for himself in the present instance.

Notes on Taaffe's Deposition (1822)

[1.] Deposition of J. Taaffe Esq.re Original.

[2.] Note by Lord Byron.

This being Mr. Taaffe's testimony as to his own impressions I cannot and do not wish to controvert them—as he must be the best judge of his own feelings.—But I must declare that the impression of the moment on my mind—from the *words*—the *tone*—the *starting* of *his horse*—and the nearness and rapidity with which the dragoon rushed past him—was—that he had received and *felt* that he had received an insult. With regard to the rest as I saw no more of him till some time after the close of the whole business—I have nothing to observe.—

Memo on Shelley's Cremation (1822)

+ Ld Byron was not present at the burning of Mr. Shelley's body—some delay having taken place in the exhumation Ld. B took the opportunity of bathing in the interim and having swum to the Schooner which lay in the Offing the operation was finished before his return.—

4 Note * I] Note * ⟨Note * The Man put out his hand *first* to me which I took ⟨as a pledge⟩ ⟨it⟩ either as a sign of hostility (as customary on the continent,) or of his repentance, mistaking him for⟩ mistook this] mistook ⟨him for⟩ 5–6 the moment] the ⟨time⟩ 18 rushed past] rushed ⟨by⟩ 23 exhumation Ld. B] exhumation ⟨of the⟩

Queries concerning the Greeks (1823)

QUERIES.

1. If they have anything they wish to be *immediately* communicated to the C. in England?
2. Their force—their mode of payment and it's amount per man—also it's average per thousand men—*i.e.* the whole expence of their maintenance?
3. Their fleet and it's object in not coming out?
4. The price of provision forage and living &c. also the exchange &c?
5. Their prisoners and their mode of treating them.
6. The *actual* and effective power of the executive Government—*so-called* at *least*—and how far it is respected & obeyed by the people. . . .
7. Their Chiefs—*who*—*which*—and *what*—I mean as 'good men and true.'
8. The state of the Islands as in connection with the peninsula & how far they are likely or liable to unite under the same Institutions.

A Note in Count Teotoky's Letter (1823)

* It appears that Count Teotoky—(a septinsular Chief now in the Morea) exaggerates the means of L.B. and probably those of the committee—in this L.B. is not to blame for he stated the exact amount of both to the principal Greeks on his arrival here (in Cephalonia)—on purpose to prevent such possible exaggeration—viz—1^{stly} the amount of the Committee's subscription and it's intention—and 2dly the sum in his own cash and credits (between forty and fifty thousand dollars) which L.B. could command personally at this present period—i.e. during the current year.—

N.B. 8bre 16. 1823.—

26 the current] the ⟨present⟩

Replies to Stanhope's Questionnaire (1824)

1st.—Will your Lordship allow me to make over a certain quantity of Greek and Roman types to the editor of the Greek Chronicle?—

Yes.

2d. —Will your Lordship subscribe £50 for the support of the Greek paper?—

Yes.

3d. —Will your Lordship allow me to take round the printing press, &c. to the seat of the Greek government, *i.e.* of the legislative body?—

We will talk over this article.

4th.—Will your Lordship subscribe £100 towards the support of the German artillery?—

Yes.

5th—Will your Lordship allow £100 of your loan to the Greek government to be made over to the German Committee, they having advanced that sum to the said government on my guaranteeing its repayment?—

Yes.

6th.—Would your Lordship approve of Mr. Hesketh being appointed Sub-intendant of Stores?—

Yes.

7th.—Would your Lordship approve of my exchanging the Greek Committee's press for the one belonging to the editor here?—

This article I do not quite understand, but will talk it over with you.

Directives to Lega Zambelli (1824)

F° 2. 1824.

1.

Il Thè non è bevanda Greca—dunque il Signor Luca può bever dell Caffè in veece—o aqua—o niente.—

2.

La paga del' detto Luca sarà di cinque talloni per mese pagati come gli altri di casa.—Egli mangiarà coi Sulioti—o dove vuole.———

3.

Il tenente di Drako può mangiare coi miei di casa——altri no—senza almeno chio si sà prima.—

Two Notes in Stanhope's Letter (1824)

[1.] On the 21st February I bivouacked in the tent of the Prefect of the Lepanto district. He had just had a conference with the garrison of that place, and said that if your Lordship appeared there with a considerable force, and the arrears due to the troops, amounting to 25,000 dollars, could be paid, the fortress would be surrendered. Most anxiously do I hope your Lordship will proceed thither, terminate the negotiation, and take possession of the place. This conquest would almost secure the independence of Greece, and would shorten her struggle, perhaps, by many years.*

* The Suliots declined marching against Lepanto, saying, 'that they would not fight against stone walls.' Colonel Stanhope also knows their conduct here in other respects lately.—N.B.

[2.] He has established two schools here, and has allowed me to set the press at work.*

6 talloni per] talloni ⟨il⟩ 10 chio si] chio ⟨sio⟩

* I hope that the press will succeed better there than it has here. The Greek newspaper has done great mischief both in the Morea and in the islands, as I represented both to Prince Mavrocordato and to Colonel Stanhope that it would do in the *present* circumstances, unless *great caution* was observed.—N.B.

APPENDIX: SALE CATALOGUES (1816 *and* 1827)

Sale Catalogue (1816)

FIRST DAY'S SALE.

Octavo et Infra.

1	A Lot of Pamphlets.	Martin
2	A Collection of odd Volumes.	Lowe
3	Ducarel's Poems.—Kirke White's Poems.—Girdlestone's Anacreon.—Baker's Poems.—Royal Eclipse,—in al [*sic*] 5 vol. *russia.*	Allen
4	Lord Chatham's Letters.—Penn's Bioscope.—Butler's Lives of Fenelon and Bossuet.—4 vol.	Plunkett
5	Translations from the Greek Anthology.—Xenophon's Expedition of Cyrus.—Rejected Addresses.—Licida da Mathias.—Œuvres de Cazotte, 3 vol.—in all 7 vols.	Lowe
6	Bacon's Essays.—Man of Feeling.—Lord Lyttelton's Letters, 2 vol.—in all 4 vol.	Sheldon
7	~~Poetical Register, 2 vol.~~—Oldham's Works, 2 vol.—Letters of a Mameluke, 2 vol.—Williams's State of France, 2 vol. Spirit of the Journals.—Flowers of Literature.—Hobhouse on the Origin of Sacrifices, six copies.—Macauley's Poetical Effusions.	E. Littledale
8	Cornelius Nepos, *Oxon.* 1803. Salustii Opera, *Glasg.* 1777. Horatius, *Eton*, 1791.	Murray
9	Coleridge's Poems. Milton's Paradise Lost. Edgeworth's Modern Griselda.	Wiltshire
10	Akenside's Poems. Poems of Addison, Pomfret, Mallet, Collins, Smollet, Gray, Goldsmith, Armstrong, &c.	Murray
11	Parsey's Poems. Bowles's Missionary. Irving's Fair Helen.	Lowe
12	Shee's Commemoration of Reynolds, 1814. Lord Thurlow's Poems, 1813, and 10 more.	Wiltshire
13	Conjuration du Duc d'Orleans, 3 vol. *Par.* 1796.	

	Levis, Souvenirs et Portraits, 1813. Mémoires de la Margueritte de Bareith, 2 vol. and 7 more.	Lowe
14	Biographical Dictionary, 11 vol. wanting vol. 8, and various others.	Do
15	Saugnier and Brisson's Voyage to Africa, 1792. Walker's Voyages, 2 vol. 1760. Memoir of the Queen of Etruria, 1814. Journey to Paris, 1814. Penrose's Journal, 4 vol. 1815.	Sheldon
16	Despotism, or Fall of the Jesuits, 2 vol. 1811. Anecdotes of the French Nation, 1794, and 12 more.	Smith
17	Veneroni's Italian Grammar, 1812, and 9 School Books.	Murray
18	Xenophontis Cyropœdia Hutchinsoni, 1797. Ciceronis Orationes Selectæ, Delphini, 1803. Demosthenis Orationes Selectæ, 1791.	Sheldon
19	Italian and English Dictionary, 1806. Veneroni's Italian Grammar, 1806. Graglia's Guide to Italian, 1803. Zotti's Italian Vocabulary.—4 vol.	Murray
20	Anquetil, Louis XIV. La Cour et le Regent, 4 vol. *Par.* 1789.	Do
21	Art of Tormenting, *russia*, 1806.	Do
22	Adams's Summary of Geography and History, *russia*, 1802.	Lacon
22*	Ancient British Drama, 3 vol. 1810.	Findley
23	Arabian Nights, by Scott, 6 vol. LARGEST PAPER, *with an additional set of plates inserted*, *green morocco*, 1811.	Cotton
23*	Anderson's British Poets, 14 vol. 1795.	J. Mason
24	Alciphronis Epistolæ, Gr. et Lat., Bergleri, *Lips.* 1715.	Murray
24*	Æschylus a Porson, 2 vol. *russia*, *Glasg.* 1806.	Do
25	Æschylus a Schutz, 3 vol. *russia*, *Halæ*, 1798.	Foster
25*	Aristotelis Poetica a Tyrwhitt, *Oxon.* 1794.	Murray
26	Anacreon a Forster, *morocco*, *Lond.* 1802.	Do
26*	Anacreon by Moore, 2 vol. *russia*, 1806.	Murray
27	Account of the most celebrated Pedestrians, 1813.	Plunkett
28	Ariosto, Orlando Furioso, 4 vol. *Livorn.* 1797.	J. Mason
29	——————— 5 vol. *Par.* 1786.	Do
30	Byron's (Lord) Hebrew Melodies, 1815.	Broadhead
31	Another Copy, 1815.	Brumby
32	Another Copy, 1815.	Evans
33	Another Copy, 1815.	Allen

34	Beaumont and Fletcher's Works, with notes by Weber, 14 vol. 1812.	Naghton
35	British Drama, 5 vol. 1804.	Smith
36	British Novelists, with prefaces by Mrs. Barbauld, 50 vols. 1810.	Lacon
37	British Essayists, by Chalmers, 45 vol. 1808.	Do
38	Beloe's Anecdotes of Literature, 2 vol. 1807.	Triphook
39	Boswell's Life of Johnson, 4 vol. 1807.	Murray
40	Burns' Works, 5 vol, 1806.	Murray
41	Burton's Anatomy of Melancholy, 2 vol. *russia*, 1806.	Do
42	Blackstone's Commentaries, by Christian, 4 vol. *russia*, 1803.	E. Little
43	Bisset's History of George III. 6 vol. *russia*, 1803.	Giles
44	Buffon's Natural History, by Smellie, 18 vol. *russia*, 1792.	Lacon
45	Beauties of England and Wales, 11 vol. 1801, &c.	Allen
46	Bonnycastle's Astronomy, *russia*, 1807.	Wiltshire
47	Bruce's Travels, 8 vols. LARGE PAPER, 1805.	Do
48	Browne's British Cicero, 3 vol. 1808.	W. Mason
49	Bisset's Life of Burke, 2 vol. 1800.	Plunkett
50	Biographical Dictionary, by Chalmers, 25 vol. 1812.	Wiltshire
51	Bland's Collections from the Greek Anthology, 1813.	Murray
52	Bland's Collection of Proverbs, 2 vol. 1814.	Naghton
53	Baretti's Italian Dictionary, 2 vol. 1813.	Dowding .
54	Biographie Moderne, or Lives of Eminent Persons, 3 vol. 1811. Grimm's Literary Memoirs, 2 vol. 1814.—5 vol.	Do
55	Bandello, Novelle, 8 vol. wanting vol. 9, *Livorn.* 1791.	Murray
56	Cobbett's Parliamentary History of England, 13 vol. 1806.	Ld Ebrington
57	Cobbett's Parliamentary Debates, from the commencement in 1803 to 1815, 31 vol.	Giles
58	Cobbett's Collection of State Trials, 21 vol. 1809.	Wiltshire
59	Chardin, Voyages en Perse, 10 vol. and Atlas, *Par.* 1811.	Holland
60	Cibber's Apology for his Life, 2 vol. 1756.	Murray
61	Carleton's Memoirs, 1808.	Plunkett
62	Chesterfield's Miscellaneous Works, 4 vol. *russia*, 1779.	Naghton

No.	Item	Buyer
63	Cumberland's Memoirs of his Life, 2 vol. *russia*, 1807.	Plunkett
64	Churchill's Poetical Works, 2 vol. *russia*, 1804.	Murray
65	Catullus, Tibullus, et Propertius, Variorum, *Tr. ad Rhen.* 1680.	Do
66	Creed, Grammatica Linguæ Græcæ Hodiernæ, *Veronæ.* 1782.	Do
67	Cumberland's John de Lancaster, 3 vol. 1809.	Do
68	Count Fathom, Humphry Clinker and Launcelot Greaves, 5 vol.	Wiltshire
69	Crabbe's Poems, 2 vol. 1809.	Do
70	Cowper's Poems, 2 vol.	Murray
71	Citizen of the World, 2 vol. 1790.	Lowe
72	Camilla, 5 vol. *russia*, 1802.	Fortescue
73	Corinna, or Italy, 3 vol. 1807.	Wiltshire
74	Critical Review, from 1795 to 1807, 38 vol. wanting vol. 34.	W. Mason
75	Dryden's Works, by Scott, 18 vol. LARGE PAPER, *russia*, 1808.	Allen
76	Drake's Literary Hours, 2 vol. 1800.	Naghton
77	D'Israeli's Curiosities of Literature, 2 vol. 1807.	Murray
78	——— Calamities of Authors, 2 vol. 1812.	Do
79	——— Quarrels of Authors, 3 vol. 1814.	Ewing
80	Dunlop's History of Fiction, 3 vol. 1814.	Wiltshire
81	Another Copy, 3 vol. 1814.	Evans
82	Discipline, a Novel, 3 vol. 1814.	Murray
83	De Staël's Germany, 3 vol. 1813.	Wiltshire
84	Dibdin's Metrical History of England, 2 vol. Cabanel's Poems, 1814.—3 vol.	Naghton
85	Dallas's Knights, 3 vol. Dallas's Novels.—7 vol.	Money
86	Dryden's Poems, 3 vol. 18mo. Reynolds's Safie, *morocco*, 1814.	Naghton
87	Dutens's Memoirs of a Traveller, 5 vol. *russia*, 1806.	Triphook
88	Don Quixote, 4 vol. Cooke's edition, *fine paper*, and Gil Blas, 4 vol. *fine paper.*—in all 8 vol.	Lowe
89	Demosthenis Orationes Selectæ, 1799. Euripidis Medea et Phœnissæ a Piers, 1703.	Boone
90	Demosthenes ab Allen, *russia*, *Oxon*, 1807.	Giles
91	Demosthenes, by Leland, 2 vol. *russia*, 1806.	Plunkett
92	Dallas's Detection of the Conspiracy against the Jesuits, 1815.	Do
93	Dante, Divina Commedia, illustrate di Note dal Zotti, *Lond.* 1808.	Laing

94	Dictionary of Cant and Flash Language, 1795.	Murray
95	Edgeworth's Tales of Fashionable Life, 6 vol. 1809.	Cotton
96	———— Patronage, 4 vol. 1814.	Do
97	Eugene's Memoirs, 1811. Palmer's Life of Sobieski, 1815. Biographical Peerage, 2 vol. 1808.	Money
98	Elegant Extracts in Verse, 1805.	Calkin
99	Another Copy, in 2 vol. 1800.	Wiltshire
100	Edinburgh Review from the commencement, 23 vol.	Murray
101	Edinburgh Review, 25 various Numbers.	Do
102	Edinburgh Annual Register for 1810, 1811, 1812, and 1813.—7 vol.	Singer
103	Euripidis Tragœdiæ 4 a Porson, *russia*, *Lips.* 1802.	Skinner
104	———— Troades a Burges, *russia*, *Cant.* 1807.	Do
105	Epictetus, by Carter, 2 vol. 1807.	Evans
106	Elton's Specimens of the Classic Poets, 3 vol. 1814.	Plunkett
107	Euclid's Elements, by Simpson, 1762. Wood's Principles of Mechanics, 1803, 2 vol.	Brumby
108	Flim Flams, 3 vol. *russia* 1805.	Plunkett
109	Ford's Dramatic Works, 2 vol. 1811.	Laing
110	Falconer's Shipwreck, by Clarke, 1804.	Cotton
111	Fernandez's Spanish Grammar, *russia*, 1805.	Brumby
112	Granger's Biographical History of England, and Noble's Continuation, 7 vol. LARGE PAPER, 1804.	Christie
113	Gibbon's Decline and Fall of the Roman Empire, 12 vol. 1807.	Naghton
114	Gisborne's Familiar Survey of Christianity, 1801.	Wiltshire
115	Gifford's Baviad and Mæviad, 1797. Poetry of the Anti-Jacobin, 1807.	Murray
116	Grammont's Memoirs, 3 vol. *portraits*, 1809.	Brumby
117	————, 2 vol. *portraits*, 1811.	Christie
118	Grant on the Superstitions of the Highlands, 2 vol. 1811. Genlis's Siege of Rochelle, 3 vol. in all 5 vol.	Naghton
119	Grahame's Poems, 2 vol. *russia*, 1811.	Murray
120	Guy Mannering, 3 vol. 1815.	Do
121	Grose's Olio, 1796.	Christie
122	Gifford's Baviad, 1810. Elgin's Pursuits in Greece, 1811.	D[r] Sutherland
123	Hutton's Battle of Bosworth Field 1813	Murray
123*	History of the Buccaneers, 2 vol.	Do
124	Historic Gallery of Portraits and Paintings, 7 vol. wanting vol. 5. 1807.	W. Mason

125	Hooke's Roman History, 11 vol. 1810.	Murray
126	Hume's History of England, 8 vol. 1807.	Do
127	Homer's Iliad and Odyssey, by Cowper, 4 vol. *russia*, 1802.	Wiltshire
128	Hayley's Life of Cowper, 4 vol. *russia*, 1806.	Murray
129	Hardy's Life of Lord Charlemont, 2 vol. 1812.	Wiltshire
130	Herodotus, by Beloe, 4 vol. 1806.	Lowe
131	Homeri Ilias, a Clarke, 2 vol. 1760.	Murray
132	Horatius Gesneri, LARGE PAPER, *morocco*, 1806.	Dr Sutherland
133	~~Homeri Ilias, Græcè~~, LARGE PAPER, *Oxon.* 1758.	passed
134	Hume's Essays, 2 vol. 1772.	Murray
135	Hodgson's Lady Jane Grey, 1809. Virgil's Georgics, by Sotheby, 1815. Sotheby's Tragedies, 1814. 3 vol.	Singer
136	Herbert's Helga, 1815. Cunningham's De Rance, 1815. Hobhouse's Poems, and three more.	Do
137	Jane's Beauties of the Poets, 1800. Tighe's Psyche, 1811. Merivale's Orlando, 1814. 3 vol.	Murray

Quarto.

138	Ainsworth's Latin Dictionary, 1796.	Lowe
139	Aikin and Enfield's General Biography, 5 vol. 1799, &c.	Murray
140	Austin on Rhetorical Delivery, *russia*, 1806.	Dr Sutherland
141	Broughton's Letters from a Mahratta Camp 1813	Murray
142	Blair's Grave, with Blake's Designs, 1808.	Rogers
143	Brown's Travels in Africa, 1807.	Wiltshire
144	Bloomfield's General View of the World, 2 vol. 1804.	Murray
145	Bonaparte (Lucien) Charlemagne, où l'Eglise Delivrée, 2 vol. LARGE PAPER. 1814.	Do
146	Bonaparte's Charlemagne, translated by Butler and Hodgson, 2 vol. LARGE PAPER. 1815.	Do
147	Black's Life of Tasso, 2 vol. 1810.	Murray
148	Clarke's Travels, vol. 2 and 3.	Do
149	Carr's Stranger in France, 1803.	Lyttelton
150	Carr's Travels through Denmark, Sweden, &c. 1805.	Do
151	Carr's Tour through Scotland, 1809.	Do
152	Chaucer's Canterbury Tales, by Tyrwhitt, 2 vol. LARGE PAPER, *Oxf.* 1798.	Sutherland

153	Coxe's History of the House of Austria, 3 vol. 1807.	Lyttelton
154	Coxe's Memoirs of the Bourbon Kings of Spain, 3 vol. 1813.	Cotton
155	——— ——— of Sir R. Walpole, 3 vol. 1798.	Wiltshire
156	Culloden Papers, 1815.	Ewing
157	Campbell's Gertrude of Wyoming, 1809. Colman's Poetical Vagaries, 1802, 2 vol.	Murray
158	Croker's Talavera, 1812. Childe Alarique, 1813. Chevy Chase, 1813, 3 vol.	Singer
159	Clifford's Tixall Poetry, 1813.	Do
160	Costume of Turkey, *red morocco*, 1802.	Wiltshire
161	Decker's Gull's Hornbook, by Nott, 1812.	Triphook
162	Davila, Historia delle Guerre Civili di Francia, 2 vol. *Lond.* 1755.	Scrope Davies
163	Edinburgh Encyclopædia, 4 vol. and vol. 5 part I.	Murray
164	Fox's History of James the Second, ELEPHANT PAPER, *russia*, 1808.	Do
165	Elphinstone's Account of Caubul, 1815.	Cotton
166	Gibbon's Miscellaneous Works, 3 vol. 1796.	Calkin
167	Galt's Life of Wolsey, LARGE PAPER, 1812.	Wiltshire
168	Hodgson's Juvenal, 1807.	Singer
169	Holinshed's Chronicles, 6 vol. 1807.	Shairpe
170	Hope's Costume of the Ancients, 2 vol. 1809.	Duncomb
171	Hederici Lexicon Græcum, *russia*, 1803.	Christie
172	Juvenal, by Gifford, 1802.	Murray
173	Illustrations of Northern Antiquities, 1814.	Sir S. Shairpe
174	Thurston's Illustrations of Lord Byron's Corsair, *on India paper*, 1814.	Dr Sutherland
175	Another Copy, *on India paper*, 1814.	Wiltshire
176	Another Copy, *on India paper*,	Allen
177	Another Copy, *on India paper*,	Charnier
178	Two Copies, *on India paper*,	Murray
179	Kinneir's Memoir of a Map of the Persian Empire, *with a map*, 1813.	Sutherland
180	Another Copy, *without the map*, 1813.	Shairpe
181	Kelsall's Phantasm of an University, 1814. Kelsall's Letters from Athens, 1812.	Triphook
182	Lucretius, by Busby, 2 vol. 1813.	Singer
183	Langsdorff's Voyages and Travels, 1813.	Ewing
183*	Lempriere's Universal Biography, 1808.	Scrope Davies
184	Lavater's Physiognomy, by Hunter, 5 vol. *blue mor.* 1789.	Boone

185 Malcolm's Manners and Customs of London, during the 18th Century, 1808. — Sir S. Shairpe
186 Macartney's Embassy to China, 2 vol. 1798. — Wiltshire
187 Maps to Cellarius's Geography, 1806. — Evans
188 Memoirs of Colonel Hutchinson, *russia*, 1806. — Shairpe

Folio.

189 Biographia Britannica, by Kippis, 5 vol. 1778, &c. — Sir S. Shairpe
190 General Dictionary, Historical and Critical, including Bayle, 10 vol. half bound, uncut, 1734. — Murray
191 Herbelot Bibliothèque Orientale, *Maest.* 1776. — Singer
192 Meletii Geographia antiqua et moderna, *in* Lingua Græca, Hodierna, *russia*, *Ven.* — Murray
193 Athenæus, Gr. et Lat., Casauboni, *Lugd.* 1657. — Scrope Davies
194 Stephani Thesaurus Linguæ Græcæ, a Valpy, part the first, 1815. — Singer
195 Nathan, Collection of Music adapted to Poetry of Lord Byron, *blue morocco.* — Murray

SECOND DAY'S SALE.

Octavo et Infra.

196 Brydges's Ruminator, 2 vol. 1813. D'Israeli's Literary Miscellanies, 1801, and 12 more. — Lowe
197 Playfair's Political Portraits, 2 vol. 1813. Intercepted Letters, 1814, and nine more. — Davenport
198 History of Pugilism, 1812. Boxiana, 1812. History of Pedestrianism, 1813. — Finlay
199 Gilchrist's Collection of Scottish Ballads, 2 vol. 1815. Burns' Select Scottish Songs, 2 vol. 1810. — Evans
200 Cottages of Glenburnie, 1810. Florian's Gonsalvo of Cordova, 3 vol. 1792. Carlisle's Poems, 1807. Two-penny Post Bag, And Jacqueline. — Murray
201 Duclos Mémoires Secrets de Louis XIV. et XV. 2 vol., and twelve more. — Evans
202 Hurd's Horace, 2 vol. 1766. Ovid's Metamorphoses, by Garth. Salluste, par Delamelle. 2 vol. Lettres de Ganganelli, 2 vol. — Mrs Priestley
203 Hay's History of the Insurrection at Wexford, 1803. Gazetteer of Scotland, and twelve more. — Murray

204	History of Pedestrianism, 1813. Angelo's School of Fencing, 1787, and nine more.	Mrs Priestley
205	Lord Baltimore's Tour. Voltaire's Henriade in English. Opie's Father, and Daughter, and seven more.	Murray
206	Junius's Letters, 2 vol. *russia*, 1806.	Davenport
207	Junius's Letters, by Woodfall, 3 vol. LARGE PAPER, 1812.	Allen
208	Johnson's Dictionary, 4 vol. *russia*, 1805.	Wiltshire
209	Johnson's Lives of the Poets, 3 vol. *russia*. 1806.	Murray
210	Juvenal and Persius, by Madan, 2 vol. 1807.	Plunkett
211	Juvenal and Persius, Variorum, *L.Bat.* 1664.	Findlay
212	Inchbald's British Theatre, 25 vol. FINE PAPER, 1808.	Murray
213	Inchbald's Collection of Farces, 7 vol. wanting vol. 2, FINE PAPER, 1808.	Do
214	Kaim's Elements of Criticism, 2 vol. *russia*, 1805.	Abercromby
215	Knight on Taste, *russia*, 1808.	Murray
216	Klopstock, and his Friends, 1814. Bidlake's Year, 1813. Paterson's Legend of Iona, 1614. Lewis's Romantic Tales, 4 vol. in all 7 vol.	Evans
217	Labaume's Account of the Campaign in Russia, 1815. Rocca's Memoirs of the War in Spain, 1815, 2 vol.	Abercrombie
218	Lebrun's Barons of Felsheim, 3 vol. Lebrun's My Uncle Thomas, 4 vol. 1801, in all 7 vol. *in russia.*	Evans
219	Locke on the Understanding, 2 vol. *russia*, 1805.	Abercrombie
220	Lempriere's Classical Dictionary, *russia*, 1801.	Lowe
221	Luciani Opera, 10 vol. *Bipont*, 1789.	Murray
222	Lyre of Love, 2 vol. *russia.*	Evans
223	Letters from the North of Scotland, 2 vol. 1815.	Wiltshire
224	Lara and Jacqueline, 1814. Little's Poems, 1806. Strangford's Camoens, in all 3 vol.	Murray
225	Memoirs of Talleyrand, 2 vol. 1805. Biographical anecdotes of the founders of the French Republic, 2 vol. Barre's History of the French Consulate, in all 5 vol.	Evans
226	Meiner's History of the Female Sex, 4 vols. 1808.	Plunkett
227	Miseries of Human Life, 2 vol. *plates*, *russia*, 1807.	Wiltshire
228	Montaigne, Essais de, 3 vol. 1802.	Sullivan
229	Mrs. Moore's Cælebs, 2 vol. 1808.	Wiltshire
230	Memoirs of the Margravine of Bareith, 2 vol. 1812.	Murray
231	Middleton's Life of Cicero, 3 vol, *russia*, 1804.	Do

232	Milton's Prose Works, 7 vol. LARGE PAPER, wants vol. 3. 1806.	Smedley
233	Montaigne's Essays, 3 vol. 1811.	Mrs. Priestley
234	Mirabeau de la Monarchie Prussienne sous Frédéric le Grand, 7 vol. and Atlas in folio. 1788.	Murray
235	Mitford's History of Greece, 6 vol. *russia*, 1795.	Do
236	Murphy's Life of Garrick, 2 vol. *russia*, 1801.	Cotton
237	Montesquieu's Spirit of Laws, *russia*, 1793.	Murray
238	Memoirs of Comines, 2 vol. 1723.	Graham
238*	Massinger's Plays by Gifford, 4 vol. 1805.	Giles
239*	Another copy, 4 vol. 1813.	Wiltshire
239	Machiavelli, Opere di, 13 vol. *in russia*, *Milan*. 1804.	Murray
240	Mémoires de Goldoni, 2 vol. *Par.* 1814.	Payne & Foss
241	Museum Criticum, parts 2, 3, 4, and 5.	Evans
242	Memoirs of Cooke, by Dunlap, 2 vol. 1813.	Plunkett
243	Naylor's History of Germany, 3 vol. 1816.	Do
244	Nichols's Literary Anecdotes of the 18th Century, 7 vol. 1812.	Cotton
245	Nelson's (Lord) Letters to Lady Hamilton, 2 vol. 1814.	Plunkett
246	Novum Testamentum Græcum, *russia*, *Oxon*. 1805.	Wiltshire
247	Opie's Simple Tales, 4 vol. Opie's Tales of Real Life, 3 vol. in all 7 vol.	Maynard
248	Ossian's Poems, 3 vol. *russia*, 1803.	Wiltshire
249	Ossian's Poems, Gaelic and Latin, 3 vol. *russia*, 1807.	Murray
250	Poets of Great Britain from the time of Chaucer to Sir William Jones. Bagster's edition, bound in 61 vol. *russia*, in a travelling case, 1807.	Giles
251	Poetry of the Anti-Jacobin, 1807. Hunt's Feast of the Poets, 1814. Poetical Epistles, 1813. Lay of the Scottish Fiddle, 1814, 4 vol.	Plunkett
252	Percy's Reliques of Ancient Poetry, 3 vol. 1775.	Murray
253	Peregrine Pickle, 4 vol. 18mo. FINE PAPER, Roderic Random, 2 vol. in all 6 vol.	Sir J Abercromb.
254	Peter Pindar's Works, 5 vol. 1792.	Davies
255	Public Characters, 8 vol. *russia*, 1799.	Davenport
256	Pinkerton's Modern Geography, *russia*, 1803.	Davenport
257	Pope's Works by Bowles, 10 vol. 1806.	Sir J. Abercromby
258	Poetical Register, 4 vol. *russia*, and vol. 5 and 6, *in boards*, 1802.	Charnier
259	Paley's Philosophy, 2 vol. *russia*, 1806.	Boone

260	Parkes's Chemical Catechism, 1808.	W. Mason
261	Pursuits of Literature, 1808.	Murray
262	Port Royal Greek Grammar, *russia*, 1797.	Murray
263	Plutarch's Lives by Langhorne, 6 vol. 1809.	Boone
264	Potts's Gazetteer of England, 1810.	Wiltshire
265	Polybius by Hampton, 3 vol. 1809.	W. Mason
266	Porteus's Lectures, 2 vol. 1813.	Murray
267	Paradise of Coquettes, 1814. Hunt's Feast of the Poets, 1814. Pratt's Poems, 1807. Philosophy of Nature, 2 vol. 1813, 5 vol.	Evans
268	Petronius Arbiter, Variorum, *Amst.* 1669. Martialis Opera, Variorum, *L.Bat.* 1670, 2 vol.	Murray
269	Quarterly Review, 11 odd numbers.	Lowe
270	Ring and the Well, 4 vol. 1808. Magic of Wealth, 4 vol. 1815.	Lowndes
271	Rogers's Poems, 1812.	Murray
272	Rogers's Poems, *yellow morocco*, 1812.	Murray
273	Rousseau's Confessions, 5 vol. 1796.	Wiltshire
274	Roscoe's Life of Lorenzo de Medici, 3 vol. 1806.	Graham
275	Rolliad and Probationary Odes, 1799.	Singer
276	Another Copy. 1812.	Plunkett
277	Rabelais's Works, 4 vol. LARGE PAPER, 1807.	Rogers
278	Revolutionary Plutarch, 3 vol. 1806. Secret History of the Court of St. Cloud, 3 vol. 1806. Secret History of Bonaparte's Cabinet, 1811, 7 vol.	Giles
279	Ripperda's Life if Alberoni, 2 vol. Laing's History of Scotland. Roche on the Author of Junius.	Murray
280	Richardson on Eastern Literature, *russia*, 1778.	Murray
281	Ritson's Scottish Songs, 2 vol. 1794.	Findlay
282	Shakespeare's Plays, 20 vol. Bell's edition, FINE PAPER, 1788.	Murray
283	Swift's Works, by Scott, 19 vol. 1814.	Wellesley
284	Southey's Madoc, 2 vol. 1807. Shakespeare's Poems, 2 vol. 1804, in all 4 vol.	Murray
285	St. Pierre's Studies of Nature, 3 vol. 1799.	Christie
286	Scott's Lay of the Last Minstrel, *russia*, 1807.	Sir J Abercrombie
287	Scott's Ballads, *russia*, 1806.	Ewing
288	Scott's Border Minstrelsy, 3 vol. 1802.	Evans
289	Sheridan on Elocution, *russia*, 1798.	Wiltshire
290	Sevigné, Lettres de, 11 vol. *in russia*, *Par.* 1806.	Holland
291	Œuvres de Saint-Simon, 13 vol. *Strasb.* 1791.	J. Hunter
292	Sismondi, de la Littérature du Midi, 4 vol. *in russia*, *Par.* 1813.	Keysall
293	Sinclair's Code of Health, 4 vol. 1807.	Wiltshire

294	Another Copy, 4 vol. 1807.	Evans
295	Smither's Poems, *russia*, 1807.	Ewing
296	Stephens's Life of Horne Tooke, 2 vol. 1813.	G. Chalmers
297	Stewart's Philosophy of the Human Mind, *russia*,	Murray
298	Stewart's Outlines of Moral Philosophy, *russia*,	Do
299	Spalding's History of the Troubles in Scotland, 2 vol. 1792.	Holland
300	Segur's History of Frederic II. vol. [*sic*] Segur on Women, 2 vol. Rival Roses, 2 vol. in all 7 vol.	Richard
301	Thiebault's Anecdotes of Frederic the Second, 2 vol. 1805. Correspondence of Grimm and Diderot, 2 vol. 1814, in 4 vol. [*sic*]	Wiltshire
302	Turnbull's Voyage round the World, 3 vol. *russia*, 1805.	S. Davies
303	Tasso's Jerusalem, by Hoole, 2 vol. *russia*, 1803.	Murray
304	Tom Jones, 3 vol. *Cooke's edition*, *fine paper*.	Binder
305	Taylor's Travels to India, 2 vol. 1799. Galt's Letters from the Levant, 1813.	G. Chalmers
306	Tyers's Tracts, History of Pedestrianism, and six more.	Miller
307	Tacitus, by Murphy, 8 vol. 1807.	S. Davies
308	Tales of the East, 3 vol. 1812.	Do
309	Tasso, Gerusalemme Liberata, 2 vol. *mor. Lond.*	Murray
310	Tasso, Gerusalemme Liberata, 2 vol. *Par.* 1776. Tasso, Gerusalemme Liberata, 3 vol. 1813. Dante, 3 vol. 1808.	Murray
311	Tasso, Gerusalemme Liberata, 2 vol. *Par.* 1785. Petrarca, *Ven.* 1800. Dante, 3 vol. *Par.* 1787.	Boone
312	Vathek, par Beckford, 1815.	Quillinan
313	Voltaire's Works, by Francklin, Smollett, &c. 35 vol. 1778.	Wiltshire
314	Vigerus de Idiotismis Græcis, *russia*, *Lips.* 1802.	Plunkett
315	Van-Ess's life of Bonaparte, 6 vol. 1808.	W. Mason
316	Williams's (Miss) Narrative of the late Events in France. 1815.	G. Chalmers
317	Watson's Apology for the Bible and for Christianity, 2 vol.	Murray
318	Wordsworth's Lyrical Ballads, 2 vol. *russia*. Wordsworth's Poems, 2 vol. *russia*, 1807.	Holland
319	Walsingham, by Mrs. Robinson, 4 vol. *russia*, 1805.	Ld Elmley
320	Warton on the Genius of Pope, 2 vol. 1806.	Holland
321	Wanley's Wonders of the Little World, 2 vol. 1806.	Lowe
322	Wraxall's Memoirs of his Own Time, 2 vol. 1815.	Wiltshire
323	Wakefield's Correspondence with Fox, 1813.	Murray

324	Kirke White's Remains, 2 vol. Dutens Memoirs, 5 vol. Goldoni's Memoirs, 2 vol. in all 9 vol.	S. Davies
325	Zimmermann's Reflections Seward's Memoirs of Darwin, and Sturm's and Reflections [*sic*], in all 4 vol.	Boone
326	Erskine on the War, Duppa on Junius. Duppa's Memoirs of a Political and Literary Character, in all 3 vol.	Murray

Quarto.

327	Malcolm's History of Persia, 2 vol. *russia*, 1815.	Fletcher
328	Macdiarmid's Lives of British Statesman [*sic*], *russia*, 1807.	Wiltshire
329	Moore's Poems, *russia*, 1806.	Murray
330	Lord Orford's Works, 5 vol. *green morocco*, 1798.	Do
331	Park's Travels in Africa, vol. 2, 1815.	Wiltshire
332	Plates to illustrate Lord Byron's Poems, LARGE PAPER, *proof impressions.*	Allen
333	Painter's Palace of Pleasure, 3 vol. 1813.	Ewing
334	Potter's Travels in Russia and Sweden, 2 vol. 1809.	Evans
335	Playfair's British Family Antiquity, illustrating the Histories of the Noble Families of the United Kingdom, with chronological Charts, 5 vol. 1809.	S. Davies
336	Petrarca, con le Osservazioni di Muratori, *Modena*, 1811.	Murray
337	Pauli (Demetrii) Lexicon Tripartitum Linguæ Græcæ Hodiernæ, Italicæ et Gallicæ, 3 vol. *russia*, *Vien.* 1790.	Do
338	Roscoe's Life of Leo the 10th, 4 vol. 1805.	Do
339	Sonnini's Travels in Egypt, 1800.	S. Davies
340	Scott's Marmion, 1808.	Wiltshire
341	Another Copy, 1808.	Sir J. Abercrombie
342	Southey's Roderick, 1814.	Wiltshire
343	Stewart's Philosophical Essays, *russia*, 1810.	Murray
344	——— Philosophy of the Human Mind, vol. 2. 1814.	Duncombe
345	Stewart's History of Bengal, 1813.	S. Davies
346	Sotheby's Saul, 1807. Galt's Tragedies, 1812, 2 vol.	Wiltshire
347	Stark's Medical Works, 1788.	} Duncomb
348	Smith's General Atlas, 1808.	}
349	Sophocles a Brunck, 2 vol. *russia*, *Argent.* 1786.	Hawkins
350	Sallust's Works, by Stewart, 2 vol, 1806.	Sutherland

351 Turner's History of England, vol. 1. 1814. Evans
352 Tweddell's Remains 1815. Ewing
353 Townsend's Armageddon, 1815. The Trident, 1802. Murray
354 Von Buch's Travels through Norway and Lapland, 1813. Wiltshire
355 Thornton's Sporting Tour through England, *russia*, 1804. Bender
356 Veniere, Compendio di Grammatica in Dialetto Greco Volgare, con la traduzione, *russia*, *Triest.* 1799. Triphook
357 Varchi, l'Ercolano, *Fir.* 1730. Bender
358 Virgilius Heynii, 8 vol. LARGE PAPER, *red mor. Lond.* 1793. Ld Keith
359 Virgil's Æneid, by Beresford, *russia*, 1794. Miller
359* Ulachi Thesaurus Encyclopædicæ Basis Quadrilinguis, *Ven.* 1659. Triphook
360 Woodhouslee's Life of Lord Kames, 2 vol. *russia*, 1807. Singer
361 Wordsworth's Excursion, a poem, 1814. Ryan
362 ———— White Doe of Rylstone, 1815. Singer
363 Thurston's Illustrations of Lord Byron's Corsair, *on India paped* [*sic*], 1814. Ld Keith
364 Another Copy, *on India paper*, 1814. Bender
365 Another Copy, *on India paper*, 1814. J. Hunter
366 Another Copy, *on India paper*, 1814. Ewing
367 Three Copies, *on India paper*, 1814. Murray
368 Two Copies, *on India paper*, 1814. Plunkett

Folio.

369 Thomson's Collection of Original Scottish Airs, 4 vol. in 2. Violincello Accompaniment, and Violin Accompaniment. Triphook
370 Thomson's Collection of Original Welch [*sic*] airs, 2 vol. and Violin and Violincello Accompaniment. Do
371 Tindal's Continuation of Rapin, 2 vol. 1751. Martin
372 Grimestone's Historie of the Netherlands, 1609. Murray
373 Moreri, Dictionnaire Historique, 10 vol. *Par.* 1759. Nornaville
374 The *Large Plates to Boydell's Shakspeare*, engraved by the first Artists, VERY BEAUTIFUL PROOF IMPRESSIONS, *bound in red morocco.* Fletcher

375	Portrait of the Rev. Dr. Parr, engraved by Turner after Hall. *Proof Impression, in a gilt frame.*	Singer
376	Portrait of Bonaparte, engraved by Morghen, *very fine impression, in a gilt frame.*	Singer
377	Portrait of Machiavel, engraved by Cipriani, *in a gilt frame.*	Do
378	Portrait of Campbell (Author of the Pleasures of Hope,) after Laurence [*sic*], *in a gilt frame.*	Wiltshire
379	Portrait of Kean, in Richard III., engraved by Turner.	Singer
380	Portrait of the Right Hon. W. Pitt, from the Statue by Nollekens, engraved by Heath. *Proof impression.*	Colnaghi
381	Portrait of Jackson, the Pugilist, a Crayon Drawing, *in a gilt frame.*	Murray
382	A Skreen six feet high, covered with NUMEROUS PORTRAITS OF ACTORS, Scene Prints, Portraits of Pugilists, and Representations of Boxing Matches, &c.	Do
383	A Silver Cup and Cover, elegantly chased. The weight is 29oz. 8dwts.	[no purchaser]

Sale Catalogue (1827)

Octavo et Infra.

1	Aucher, Dictionnaire Arménien et François, 2 vol. 1812.	Behn
2	Adamson's Life of Camoens, 2 vol. 1820.	Hunter
3	Aristophanes by Mitchell, vol. 2, 1822.	James
4	Achilles Tatius, Amours de Leucippe et de Clitophon, 2 vol. *Par.* 1797. Chariton, Amours de Chércas et Callirrhoé, 2 vol. *Par.* 1797. Heliodore, Amours de Theagénes et Chariclée, 2 vol. 1796. Eustathe, Amours d'Ismene et d'Ismenias, 1796. Longus, Amours de Daphnis et Chloe, 1797. Lucian, l'Asne, 1797. Prodromus, Amours de Rhodante, 1797. Parthenius, Affections d'Amour 1797. Xenophon, Abrocome et Anthia, 1797, 12 vol.	Payne
5	Atherstone's Last Days of Herculaneum, *Presentation copy to Lord Byron.* 1821.	Brumby
6	Anecdotes de la Cour de France pendant la faveur de la Marquise de Pompadour, *Par.* 1802.	Badeley

7	Lord Aberdeen's Principles of Beauty in Grecian Architecture, 1822.	Fletcher
8	Anacreon, Gr. et Lat. *with the Autograph of Percy Bysshe Shelly* [*sic*], *Glasg.* 1783.	Brumby
9	Aulus Gellius, *Aldus*, 1515.	Henniker
10	Anquetil, Esprit de la Ligue, 3 vol. *Par.* 1808.	Payne
11	Antar, a Bedoueen Romance by Hamilton, 4 vol. 1819.	Do
12	Aristophanes by Mitchell, vol. 2, 1822.	Singer
13	Bayle, Dictionnaire Historique et Critique, vol. 1 to 12. *Par.* 1820.	Dalan
14	Another copy, vol. 1 to 11, *ib.* 1820.	Do
15	Biographie des Hommes Vivants, 5 vol. vol. 1 imperfect, *Par.* 1816.	Badeley
16	Bassompierre's Embassy to England, with Notes, 1819.	Herald
17	The Banquet, 1819. The Dessert, 1819, 2 vol.	Thornton
18.	Butler's Reminiscences, 1822.	Brumby
19	——— History of the English Catholics, vol. 3 and 4, *Presentation copy*, 1821.	Do
20	Beyle, Histoire de la Peinture en Italie, 2 vol. *Par.* 1817.	Badeley
21	Birbeck's Notes of a Journey in America, 1818. Birbeck's Letters from Illinois, 1818. 2 vol.	Brumby
22	L. Bonaparte, Documents Historiques sur la Hollande, 3 vol. *Lond.* 1820.	Lewin
23	Beloe's Sexagenarian, 2 vol. 1817.	Badeley
24	Baillie's Metrical Legends, 1821.	Watson
25	Lord Byron's Werner, 1823.	Ogden
26	Lord Byron to Bowles on Pope, 1821. Antologia, No 2, 5, and 16. Brooke's Retrospection, 1822.	Brumby
27	Byron, Oeuvres Completes, vol. 2, 4, and 6, *Par.* 1821.	Ogden
28	Barrow's History of Voyages to the Arctic Regions, 1818.	Hunter
29	Bibliotheca Pisanorum Veneta, 2 vol. stained, *Ven.* 1807.	Brumby
30	Baldi, Vita di Guidobaldo Duca d'Urbino, 2 vol. *Mil.* 1821.	Do
31	Beauties of English Poetry, *Paris*, 1818.	Hunter
32	Bibliotheque Universelle pour Jan. Fev. et Mars, 1819, *Gen.* 1819.	Badeley
33	Bottani, Storia della Citta de Caorle, *Ven.* 1811.	Brumby

34	Beaumarchais, Oeuvres choisies, 4 vol. *Par.* 1818. Memoires de Bussy Rabutin, 4 vol. *Par.* 1696.	Way
35	Cramer on Hannibal's Passage over the Alps, 1820.	Payne
36	Cottin, Malvina, 3 vol. Amélie Mansfield, 3 vol. Claire d'Albe. Mathilde, vol. 3 and 4, in all 9 vol.	Brumby
37	Casti's Court of Beasts, 1819. Croly's Angel of the World, 1820. Croly on the Death of the Princess Charlotte, 1818. Chafin's Anecdotes of Cranbourn Chase, 1818.	Do
38	Coxe, Histoire de la Maison d'Autriche, 5 vol. *Par.* 1810.	Bossange
39	Crebillon le fils, Œuvres, 7 vol. 1779.	Way
40	Campbell's Specimens of the British Poets, 7 vol. 1819.	Brumby
41	Crabbe's Tales of the Hall, 2 vol. 1819.	Do
42	Curran's Life of Curran, 2 vol. 1819.	Hunter
43	Castéra, Histoire de Catherine II. 4 vol. *Par.* 1809.	Brumby
44	Barry Cornwall's Flood of Thessaly, 1823. Barry Cornwall's Dramatic Scenery, 1819.	Fletcher
45	Cobbett's Year's Residence in America, 3 vol. 1819.	Money
46	Chaboulon, Memoires de Napoleon, 2 vol. *Lond.* 1819.	Dalan
47	Chénier, Poesies Diverses, *Par.* 1818. Pigault Le Brun, le Beau-Pere et le Gendre, 2 vol. 1822.	Brumby
48	Coleridge's Biographia Literaria, 2 vol. *with Lord Byron's Autograph*, 1817.	Brumby
49	Catullus by Lamb, 2 vol. 1821.	Singer
50	Consciences Littéraires d'à-présent, *Par.* 1818.	Walther
51	Criminal Trials, illustrative of the Heart of Mid Lothian, 1818.	Money
52	Diedo, Storia di Venezia, 15 vol. in 7, *Ven.* 1792.	Brumby
53	Diodoro Siculo, volgarizzato di Compagnoni, 7 vol. *Milan*, 1820.	Do
54	D'Epinay, Memoires et Correspondance, 3 vol. *Par.* 1818.	Do
55	Dallas's Poems, 1819.	Do
56	D'Israeli on the Literary Charater, 1818.	Badeley
57	De Bosset's Proceedings in Parga and the Ionian Islands, 1819.	Brumby
58	Davies's Life of Garrick, 2 vol. 1808.	Warder
59	Daru, Histoire Venise, 7 vol. *Par.* 1819.	Hobhouse
60	D'Israeli's Curiosities of Literature, vol. 3, 1817.	Rainford

61	Du Cygne, Fons Eloquentiæ, *Ven.* 1713. Benzone Nella, Poema, *Ven.* 1820. Buxton on Prison Discipline, 1818. Erskine du Christianisme, *Par.* 1822, 4 vol.	Singer
62	Erodoto, da Mustoxidi, vol. 1, *Mil.* 1820.	Do
63	Edgeworth's Memoirs of Lovel Edgeworth, 2 vol. 1820.	Lackland
64	———— Harrington and Ormond, vol. 2 and 3, *with Lord Byron's Autograph*, 1817.	Brumby
65	Frederic Roi de Prusse, Oeuvres, 13 vol. wanting vol. 2 and 3, 1789.	Do
66	Firenzuola, Opere, 6 vol. *Pisa*, 1816.	Do
67	Fearon's Sketches of America, 1818. Cause e Effetti della Confederazione Renana, 2 vol. vol. 1 a little stained, *Ital.* 1819.	Warder
68	Fouqué's Sintram, 1820. Undine, by Soane, 1818.	Rainford
69	Forsyth's Remarks on Italy, 1816.	Miss Wilson
70	Faber on the Mysteries of the Cabiri, 2 vol. 1803.	Warder
71	Fortiguerri's Ricciardetto, First Canto, by Lord Glenbervie, 1822.	Fletcher
72	Franceschinis, Morte di Socrate, *Ven.* 1820.	Rainford
73	Foscolo, Ricciarda, Tragedia, *Lond.* 1820.	Pickering
74	Franceschinis, Morte di Socrati [*sic*], *Ven.* 1820.	With No. 72
75	Giuseppe tradotto dall' Angiolini, 7 vol. *Milan*, 1821.	Bossange
76	Galiffe's Italy and its Inhabitants, 2 vol. 1820.	Brumby
77	Gibbon's Life and Miscellaneous Works, 7 vol. *Basil.* 1796.	Do
78	Greek Tragic Theatre, 7 vol. *Lond. Lord Byron has occasionally pencilled some of the most striking passages.* 1779.	Webb
[no lot numbered 79]		
80	Ginguené, Histoire Litteraire d'Italie, 9 vol. *Par.* 1811.	Brumby
81	Another copy, vol. 7, 8, and 9, *Par.* 1819.	Dalan
82	Geoffroy, Cours de Litterature Dramatique, 5 vol. *Par.* 1819.	Hunter
83	Georgel, Memoires de la fin du XVIII siecle, 6 vol. *Par.* 1817.	Brumby
84	Galiani, Correspondance Inédite, 2 vol. *Par.* 1818.	Lackland
85	Grimm, Correspondance Littéraire, 16 vol. *Par.* 1813.	Brumby
86	Godwin's Mandeville, 3 vol. 1817.	Rainford

87 Gleanings in Buenos Ayres, 1818. Guigou, Topographie de Livourne, *Liv.* 1814. Galignani's Magazine, 3 odd numbers. — Badeley
88 Galt's Annals of the Parish, 1821. Vie Polemique de Voltaire, 1802. Fontaine, Contes, 2 vol. *Par.* 1813. — Brumby
89 Gourgaud, Campagne de 1815, *Lond.* 1818. Letters from St. Helena, 1818. — Rainford
90 Giannotti, Opere, 3 vol. *Pisa*, 1819. — Brumby
91 Guidi, Poesie, 1726. Mayeux, Sept Journées, 2 vol. 1818. Jeunesse de Florian, 1812. — Ogden
92 Hackett's Narrative of the Expedition to South America, 1818. Dono all' Amicizia, *presentation to Lord Byron*, *Vicenz.* 1817. — Brumby
93 Holland's Life of Lope de Vega, 2 vol. *presentation copy*, 1817. — Joy
94 Holcroft's Memoirs, 3 vol. 1816. — Lackland
95 Lady Hervey's Letters, 1821. — Brumby
96 Haslam on Madness and Melancholy, 1809. — Badeley
97 Hogg's Brownie of Bodsbeck, 2 vol. 1818. — Duncan
98 Hodgson's Friends, a Poem, 1818. Hoare's Hints to Travellers in Italy, 1815. — Brumby
99 Hazlitt's Lectures on the English Poets, 1818. — Rainford
100 Sir B. Hobhouse's Travels in France, Italy, &c. 1796. — Hunter
101 Hobhouse's Last Reign of Napoleon, 2 vol. 1817. — Brumby
102 Hayley's Life of Milton, *Basil.* 1799 — E. L. Badeley
103 Histoire de la Nouvelle Russie, 3 vol. *Par.* 1820. — Brumby
104 Histoire du Prince Eugene, 5 vol. *Vien.* 1790. — Do
105 ——— de Pierre III. de Russie, 2 vol. *Par.* 1799. — Do
106 Karamsin, Istoria di Russia, 6 vol. *Ven.* 1820. — Do
107 King's Anecdotes of his Own Times, 1818. — E. L. Badeley
108 Keate's Account of the Pellew Islands, *Basil.* 1789. — Brumby
109 Keat's [*sic*] Endymion, 1818. Keat's [*sic*] Poems, 1817. — Rainford
110 Luchet, Histoire Littéraire de Voltaire, 6 vol. *Cassel.* 1780. — Bossange
111 Laugier, Istoria di Venezia, 12 vol. *Ven.* 1778. — Brumby
112 ——————————— vol. 3 to 12, 1778. — Money
113 Pigault Le Brun, Jerome, 4 vol. 1818. Adelaide de Méran, 4 vol. 1820. La Famille Luceval, 4 vol. 1819. Enfant du Carnaval, 3 vol. 1818. Folie Espagnole, 4 vol. 1820. — Brumby

114	Pigault Le Brun, l'Officieux, 2 vol. 1819. Garçon Sans Souci, 2 vol. 1818. L'Egoisme, 2 vol, 1819. Melanges, 2 vol. 1816. Angelique et Janneton, 2 vol.	Do
114*	Hunt's Foliage.	Drane
115	Pigault Le Brun, Une Macedoine, 4 vol. Tableaux de Societé, 4 vol. 1811. Cent Vingt Jours, 4 vol. Monsieur Martin, 2 vol.	Bossange
116	——— l'Officieux, 2 vol. 1819. Le Citateur, 2 vol. 1811. L'Homme à Projets, 4 vol. 1819. Théatre, 6 vol. 1818.	Do
117	——— Monsieur de Robeville, 4 vol. 1818, and 4 more.	Do
118	Leake's Topography of Athens, 1821.	Webb
119	La Harpe, Œuvres Posthumes, 4 vol. 1806. Annuaire Historique Universel, 1820. Lucien, par D'Ablancourt, 2 vol. in 1, 1697.	Mitchell
120	Le Sage, Histoire de Gil Blas, 4 vol. *Par.* 1818.	Warder
121	Luciano, Opere, tradotte da Manzi, 3 vol. *Losan.* 1819.	Singer
122	Lamb's Works, 2 vol. 1818. Luttrell's Letters to Julia, 1822. Lake's Poems, 1823.	Glynn
123	Lyndsay's Dramas of the Ancient World, 1822.	W. Clarke
124	Las Casas's Memoirs, 1818. Letters from the Cape of Good Hope, 1817. Manuscript de l'Isle de l'Elbe, 1818, 3 vol.	Rainford
125	Levati, Viaggi di Petrarca in Francia, Germania ed in Italia, 5 vol. *Milan*, 1820.	Behn
126	Mémoires du Duc de Richlieu, 9 vol. *Par.* 1790.	Bossange
127	Morellet, Melanges de Littérature, 4 vol.: vol. 1 slightly damaged by a nail, *Par.* 1818.	Swainston
128	Le Mercier, Cours Analytique de Littérature, 4 vol. *Par.* 1817.	Behn
129	Montbron sur la Littérature des Hebreux, 3 vol. in 4, *Par.* 1819.	Nowell
130	Middleton's Life of Cicero, 3 vol. 1755.	Brumby
131	Matthiæ's Greek Grammar, 2 vol. 1818.	Payne
132	Marc Aurele ou Histoire Philosophique de Marc Antonin, 4 vol. and Atlas in 4to. *Par.* 1820.	Bossange
133	Morgan's France, 2 vol. 1818.	Mark
134	——— Florence Macarthy, 4 vol. 1818.	Do
135	Matthews's Diary of an Invalid, 1820.	Pickering

136 M'Leod's Voyage to Lewchew, 1818. Rainford
137 Mirabeau, Discours et Opinions, par Barthe, 3 vol. *Par.* 1820. Bossange
138 Murray's History of Discoveries in Africa, 2 vol. 1817. Hunter
139 Mosca, Geografia Moderna, 2 vol. *Bol.* 1819. Warder
140 Mémoires de Retz et de Joli, 6 vol. *Gen.* 1777. Payne
141 Marmontel, Mémoires, 4 vol. *Par.* 1807. Marmontel, Nouveaux Contes Moraux, 5 vol. 1801. Rainford
142 Melincourt, 3 vol. 1817. Montgomery's Greenland, 1819. Polidori's Ernestus Berchtold, 1819. Mirabeau, Lettres à Sophie, 4 vol. 1818. Do
143 Lady Montague, Œuvres, 4 vol. *Par.* 1804. Wraxall, Mémoires Historique, 2 vol. 1817. Cobbett, Maitre Anglais, 1815. Rainford
144 Mathias, Poesie Liriche Toscane, *presentation copy*, *Napol.* 1818. Longman
145 Morelli, Operette, 3 vol. *Ven.* 1820. Cooney
146 Molina, Memorie di Storia Naturale, 2 vol. *Bol.* 1821. Critique des Mémoires de Bonneval, 1738. Singer
147 Mémoires de Napoleon, livre 9, 1820. O'Meara, Napoleon en Exil, 2 vol. *Par.* 1822. Manuscrit venu de St. Helene, 1817. Macirone's Facts relating to Murat, 1817. Mark
148 Nodier, Melanges de Littérature, 2 vol. 1820. Odeleben, Campagne de 1813 en Saxe, 2 vol. 1817. Swainston
149 Omero, Iliade, da Monti, 2 vol. *Milan.* 1820. North
150 Ossian, Nuovi Canti, da Leoni, 3 vol. *with Lord Byron's Autograph*, *Ven.* 1818. Brumby
151 Osservatore Fiorentino sugli Edifizi della sua Patria, 8 vol. in 4, *Firenz.* 1821. Singer
152 Onguant pour la brulure. *Col.* (*Elz.*) 1669. Boussole des Amans, (*Eliz.*) 1668, and other tracts in the volume. Money
153 Pope's Works, by Warton, 9 vol. *Basil.* 1803. Hobhouse
154 Pitaval, Cause Celebri ed Interessanti con le Sentenze che le hanno decise, 20 vol. *Par.* 1757. Processo contro li Gesuiti, *Par.* 1760. Brumby
155 Plumtre's Letters from the Continent, 1799. Payne
156 Priestley's Memoirs, 1805. Rainford
157 Philostratus's Life of Apollonius of Tyana, 1809. James
158 Poetic Mirror, *with Lord Byron's autograph*, 1816. Longman
159 Petronius Arbiter, Variorum, 1669. F North

160 Pindaro, Odi, tradotte ed illustrate da Mezzanotte, 2 vol. *Pisa*, 1819. Singer
161 Prévost, Mémoires d'un Homme de Qualité, 3 vol. 1808. Voltaire, Romans, 3 vol. *Par.* 1800. Frost
162 Regnard, Œuvres, avec des remarques par Garnier, 6 vol. *Par.* 1810. Rainford
163 Rousselin, Vie du General Hoche, 2 vol. *Par.* 1798. Money
164 Ramsay, Histoire de la Revolution d'Amérique, 2 vol. *Par.* 1787. Rainford
165 Ricci, l'Italiade, Poema, *Livorn.* 1819. Money
166 Histoire de la Vie et des Ouvrages de Rousseau, 2 vol. *Par.* 1821. Badeley
167 Rousseau, la Nouvelle Heloise, 3 vol. 1792. Rousseau, Confessions, 6 vol. 1782. Payne
168 Rakitsch, il Dialoghista Illirico-Italiano, *Ven.* 1810. Singer
169 Ramsay's Travels of Cyrus, *Par.* 1814. Rhododaphne, a Poem, 1818. Money
170 Southey's Life of Wesley, 2 vol. 1820. Hunter
171 Sterne's Tristram Shandy, 2 vol. *Basil.* 1803. Payne
172 Stendhal, Rome, Naples et Florence, en 1817, *Par.* 1817. Bossange
173 Schlegel's Lectures on the History of Literature, 2 vol. 1818. Nicol
174 Spence's Anecdotes, by Malone, 1820. Money
175 Senofonte, la Cyropedia, da Regis, 2 vol. *Milan*, 1821. Senofonte, Storie Greche, da Gandini, *Mil.* 1821. Behn
176 Saabye's Greenland, 1818. Sketch of the Military Power of Russia, 1817, 2 vol. Nattali
177 Bysshe Shelley's Prometheus Unbound, 1820. Fletcher
178 Another copy, 1820. Glynn
179 Sismondi, Storia dei Francesi, vol. 1, *Milan*, 1822. Sartorius dei Popoli d'Italia sotto li Gotti, 1820. Saggio di Estetica, stained, 1822. Schiller, il Visionario, 1819. Singer
180 Sir W. Scott's Halidon Hill, *presentation copy, with an inscription on the fly-leaf*, 1822. Pratt
181 Smith's Philosophical Essays, *Basil.* 1799. Vigors on Poetic Licence, 1813. Singer
182 Senecæ Tragœdiæ, 1589. Theodosii et Valentiniani 3 Novellæ Leges, 1766. Hobhouse
183 Taciti Opera, notis Variorum, 2 vol. *Elzev.* 1672. Do
184 Tooke's View of the Russian Empire, 3 vol. 1799. Hunter

185	Tasso's Jerusalem, by Fairfax, vol. 2, 1818. Hogg's Winter Evening Tales, vol. 2, 1820.	Money
186	Vestriad, 1819. Unknown of the Pyrenees, 1817. Vasselier, Contes Gais et Badins, 1819, 3 vol.	Fletcher
187	Urquhart's Commentaries on Classical Learning, 1803.	Money
188	Vasi, Itinéraire Instructif de Rome, 2 vol. *cuts*, *Rome*, 1816.	Do
189	Vie de Voltaire, 1789. Varillas Anecdotes de Florence, 2 vol. 1787.	E. L. Badeley
190	Wraxall's Memoirs of his Own Time, 3 vol. 1818.	Hunter
191	Sir C. Hanbury Williams's Works, 3 vol. 1822.	Do
192	Wieland, Aristippe et ses Contemporains, 7 vol. *Par.* 1805.	Bossange
193	Women, or pour et contre, 3 vol. 1818. Whistlecraft's Poem, Cantos [*sic*], 1818, and 2 copies of Cantos 3 and 4.	Singer
194	Warton on Pope, 2 vol. much damaged, 1762. Warden's Letters respecting Bonaparte, 1816.	Michael
195	Wishart's Memoirs of the Marquis of Montrose, 1819.	Duncan
196	Lot of Odd Volumes.	Money
197	—— Odd Volumes.	Singer

Quarto.

198	Biblia Sacra Armena, *with Lord Byron's autograph*, 1805.	Brumby
199	Belzoni's Travels in Egypt and Nubia, with the Appendix, 1820.	Lackland
200	Burckhardt's Travels in Nubia, 1819.	Borne
201	———— Travels in Syria and the Holy Land, 1822.	O Martin
202	Bowdich's Mission to Ashantee, 1819.	Rainford
203	Baruffaldi, Vita di Ariosto, *Ferrar*, 1807.	Singer
204	Bell's Account of the Huntingdon Peerage, 1820.	Lackland
205	Bertolonii Amoenitates Italicæ, opuscula de Re Herbaria, *Bonon.* 1819.	Singer
206	Berry's Life of Lady Rachel Russell, 1819.	Rainford
207	Comment on Dante, vol. 1, *London*, (*Italy*), 1822.	Pickering
208	Clarke's Travels. Part the Third, Section the First, Scandinavia, 1819.	Borne

209	Coxe's Life of the Duke of Marlborough, 3 vol. 1818.	Do
210	Ciakciak, Dizionario Italiano-Armeno-Turco.	Brumby
211	Foscarini, Discorso, *Ven.* 1819.	Singer
212	Fitzclarence's Journey from India to England, 1819.	Beckley
213	Hume's Correspondence, 1820.	Badeley
214	Hardy's Life of Lord Charlemont, 1810.	W. Clarke
215	Hope's Costume of the Ancients, 2 vol. 1812.	Burnett
216	Johnstone's History of the Rebellion of 1745, 1820.	Duncan
217	Lockhart Papers, 2 vol. 1817.	Hunter
218	Macmichael's Journey from Moscow to Constantinople, 1819.	Badeley
219	Lord Orford's Memoirs of the last 10 years of George the Second, 2 vol. 1822.	Behn
220	Pulci, Morgante Maggiore, *Firenz.* 1732.	Joy
221	Parry's Voyage to Discover a North West Passage, 1821.	Warder
222	Rogers's Human Life, a Poem, 1819.	Singer
223	Sotheby's Farewell to Italy, 1818. Fitzpatrick's Lines Written at Ampthill Park, 1819.	Do
224	Suetonii Opera, notis Pitisci, 2 vol. *Leov.* 1714.	Behn
225	Sanazarii Poemata, *ap. Cominum*, 1731.	Singer
226	Watson Taylor's Profligate, a Comedy, PRIVATELY PRINTED, *Presentation copy, very scarce*, 1820.	Glynn
227	Vite e Ritratti de Illustri Italiani, 2 vol. *numerous portraits*, *Pad.* 1812.	Joy
228	Valperga in Horatii Epistolam de Morte Mæcenatis, *Aug. Taur.* 1812, and 4 more.	Singer
229	Waldegrave's Memoirs, *portraits*, 1821.	Pybus
230	Walpole's Travels in various Countries of the East, 1820.	Borne
231	Watt's Bibliotheca Britannica, Part 1 and 2, 1819.	Rainford
231*	Sandi, Storia di Venezia, 9 vol. *Ven.* 1755.	Behn

Folio.

232	Horatii Opera, cum Quatuor Commentariis, stained, *cuts*, *Ven.* 1509.	Badeley
233	Moreri, Dictionnaire Historique, 8 vol. *Amst.* 1740.	Pickering

NOTES

READING LIST
(1807)

Text: MS Murray. First published (in part) in Moore i. 100–1, 95–8. Thereafter published (in part) in *Works* (1832), i. 146–8, 140–4.

B wrote this list during his last month at Trinity College, Cambridge. It is a list of the works he had read up to that time. Thomas Moore, his friend and biographer, was extremely impressed by it: 'The list is, unquestionably, a remarkable one' (Moore i. 95). His closest friend John Cam Hobhouse, on the other hand, was not. In the margins of his copy of Moore, he wrote against it: 'Certainly he did *not* read these books', and again, less assertively, 'As Lord Byron says he read these volumes I am inclined to believe the fact, but it is certain he never gave any sign of this knowledge afterward' (Marchand i. 85). These seem very curious observations coming from such a quarter, but he maintained his doubts later in the margins of his Moore. In a letter to Robert Charles Dallas of 21 Jan. 1808, B had written: 'As to my reading, I believe I may aver without hyperbole, it has been tolerably extensive in the historical department, so that few nations exist or have existed with whose records I am not in some degree acquainted from Herodotus down to Gibbon' (*BLJ* i. 147–8). Against this Hobhouse wrote with a little more clemency: 'I am afraid that is not true to the extent which Byron would wish us all to believe.' (Harold Nicolson, *Byron: The Last Journey*, new edn. (1940), p. 297.)

Hobhouse appears to have been somewhat proprietorial over learned matters and his scepticism is amply refuted by B's entire *œuvre*. Moreover it was not apparently shared by other of B's contemporaries. In his 'Detached Thoughts' (1821–2), for instance, B recalled that 'while at Harrow my general information was so great on modern topics as to induce a suspicion that I could only collect so much information from *reviewers*—because I was never *seen* reading—but always idle and in mischief—or at play.—The truth is that I read eating—read in bed—read when no one else read—and had read all sorts of reading since I was five years old' (*BLJ* ix. 42).

B was unquestionably not only a voracious reader, but also an extremely attentive and discerning one; but he did not make an ostentatious display of learning in convivial company (and least of all in Hobhouse's). See also, e.g., Marchand i. 84–5, 138; *BAP*, p. 46.

In the following notes I have annotated only those authors or productions, about which I have felt it helpful or necessary to clarify B's reference. In many cases it is also worthwhile consulting the Sale Catalogues in the Appendix.

Besides the classics (Latin and Greek), B would have had, at the time of drawing up this list, an adequate reading knowledge of French, Italian, and Spanish, but not of German, or other Asiatic languages.

1. *England.* Moore omits the whole of the passage from here down to Metastasio, and begins at Arabia.

2. *Ossian or Macpherson.* James Macpherson (1736–96), historian, poet, scholar, and MP for Camelford, published *Fragments of Ancient Poetry, Collected in the Highlands of Scotland* (1760); *Fingal, an Ancient Epic Poem* (1762); and *Temora, an Epic Poem* (1763). These were corporately known as the 'Poems of Ossian', since they purported to be by that bard. Their authenticity was hotly disputed, particularly by Johnson. However, they were greatly admired by, for instance, Goethe, who incorporated the whole of 'The Songs of Selma' into the second book of his *Sorrows of Young Werther.* B himself published two Ossianic pieces in *Hours of Idleness* (1807): 'Oscar of Alva' and 'The Death of Calmar and Orla', besides writing 'Ossian's Address to the Sun in "Carthon"' (see *CPW* i. 4–5, 54–66, 112–16, 356, 368–9, 374–5).

3. *Ramsay.* Allan Ramsay (1686–1758), poet and bookseller, and institutor of the circulating library in Scotland. Friend of Pope and John Gay. Wrote satirical elegies, his principal work being the pastoral drama *The Gentle Shepherd* (1725).

4. *Macneill.* Hector Macneill (1746–1818), poet, author of *The Harp, a Legendary Tale* (1789) and other ballads. B favoured in particular Macneill's highly popular ballad 'Scotland's Scaith, or the Waes of War' (1795), which went through fourteen editions within the first year of publication. See *EBSR*, l. 818 (*CPW* i. 255, 415).

5. *Home Author of Douglas.* John Home (1722–1808), Presbyterian minister and dramatist, author of the immensely popular tragedy *Douglas* (1756).

6. *Taliessin and the Bards.* Taliesin (*fl.* 550), Celtic bard, though probably a mythical figure, to whom a mass of poetry of doubtful origin and date has been ascribed. *The Book of Taliesin* (14th century) comprises a collection of poems known to be by different authors and of different dates, but ascribed none the less to Taliesin.

7. *Chaulieu.* Guillaume Amfrye, Abbé de Chaulieu (1639–1720), poet and member of the free-thinking *cénacle* known as Le Temple, whose members also included Voltaire. Chaulieu's sobriquet was 'L'Anacréon du Temple', and his works were collected and published as *Œuvres de l'abbé de Chaulieu* (Amsterdam, 1757).

8. *DeLille.* Jacques, Abbé Delille (1738–1813), poet, scholar, and friend of Voltaire. Translated Virgil's *Georgics* (1770)—an immensely successful work—and *Aeneid* (1804); also Milton's *Paradise Lost* (1805), and Pope's *Essay on Man* (posthumously published). His own works include *Les Jardins* (1782) and *L'Imagination* (1788).

9. *Lope de Vega.* Lope Felix de Vega Carpio (1562–1635), poet and founder of Spanish drama. Wrote a considerable number of poems, plays, and romances, and took part in the Armada (1588). B's reference here is most probably to his reading of Lord Holland's *Some Account of the Life and Writings of Lope Felix de Vega Carpio*, which appeared anonymously in 1807. See *EBSR* l. 551 (*CPW* i. 246, 410); see also *BLJ* v. 206 and n.

10. *Cervantes . . . Don Quixote.* Miguel de Cervantes Saavedra (1547–1616), soldier, novelist, poet, and dramatist. *Primera parte de la Galatea, diuidida en seys libros* was published in 1585.

11. *Camoens . . . effort.* Luiz de Camoens (1524–80), soldier and poet, author of the epic *Os Lusiadas* (1572). See also n. 28 to B's review of Spencer's *Poems*, below.

12. *Gesner.* Salomon Gessner (1730–88), poet, author of the highly popular pastorals *Idyllen* (1756), and the prose epic *Der Tod Abels* (1758). The latter was translated into English by Mary Collyer (*The Death of Abel*, 1761), and went through twenty editions before 1799. See, in particular, B's preface to *Cain* (1821).

13. *Ferdausi.* Abul Kasim Mansur Firdusi (*c.*950–1020), satirical and epic poet of Persia, author of the great epic *The Shahnameh.*

14. *Sadi.* Muslihu-'d-Din Sadi (*c.*1200), moral poet of Persia, honoured by his countrymen as a saint, and author of *Gulistan* (*The Rose Garden*) and *Bustan* (*The Orchard*).

15. *Hafiz.* Shams-Ed-Din Muhammed Hafiz (?1326–90), philosopher and great Persian lyric poet. His *Diwan* (*Collection of Odes*) comprises *ghazals* (lyrics or odes) of an Anacreontic nature. Edward Scott Waring recorded: 'The tomb of this celebrated poet is of white marble, built by the munificence of the Vakeel, and is situated in a small garden called the Hafizeen. On the tablet are two of his odes, very beautifully cut' (*A Tour to Sheeraz* (1807), p. 37).

16. *Greece.* Moore omits the whole of the passage from here down to Seneca.

17. *Barlow.* Joel Barlow (1754–1812), statesman and poet, whose main ambition was to write an American epic. In 1787 he published *The Vision of Columbus* (a poem in nine books, over five thousand lines long). This he revised and rewrote over subsequent years and republished as *The Columbiad* in 1807. In his journal for 20 June 1815, George Ticknor recorded that on his first visit to B: 'He talked, of course, a great deal about America; wanted to know what was the state of our literature, how many universities we had, whether we had any poets whom we much valued, and whether we looked upon Barlow as our Homer' (*Life, Letters, and Journals of George Ticknor*, 2 vols. (1909), i. 59).

18. *Lodbrog.* Moore misreads as 'Lodborg'. In his *History of English Poetry* (3 vols., 1774), Thomas Warton wrote: 'the Goths imported into Europe a species of poets or singers, whom they called SCALDS or POLISHERS of

LANGUAGE' (vol. i, p. xxxii). He continued: 'The earliest scald now on record is not before the year 750. From which time the scalds flourished in the northern countries, till below the year 1157. The celebrated ode of Regner Lodbrog was composed about the end of the ninth century' (vol. i, p. lvii). *The Death-Song of Ragnar Lodbrog* was translated by Thomas Percy and published in his *Five Pieces of Runic Poetry* (1763).

19. *Emperor Kien Long . . . Tea.* Kien Long, Emperor of China (1735–95) and poet. His reign was considered the most glorious of the Manchu dynasty, and by many the most glorious in the whole of Chinese history. His *Ode to Tea* (1746) comprises a recipe for the making of tea and a somewhat Proustian meditation on that infusion, which, he claims, reposes and contents its consumer, recalling to him the 'Sages of Antiquity'. See also Peter Pindar's *Odes to Kien Long* (1792), which are dedicated to that emperor, praising him and his *Ode* in a jovial and facetious manner.

20. *these.* Moore misreads as 'their'.

21. *or Thomson.* Omitted in Moore.

22. *Churchill.* Charles Churchill (1731–64), poet and satirist, author of *The Rosciad* (1761), *The Prophecy of Famine* (1763), *The Duellist* (1763), *The Times* (1764), and other satires of a social or political nature. He was a friend of the radical, John Wilkes (1727–97) and helped him to found the *North Briton*, to which he also contributed. See B's poem 'Churchill's Grave' (1816) (*CPW* iv. 1–2); see also *BLJ* ii. 207; ix. 11.

23. *"voces & praeterea nihil".* 'Voices and nothing more': Latin proverb.

24. *Chaucer . . . contemptible.* For other references to Chaucer see *BLJ* vi. 91, 94 (cited by B in defence of *DJ*); viii. 101–2 (favourably mentioned); and ix. 62 (*The Wife of Bath's Tale* cited by B in defence of *The Vision of Judgment* (1822)).

25. *Thomas of Ercildoune.* Thomas of Erceldoune (also called Thomas the Rhymer) (?1220–?97), poet and visionary, is supposed to have predicted many major historical events and to have written a poem on the Tristan story (which Walter Scott believed to be authentic).

26. *Taste . . . mankind.* This early private expression of B's low opinion of contemporary English literature takes on more urgent argumentative force in the prose written for publication in 1820–1 (see *post* in this volume). It is also worth noting here how B seems to regard 'Taste' as a monitor not only of literature but also of national identity ('our name') and power ('Empire').

27. *Hume.* Moore omits the whole of the passage from here down to heads. David Hume (1711–76), philosopher, historian, and political economist, author of *A Treatise of Human Nature* (1739–40), *Essays Moral and Political* (1741–2), *An Enquiry concerning Human Understanding* (1748), and many other such works. His *History of Great Britain* (1754–61) was a controversial but standard work.

28. *Robertson.* William Robertson (1721–93), Presbyterian minister and historian, Principal of Edinburgh University, Moderator of the General Assembly, and historiographer of Scotland. His works include *History of Scotland during the Reigns of Queen Mary and of James VI* (1759), *History of Charles V* (1769), and *History of America* (1777–96).

29. *Orme.* Robert Orme (1728–1801), member of the Society of Antiquaries, historian of India, and historiographer to the East India Company. His works include *A General Idea of the Government and People of Indostan* (1752, but first published 1805), *A History of the Military Transactions of the British Nation in Indostan from the year 1745* (1763–78), and *Historical Fragments of the Mogul Empire, of the Morattoes, and of the English Concerns in Indostan from the year 1659* (1782).

30. *Voltaire.* François-Marie Arouet Voltaire (1694–1778), historian, philosopher, poet, novelist, dramatist, and encyclopaedist. Of his numerous writings, those of relevance here are *Histoire de Charles XII* (1731), *Siècle de Louis XIV* (1751), and *Histoire de l'Empire de Russie sous Pierre le Grand* (1759–63). He also wrote, in English, his *Essay upon the Civil Wars of France, extracted from Curious Manuscripts* (London, 1728).

31. *Rollin.* Charles Rollin (1661–1741), historian and Rector of the University of Paris. His works include *Traité des Etudes* (1726–8), the thirteen-volume *Histoire ancienne des Égyptiens, des Carthaginois, des Assyriens, des Babyloniens, des Mèdes, et des Perses, des Macédoniens, des Grecs* (1730–8), and *Histoire romaine* (1738).

32. *Rapin.* Paul de Rapin de Thoyras (1671–1725), historian, author of *Histoire d'Angleterre* (1724), translated into English by Nicholas Tindal between 1725 and 1731. See n. 39 below.

33. *Smollet.* Tobias George Smollett (1721–71), novelist and author of *A Complete History of England* (1757–8), which went through numerous editions.

34. *Henry.* Henry of Huntingdon (?1084–1155), Archdeacon of Huntingdon and historian who, at the request of Bishop Alexander of Lincoln, compiled *Historia Anglorum* (which extended to 1154).

35. *Knolles.* Richard Knolles (?1550–1610), historian, and author of the first definitive study of the Ottoman Empire in English, *The Generall Historie of the Turkes* (1603).

36. *Cantemir.* Count Demetrius Cantemir (1673–1723), Hospodar of Moldavia, and author of *The History of the Growth and Decay of the Othman Empire* (written in Latin and translated into English under this title by Nicholas Tindal in 1734–5). See n. 39 below.

37. *Paul Rycaut.* Sir Paul Rycaut (1628–1700), traveller and historian, and author of *The Present State of the Ottoman Empire* (1668), and *The Historie of the Turkish Empire from 1623 to 1677* (1680)—a continuation of Knolles's *Historie* (see n. 35 above).

38. *Vertot.* René Aubert de Vertot (1655–1735), historian, and author of *Histoire de la conjuration de Portugal* (1689), which continued under the titles of *Histoire des révolutions de Portugal* and *Révolutions de Portugal* (new editions printed repeatedly between 1712 and 1734), *Histoire des révolutions du Suède* (1695), *Histoire des révolutions arrivées dans le gouvernement de la Republique Romaine* (1719), and *Histoire des chevalier hospitaliers de Saint-Jean de Jerusalem* (1726)—which was translated into English as *History of the Knights of Malta* (1728). See n. 55 below.

39. *Tindal.* Nicholas Tindal (1687–1774), historian and translator. See nn. 32 and 36 above. Tindal continued Rapin's *Histoire* (which ended with the Revolution of 1688), and brought it down to the accession of George II (1727) in two further volumes (1744–5).

40. *Belsham.* William Belsham (1752–1827), Unitarian minister, historian, and author of *History of Great Britain to the Conclusion of the Peace of Amiens in 1802* (1806).

41. *Bisset.* Robert Bisset, LLD. (1759–1805), biographer and historian, author of *Life of Burke* (1798), and *History of George III to the Termination of the late War* (1804).

42. *Adolphus.* John Adolphus (1768–1845), historian, lawyer, and writer, known chiefly for his *History of England from the Accession of George III to the Conclusion of Peace in 1783* (1802).

43. *Buchanan.* George Buchanan (1506–82), poet, scholar, historian, and sometime tutor of Montaigne, whose works include *Rerum Scoticarum Historia* (1582).

44. *Boethius.* Hector Boethius (?1465–1536), historian and professor at the University of Paris, whose *Scotorum Historiae a Prima Gentis Origine* (1526) was the first printed history of Scotland.

45. *Gordon.* The Reverend James Bentley Gordon (1750–1819), author of *A History of the Rebellion in Ireland in 1798* (1801) and *A History of Ireland* (1805).

46. *Hooke.* Nathaniel Hooke (d. 1763), Roman historian, friend of Pope and Martha Blount. Besides numerous dissertations on the Roman Senate, he wrote *Roman History, from the Building of Rome to the Ruin of the Commonwealth* (1738–71).

47. *Cornelius Nepos.* Cornelius Nepos (1st century BC), Latin historian who flourished during the reigns of Julius Caesar and Augustus Caesar. Friend of Cicero, Pomponius Atticus, and Catullus (whose *Carmina* are dedicated to Nepos: see *Carmina* I). His chief work was *Vitae Excellentium Imperatorum.*

48. *Mitford's Greece.* William Mitford (1744–1827), historian and author of *History of Greece* (1784, 1790, 1810). B reread Mitford, and drew from him, when writing *Sardanapalus.* See *BLJ* viii. 13–15, 18, 26–7, 129n.

49. *Lelands Philip.* Thomas Leland (1722–85), historian and translator,

published *The History of Philip, King of Macedon* (1758) and *The Orations of Demosthenes against Philip* (1754–61).

50. *Potters Antiquities.* John Potter (?1674–1747), successively Bishop of Oxford and Archbishop of Canterbury, and author of *Archaeologicae Graecae: or The Antiquities of Greece* (1697–8).

51. *Mezeray.* François Eudes de Mézeray (1610–83), historian and *Académicien*, whose most celebrated work was *Histoire de France* (1643–51).

52. *Alberoni.* Jules Alberoni (1664–1752), Italian adventurer and intriguer, who rose to favour in France, became Minister of State in Spain (1714), and eventually Cardinal legate in the Romagna (1734–9). See also *BLJ* iii. 213 and n.; vi. 181 (and ix. 231 for correction); and viii. 36 and n., 39.

53. *Prince of Peace.* Manuel de Godoy (1767–1851), a Spanish guard in the service of Charles IV of Spain. He gained the Queen's attention and became her paramour. He was raised to the title of Marquis of Alcudia and appointed prime minister (in effect, ruler of Spain). He negotiated peace between France and Spain in 1795, which earned him the sobriquet of 'Principe de la Paz', and later negotiated the Treaty of Fontainebleau (1807), which resulted in France's invasion of Spain. He was execrated by his countrymen. See also *CHP* I. 48 (*CPW* ii. 28, 188, 279).

54. *their connection.* Moore misreads as 'its connexion'.

55. *From Vertot . . . totally different.* See n. 38 above. Cf. Walpole's anecdote: 'In writing the History of the Knights of Malta, Vertot had sent to Italy for original materials concerning the siege of Rhodes: but, impatient of the long delay, he completed his narrative from his own imagination. At length the packet arrived, when Vertot was sitting with a friend: he opened it, and threw it contemptuously on the sopha behind him, saying coolly, *Mon siege est fait*' (*Walpoliana*, 2 vols. (1800), i. 134).

56. *Tangralopix.* Moore misreads as 'Tangralopi'. Tangralopix (Togra Mucalet) (*fl.* during 11th century), Turkish chieftain of the Selzuccian dynasty. At the Battle of Ispahan (1030) between the Turks and the Persians, the Sultan of Persia fell from his horse and broke his neck. By the common consent of both Turkish and Persian soldiers, Tangralopix was immediately proclaimed Sultan of Persia. Thus the first kingdom of the Turks was established. See Knolles, *Generall Historie of the Turkes* (1603), p. 4.

57. *Othman 1st* The Ottoman Empire received its name from its founder, Osman (or Othman), who reigned from 1280 to 1324.

58. *Passarowitz . . . 1718.* By the Treaty of Passarowitz between Austria and Turkey, Austria extended its empire in the Balkans as far as it ever would under the *ancien régime*: Turkey ceded Belgrade, the Banat of Tamesvar, and parts of Bosnia, Wallachia, and Serbia. See also n. 59.

59. *Battle of Crotzka in 1739.* Moore misreads as 'Cutzka'. A decisive battle

between Turkey and Austria, in which the latter was defeated. By the subsequent Treaty of Belgrade (1739) between Austria, Russia, and Turkey, the Turks regained all that they had lost by the Treaty of Passarowitz (1718), except the Banat of Tamesvar. See n. 58.

60. *the treaty . . . 1790.* Between 1787 and 1792, Russia and Austria were at war with Turkey. Hostilities ended between Austria and Turkey with the Treaty of Sistova (1791); and between Russia and Turkey with the Peace of Jassy (1792).

61. *Tookes . . . Catherine 2d.* William Tooke (1744–1820), Russian historian. Author of *The Life of Catharine II* (1798) and *A View of the Russian Empire during the Reign of Catharine II and to the Close of the Present Century* (1799).

62. *Norberg's Charles 12th.* Göran Andersson Nordberg (1677–1744), Chaplain to, and historian of Charles XII of Sweden. Author of *Konung Carl den XII: tes historia* (Stockholm, 1740), of which there is apparently no English translation. B probably therefore read the French translation by C. G. Warmholtz, *Histoire de Charles XII: Roi de Suède* (La Haye, 1742). Charles XII, King of Sweden 1682–1718 and great military commander, suffered a total defeat at the Battle of Poltava (1709). See particularly B's *Mazeppa* (1818); also Samuel Johnson's *The Vanity of Human Wishes*, in which '*Swedish Charles*' is the very man who 'left the Name, at which the World grew pale, / To point a Moral, or adorn a Tale' (ll. 221–2).

63. *Translation . . . thirty years war contains.* Moore misreads as 'war which contains'. Schiller's *Geschichte des Dreissigjahrigen Kriegs* (1789–93) was translated into English by Captain Blaquiere and published as *The History of the Thirty Years War in Germany* (1799).

64. *Harte's Life . . . Prince.* Walter Harte (1709–74), writer and historian. Friend of Pope, Warton, and Johnson, and author of *History of the Life of Gustavus Adolphus, King of Sweden, surnamed the Great* (1759). Gustavus Adolphus (1594–1632) reigned from 1611 to 1632, and was celebrated for his campaigns during the Thirty Years War (1618–48).

65. *I have somewhere read . . . Gustavus Vasa.* Moore misreads as 'somewhere too read'. Gustavus Vasa (1496–1560) liberated the Swedes from Danish yoke in 1521, and ascended the throne of Sweden as Gustavus I in 1523. B may have read an account of his life in Vertot's *Histoire des révolutions de Suède* (1695) (see n. 38 above). Alternatively or additionally, he may have read the notorious tragedy by Henry Brooke, *Gustavus Vasa, the Deliverer of his Country* (1739).

66. *Gillies.* John Gillies (1747–1836), classical scholar and historian, and author of a very popular *History of Greece* (1786). He also published *A View of the Reign of Frederick II of Prussia* (1789) and *The History of the World, from the Reign of Alexander to that of Augustus* (1807).

67. *His own works.* Frederick II ('the Great') of Prussia (1712–86) ascended the throne in 1740 and raised Prussia into a powerful state. A man of great intel-

lectual and military capabilities, and a prolific writer on numerous subjects; for instance *Anti-Machiavel: or, an Examination of Machiavel's Prince* (1741), *Memoirs of the House of Brandenburg* (1758–68), *De la littérature Allemande* (1780), and *The Art of War: a Poem in Six Books* (1782). His works were first collected and published under the title of *Oeuvres de Frédéric II., Roi de Prusse* (4 vols., 1789).

68. *Thiebault.* Dieudonné Thiébault (1733–1807), Frenchman of letters who spent some time at the court of Frederick II and later published *Mes Souvenirs de vingt ans de séjour à Berlin, ou Frédéric le Grand, sa famille, sa cour, son gouvernement, son académie, ses écoles, et ses amis, littérateurs et philosophes* (1804).

69. *Houses of Swabia.* Moore misreads as 'House'. B had certainly read William Coxe's *History of the House of Austria* (3 vols., 1807) (see *BLJ* iv. 161: 'Coxe's Spain & Austria are dry enough'). He may also have read Godefroy's *De la vraye origine de la maison d'Austriche* (1624), and three other anonymous works: *Mémoires historiques et politiques* (1670), *The History of the Imperial & Royal Families of Austria & Bourbon* (1708), and *Histoire de la dernière guerre de Bohème* (3 vols., 1745). See also *CHP* IV. 12 (*CPW* ii. 128, 320). See also nn. 70, 71.

70. *Wenceslaus.* There were four Kings of Bohemia so named, living, respectively 1205–53, 1271–1305, 1289–1306, and Wenceslaus IV was also King of Germany. See n. 69 for B's sources.

71. *Rudolph ... Descendants.* Rudolph, Count of Habsburg (1218–91) was elected Holy Roman Emperor in 1273, thus becoming Rudolph I and founder of the Austrian monarchy. The phrase '*thick lipped*' refers to the protruding lower jaw and lip, which was a physical peculiarity of the House of Habsburg from Frederick III (1415–93) onwards. See n. 69 for B's sources.

72. *William Tell... Morgarten.* William Tell (*fl.* early 14th century), the legendary Swiss hero. He is said to have been a leader in the Swiss revolution of 1307 and to have taken part in the Battle of Morgarten (1315) (the first battle for Swiss independence from the yoke of Austrian Habsburg domination). Schiller's *Wilhelm Tell* was first published in 1804; Rossini's opera *Guillaume Tell* was first produced in Paris in 1829.

73. *Burgundy was slain.* I think B is mistaken here; there is no reference to any Duke of Burgundy being present at the Battle of Morgarten (see n. 72). He probably meant Charles the Bold, Duke of Burgundy 1467–77, who was severely defeated by the Swiss at Granson and Morat (1476) and at Nancy (1477) where he 'was slain'. See *CHP* III. 64 (*CPW* ii. 100–1, 307); also *BLJ* v. 78; viii. 20 and n.

74. *Davila.* Enrico Caterino Davila (1576–1631), Italian historian, author of the immensely successful *Istoria delle Guerra Civile di Francia* (Venice 1630). See also *BLJ* iv. 161 and n.

75. *Guiccadini.* So spelt by B. Francesco Guicciardini (1483–1540), Italian statesman and historian, author of *Storia d'Italia* (1561). See also *BLJ* iv. 161 and n.

76. *Guelphs . . . Gibellines.* The two great factions in medieval Italian politics. The Guelphs supported the authority of the popes, the Ghibellines that of the emperors. See nn. 74 and 75 for B's sources.

77. *the Battle of Pavia.* The Battle of Pavia (1525) between France and Spain, in which Francis I was defeated and captured by Charles V. See also *BLJ* iii. 256; viii. 118; and *CPW* iii. 261–2, 457.

78. *Massaniello . . . &c &c.* Tommaso Aniello (1622–47), a fisherman from Amalfi who led the temporarily successful Neopolitan revolt of 7 July 1647. He inspired the people, but did not seek power for himself. None the less he was assassinated, probably by his own supporters, on 16 July 1647, his dying words being 'Ah traditori, ingrati'. B may well have read Midon's *The History of the Rise and Fall of Masaniello* (1729) and de Lusan's *Histoire de la révolution du royaume de Naples dans les années 1647 et 1648* (4 vols., 1757). Auber's opera *Masaniello* (or *La Muette de Portici*) was first produced in Paris in 1828.

79. *Cambridge.* Richard Owen Cambridge (1717–1802), poet, wit, and scholar, author of *History of the War upon the Coast of Coromandel* (1761), and a contributor of twenty-one papers of great erudition to Edward Moore's *World* (1753–6).

80. *Andrews . . . War.* John Andrews (1736–1809), historian, author of *History of the War with America, France, Spain, and Holland, Commencing in 1775 and Ending in 1783* (1785–6).

81. *Parke.* Mungo Park (1771–1806), surgeon and traveller, who explored the course of the river Niger and published *Travels in the Interior of Africa* (1799).

82. *Bruce.* James Bruce (1730–94), traveller and explorer, who discovered the source of the Blue Nile and later published *Travels to Discover the Source of the Nile* (1790).

83. *Marlborough & Eugene.* John Churchill, first Duke of Marlborough (1650–1722), English general, most famous for his victory at the Battle of Blenheim (1704) where he and Eugène were highly compatible allied commanders. François de Savoie, Prince Eugène (1663–1736), the greatest of Austrian generals and President of the Supreme Council of War from 1703. Amongst other works, B may well have read the anonymous *The Lives of the Two Illustrious Generals, John, Duke of Marlborough, and Francis Eugene, Prince of Savoy* (1713), Rousset and Dumont's *Histoire militaire du Prince Eugène* (1729), Lediard's *The Life of John, Duke of Marlborough* (1736), and Banks's *The History of Francis-Eugene, Prince of Savoy* (1741). See also n. 91.

84. *Tekeli.* Count Emeric Tekeli (1658–1705), Hungarian general, took part in the Hungarian-Ottoman campaign against Austria in 1683, and fought again with the Ottomans in a disastrous campaign against Prince Eugène at the Battle of Zenta (1699), after which the Treaty of Carlowitz was signed. B may well have read *An Account of the Defeat of Count Tekely* (1683) and Leclerc's *Histoire d'Emeric Comte de Tekeli, ou Mémoires pour servir à sa vie* (1693). See also n. 83.

85. *Bonneval.* Moore misreads as 'Bonnard'. Claude Alexandre, Comte de Bonneval (1675–1747), military commander and somewhat of an adventurer. Having served his own country (France) from 1698 to 1704, he joined Prince Eugène in 1706, and fought with him in the Austrian campaigns against the French (1706–12) and the Turks (1715–18). Having fallen out with Eugène, he later joined the Turks, became a Muslim, rejuvenated their army, and fought with them against the Austrians and Russians in the campaign of 1736–9. He received the title of *Pasha* from the Sultan, and died at Constantinople. B appears to have admired him (see *BLJ* iii. 213), and, amongst other works, may well have read the spurious *Mémoires du Comte de Bonneval* (1737), repudiated by Bonneval himself. See also n. 83.

86. *Buonaparte.* At the time of B's writing there were already several books about Napoleon: e.g. Burdon's *The Life and Character of Bonaparte* (1804), and the anonymous *Authentic Memoirs of Napoleon* (?1802), *Life of Bonaparte* (1804), *Bonaparte, and the French People under his Consulate* (1804), and a *History of Buonaparté* (*c.* 1805).

87. *Anderson.* Robert Anderson, MD (1750–1830), surgeon and man of letters, compiled *A Complete Edition of the Poets of Great Britain* (13 vols., 1792–5; vol. 14, 1807).

88. *Cromwell.* Oliver Cromwell (1599–1658), Lord Protector of England 1653–8. B may well have read Isaac Kimber's *The Life of Oliver Cromwell, Lord Protector of the Commonwealth* (1724), Richard Burton's *The History of Oliver Cromwell* (1728) and/or John Banks's *A Short Critical Review of the Political Life of Oliver Cromwell* (1739).

89. *British Plutarch.* B had probably read one or all of the three major translations of Plutarch: T. North's *The Lives of the Noble Grecians and Romanes* (1579), Dryden's *Plutarch's Lives* (1683–6), and J. and W. Langhorne's *Plutarch's Lives* (1770).

90. *British Nepos.* Cornelius Nepos (see n. 47). B may well have read L. W. Finch and Others' *The Lives of the Illustrious Men: Written in Latin by C. Nepos and done into English by Several Hands* (1684) and J. W. Clarke's *Cornelius Nepos's Lives of the Excellent Commanders* (1723).

91. *Campbell's . . . Admirals.* John Campbell, LLD. (1708–75), writer, author of *Lives of the Admirals, and other Eminent British Seamen* (1742–4). He also wrote *Military History of the late Prince Eugene of Savoy and the late John, Duke of Marlborough* (1721), which B may well have read (see n. 83).

92. *Henry Ld Kames.* Moore misreads as 'Kaimes'. Henry Home, Lord Kames (1696–1782), Scottish judge and writer of many works on law, morality, and antiquities. B had certainly read *Memoirs of the Life and Writings of the Honourable Henry Home of Kames* (1807) by Alexander Fraser Tytler (Lord Woodhouselee). See *BLJ* i. 112.

93. *Marmontel.* Jean-François Marmontel (1723–99), prolific poet, novelist, and critic. B had certainly read his *Mémoires d'un Père* (1807) and his *Nouveaux contes moraux* (1801). Marmontel also wrote a historical romance entitled *Bélisaire* (1767) which, despite being somewhat mediocre, was condemned by the Sorbonne for its liberal religious views, and thus gained some notoriety. See n. 96.

94. *Teignmouth's . . . Jones.* Sir William Jones (1764–94), linguist, philologist, orientalist, and jurist. His works were collected and edited by Anna Maria Jones, and published as *The Works of Sir William Jones* (6 vols., 1799) and to which John Shore, Baron Teignmouth, contributed a 'Discourse on the Life and Writings of Sir W. Jones'. Teignmouth also wrote *The Literary History of the late Sir W. Jones* (1795) and *Memoirs of the Life, Writings and Correspondence of Sir William Jones* (1804). See *CPW* i. 342–4 for B's 'Parody on Sir William Jones's Translation from Hafiz'.

95. *Life of Newton.* Sir Isaac Newton (1642–1727), scientist, philosopher, and discoverer of the laws of gravity. B may have read Bernard Le Bovier de Fontenelle's *The Life of Sir Isaac Newton* (1728).

96. *Belisaire.* Belisarius (*fl.* 527–63), the greatest military commander of the Emperor Justinian. B may have read John Oldmixon's *The Life and History of Belisarius* (1713) or A. Richer's *The Life of Belisarius* (1759). In view of the French spelling, however, it is very likely that he had read Marmontel's *Bélisaire* (1767) in the original (though this was translated into English in the same year as *Belisarius*). See n. 93.

97. *Blackstone.* Sir William Blackstone (1723–80), jurist, author of the famous *Commentaries on the Laws of England* (1765–9). He was made a judge in 1770.

98. *Drummond.* William Drummond of Hawthornden (1585–1649), poet, historian, and man of letters, author of *The Cypresse Grove* (1623) and *The History of Scotland* (1655).

99. *Beattie.* James Beattie (1735–1803), poet and professor of moral philosophy at Marischal College in Aberdeen. His most famous work is perhaps the poem *The Minstrel* (1771–4); but he also wrote such works as *An Essay on the Nature and Immutability of Truth* (1770), *Dissertations Moral and Critical* (1783), *Evidences of the Christian Religion* (1786), and *Elements of Moral Science* (1790).

100. *Bolingbroke.* Henry St John, first Viscount Bolingbroke (1678–1751), statesman, orator, architect, and great friend and patron of Pope. He was a prolific writer on history, philosophy, politics, and religion, and his works were collected and edited by D. Mallet and G. Parke, and published as *The Works of the Right Hon. Henry St. John, Lord Viscount Bolingbroke* (1754–98).

101. *Hobbes.* Thomas Hobbes (1588–1679), philosopher and author of amongst other works the famous *Leviathan* (1651). B may have read *The Moral and Political Works of Thomas Hobbes* (1750), which were collected and edited by John Campbell (see n. 91).

102. *Cellarius.* Christophorus Cellarius (1638–1707), geographer, historian, and philologist, author of *Geographia Antiqua* (1692), of which there appears to be no English translation. B may also have seen *General View of Geography, Ancient and Modern* (1789), which was specially prepared for Rugby School as an introduction to the geographical ideas put forward by Cellarius and Guthrie (for whom see n. 105).

103. *Adams.* John Adams (*fl.* 1680), topographer and barrister, published *Index Villaris* (1680), and *Angliae Totius Tabula* (1685) which was later reissued as *A New Map of England* (1693).

104. *Pinkerton.* John Pinkerton (1758–1826), historian and antiquary, who published amongst numerous other works *The History of Scotland* (1797) and *Modern Geography* (1802).

105. *Guthrie.* William Guthrie (1708–70), writer, author of *A New Geographical, Historical, and Commercial Grammar* (1770), which went through numerous editions and later appeared under the title *A New System of Modern Geography* (1786). See also n. 102.

106. *Cid . . . favourite. Le Cid* (1637) by Pierre Corneille (1606–84), marked a turning-point in the history of French drama, and was condemned by the Académie (see, for instance, *Sentiments de l'Académie sur le Cid* (1638)).

107. *a little Italian.* Moore omits 'a'.

108. *translated . . . verse . . . prose.* As far as 'verse' is concerned, see *CPW* i. 8–11, 69–92, 153, 155–6; the 'prose' probably refers to school exercises.

109. *Sheridan.* Thomas Sheridan (1719–88) (father of Richard Brinsley Sheridan, the playwright), whose works on elocution and the English language include *A Course of Lectures on Elocution: Together with Two Dissertations on Language* (1762), *A Rhetorical Grammar of the English Language* (1781), and *Elements of English* (1786).

110. *Austin's Chironomia.* Gilbert Austin (no dates), author of *Chironomia; or, a Treatise on Rhetorical Delivery* (1806).

111. *Elocution . . . Speaker.* Omitted in Moore. William Enfield (1741–97), theologian, published numerous sermons and other learned works, amongst which was the very popular *The Speaker, or Miscellaneous Pieces selected from the best English Writers* (1774).

112. *Blair.* Robert Blair (1699–1746), poet and Presbyterian minister, author of the celebrated poem *The Grave* (1743).

113. *Porteus.* Beilby Porteus (1731–1808), successively Bishop of Chester and of London, published such works as *Sermons on Several Subjects* (1770), *The Works of T. Secker* (1775), *Select Discourses* (1786), and *Tracts on Various Subjects* (1807).

114. *Tillotson.* John Tillotson (1630–94), Archbishop of Canterbury. His

numerous writings and sermons were edited by Ralph Barker and published as *The Works of the Most Reverend Dr. John Tillotson* (1695–1704), and also by T. Birch under the same title in 1752.

115. *Hooker.* Richard Hooker (?1554–1600), theologian and professor of Hebrew at Oxford, author of *Of the Laws of Ecclesiastical Politie* (1594–7), to the 1665 edition of which Izaak Walton (1593–1683) contributed a biography of him.

116. *I abhor Religion.* In Moore this reads 'I abhor books of religion'. By interpolating 'books of', Moore was clearly trying to tone down B's strong views on religion and to redirect the force of his criticism.

117. *without . . . Sectaries.* For this clause and B's erasures, cf. 'I have refused to take the Sacrament because I do not think eating Bread or drinking wine from the hand of an earthly vicar, will make me an Inheritor of Heaven' (to R. C. Dallas, 21 Jan. 1808, *BLJ* i. 148).

118. *or a belief.* Moore omits 'a'.

119. *thirty nine articles.* The thirty-nine articles of faith to which those taking orders in the Church of England have, since 1571, been obliged to subscribe.

120. *Miscellanies . . . over.* This direction is written about two-thirds of the way down the penultimate page (recto) and is followed by a flourish of the pen.

121. *Spectator.* A periodical conducted by Richard Steele and Joseph Addison from Mar. 1711 to Dec. 1712, and revived by Addison alone in 1714 for eighty numbers. Addison, Ambrose Philips, Pope, Steele, and Thomas Tickell were its principal contributors.

122. *Rambler.* A periodical conducted by Samuel Johnson in 208 numbers from Mar. 1749 to Mar. 1750, and again from Mar. 1751 to Mar. 1752. Johnson himself wrote most of the articles, though Samuel Richardson and others contributed to the later numbers.

123. *World.* A periodical managed by the poet, dramatist, and bookseller Robert Dodsley (1703–64) and edited by the dramatist and fabulist Edward Moore (1712–57). It was highly successful and ran between the years 1753 and 1756. Amongst its contributors were Lord Chesterfield, Horace Walpole, and Richard Owen Cambridge (see n. 79).

124. *since I left Harrow.* B left Harrow in the summer of 1805, and took up residence at Trinity College, Cambridge, in Oct. the same year.

125. *Mackenzie.* Henry Mackenzie (1745–1831), novelist and author of the successful sentimental novel *The Man of Feeling* (1771), to whom B sent a copy of his *Poems on Various Occasions* (1807) and from whom B received 'Encomiums' (see *BLJ* i. 111).

126. *"Burton's . . . Melancholy".* Robert Burton (1577–1640), scholar and clergyman, whose principal work was the immensely influential *The Anatomy of*

Melancholy (1621). Although in purpose a medical treatise, it draws examples from such a vast literary fund that it is rather more a storehouse of miscellaneous learning (as B here suggests).

REVIEWS

Wordsworth's *Poems* (1807)

Text: *Monthly Literary Recreations*, xiii (July 1807), 65–6. Thereafter published in *Works* (1832), vi. 293–5, and Prothero i. 341–3.

B wrote this review in mid-July 1807, and seems to have offered it gratuitously to Ben Crosby in his letter to him of 21 July 1807 (*BLJ* i. 129):

> I have sent you a critique on Wordsworth's poems, for 'Literary Recreations,' insert or not as you please, or rather the editors. Of course they must alter or expunge what they disapprove. If it is not deemed worthy of publication, you need not trouble yourself to return the manuscript, but commit it to the flames.

Ben Crosby was the London bookseller who not only published *Monthly Literary Recreations*, but also acted as the agent for John Ridge (B's printer at Newark) in his dealings with the sale of B's *Hours of Idleness* (1807), which was favourably reviewed in the same number of the periodical immediately after B's review of Wordsworth (pp. 67–71). See also *BLJ* i. 129n., 130; Marchand i. 134–5 and n.; *BAP*, p. 45.

Poems, in Two Volumes, was Wordsworth's first publication since *Lyrical Ballads* (1798). B has added the total pagination of the two volumes (vol. i: 158 pp.; vol. ii: 170 pp.). His review is restrained and even generous, though not without some covert irony. The tone may have been prompted by his apprehension for the reception of his own publication; but it was his first review, and he was clearly aware that he was reviewing the work of an established, influential, and respected poet. Later, however, in his 'Detached Thoughts' (1821–2), he recalled bluntly: 'In 1807—in a Magazine called "Monthly Literary Recreations" I reviewed Wordsworth's trash of that time' (*BLJ* ix. 42). Although this opinion may well have been coloured by Wordsworth's subsequent publications, and by B's own antagonism to the poetical trend of the day, only two years after writing this review B was to begin the first of his many sallies against Wordsworth. See *EBSR*, ll. 235–54, 903–5 (*CPW* i. 236, 257, 404).

1. *Lyrical Ballads . . . applause.* By the time of B's writing this review, *Lyrical Ballads* had already gone into its fourth edition (1805). Francis Jeffrey, editor of the *Edinburgh Review*, reviewing *Poems, in Two Volumes* in the first of the *Edinburgh Review*'s notices to devote itself exclusively to any of Wordsworth's productions (vol. xi, no. xxi (Oct. 1807), art. xiv, pp. 214–31), concurred with B's appreciation: 'The Lyrical Ballads were unquestionably popular; and, we

have no hesitation in saying, deservedly popular; for in spite of their occasional vulgarity, affectation, and silliness, they were undoubtedly characterised by a strong spirit of originality, of pathos, and natural feeling' (p. 214).

2. *cotemporary sonneteers.* Such as William Thomas Fitzgerald (*c.*1759–1829) and William Lisle Bowles (1768–1850), the two sonneteers B castigates in *EBSR* ll. 1–2 and ll. 327–84 respectively. See *CPW* i. 229, 239–41, 400, 405.

3. *the present crisis.* On the one hand, the Napoleonic wars on the Continent: Napoleon had recently defeated the Prussians and the Russians at Eylau (8 Feb. 1807), and at Friedland (14 June 1807); and on the other, the collapse of the Grenville administration (the 'Ministry of All Talents') on 24 Mar. 1807.

4. *genuine poet . . . writes.* While this sentiment echoes much of what Wordsworth himself expresses in his prefaces to *Lyrical Ballads* of 1800 and 1802, the phrase certainly glances at Horace's 'si vis me flere, dolendum est primum ipsi tibi' (*Ars Poetica*, ll. 102–3), which B himself reflects in *Hints from Horace* (written 1811), ll. 141–2 (*CPW* i. 294), and gives trenchant poetic form in *EBSR* (1809), l. 814: 'Feel as they write, and write but as they feel' (*CPW* i. 255).

5. *"Another year . . . understand."* The occasion of this sonnet was the defeat of the Prussians by Napoleon at Jena (14. Oct. 1806). Apart from minor details in punctuation and capitalization B quotes the sonnet verbatim.

6. *"Ah! little . . . less."* Apart from minor details in punctuation and capitalization B quotes stanza 4 verbatim.

7. *"Moods . . . Mind".* A sequence of thirteen poems in the second volume: 'To a Butterfly' ('Stay near me—do not take thy flight!'); 'The Sun has long been set'; 'O Nightingale! thou surely art'; 'My heart leaps up when I behold'; 'Written in March, while resting on the Bridge at the Foot of Brother's Water'; 'The Small Celandine'; 'I wandered lonely as a Cloud'; 'Who fancied what a pretty sight'; 'The Sparrow's Nest'; 'Gypsies'; 'To the Cuckoo'; 'To a Butterfly' ('I've watched you now'); and 'It is no spirit who from Heaven hath flown'.

8. *"abandoning" his mind.* Sir Joshua Reynolds informed Boswell that 'Johnson thought the poems published as translations from Ossian, had so little merit, that he said, "Sir, a man might write such stuff for ever, if he would *abandon* his mind to it"' (*Boswell's Life of Johnson* iv. 183).

9. *namby-pamby.* Mawkishness, puerility. This was the sobriquet of the poet Ambrose Philips (?1675–1749), first applied to him by Henry Carey in his poem 'Namby-Pamby. A Panegyric on the New Versification, Address'd to A—— P—— Esq.' (1725). See Frederick T. Wood, *The Poems of Henry Carey* (1930), pp. 112–14. In his review (see n. 1 above) Jeffrey also ridiculed *Poems, in Two Volumes* as 'namby-pamby' (p. 220).

10. *"The cock . . . hill."* B quotes verbatim all but the final six lines of 'Written in March, while resting on the Bridge at the Foot of Brother's Water'.

11. *exquisite measure.* B gives the misleading impression that this line is from another poem, whereas it is merely the first of the final six lines which he omitted from his last question (see n. 10 above).

12. *"Hey . . . spoon."* An English nursery rhyme.

13. INNOCENT . . . *canamus."* The final poem of Wordsworth's volumes is entitled simply 'Ode', and bears the motto '*Paulo majora canamus*' (Virgil, *Ecloga* iv. 1: 'Let us sing of greater things'). This 'Ode' was later retitled 'Ode: Intimations of Immortality from Recollections of Early Childhood'.

14. *genius . . . excel.* B maintained this view throughout his life. In a letter to Leigh Hunt of 30. Oct. 1815, for instance (the whole of which is worth consulting in this context), he wrote: 'I take leave to differ from you on Wordsworth as freely as I once agreed with you—at that time I gave him credit for promise which is unfulfilled—I still think his capacity warrants all you say of *it* only—but that his performances since "Lyrical Ballads"—are miserably inadequate to the ability which lurks within him' (*BLJ* iv. 324).

Spencer's *Poems* (1812)

Text: *Monthly Review* (Enlarged Series), vol. lxvii (Jan.–Apr. 1812), art. vii, pp. 54–60. Thereafter published in Prothero ii. 413–20.

This review appeared in the *Monthly Review* for Jan. 1812. B wrote it between 19 Dec. 1811 and the end of the year at home at Newstead, where his friends William Harness and Francis Hodgson (the principal editor of the *Review*, and then occupied with getting ready the Jan. number) were guests at the time. See A. G. L'Estrange, *The Literary Life of the Rev. William Harness* (1871), pp. 12–13, and B. C. Nangle, *The Monthly Review: Second Series, 1790–1815* (1955), pp. 13, 207. See also *BLJ* ii. 156, and ix. 42.

The Honourable William Robert Spencer (1770–1834) was the younger son of Lord Charles Spencer, the second son of the third Duke of Marlborough. He was a poet, wit, and dandy, a frequent guest at Carlton House, home of the Prince Regent, and highly popular in London society. From 1797 to 1826 he was a Commissioner of Stamps; but owing to financial embarrassments he removed to Paris where he spent the remaining eight years of his life in poverty and ill-health. Other of his works not mentioned in the notes below include *Urania; or, The Illuminé: A Comedy, in Two Acts* (1802), and *Miscellaneous Poems* (1812).

Spencer was involved in the duel between Thomas Moore and Francis Jeffrey of 1806 (to which B alludes in *EBSR*, ll. 460–71 (*CPW* i. 243–4, 407)), lending the former his pistols. Of that occasion Samuel Rogers recalled that, when asked to bail Moore out of custody afterwards, Spencer refused, because 'he could not well go out, for it was *already twelve o'clock*, and he had to be dressed *by four!*' (Morchard Bishop (ed.), *Recollections of the Table Talk of Samuel Rogers* (1952), p. 228).

B liked Spencer, dined with him, and met him often in society during his London days. See *BLJ* iv. 116; ix. 22, 29. Lady Blessington records his saying (*Lady Blessington's Conversations*, p. 133):

> Did you know William Spencer, the Poet of Society, as they used to call him? . . . His was really what your countrymen call an elegant mind, polished, graceful, and sentimental, with just enough gaiety to prevent his being lachrymose, and enough sentiment to prevent his being too anacreontic. There was a great deal of genuine fun in Spencer's conversation, as well as a great deal of refined sentiment in his verses. I liked both, for both were perfectly aristocratic in their way; neither one nor the other was calculated to please the *canaille*, which made me like them all the better.

Nevertheless, as can be seen, B's review (which was, of course, anonymous) is written with considerable irony, and, although genial and bantering in tone, does occasionally give way to sardonic criticism.

1. *"mob . . . ease"*. Pope, *Imitations of Horace*, 'The First Epistle of the Second Book of Horace', l. 108.

2. *"Vers de Société"*. Society verses; about, addressed to, and popular amongst the fashionable circle.

3. *Bellman . . . allowed.* The 'Bellman' was the town crier. See, for example, B's letter to Moore of 25 Dec. 1820: 'I conclude poetically, with the bellman, "A merry Christmas to you!"' (*BLJ* vii. 255). In Spencer's 'Christmas Carol', the chorus twice repeated runs:

> Be merry all, be merry all,
> With holly dress the festive hall,
> Prepare the song, the feast, the ball,
> To welcome merry Christmas.

4. *Of 'Leonora,' . . . p. 451.*). Gottfried August Bürger's ballad *Lenore* (first published in the *Göttinger Musenalmanach* in 1774) struck the English imagination in 1796, when no less than five translations of it were published. Amongst these was *Leonora: Translated from the German of Gottfried Augustus Bürgher, By W. R. Spencer, Esq. With Designs by the Right Honourable Lady Diana Beauclerc. 1796.* The earlier 'report' was the review of this by John Aiken (May–Aug. 1796, art. xiii), in which he transcribed eight stanzas (none of which B reproduces here), merely commenting: 'This publication is a splendid piece of typography, having the German printed on one side of the page' (p. 453). In *Poems* also, 'Leonora' appears with her German original on the facing page. It is by far the weightiest poem in the volume, where it appears in a slightly revised version.

5. *'See . . . dead!"'* Stanzas 25–7 of Spencer's text. In the German, the final line of the third stanza here is enclosed within separate question-marks, being spoken by Lenore herself; Spencer gives the whole speech to her lover.

6. *'Reviving Friendship' . . . character.* In the first edition of *Leonora* (see n. 4 above), the last six lines of stanza 2 run:

> Their arms relenting friendship leagued,
> And heal'd the bleeding world with Peace.
> They sing, they shout, their cymbals clang,
> Their green wreaths wave, they come, they come;
> Each war-worn Hero comes to hang
> With trophies his long wept for home.

In *Poems*, the same lines stand:

> Their arms reviving friendship leagued,
> And heal'd the bleeding world with Peace.
> They shout, they sing, their cymbals ring,
> Their green wreaths wave, they come, they come;
> Ten thousand furlow'd heroes bring
> Or wounds, or wealth, or trophies home.

7. *"otium cum dignitate".* Ease with dignity. See Cicero, *Pro Publio Sestio Oratio*, 45: 'Id quod est praestantissimum, maximeque optabile omnibus sanis et bonis et beatis, cum dignitate otium.' (What stands out first and is most to be desired by all healthy, good, and happy people, is ease with dignity.) The point which B is humorously exploiting here is the ineptitude of associating a soldier with his 'furlow' ('furlough', leave of absence from duty), rather than his soldierly occupation of fighting. Spencer's original epithet of 'war-worn' was both appropriate and poetically superior (the image, alliteration, and assonance).

8. *Why . . . aspirate?* B's error in miscopying 'horsemen' for 'horseman'. In the first edition of *Leonora* (see n. 4 above), the final line of the second stanza quoted here by B runs 'And horse and horseman pant for breath.'

9. *The next . . . p. 288. The Year of Sorrow: Written in the Spring of 1803, By W. R. Spencer*, and tracing in rhyming couplets the 'anguish of domestic woe', was first published in 1804. The earlier 'tribute of praise' was the review of this by Lockhart Muirhead (Sept.–Dec. 1804, art. ix), who wrote: 'In paying a melancholy tribute to the memory of those friends and relatives, who, in the course of a single year, were severed from him by death, Mr. Spencer has contrived to interest our feelings; and to recommend his elegaic pages to every reader of taste and sensibility.'

10. *We are . . . fact.* On p. 15 of the first edition of *The Year of Sorrow* (see n. 9 above), to the lines 'Have ye not seen, ye plains of Stafford, say, / A new Etruria mould your native clay, / Rough British hands light Grecian forms prepare, / And every mart demand the classic ware?', the following note (which remains unchanged on p. 50 of *Poems*) is appended:

It is generally known that Mr. Wedgewood's Etruria owes its name and the perfection of its *forms* to the exquisite *Etruscan* or *Grecian* models first introduced into this country by Sir William Hamilton; and a late traveller observes, that 'the demand for this elegant manufacture is now so universal, that an Englishman in journeying from Calais to Ispahan, may have his dinner served every day upon *Wedgewood's ware.*'

Josiah Wedgwood (1730–95) was the founder of the famous pottery at Etruria, a village which he built for his workers near Stoke-on-Trent in Staffordshire. He developed new techniques in the manufacture of chinaware, which was (and is) immediately recognizable from its Greek ornamentation.

11. *It has . . . department.* This of course is B himself.

12. *Passing . . . school-exercises.* B refers to 'Chorus from the Iphigenia in Aulis of Euripides. Written at Harrow School, in the Year 1784.' There are no other such 'school-exercises' included in the volume; B means that this one should not have been included either.

13. *poems.* B quotes the following two poems verbatim and in full.

14. *It is happy . . . anonymous.* The quantity of poems addressed to the nobility is somewhat overwhelming and ostentatious. Eight of the titles include the names of duchesses, marchionesses, countesses and viscountesses. There are also twelve anonymous blanks, ennobled or otherwise; but there is no 'Lady Asterisk'.

15. *'What ails . . . you.'* B quotes verbatim the first three of the poem's five stanzas.

16. *killing partridges . . . quinsey.* The shooting season (pheasant and partridge) opens in Sept. (Cf. *DJ* XIII. 48: 'But there's no shooting (save grouse) till September', *CPW* v. 539)). B points up the ludicrousness of Spencer's comparison by continuing the 'choking' imagery in 'quinsey' (a severe throat infection).

17. *"the song . . . quality;".* This is not the title of one of Spencer's poems. The reference is to 'Song. By a Person of Quality', collected in *Miscellanies* by Swift and Pope, with contributions by Arbuthnot and Gay. See for example *Miscellanies*, 4 vols. (1747), iv. 141–2.

18. *'When . . . wire.'* This and the following two stanzas, quoted verbatim by B, comprise stanzas 1, 4, and 5 of 'On the Sounds produced by the Wind passing over the Strings of a Pedal Harp in a Garden'.

19. *If . . . "preferred for wit."* Pope, *The Dunciad* iii. 326. See also n. 9 to B's review of Wordsworth's *Poems* above.

20. *Castle of Indolence.* For James Thomson's lines on the Aeolian harp, see *The Castle of Indolence*, stanzas 40–1. (B asks us to contrast Thomson's dignified, decorous, and polished description in Spenserian stanzas with Spencer's trite, fanciful, and extravagant quatrains.) The figure—a harp or lyre over which the wind blows producing natural music unmediated by the art of man—became an important emblem or metaphor for the operation of the imagination in Romantic poetry. See, e.g., Coleridge's 'The Eolian Harp', and 'Dejection: An Ode'.

21. *Cruscanti.* A group of English poets better known as the 'Della Cruscans'. For fuller details, see n. 100 to 'Some Observations' (1820) below.

22. *"Poor . . . cold!" King Lear* III. iv. 140.

23. *One . . . lines.* B transcribes the lines verbatim. The poem was written in Dec. 1808. In 1806, Moore had addressed an Epistle 'To the Honourable W. R. Spencer.' (See *Epistles, Odes, and Other Poems* (1806), 'Epistle VIII'.)

24. *We have . . . former.* There are thirteen poems in French, and three Italian 'Canzonetta'. B quotes two of the former verbatim and in full. With regard to the second of these, Gillwell House was the residence of Mrs Chinnery, to whom Spencer addresses several other of his poems. This poem is decorated, as B mentions later, with an urn inscribed 'W.R.S.'.

25. *Mr. Mathias.* Thomas James Mathias (?1754–1835), satirist, linguist, and Italian scholar, was a Fellow of Trinity College, Cambridge, and sometime Treasurer and Librarian at Buckingham Palace. He published *The Pursuits of Literature* (1794–7), which was a highly provocative satire on contemporary writers, and edited *The Works of Thomas Gray* (1814). He also published *Canzone Toscane* (1806), and *Canzone e Prose Toscane* (1808), to both of which B refers here. See also *BLJ* ii. 86–7, 171, 176, 178.

26. *concetti.* Conceits (Italian): far-fetched comparisons, or affectations in style.

27. *Shenstone . . . Leasowes.* William Shenstone (1714–63), poet, and landscape gardener of his own estate at The Leasowes, near Halesowen. Cf. B's 'Verses found in a Summer House at Hales-Owen' (*CPW* i. 226, 392). The anonymous author of *Promenade ou Itinéraire des Jardins d'Ermenonville* (Paris, 1788) writes that in the gardens at Ermenonville, which belonged to the Marquis de Gérardin (an enthusiastic admirer of Shenstone), there was the inscription (I give the first six lines only):

This plain stone
To William Shenstone
In his verses he display'd
His mind natural
At Leasowes he lay'd
Arcadian greens rural.

28. *Lord Strangford.* Percy Clinton Sydney Smythe, sixth Viscount Strangford, and first Baron Penshurst (1780–1855), poet and diplomat, was renowned for his *Poems, from the Portuguese of Luis de Camoens: With remarks on his Life and Writings* (1803). See also *EBSR*, ll. 295–308, 921–2 (*CPW* i. 238, 258, 404).

Ireland's *Neglected Genius* (1813)

Text: *Monthly Review* (Enlarged Series), vol. lxx (Jan.–Apr. 1813), art. xv, pp. 203–5. Thereafter published in Prothero ii. 420–3.

This review appeared in the *Monthly Review* for Feb. 1813. Although B had written to Francis Hodgson on 3 Jan. saying 'I cannot review in the "*Monthly*;" in fact I can just now do nothing, at least with a pen' (*BLJ* iii. 7), he must have been persuaded to do so either by Hodgson himself, or possibly by Lady Oxford—with whom he was deeply involved at the time. Accordingly, he wrote the review, either at Eywood, the country home of the Oxfords near Presteign, or in London, some time between 3 Jan. and the end of the month. No doubt his involvement with Lady Oxford accounts for his initial reluctance to undertake it, and, in part at least, for its brevity when he eventually did. It was the last review he was to contribute to the *Monthly.* For further details, see B. C. Nangle, *The Monthly Review: Second Series, 1790–1815* (1955), p. 145.

William Henry Ireland (1777–1835), poet and dramatist, achieved great notoriety in 1795 and 1796 as a forger of plays by Shakespeare. He managed to deceive most of the leading literati of the day, including Joseph Warton, James Boswell, Richard Sheridan, and William Pye (the Poet Laureate), though Richard Porson, the classical scholar and Professor of Greek at Cambridge, was not convinced. After confessing to forgery in Apr. 1796, Ireland left London, and rambled penniless around the Bristol area, identifying with Chatterton with whose history he had been obsessed from an early age. He married in 1797, and opened a circulating library in Kensington the following year. Other of his publications, not noted in the notes below, include the two dramas originally represented as Shakespeare's—*Vortigern* (1796) and *Henry the Second* (1799)—*Gondez, the Monk* (1805), *Chalcographimania* (1814), *Jack Junk* (1814), *Scribbleomania* (1815), many volumes of prose, and a *Life of Napoleon Bonaparte* (1823). See also Bernard Grebanier, *The Great Shakespeare Forgery: A New Look at the Career of William Henry Ireland* (1966).

It is highly unlikely that B was aware of Ireland's history, otherwise he would almost certainly have alluded to it, or exploited it in some way in his review. As can be seen, the review is written with heavy irony, and, while amusing and good-natured in tone, is thoroughly dismissive of Ireland's volume—the title of which was without doubt borrowed from B (see *EBSR*, l. 800: 'Neglected Genius! let me turn to you' (*CPW* i. 254); though cf. Pope's *Epistle to Dr. Arbuthnot*, ll. 257–8).

1. *Neglected Genius . . . 1812.* B gives the title-page verbatim and in full, except that 'Fall' should read 'Fate'. Ireland published under the pseudonym of 'H. C. Esq.' *The Fisher-Boy* (1808), *The Sailor-Boy* (1808), and *The Cottage-Girl* (1809).

2. *The book . . . eulogized.* Ireland's Dedication, 'To the Most Noble William Spencer Cavendish, Marquis of Hartington', opens: '*As the language of adulation and flattery would be repugnant to your enlightened understanding, permit me to assure your Grace, that, in soliciting the enviable patronage of your name, I was prompted only by feelings of respect for your mental acquirements*.' And it continues: '*In contemplat-*

ing the unvarying conduct of your Grace, I cannot but call to mind the dignified independance which uniformly characterized your illustrious father's career.' William George Spencer Cavendish (1790–1858), sixth Duke of Devonshire (the 'present' Duke, and Dedicatee of *Neglected Genius*), was the only son of William Cavendish (d. 1811), fifth Duke of Devonshire (the 'late' Duke, and subject of the 'Monody'). The latter left a widow, Elizabeth (his second wife), to whom the 'Monody' is addressed (see n. 3 below).

3. *Lest . . . Duchess.* B quotes verbatim stanzas 6–10 of 'Monody Upon the Death of the Most Noble William Cavendish, Late Duke of Devonshire. Inscribed (By Permission) to Elizabeth, Duchess of Devonshire' (see also n. 2). The poem is sixteen stanzas long, and is framed throughout its six pages, as B says, by a black margin.

4. *Milton.* B quotes verbatim the whole of 'John Milton'.

5. *We must . . . original.* B quotes verbatim the whole of 'Naham Tate' (so spelt by Ireland). B's comment on Ireland's 'imitative' approximation to 'his original' is splendidly ironic. Nahum Tate (1652–1715), poet, dramatist, and friend of Dryden, was appointed Poet Laureate in 1692, after the death of Thomas Shadwell. He is perhaps best known for his versification of the Psalms (*A New Version of the Psalms*, 1696), for writing the libretto of Purcell's opera *Dido and Aeneas* (*c.* 1690), and for his alterations to Shakespeare's plays (most notably *King Lear*, in which the Fool is entirely omitted, and Cordelia survives Lear to marry Edgar). Pope gives him short shrift in *The Dunciad* i. 105, 238, and in his *Epistle to Dr. Arbuthnot*, ll. 189–90.

6. *Where . . . &c.* These cacophonous rhymes occur in 'Imitation of the Style of Butler'. John Lemprière (?1765–1824), classical scholar and schoolmaster, is most renowned for his *Bibliotheca Classica; or, a Classical Dictionary containing a full Account of all the Proper Names mentioned in Antient Authors* (1788). Deucalion was the Greek equivalent to Noah. A son of Prometheus, he ruled over part of Thessaly. During his reign, Jupiter in his wrath with man caused an inundation, and Prometheus advised Deucalion to build a boat.

7. *as . . . runs.* John Bannister (1760–1836), comedian, and the manager of the Drury Lane Theatre in 1802 and 1803. B refers to the song 'Captain Wattle and Miss Roe', ll. 1–2 of which run: 'Did you ever hear of Captain Wattle, / He was all for love and a little for the bottle.' It was composed by Charles Dibdin (1745–1814), song-writer and dramatist. See *A Collection of Songs, Selected from the Works of Mr. Dibdin*, 2 vols. (1814), ii. 241–2.

8. *Chatterton . . . Ireland.* This is so. More than forty pages of indifferent verse are devoted to Thomas Chatterton (1752–70), the poet and fabricator of the Rowley poems, who was born and bred in Bristol and committed suicide in London. These items include imitations of the 'Rowleian' style, with modern versifications of the same, as well as a long 'Elegy' on, and an 'Address' to Chatterton—all intermingled with much abuse of Bristol.

9. *The notes . . . page.* In a note to one of his lines concerning Horace Walpole (1717–97), fourth Earl of Orford, author and patron of the arts, Ireland wrote (p. 145):

> Chatterton began a correspondence with the late Lord Orford, (then Sir Horace Walpole) and remitted to him several of the supposed Rowley productions; but, upon Sir Horace communicating the papers to his friends *Mason* and *Gray*, they pronounced them to be forgeries. Chatterton had formed very great expectations from the patronage of Sir Horace, but, finding himself shamefully neglected, he wrote a very spirited and indignant letter, demanding the restitution of his MSS. and thus terminated the intercourse.

Had Ireland perused more attentively the life of Chatterton in the very work to which he himself refers, he would not have made this blunder. See G. Gregory, *The Works of Thomas Chatterton*, 3 vols. (1803); Chatterton's life is in the first volume, and Walpole is referred to throughout as 'Mr.'.

10. *and we . . . better.* Printer's devil, an errand-boy in a printing house.

SPEECHES

Although B spoke only three times in the House of Lords, he sat on many other occasions. The dates of these attendances are given below. They are taken from *The Journals of the House of Lords*, vols. xlvii (1809–10), xlviii (1810–12), xlix (1813–14), l (1814–16). An asterisk denotes that on that date B was also amongst those appointed to a select committee to consider various bills (e.g. an enclosure bill, a road bill, or a bill to naturalize an alien); italicization merely draws attention to the date of his speaking.

1809	13, 14, 15, 21* Mar.; 28* Apr.; 10*, 15* May.
1812	15, 16, 20*, 27, 28, 31 Jan.; 13, 17*, 20*, 24*, *27**, 28 Feb.; 2, 19 Mar.; 16, 20, *21* Apr.; 19 June; 1, 3, 6, 7, 10, 14 July.
1812 (New Session)	3*, 7* Dec.
1813	23*, 25*, 26 Feb.; 4*, 12 Mar.; 14* May; *1*, 18, 22 June; 15 July.
1814	29 Apr.; 10 May.
1815	23 May.
1816	19 Feb.; 2 Apr.

In addition on 1 June 1814 'Several Petitions for facilitating the introduction of Christian Knowledge into India, were presented by Lord Viscount Sidmouth and Lord Byron. Ordered to lie on the table [i.e. ordered to be submitted for future discussion]' (*Morning Chronicle*, Wed. 2 June 1813; similarly reported in *The Times* and the *London Gazette* of the same date. See also *The Journals of the House of Lords*, xlix (1813–14), 461–2).

B attended the House of Lords 48 times in all. Many of the above debates were of such minor interest that they were not reported in *Cobbett's* or in Hansard, and B was often absent from debates that were of major import. The few that he attended in 1814, 1815, and 1816 were, however, crucially important, which suggests that his presence on those occasions may have been merely dutiful.

The principal issues discussed in parliament at the time were: addresses from the Prince Regent, the state of the king's health, the conduct of the war in the Peninsular, domestic disturbances (exemplified by the frame-breakers), and the state of Ireland (including the claims of the Roman Catholics). B did speak on two of the major topical concerns, and in each case in support of the liberty of a particular oppressed group or individual. That he did not speak more often, and that the number of his attendances progressively diminished, are fairly reasonably accounted for by himself. Some years later in Italy he confessed to Thomas Medwin: 'I am not made for what you call a politician, and should never have adhered to any party. I should have taken no part in the petty intrigues of cabinets, or the pettier factions and contests for power among parliamentary men' (*Medwin's Conversations*, p. 228).

The Tory stronghold in parliament at the time was virtually unassailable, and opposition to it, though not entirely useless, was scarcely effectual. (See *BLJ* v. 19; ix. 17.) Moreover, B lacked both the stimulus and the encouragement he required to pursue a parliamentary career. (See, e.g., *BLJ* iii. 206, 229; ix. 16.) He also found the House of Lords 'dull' (*BLJ* v. 19; vii. 205). This last observation is understandable enough and can be adequately attested by briefly comparing his speeches with those of other lords. In general, lords' speeches were characterized by a laboured rehearsal of historical fact, Acts of parliament, and references to former debates and speakers; high rhetoric and gravity (though sometimes spiced with wit); and, while including citations from the classics and some English poets (principally Shakespeare and Milton), avoided imagery of any kind—rarely descending even to a metaphor. B's speeches, while attempting to adopt some of these features, are lively, provocative, ironic, sardonic, allusive, highly metaphorical, and eminently readable, revealing perhaps too readily his literary cast of mind (see Marchand i. 313–46; *BAP*, pp. 112–26). For two recent studies of B's politics, see Malcolm Kelsall, *Byron's Politics* (1987), and Michael Foot, *The Politics of Paradise: A Vindication of Byron* (1988).

It will be seen in the following notes that reference is made to *Cobbett's Parliamentary Debates*, with respect to B's first two speeches, and to Hansard with respect to his 'Presentation of Major Cartwright's Petition'. The explanation is simply that *Cobbett's Parliamentary Debates* were issued by William Cobbett and printed by Thomas Curzon Hansard under this title from 1800 to 4 May 1812 (vols. i–xxii), but in 1811 Hansard took over their publication, and from 5 May 1812 (vol. xxiii) the title became simply *The Parliamentary Debates* (more familiarly known as Hansard).

Frame Work Bill Speech: Draft Notes (1812)

Text: MS Bodleian (Dep. Lovelace Byron 154, f. 215v). Unpublished.

These draft notes are written in three columns (numbered by B 1–7, 8–15, and 16–22 respectively) on the title-page of his copy of the Frame Work Bill (printed according to the order of the House of Lords on 21 Feb. 1812). B obviously jotted them down soon after that date and later worked them up into the full body of his speech, which is discussed below. I have here annotated only those items not mentioned in the notes to his main text.

1. *M^{s}:* This, and the 'M^{s}:' in item 9, is a contraction of 'Manufacturers', that is, the frame-workers themselves.

2. *Bankruptcy . . . pardoned.* A 'Motion Respecting Members Becoming Bankrupts' was moved in the House of Commons on 31 Jan. 1812, but was negatived (*Cobbett's* xxi (1812), 478–82). The case of Walsh was notorious at the time. Benjamin Walsh, a stockbroker and MP, had been expelled from the Stock Exchange in 1809 for malpractice. On 5 Dec. 1811 he misappropriated a money order of considerable value from a client. On 14 Jan. 1812 he was convicted by a jury at the Old Bailey of the 'felony' of stealing the money order. However, in a letter of 15 Feb. 1812 to Mr Secretary Ryder of the House of Commons, the Lord Chief Baron (who had sat on the case) asserted that the facts proved at Walsh's trial did not constitute a 'felony'. He therefore recommended a pardon from the crown, which was soon afterwards granted. The House of Commons, however, was not mollified: it moved that the issue should be discussed and that Walsh should be ordered to appear before the House with a view to his expulsion. The date appointed was 27 Feb. 1812 (the day of B's speech); but Walsh excused himself. He was ordered to appear on 2 Mar. (which he failed to do) and again on 3 Mar. (which he again failed to do). On 5 Mar. his case was debated in his absence and he was by a large majority expelled from the House (*Cobbett's* xxi (1812), 933–43, 982–8, 1088–92, 1174–201). See also n. 18 to B's 'Frame Work Bill Speech' below.

3. *Arnold.* This town in Nottinghamshire had been the focus of a major frame-breaking attack in Mar. 1811. See John Blackner, *The History of Nottingham* (1815), p. 402.

4. *B. . . . J.* That is, 'butchers' and 'Jefferies'. See the final sentence of B's 'Frame Work Bill Speech' and n. 46 thereto.

Frame Work Bill Speech (1812).

Text: MS BL Egerton 2030. First published 'as spoken' (*BLJ* ii. 167) in *Cobbett's Parliamentary Debates* xxi (1812), 966–72. Thereafter published from *Cobbett's* (despite the claim in its subtitle) in *The Parliamentary Speeches of Lord Byron: Printed from the Copies prepared by his Lordship for Publication* (1824), pp. 5–16. Thereafter, published from this last source in *Works* vi (1832), 314–21, and Prothero ii. 424–30. First published from MS by R. C. Dallas in *Recollections of the Life of Lord Byron* (1824), pp. 205–18.

Dallas introduced his transcription as follows: 'A short time afterwards, he made me a present of the original manuscript of his speech *which he had previously* written,–and *from that manuscript*, I now insert it here as a literary curiosity, not devoid of interest' (p. 205). This statement, together with the slightly different shading in the ink from the text of the speech, would seem to confirm that the superscribed note and date on the first page of the MS was added by B the day after its delivery.

None of the secondary sources is reliable. *Cobbett's* committed several major errors (plausibly aural ones), which were perpetuated in *The Parliamentary Speeches of Lord Byron*, and so in *Works* and Prothero. Dallas, whose text one might reasonably suppose to be the most dependable, has been thoroughly unscrupulous. Apart from misreading in places, he has tampered with the MS to make it agree with the text of the speech as given in *Cobbett's*. His amendments on the MS are both in pencil (see nn. 3 and 9 below) and in ink (see nn. 2, 4, 8, 13, 42). Although *Cobbett's*' mistakes and Dallas's alterations to the MS may possibly reflect what B delivered in the Lords on the occasion, they do not represent what he originally wrote. All the variants are detailed in the notes below.

The speech was also reported 'very incorrectly' in the *Morning Post*, the *Morning Herald*, the *Day*, and the *British Press* on 28 Feb. 1812 (*BLJ* ii. 166–7).

This was B's maiden speech, delivered on 27 Feb. 1812 in the House of Lords. It was excogitated over the period 4–21 Feb., but in the light of his 'Draft Notes' (see above), was very probably only written out at length between 21 Feb. and its delivery.

He had originally intended making his maiden speech in the Roman Catholic Claims debate. On 1 Feb. 1812 he wrote to Francis Hodgson: 'The Catholic Question comes on this month, and perhaps I may then commence. I must "screw my courage to the sticking place," and we'll *not* fail' (*BLJ* ii. 160). This is confirmed by the existence of the partial draft MS of his 'Roman Catholic Claims Speech', the first four sentences of which, though scored out, clearly show that that MS predates the MS of the present speech (see below). However, by 4 Feb., B's interest had already turned to the more pressing and equally topical issue of frame-breaking. Writing to Samuel Rogers on that date, B said:

With my best acknowledgements to Lord Holland, I have to offer my perfect concurrence in the propriety of ye. question previously to be put to Ministers.—If their answer is in ye. negative, I shall with his Lordship's approbation, give notice of a motion for a committee of enquiry.—I would also gladly avail myself of his most able advice, & any information in documents with which he might be pleased to entrust me, to bear me out in the statement of facts it may be necessary to submit to the house.—From all that fell under my own observation during my Xmas visit to Newstead, I feel convinced that if *conciliatory* measures are not very soon adopted, the most unhappy consequences may be apprehended.—Nightly outrage & daily depredation are already at their height, & not only the masters of frames who are obnoxious on account of their occupation, but persons in no degree connected with the malcontents or their oppressors, are liable to insult & pillage. (*BLJ* ii. 160–1)

In his memoirs, Lord Holland, Recorder of Nottingham and Leader of the Whig Opposition in the House of Lords, recalled the occasion and his introduction to B as follows:

Mr. Rogers . . . informed me that Lord Byron wished to speak in Parliament against the Frame-breaking Bill, and that he was anxious to learn the forms and to consult some peer in Opposition. Mr. Rogers asked me if I would allow him to introduce me to the young poet. I willingly and warmly acquiesced, gave him what assistance I could, and received from him a very handsome and well-written letter. His speech was full of fancy, wit, and invective, but not exempt from affectation nor well reasoned, nor at all suited to our common notions of Parliamentary eloquence. His fastidious and artificial taste and his over-irritable temper would, I think, have prevented him from ever excelling in Parliament. This accidental intercourse about his first speech led to our acquaintance and even friendly familiarity, which was never interrupted. I have mentioned it because everything relating to him excites curiosity; and the uniformly courteous, I might almost say grateful, manner in which he acknowledged and returned my trifling services, amounting to little more than ordinary civility, shows a sensibility and kindness for imaginary favours in one who was unhappily too often suspected, with reason, of an extreme susceptibility to slight, and even imaginary, injuries. His speech and his verses on Princess Charlotte's tears ['Lines to a Lady Weeping', *CPW* iii. 10, 391–2] fixed his politics, and he was upon system invariably attached to the party and principles of the Whigs. (Henry Richard Vassall, Third Lord Holland, *Further Memoirs of the Whig Party 1807–1821, With Some Miscellaneous Reminiscences*, edited by Lord Stavordale (1905), pp. 122–4)

The 'handsome and well-written letter' to which Lord Holland here referred was that sent to him by B on 25 Feb. in which the following important passage appeared:

For my own part, I consider the manufacturers as a much injured body of men sacrificed to ye. views of certain individuals who have enriched themselves by those practices which have deprived the frame workers of employment.—For instance;—by the adoption of a certain kind of frame 1 man performs ye. work of 7—6 are thus thrown out of business.—But it is to be observed that ye. work thus done is far inferior in quality, hardly marketable at home, & hurried over with a view to exportation.—Surely, my Lord, however we may rejoice in any improvement in ye. arts which may be beneficial to mankind; we must not allow mankind to be sacrificed to improvements in Mechanism. The maintenance & well doing of ye. industrious poor is an object of greater consequence to ye. community than ye. enrichment of a few monopolists by any improvement in ye. implements of trade, which deprives ye workman of his bread, & renders ye. labourer 'unworthy of his hire.'—My own motive for opposing ye. bill is founded on it's palpable injustice, & it's certain inefficacy.——I have seen the state of these miserable men, & it is a disgrace to a civilized country.—Their excesses may be condemned, but cannot be subject of wonder.—The effect of ye. present bill would be to drive them into actual rebellion.—The few words I shall venture to offer on Thursday will be founded upon these opinions formed from my own observations on ye. spot.—By previous enquiry I am convinced these men would have been restored to employment & ye. county to tranquillity.—It is perhaps not yet too late & is surely worth the trial. It can never be too late to employ force in such circumstances. . . . Condemning, as every one must condemn the conduct of these wretches, I believe in ye. existence of grievances which call rather for pity than punishment.

And he added the jocular though somewhat uneasy postscript: 'I am a little apprehensive that your Lordship will think me too lenient towards these men, & *half* a *framebreaker myself*' (*BLJ* ii. 165–6). As can be seen, many points and even phrases and allusions, both in this letter and in his letter to Rogers, crop up in the speech itself; and it is certainly clear that however history may regard the practice, B himself regarded (or chose to regard) frame-breaking as a symptom of capitalism and oppression.

The immediate aftermath of B's speech is captured vividly, though somewhat ludicrously, by R. C. Dallas:

It produced a considerable effect in the House of Lords, and he received many compliments from the Opposition Peers. When he left the great chamber, I went and met him in the passage; he was glowing with success, and much agitated. I had an umbrella in my right hand, not expecting that he would put out his hand to me—in my haste to take it when offered, I had advanced my left hand—'What,' said he, 'give your friend your left hand upon such an occasion?' I showed the cause, and immediately changing the umbrella to the other hand, I gave him my right hand, which he shook and pressed warmly. He was greatly elated, and repeated some of the compliments which had been paid him, and mentioned one or two of the Peers who had desired to be introduced to him. He concluded with saying, that he had, by his speech, given me the best advertisement for Childe Harold's Pilgrimage. (Dallas, *Recollections of the Life of Lord Byron*, pp. 203–4)

B himself wrote ebulliently of his performance to Hodgson on 5 Mar. 1812:

Lds. Holland & Grenville, particularly the latter paid some high compts. in the course of their speeches [see nn. 25, 26, 39, 43 below] as you may have seen in the papers, & Ld. Eldon & Harrowby answered me.——I have had many marvelous eulogies repeated to me since in person & by proxy from divers persons *ministerial—yea ministerial*! as well as oppositionists, of them I shall only mention Sir F. Burdetts.—*He* says it is the best speech by a *Lord* since the 'Lord knows when' probably from a fellow feeling in ye. sentiments.—Ld. H[olland] tells me I shall beat them all if I persevere, & Ld. G[renville] remarked that the construction of some of my periods are very like *Burke's*!!—And so much for vanity.——I spoke very violent sentences with a sort of modest impudence, abused every thing & every body, & put the Ld. Chancellor [Eldon] very much out of humour, & if I may believe what I hear, have not lost any character by the experiment.—As to my delivery, loud & fluent enough, perhaps a little theatrical.——I could not recognize myself or any one else in the Newspapers. (*BLJ* ii. 167)

Cf. *The Annual Register* (1812), p. 38. See also 'An Ode to the Framers of the Frame Bill', and 'The Waltz', l. 165 (*CPW* iii. 9, 28, 390–1, 401).

The history of frame-breaking and of Luddism in Nottinghamshire have been ably studied in Malcolm I. Thomas, *Politics and Society in Nottingham 1785–1835* (1969) (esp. pp. 78–90, and cf. E. P. Thompson, *The Making of the English Working Class* (1963), pp. 530–602); Malcolm I. Thomas, *The Luddites: Machine-breaking in Regency England* (1970), and id. (ed.), *Luddism in Nottinghamshire* (1972) (a selection of the Home Office papers of the time). See also Frank Ongley Darvall, *Popular Disturbances and Public Order in Regency England* (1934); John Blackner, *The History of Nottingham* (1815); William Felkin, *A History of the Machine-Wrought Hosiery and Lace Manufactures* (1867), and Stanley D. Chapman (ed.), *Henson's History of the Framework Knitters* (1970) (though this last source, being unfinished, is deficient in details of the period with which B is connected). Felkin's work is of particular interest since he himself was a Special Constable in the locality at the time of the disturbances to which B alludes, and speaks from first-hand experience. Other useful references are:

The Annual Register (1811, 1812); *Cobbett's Parliamentary Debates* xxi (1812), and *Reports from Committees* (1812), ii (Jan.–July), 203–304. This last source is especially informative since it records the various grievances of the frame-workers generally, as elicited from their representatives (such as John Blackner and Gravenor Henson) who were interviewed before the House of Lords' Committee on the Framework Knitters Petitions (which sat in May and July 1812). In summary, the principal complaints and demands were as follows:

1. *Wide frames.* Although it appears that the machines themselves were not the objects of the frame-workers' aggravation, but rather the *use* to which they were put, 'wide frames' were regarded as producing the poorest work and were associated specifically with 'cut-ups' and 'single press'. 'Cut-ups' were articles such as gloves or stockings manufactured of large pieces of material, cut out and sewn to the shape of the hand or foot. They were easy, quick, and cheap to make, but of poor quality and not durable. The same applies to 'single press', which comprised articles made from single-thread material in imitation of 'double press' (i.e. double-thread work and the genuine thing). There was the additional irritation here in that unscrupulous workers could, and frequently did, pass off 'single press' as 'double press' items to the purchaser. As the difference between the two was difficult to detect (even to the eye of an experienced worker), the unwitting customer was thus easily defrauded. (The term 'spider work' (see n. 7 below) seems to refer to either or both of these two practices). In the frame-workers' view, the effects of such practices were that less skilled labour was required (hence 'colting', see below) and many were thrown out of employment; output doubled, and the market became glutted; the workers' credit was destroyed, and the trade brought into disrepute.

2. *Colting.* Trade cant for the taking on of (cheap) unskilled labour, such as workers not brought up to the trade or not having served a regular apprenticeship.

3. *Truck.* Trade cant for being paid in goods rather than money.

4. *The rack.* A worker was paid by the yard. The 'Rack' measured *exactly* how much he had produced. The frame-workers demanded the compulsory use of this instrument, as without it they felt they could be too easily defrauded by their employers.

5. *Schedule of payment.* Unscrupulous employers often failed to pay their employees the wages originally agreed upon. The demand for a compulsory 'schedule' aimed at binding both employer and employee to the original contractual terms of employment.

6. *Fixed frame-rents.* A frame-worker was not in a position to buy his own frame; he generally hired one. Many capitalists who had no interest in the trade (e.g. butchers, millers) bought new frames merely to let them out at exorbitant rents. A fixed frame-rent would ensure that every worker paid only the statutory rate.

The full title of the Frame Work Bill, as amended in the Committee of the House of Commons on 18 Feb. was: 'A Bill for the more exemplary Punishment of Persons destroying or injuring any Stocking or Lace Frames, or other Machines or Engines used in the Framework Knitted Manufactory, or any Articles or Goods in such Frames or Machines.' In its preamble, the Bill referred to an earlier Act of 1788, the provisions of which, it stated, 'have been found ineffectual'. That Act had made frame-breaking a felony, carrying the penalty of transportation for not less than 7 and no more than 14 years (*The Statutes at Large*, vol. xxxvi (1787–9), pt. ii, ch. lv, pp. 550–3). After detailing the nature of the offence, the Bill provided for the death penalty for all frame-breakers, without benefit of clergy (i.e. without special claims or privileged exemptions), and proposed that those persons in whose name or custody machines destroyed were registered should give notice of such destruction to the owners and should appear before magistrates to be examined as to their knowledge of the offenders. The Bill was to remain in effect until 1 Mar. 1814. For the full title, preamble and articles of the Bill, see *Public Bills* (1812), i (Session 7 Jan.–30 July), 325–8. For the passage of the Bill through both Houses of Parliament, see *Cobbett's* xxi (1812), 602–1168 *passim*, and *Journals of the House of Lords* xlviii (1810–12), 593, 614. It received the Royal Assent on 20 Mar. 1812 (*Journals of the House of Lords* xlviii (1810–12), 654).

1. *on the day . . . detection.* B left Newstead, his estate in Nottinghamshire, for London on 11 Jan. 1812 (Marchand i. 310). Felkin states that a number of frames were broken throughout Nottinghamshire 'in the first fortnight of 1812; also fifteen frames were destroyed at New Radford, nine at Basford, nine at Hucknall, five in Nottingham, and three at Bulwell' (*A History*, p. 234). No doubt B alludes in particular to these last 41 breakages since all these towns are in the vicinity of Newstead.

2. *then.* Dallas has crossed out this word in B's MS, and has then reinstated it in his own hand; it appears in all editions.

3. *populace.* Deleted by Dallas in B's MS with two vertical slashes, and 'people' overwritten in pencil; 'people' in all editions.

4. *&.* Deleted by Dallas: 'yet' substituted; 'yet' in all editions.

5. *At the time . . . Nothing.* Cf. Felkin:

> An effective military force of about 800 horse and 1000 foot, was concentrated chiefly in and near Nottingham, under the direction of several experienced military officers who had orders to consult with the local magistrates and two London police magistrates, specially sent down by government, to assist in every way practicable. Money was secretly offered for information; and a royal proclamation was issued offering £50 reward for the apprehension of any offender. Notwithstanding all these measures, the devastation increased in extent and violence as the winter [of 1811] came on. (*A History*, p. 232)

6. *By the adoption . . . employment.* B probably alludes here to the 'Old Loughborough', a traverse bobbin net machine (invented by John Heathcoat

(1783–1861) and patented by him in July 1809), which could make net of any width. Felkin remarks that this machine was regarded by some as providing employment for many, but that by others it was 'looked upon as shortening labour . . . and disliked and decried accordingly' (*A History*, p. 204).

7. *Spider work.* B himself appears to have given currency to this term. Both the *OED* and the *English Dialect Dictionary* cite this passage as their only example of its usage. It is defined by the latter as denoting 'an inferior class of goods produced by machinery'. See general note above.

8. *well doing & maintenance.* Dallas has marked 'well doing' and 'maintenance' to be transposed and has parenthesized the ampersand; 'maintenance and well doing' in all editions.

9. *was an object.* Grammatically corrected by Dallas in pencil: he has scored out 'was an', overwritten the word 'were', and added an 's' to the word 'object'; 'were objects' in all editions.

10. *labourer . . . hire.* Luke 10: 7.

11. *yet in . . . exportation.* Cf. Felkin: 'the fear of an entire cessation of demand in the markets of North America, the heavy burden of war taxation and the loans necessary for national purposes, left manufacturers everywhere only confined means, and lowered credit. In the hosiery districts the warehouses were full of goods' (*A History*, p. 230).

12. *construction.* This reads 'description' in all editions except Dallas's.

13. *but their.* Dallas has inserted an 'of' between these two words in B's MS; 'but of their' in all editions.

14. *warfare . . . eighteen years.* With periodic intermissions of peace, England had been at war with France since 1793.

15. *"great statesmen now no more".* In a debate on the Roman Catholic petition on 27 May 1808, Lord Grenville spoke of Pitt as 'that great statesman, now no more' (*Cobbett's* xi (1808), 648).

16. *third & fourth generation.* Exodus 20: 5.

17. *daily bread.* Matthew 6: 11, and see also Felkin: 'How many thousands of times was that cry repeated—"Give us work at any price; half a loaf is better than no bread!" It was a heavy cry uttered too often ever to be forgotten' (*A History*, p. 230).

18. *Can you . . . Lordships.* B refers to the various cases of public defalcations, bankruptcy, and dubious financial dealings amongst members of the lower House currently under consideration. See *Cobbett's* xxi, 478–82, 1315–16; xxii. 106–7, 146–8, 371–4, 1068–9. See also n. 2 to B's 'Draft Notes' above, and n. 26 to B's 'Roman Catholic Claims Speech' below.

19. *to dig . . . to beg.* Luke 16: 3.

20. *It has been stated . . . destruction.* Introducing the Frame Work Bill in the

House of Commons on 14 Feb. 1812, Mr Secretary Ryder informed the House that:

They were not, perhaps, aware, that the machinery, which had been destroyed, did not belong to the houses in which they were, but were either hired by the masters to the operative manufacturers, or were the property of a middle class, who vested their capitals in the purchase of frames which they hired. The consequence had been that those persons to whom the frames belonged, had been most active accomplices in their destruction, and they had a direct interest in preventing the discovery of the delinquents. (*Cobbett's* xxi. 809)

21. *seem formed on.* This reads 'seemed on' in all editions except Dallas's.

22. *Major Sturgeon . . . Mansfield.* See Samuel Foote, *The Mayor of Garratt* (1764), Act I: 'Oh! such marchings and counter-marchings, from Brentford to Elin, from Elin to Acton, from Acton to Uxbridge; the dust flying, the sun scorching, men sweating—' (Major Sturgeon himself speaking). For these towns in Middlesex, B has substituted those most inflamed towns in Nottinghamshire within the vicinity of Newstead: Basford and Bulwell being respectively 7 and 5 miles to the south, and Mansfield 4 miles to the north of Newstead. Basford is the correct orthography: Dallas has 'Bareford'; it is 'Banford' in all other editions. Bulwell (the correct orthography) becomes 'Bulnell' in Dallas, and 'Bullwell' in all other editions.

23. *"the pride . . . war". Othello* III. iii. 356.

24. *"spolia opima".* The spoils of war, the choicest booty from the battlefield. See Livy, *Ab Urbe Condita* iv. 20.

25. *Now . . . made ridiculous.* Lord Holland concurred with this point: 'He agreed with his noble friend in disapproving the manner in which the military had been employed, and urged the propriety of an inquiry to open the eyes of the deluded multitude' (*Cobbett's* xxi. 973).

26. *As the Sword . . . Scabbard.* This image, of which B was fond (see, e.g., *BLJ* ix. 191), echoes the Earl of Clarendon's comment about John Hampden (1594–1643), who opposed the imposition of Ship money, and was mortally wounded in a skirmish near Oxford: 'when he first drew his sword he threw away the scabbard' (see Clarendon, *The History of the Rebellion*, ed. W. Dunn Macray, 6 vols. (1888), iii. 63). Lord Grenville adverted to B's point with some enthusiasm: 'There never was a maxim of greater wisdom than that uttered by the noble lord (Byron), who had so ably addressed their lordships that night for the first time, that the military ought never to be employed except in extreme cases, and then they should be effectual, if possible, rather by the terror of their appearance, than their power of execution' (*Cobbett's* xxi. 977).

27. *"good easy men . . . ripening". Henry VIII* III. ii. 357–8.

28. *your land divides against itself.* Mark 3: 25.

29. *"Bellua multorum capitum".* The many-headed monster. See Horace, *Epistulae* I. i. 76. The phrase was proverbial even in Horace's time. See also Pope,

The First Epistle of the Second Book of Horace, l. 305: 'The many-headed monster of the pit'.

30. *the parish.* Before the arrival of the welfare state, the 'dole' (or poor relief) was dispensed by the 'parish', a local civil authority constituted to administer the Poor Law. At the time of B's speech, nearly half the population of Nottingham was receiving such relief. See Felkin, *A History*, p. 231.

31. *the widow's mite.* Mark 12: 41–4. This biblical saying is proverbial for giving one's all, though it be but little. See also *DJ* VI. 6.

32. *When the Portuguese . . . granaries.* On 21 Aug. 1808 the French under Junot were defeated by the English under Wellesley (later the Duke of Wellington) at Vimiero. Since 1808 England had granted an annual sum of £2 million as aid to Portugal.

33. *Charity . . . at home.* Although the phrase 'Charity begins at home' is proverbial, B may also have had in mind here the exchange between Rowley and Sir Oliver Surface in Sheridan's *The School for Scandal* V. i. Speaking of Joseph Surface, Rowley says: 'I believe there is no sentiment he has such faith in as that *Charity begins at home.*' To which Sir Oliver replies: 'And his, I presume, is of that domestic sort which never stirs abroad at all.'

34. *tender mercies . . . gibbet.* Cf. Proverbs 12: 10 and Luke 1: 78.

35. *funds.* This reads 'friends' in all editions except Dallas.

36. *Draco.* Draco (*fl.* 621 BC), author of the first written Athenian laws (621 BC). He affixed the death penalty to virtually every offence, from the merest misdemeanour to the gravest of crimes, which gave rise to the famous comment of Demades that 'Draco's code was written not in ink but in blood' (Plutarch, *The Rise and Fall of Athens*, trans. Ian Scott-Kilvert (1960), p. 59).

37. *After feeling . . . Sangrados.* Dr Sangrado is a quack physician in A.-R. Le Sage's *Gil Blas de Santillane* (1715–35). Gil Blas becomes apprenticed to Dr Sangrado, who reveals the secret of his profession to him thus:

> Know, my friend, all that is required is to bleed the patients, and make them drink warm water. This is the secret of curing all the distempers incident to man. Yes! that wonderful secret which I reveal to thee, and which nature, impenetrable to my brethren, hath not been able to hide from my researches, is contained in these two points, of plentiful bleeding and frequent drafts of water. I have nothing more to impart . . . (*The Adventures of Gil Blas*, trans. T. Smollet (3 vols., 1802), I. ii. 137)

38. *inefficacy.* This reads 'inefficiency' in all editions including Dallas.

39. *blood enough upon your penal code.* Cf. Leviticus 20: 9–16, 27; Deuteronomy 19: 10; Joshua 2: 19; Ezekiel 18: 13; 33: 5. Lord Grenville shared the sentiments expressed by B in this passage (see n. 43 below).

40. *testify against you.* Cf. Psalms 50: 7; Isaiah 59: 12; Jeremiah 14: 7.

41. *Sherwood forest . . . Outlaws.* Sherwood forest (4 miles to the north of Newstead, abutting the town of Mansfield) was crown property long

preserved by royal charter. At the time of B's speaking it was the site of a military encampment (stationed there to quell the current disturbances). It is perhaps most celebrated for its connection with the legendary hero/outlaw Robin Hood. See Blackner, *The History*, p. 37; also John Throsby, *Thoroton's History of Nottinghamshire*, 3 vols. (1797), ii. 157–76.

42. *"Jack Ketches?* The closing quotation marks are missing in the original. Dallas has stroked through these two words with several vertical slashes and has substituted 'Executioners?' in B's MS; 'Executioners?' appears in all editions. 'Jack Ketch' had been the sobriquet for the common hangman since the seventeenth century. It derived from John ('Jack') Ketch (d. 1686), the public executioner from 1663 to 1686 who was renowned for his brutality and who carried out many of the sentences of Judge Jeffreys (see n. 46 below).

43. *That most . . . in this.* Lord Grenville echoed B's argument:

> he hoped their lordships were familiar with the wise maxim of a great authority 'de vita hominis nulla est cunctatio longa.' When the question was about the life of man, he should have expected that ministers . . . would have willingly acceded to the delay, if there was the smallest doubt in the mind of any noble lord, whether it was necessary to add to the horrible and sanguinary catalogue of our capital punishments. (*Cobbett's* xxi. 976)

The Latin tag here is adapted from Juvenal, *Satire* vi. 221: 'nulla umquam de morte hominis cunctatio longa est' ('no delay is too long when the life of a man is at stake'). The 'recent instances' to which B refers here would include the other two major parliamentary issues of the time: the abolition of the slave trade, and the Roman Catholic claims (the 'emancipate or relieve' respectively of the following sentence).

44. *framers.* B is enjoying the pun here on 'frame' (as it relates to the frame-workers), and 'frame' (as the technical term used in parliamentary circles for the drawing up of a Bill). Cf. 'An Ode to the Framers of the Frame Bill' (*CPW* iii. 9). (The derogatory senses of 'frame' (as in 'frame-up', or 'framed') are of twentieth-century origin.)

45. *Athenian lawgiver . . . blood.* This is Draco (see n. 36 above).

46. *twelve butchers . . . Judge.* An English jury consists of twelve commoners who pass the verdict (but not the sentence) on the accused. George ('Judge') Jeffreys, first Baron Jeffreys of Wem (1648–89), was notorious for his severity as a judge. In 1683 he was appointed Lord Chief Justice, and in 1685 Lord Chancellor. His notoriety stems principally from the 'Bloody Assizes' (1685), which were held after the battle of Sedgemoor (1685), at which Jeffreys sentenced more than 300 people to execution, and 1,000 to transportation.

Roman Catholic Claims Debate: Draft Speech and Notes (1812)

Text: MS Murray. Unpublished.

The existence of this draft MS proves conclusively that B had not merely contemplated making his maiden speech on the Catholic question, but had actually started to compose it. For this reason I have not edited to the foot of the page the first four erased sentences, which should be compared with the opening of his 'Frame Work Bill Speech' and particularly its third sentence.

On 16 Jan. 1812 B wrote to Hobhouse, who was then with his regiment at Enniscorthy in Ireland: '*Do* leave Ireland, I fear your Catholics will find work for you, surely *you* wont fight against them.—Will you? I went down to the house & resumed my seat yesterday, I mean to try a speech but have not yet determined on my subject' (*BLJ* ii. 155). The promise of a debate on the state of Ireland hung over the proceedings in the House of Lords during the whole of Jan. 1812; and without a doubt this prompted B to turn his attention at first to the affairs of that country as a subject for a speech. After several postponements, a motion for a debate on the state of Ireland was tabled by Earl Fitzwilliam on 31 Jan. 1812. Although the motion was eventually rejected, it gave rise to a long debate (the whole of which is reported in *Cobbett's* xxi (1812), 408–77) which did not end until 6.30 on the morning of 1 Feb., by which time B had already paired off and left the House. (To pair off is parliamentary parlance for the agreement between two members of opposing parties that neither shall vote in a debate.) He wrote to Hodgson that day:

> I am rather unwell with a vile cold, caught in the House of Lords last night. Lord Sligo and myself, being tired, *paired off*, being of opposite sides, so that nothing was gained or lost by *our* votes. I did not speak: but I might as well, for nothing could have been inferior to the Duke of Devonshire, Marquis of Downshire, and the Earl of Fitzwilliam. The Catholic Question comes on this month, and perhaps I may then commence. I must 'screw my courage to the sticking place,' and we'll *not* fail. (*BLJ* ii. 160)

As it happened, no notice was given at all for such a debate on the Catholic question in Feb.; and by 4 Feb. B had determined to make his maiden speech on the Frame Work Bill. Hence this draft was almost certainly written between 1 and 3 Feb. 1812; but it is clear that B returned to it later when drafting his speech (see below).

1. *"Non . . . &c"* (*quote*). B's parenthetical direction to himself is written underneath the Latin quotation (for which see n. 1 to his speech below).

2. *The enemy . . . within.* B refers to the continuing wars on the Continent (Napoleon's Russian campaign was imminent), and to the growing hostility between America and England (war was declared in June 1812).

3. *Thirty nine articles.* See n. 119 to 'Reading List' above.

4. *We have . . . whatsoever.* The phrase 'within & without doors' is parliamentary parlance for what is said or done inside or outside the Houses of Parliament. Although the cliché 'Church and State' was bandied about by supporters and antagonists of the Roman Catholic claims, strictly speaking the allusion is to Burke: 'Church and state are ideas inseparable in their minds [those of the

English], and scarcely is the one ever mentioned without mentioning the other' (Edmund Burke, *Reflections on the Revolution in France* (1790), p. 148). For the phrase 'church militant' see n. 4 to B's speech below.

5. *"our eggs . . . end."* Swift, *Gulliver's Travels*, pt. i, ch. 4. (This idle dispute between the 'Big-Endians' and the 'Little-Endians' was itself a satire on the religious controversies of the time.)

6. *"Fear God . . . King" . . . will.* This is a conflation of I Peter 2: 17 ('Honour all men. Love the brotherhood. Fear God. Honour the king') and Luke 2: 14 ('Glory to God in the highest, and on earth peace, good will toward men').

7. *"To the . . . generation".* Exodus 20: 5.

8. *Pharisees of Christianity.* The Pharisees were one of the three Jewish sects (the other two being the Sadducees and the Essenes) who opposed Christ's teachings, and who were renowned for their strict observance of religious law and for their sanctimoniousness. See, e.g., Matthew 15: 1–20; 16: 1–12; 22: 15–46; and 23. 'Pharisee' is synonymous with 'hypocrite'.

9. *It was said . . . Jews?* B must be referring here to Viscount Sidmouth's comment in his speech in the debate on Earl Fitzwilliam's Motion respecting the State of Ireland on 31 Jan. 1812:

> Was not the House called on to protect the true religion, established by law in this country? And must they not greatly detract from that estimation in which it was essential that it should be held, by allowing it to be supposed that they so far countenanced mass, as to put it on a level with the established religion of the country—allowing it to be regarded as a matter of indifference whether persons went to the church, to mass, or to the synagogue. (*Cobbett's* xxi (1812), 428)

10. *"Would any . . . Catholic?* B misspells Barabbas and omits the closing quotation marks. This is a paraphrase of Shylock in *The Merchant of Venice* IV. i. 297–8.

11. *"beam . . . neighbours."* Matthew 7: 3–5.

12. *It has . . . they are.* For example, in the debate on Earl Fitzwilliam's Motion respecting the State of Ireland on 31 Jan. 1812, Viscount Sidmouth alluded to the majority of the Catholic population in Ireland as 'the great mass of the people, who were not at all interested, nor seemed to be in the contemplation of the noble earl [Fitzwilliam], while he set up the right of the higher ranks [of the Roman Catholics] to the privileges which it was the object of his present motion to obtain for them'. And the Earl of Westmoreland, in the same debate, expressed a similar view: 'That the concession of the Catholic claims would not at all affect the great mass of Catholic population in Ireland, he was persuaded' (*Cobbett's* xxi (1812), 425, 456). See also n. 37 to B's speech below.

13. *"house of bondage".* Exodus 13: 14; 20: 2.

14. *you might . . . purport.* This was indeed so. The Slave Trade Abolition Bill was passed in the House of Lords on 23 Mar. 1807, and received the royal

assent on 25. Mar. However, a petition against the bill had been presented in the House of Commons on 27 Feb. 1807, and was again presented in the House of Lords on 23 Mar. *Cobbett's* records:

> The Earl of *Westmoreland* presented a petition from certain planters, mortgagees, merchants and others, interested in the West India islands, against a clause added by the house of commons to the Slave Trade Abolition bill, enacting that negroes seized in consequence of illicit trade, should be declared free, which they stated would be productive of great danger to the colonies. (*Cobbett's* ix (1807), 168)

See also *Journals of the House of Commons* lxii (15 Dec. 1806–17 Dec. 1807), 188–9; *Journals of the House of Lords* xlvi (1806–8), 128; and *Cobbett's* ix (1807), 168–70, 187.

15. *the.* The MS breaks off here at the foot of the page.

16. *and . . . subjects?* B almost certainly refers to Ferdinand VII (1784–1833), King of Spain (Mar.–May 1808, 1814–33), who had been imprisoned by Napoleon at Valençay since 1808. See n. 17; see also nn. 60, 61 to B's speech below.

17. *Usurper.* See also B's erasure. B refers to Charles-Maurice de Talleyrand-Périgord (1754–1838), who was responsible for the custody of Ferdinand VII and the Spanish princes at Valençay. See n. 16 above, nn. 60, 61 to B's speech below, and 'A Letter on the State of French Affairs', *post.*

18. *and . . . body——.* This fragment of MS represents four and a half lines written at the head of a separate sheet of paper from the foregoing MS. Unfortunately the intervening pages of the MS are no longer extant. See also n. 19 below.

19. [*Draft Notes*]. The jottings that follow are on the verso of the fragment of MS of this draft speech (see n. 18), and were doubtless intended as memoranda for its continuation.

20. *Disputes . . . Constantinople.* B refers to the disputes between the Latin and Greek churches during the siege of Constantinople by Mahomet II in the spring of 1453, which greatly contributed to the capture of the city and thus to the downfall of the Roman empire. See Gibbon, *The History of the Decline and Fall of the Roman Empire*, chs. lxvii, lxviii.

21. *Ld P. . . . &^{c}.* Lord Peterborough. See n. 5 to B's speech below.

22. *Paley. &^{c}.* See n. 36 to B's speech below.

23. *I.^{h} D.^{rum}.* Irish Drummer. See n. 40 to B's speech below.

24. *Maltese . . . &^{c}.* In July 1811 the Maltese (for the administration and defence of whom England was responsible) had petitioned the King for their own parliament, a free press, trial by jury, and the restoration of various ancient Maltese rights. A commission of inquiry was set up in 1812 and sent out to investigate. The result was that Sir Thomas Maitland (?1759–1824) was appointed Governor and Commander-in-Chief of Malta in 1813. By the terms of the Sicilian treaty of 1808, England had agreed to grant Sicily (for whose

defence she was also responsible) an annual sum of £400,000. The House of Commons had last voted for the annual renewal of the subsidy on 1 May 1811, and would do so again on 25 Mar. 1812 (*Cobbett's* xix (1811), 782–5; xxii (1812), 187–92). See also n. 57 to B's speech below.

25. *Mice—mountains.* See n. 49 to B's speech below.

26. *D.r Johnson . . . &c.* For B's references to Dr Johnson and to the Union see, respectively, nn. 45 and 24 to his speech below.

Roman Catholic Claims Speech: Notes

Text: MS Bodleian (Dep. Lovelace Byron 154 f. 212r and v). Unpublished.

These 'Notes' were written in four columns on a single folded half-sheet folio. It seems most probable that B began to draft them after he had received the following letter (and enclosure) from his friend John Cam Hobhouse, written in Mar. 1812 but dated merely 'Wednesday 2 O'clock':

> I am going to my Father's mansion again this day and am so much the more chagrined that I did not see you yesterday. Saturday however will see me again in London & of course at n 8—Inclosed is a long letter from B L Ryan for your use—What he says is very strong & you may depend upon his facts—you will I trust be able to make some use of this information which as far as it goes appears to me to be curious and not already made public but which I wish were more detailed, as believe me, that I am most interested as to the part you are to act on the important tenth of April—(*Byron's Bulldog*, p. 99)

In his note to this letter (p. 99n.), Peter Graham makes the sound suggestion that the enclosed letter of Dr Ryan (the Catholic titular Bishop of Ferns) may have 'contained some of the specific instances of British abuse of the Irish Catholics, such as the disbanding of the congregation at Newton Barry, Wexford, and the acquittal of a Protestant yeoman who shot and killed a Catholic', to which B refers in his speech (see respectively nn. 15 and 18 below). If this is so, then the most likely date of Hobhouse's letter is Wednesday 18 Mar. (It cannot have been Wednesday 11 Mar., the only Wednesday in March on which Hobhouse distinctly states in his diary that he 'went down to Whitton', because he had seen *Julius Caesar* with B and Moore the preceding evening (Broughton Papers, BL Add. MS 56530, f. 39). Nor can it have been Wednesday 25 Mar., for Hobhouse was 'writing hard' in London that day, and only went down on Thursday 26 to Whitton, where he remained until the following Tuesday, 31 Mar. (ibid., f. 40v).) Although he does not specifically state that he went to Whitton on 18 Mar., he did at least dine there on Thursday 19 Mar., had *not* seen B the previous Tuesday 17 Mar. (on which day, though, he had repaid his outstanding debt to B through his brother Benjamin), and *did* dine in B's company at Wedderburn Webster's in London before going off to Lady Mountnorris's ball on Friday 20 Mar. (ibid.). Hence these 'Notes' were almost certainly written out between 18 Mar. and 10 Apr., the original date set for the Roman Catholic Claims debate (hence Hobhouse's reference to 'the important tenth of April'). It was subsequently postponed to 21 Apr. 1812 (*Journals of the House of Lords* xlviii (1810–12), 624, 684, 741).

I do not wish to suggest, however, that inordinate weight should be given to Dr Ryan's letter as regards the content of either these 'Notes' or B's speech. Assuredly it may have supplied him with one or two local details, on which he was able to capitalize (see nn. 15, 18, 20, 33 below); but it is quite evident that B had done a considerable amount of research into the subject himself, and some of the sources he may have consulted are given below. What is perhaps most valuable to note is the shift in B's approach to the issue of Catholic emancipation, from the generalized rhetoric of his 'Draft Speech and Notes', to the more informed and incisive argument (rich in detail, relevant fact and precise examples) that characterizes these 'Notes' and his eventual speech.

As B raised each item in these 'Notes' in his speech as received, I have resisted annotating here, and refer the reader to the notes to B's speech below. To prevent any misunderstanding, however, I have expanded his abbreviations in the following notes.

1. *C*^{c} Catholic.
2. *M*^{a} . . . *B's Ad*^{m} Militia . . . Bedford's Administration. (See nn. 10, 11, 23 to B's speech.)
3. *Sus Cler* . . . *J*^{e} . . . *G*^{d} Suspended Clergyman . . . Justice . . . Grand. (See n. 20 to B's speech.)
4. *Com*^{ers} Commissioners. (See n. 22 to B's speech.)
5. *C.* Camden. (See n. 23 to B's speech.)
6. *L*^{n} Legion. (See n. 78 to B's speech.)

Roman Catholic Claims Speech

Text: *Cobbett's Parliamentary Debates* xxii (1812), 642–53. Thereafter published from *Cobbett's* in *The Parliamentary Speeches of Lord Byron* (1824), pp. 17–39, from which it was published in *Works* vi (1832), 321–35, and Prothero ii. 431–43.

Although B clearly returned to his original draft of this speech, begun between 1 and 3 Feb. (see 'Draft Speech and Notes' above), he must have worked up another draft (no longer extant) for the text of this speech from the foregoing 'Notes'; and, as with those 'Notes', it must have been composed between 18 Mar. and 10 Apr. 1812. There is no reference whatsoever to the writing or the delivery of this speech in B's correspondence.

Since the Union of England with Ireland (effective from 1 Jan. 1801), there had been four major debates in parliament on the Roman Catholic petitions, in 1805, 1808, 1810, and 1811. On none of these occasions were the Roman Catholics yielded the least relief. However, although they make somewhat turgid and bigoted reading, these debates provide an instructive background both in spirit and in matter to the current debate and to B's speech: certainly B appears to have studied them with some care.

In the relevant session of parliament, amongst the numerous other petitions that had been accumulating, the Earl of Donoughmore presented 'The General Petition of the Roman Catholics of Ireland' on 20. Apr. (The text is given in full in *Journals of the House of Lords* xlviii (1810–12), 741–3; see also *Cobbett's* xxii (1812), 452–63). The following extract from this epitomizes the full nature and extent of the Roman Catholic claims for which B was pleading:

> Our object is avowed and direct; earnest, yet natural: it extends to an equal participation of the civil rights of the constitution of our country, equally with our fellow-subjects of all other religious persuasions: it extends no further. We would cheerfully concede the enjoyment of civil and religious liberty to all mankind; we ask no more for ourselves. We seek not the possession of offices, but mere eligibility to office, in common with our fellow-citizens; not power or ascendency over any class of people, but the bare permission to rise from our prostrate posture, and to stand erect in the empire. (*Cobbett's* xxii (1812), 457)

The debate itself took place in a full House of Lords on Thursday 21 Apr. 1812. It is reecorded in its entirety in *Cobbett's* (xxii (1812), 509–704) under the title 'The Earl of Donoughmore's Motion for a Committee on the Civil Disabilities of the Roman Catholics'. There were eleven speakers; B spoke eighth, and no one alluded to any part of his speech. However, Hobhouse recorded in his diary for the day that he had 'staid up all night at the House of Lords—debate on the catholic question heard Byron—who kept the House in a roar of laughter' (Broughton Papers, BL Add. MS 56530 f. 41v; *Recollections* i. 38. See also Marchand i. 345; *BAP*, pp. 125–6).

As for B's concern for the Roman Catholics of Ireland, perhaps the following is indicative of its strength. In his *Fugitive Pieces and Reminiscences of Lord Byron* (1829), Isaac Nathan, the musician with whom B collaborated over *Hebrew Melodies* in 1815, records:

> This liberality of sentiment of Lord Byron was not confined to the Jews alone, but his Lordship often regretted the truly distressed state of Ireland: 'two thirds of that unhappy country,' he observed, 'had laboured for ages to obtain that liberty which was only extended to one third part of its population, and he hoped a time would arrive, when religious distinctions in political matters, would not prove a barrier to preferment in that country: till which period, Ireland would never cordially coalesce with Great Britain, but continue as it had been the scene of bloodshed, anarchy and confusion.' (p. 25)

(For B's comparison of the oppression of the Roman Catholics and the Jews with that of the Greeks, see his own notes to stanza 73 of *CHP* II (*CPW* ii. 201, 202).)

Apart from the debates mentioned above and various other works referred to in the notes to his 'Draft Speech and Notes' (above) and to his speech below, B may have also consulted the following sources (their short titles, used in the notes below, are given in square brackets).

Francis Plowden, *The History of Ireland, from its Union with Great Britain in January 1801, to October 1810*, 3 vols. (1811) [Plowden, *History of Ireland*].

A Statement of the Penal Laws, which aggrieve the Catholics of Ireland. (2nd edn. 1812) [*A Statement*].

A Summary View of the Rights and Claims of the Roman Catholics of Ireland (Edinburgh, 1808). This is a reprint of Jeffrey's important, influential and sympathetic article on various 'Pamphlets on the Catholic Question', which first appeared in the *Edinburgh Review*, vol. xi, no. xxi (Oct. 1807), art. viii, pp. 116–44.

Thomas Newenham, *A View of the Natural, Political, and Commercial Circumstances of Ireland* (1809). (See particularly pt. iv, sections i–iv, viii).

Edward Wakefield, *An Account of Ireland, Statistical and Political*, 2 vols. (1812), ii.

1. *"Non tempore . . . hostis."* Virgil, *Aeneid* xi. 303–4: 'Such is not the time to hold a counsel while the enemy besiege our walls.' This forms part of the opening sentence of Latinus' speech which B recited at the Harrow speech day on 5 July 1804 (see Marchand i. 84).

2. *The enemy . . . religion.* See n. 2 to B's 'Draft Speech' above. By the time of B's speaking, Napoleon had concluded treaties of alliance with Prussia (Feb. 1812) and Austria (Mar. 1812), and had declared war on Russia (Apr. 1812).

3. *Much . . . State.* See n. 4 to B's 'Draft Speech' above.

4. *Church militant.* B echoes 'the whole state of Christ's Church militant here in earth' (*Book of Common Prayer*, 'Prayer for the Church Militant').

5. *"Parliamentary . . . religion."* At the second reading of the Bill against Blasphemy and Prophaneness on 2 May 1721 the Earl of Peterborough said that 'Though he was for a parliamentary king, yet he did not desire to have a parliamentary God, or a parliamentary religion: and, if the House were for such a one, he would go to Rome and endeavour to be chosen a cardinal; for he had rather sit in the conclave, than with their lordships upon those terms' (*Cobbett's Parliamentary History of England* vii (1811), 894–5).

6. *"eggs . . . end."* See n. 5 to B's 'Draft Speech' above.

7. *The opponents . . . happy.* This is B's own interpretation and categorization of the major arguments of those opposed to the claims of the Roman Catholics, and it has much validity. For example, in the debate on Earl Fitzwilliam's Motion respecting the State of Ireland on 31 Jan. 1812, Lord Mulgrave asked: 'if every thing were granted to the Roman Catholics which they now demand, was it in human nature that they should stop short there?' (*Cobbett's* xxi (1812), 461). And he reiterated this question in a debate on Lord Boringdon's Motion respecting an efficient Administration on 19 Mar. 1812, saying of the Roman Catholic claims: 'Were we sure that when these claims were conceded, fresh claims would not be advanced?' (*Cobbett's* xxii (1812), 86). Also, Sir John Nicholl, speaking in a debate in the House of Commons on Lord Morpeth's Motion respecting the State of Ireland on 3 Feb. 1812 said: 'Suppose that all

the demands now made were conceded; would the measure stop here? would the Catholics be satisfied?—That is hardly possible; for other measures, some of smaller, some of greater importance, must follow' (*Cobbett's* xxi (1812), 510). See also n. 12 to B's 'Draft Speech' above, and n. 37 below.

8. *house of bondage.* See n. 13 to B's 'Draft Speech' above.

9. *it might . . . effect.* See n. 14 to B's 'Draft Speech' above.

10. *They are . . . own?* Article XI of An Act for the Relief of His Majesty's Popish, or Roman Catholic Subjects of Ireland (1793) provided 'That no papist or person professing the popish, or Roman catholick religion, shall be liable to, or subject to any penalty for not attending divine service on the sabbath day, called Sunday, in his or her parish church' (*Statutes at Large* [Ireland] xvi (1796), 690). However, by way of the Mutiny Act (1811), Catholics serving in the regular army were still compelled to attend Protestant services, since disobeying any order so to do could easily be construed as mutinous.

Henry Brooke Parnell raised the matter in the House of Commons on 11 Mar. 1811, when he tried unsuccessfully to have a clause added to the Mutiny Bill providing that 'no person professing the Roman Catholic religion serving in his Majesty's regular forces, or in the militia of the united kingdom, should be subjected by the articles of war to any punishment for not frequenting divine service as performed according to the rites and ceremonies of the established church' (*Cobbett's* xix (1811), 351). His object was to give legislative force to general orders of the same construction issued in May 1806 during the Bedford administration (see n. 23 below), by the Earl of Harrington, Commander-in-Chief in Ireland (1805–12), and circulated in the army repeatedly after that time but ignored. Earl Stanhope, with the same lack of success, moved a clause to a similar effect at the second and third readings of the Mutiny Bill in the House of Lords on 15 and 18 Mar. 1811 (*Cobbett's* xix (1811), 367–71, 383–7). At the report stage of the British and Irish Militias Interchanges Bill on 30 May 1811, Parnell put the issue succinctly: 'though the Irish Act of 1793 enabled the Catholic to serve in the army, the constructive privilege conferred by that act as to religious worship, was taken away by the mutiny act' (*Cobbett's* xx (1811), 365). Hence, despite what B says, even if a Catholic was 'quartered in Ireland or in Spain' (or for that matter in Portugal, Sicily or South America), he could still be prevented, and had been prevented, from exercising his religion and from having access to a Catholic chaplain. See *A Statement*, pp. 126–33, and Plowden, *History of Ireland* iii. 777–86. See also following n. 11.

11. *The permission . . . right.* The Act of 1793 (see foregoing n. 10) made no express provision for such permission. Indeed, one of the complaints registered in *A Statement* was that the Act was 'profoundly silent respecting any legal enactment, securing the appointment of Catholic regimental chaplains, or any other provision for the free exercise of the Catholic Religion in

the army or navy' (p. 131). In fact, Article X of the Act debarred Catholics from presenting to an ecclesiastical benefice, thus effectively depriving them of any statutory authority for the appointment of their chaplains to the army or militia (*Statutes at Large* [Ireland] xvi (1796), 690).

12. *Can the Church . . . betrayed.* Owing to the continued effect of innumerable obsolete statutes, the Catholic church was unable to purchase land in mortmain; no chapel could be permanently endowed nor any long lease be granted. Moreover, by Article V of An Act to Relieve, upon Conditions, and under Restrictions, the Persons therein described, from certain Penalties and Disabilities to which Papists, or Persons professing the Popish Religion, are by Law Subject (1791), Catholics were denied any 'place of congregation, or assembly for religious worship . . . until the place of such meeting shall be certified to the justices of the peace, at the general or quarter sessions of the peace for the county, city, or place in which such meeting shall be held, and until the place of such meeting shall be recorded at the said general or quarter sessions' (*Statutes at Large* [England] xxxvii (1790–2), 314).

13. *Protestant . . . people.* While there were numerous petitions from Catholics and Protestants in support of the Catholic claims, there were many Protestant petitions against them, most notably perhaps from the universities of Oxford and Cambridge.

14. *peace . . . men.* See n. 6 to B's 'Draft Speech' above.

15. *This has happened . . . disturbances.* I have been unable to find any reference to this particular example of abuse in the newspapers or records of the time. Perhaps it was mentioned in Dr Ryan's letter which Hobhouse enclosed with his own to B in Mar. 1812 (see general note, and *Byron's Bulldog*, p. 99 and n.). The Chief Secretary to the Lord Lieutenant (the Duke of Bedford) at Dublin Castle in 1806 was the Right Honourable William Elliott.

16. *"pelting . . . heaven". Measure for Measure* II. ii. 112, 121 (Isabella speaking).

17. *Have . . . under-sheriffs.* Article IX of the Act of 1793 (see n. 10 above) debarred Catholics from holding the offices of Sheriff or Sub-Sheriff who alone could select juries (*Statutes at Large* [Ireland] xvi (1796), 689; see also *A Statement*, pp. 213–15).

18. *Of this . . . Catholics.* This case received much coverage in the Irish press, though B's informant may have been Dr Ryan (see n. 15 above). The *Freeman's Journal* (vol. liii, 20 Mar. 1812) reported that the case of the King v. James Kittson and others had been brought before Mr Justice Osborne (Assize Judge on the Leinster circuit) at the Enniskillen Assizes on 16 Mar. 1812. Kittson (a Protestant) was accused of the murder of Denis Murvournagh (a Catholic), who had been shot and battered to death at the Derrygonnelly fair on 10 July 1811. Despite the evidence of several witnesses and Mr Justice Osborne's clear directions to the jury, it none the less returned a verdict of 'Not guilty'.

See also *Ramsey's Waterford Chronicle*, no. 11266, 24 Mar. 1812, though here the trial is dated 10 Mar. 1812.

19. *By a late . . . jails.* Article XLVII of An Act for Repealing the Several Laws Relating to Prisons in Ireland (1810) provided that courts could require the appointment of Roman Catholic chaplains to prisons (*Statutes at Large* [England] l (1810), 307).

20. *but in . . . contrary.* Again B's informant here may have been Dr Ryan (see n. 15 above). However, *Ramsey's Waterford Chronicle* (no. 11111, 28 Mar. 1811) reported that at the Enniskillen Assizes before Mr Justice Fletcher the Grand Jury had presented the Revd James M'Gir to be Catholic Chaplain of the Enniskillen gaol, even though he lived ten miles away and was somewhat elderly. His presentation was opposed by the Revd Edward Kernan in whose parish the gaol was. Mr Justice Fletcher suggested that it was impossible for such a man as M'Gir at such a distance to discharge his duties adequately; but the Grand Jury persisted in their presentation of him. Although Mr Justice Fletcher finally acquiesced, he ordered that at the subsequent Assizes there should be an investigation as to whether the duties of the chaplain had been fully discharged. See also *A Statement*, pp. 34–7.

21. *It has . . . priesthood?* The phrase 'another place' is parliamentary parlance for one House speaking of the other. In the Irish Miscellaneous Services debate in the House of Commons on 9 Mar. 1812, the Lord Chancellor asked 'Why did not the wealthy Catholics come forward and educate their clergy without calling on the state?' (*Cobbett's* xxi (1812), 1229).

22. *Why . . . donations?* The Commission of Charitable Bequests was constituted by An Act to amend an Act passed in the third year of his present Majesty, King George the Third, entitled, An Act for the better Discovery of Charitable Donations and Bequests (1800). Article I provided that the commissioners should comprise (Protestant) archbishops, bishops, judges and commissaries; Article IV provided that annual returns of all bequests should be made by officers upon oath and sent to the secretary of the commissioners during a specific period in the year (*Statutes at Large* [Ireland], xx (1801), 858–60). At the time of B's speaking, Dr Duigenan was one such commissioner (see n. 44 below). B may have had in mind here the case of Mrs Power, a Catholic widow of County Waterford, who left a substantial bequest to two Catholic bishops and to the poor '*without distinctions of religious persuasions*' (*Cobbett's* xxi (1812), 607). The bequest had been set aside by the commissioners. Sir John Newport made much of this issue in the debate in the House of Commons on Lord Morpeth's Motion respecting the State of Ireland on 4 Feb. 1812, as he did again in the debate on the Irish Miscellaneous Services Bill on 9 Mar. 1812 (*Cobbett's* xxi (1812), 607–8, 1224–6).

23. *As to . . . encouraged.* Maynooth College (St Patrick's College, Maynooth, County Kildare) was the first seminary in Ireland for the exclusive education

of Roman Catholic clergy. It was established under the terms of An Act for the better Education of Persons professing the Popish, or Roman Catholic Religion (1795). John Jeffreys Pratt, second Earl and first Marquis Camden (1759–1840), was appointed Lord Lieutenant of Ireland in 1795. He was a vigorous opponent of the Catholic claims and his lieutenancy was highly repressive. However, he laid the foundation-stone of Maynooth College and encouraged that institution, on the assumption and with the ulterior motive that such state-endowed education would diminish the influence of the Catholic clergy and induce its subservience to the crown. The dukes of Bedford were distinguished for their liberal views. B alludes to three of them in particular: John Russell (1710–71), fourth Duke, Lord Lieutenant of Ireland 1755–61 and greatly in favour of the relaxation of the penal laws against the Catholics; Francis Russell (1765–1802), fifth Duke, friend and colleague of Charles James Fox and Lord Holland, and opposed to all the repressive measures of his time (in 1798 he signed two protests against the methods used to suppress the Irish Rebellion of that year); John Russell (1766–1839), sixth Duke, appointed Lord Lieutenant of Ireland in 1806, but resigned with his colleagues (the 'Ministry of All Talents') in 1807. Thereafter he held no office but was a strong vocal supporter of the Roman Catholic claims.

24. *There was . . . obscurity.* An Act for the Union of Great Britain and Ireland was passed on 30 June 1800 and received the royal assent on 2 July 1800; it took effect from 1 Jan. 1801. Articles III and IV provided for the joint representation of the English and Irish people at Westminster; Article V united the churches of England and Ireland. However, nowhere does the Act provide for or even mention the Roman Catholics (*Statutes at Large* [England] xlii (1799–1800), 648–79). That 'the Union would do every thing' for the Catholics was so understood by Whig and Tory, Protestant and Catholic alike. For example, the Duke of Norfolk in a debate on the Roman Catholic Petitions on 13 May 1805 said: 'I have been very credibly informed, that under that administration [that of the Marquis of Cornwallis at the time of the Union], assurances were held out to the catholics of Ireland, from the highest authority, that their final claims should be ceded, as a condition for their acquiescence to that measure; for, otherwise, the union could not have been carried' (*Cobbett's* iv (1805), 770–1). That 'highest authority' was none other than the Prime Minister, William Pitt. In a speech in the House of Commons on 3 Jan. 1799, in which he proposed various resolutions to form the basis for the terms of union between England and Ireland, Pitt asserted that 'two propositions are indisputable':

> First, When the conduct of the Catholics shall be such as to make it safe for the Government to admit them to the participation of the privileges granted to those of the Established Religion, and when the temper of the times shall be favourable to such a measure;—When these events take place, it is obvious that such a question may be agitated in an United, Imperial Parliament, with much greater safety, than it could be in a separate Legislature. In the second place, I think it certain that, even for whatever period it may be thought necessary, after the Union, to withhold from the Catholics the

enjoyment of those advantages, many of the objections which at present arise out of their situation would be removed, if the Protestant Legislature were no longer separate and local, but general and Imperial; and the Catholics themselves would at once feel a mitigation of the most goading and irritating of their present causes of complaint.

How far, in addition to this great and leading consideration, it may also be wise and practicable to accompany the measure by some mode of relieving the lower orders from the pressure of Tithes, which in many instances operate at present as a great practical evil, or to make, under proper Regulations, and without breaking in on the security of the present Protestant Establishment, an effectual and adequate provision for the Catholic Clergy, it is not now necessary to discuss. It is sufficient to say, that these, and all other subordinate points connected with the same subject, are more likely to be permanently and satisfactorily settled by an United Legislature, than by any local arrangements. (*Speech of the Right Honourable William Pitt* (1799), pp. 39–41.

See also *Substance of the Speech of the Right Honourable Henry Addington . . . On the 12th of February, 1799* (Dublin, 1799), pp. 25–6, and *Cobbett's* iv (1805), 422, 659–60, 849.

25. *In the conduct . . . oath.* Article VIII of the Act of 1795 (see n. 23 above) provided that all pupils, teachers, members and employees at such a Catholic educational institution should take the Oath of Allegiance; Article IX provided that the expenditure of the grant had to be accounted for before the commissioners of imprest accounts (*Statutes at Large* [Ireland] xvii (1796), 511–15). Since 1801, the grant to Maynooth College had been £8973. In the debate on the Irish Miscellaneous Services Bill in the House of Commons on 9 Mar. 1812 Sir John Newport attempted to increase the grant to £13000, but with no success (*Cobbett's* xxi (1812), 1226–34).

26. *Hunts . . . Chinnerys.* See also n. 18 to B's 'Frame Work Bill Speech' above. Mr Chinnery had been private secretary to Lord Thurlow during his chancellorship, and was later appointed First Clerk of the Treasury. In order to support his highly extravagant life-style, he syphoned off funds from the Treasury to the extent of something in excess of £80,000. This was brought to the attention of the House of Lords by Earl Grosvenor on 23 Mar. 1812, and to that of the House of Commons by Mr Bankes on 25 Mar. 1812 (*Cobbett's* xxii (1812), 106–7, 192–5). In the House of Commons on 15 Apr. 1812 Sir John Newport raised the issue of public defaulters, amongst whom was Mr Hunt, whose defalcation amounted to £93,000 (*Cobbett's* xxii (1812), 371–4).

27. *"gilded bugs".* See Pope, *Epistle to Dr Arbuthnot*, ll. 309–10.

28. *"To John . . . quit."* Matthew Prior, 'Epigram' (slightly adapted).

29. *Some persons . . . Gil Blas.* In a debate on Lord Boringdon's Motion for an Address to the Prince Regent, beseeching His Royal Highness to form an efficient Administration on 19 Mar. 1812, Lord Mulgrave said slightingly of the Catholics: 'Their demands indeed now, were something like those of the beggar in Gil Blas, who levelled a musquet to enforce the charity he solicited' (*Cobbett's* xxii (1812), 86). For the allusion here, see, for example, *The*

Adventures of Gil Blas, of Santillane, translated from the French of Le Sage, by T. Smollett, 3 vols. (1802), vol. i, bk. i, ch. 2, pp. 5–6.

30. *As a contrast . . . 41,000l.* The Protestant Charter Schools in Ireland had been awarded a grant of £41,539 in the Irish Miscellaneous Services debate on 9 Mar. 1812—an increase of £2,500 on the previous year (*Cobbett's* xxi (1812), 1221).

31. *Montesquieu . . . woods".* Montesquieu wrote: 'Si l'on veut lire l'admirable ouvrage de *Tacite* sur les moeurs des Germains, on verra que c'est d'eux que les *Anglois* ont tiré l'idée de leur gouvernement politique. Ce beau systême a été trouvé dans les bois' (*De l'Esprit des Loix*, 4 vols. (1757), vol. i, bk. xi, p. 333: 'If one reads that fine work of Tacitus on the manners of the Germans, one will see that it is from them that the English have taken their practice of government. This beautiful system, then, was discovered in the woods'). The allusion is to Tacitus, *De Origine et Situ Germanorum* XI. i: 'De minoribus rebus principes consultant, de maioribus omnes, ita tamen, ut ea quoque, quorum penes plebem arbitrium est, apud principes praetractentur.' ('Minor matters are considered by the chief men, major matters by all; though even here, where the decision rests with the whole community, such matters are first discussed by the chiefs.) The reference to 'woods' arises because Tacitus found Germany either bristling with trees or disfigured by bogs ('aut silvis horrida aut paludibus foeda', V. i).

32. *janissaries . . . Amurath.* Of the institution of the 'Janissaries' (*Yengi Cheri* or New Soldiers), Gibbon gives an account in *The History of the Decline and Fall of the Roman Empire*, ch. 65. Christian children were removed from their parents and harshly trained for public service in the Ottoman empire. Amurath I, in whose reign this system originated, is more commonly known as Murad I, Ottoman Sultan (1360–89).

33. *The sister . . . school.* I have been unable to trace this particular case, and perhaps B's informant was Dr Ryan (see n. 15 above). However, *A Statement* also complained that Catholic orphans were forced into Protestant Charter Schools (pp. 267–8), and points out, with an example similar to that given here by B, that no Catholic was permitted to be a guardian (pp. 279–85).

34. *A catechism . . . Papists! A Protestant Catechism: Shewing the Principal Errors of the Church of Rome* (24pp., 1800), has: 'Q. *Where was the Protestant Religion before the Reformation*? A. In the Bible; where it is now, and where alone all true Religion is to be found' (p. 9). This is actually a variation of an anecdote recorded by Isaac Walton in his life of Sir Henry Wotton. Walton wrote that Wotton:

> Having at his being in Rome made acquaintance with a pleasant priest, who invited him one evening to hear their vesper-music at church: The priest seeing Sir Henry stand obscurely in a corner, sends to him by a boy of the choir this question, written in a small piece of paper, 'Where was your religion to be found before Luther?' To which question Sir Henry presently underwrit, 'My religion was to be found then, where yours is not to

be found now, in the written word of God.' (*Lives of Dr. John Donne; Sir Henry Wotton, etc* (1796), pp. 165–6)

35. *"Peace . . . God?"* Luke 2: 14. (See n. 6 to B's 'Draft Speech' above.)

36. *"I perceive . . . ethics!"* William Paley (1743–1805) had been a Fellow of Christ's College, Cambridge, and was a highly respected theologian and moral philosopher. In his essay 'Of Religious Establishments and of Toleration' he wrote:

> When we examine, however, the sects of Christianity which actually prevail in the world, we must confess that, with the single exception of refusing to bear arms, we find no tenet in any of them which incapacitates men for the service of the state. It has indeed been asserted that discordancy of religions, even supposing each religion to be free from any errors that affect the safety or the conduct of government, is enough to render men unfit to act together, in public stations. But upon what argument, or upon what experience, is this assertion founded? I perceive no reason why men of different religious persuasions may not sit upon the same bench, deliberate in the same council, or fight in the same ranks, as well as men of various or opposite opinions upon any controverted topic of natural philosophy, history, or ethics. (*The Works of William Paley*, 5 vols. (1819), ii. 55)

(The exact passage which B cites here was often quoted. See, e.g., Thomas Newenham, *An Obstacle to the Ambition of France* (1803), p. 20; Charles James Fox, in his speech in the debate on the petition of the Roman Catholics of Ireland in the House of Commons on 13 May 1805 (*Cobbett's* iv (1805), 845); and *A Statement*, p. 117.)

37. *I shall not . . . family.* This was a persistent and aggravating issue. Catholics were obliged to pay double tithes—to the Protestant and to their own clergy. This was exacerbated by the (Protestant) clergy appointing proctors, for the collection of the tithes, who charged the peasant an arbitrary sum for their services. In an Examination before the Secret Committee of the House of Lords on 7 Aug. 1798, Dr William James M'Neven was asked: 'Do you think the mass of the people in the provinces of Leinster, Munster, and Connaught care the value of this pen, or the drop of ink which it contains, for Parliamentary Reform or Catholic Emancipation?' M'Neven replied: 'I am sure they do not; but they wish much to be relieved from the payment of Tithes.' On 11 Aug. 1798, Thomas Addis Emmett said in reply to a similar question from the committee: 'I believe the mass of the people do not care a feather for Catholic Emancipation, neither did they care for Parliamentary Reform, till it was explained to them as leading to other objects which they looked to, principally the abolition of tithes' (*Report from the Secret Committee of the House of Lords* (Dublin, 1798), pp. 45, 55–6). The evidence of M'Neven and Emmett, leading figures in the United Irishmen movement, was frequently referred to in the various debates on the Roman Catholic claims or petitions after 1800. See, e.g., Lord Hawkesbury in his speech in the debate on the Roman Catholic Petition in the House of Lords on 10 May 1805 (*Cobbett's* iv (1805), 684; and

The State of Ireland Considered (Dublin, 1810), pp. 18n., 41n.). See also the second paragraph of the extract from Pitt's speech cited in n. 24 above.

38. *Amongst . . . privates.* Orange Lodges were founded in 1795, and were so named in commemoration of the defeat of King James II's troops by William of Orange at the Battle of the Boyne in 1690. Orangemen were an extreme Protestant group, loyal to England and the crown, and hostile to any form of Catholic emancipation or relief. Although their existence in the army was considered unlawful by government, they were none the less connived at and even encouraged by some officers. Henry Stanton (Orange Grand Master of Middlesex) wrote to Colonel Gordon on 3 Oct. 1809: 'There are generals and colonels who allow and encourage lodges of Orangemen in their Regiments.' See Hereward Senior, *Orangeism in Ireland and Britain, 1795–1836* (1966), p. 161.

39. *Generous . . . declaimers!* This Shylockian outburst echoes Cicero in sentiment: 'Nihil est liberale, quod non idem justum' (*De Officiis* I. xiv. 43: 'Nothing is generous if it be not also just').

40. *Those personnages . . . will!"* BM's source for this story was Sheridan. In his speech in the debate on the State of Ireland in the House of Commons on 13 Aug. 1807, Sheridan said:

> The fact is, that the tyranny practised upon the Irish has been throughout unremitting. There has been no change but in the manner of inflicting it. They have had nothing but variety in oppression, extending to all ranks and degrees of a certain description of the people. If you would know what this varied oppression consisted in, I refer you to the penal statutes you have repealed, and to some of those which still exist. There you will see the high and the low equally subjected to the lash of persecution; and still some affect to be astonished at the discontents of the Irish! But, with all my reluctance to introduce any thing ludicrous upon so serious an occasion, I cannot help referring to a little story which those very astonished persons call to mind. It was with respect to an Irish drummer, who was employed to inflict punishment upon a soldier. While he was flogging the soldier, the poor fellow, writhing with pain, intreated him to change his mode of lashing him. Sometimes he called to him to strike a little higher, and sometimes a little lower. The drummer endeavoured to accommodate him as far as it was in his power; but finding it to no purpose, at last cried out, 'Upon my conscience, you are a discontented fellow, for whether I strike high or low, there is no such thing as pleasing you.' This is precisely the case with respect to Ireland. Notwithstanding the infinite variety of oppression exercised against them, there are still a number of them who are so unreasonable as to be discontented. (*Cobbett's* ix (1807), 1192–3.

For a revised version of this speech see *Speeches of the Right Honourable Richard Brinsley Sheridan*, 5 vols. (1816), v. 351–2. B also refers to this story in his letter to Francis Hodgson of 4 Dec. 1811 (*BLJ* ii. 136).

41. *rod . . . posterity.* An irresistible pun.

42. *It was . . . Jews?* See n. 9 to B's 'Draft Speech' above.

43. *"Would any . . . Christian."* B misspells Barabbas. See n. 10 to B's 'Draft Speech' above.

44. *Dr. Duigenan.* Patrick Duigenan (1735–1816), barrister, writer, and politician, was brought into the Irish House of Commons in 1790 and became a privy councillor. He was also Professor of Civil Law at Trinity College, Dublin, and a member of the board of the Commission of Charitable Bequests (see n. 22 above). He was elected MP for Armagh to the first united Parliament of England and Ireland, and was a vigorous opponent of all demands for Catholic emancipation or relief. Indeed, he spoke and wrote on hardly any other topic. His numerous publications include his speech in favour of the Union, *The Speech of Patrick Duigenan, Esq. L.L.D. in the House of Commons of Ireland, February 5, 1800* (Dublin, 1800), and the extensive and influential pamphlet, *The Nature and Extent of the Demands of the Irish Roman Catholics fully Explained* (1810). In a debate in the House of Commons on a change of Administration on 9 Apr. 1807, he denounced the Catholics with such virulence and made such sweeping allegations against them as to provoke an uproar (*Cobbett's* ix (1807), 324–7). B's ironic designation of him as 'the gentle apostle of intolerance' is extremely apt.

45. *"cried ... deluge."* During their tour of Scotland, Boswell and Johnson stopped for tea at Cupar and fell into a debate on politics. Boswell recorded Johnson saying to him: '"You are frightened by what is no longer dangerous, like Presbyterians by Popery."—He then repeated a passage, I think, in Butler's *Remains*, which ends, "and would cry, Fire! Fire! in Noah's flood"' (*Boswell's Life of Johnson* v. 57). In his character of 'The Assembly Man', Samuel Butler wrote: 'He preaches indeed both in Season and out of Season; for he rails at Popery, when the Land is almost lost in Presbytery; and would cry out, *Fire*, *Fire*, in *Noah's Flood*' (see Butler, *Posthumous Works in Prose and Verse* (1715), pp. 122–3).

46. *with fire ... thence?"* The particular disease B has in mind here is hydrophobia (rabies), one of the most common and most feared of fatal diseases of the time. The word 'rabies' is from the Latin *rabere*, to rave; and B has subtly played on this 'raving' by conflating allusions to Rochester, 'Reason, an *ignis fatuus* of the mind' (*A Satire Against Mankind*, l. 11); Johnson, 'And Swift expires a Driv'ler and a Show' (*The Vanity of Human Wishes*, l. 318); and *Macbeth* V. iii. 55–6: 'What rhubarb, senna, or what purgative drug / Would scour these English hence?' (See also n. 47.)

47. *"Caput ... Anticyrus."* Horace, *Ars Poetica*, l. 300. At this point in the poem Horace is satirizing the slovenly and uncleanly habits of the aspiring pseudo-poet. The whole sentence runs: 'Nanciscetur enim pretium nomenque poetae, / si tribus Anticyris caput insanabile nunquam / tonsori Licino commiserit' (ll. 299–301: 'He believes he will easily obtain the honour and name of Poet, so long as his head, which the three Anticyras would not be able to cure, is never committed to Licinus the barber'). Anticyra was the name of three different towns in Greece, two of which were renowned for hellebore, the ancient cure for insanity. The name also gave rise to the proverb 'Naviget Anticyram'

('He's going to Anticyra'), which was applied to anyone who spoke or behaved in a senseless or irrational manner. Elsewhere Horace referred to one Anticyra as being also the reserve of the greedy or covetous ('avari'). See *Satires*, II. iii. 83, 166. For B's own rendition of the above lines, see *Hints from Horace*, ll. 469–74 (*CPW* i. 306).

48. *Like Bayle . . . whatsoever.* Pierre Bayle (1647–1706), philosopher and lexicographer, began life as a Protestant, changed to Catholicism, then reverted to Protestantism. For some time he held the Chair of Philosophy at Rotterdam, and his most notable work is the *Dictionnaire historique et critique* (1697–1706). In his *Lettres à son Altesse Monseigneur Le Prince de* **** (1768), Voltaire related the anecdote (which he refuted as apocryphal) that the Cardinal de Polignac asked Bayle whether he was an Anglican, a Lutheran or a Calvinist, to which Bayle replied, 'Je suis protestant, car je proteste contre toutes les religions' (p. 65: 'I am a protestant, because I protest against all religions').

49. *These . . . mountains.* B alludes to Horace, *Ars Poetica*, l. 139: 'Paturient montes, nascetur ridiculus mus' ('The mountains labour, and a ridiculous mouse is born'). Notice B's pun on 'conceive'.

50. *bull.* An Irish blunder, a paradoxical statement. B may also be enjoying a pun on 'bull' as a papal edict. See also Richard Lovell Edgeworth and Maria Edgeworth, *Essay on Irish Bulls* (1802).

51. *You . . . Irish militia.* An Act to permit the Interchange of the British and Irish Militias respectively had been passed on 1 July 1811. Ostensibly its object was, according to Lord Liverpool, to consolidate the connection between England and Ireland 'not only on extraordinary but on ordinary occasions' (*Cobbett's* xx (1811), 645). Effectively, however, it facilitated the deployment of the Irish Militia in England, when and where necessary at the government's discretion. Moreover, in the debate on Lord Boringdon's Motion for an Address to the Prince Regent, beseeching His Royal Highness to form an efficient Administration on 19 Mar. 1812 the Earl of Moira, attacking the government for not conceding the Roman Catholic claims, pointed out that 'The population of Ireland furnished one half of the forces of the empire' (*Cobbett's* xxii (1812), 88).

52. *At this . . . general.* B alludes to Arthur Wellesley, first Duke of Wellington (1769–1852), the famous field-marshal for whom B never entertained much respect. See, e.g., *DJ* IX. 1–12 (*CPW* v. 409–12). At the time of B's speaking he had recently taken Cuidad Rodrigo (19 Jan. 1812), for which both Houses of Parliament had voted him thanks on 10 Feb. 1812 (*Cobbett's* xxi (1812), 703–7, 707–13).

53. *it is . . . army.* By Article IX of the Act of 1793 (see n. 10 above), Catholics were debarred from holding any of the higher offices of state, civil or military. In the army a Catholic could not rise above the rank of non-staffed general (*Statutes at Large* [Ireland] xvi (1796), 689). While many speakers in the various

debates on the Roman Catholic claims and petitions alluded to this disability, B was the only one to make such an imaginative supposition.

54. *his. . . panegyric.* Richard Colley Wellesley, Marquis Wellesley (1760–1842), brother of Arthur (see n. 52 above) and of William (see n. 55), had been Governor-General of India (1796–1806) and Ambassador-extraordinary to Spain (1809). He was Foreign Secretary 1809–12, and on the death of Perceval was invited by the Regent to form an Administration which he was unable to do. He refused the office of Lord Lieutenant of Ireland in 1812 (though he accepted it in 1821). He was an active and well-respected politician, and a vociferous supporter of the Roman Catholics. He spoke fifth in the present debate, and throughout his speech in favour of the motion was 'repeatedly and loudly cheered' (*Cobbett's* xxii (1812), 611). In his journal for the early hours of 6 Dec. 1813, B mentions Wellesley as being 'a clever man' (*BLJ* iii. 232).

55. *whilst . . . statutes.* B refers to William Wellesley-Pole, third Earl of Mornington (Irish peerage) and first Baron Maryborough (United Kingdom peerage) (1763–1845), the brother of Arthur and Richard (see nn. 52 and 54 above). He was a member of the Irish and English Houses of Commons, and had been Secretary to the Admiralty in 1807. He was Chief Secretary for Ireland (1809–12), and a bitter opponent of all relief or claims of the Roman Catholics. The matters to which B alludes here were topical and highly contentious. With the aim of making Catholic petitioning more effective, a letter dated 1 Jan. 1811 had been sent to the Catholics throughout Ireland by Edward Hay, Secretary to the General Committee of the Catholics in Ireland, sitting in Dublin. It urged each county to appoint a committee of ten persons to act as managers of the county's petition. This prompted Wellesley-Pole to issue, on 11 Feb. 1811, a circular letter instructing magistrates to arrest and commit to prison any persons who assembled to nominate or appoint such a committee. This was first brought to the attention of both Houses of Parliament on 18 Feb. 1811, and in the House of Lords a motion ordering a copy of the letter to lie upon the table (i.e. to be submitted for future discussion) was carried (*Cobbett's* xviii (1810–11), 1224–36, 1239–41). The issue was later discussed in both Houses on 22 Feb. 1811, and although Wellesley-Pole was severely censured by the Opposition, motions requiring the production of papers relating to the letter were rejected (*Cobbett's* xix (1811), 1–18, 18–55: the texts of both Wellesley-Pole's and Hay's letters are printed as footnotes on 1–6). On 30 July 1811 Wellesley-Pole issued a proclamation declaring illegal the election of deputies, managers or delegates to a Catholic committee. In pursuance of this, two delegates, Dr Sheridan and Mr Kirwan, were arrested on 9 Aug. 1811. Dr Sheridan was tried and acquitted on 21–22 Nov. 1811, while Mr Kirwan was tried and found guilty (though fined a nominal penalty only) on 3 Feb. 1812. Meanwhile, at an assembly of the Catholic Committee in Dublin on 23 Dec. 1811, Lord Fingal and Lord Netterville had been arrested and the meeting dispersed. The statute under whose authority Wellesley-Pole

had issued both his circular letter and his proclamation was An Act to prevent the Electon or Appointment of unlawful Assemblies, under Pretence of preparing or presenting public Petitions, or other Addresses to His Majesty, or the Parliament (1793) (*Statutes at Large* [Ireland] xvi (1796), 794–5). This Act was regarded by most thinking politicians as, in the words of the Earl of Moira, 'an obsolete and long inoperative law' (*Cobbett's* xviii (1810–11), 1226). The closing phrase of B's sentence here echoes ironically Ephesians 6: 11: 'Put on the whole armour of God, that ye may be able to stand against the wiles of the devil' (see also Ephesians 6: 12–14, and Romans 8: 11–14).

56. *Saviour . . . Delegates.* These are respectively Wellington (see n. 52; cf. also *DJ* IX. 5 (*CPW* v. 410)), and Wellesley-Pole (see n. 55).

57. *king of . . . him.* On the annexation of the Kingdom of Naples by Napoleon in 1806, Ferdinand IV of Naples (1751–1825) had fled to Sicily where he established his court under British protection. His rule was absolutist and repressive, and he himself was dominated by his wife Maria Carolina of Austria. In 1812 pressure from England forced him to remove Maria Carolina from his court, appoint his son Francis (1777–1830) as Regent, and grant the Sicilians a constitution. At the time of B's speaking, the annual Sicilian subsidy of £400,000 had recently been renewed (25 Mar. 1812). See n. 24 to B's 'Draft Speech and Notes' above; see also *Cobbett's* xxii (1812), 187–92.

58. *away goes . . . allies.* B refers to the continuing war in the Peninsular (see n. 52 above and n. 32 to B's 'Frame Work Bill Speech'); to Marquis Wellesley, Ambassador-extraordinary to Spain in 1809 (se n. 54 above); to the Convention of Cintra (1808) (see *CHP* I, 24–6 (*CPW* ii. 19–21)); and to the Portuguese subsidy. With respect to the last, on 16 Mar. 1812 a resolution was passed in both Houses of Parliament granting the sum of £2 million to the Portuguese government (*Cobbett's* xxi (1812), 1294–310).

59. *"father's . . . mansions".* John 14: 2.

60. *Allow . . . bigot.* B refers to Ferdinand VII of Spain (see n. 16 to B's 'Draft Speech' above). Ferdinand was the son of Charles IV of Spain (reigned 1788–1808), whose powerful prime minister, Manuel de Godoy, excluded him from any share in his father's government. However, in Mar. 1808 Godoy was overthrown and Charles abdicated in favour of Ferdinand. In May 1808 Ferdinand was summoned to France by Napoleon who forced him to return the crown to his father (who duly gave it to Napoleon). He was imprisoned by Napoleon at Valençay between 1808 and 1814, during which time the Spanish revolutionaries rallied round his name. See also *CHP* I. 48 (*CPW* ii. 27–8, 188, 279).

61. *usurper.* That is, Charles-Maurice de Talleyrand-Périgord, the gaoler of Ferdinand VII at Valençay. See foregoing n. 60; also nn. 16 and 17 to B's 'Draft Speech' above; and B's 'A Letter on the State of French Affairs', *post.*

62. *fetters . . . body.* Echoes Publilius Syrus, *Sententiae*, no. 166: 'Dolor animi gravior est quam corporis' ('The pain of the mind is worse than that of the body').

63. *"Lucus a non lucendo,"*. Literally, 'a grove from not shining with light'. This is a complicated pun on *lux* (light), *lucere* (to shine) and the supposed derivation of *lucus* (a grove). It is explained by Quintilian as follows: 'Lucus, quia, umbra opacus, parum luceat' ('A grove is so called because owing to its dense shade there is little light there') (*De Institutio Oratoria* I. vi. 34). The 'a non' principle is applied to many paradoxical derivations or jocular constructions, e.g. 'canis a non canendo' ('a dog from not singing'); see B's own example in his letter to John Cam Hobhouse of 2 July 1811: 'I wrote to you from Malta, during my Fever, my Terzana, or rather Quotidiana, for it was called intermittent "a *Non* Intermittendo"' (*BLJ* ii. 56; for another example see ii. 204). See also *DJ* VI. 55 and n. (*CPW* v. 316, 722).

64. *The esteem . . . House.* In the recent debate in the House of Lords on Lord Boringdon's Motion for an Address to the Prince Regent, beseeching His Royal Highness to form an efficient Administration (19 Mar. 1812), Viscount Grimston had asserted:

> His Majesty's arms had been eminently successful under the administration of the present ministers, during the time that the Prince Regent had been at the head of the government. During that time the country had to boast the conquest of the islands of Mauritius and of Java, the total expulsion of Massena and the French from Portugal, the repulse of the enemy at Tarifa, and lastly, the capture of Cuidad Rodrigo. Ministers, under whom the arms of the country had been so successful, ought still to be required to guide the vessel of the state. He did not conceive those successes to be the effect of chance, but of the energetic policy of ministers. He believed that the country was of the same opinion, and did not wish for any change of administration at present. (*Cobbett's* xxii (1812), 55–6)

65. *"No one . . . goeth"*. John 3: 8.

66. *If they plunge . . . approbation?* B refers in particular to the plight of the frame-workers throughout England and Scotland. See his 'Frame Work Bill Speech' above, and nn. thereto.

67. *Temple Bar . . . gateway.* Temple Bar was the gateway marking the western limit of the City of London's jurisdiction. The heads of criminals were arrayed on pikes in its niches—a monitory sight to the potential malefactor. (Temple Bar was removed to Cheshunt in 1878.)

68. *"not . . . deep"*. *Macbeth* V. iii. 27.

69. *bankrupt . . . stock-holders.* See n. 26 above. See also n. 18 to B's 'Frame Work Bill Speech', and n. 2 to his 'Draft Notes' to that speech above.

70. *If they . . . Walcheren.* The Walcheren Expedition (1809) was intended to divert Napoleon's forces northwards, destroy his base at Antwerp, and cause a Dutch revolt. It was a disaster. On 28 July 1809, 40,000 men embarked from England, reaching Walcheren (an island at the mouth of the river Scheldt well known for its unhealthy conditions) on 29 July. On 13 Aug. they took Flushing, before being obliged to withdraw. There were considerable losses, mostly

from fever, and only a remnant of the expedition returned. Laurel and nightshade are respectively emblems of victory and of death.

71. *'cloud of witnesses'.* Hebrews 12: 1. Cf. also Henry Vaughan, 'The World', stanza 2: 'And Clouds of crying witnesses without / Pursued him ['The darksome States-man'] with one shout.'

72. *"noble army of martyrs".* From the 'Te Deum', *Book of Common Prayer*.

73. *in which . . . own.* B refers to Caligula's single and futile military campaign, which was merely a piece of melodramatic staging. Suetonius recorded:

> In the end, he drew up his army in battle array facing the Channel and moved the siege-engines into position as though he intended to bring the campaign to a close. No one had the least notion what was in his mind when, suddenly, he gave the order: 'Gather sea-shells!' He referred to the shells as 'plunder from the sea, due to the Capitol and to the Palace', and made the troops fill their helmets and tunic-laps with them; commemorating this victory by the erection of a tall lighthouse, not unlike the one at Pharos, in which fires were to be kept going all night as a guide to ships. (*The Twelve Caesars*, trans. Robert Graves (1957), p. 172)

74. *Saracen's head.* This was a common inn-sign (such as that at Southwell) since the time of the Crusades.

75. *There is . . . Emancipation.* Ths line of argument was frequently raised in the various debates on the Roman Catholic petitions, the point being that so long as the Catholics remained oppressed, they represented to Napoleon a potential ally within the United Kingdom against England.

76. *no line . . . Ireland.* B here paraphrases the celebrated motion of John Dunning 'that the Influence of the Crown has increased, is increasing, and ought to be diminished' (see n. 1 to B's 'Presentation of Major Cartwright's Petition', *post*).

77. *as he . . . seve-china.* Napoleon's continental blockade ('Le Blocus continental'), by which trade with England was prohibited, had been in operation since 21 Nov. 1806. There were numerous loopholes, but the strain on both French and English economies became so intense that in Nov. 1811 trade restrictions were relaxed, and a system of licensing was introduced on both sides of the Channel. A 'cartel' is an exchange agreement. Sèvres porcelain had been manufactured at Sèvres, near Versailles, since 1756. It superseded Meissen china and was patronized by Madame de Pompadour. During the Napoleonic period it adopted Neoclassical and Egyptian designs.

78. *blue ribbands . . . disciples.* The Legion of Honour ('La Légion d'honneur') was instituted by Napoleon on 19 May 1802 as a reward for both military and civil services to the state. (See B's 'On the Star of "The Legion of Honour"', *CPW* iii. 317–18.) In fact its ribbon was *red*, not blue; and B may have been alluding here to 'The Most Illustrious Order of St. Patrick' (KP), which had been instituted by George III in 1783 as an award for distinguished services. The Order consisted of the King, the Lord Lieutenant of Ireland, and twenty-

two knights, and its mantle, sash, and ribbon were sky-blue. Cf. *DJ* XI, unincorporated stanza 76 (*CPW* v. 494; and *Lord Byron: Don Juan*, ed. T. G. Steffan, E. Steffan, and W. W. Pratt (1977), p. 704). With regard to Dr Duigenan (for whom see n. 44 above), the implication is that by opposing the claims of the Roman Catholics he served to promote the cause of Napoleon (in the manner outlined in n. 75 above).

Presentation of Major Cartwright's Petition (1813)

Text: Hansard, *Parliamentary Debates* xxvi (1813), 479–80, 483. Thereafter published in *The Parliamentary Speeches of Lord Byron* (1824), pp. 40–4. Thereafter published from this last source in *Works*, vi (1832), 335–8, and Prothero ii. 443–5.

B presented this petition on Tuesday 1 June 1813, and it was the last occasion of his speaking in the House of Lords. He wrote to Murray the following day: 'I presented a petition to the house yesterday—which gave rise to some debate—& I wish you to favour me for a few minutes with the *Times* & Herald to look on their *hostile* reports—You will find if you like to look at my *prose*—all my words nearly verbatim in the M[orning] Chronicle' (*BLJ* iii. 55). In fact, *The Times* for Wednesday 2 June 1813 carried no such 'hostile' report but merely a summary of B's presentation speech and a short outline of the debate. However, both the *Morning Chronicle* and the *London Gazette* for that date printed B's speech in full; and, except for one interpolation and the mere mention of B's reply (both noted below), and some differences in capitalization, their texts match verbatim the text printed here from Hansard.

Of this occasion Thomas Moore recalled:

> In his way home from the House that day, he called, I remember, at my lodgings, and found me dressing in a very great hurry for dinner. He was, I recollect, in a state of most humorous exaltation after his display, and, while I hastily went on with my task in the dressing-room, continued to walk up and down the adjoining chamber, spouting forth for me, in a sort of mock-heroic voice, detached sentences of the speech he had just been delivering. 'I told them,' he said, 'that it was a most flagrant violation of the Constitution—that, if such things were permitted, there was an end of English freedom, and that——' 'But what was the dreadful grievance?' I asked, interrupting him in his eloquence.—'The grievance?' he repeated, pausing as if to consider—'Oh, *that* I forget.' (Moore i. 402)

This was, of course, merely a display of bravado on B's part, in the wake of his nervousness and agitation at presenting a petition which he almost certainly knew beforehand would not be favourably received by the House (see Marchand i. 390–1; *BAP*, p. 143). Moreover he was no doubt conscious that he was following in the illustrious footsteps of those who had presented Cartwright's petitions on former occasions: Charles James Fox (1795), Earl Stanhope (1808), the Earl of Moira (1810), and Samuel Whitbread (1810). Despite his courageous efforts, however, the petition was not received for various reasons, though principally because it did not contain a 'prayer' (see nn. 4, 7, and especially 8 below).

The petition itself, written out in John Cartwright's meticulous and formal longhand, is in the Records Office of the House of Lords. It is extremely long and verbose, and is couched in strong, even virulent, language. Apart from the specific instance of abuse to which B alludes in his presentation (see n. 3), the petition complains generally of the existence of 'an active System of oppression for obstructing the People in the free exercise of the sacred right of Petitioning'.

John Cartwright (1740–1824) was the politically embarrassing, indefatigable grand old father of reform. He joined the Navy in 1758 and saw active service under Admiral Howe. As First Lieutenant he was posted to Canada in 1766, where he remained until his return to England in 1770. In 1775 he was appointed Major in the Nottinghamshire Militia, a post he held till his dismissal in 1792. It was during this period that he began his hyperactive career in politics, electioneering, publishing numerous pamphlets on the constitution and parliamentary reform, and founding 'The Society for Constitutional Information' in 1780. In 1792 he founded 'The Society of the Friends of the People' (expressly associated for the purpose of obtaining parliamentary reform), and 'The Society of Friends to the Liberty of the Press', both of which were intended to counteract the principles of absolute republicanism propagated by Thomas Paine. Cartwright was less extreme: he favoured the monarchy and parliament, and sought reform of parliament through constitutional means (petitioning). His principal demands were for annual parliaments and the franchise for all tax-payers. He was elected to the Hampden Club, founded in Apr. 1812 and to which B belonged (Marchand i. 351; *BAP*, p. 128), and remained its most active member until it ceased to exist in 1819. His first major publication was *American Independence the Interest and Glory of Great Britain* (1774), and amongst his numerous later writings those nearest to the time of B's speaking include *Reasons for Reformation* (1809), *The Comparison: in which Mock Reform, Half Reform, and Constitutional Reform, are considered* (1810), and *Six Letters to the Marquis of Tavistock on Reform of the Commons House of Parliament* (1812). See *The Life and Correspondence of Major Cartwright*, ed. F. D. Cartwright, 2 vols. (1826), and John W. Osborne, *John Cartwright* (1972).

In presenting (successfully) Cartwright's petition against the introduction of the Seditious Meetings and the Safety of His Majesty's Person bills on 27 Nov. 1795, Charles James Fox said of him: 'He was one whose enlightened mind and profound constitutional knowledge, placed him in the highest rank of public character, and whose purity of principle and consistency of conduct through life, commanded the most respectful attention to his opinions' (*Life* i. 233; see also *Journals of the House of Commons* li (29 Oct. 1795–19 May 1796), 134–7).

On 18 June 1808 Earl Stanhope presented Cartwright's petition against the establishment of a permanent local Militia force as a means of defence, and on 20 June wrote to him: 'On Saturday I had the pleasure to present your petition to the Lords; and in order to shew them my approbation, I read the whole very loudly and distinctly myself. They wished not to receive it, because it was not addressed to the Lords *Spiritual* and *Temporal*; but I got it received, notwithstanding' (*Life* i. 367; see also *Journals of the House of Lords* xlvi (1806–8), 735).

B himself was later to speak very unfavourably of Cartwright and the sort of reform for which he stood (see *BLJ* vi. 165, 211–12; viii. 240); and Hobhouse, in a letter to B of 31 March 1820, dubbed him 'Old Prosy' (*Byron's Bulldog*, p. 286).

1. *against . . . diminished.* B provocatively echoes the celebrated motion in the House of Commons tabled by John Dunning, first Baron Ashburton (1731–83), an eminent barrister, politician, and sometime Solicitor-General, and passed on 6 Apr. 1780, 'that the Influence of the Crown has increased, is increasing, and ought to be diminished' (*Journals of th House of Commons* xxxvii (Nov. 1778–Aug. 1780), 763).

2. *"frangas non flectes".* 'You may break, but you will not bend him.' Cf. Seneca, *Thyestes*, ll. 199–200: 'Novi ego ingenium viri / indocile; flecti non potest—frangi potest.' ('I know the stubborn nature of the man—he may be broken but may not be bent.')

3. *The petitioner . . . granted.* These events occurred during Cartwright's 29-day tour through the northern and western parts of England, when he visited more than 30 major towns, founding Hampden Clubs and gaining signatories to his petitions for reform of parliament. In a letter to his wife of 22 Jan. 1813 he wrote 'Last night I was annoyed by a very rude interference of civil and military professors of loyalty, and required to appear before a magistrate, and after admitting that petitions to the House of Commons were found in my possession, dismissed' (*Life* ii. 49). In the Petition he rehearsed the details at length.

4. *inferior court . . . himself.* During the debate Earl Fitzwilliam objected to this very point: 'There were charges and complaints in the present Petition, which, if they could be supported by proof, were remediable, and ought to be redressed, by the inferior tribunals' (Hansard xxvi (1813), 481).

5. *measure fully.* In both the *Morning Chronicle* and the *London Gazette* (2 June 1813) this reads 'measure as fully'.

6. *representatives.* Immediately after this part of the presentation of the Petition, Hansard runs: 'His lordship then presented the Petition from major Cartwright, which was read, complaining of the circumstances at Huddersfield, and of interruptions given to the right of petitioning, in several places in the northern parts of the kingdom, and which his lordship moved should be laid on the table [i.e. submitted for future discussion]' (480–1). Some discussion then ensued, in the course of which various objections against receiving the petition were raised.

7. *Lord Byron . . . consideration.* B's only supporter on this occasion was Earl Stanhope, with whom, he recalled in his journal for 1 Dec. 1813, he 'stood

against the whole House, and mouthed it valiantly—and had some fun and a little abuse for our opposition' (*BLJ* iii. 229). Charles, third Earl Stanhope ('Citizen' Stanhope) (1753–1816), politician, scientist, and inventor, had been a close associate of Pitt, but his active and vociferous sympathy for the French Revolution and the rise of the Republic soon alienated him from both sides of the House. In the present instance he challenged Earl Fitzwilliam's objection to the petition (see n. 4 above):

> Did the noble earl suppose that redress could always be obtained before other tribunals? It very often happened that the sufferers were so poor that they could not redress their wrongs. He would, however, contend that the laws of this country ought to be so framed that the rich should not only enjoy protection, but that it should be equally extended to the poor. There was certainly great oppression here complained of, and the very reason alleged in the Petition itself was, that the sufferers were poor persons, and could not procure redress. For this purpose, the petitioner approached their lordships, and prayed their interference, that the law might be altered. And could any man dispute that it was a fair subject of petition, to desire that this House, with the consent of the other two branches of the legislature, would make laws to redress the existing grievances of the poor? (481)

Other objections to receiving the petition were raised by the Earl of Lauderdale, who doubted the accuracy of the charges in the petition and deplored the absence of a 'prayer' (see n. 8 below). The Duke of Norfolk (himself a member of the London Hampden Club; see also *BLJ* ix. 27), took exception to the 'censure on the conduct of a most respectable magistrate (Mr. Ratcliffe)'. After B had made his reply (which was briefly noted in one short sentence in *The Times*, the *Morning Chronicle* and the *London Gazette*), Viscount Sidmouth, who had taken his seat late in the debate, denied the existence of any oppressive conduct on the part of the military and civil authorities, and also objected to the impugnment of Mr Ratcliffe's character (482–4).

8. *The noble earl. . . received.* The Earl of Lauderdale stated that 'he never knew any petition received by their lordships without a prayer'; 'he did not denominate the statement which had been read a petition, but the written speech of the individual who had signed it' (Hansard, 482, 483). Unfortunately for B, this was a perfectly valid point; a 'prayer' was a necessary formality. According to Erskine May 'The general allegations of the petition are concluded by what is called the "prayer," in which the particular object of the petitioner is expressed. To the whole petition are generally added these words of form, "And your petitioners, as in duty bound, will ever pray;" to which are appended the signatures or marks of the parties' (Thomas Erskine May, *A Treatise upon the Law, Privileges, Proceedings and Usage of Parliament* (1844), p. 303). After stating his general allegations, Cartwright expressed no such particular object of his petition, but merely dated it (31 May 1813) and signed his name.

WRITINGS

Bramblebear and Lady Penelope (1813)

Text: R. C. Dallas, *Recollections of the Life of Lord Byron* (1824), pp. 259–63. First published with certain variations in *Sir Francis Darrell; or, The Vortex: A Novel*, by R. C. Dallas, 4 vols. (1820), i. 1–6. (Title supplied by me.)

Dallas introduced this letter as follows:

I was highly gratified, allowing it even to be flattery, at his [B's] acknowledgement of being pleased with the novels I had written; and I was still more flattered when he proposed to me to write one jointly. I thought the proposal made on a transient thought; and was rather surprised, when I next saw him, to receive from him two folio sheets of paper, accompanied with these words, 'Now, do you go on.' On opening the paper I read, 'Letter I. Darrell to G.Y.' and found it to be the commencement of a novel. I was charmed to find his intention real; but my pleasure, which continued through the perusal, forsook me when I reflected on the impossibility of my adopting either the style or the objects he had in view, as he dwelled upon them. I told him I saw that he meant to laugh at me, but I kept the manuscript, though, at the time, I had no intention of using it; however, in writing another novel, I was tempted to build a very different structure upon it than was originally planned, and it stands the first letter in my novel of Sir Francis Darrell. (*Recollections of the Life of Lord Byron*, pp. 257–8)

In his preface to that novel he wrote:

I think it right to acknowledge that the first letter of the Novel was not written by me. It was written and given to me, some years ago, by a friend, for the purpose of inducing me to continue it. Conscious that I could not keep up the spirit which it broached, I owned my inability; and the letter lay, among other papers, in my desk, till last Christmas, when . . . I re-perused it, and conceived the idea of adapting it to the object I have stated ['not only to expose vice and folly, but to counteract the impiety and blasphemy which disgrace the age']. I hope I have made so good a use of it, that if it ever meets the eye of the writer, he will be induced to read to the end of the work, and to overlook its defects, in consideration of its tendency. (*Sir Francis Darrell* i, pp. vii [v–vi])

Although B wrote to Murray on 1 Mar. 1820 that he had received 'a scrubby letter' from Dallas, 'accusing me of treating him ill' (*BLJ* vii. 47–8), there is no evidence to suggest that he ever saw or read *Sir Francis Darrell*, and it was not among his books sold after his death (see Sale Catalogue (1827), *post*).

Dallas supplied no date to this letter, but it was almost certainly written in Nov. 1813, during or shortly after the composition of *The Bride of Abydos*, both productions being prompted by the same impulse (the letter assuming the mask of comedy). It is, as far as it goes, the commencement of a very thinly disguised skit on B's own unconsummated affair with Lady Francis Webster, when he was a guest of Wedderburn Webster's at Aston Hall in Oct. 1813. (For the full details, see Marchand i. 412–17; *BAP*, pp. 151–4; *BLJ* ii. 287.) The style and tone of the letter bear favourable comparison with B's real letters to Lady Melbourne during the same month, which keep up a running commentary on the progress and development of that affair (*BLJ* iii. 132–55).

On 14 Nov. 1813 B recorded in his journal that he had 'some idea of expectorating a romance, or rather a tale in prose' (*BLJ* iii. 205). By 17 Nov., however, he was less confident: 'I began a comedy and burnt it because the scene ran into *reality*;—a novel, for the same reason. In rhyme, I can keep more away from facts' (*BLJ* iii. 209). He reiterated this sentiment in his entry for 23 Nov.: 'I have burnt my *Roman*—as I did the first scenes and sketch of my comedy . . . I ran into *realities* more than ever; and some would have been recognized and others guessed at' (*BLJ* iii. 217).

Quite evidently this letter was just one such piece of prose; and had it been continued by B, no doubt it would have become further entrenched in 'reality'. For Darrell is clearly a fictional self-projection of B, while Bramblebear and Lady Penelope are obviously fictional representations of Webster and Lady Francis respectively. However, although there were indeed two others of the party at Aston Hall ('a Mr. Westcombe very handsome but silly—& a Mr. Agar frightful but facetious' (*BLJ* iii. 133)), it would be misleading to suggest that Veramore and Asply were fictional representations of *them.* Veramore, whose character certainly has potential for further development, is clearly the foil or *alter ego* of the narrator (Darrell). Hence B represents himself under the double aspect of observed and observer, spectator and participator (cf. *BLJ* iii. 240: 'How I do delight in observing life as it really is!—and myself, after all, the worst of any'). It is also noteworthy that B should have chosen the epistolary form of the novel and should have intended that the 'replies' be indeed written by another person (Dallas). This is an extraordinarily original conception: to realize a fictional correspondence, or perhaps rather to fictionalize a 'real' correspondence.

The variant readings in *Sir Francis Darrell* (*Sir F.D.*) are given in the footnotes on the page.

1. (*The first . . . lost.*) It is not possible to say with absolute certainty whether this parenthesis is part of B's fiction, or Dallas's editorial interpolation; but the balance seems to be in favour of the former. The parentheses are square in Dallas's text.

2. *'lack of argument.' Henry V*, III. i. 21.

3. *Sackcloth . . . Soliloquy.* No doubt B has in mind the great soliloquies of Hamlet, and those of Jaques in *As You Like It* II. vii.

4. *'Rebellion . . . it.' Henry IV, Part I*, V. i. 28.

5. *'beau garçon.'* A fine fellow, a fop.

6. *Cortejos . . . Cicisbei.* The plural forms respectively of the Spanish and Italian words for 'lover'.

7. *enthusiasm . . . way.* B uses 'enthusiasm' in its eighteenth-century sense of 'Ill-regulated or misdirected religious emotion', the false feeling of divine presence, or, as Johnson defines it, 'a vain confidence of divine favour or communication' (*OED*).

8. (*as . . . says*). Scrub, in Farquhar's *The Beaux' Strategem*, is in the habit of giving multiple reasons when accounting for his asseverations (see III. i; IV. i).

9. *sentimental harlequin.* According to B, this was Samuel Rogers's phrase (see *BLJ* ix. 27).

Leake's *Researches in Greece* (1815)

Text: MS Bodleian (Dep. Lovelace Byron 154, ff. 189–91). Unpublished.

This is a draft of what was to have been B's contribution to his and John Cam Hobhouse's projected collaborative review of William Martin Leake's *Researches in Greece* (1814). It was written at Seaham, Annabella's home, in Feb. 1815, shortly after their marriage (2 Jan. 1815), but eventually formed no part of the review which was written solely by Hobhouse.

As early as 31 Aug. 1814, Francis Jeffrey (editor of the *Edinburgh Review*) had written to Thomas Moore saying, 'I wish you would make Lord B. write a review' (*Memoirs* ii. 39). Moore had passed on this proposal to B; but by 18 Sept. B was engaged, and thereafter was involved in all the bustle of his wedding preparations. However, in their journey up to Seaham for the ceremony, B suggested to Hobhouse that they should collaborate in a review of Leake's *Researches*—Hobhouse doing the more detailed, academic part, and B dealing with more general aspects (*Byron's Bulldog*, p. 155). On this hint Hobhouse set to work. According to his diary, he began his share on 23 Jan. 1815 and completed it on 12 Feb. (Broughton Papers, BL Add. MS 47232, ff. 59–61). The following day he sent it to B, saying: 'It breaks off just where a disquisition on general topics without a reference to Leake may well begin, and will begin well if you put pen to paper' (*Byron's Bulldog*, pp. 163–4). To this B replied on 17 Feb.: 'I like your review vastly—but it is long enough in itself—without any additions from me—I shall write to J[effrey] and do all I can about insertion' (*BLJ* iv. 272). B must have sent the review to Jeffrey on 21 Feb.; for on 22 Feb. he wrote to Moore:

> Yesterday I sent off the packet and letter to Edinburgh. It consisted of forty-one pages, so that I have not added a line; but in my letter, I mentioned what passed between you and me in autumn, as my inducement for presuming to trouble him either with my own or [Hobhouse]'s lucubrations. . . . I hope J[effrey] won't think me very impudent in sending [Hobhouse] only; there was not room for a syllable. I have avowed [Hobhouse] as the author, and said that you thought or said, when I met you last, that he (J[effrey]) would not be angry at the coalition (though, alas! we have not coalesced) . . . (*BLJ* iv. 273–4)

In the meantime Hobhouse replied on 21 Feb. to B's letter of 17 Feb., saying:

> You rogue you have not read the review—by the lord I know it as well as if I were at your elbow. So you wont say a good word for me—well, well! If you had only filled up the odd sheet with a few sentences purporting 'we have taken some pains to enquire from those

who have travelled in Greece & find Mr. H's narratives &c. &c.—' This coming from you in your hand would have been worth twenty other eulogies—and would have produced an octavo edition in a year. (*Byron's Bulldog*, p. 172)

Hobhouse refers here to his *Journey through Albania*, published in quarto in May 1813, which Leake criticized in his *Researches* (see below). However, B maintained his position in his letter of 24 Feb., arguing: 'I think you will see on a little reflection that it was much better for me to be silent altogether about your "Behemoth"—for obvious reasons—J[effrey] would have looked upon it as an attempt rather to review *you* than the philologer' (*BLJ* iv. 275).

On 28 Feb. B informed Hobhouse of the acceptance of his review (*BLJ* iv. 276; see also *BLJ* iv. 277, and *Byron's Bulldog*, p. 179); and it was published in the *Edinburgh Review*, vol. xxiv (Feb. 1815), art. v, pp. 353–69. The article is wry, witty, and extremely erudite, and would not have been enhanced by additional material furnished by B which, as he shrewdly judged, would have deflected the focus of its attention.

Lieutenant-Colonel William Martin Leake (1777–1860) was a classical topographer and numismatist of international repute. He was commissioned in 1794 and was sent on various military missions to the East, travelling, surveying, and researching in Turkey, Syria, Egypt, and Palestine. He persuaded Ali Pacha, the despotic ruler in Western Greece, to negotiate a reconciliation between England and the Ottoman empire, which was successfully effected and led to the Peace of the Dardanelles (1809). He was the official English Resident at Ioannina (1809–10) when B and Hobhouse first met him. See Marchand i. 204–5, 208–9, 212; *BAP*, pp. 69, 71, 73; *BLJ* i. 227, 237. He was promoted to Major in 1810 and to Lieutenant-Colonel in 1813. His last military assignment was in May 1815, when he was sent to assist in reconstructing the Swiss corps. Thereafter, he devoted himself to literary and classical labours. He was a member of the Society of Dilettanti, a Fellow of the Royal Society and of the Royal Geographical Society, and Vice-President of the Royal Society of Literature. On the continent, he was an honorary member of the Royal Academy of Sciences at Berlin, and a Correspondant of the Institut de France. See John Howard Marsden, *A Brief Memoir of the Life and Writings of the late Lieutenant-Colonel William Martin Leake*, 1864. Leake also published a *Topography of Athens* (1821), *Travels in the Morea* (1830), and *Travels in Northern Greece* (1835), which last two works may be regarded as the second and third volumes of his *Researches in Greece.*

In his preface to his *Researches*, Leake advised his readers that as author:

His principal object was a comparison of the ancient and modern geography, by confronting the information contained in the ancient authors with the actual state of the country. The vernacular tongues (the only key to the attainment of accurate intelligence in foreign countries) having been one of his earliest objects of inquiry, some remarks upon them may form a suitable introduction to the other branches of research. (*Researches*, p. ii)

In effect, this linguistic 'introduction' forms the whole of the volume. It is divided into three chapters (each containing several parts) entitled respectively 'Of the Modern Greek Dialect', 'Of the Albanian Language', and 'Of the Wallachian and Bulgarian Languages'. Essentially it is exactly as B describes it, 'a Polyglott Grammar', dealing with the vocabulary, 'moods & tenses' of the various 'tongues and dialects' currently to be found in Greece. It provides examples of commonly used words and phrases and specimens of the literature, and includes Leake's observations on the Greek system of education. In the second and third chapters Leake outlines the history of Albania, Wallachia, and Bulgaria.

In his first appendix (pp. 403–42), Leake extensively criticised Hobhouse's *Journey through Albania* (1813), which had only come to his notice during the completion of his work. He attacked Hobhouse for giving misleading information concerning the language, the geographical sites, and other details of circumstantial import. More importantly, however, Leake disputed Hobhouse's dating of the currency of the Romaic language. Hobhouse had claimed that 'the use of the auxiliary verbs, and the rejection of the simple infinitive mood', which were 'characteristics of the Romaic', were not current prior to the Turkish conquest of Albania, nor yet even formed in 1528. He therefore suggested that the Romaic became current at the earliest a hundred years after the inception of Turkish rule (see *Journey through Albania*, pp. 555–6, 1085, 1087). Leake agreed with Hobhouse's linguistic argument ('auxiliary verbs' and 'infinitive mood', etc.), but maintained that the Romaic originated long before even the twelfth century (see *Researches in Greece*, pp. 169n., 404). All this may be valuably compared with the notes to *CHP* II (*CPW* ii. 189–217, 282–97).

According to Marsden (*Brief Memoir*, p. 32), Leake used to say that when B was in Greece, he 'turned aside from the contemplation of nearer objects and from the conversation of those about him, to gaze with an air *distrait* and dreamy upon the distant mountains'. After calling upon him on 22 Feb. 1828, Moore recorded in his journal that Leake 'never saw anything of Byron, but at the time he was at Tepelene: seemed to him to have some weight on his mind' (*Memoirs* v. 268). This is curious; for B wrote to Hobhouse on 20 Sept. 1811: 'I had a visit lately from Major (Capt.) Leake "en passant" he talks of returning to Ali Pacha . . . he is grown less taciturn, better dressed, & more like an (English) man of this world than he was at Yanina' (*BLJ* ii. 102).

B himself (despite the tenor of this draft review) seems to have had much respect for Leake and his knowledge of Greece (see *BLJ* ii. 125, 134, 261). Indeed, in his letter to Moore of 22 Feb. 1815 concerning Hobhouse's review, he admits 'I should have been less severe upon the Reviewée' (*BLJ* iv. 274).

B's notice of Leake's work itself is only cursory, but it allows him to turn his attention to the issue of Greek independence. At the time Greece was part of the Ottoman empire, governed by, and paying tribute ('haratch') to the Porte (the Sultan and his court at Constantinople). The inhabitants comprized Greeks, Turks, Albanians, and numerous tribes and factions frequently hostile to one another. They knew little or nothing, and cared even less, about the idea of a united sovereign and independent nation: Greece had never been one. This was a European concept, nurtured by the Franks (a term commonly applied to any Western people), and exploited by such enlightened or Europeanized Greeks who knew of the upheavals in Europe, the American War of Independence, the French Revolution, and the liberation movement of the South American colonies from Spanish dominion by Simon Bolivar (1783–1830). The gist of B's argument is that interference by the European powers in the affairs of Greece would meet with extreme hostility from the Porte, and that the only real chance of Greek liberation from Ottoman domination lay in the emergence of a strong leader, who could unite the disparate factions into an organized force (*not* a regular army), and co-ordinate and direct their native guerrilla skills towards the common aim of independence. These are very much the sentiments B expresses in his poetry. See, e.g., *CHP* II. 73–6 (*CPW* ii. 68–9), and *DJ* III, 'The Isles of Greece', esp. stanza 14 (*CPW* v. 188–92). See also 'The Present State of Greece', *post.*

1. *Russian Alexander . . . Poland.* By the Treaty of Reichenbach (1813) Russia, Prussia, and Austria had agreed to partition Poland amongst themselves. However, during negotiations at the Congress of Vienna (Sept. 1814–June 1815), the Tsar Alexander had peremptorily demanded the whole of the Grand Duchy of Warsaw and said that Prussia should be compensated by the annexation of Saxony. The issue, which was a highly delicate one and nearly precipitated another war, was finally resolved in Feb. 1815 (and ratified in June); Russia did indeed gain the greater part of the Grand Duchy of Warsaw and Prussia a part of Saxony.

2. *At a time . . . permit.* See general note above. B refers here to the first stirrings of the Greek Revolution (which finally broke out in 1821), and to the then-current British and Austrian fears of Russian expansion in the Turkish provinces. The shared orthodox religion of the Russian and Greek churches, and the influence of highly placed Greeks in the tsar's government, made this appear all the more likely. For Tsar Alexander's 'waltzing' capabilities, see B's *The Age of Bronze* (1823), x. 434–5: 'Resplendent sight! Behold the coxcomb Czar, / The Autocrat of waltzes and of war!'

3. *The obstacles . . . expulsion.* Although B may be alluding to the protracted wars in the Peninsular, which had finally ended with the French evacuation of Spain after their defeat by Wellington and the Spanish guerrillas at the Battle of Vittoria (1813), the context suggests that the may have in mind the independence movement in the Spanish colonies in South America. Venezuela had declared her independence on 5 July 1811, but an armistice of 1812 had left her at the mercy of Spain again. In 1813, Simon Bolivar (1783–1830), the 'Liberator' ('El Libertador'), had defeated the Spanish and regained the capital, but had himself been defeated by the Spanish in 1814.

4. *Austria . . . triumph.* Prince Eugène of Austria (see n. 83 to 'Reading List' above) defeated the Turks under Ali Kumurgi at the Battle of Peterwaradin (1716). The following year he besieged and eventually captured Belgrade, with an army one fifth the size of that of the Turks. (The Bosnian forces held out for a long time against him, but were beaten when the Venetians eventually attacked them from the rear.) This was considered his greatest achievement. (See also n. 58 to 'Reading List' above).

5. *"the battle . . . strong'.* Ecclesiastes 9: 11.

6. *But . . . unjust.* By a treaty of 1726 between Russia and Austria, Austria was drawn reluctantly into the Russo-Turkish war of 1736–9. Prince Eugène (see n. 4 above) had died on 1 Apr. 1736, and Austria had no other such accomplished general. The war lingered on in a desultory way until the decisive defeat of the Austrians at the Battle of Crotzka (1739). (See n. 59 to 'Reading List' above.) In Feb. 1788 the Emperor Joseph II of Austria joined Catherine II of Russia in a campaign against the Turks. They suffered ignominous defeats in the Carpathian Mountains and Transylvanian Alps during 1788–9, before finally taking Belgrade. At the subsequent Peace of Sistova (1791) between Austria and Turkey, Austria surrendered her conquests in Bosnia, Serbia, and the Principalities. (See n. 60 to 'Reading List' above.) The town of Caransebes was situated in the Transylvaian Alps, east of Peterwaradin and north-east of Belgrade, in the Banat (province) of Temesvar—the 'Bannat' to which B refers here.

7. *Kuperli . . . Bonneval.* Kuperli (Kiuperli, Koprülü) was the name of a Turkish family of great repute. B probably has in mind Fazil Ahmet Kuperli, Grand Vizier (1661–76), who commanded the besieging army at the siege of Candia (1666–9) and to whom Morosini, the Venetian commander, eventually surrendered. For Bonneval, see n. 85 to 'Reading List' above: 'enterprising Renegade' seems to be B's euphemism for an apostate.

8. *Junot.* Jean-Andoche Junot, Duke of Abrantes (1771–1813), was ADC to Napoleon and later his ambassador in Lisbon. In 1807 he invaded Portugal, which earned him both his title and the position of Governor of Portugal. However, on signing the Convention of Cintra after the defeat of the French at the Battle of Vimiero (1808), he fell from favour. Although he fought again in Spain, Germany, and Russia, he never fully regained Napoleon's confidence, and was eventually sent to govern the Illyrian provinces, where he went mad and committed suicide.

9. *These are . . . Medditeranean.* B misspells 'Mediterranean'. Cf. *CPW* ii. 210: 'The Ottomans, with all their defects, are not a people to be despised. . . . Were they driven from St. Sophia to-morrow, and the French or Russians enthroned in their stead, it would become a question, whether Europe would gain by the exchange. England would certainly be the loser.'

10. *America . . . Atlantic.* America was at war with England from 1812 to 1814, the origin of the dispute being chiefly England's claim to the Freedom of the Seas (an euphemism for her right to search neutral merchant ships in time of war). In 1813, the American navy had had several unexpected successes against the English in the Atlantic, which caused much sensation in both countries. Although the war ceased with the Treaty of Ghent (24 Dec. 1814), the terms of that agreement were inconclusive, and relations between the two countries remained strained.

A Letter on the State of French Affairs (1815)

Text: MS Bodleian (Dep. Lovelace Byron 154, ff. 216–17). First published in Prothero iii. 209n.

Although B never sent this letter, he may have envisaged its addressee as being either James Perry, editor of the *Morning Chronicle*, or Leigh Hunt, editor of the *Examiner*. On the day preceding its composition he had written to Hunt, enclosing his poem 'Napoleon's Farewell' for anonymous publication in his paper, and requesting him to return some letters of John Cam Hobhouse (*BLJ* iv. 306–7; see also *CPW* iii. 312–13, 473). These letters had been written by Hobhouse to B from Paris, where he had gone for the sole purpose of seeing Napoleon. They cover the period 13 Apr.–12 July 1815 (i.e. Napoleon's Hundred Days, Waterloo, and Louis XVIII's second restoration), and form a vivid background to this letter. See *Byron's Bulldog*, pp. 192–220. On 23 July Hobhouse returned from France, and saw B on 27 and 28 July. On 28 July he recorded in his diary: 'Before I came out of London, heard the *Gazette Officielle* from France to-day contains what I dreaded, a list of proscribed: nineteen for their lives, others banished' (*Recollections* i. 322).

It was clearly two numbers of the French *Gazette Officielle* which prompted B to compose this letter. The *Gazette Officielle*, no. 6 (24 July 1815), p. 3, announced, under the general superscription of 'Ordonnances du Roi', the nomination of Talleyrand as honorary Counsellor of State ('Le sieur de Talleyrand, préfet du Loiret, est nommé conseiller-d'état honoraire'). The following day it published three lists of persons denounced by the king: the first listed 29 peers proscribed from the Chambre des Pairs, signed by Talleyrand, who as President of the Council of Ministers was charged with the execution of the order. The second listed 18 officers and generals (amongst whom were Ney, Grouchy, and Bertrand) who were to be court-martialled; the third named 38 persons who were instructed to leave Paris within three days, and to remain under close surveillance in the interior of France pending trial or banishment. These last two lists were signed by Joseph Fouché (1759–1820), Duke of Otrante, the former regicide, Napoleon's and now Louis's Minister of Police (*Gazette Officielle*, no. 7 (25 July 1815), pp. 1–3).

Napoleon had escaped from Elba on 26 Feb. 1815 and had entered Paris on 20 Mar. (Louis XVIII having hurriedly departed for Ghent the preceding night). The Battle of Waterloo took place on 18 June, and Napoleon abdicated for the second time on 22 June. On 25 June he left Paris, embarked on the *Bellerophon* on 15 July, arrived at Torbay on 24 July, and at the time of B's writing was in Plymouth Sound. (For the variety of B's feelings over this period, see *BLJ* iv. 284–5, 295, 300, 302.) Meanwhile, Louis returned from Ghent and on 8 July, accompanied by Talleyrand and Fouché, re-entered Paris (which was filled with English, Russian, Prussian, and Austrian troops). On 9 July he issued a royal proclamation appointing Talleyrand his 'Président du conseil des ministres' (or prime minister), and on 14 July 1815 the first number of the *Gazette Officielle*, which thenceforward carried all his proclamations or 'Ordonnances', was published.

Louis-Stanislas-Xavier, Comte de Provence (1755–1824), brother of the guillotined Louis XVI, had declared himself Louis XVIII in 1795, but in the event only reigned from 1814 to 1824. Between 1795 and 1814 he led a vagrant life of exile, settling for periods in Prussia, Russia, and England, from where he was invited to return to France by Talleyrand. His official restoration as King took place on 3 May 1814. 'Louis le Désiré' as his supporters called him, or 'Louis the Gouty' as he was less romantically styled by B (*BLJ* iv. 100), was a kindly, good-humoured, intelligent, and judicious man, whose singular interest was gastronomy. He was continually afflicted with gout, and was so obese that he could hardly stand.

Charles-Maurice de Talleyrand-Périgord (1754–1838) began his career as a court cleric. He was appointed Agent General of the French clergy in 1780, and Bishop of Autun in 1788. In 1789 he was elected by his fellow clergymen as their deputy in the National Assembly. His revolutionary reorganization of the church in 1790 led to his excommunication by the Pope, and in 1791 he resigned all his clerical offices. In 1793 he was denounced for a secret correspondence with Louis XVI and sought asylum in England. He was expelled from England in 1794 and emigrated to America, where he remained for two years amassing a fortune. He returned to France in 1796, and became Foreign Minister under the Directoire and Napoleon (1797–1807). He was created Prince de Benevento in 1806. However, his growing alarm at Napoleon's ambition prevented him from serving him in any official capacity after 1807, though he remained an adviser and negotiated Napoleon's marriage with Marie-Louisa of Austria in 1810. On 1 Apr. 1814, during the occupation of Paris by the allies, he convened the Senate and had himself elected 'Président' (only 64 of the 140 members being present). The following day he announced Napoleon's deposition, and formally invited Louis XVIII to return as King to France. He became Louis's prime and foreign minister, and skilfully negotiated on the part of France at the Congress of Vienna (1814). He resigned from political life on 24 Sept. 1815, under pressure from the ultra-royalists. See J. F. Bernard, *Talleyrand: A Biography* (1973); see also F. de

Bourrienne, *Memoirs of Napoleon Bonaparte*, ed. Edgar Sanderson (1904), pp. 507–13; Jean Tulard, *Napoleon: The Myth of the Saviour* (1984), pp. 328–42.

The immense value of this letter lies in its revelation of B's vitriolic feelings towards Talleyrand, to whom there is otherwise merely a single reference in the whole of his correspondence, and that a brief though telling one: 'I am obliged to be as treacherous as Tallyrand [*sic*]' (*BLJ* ii. 195–6; see also, though, n. 61 to B's 'Roman Catholic Claims Speech' above).

1. *"Shed . . . Renault"*. Thomas Otway, *Venice Preserved* III. ii. 341 (Jaffeir speaking). The suggestion is that Louis's measures were unwarrantably extreme and vengeful.

2. *Castlereagh . . . Minister.* Robert Stewart Castlereagh (1769–1822), second Marquis of Londonderry, Viscount Castlereagh, was appointed Foreign Secretary in 1812, which post he held until his death. As British minister plenipotentiary, he negotiated at the Treaty of Paris (1814), which restored the Bourbon dynasty after the fall of Napoleon, and at the Congress of Vienna (1814–15), which redrew the map of Europe after Napoleon's Hundred Days (Mar.–June 1814), and opened the Continent to travellers. He was B's abomination (see, e.g., *DJ* 'Dedication', 11–16 (*CPW* v. 6–8)). In the present connection, see also *BLJ* iv. 302.

3. *newspapers . . . France.* Cf. Hobhouse's letter to B of 31 May 1815, written from Paris during Napoleon's Hundred Days:

> As to the News Papers they are so far from being at the disposal of government that more than one are actually suspected of being in the pay of the Bourbons and the Gazette de France is, as well as the Journal General, called 'Le Journal de l'Eteignoir'—This extinguisher is the imputed symbol of royalism—and as you may conceive, means 'extinguisher of les nouvelles lumières.' A newspaper called the Independant is the journal of the republicans and not at all devoted to the court. (*Byron's Bulldog*, p. 211)

4. *premier . . . individual.* Charles-Maurice de Talleyrand-Périgord. See general note above.

The Tale of Calil (1816)

Text: MS Murray. First published in the *Times Literary Supplement*, 17 May 1985, pp. 541–2.

There is nothing in B's correspondence or elsewhere to suggest that he was engaged in writing this story; but it was written in the midst of proceedings leading to his separation from his wife, and in the aftermath of the fall of Napoleon—both of which circumstances form its point of departure. Whether or not B ever envisaged publishing it must remain a matter for conjecture; but he would have found a very ready publisher in Leigh Hunt, whose 'ACCOUNT of the remarkable RISE and DOWNFALL of the late GREAT KAN OF TARTARY, with the still more remarkable fancies that took possession of the heads of some of his

Antagonists', had recently appeared in the *Examiner* (no. 420, 14 Jan. 1816). Hunt's piece is a very thinly veiled, light-hearted satire on the rise and fall of Napoleon, the restoration of the Bourbons, and the victory celebrations after Waterloo. It is set in China, with Tartary representing France, and Samarcand Paris, and features other such *dramatis personae* as 'KAN LOO-HISS' (Louis XVIII), 'KAH-STLEE-RA' (Lord Castlereagh, British Foreign Minister), and 'VEL-HING-TONG' (Wellington). It is not a particularly subtle piece, but it is more sympathetic towards Napoleon than it is towards his 'Antagonists', who merely ape his actions once they are in power, and reach a delusional state of intoxication at the 'Feast of Lanthorns' (the victory celebrations after the Battle of Waterloo). B's story quite clearly glances at this and, in a friendly manner, competes with it. But other circumstances form the immediate backdrop to his story. The principal topics being discussed in the newspapers at the time were the continuing witch-hunts on the Continent of Napoleon's supporters by the restored Bourbon regime (Marshal Ney had been executed on 7 Dec. 1815: see also general note to 'A Letter on the State of French Affairs'), and the Property Tax question which was under discussion in parliament. This tax had been imposed for the duration and the funding of the war, but the government was eager to extend it into peace-time. The issue had initially been raised in the debate on the Prince Regent's speech at the opening of the parliamentary session on 1 Feb. 1816, and it was debated with much rancour and numerous petitions against the imposition throughout Feb. and early Mar., until on 18 Mar. 1816 the Tory 'Motion for the Continuance of the Property Tax' was defeated in the House of Commons by a majority of 38. See *Hansard* xxxii (Feb. to Mar. 1816), *passim*, and xxxiii (Mar. to Apr. 1816), 1–455 *passim.* See also, for example, the *Examiner*, no. 427 (3 Mar. 1816); no. 428 (10 Mar. 1816); no. 429 (17 Mar. 1816). The news of Napoleon's arrival in St Helena on 16 Oct. 1815 first reached England on 12 Dec. 1815, and thereafter reports of his welfare and manner of living appeared regularly in the press. Moreover, Waterloo was still fresh in the public mind. Wordsworth's two sonnets 'Occasioned by the Battle of Waterloo', and the sonnet on 'The Siege of Vienna raised by John Sobieski' (composed in Jan. 1816, and first published in the *Champion* on 4 Feb. 1816), were reviewed by Hunt in the *Examiner*, no. 425, 18 Feb. 1816; and B himself had sent Perry, the editor of the *Morning Chronicle*, on 26 Feb. 1816 his recently composed 'Ode (From the French)', which was first published in the *Morning Chronicle*, no. 14,623 (15 Mar. 1816). See *BLJ* v. 33–4, and *CPW* iii. 375–9, 491–3). These circumstances inform and colour B's story, which simultaneously of course reaches back to the events of the summer of 1815.

Of this story, Leslie Marchand, in his introductory note to its first publication, suggests (p. 541): 'It can be taken as a satire on the inane savagery of war as pictured in the description of the battle of Ismael in the seventh and eighth cantos of *Don Juan*.' Michael Foot, in a 'Postscript' to his review of Peter Graham's *Byron's Bulldog* (1984) in the *Byron Journal* (xiv (1986), 61), remarks that 'one topical event in the story was the way in which Prince Talleyrand had betrayed Napoleon'.

> The immaculate and faithful ambassador who deserts his master with such coolness was one of Byron's special bête-noirs. He had no love for some other foreign ministers, such as Metternich or Castlereagh, but neither of these could be accused of quite so flagrant a piece of treachery as *The Tale of Calil* describes.

See also Michael Foot, *The Politics of Paradise* (1988), pp. 169–70.

Unquestionably, B's story is a satire on the contemporary political scene, and Talleyrand can indeed be regarded as one of its principal targets (especially in the light of 'A Letter on the State of French Affairs' above). Moreover, an analogy might fairly be drawn between Napoleon and Tamerlane, since B himself draws it in stanza 15 of his *Ode to Napoleon Buonaparte* (1814) (*CPW* iii. 264), and does so again in a letter to Sir Walter Scott of 4 May 1822, where he writes of their times 'having seen Napoleon begin like Tamerlane and end like Bajazet' (*BLJ* ix. 155). All the same, the story is not a straightforward allegory, and I think it would be a mistake to look for a definite key. Of singular interest, however, is the way B manoeuvres the story from the private sphere of the domestic quarrel between Calil and Sudabah (or Subadah, as he later calls her), over the naming of their son (naming, or the application of the signifier, representing power over the other), to the public arena of civil dissension, political intrigue, apostasy, and war—the two aspects seemingly reflecting each other. Furthermore, behind this ostensibly insignificant squabble B appears to be playing with a feature of the Turkish language and thereby widening his range of historical allusion: the names of Calil, Bash, and Tash were plausibly chosen with more conscious intent than might at first be credited. (Even 'Subahdar' means master, or a governor of a 'Subah' (province) in Indian.)

Before the final standardization of the Turkish language in 1977, various letters in its alphabet were interchangeable, for example, 'p' and 'b', 'g' and 'v', and 't' and 'd' (*Oxford Turkish–English Dictionary* (1984), p. xii). Hence 'Pashaw'/'Bashaw', chief, and 'Timur'/'Demir', iron. The word 'baş' means head, and 'taş' stone (the 'ş' being pronounced 'sh'). So, 'Demir Bash', Iron Head, and 'Demir Tash', Iron Stone.

'Demir Bash' was the sobriquet given to Charles XII of Sweden (1682–1718) by the Turks for his obstinate nature, when he was in retirement at Bender in his Turkish provinces, after his defeat by Peter the Great at Poltova in 1709 (A. L. Castellan, *Moeurs, Usages, Costumes des Othomans, et Abrégé de leur histoire*, 6 vols. (1812), ii. 152; see also pp. 143–57). During this period of retirement (1709–14), he was the object of numerous Turkish intrigues, and in 1713 was compelled to fight the Turks in order to avoid a plot to hand him over to Augustus of Saxony. He returned to Sweden in 1714 and was killed at the siege of Halden (1718), at the start of his invasion of Norway. He is the subject of Johnson's *The Vanity of Human Wishes* (ll. 190–222), which is itself an 'imitation' of Juvenal's *Satire X*, of which B cites ll. 147–8 as his first epigraph to the *Ode to Napoleon Buonaparte* (*CPW* iii. 259; cf. B's journal entry for 9 Apr. 1814 (*BLJ* iii. 256); see also B's *Mazeppa* (1819) (*CPW* iv. 173–200, 493–4)).

Timur Tash (d. 1328) was the son of Amir Chupan (or Choban), the Regent during the minority of Abu Said, Il-Khan of Persia (1316–35). He was appointed by his father Viceroy of Rum, but in 1322 revolted against him, proclaiming himself an independent ruler and claiming to be the *Madhi* (the Muslim messiah). Chupan (though grievously afflicted with gout) suppressed the rebellion, reprieving Timur Tash and even restoring him to his former position of Viceroy. Chupan and Abu Said were on good terms with each other (Chupan had married Said's sister) until the latter desired to marry Chupan's daughter. His persistent requests for her hand being met by Chupan's equally persistent refusals led to open hostilities between them and eventually to Chupan's execution. On hearing of his father's death, Timur Tash fled to the Mameluke Sultan at Cairo, where he was at first well received. But the Sultan, wishing to keep on good terms with Abu Said, later killed him. It is said that had Timur Tash survived, he might have delayed or even have prevented the rise of the Ottoman empire. See *The Cambridge History of Iran*, 8 vols., v (1968), 409–12; see also Brigadier-General Sir Percy Sykes, *A History of Persia*, 2 vols. (1958), ii. 115).

On the death of Tamerlane (see below), his grandson Khalil (or Calil) Sultan (1384–1411), son of Miran Shah, took possession of Samarcand and appropriated the succession to the empire from his cousin, Pir Mohammed, whom Tamerlane had named as his successor. Khalil was a man of literary and artistic leanings, generous and liberal, but weak and gullible, and he aggravated the nobles by squandering all the wealth accumulated by Tamerlane on his wife, 'Shad Mulk' ('Joy of the State'), of whom he was devotedly fond. He was dethroned in 1409, and later appointed Governor of Ray where he died in 1411. On his death, 'Shad Mulk' took her own life.

As for Tamerlane (Timur Lenc) (1336–1405), the great Mogul Emperor (1369–1405) (who did not in fact suffer from gout but was an energetic old man to the last), he out-did in many ways even Genghis Khan and Alexander the Great. ('Lenc', lame, was a title of contempt applied to him by his enemies, though he was indeed lame.) He mastered the whole of Asia from Mongolia to the Mediterranean, overruning Persia, Mesopotamia, and parts of Russia, before invading India and taking Delhi in 1398–9 (AH 800–1 (see n. 1 below)). While in Delhi he was informed of disturbances and uprisings in Georgia and Anatolia, and of the designs of Bajazet, Sultan of Turkey (1389–1402), who was then besieging Constantinople and was ambitious to extend the bounds of the Ottoman empire. Tamerlane therefore returned to Samarcand in 1400, and in 1401 set out on his leisurely and circuitous campaign against Bajazet, taking Damascus, Aleppo, and Bagdad, and reducing the Mamelukes in his way, before finally meeting the full Ottoman force on the fields of Ankara in 1402, where he defeated and captured Bajazet (who was severely hampered in his flight by gout). He died of fever on his expedition to invade China in 1405. See Edward Gibbon, *The History of The Decline and Fall of the Roman Empire*, ch. 65. For Tamerlane and Khalil (Calil), see Sykes, *History of Persia* ii. 118–37; *The Cambridge History of Iran*, vi (1986), 42–101; Hilda Hookham, *Tamberlaine the Great* (1962).

The above recital is not intended to imply any historical foundation for what is after all a wonderful piece of satirical fiction. But I do suggest that there are resonances at play within the text which B was consciously exploiting, and which give the satire a broader perspective than may at first be apparent, along the lines of his assertion in *CHP* IV. 108: 'There is the moral of all human tales; / 'Tis but the same rehearsal of the past', 'And History, with all her volumes vast, / Hath but *one* page' (*CPW* ii. 160). For the story might be considered (in addition to the above suggestions by Marchand and Foot) as part of B's sustained indictment of ambition, tyranny, and war generally, as traced for instance in the more proximate *Ode to Napoleon Buonaparte* (1814), *CHP* III. 17–45; IV. 83–114 (*CPW* iii. 259–66; ii. 82–93, 152–62).

1. *Hegira.* (migration). The flight of Mahomet (*c.* AD 570–632) from Mecca to Medina took place in AD 622, from which year the Muslim era is dated (cited as AH, *anno Hegirae*).

2. *Bile . . . of it.* B is punning here on 'bile' as the medical word for the digestive juice secreted by the liver (a derangement of which would indeed result in ill-health or biliousness), and 'bile' as one of the four humours, whose manifestation was bad temper or peevishness, which Sudabah certainly does not appear to 'want' (lack).

3. *Tomans.* Persian gold coins. (1 toman was worth approximately £2 in B's day).

4. *Heron's tail.* See also B's erasure. It is a shame that B should have made this alteration, for the peacock is indigenous to India and was the symbol of Mogul hegemony. The highly ornamented throne of the kings of Delhi, which imitated the peacock's fantail, was called 'the Peacock throne'.

5. *Balaam's ass . . . Mecca.* For Balaam and his (speaking) ass, see Numbers 22. The closing quotation marks were omitted by B.

6. *Bairam.* The name of the Muslim festivals: the Lesser Bairam, which follows immediately after Ramadan (the fasting period in the ninth month of the Muslim calendar) and lasts three days; and the Greater Bairam, which follows seventy days later and lasts for four days.

7. *demands.* Closing quotation marks omitted by B.

8. *peccant part.* The offending or injurious part ('peccant' means malignant, or the cause of disorder to the system). Cf. Pope, *Essay on Man* ii. 141–4; and Dryden, 'The Tenth Satyr of Juvenal', ll. 489–90.

9. *Sophi of Persia.* Sophi (or sophy) means shah or ruler, or king.

10. *Opodeldoc ... exported.* 'Opodeldoc' was the name of various plasters invented and compounded by Paracelsus before 1541, which later became the general term for a soap liniment or embrocation. B himself had recourse to opodeldoc for 'the rheumatics' and '*chilblains*' in 1822 and 1823. See *BLJ* ix. 216; x. 82.

11. *Cadi... orthography.* Cadi (Cadhi), a civil judge or magistrate.

12. *pyramid ... edifice.* It was Tamerlane's custom after a battle to have the heads of the vanquished piled into columns or pyramids. At Aleppo, for instance, twenty thousand heads were piled into a pyramid.

13. *Before... Delhi.* This, and the following paragraph, might bear happy comparison with the Stranger's musings on his mule in 'Slawkenbergius's Tale' in Sterne's *Tristram Shandy*, vol. iv.

14. *mulct.* A fine, or an impost.

Augustus Darvell: A Fragment of a Ghost Story (1816)

Text: MS Brotherton Collection, University of Leeds. First published at the end of B's *Mazeppa* (1819), pp. 59–69. Thereafter published in *Works* vi (1832), 339–45, and Prothero iii. 449–53. (Title supplied by me.)

B wrote this story at Diodati in June 1816 when he, Shelley, Mary Shelley, Claire Clairmont, and John Polidori (B's physician) were constantly in each other's company. It was begun as part of a contest between all of them except Claire, after they had been reading together a collection of ghost stories entitled *Fantasmagoriana, ou Recueil d'Histoire d'Apparitions de Spectres, Revenans, Fantômes, etc.; Traduit de l'allemand, par un Amateur*, 2 vols. (Paris, 1812). Perhaps the best account concerning the occasion of its composition was given by Mary who, in her preface to the third edition of *Frankenstein* (issued by Colburn and Bentley as the first part of no. ix of their *Standard Novels* (1831)), wrote of that memorable summer:

In the summer of 1816, we visited Switzerland, and became the neighbours of Lord Byron.... But it proved a wet, ungenial summer, and incessant rain often confined us for days to the house. Some volumes of ghost stories, translated from the German into French, fell into our hands. There was the History of the Inconstant Lover, who, when he thought to clasp the bride to whom he had pledged his vows, found himself in the arms of the pale ghost of her whom he had deserted ['La Morte Fiancée' ii. 1–101]. There was the tale of the sinful founder of his race, whose miserable doom it was to bestow the kiss of death on all the younger sons of his fated house, just when they reached the age of promise ['Les Portraits de Famille' i. 117–225]....

'We will each write a ghost story,' said Lord Byron; and his proposition was acceded to. There were four of us. The noble author began a tale, a fragment of which he printed at the end of his poem of Mazeppa. Shelley, more apt to embody ideas and sentiments in the radiance of brilliant imagery, and in the music of the most melodious verse that adorns our language, than to invent the machinery of a story, commenced one founded on the experiences of his early life. Poor Polidori had some terrible idea about a skull-headed lady, who was so punished for peeping through a key-hole—what to see I forget—something very shocking and wrong of course; but when she was reduced to a worse condition than the renowned Tom of Coventry, he did not know what to do with her, and was obliged to despatch her to the tomb of the Capulets, the only place for which she was fitted. The illustrious poets also, annoyed by the platitude of prose, speedily relinquished their uncongenial task. (pp. vii–viii)

She goes on to speak of the conception on that occasion of her *Frankenstein; or, The Modern Prometheus*, which was published anonymously in three volumes in 1818. Of Shelley's story there is nothing extant, and Polidori must indeed have despatched his 'skull-headed lady . . . to the tomb of the Capulets', for nothing survives of her either. His contribution was in fact twofold, his own original composition being *Ernestus Berchtold; or, The Modern Œdipus* (1819). In the preface to this work he wrote:

The tale here presented to the public is the one I began at Coligny, when Frankenstein was planned, and when a noble author having determined to descend from his lofty range, gave up a few hours to a tale of terror, and wrote the fragment published at the end of Mazeppa. (p. v)

To the last phrase here he appended the following note:

The tale which lately appeared, and to which his lordship's name was wrongfully attached, was founded upon the ground-work upon which this fragment was to have been continued. Two friends were to travel from England into Greece; while there, one of them should die, but before his death, should obtain from his friend an oath of secrecy with regard to his decease. Some short time after, the remaining traveller returning to his native country, should be startled at perceiving his former companion moving about in society, and should be horrified at finding that he made love to his former friend's sister. Upon this foundation I built the Vampyre, at the request of a lady, who denied the possibility of such a ground-work forming the outline of a tale which should bear the slightest appearance of probability. In the course of three mornings, I produced that tale, and left it with her. From thence it appears to have fallen into the hands of some person, who sent it to the Editor in such a way, as to leave it so doubtful from his words, whether it was his lordship's or not, that I found some difficulty in vindicating it to myself. (pp. vn.–vi n.)

This disingenuous explanation refers to *The Vampyre* (1819) which was spuriously attributed to B by Polidori himself. He may perhaps have 'vamped up his strange novel of the Vampire' (Moore ii. 31 n.) from B's outline, for there is some slight resemblance between the initial part of it and B's fragment; but the work is entirely his own.

The Vampyre; A Tale, By the Right Honourable Lord Byron, was printed for Sherwood, Neely, and Jones, and entered at the Stationers' Hall on 27 Mar. 1819. The volume contains: 'Extract of a Letter from Geneva', the title story, and 'Extract of a Letter containing an account of Lord Byron's Residence in the Island of Mitylene'. The first 'Extract', together with *The Vampyre*, appeared in the *New Monthly Magazine*, vol. xi, no. 63 (1 Apr. 1819), pp. 193–206, and included the following paragraph (p. 195), which recurs verbatim in *The Vampyre*:

Among other things which the lady, from whom I procured these anecdotes, related to me, she mentioned the outline of a ghost story by Lord Byron. It appears that one evening Lord B., Mr. P. B. Shelly, the two ladies and the gentleman before alluded to [Polidori himself], after having perused a German work, which was entitled Phantasmagoriana, began relating ghost stories; when his lordship having recited the beginning of Christabel, then unpublished, the whole took so strong a hold of Mr. Shelly's mind, that he suddenly started up and ran out of the room. The physician and Lord Byron followed, and discovered him leaning against a mantle-piece, with cold drops of perspiration trickling down his face. After having given him something to refresh him, upon enquiring into the cause of his alarm, they found that his wild imagination having pictured to him the bosom of one of the ladies with eyes (which was reported of a lady in the neighbourhood where he lived) he was obliged to leave the room in order to destroy the impression. It was afterwards proposed, in the course of conversation, that each of the company present should write a tale depending upon some supernatural agency, which was undertaken by Lord B., the physician, and Miss M. W. Godwin. My friend, the lady above referred to, had in her possession the outline of each of these stories; I obtained them as a great favour, and herewith forward them to you, as I was assured you would feel as much curiosity as myself, to peruse the *ebauches* of so great a genius, and those immediately under his influence. (*The Vampyre*, pp. xv–xvi)

Murray sent B *The Vampyre* and this number of the *New Monthly Magazine* (whose proprietor was Henry Colburn), which clearly prompted B to publish his fragment and elicited from him the following letter to Murray of 15 May 1819:

I have got yr. extract, & the 'Vampire'. I need not say it is *not mine* ... The Story of Shelley's agitation is true—I can't tell what seized him—for he don't want courage.... [But he] certainly had the fit of phantasy which P[olidori] describes—though *not exactly* as he describes it. The story of the agreement to write the Ghost-books is true ... Mary Godwin (now Mrs. Shelley) wrote 'Frankenstein' ... methinks it is a wonderful work for a Girl of nineteen—*not* nineteen indeed—at that time.—I enclose you the beginning of mine—by which you will see how far it resembles Mr. Colburn's publication.—If you choose to publish it in the Edinburgh Magazine (*Wilsons* & *Blackwoods*) you may—*stating why*, & with such explanatory proem as you please.—I never went on with it—as you will perceive by the date.—I began it in an old account-book of Miss Milbanke's which I kept because it contains the word '*Household*' written by her twice on the inside blank page of the Covers—being the only two Scraps I have in the world in her writing, except her name to the deed of Separation.... I have torn the leaves containing the part of the tale out of the book & enclose them with this sheet. (*BLJ* vi. 125–7)

These are the (eight) 'leaves' which are in the Brotherton Library, and from which the present text is taken. Murray did not 'choose to publish it in the Edinburgh Magazine', but published it as 'A Fragment' with *Mazeppa* and 'Venice. An Ode' on 28 June 1819—much to B's displeasure (see *BLJ* vii. 58).

B wrote to Murray on 2 Apr. 1817: 'I hate things *all fiction* ... there should always be some foundation of fact for the most airy fabric—and pure invention is but the talent of a liar' (*BLJ* v. 203). Although this fragment is merely a ghost story and certainly fictitious, it may well have had some 'foundation of fact'. For in Sept. 1810, B was seriously ill with a fever in Patras (see Marchand i. 260; *BLJ* ii. 14–16, 18–19, 44). In a letter to Murray of 6 Oct. 1820, B told him of a curious incident that had occurred to Robert Peel, his old school-friend, during that time:

He told me that in *1810* he met me as he thought in St. James's Street, but we passed without speaking.—He mentioned this—and it was denied as impossible—I being then in Turkey.—A day or two after he pointed out to his brother a person on the opposite side of the way—'there'—said he 'is the man I took for Byron'—his brother instantly answered 'why it *is* Byron & no one else.'—But this is not all—I was *seen* by somebody to *write down my name* amongst the Enquirers after the King's health—then attacked by insanity.—Now—at this very period, as nearly as I could make out—I was ill of a *strong fever* at Patras, caught in the marshes near Olympia—from the *Malaria.*———If I had died there this would have been a new Ghost Story for you. (*BLJ* vii. 192)

Robert Peel confirmed his experience to Moore when the latter called upon him on 20 Feb. 1829. See Moore, *Memoirs* vi. 14. Referring to his fever a few years later, B told Thomas Medwin:

I had no intention of dying at that time; but if I had died, a similar thing would have been told of me to that related as having happened to Colonel Sherbrooke in America. On the very day my fever was at the highest, a friend of mine declared that he saw me in St. James's Street; and somebody put my name down in the book at the Palace, as having enquired after the King's health! Everybody would have said that my ghost had appeared.... I mean to return to Greece, and shall in all probability die there. (*Medwin's Conversations*, p. 91)

On this last remark, his wife Annabella commented: 'He had often said before leaving England "I *must* go to the East—to die"' (ibid., p. 92n.).

The incident that occurred to (Colonel) Sir John Coape Sherbrooke (1764–1830), the Governor-General of Canada in 1816, took place when he was serving in Sicily in 1805–7, and was known as the 'Wynyard Story'. Sherbrooke and Lieutenant George Wynyard had both seen an apparition of the latter's brother at exactly the moment of that brother's death in England. (See A. Patchett Martin, *Life and Letters of the Right Honourable Robert Lowe, Viscount Sherbrooke, G.C.B., D.C.L. etc. With a Memoir of Sir John Coape Sherbrooke, G.C.B.*, 2 vols. (1893), ii. 594–5.)

While *Fantasmagoriana* (and particularly the story 'L'Heure Fatale' (see n. 10 below), in which Séraphine appears under her earthly and her spiritual aspect simultaneously), may indeed form a marginal part of the influential background to B's composition, greater credit should, I suggest, be given to the above two occurrences and to B's own comments.

In addition to the works referred to above, see *Tales of the Dead. Principally Translated from the French* (1813) (which is only a selection from *Fantasmagoriana*, but includes 'L'Heure Fatale' translated as 'The Fated Hour'); William Michael Rossetti (ed.), *The Diary of Dr. John William Polidori* (1911); Samuel C. Chew, *Byron in England*, ch. 10 ('The Byron Apocrypha'); and P. B. and M. W. Shelley, *History of a Six Weeks' Tour through a part of France, Switzerland, Germany, and Holland, etc.* (1817).

1. *I had heard.* Prothero has 'I heard'.

2. *arrangements.* Prothero has 'arrangement'.

3. *Serrugee . . . Janizary.* 'Serrugee' (Turkish, *Sürücü*), a driver, or man in charge of post-horses; 'Janizary', a soldier escorting travellers.

4. *Caravansera.* A hostel, or an inn (Persian).

5. *"City . . . Dead".* Cf. 'On the Star of "The Legion of Honour"', stanza 7, ll. 37–8: 'And Freedom hallows with her tread / The silent cities of the dead' (*CPW* iii. 318).

6. *he said . . . water.* The phrase here is Turkish: *Ver*, give; *bana*, to me; and *su*, water. B may well be recalling Suliman, the name of his and Hobhouse's guide when they visited the ruins of Ephesus together in Mar. 1810. According to Hobhouse, when they were eager to return speedily from the ruins to Smyrna, 'Suliman was not to be persuaded to participate in our impatience; he would not quit his smoking pace (for he had a pipe in his mouth during nearly the whole journey)' (J. C. Hobhouse, *A Journey through Albania* (1813), p. 667). See also Marchand i. 234–5.

7. *he returned.* In all editions this has been changed to 'I received'.

8. *to request to make.* In all editions this has been changed to 'a request to make'.

9. *9th . . . month.* All editions read 'ninth day of the month' (without emphasis).

10. *9th . . . month.* All editions read 'ninth day of the month'. The choice of this particular date may well have been influenced by the story 'L'Heure Fatale' in *Fantasmagoriana* (ii. 105–60), in which the 'fatal hour' is nine o'clock. But see also Schiller's *The Ghost-Seer*, where the Armenian at the Venetian Carnival tells the Prince of W—, 'Wish yourself joy, Prince . . . *at nine o'clock he died*' (*The Ghost-Seer.* Colburn and Bentley, Standard Novels, no. ix (1831), pt. ii, p. 11). Cf. also B's letter to John Murray of 2 Apr. 1817, in which he mentions 'Schiller's "*Armenian*"—a novel which took a great hold of me when a boy—it is also called the "Ghost Seer"—& I never walked down St. Mark's by moonlight without thinking of it &—"at nine o'clock he died!"' (*BLJ* v. 203).

11. *a Stork . . . us.* The antagonism between storks and snakes is an old belief perhaps of Jewish origin. This image, however, has multiple significations of which the most pertinent to the present context appear to be the following. According to Pliny, storks were so highly regarded for their utility in destroying snakes that in Thessaly it was a capital crime to kill one (*Natural History*, X. xxxi). A stork augurs death, is the form assumed by the soul after death, and, in Egyptian mythology, storks were previously men who became men again in winter. The more familiar image of the stork with a child in its beak may also be relevant here, since as long as the stork holds the child in its beak the child is not yet born. Snakes also are transformed into men in Indian, Hindu, and Buddhist mythology. Evil-doers are reborn as snakes; birds attack snakes because they are produced by demons; snakes choose to die beside a spring, and never die before sunset. See, for example, Angelo de Gubernatis,

Zoological Mythology, 2 vols. (1872). However, in *Morgenröthe* (1881, p. 69), Nietzsche also refers to this exact image—'a stork holding a snake in its beak but *hesitating* to swallow it'—as a 'Dreadful portent' which appeared to 'the Christian of the Middle Ages' (*Daybreak*, trans. R. J. Hollingdale (1982), p. 46). The allusion must therefore have a specific source, but neither Reginald Hollingdale nor I have been able to locate it.

12. *ataghan.* A variation of 'yataghan', a Turkish sword with a curved double-edged blade. See for instance the illustration facing p. 178 in *CPW* iii.

13. *some preceding.* Omitted in all editions.

ARMENIAN STUDIES (1816–1817)

B began studying Armenian under Padre Paschal Aucher (for whom see below), at the Armenian Convent on the island of St Lazaro, Venice, in late Nov. or early Dec. 1816. He first visited the Armenian Convent on 27 Nov. (*Bentley's Miscellany*, v (1839), 259), and on 4 Dec. wrote to John Murray: 'I had begun & am proceeding in a study of the Armenian language—which I acquire as well as I can—at the Armenian convent where I go every day to take lessons of a learned Friar—and have gained some singular and not useless information with regard to the literature & customs of that Oriental people' (*BLJ* v. 137). By 19 Dec. he was able to tell his friend John Cam Hobhouse that he had 'about mastered thirty of the thirty eight cursed scratches of Mesrob the Maker of Alphabets and some words of one syllable' (*BLJ* v. 142). He continued his studies until the end of Feb. 1817 at the latest; for on 3 Mar. he reported to Murray: 'my Armenian studies are suspended for the present—till my head aches a little less' (*BLJ* v. 179). Throughout the month he was ill with fever, and on 25 Mar. he confessed again to Murray: 'My illness has prevented me from moving this month past—& I have done nothing more with the Armenian' (*BLJ* v. 193). In Apr. he left for Rome and does not appear to have resumed his studies on his return to Venice.

These pieces were therefore most probably written during Jan.–Feb. 1817—which coincides with the time of his translating 'The Pleasures of the Summer Houses of Byzantium' (see *CPW* iv. 110–13, 477).

Why B should have undertaken the study of such an 'out of the way language' at this time, he himself explained to his sister Augusta: 'it is Oriental & difficult—& employs me—which are—as you know my Eastern & difficult way of thinking—reasons sufficient' (*BLJ* v. 141). To Murray and Thomas Moore he was perhaps more expansive. Writing to Murray he declared: 'I found it necessary to twist my mind round some severer study—and this—as being the hardest I could devise here—will be a file for the serpent' (*BLJ* v. 137). To Moore he wrote: 'By way of divertisement, I am studying daily, at an Armenian monastery, the Armenian language. I found that my mind wanted something craggy to break upon; and this—as the most difficult thing I could discover here for an amusement—I have chosen, to torture me into attention' (*BLJ* v. 130). See also the second sentence in the second paragraph of his 'Preface'. These remarks should, I suggest, be compared with the closing passage of his 'Alpine Journal' (*BLJ* v. 104–5) and with his professed reasons for writing *The Bride of Abydos* (1813)—or indeed, for writing at all (*BLJ* iii. 157, 161, 168, 184, 205, 208, 225). With his separation from his wife and self-imposed exile still very much on his mind, he evidently required a more intellectually bracing and more challenging 'divertisement' from himself than poetry could provide.

Notwithstanding these personal reasons and his natural aptitude for and genuine interest in languages generally, it should not be forgotten that B was attempting the language of an oppressed people—a point to which he draws attention in his 'Preface'. Armenia had been the squabbling ground of Turkey and Persia since at least the seventeenth century, and Russia was to join in the quarrel in the early nineteenth century. Indeed, at the time of B's writing, Russia had already annexed the bulk of the Caucasus and had gained considerable authority over other parts of Armenia by the Treaty of Bucharest (1812, with Turkey) and the Treaty of Gulistan (1813, with Persia). Hence B's commitment to the Armenian language could reasonably be thought of as both linguistically *and* politically motivated, and these writings regarded as an endeavour to attract the attention of the English reader to the plight of the Armenians—or at the least, to register his own support for their cause. George Mackay, who visited the monastery in 1868, reports, on the authority of a certain Brother Nicholas who had known B, that:

> Padre Paschal did not approve of the preface. He said it was an attack on the Turkish Government, whose flag protected the Convent, and declined to accept it.
> —What! [exclaimed B] you refuse to print this preface because it is severe on your masters and oppressors? Slaves and cowards! You ought to have hard masters; you are not worthy of the great nation from which you sprang!
> Padre Paschal remonstrated, but Byron . . . knew no bounds to his fury and exclaimed:
> —Monks, not men! you're cowards all, and I know not what keeps me from beating you!
> (George Eric Mackay, *Lord Byron at the Armenian Convent* (Venice, 1876), p. 79)

To this same Brother Nicholas, B was also quite literally a 'Saint in Heaven': he regarded B's death at Missolonghi, in Greece, as having been as much in the Armenian as in the Greek cause for freedom (Mackay, p. 80).

Of B's advancement in his studies, Padre Aucher is reputed to have said: 'He did not make very rapid progress. He was often very pettish, and complained a good deal of the hardships he experienced in trying to learn it' (*Bentley's Miscellany*, v (1839), 260). B himself said that he found the language 'difficult but not invincible', and that he pursued his lessons 'without any rapid progress—but advancing a little daily' (*BLJ* v. 137, 156). A few years later, in his 'Detached Thoughts' (1821–2), he was to record:

> I sometimes wish that—I had studied languages with more attention . . . I set in zealously for the Armenian and Arabic—but I fell in love with some absurd womankind both times

> before I had overcome the Characters and at Malta & Venice left the profitable Orientalists for—for—(no matter what—) notwithstanding that my master the Padre Pasquale Aucher (for whom by the way I compiled the major part of two Armenian & English Grammars) assured me 'that the terrestrial Paradise had been certainly in *Armenia*'. (*BLJ* ix. 31)

None the less, to have acquired the language (and *such* a language) within three months, and with enough proficiency to accomplish these translations, is surely impressive. (For an assessment of B's acquisition of Armenian see D. B. Gregor, 'Byron's Knowledge of Armenian', *Notes and Queries*, vol. cxcvi, no. 15 (21 July 1951), pp. 316–20.)

Padre Paschal Aucher (1774–1854) was a Mechitarist priest and the librarian of the convent. He had a prodigious memory and was the master of no less than ten languages. Besides grammars and dictionaries, his many works include a translation into Armenian of *Paradise Lost* (1824). According to B, he was 'a very attentive preceptor', and 'a learned & pious soul' who 'was two years in England' (*BLJ* v. 142, 152). There are two other contemporary portraits of Aucher. Henry Matthews, who met him on 29 May 1818, wrote of him as 'a man of great learning, very extensive knowledge of the world, and most amiable manners' (*The Diary of an Invalid* (1820), p. 284). When the Morgans visited him a little later, he received them with 'the ease and address of a man of the world'—though Lady Morgan found his notions of a free press somewhat equivocal (Lady Morgan, *Italy*, 2 vols. (1821), ii. 464–5). He also appears to have been a kindly and good-humoured man, with a great affection for B whom he recorded in his diary as being 'a young man, quick, sociable, with burning eyes' (Gregor, 'Byron's Knowledge of Armenian', p. 317).

In the notes to the following pieces, reference is made to the History of Armenia by the fifth-century-AD Armenian scholar and historian, Moses of Corene, edited and translated into Latin by William and George Whiston, and published by John Whiston in 1736 under the title: *Mosis Chorenensis Historiæ Armeniacæ Libri III.* B himself refers to, and translates from, this work (see, e.g., 'Translations from the Armenian: Two Extracts' and 'Two Epistles' below), which has been abbreviated here to *W*.

The Armenian Alphabet (1816)

Text: MS Murray. Unpublished.

Although this bears no date, it clearly belongs to the very earliest stages of B's Armenian Studies (Nov.–Dec. 1816). The list consists of the 38 characters of the Armenian alphabet, written out in the correct order phonetically on the recto and verso of a foolscap sheet. To the left of the column, B has also written in Armenian script the letters to which his phonetics apply. These have not been reproduced here. All Armenian letters (with the exception of the last two listed here) also have a number value: hence B's numbering (1–10) on the right of the column. It is interesting to note that B's phonetics correspond very closely to those given by Mesrob Kouyoumdjian in *A Comprehensive Dictionary Armenian–English* (1950). See also 'The Armenian Language: A Note' below (and esp. nn. 2, 3 thereto).

1. *Hajg . . . Armeni.* This is written in the top right-hand margin of the page (verso) and translates:

> Hajg, the name of the first Armenian Hero.
> Aram, the second.
> haj. An Armenian.
> hajK, Armenians.

For 'Hajg' (Haic), the Armenian patriarch, and for 'haj' and 'hajK', see 'The Armenian Language: A Note' below (esp. n. 5). Aram was the sixth ruler of the Armenians (Haics) after Haic. His heroic deeds earned Armenia her name from her neighbours ('Armenia' being a corruption of the land or people of Aram).

The Armenian Language: A Note (1817)

Text: MS Murray. Unpublished.

Although this note is undated, and is clearly only a rough draft, B may well have intended it eventually to form part of a larger note or preface to one of Aucher's Grammars (1817 or 1819). See the general note to 'The Armenian Grammar: Two Comments' below.

1. *Veram shabuk . . . Alphabet.* St Mesrob (Mesrob-Mashtots) (354–441), the inventor of the Armenian alphabet, was the disciple of and secretary to St Nerses I ('Magnus'), the 7th Patriarch of the Armenian Church (340–74). He was ordained in 386, and later became secretary and chancellor to Vramshapuh I, King of Armenia (392–414). On the death of his close colleague and coagitator, St Isaac I (Sahag the Great) (b. *c.*340; d. 440), the 10th Patriarch of the Armenian Church (390–440), Mesrob succeeded to the Patriarchate, just six months before his own death (441).

In *c.*393, Mesrob and Isaac, with the encouragement of King Vramshapuh, initiated a religious and literary revival in Armenia, promoting in particular a movement for the systematizing of the vernacular language and the elimination of all pagan or idolatrous forms of worship. In 406 Mesrob invented the first 36 characters of the Armenian alphabet (from 'Ayp', 'Aip', or 'Ipe', to 'K' or 'Ka') following the Greek arrangement. By 410, Mesrob and Isaac, using this alphabet, had produced a Bible in the written vernacular translated principally from Greek and Syriac MSS.

The significance of the creation of this alphabet to the Armenians at the time should not be underestimated. Although they had their own king, they continued to be a vassal state of Persia. Their official adoption of Christianity in *c.*280 signalled their initial resistance to cultural and religious assimilation by Persia; the alphabet gave them a national identity. See also n. 4 below.

2. *Syriac . . . character.* Before the invention of the alphabet by Mesrob the Armenians possessed no native *written* language. According to Moses, the clergy used the Greek characters, while Persian characters were in general use (bk. III, chs. xxxvi and lii; *W.* pp. 273, 297). After the partitioning of Armenia in 384 (between the Romans and the Persians—the latter gaining by far the greater territory), Syriac was the only authorized language (bk. III, ch. liv; *W.* p. 300). This may explain why B has subnumbered 'Persian' ('*1*') and 'Syriac' ('*2*'), intending this to mean 'at first and then', or 'firstly and secondly', or perhaps even 'primarily and secondarily'.

3. *in the . . . introduced.* The repetition of 'to' here is B's error. The last two characters of the 38 letters of the Armenian alphabet were introduced in the twelfth century (by whom is not known), thus completing what B referred to as 'a Waterloo of an Alphabet' (*BLJ* v. 131).

4. *many M.S.S. . . . Paganism.* The destruction of manuscripts and libraries by Christian clergy and others took place during the fourth and fifth centuries. However, the Christians were systematically persecuted by Shapur II, King of Persia (309–79), who, in 356, sacked and destroyed every major town in Armenia. His agent, one Meruzanus, imprisoned and deported all priests and bishops, and ordered the burning of all Greek texts (Greek being associated with Christianity and hence with disaffection; see nn. 1, 2 above). This is recounted by Moses in bk. I, chs. xxxv, xxxvi, and lii of his History (*W.* pp. 270–3, 300).

5. *The Armenians . . . an Armenian.* Haic (Haicus), whom the Armenians regard as their first king, is reputed to have been the great-great-great-grandson of Noah, descending from him through his third son Japheth (for whom see Genesis 10). He is said to have come from Babylon, and to have established himself and his family in Armenia in 22 BC. The Armenians thus designate themselves 'Haics' or 'Haykh' (the plural form of 'Hay'). This is discussed by Moses in bk. I, chs. ix and x of his History (*W.* pp. 25–30).

6. *The Armenians . . . copiousness.* In Aucher's *Grammar* (1819), for instance, there are some verse extracts from Nierses Claensis (twelfth century), two of which consist respectively of 32 lines ending in '*in*', and 16 lines ending in '*is*'—yet none of the *words* is the same (pp. 310–11).

The Armenian Grammar: Two Comments (1817)

Text: MS Murray. Unpublished.

These two comments were written by B on the proof sheets of Padre Paschal Aucher's *Grammar English and Armenian* (1817), which was printed at the press of the Armenian Academy at Venice during Dec. 1816 and Jan. 1817. There are eight sheets altogether, being the first sixteen pages of the *Grammar* itself. The first comment appears on page 1, the second on page 11. ('Orinag' transliterates the Armenian for 'Example'.)

B sent these sheets to Murray on 2 Jan. 1817, saying (*BLJ* v. 156):

I send you some sheets of a grammar English & Armenian for the use of the Armenians—of which I promoted & indeed induced the publication; (it cost me but a thousand francs of French livres) . . . Padre Paschal—with some little help from me as a translator of his Italian into English—is also proceeding in an M.S. grammar for the *English* acquisition of Armenian—which will be printed also when finished.—We want to know if there are any *Armenian types* or letter-press in England—at Oxford—Cambridge or elsewhere?—You know I suppose that many years ago the two Whistons published in England an original text of a history of Armenia with their own Latin translation.—Do these types still exist? & where.—Pray enquire among your learned acquaintance.—When this grammar—(I mean the one now printing) is done will you have any objection to take 40 or fifty copies which will not cost in all above five or ten guineas—& try the curiosity of the learned with the sale of them.—Say yes or no as you like.—I can assure you that they have some very curious books & M.S. chiefly translations from Greek originals now lost.

Murray replied to this most enthusiastically on 22 Jan. 1817:

Frere . . . likes the 'Armenian Grammar' very much, though he would prefer the English part of it. . . . He says that the type is not so large as it ought to be for a language which is not to be whipped into one, but coaxed in by the most enticing appearances. I will most willingly take fifty copies even upon my love of letters; so they may be sent as soon as completed. We are all much interested with 'the very curious books and MSS. *chiefly translated from Greek originals now lost*,' and I am desired to entreat that you will gain every particular respecting their history and contents, together with the best account of the Armenian language, which may form a very interesting introduction to the copies which you send here, and which preface I will print myself; unless as a curiosity you print it there also; or if you would review the 'Grammar' for me and insert all this knowledge in the article, which would certainly be the very best way of making the 'Grammar' known to the public. . . . I have as yet ascertained only that there are no Armenian types at Cambridge. (Samuel Smiles, *A Publisher and His Friends*, 2 vols. (1891), i. 370–1)

B did not respond to this immediately, but it is more than likely that he wrote the 'Preface to the Armenian Grammar', and drafted 'The Armenian Language: A Note', as a response to Murray's letter. By 3 Mar. 1817 the *Grammar* had been published (*BLJ* v. 179), and on 8 June 1817 B wrote to Murray: 'The present letter will be delivered to you by two Armenian Friars—on their way by England to Madras—they will also convey some copies of the Grammar, which I think you agreed to take' (*BLJ* v. 235). These friars arrived at Murray's while he was writing to B on 5 Aug. 1817: 'Your Armenian friends have this moment presented themselves with your letter. I will take all their grammars and do all otherwise to serve and assist them' (*A Publisher and His Friends* i. 386). Thereafter, however, interest in the enterprise appears to have lapsed. There was no review of the *Grammar*, nor advertisement of its publication, in any of the periodicals of the day, and neither Murray nor B referred to it again in their correspondence with each other.

As B says, the *Grammar* was expressly intended for the use of the Armenian reader—a point which Aucher also made clear in his introduction to the volume, and again in his introduction to *A Grammar Armenian and English* (1819), which was expressly intended for the use of the English reader. Although Aucher, in his introduction to the *Grammar*, paid a very handsome tribute to B for his assistance and generosity in its preparation, at the time B claimed only a modest share in its compilation (see, e.g., his preface, and *BLJ* v. 142, 152, 156). Some years later, however, in his 'Detached Thoughts', he recorded that he had 'compiled the major part of two Armenian & English Grammars' (*BLJ* ix. 31). In the light of this, it is perhaps worth noting that the 1873 edition of *A Grammar Armenian and English* (which is quite simply a grammar, containing none of B's exercises, and no other extracts), bears on its title-page 'By P. Paschal Aucher and Lord Byron'. This would suggest that B was indeed responsible for a greater share in the compilation of both grammars than he professed at first.

For details concerning the presentation and typography of the text and comments here, see the Editorial Introduction above. Briefly, B's comments are in the usual size of type, the *Grammar*'s text in smaller type. I have not attempted to reprint the Armenian of the *Grammar*.

Preface to the Armenian Grammar (1817)

Text: Moore ii. 69n. First published in Moore. Thereafter published in *Works*, iii (1832), 336–7; *Beauties of English Poetry* (Venice, 1852), pp. iv–vi; *Lord Byron's Armenian Exercises and Poetry* (Venice, 1870), pp. 4–10; George Eric Mackay, *Lord Byron at the Armenian Convent* (Venice, 1876), pp. 34–6; Prothero iv. 44–5; *BLJ* v. 157n.

The preface was not published during B's lifetime because Aucher objected to its ostensible political nature (see general note on Armenian Studies above). The text is taken from Moore because Prothero gives no indication that he was transcribing from an original MS. Indeed, his brief introduction to the text almost exactly echoes that of Moore (cf. Moore ii. 69n. and Prothero iv. 43n.).

1. *2 January 1817.* This date is supplied from *Beauties* (p. 3), and is almost certainly conjectural (see general note to 'The Armenian Grammar: Two Comments', above).

2. *The English . . . led to it.* This passage is not in *Beauties*. In that volume the text begins at 'On my arrival . . .'.

3. *On my arrival . . . pursuit.* Cf. *BLJ* v. 130, 137, 141. See also the general note on Armenian Studies above.

4. *At this period . . . vices.* The Armenian monastery is situated on the island of St Lazaro, near the Lido, about two miles from the Piazza San Marco. Its

founder was Peter Mechitar (1672–1749), an Armenian doctor born in Sebaste in Armenia Minor, who instituted a literary academy called the Mechitaristican Society at Constantinople in 1701. Persecution drove the Society first into the Morea and then to Venice, where the authorities eventually granted it the island of St Lazaro (a former hospital for lepers) as a permanent home in 1717.

5. *'there is . . . better'.* Kotzebue, *The Stranger* (trans. Benjamin Thompson, 1800), I. i (Toby speaking): 'To be sure I can expect but little joy before I die. Yet, there is another, and a better world.'

6. *'the House of Bondage . . . many mansions.* This is a conflation of Exodus 20: 2 and John 14: 2.

7. *If the Scriptures . . . placed.* Cf. *BLJ* ix. 31. For the site of the Garden of Eden (or Paradise), see Genesis 2: 8–14; for commentaries on its supposed site, see John Skinner, *A Critical and Exegetical Commentary on Genesis* (1980), pp. 59–66; *The Interpreter's Dictionary of the Bible*, 4 vols. (1962), i. 227.

8. *It was . . . alighted.* For the abatement of the Flood and the alighting of the dove, see Genesis 8: 1–12. Ararat (Assyrian, *Urartu*; Armenian, *Ayrarat*) is or was, properly speaking, a region in the NE of Armenia. But the original name of Armenia was Urartu-Ararat. See II Kings 19: 37; Isaiah 37: 38; Jeremiah 51: 27. See also Skinner, *Commentary*, pp. 165–7; *Interpreter's Dictionary* i. 227.

9. *the satraps . . . image.* A 'satrap' was the governor or the viceroy of a province under Persian rule (a 'satrapy'). For the occupation of Armenia by the Turks and Persians (and Russians), see the general note on Armenian Studies above. For the biblical allusion here, see Genesis 1: 26, 27.

Translations from the Armenian: *Two Extracts* (1817)

Text: Paschal Aucher, *A Grammar Armenian and English* (Venice, 1819), pp. 203–9 and 209–11 respectively. First published in ibid., with no acknowledgement given to B. Thereafter published in *A Grammar* (2nd edn. 1832), pp. 161–7 and 167–9 respectively, each under the title of 'Lord Byron's Translation'; *Beauties of English Poetry* (Venice, 1852), pp. 3–13 and 15–17 respectively, under the general rubric of 'Pieces of the Armenian History Translated By Lord Byron to exercise himself in the arm. language'; *Lord Byron's Armenian Exercises and Poetry* (Venice, 1870), pp. 21–31 and 33–5 respectively, under the same general rubric. Neither piece appears in Moore or Prothero.

Corenensis in his Armenian History

1. *Corenensis. . . History.* The passage translated here occurs in bk. I, chs. vii and viii of Moses's History (*W.* pp. 20–3). In *W.* the text is given in Armenian and Latin only. The early history of Armenia is somewhat obscure and even modern historians do not always agree. Moses himself appears to have conflated the lives of several of the *dramatis personae* who figure here (see nn. 2, 3, 4 below).

2. *Arsaces . . . Macedonians.* The Parthian Arsacid dynasty was established by Arsaces I ('Fortis') in *c.*249 BC, when he overthrew the Seleucid satrap (governor) Andragoras in the reign of Antiochus II ('Theos'), King of Syria (261–46 BC). Elsewhere Moses says (logically) that it was he who revolted from the Macedonians (bk. II, ch. lxv; *W.* p. 188). He reigned for two years only (d. *c.*247 BC).

The *Armenian* Arsacid dynasty was founded by Artaxias (who was related to the Parthian Arsacids), a general of Antiochus the Great, King of Syria (223–187 BC), who eventually revolted against him in *c.*188 BC and established Armenia as an independent sovereignty. It was, however, Mithridates I (Arsaces VI) (d. *c.*130 BC), who greatly expanded the Parthian empire and also captured, in *c.*138 BC, Demetrius Nicator, King of Syria (*c.*146–128 BC). See also n. 3 below.

3. *Antiochus. . . Nineveh.* Antiochus VII ('Sidetes'), King of Syria (*c.*137–128 BC) and brother of Demetrius Nicator (see n. 2 above), invaded Mesopotamia in *c.*128 BC, and fell in the ensuing battle against the Parthians (led by Phraates II (Arsaces VII), the brother of Mithridates I, whom he had succeeded in *c.*130 BC).

4. *Valarsaces.* Vologeses I (Arsaces XXIII, *fl.* AD 50), King of the Parthians, made his brother, Tiridates, King of Armenia. Having been later driven out of his kingdom by the Roman consul Domitius Corbulo, Tiridates received it back in AD 63 as a gift from Nero himself, the Roman emperor (AD 54–68)—a condition of peace between Nero and Vologeses I, stipulated by the latter.

5. *Nisibin.* Nisibis was the capital of the region of Mygdonia in Mesopotamia, situated on the banks of the river Mygdonius and of great importance as a military post.

6. *Thitalia.* This province does not appear on the map in *W. W.* deems the name corrupt and suggests that it may refer to the Greek 'Θαλαττα' (Attic dialect for Θαλασσα, sea), and hence be interpreted as 'oram maritimam', sea coast (*W.* p. 20n.). If he is correct, then the province would necessarily be somewhere on the coast of the Black Sea (Pontus Euxine). And this would make sense; for in the map in *W.*, the province situated along the south coast of the Pontus Euxine is called 'Pontus', sea.

7. *Atropatane.* This was a province situated along the south coast of the Caspian Sea.

8. *Maribas . . . Catina. W.* adds a note here to the effect that this means 'Lord Ibas of the town of Catina' (p. 21 n.). Catina (modern Catania) is in Sicily. Maribas (*fl.* 50 BC), was the first Armenian historian, and compiled the ancient history of the kings of Armenia from Haicus to Vahey.

9. *Satrapies. . . me.* See n. 9 to the 'Preface to the Armenian Grammar' (above).

10. *Alexander . . . Apetosthes.* Alexander the Great (356–323 BC), King of

Macedonia and the conqueror of Asia. Moses, citing an earlier authority, claims that '"Zerovanus, Titan and Japetosthes [who] ruled over the earth", seem to me to be Semus, Chamus & Japhethus' (bk. I, ch. v; *W.* p. 16). Semus was the forefather of the Hebrews, Chamus that of the Assyrians, and Japhethus that of the Armenians (*W.* p. 385). They were also the three sons of Noah—Shem, Ham, and Japheth (Genesis 10).

11. *When . . . treasures.* The passage omitted by B here eulogizes Valarsaces, and might be translated as 'that handsome hero, strong and skilled in archery, distinguished for his eloquence and discernment' (*W.* p. 23).

12. *Sardanapalus.* The last king of the Assyrian empire of Nineveh, renowned for his luxurious and effeminate way of life. See B's *Sardanapalus* (1821).

Lampronensis in his Synodical oration

13. *Lampronensis . . . oration.* The passage translated here occurs in Pasquale Aucher, *Orazione Sinodale di S. Nierses Lampronense* (Venice, 1812), pp. 24–7, where the text is given in Armenian and Italian. St Nerses of Lampron or Lambron (1153–98) was the Archbishop of Tarsus in Cilicia, and highly regarded as a church leader and theologian.

14. *It was beautiful . . . beloved.* The idea behind this—and, indeed, the whole excerpt—is the biblical analogy of Christ as the 'bridegroom' of the church (the 'beloved'). For the various echoes here see Matthew 9: 15, John 3: 29, and Revelation 21: 2.

15. *"Enlarge . . . ever".* Isaiah 53: 2–4.

16. *like the lion . . . Christ.* Cf. I Peter 5: 8 and Revelation 12: 7–17.

Translations from the Armenian: Two Epistles (1817)

Text: Moore ii. 809–13. First published in Paschal Aucher, *A Grammar Armenian and English* (Venice, 1819), pp. 177–95, with no acknowledgement given to B. Thereafter published in Moore, Works, iv (1832), 269–75, and *A Grammar* (2nd edn. 1832), pp. 145–69, under the title of 'Lord Byron's Translation'. (This edition omits all variant readings.) Republished in *Beauties of English Poetry* (Venice, 1852), pp. 19–41; *Lord Byron's Armenian Exercises and Poetry* (Venice, 1870), pp. 37–59; George Eric Mackay, *Lord Byron at the Armenian Convent* (Venice, 1876), pp. 37–46; Prothero iv. 429–33.

B was the first person ever to have translated these epistles from the Armenian into English. He first mentioned his having done so in a letter to Scrope Davies dated 7 Mar. 1817: 'I have been acquiring the Armenian Alphabet—& have lately translated into scriptural English—Chapter & verse an epistle *to* St. Paul—and an epistle *from* St. Paul to the Corinthians—which is in the Armenian version of the Scriptures—& not in ours;—this I mean to send on soon to Mr. Murray' (*BLJ* xi. 164). It appears that he enclosed the epistles in a letter to Murray on 14 Apr. 1817, just before he left Venice for Rome. This would explain the otherwise somewhat cryptic postscript to that letter, 'Enclosed are the 2 letters' (*BLJ* v. 212), and would account for the enquiry in his letter to Murray on 14 June 'by the way have you never received a translation of St. Paul? which I sent you *not* for publication—before I went to Rome?' (*BLJ* v. 238). Some years later he had apparently forgotten this *non imprimatur*; for, writing to Murray on 9 Oct. 1821, he asked: 'Another question? The Epistle of St. Paul which I translated from the Armenian—for what reason have you kept it back . . . Is it because you are afraid to print anything in opposition to the Cant of the Quarterly about 'Manicheism'? Let me have a proof of that Epistle directly. I am a better christian than those parsons of yours though not paid for being so' (*BLJ* viii. 237). B had been accused of 'a strange predilection for the worser half of manicheism' in the *Quarterly Review* of May 1820 (xxiii. 225). See also nn. 210 and 211 to 'Letter to John Murray Esq[re.]' (1821) below. Clearly he judged that the timely publication of his translations would prove an opportune riposte to such a charge. However, his peremptory demand for a proof was neither met by Murray nor followed up by himself.

These epistles (the second of which is commonly called 'The Third Epistle to the Corinthians') form part of the Acts of Paul—one of the books of the New Testament Apocrypha. According to Tertullian (*c.* 200), the book was written a little before his time (*c.* 160) by an orthodox priest of Asia Minor in honour of St Paul, whom he venerated. He was convicted of the forgery and deprived of his office, though not excommunicated (Tertullianus, *De Baptismo*, xvii). Both epistles survive in the Armenian Bible, St Ephraem's Commentary, various Armenian MSS, five Latin MSS, and one Coptic MS. See Montague Rhodes James, *The Apocryphal New Testament* (1953), pp. 270, 288, 570–1; E. Hennecke, *New Testament Apocrypha*, edited by W. Schneemelcher, English translation edited by R. McL. Wilson, 2 vols. (1963–5), ii. 326–7, 340–2; *The Interpreter's Dictionary of the Bible*, 4 vols. (1962), iii. 678–80.

The epistles, together with a brief introductory narrative not included in *W.* nor by B, are given in full in Montague Rhodes James, *The Apocryphal New Testament*, pp. 288–91, and E. Hennecke, *New Testament Apocrypha*, ii. 373–7. The text in *W.* to which B occasionally refers appears on pp. 371–83, and is given in Armenian, Greek, and Latin.

The variant readings in Aucher's *Grammar* (1819) are given by line number in the footnotes.

The Epistle of the Corinthians to St. Paul the Apostle

1. *STEPHEN*[b]. B's note here is not at all clear: there are no 'marginal verses' in *W.* For the biblical Stephen see I Corinthians 1: 16; 16: 15–17.

2. *Dabnus . . . health*[c]. For the biblical Eubulus and Theophilus see, respect-

ively, II Timothy 4: 21; and Luke 1: 3 and Acts 1: 1. There are no biblical equivalents of Dabnus, Xinon, Numenus, and Nomeson.

3. *Two men . . . Cleobus,*[d]. For the biblical Simon see Acts 8: 9–24. There is no biblical equivalent of Cleobus (or Clobeus).

4. *But we know . . . from thee.* Cf. I Corinthians 11: 2; Philippians 1: 22–6.

5. *The deacons . . . Tichus*[i]. For Thereptus (Therepus), cf. the biblical Tertius (Romans 16: 22); for Tichus (Techus), cf. the biblical Tychicus (Acts 20: 4; Ephesians 6: 21; Colossians 4: 7).

6. *to the city of the Philippians.*[j]. *W.* has 'in oppidum Phœnices' (p. 375).

7. *the wife of Apofolanus,*[l]. *W.* has 'Apollophanis uxorem' (p. 375).

8. *and said weeping.* Cf. Philippians 3: 18.

9. *"It were . . . Lord.* Cf. Philippians 1: 23.

10. *grief . . . grief.* Cf. 'sorrow upon sorrow', Philippians 2: 27.

11. *And thus . . . Epistle.—*. Cf. II Corinthians 2: 4. For the *real* itinerary and imprisonment of St Paul, see Acts 18: 1, 11, 18–23; 19: 1, 10; 20: 1–6, 13–15; 21: 1–10, 15–18, 33–40; 22–7; 28: 1, 11–16. For the reconstruction of his itinerary and imprisonment in the apocryphal Acts of Paul, see E. Hennecke, *New Testament Apocrypha* ii. 329–47 (esp. 347).

Epistle of Paul to the Corinthians

12. *Paul . . . Christ.* Cf. II Corinthians 11: 23; Ephesians 3: 1; 4: 1.

13. *health.* This greeting (rendered 'salutem' in *W.*) was not used by the early Christians, nor anywhere in the Vulgate by Paul.

14. *I nothing . . . progress.* Cf. Galatians 1: 6–9.

15. *For . . . coming.* Cf. Philippians 4: 5; II Thessalonians 2: 1–2.

16. *But . . . apostles.* Cf. I Corinthians 15: 3; Galatians 1: 11–12.

17. *And I now . . . heaven.* Cf. Luke 1: 26–35; Romans 1: 3.

18. *That Jesus . . . world,*[c]. Cf. I Timothy 1: 15.

19. *He has . . . adoption.* For the consoling testimony that man has not 'remained in perdition unsought', and for the specific sense given to the word 'adoption', see Romans 8: 15–16, 23; 9: 4; Galatians 4: 5; Ephesians 1: 5.

20. *believing readily,*[f]. Cf. Luke 1: 45 (also n. 17 above).

21. *For Jesus . . . faith.* Cf. I Timothy 3: 16.

22. *children of wrath.* Cf. Ephesians 2: 3.

23. *children of rebellion,*[i]. Cf. Ephesians 2: 2; Colossians 3: 6.

24. *That . . . falls*[j]. Cf. John 12: 24; I Corinthians 15: 35–7.

25. *Neither . . . blessing.* Cf. John 12: 24; I Corinthians 15: 42–4.

26. *Jonas . . . Amittai.* The Vulgate has 'Jonam filium Amathi'; the Authorized Version reads 'Jonah the son of Amittai' (Jonah 1: 1). For the story recounted in the following verses here (43–5) see Jonah 1–3. See also Matthew 12: 39–41.

27. *Neither . . . down.*[m]. Cf. Acts 27: 34.

28. *oh men of little faith!* This phrase appears nowhere in the writings of St Paul, but belongs specifically to the language of St Matthew. See Matthew 6: 30; 8: 26; 14: 31; 16: 8.

29. *If . . . dead.* For this incident, see II Kings 13: 20–1.

30. *Elias . . . dead.* See I Kings 17: 17–24.

31. *fetters,*[o]. *W.* finishes here with the variant B cites in his footnote as verses 53 and 54 (p. 383). Cf. also Galatians 6: 17–18.

32. *generations of vipers.* Cf. Matthew 3: 7.

33. *dragons and basilisks.* In the NT dragons appear in Revelation 12–20 *passim.* A basilisk (also called a cockatrice) was a fabulous reptile—a cock with a serpent's tail, whose breath and look were supposed to be fatal. However, there are no basilisks in the Bible.

34. *And the peace . . . upon you.*[q]. St Paul concludes all his epistles (except Romans) with 'The grace of our Lord Jesus Christ be with you' or some similar benediction.

35. *I had . . . Latin text.* In the light of B's allusions, this text was almost certainly that of *W.* See also *BLJ* v. 156.

36. *Done into English . . . omissions.* This statement (with the exception of the signature, location, and date) is here italicized in Moore (ii. 813). It is given earlier in the same volume (though not italicized, and with some slight difference in pointing), with Moore's preamble: 'Annexed to the copy in my possession are the following words, in his own handwriting' (ii. 94n.).

WRITINGS (1817–1820)

Donna Josepha (1817)

Text: Moore ii. 522–3. First published in Moore; thereafter published in *Works* xv (1833), 126n., and Prothero v. 355n.–6n. (Title supplied by me.)

This fragment is part of a very thinly veiled skit on the proceedings leading to B's separation from his wife (for the details of which see Marchand ii. 563–608; *BAP*, pp. 213–34), with B representing himself as Don Julian, Annabella (his wife) as Donna Josepha (a name which may have suggested itself to him from the Donna Josepha with whom he and Hobhouse lodged in Seville in 1809 (Marchand i. 189; *BAP*, p. 63)), and Sir Ralph Milbanke (his father-in-law) as Don Jose di Cardozo; Arragon, Andalusia, Seville, and Spain representing respectively Kirkby Mallory (the Milbankes' house in Leicestershire), London, and England.

In his letter to Moore of 3 Sept. 1821, B wrote: 'By Mr. Mawman . . . I yesterday expedited to your address, under cover one, two paper books containing the *Giaour*-nal, and a thing or two. It won't *all* do—even for the posthumous public—but extracts from it may. It is a brief and faithful chronicle of a month or so—parts of it not very discreet, but sufficiently sincere' (*BLJ* viii. 196). Since the relevant paper book is no longer extant (possibly having been burnt with B's memoirs), it is unfortunate to say the least that Moore should have followed B's suggestion of making 'extracts from it' to such a meagre extent. For in his note to this letter introducing the present fragment, Moore said somewhat casually: 'One of the "paper-books" mentioned in this letter as intrusted to Mr. Mawman for me, contained a portion, to the amount of nearly a hundred pages, of a prose story, relating the adventures of a young Andalusian nobleman, which had been begun by him, at Venice, in 1817. The following passage is all I shall extract from this amusing Fragment' (Moore ii. 522).

There is nothing concerning this piece in Moore's *Memoirs*, nor is there any further allusion to it by B. However, some more can be learnt from John Cam Hobhouse, who was with B in Venice during the period Aug. 1817 to Jan. 1818, and who noted in his diary on 4 Jan. 1818: 'read the beginning of a novel of B's—he adumbrates himself—Don Julian—Florian has made himself also a young Spaniard—there is not, however, the least plagiary or resemblance it must be said' (Broughton Papers, BL Add. MS 47234, f. 42; also *Recollections* ii. 88). The reference here is illuminating. In his posthumously published *La Jeunesse de Florian, ou Mémoires d'un Jeune Espagnol* (1807), the French fabulist, novelist, and dramatist Jean-Pierre Claris de Florian (1755–94), disguising himself as a Spaniard, describes the first 18 years of his life as set in Spain rather than in France. He also gives Spanish names to certain French celebrities with whom he was connected; so that, for instance, Voltaire becomes Lope de Vega, and the Duc de Penthièvre (Florian's patron) becomes, significantly, Don Juan. Hobhouse had read these *Mémoires* as early as 14 Aug. 1817, and recorded his impressions of them in his diary on that date:

> dined & rode with Byron—read . . . Florian's life of himself called the memoirs of a young Spaniard—F. talks with rapture of Voltaire . . . it is surprising what libertinage seems to have reigned in his youth amongst the boys—especially in the military schools—F was one of the victims of the revolution—but died before 40 not on the scaffold but in consequence of imprisonment by Robespierre—he was noble—his death caused no sensation in those days of horror. (Broughton Papers, BL Add. MS 47234, ff. 13v–14v)

The 'libertinage' is not quite as abandoned as Hobhouse might lead us to imagine, but the other biographical details are correct and apropos.

B had also read these *Mémoires*—his own copy of the 1812 edition was sold in Lot 91 at the sale of his books in 1827 (see Sale Catalogue (1827) below); but, as Hobhouse said, there is no 'plagiary' from them, nor any 'resemblance' to them in his story. However, they clearly prompted B, as Hobhouse implied, to set his own autobiographical account in Spain, with the names of the parties suitably adapted.

This piece should of course be compared with *DJ* I. 9–36 (*CPW* v. 11–20, 663, 674–6); and herein perhaps lies its principal significance. For it may fairly be regarded as a prose sketch of what was to begin to assume poetic shape on 3 July 1818. Moreover, if Florian suggested the Spanish ambiance of this piece, then he is also partially responsible for the initial setting of *DJ* (cf. Elizabeth French Boyd, *Byron's Don Juan* (1945), p. 11).

To the Editor of the *British Review* (1819)

Text: MS Murray. First published by John Hunt in the *Liberal*, vol. i, no. 1 (1822), 41–50, under the title of 'Letter to the Editor of "My Grandmother's Review"'. Thereafter published in *Works*, xv (1833), 43–54, and Prothero iv. 465–70, in both under the title of 'Letter to the Editor of "My Grandmother's Review"'.

As so often with B, he wrote this splendidly witty, Swiftian letter when he was in the lowest of spirits, and at a time when he was feeling particularly 'alone and unhappy' in the absence of Teresa Guiccioli, his mistress, who had gone to Capo-fiume for three days with her husband. (See *BLJ* vi. 214–17, 224.)

He told Hobhouse that it had been 'written in an evening & morning in haste—with ill health & worse nerves' (*BLJ* vi. 214). This must have been the evening and morning of 22–3 Aug. 1819. He had received the copy of the *British Review* from Murray on 22 Aug., and he enclosed this letter in his reply to him the following day, saying:

> I send you a letter to Roberts signed 'Wortley Clutterbuck'—which you may publish in what form you please in answer to his article.—I have had many proofs of man's absurdity but he beats all, in folly.—Why the Wolf in sheep's cloathing has tumbled into the very trap.—We'll strip him.—The letter is written in great haste and amidst a thousand vexations.—[Your] letter only came yesterday—so that there is no time to polish . . . Let Hobhouse correct the proofs— (*BLJ* vi. 215)

However, as late as 28 Mar. 1920, Murray had still not even 'alluded to' the letter (*BLJ* vii. 60); and by 12 Oct., it was '*too late*' for publication (*BLJ* vii. 201). B does not appear to have referred again to its possible publication until 5 Oct. 1821 (and then only obliquely): 'By the way you have a good deal of my prose tracts in M.S.S. Let me have proofs of them *all* again—I mean the *controversial* ones—including the last two or three years of time' (*BLJ* viii. 237). On 12 Nov. 1821, he listed it amongst those items which might form a volume of prose 'Miscellanies' he suggested Murray might publish (*BLJ* ix. 58); but on 8 July 1822 he ordered Murray to hand over 'any *prose* tracts' of his to John

Hunt (*BLJ* ix. 182). After this, there is no further reference to the letter before its publication in the *Liberal* on 15 Oct. 1822.

The occasion of this letter is as follows. On 15 July 1819 the first two cantos of *Don Juan* were published anonymously. In Canto I, B had written:

> For fear some prudish readers should grow skittish,
> I've bribed my grandmother's review—the British.
>
> I sent it in a letter to the editor,
> Who thank'd me duly by return of post—
> I'm for a handsome article his creditor;
> Yet if my gentle Muse he please to roast,
> And break a promise after having made it her,
> Denying the receipt of what it cost,
> And smear his page with gall instead of honey,
> All I can say is—that he had the money.
> (*DJ* I. 209–10; *CPW* v. 76)

This was of course quite untrue and merely a jest written in B's most playful vein. However, Roberts (the editor of the *British Review*) was so unwise as to take the accusation seriously and rose to his own defence. I give the article in full, from which B quotes at random in his letter:

> Of a poem so flagitious that no bookseller has been willing to take upon himself the publication, though most of them disgrace themselves by selling it, what can the critic say? His praise or censure ought to found itself on examples produced from the work itself. For praise, as far as regards the poetry, many passages might be exhibited; for condemnation, as far as regards the morality, all: but none for either purpose can be produced, without insult to the ear of decency, and vexation to the heart that feels for domestic or national happiness. This poem is sold in the shops as the work of Lord Byron; but the name of neither author nor bookseller is on the title page: we are, therefore, at liberty to suppose it not to be Lord Byron's composition; and this scepticism has something to justify it in the instance which has lately occurred of the name of that nobleman having been borrowed for a tale of disgusting horror published under the title of 'The Vampire'.
>
> But the strongest argument against the supposition of its being the performance of Lord Byron is this, that it can hardly be possible for an English nobleman, even in his mirth, to send forth to the public the direct and palpable falsehood contained in the 209th and 210th stanzas of the first canto of this work. No misdemeanor, not even that of sending into the world obscene and blasphemous poetry, the product of 'studious lewdness,' and 'laboured impiety,' appears to us in so detestable a light as the acceptance of a present by an editor of a review as the condition of praising an author; and yet the miserable man (for miserable he is, as having a soul of which he cannot get rid), who has given birth to this pestilent poem, has not scrupled to lay this to the charge of 'The British Review;' and that not by insinuation, but has actually stated himself to have sent money in a letter to the Editor of this journal, who acknowledged the receipt of the same by a letter in return, with thanks. No peer of the British realm can surely be capable of so calumnious a falsehood, refuted, we trust, by the very character and spirit of the journal so defamed. We are compelled, therefore, to conclude, that this poem cannot be Lord Byron's production; and we, of course, expect that Lord Byron will, with all gentlemanly haste, disclaim a work imputed to him, containing a calumny so wholly the product of malignant invention.

Lord Byron could not have been the author of this assertion concerning us (an assertion implicating himself as well as us—for to have tendered such a bribe would have been at least as mean as to have received it): not only because he is a British peer, but because he has too much discernment not to see how little like the truth such a statement must appear concerning a Review which has so long maintained, in the cause of public and private virtue, its consistency and purity, independently of all party and of all power. He knows in what a spirit of frankness and right feeling we have criticised his works, how ready we have been to do justice to their great poetical merit, and how firm and steady we have been in the reprobation of their mischievous tendency.

If Lord Byron had sent us money, and we had been so entirely devoid of honesty, feeling, and decency, as to have accepted it, his Lordship would have had sense enough to see, that to publish the fact would have been at once to release us from the iniquitous contract.

If somebody personating the Editor of the British Review has received money from Lord Byron, or from any other person, by way of bribe to praise his compositions, the fraud might be traced by the production of the letter which the author states himself to have received in return. Surely then, if the author of this poem has any such letter, he will produce it for this purpose. But lest it should be said that we have not in positive terms denied the charge, we do utterly deny that there is one word of truth, or the semblance of truth, as far as regards this Review or its Editor, in the assertions made in the stanzas above refered [*sic*] to. We really fell a sense of degradation as the idea of this odious imputation passes through our minds.

We have heard, that the author of the poem under consideration designed what he has said in the 35th stanza as a sketch of his own character:

Yet José was an honourable man,
That I must say, who knew him very well.

If then he is this honourable man, we shall not call in vain for an act of justice at his hands, in declaring that he did not mean his word to be taken when, for the sake of a jest (our readers will judge how far such a mode of jesting is defensible) he stated, with the particularity which belongs to fact, the forgery of a groundless fiction. (*British Review*, vol. xiv, no. xxvii (Aug. 1819), art. xi, pp. 266–8)

To continue the farce later into the century, Arthur Roberts (William's son) in his *Life* of his father, referred to this episode with equal gravity and ingenuousness. (*Life, Letters, and Opinions of William Roberts, Esq.* Edited by his Son, Arthur Roberts, M.A. (1850), pp. 49–51.) He also claimed that his father never read B's letter when it was published in the *Liberal*, a claim confirmed by William Roberts himself in the postscript to a review of the poetry of Bernard Barton, where he assured his readers–

We can undertake to say, upon the surest grounds of knowledge, that not a word of the letter written by the noble lord . . . to the editor of this journal has ever been read by him; so little has been his curiosity concerning it, and so ineffectual the vengeance intended to be executed upon him. (*British Review*, vol. xx, no. xl (Dec. 1822), p. 420)

The outcome of all this was that B's designation of 'my grandmother's review' stuck; and Roberts, finding himself a figure of ridicule, soon afterwards resigned his post.

The *British Review* was founded in 1811 by John Weyland, a lawyer, who edited it for one or two numbers before handing over the responsibility to

Roberts. It was a quarterly journal, Tory in politics and evangelical in religious matters. It closed in 1825.

William Roberts (1767–1849) had been educated at Corpus Christi College, Oxford, and was a barrister and writer on legal matters of some high repute. In 1792 he had begun a journal called *The Looker-on* which he edited under the pseudonym of 'the Rev. Simeon Olivebranch'. It went through 86 issues before closing in 1793. The first article which he contributed to the *British Review* was on the Catholic question, on which 'Lord Eldon enquired whether its author was a clergyman, that he might present him to a living' (*Life*, p. 41). Under Roberts's editorship the journal reviewed all B's publications from *CHP* I and II onwards. Each of these reviews was written by Roberts himself. On the whole they are very balanced and reasonably fair: they generally deplore B's gloom and morality whilst praising the poetry.

B never met Roberts, nor did he bear any malice against him. On the contrary he found his 'critique' of *CHP* I and II (in the *British Review*, vol. iii, no. vi (June 1812), pp. 275–302) 'very gratifying', and asked Longman 'to transmit his best thanks' to Roberts (*BLJ* ii. 181).

It is possible that B's continual reference in the text to Roberts as a clergyman (he was not one, but he was a devout Christian) may have been influenced by the latter's earlier assumption of a clerical editorial pseudonym (as above). But it seems much more likely that B either mistook him for a clergyman from the tone and nature of his review, or else referred to him as such intentionally.

Variants and omissions in the *Liberal* and Prothero are given in the notes below (*L* = the *Liberal*, P = Prothero).

1. *admirer . . . Review.* This reads 'admirer of, though not a subscriber to, your Review, which is rather expensive' in *L* and P.

2. *article. L* and P have 'part'.

3. *eleventh . . . appearance.* This reads 'eleventh article of your twenty-seventh number made its appearance' in *L* and P.

4. *manfully. L* has 'vigorously'.

5. *Clergyman. L* has 'barrister'.

6. *circulation . . . expect.* There is no evidence to suggest that the circulation of the *British Review* was poor. B is probably implying with considerable irony that in the (cant) moral climate of the day it should be wider.

7. *generously. L* has 'frankly', P has 'generally'.

8. *thirty nine articles . . . degrees.* See n. 119 to 'Reading List' above.

9. *Statesman. L* has 'lawyer'.

10. *veracity . . . say.* Counsellor Charles Phillips (?1787–1859) was a writer of miscellaneous prose, and a barrister renowned for his florid oratory. He would certainly get full marks for alliteration (which is why B refers to him here). See, for example: the 'wild witchery of wine, and viands of vulgar

victuals', 'the sickening scene of senatorial servility', and 'where Wisdom watched with wonder the wild and wanton wing of Eloquence' (*Calumny Confuted* (1817), pp. 22, 27, 29).

11. *tragedian . . . "I love a row".* John Liston (?1776–1846) was an actor especially renowned for his portrayal of *comic* parts (e.g. Tony Lumpkin, in Goldsmith's *She Stoops to Conquer*). Hence 'tragedian' is ironic here. B was fond of quoting Liston and this quip of his in particular. See *BLJ* vi. 229, 230; ix. 71.

12. *"breaks no bones".* B is adapting the old proverb, 'Hard (or soft, or fair) words break no bones.'

13. *Lord Mayor.* The paragraph concludes here in *L* (omitting 'Atkins . . . Thames.').

14. *Atkins . . . Thames.* Alderman John Atkins, Chief Magistrate, was elected Lord Mayor of London in 1818. He held the office over a particularly turbulent year, which included the 'Peterloo Massacre' on 16 Aug. 1819 (which had repercussions in London by which he was affected), and was not a popular figure. See *The Annual Register*, 1819 (1820), ch. 7, pp. 112–13. Towards the end of his mayoralty, he made the 'unexplained assertion of the existence of a plot to burn the city and murder all its peaceful inhabitants', which assertion provoked much derision (*The Times*, 10 Nov. 1819). B has subtly exploited here both Atkins's allegation and the saying 'to set the Thames on fire' (to do something astonishing, and/or to gain notoriety).

15. *Fellow. L* has 'Roberts'.

16. *description . . . first.* Sheridan, *The Critic* (1779), I. ii. Puff, who has reduced the art of 'puffing' (i.e. flattering, or extravagantly praising) a literary work to a science, details its various sorts as 'the puff direct, the puff preliminary, the puff collateral, the puff collusive, and the puff oblique, or puff by implication'. The 'puff collusive', he goes on to say, 'is the newest of any; for it acts in the disguise of determined hostility. It is much used by bold booksellers and enterprising poets.' Having given an example, he continues: 'Here you see the two strongest inducements are held forth: first, that nobody ought to read it; and secondly, that everybody buys it: on the strength of which the publisher boldly prints the tenth edition before he has sold ten of the first.'

17. *studious lewdness . . . dont? L* has 'doesn't!', P has 'don't!'. The phrases 'studious lewdness' and 'laboured impiety' are borrowed by Roberts from Johnson. 'The wickedness of a loose or profane author is more atrocious than that of the giddy libertine . . . for the frigid villainy of studious lewdness, for the calm malignity of laboured impiety, what apology can be invented?' (*Rambler*, no. 77, 11 Dec. 1750).

18. *divine. L* has 'barrister'.

19. *transpose. L* has 'transplant'.

20. *sermon. L* has 'brief'.

21. *"the more... speed".* B slightly refines the proverb, 'the more haste, the less speed'.

22. *Mr. S. the poet.* William Sotheby (1757–1833), poet, dramatist, and highly acclaimed translator of Virgil's *Georgics* (1800). He published *Saul; A Poem, in Two Parts* in 1807, and *Five Tragedies* in 1814. His *Farewell to Italy* appeared in 1818. By this time B had taken a distinct dislike to the 'old rotten Medlar of Rhyme' (*BLJ* vii. 172), for reasons that are discussed in the general note to 'Italy, or *not* Corinna' (see below). See also n. 24 below.

23. *of "Saul".* Omitted in *L.*

24. *one instance... performance.* B promoted Sotheby's *Ivan* when he was on the Committee of the Drury Lane Theatre in 1815. He managed to persuade the committee to accept it, but 'lo! in the very heart of the matter—upon some *tepid*-ness on the part of Kean—or warmth upon that of the Authour—Sotheby withdrew his play' (*BLJ* ix. 35). See also *BLJ* iv. 311, 313–14, 316, 323, 334.

25. *sheets... as he says. L.* has 'sheets of some new poems on Italy' (*tout court*).

26. *some. L* and P have 'a few'.

27. *"British Critic'.* Indeed, in a review of *Don Juan* I and II in the *British Critic* (vol. xii (Aug. 1819), art. ix, pp. 195–205), the reviewer, having quoted stanzas 209 and 210, commented:

> Whether it be the British Critic, or the British Review against which the Noble Lord prefers so grave, or rather so facetious an accusation, we are at a loss to determine. The latter, we understand, have thought it worth while, in a public paper, to make a serious reply. As we are not so *seriously* inclined, we shall leave our share of the accusation to its fate—simply remarking, that authors who write for their bread, have too many calls for their money to waste it upon Editors, or their Reviews. (pp. 200–1)

28. *as people ... synonimous.* B omits opening quotation marks before 'Gifford's', and spells synonymous idiosyncratically. Francis Jeffrey (1773–1850) was the editor of the liberal *Edinburgh Review* from its foundation in 1802 until 1829. William Gifford (1756–1826) was the editor of the Tory *Quarterly Review* from its foundation in 1809 (by Murray, to rival the *Edinburgh Review*), until 1824. He was Murray's literary adviser whom B regarded as his '*literary* father' (*BLJ* xi. 117).

29. *Pontiff... Joan.* This refers to the fabled Pope Joan, who was said to have held the pontificate as John VIII between that of Leo IV and that of Benedict III in the ninth century, and to have died in childbirth during a papal procession.

30. *many ... difference.* No such attribution was made before B's letter: B is merely lending credence to his own imputation.

31. *your correspondent. L* and P have 'your public correspondent'.

32. *place place... prodigies.* B's repetition of 'place'. To Hercules, the celebrated

undertaker of the twelve labours, almost every possible feat imaginable, in both infancy and manhood, has been ascribed.

33. *Ld B. . . . Child.* All these works, of which B has taken some liberty with the titles, were falsely attributed to him. See Samuel C. Chew, *Byron in England* (1924), ch. 10, 'The Byron Apocrypha', and *CPW* i. pp. xlv–xlvii. See also n. 2 to 'Some Observations' below.

34. *fellow. L* has 'friend'.

35. *Partridge . . . Almanacks.* B alludes to the famous Bickerstaff–Partridge controversy (in the vein of which his own letter is itself very much written). John Partridge (1644–1715) was an astrologer and almanack-maker of great renown. In 1707 Swift published, under the pseudonym of Isaac Bickerstaff, *Predictions for the Year 1708*, in which he foretold the death of Partridge: 'I have consulted the Stars of his Nativity by my own Rules, and find he will infallibly die upon the 29th of *March* next, about Eleven at Night, of a raging Fever; therefore I advise him to consider of it, and settle his Affairs in Time.' On 30 Mar. 1708 he published *The Accomplishment of the First of Mr. Bickerstaff's Predictions, being an Account of the Death of Mr. Partridge the Almanack-maker upon the 29th inst.* The result of this was that Partridge was struck off the rolls of the Stationers' Company and everyone believed him dead. Partridge struggled hard (by advertising in the papers) to convince the world that he was 'not only now alive, but was also alive upon the 29th of March in question'. Swift parried this with his *Vindication of Isaac Bickerstaff* (1709), and gave further testimony to Partridge's death and the futility of his attempting to prove himself alive in *Bickerstaff's Almanack for the Year 1710.* Poor Partridge was so perplexed that he published nothing until 1714, after he had discovered his executioner. He died the following year. See [Swift, Pope,] *Miscellanies in Prose and Verse*, 4 vols. (1727), i. 261–315; also Jonathan Swift, *Bickerstaff Papers*, ed. Herbert Davies (1957).

36. *"In King Cambyses' vein". Henry IV, Part I*, II. iv. 387.

37. *Charley Incledon's . . . eloquence.* Charles Incledon (1763–1826) began his career as a sailor and then became a vocalist. He first performed at Covent Garden Theatre in 1790, continuing there until 1815. He took parts in William Shield's operas, John Gay's *Beggar's Opera* and Thomas Arne's *Artaxerxes*, for instance, and often sang sailor songs in the intervals between acts. His main *forte* was ballad singing. B was fond of quoting Incledon. See *BLJ* v. 182 and n.; viii. 97.

38. *Wortley Clutterbuck.* The choice of this pseudonym presents us with an interesting example of literary synchronism. It was first used here (1819) by B, and again later by him as one of the characters in 'Italy, or *not* Corinna' (1820, *post*). At the same time however, Walter Scott, in his prefaces to *The Monastery* and *The Abbot* (both published anonymously in 1820), represented his own fictional creation, Captain Cuthbert Clutterbuck, as having supplied 'The

Author of Waverley' (i.e. Scott himself) with the original material for those works. Accordingly, when the publication of this letter was under reconsideration in 1821, B wrote to Murray on 12 Nov.: 'You must recollect however that the letter on the British review signed *Clutterbuck* must have a note stating that the name of *Clutterbuck* was adopted long before (a year I think) the publication of the Monastery & Abbot.—If you don't do this—I shall be accused (with the usual justice) of plagiarism from Walter Scott' (*BLJ* ix. 58).

39. *Septr 4.th 1819*. *L* has 'Sept.—, —.'.

40. *though not . . . hope.* Omitted in *L*.

41. *a*. *L* has 'some'.

42. *P.S. 2nd. . . . W.C.* This postscript is printed from *L* (p. 50), there being no MS extant *now* nor in Prothero's time (Prothero iv. 470n.). Undoubtedly the two words 'bar' and 'clients' would have read 'pulpit' or 'church' and 'congregation' in the original MS, to coincide with B's conception of Roberts as a clergyman.

Italy, or *not* Corinna (1820)

Text: MS Murray. First published in Prothero iv. 452–3.

There is no immediate indication as to why B should have begun this piece at this particular time. However, since 1817 he had been harbouring resentment against Sotheby (Solemnboy) whom, as he told Murray in a letter of 15 July 1817, he believed to be the author of 'an *anonymous* note containing some gratuitously impertinent remarks' concerning *The Prisoner of Chillon*, sent to him from Rome. (*BLJ* v. 252; see also vi. 18, 24, 33, 35–6). As he also made clear in this letter, he was determined to take his revenge:

> So—let him look to it—he had better have written to the Devil a criticism upon Hell-fire—I will raise him such a Samuel for his 'Saul' as will astonish him without the Witch of Endor.—An old tiresome blockhead—blundering through Italy without a word of the language—or of any language except the wretched affectations of our own which he called English—to come upon poor dear quiet me with his nonsense—but never mind—we shall see.——If he had attacked me in print—that's all fair—'*foul* is fair' at least among authors—but to come upon me with his petty—mincing—paltry—dirty—notes—& nameless as he will be himself years hence—Sunburn me! if I don't stick a pin through this old Blue-bottle. (*BLJ* v. 253)

Although Sotheby denied the charge, B continued to regard him as 'a vile—stupid—old Coxcomb' whom he intended to 'weed . . . from the surface of the society he infests & infects' (*BLJ* vi. 33). In this light then, this piece may be regarded as a part of that process of 'weeding' which B had already begun in *Beppo* (1818), stanzas 72–4 (*CPW* iv. 152, 489), *DJ* (1819), I. 206 (*CPW* v. 75, 681), and the letter 'To the Editor of the *British Review*' above (see nn. 22, 24 thereto), and which he was to pursue in *The Blues* (1821). See also *EBSR*, l. 818 (*CPW* i. 255, 414–15, and cf. iv. 126, 127, 481).

The initial prompting of B's story appears to be the following. In May 1816, Sotheby left England with his wife and family accompanied by Professor Elmsley and Dr John Playfair (1748–1819), for a tour through France, Switzerland, and Italy, returning via Germany towards the close of 1817. In 1818 he published his poetical impressions of the tour under the title *Farewell to Italy, and Occasional Poems*. This short volume contains poems celebrating various sites and cities visited (Venice, Virgil's tomb), and poems addressed to friends or acquaintances met by the way. The poet takes himself somewhat seriously and the whole is of very uneven, not to say little merit. B first referred to it in his verse epistle to Murray of 8 Jan. 1818 (*BLJ* vi. 3–4, stanzas 4–6; see also *CPW* iv. 161–2, 490).

However, although Sotheby is clearly the central target here, the satire appears to have a broader application. For the title alone has certainly one, if not a second, parodic aspect. In the first place it parodies the title of Madame de Staël's hugely successful novel *Corinne, ou l'Italie* (1807; 8th edn. 1819), which B greatly admired and which he had only recently reread (Aug. 1819) (*BLJ* vi. 215). In the second place it appears to parody the furore caused by Lady Morgan's *France*.

In 1817 Lady Morgan published her travelogue *France*, which was most virulently attacked by John Wilson Croker and William Gifford in the *Quarterly Review* (vol. xvii, no. xxxiii (Apr. 1817), pp. 260–86), where she was accused of almost every conceivable sin an author could commit. Even B himself (who later praised her *Italy* (1821) as 'fearless and excellent' (*BLJ* viii. 189)), thought the *Quarterly* had made unjustifiably 'cruel work' with her, and that the article was 'perhaps as bitter a critique as ever was written' (*BLJ* vi. 12, 13). Although she had two very gentlemanly and laudatory responses from across the Channel, of which B may have been aware (*Observations sur l'ouvrage intitulé: La France; Par Lady Morgan* [by A. J. B. Defauconpret] (Paris, 1817), and *Lettre à Mylady Morgan sur Racine et Shakespeare* [by Baron Charles Dupin] (Paris, 1818)—both of which engaged in civilized and respectful dialogue with her), the vituperation of the *Quarterly* was followed up as ferociously by William Playfair (1759–1823, brother of John above), in his *France As It Is, Not Lady Morgan's France* (1819, 1820).

In reversing and putting into the negative Madame de Staël's title in his own (and so parodying hers), B seems to be simultaneously deliberately echoing Playfair's (and so parodying his). This would serve to promise on the one hand that his own story was to be no such tragical romance as *Corinne*, and on the other, that it might eventually develop into an account of Italian manners (though doubtless of a more facetious nature than the Morgan and Playfair accounts of France).

As a whole then, it may well be that B intended this as a satire against the current vogue for, or the entire genre of travel-writing, and English travellers in particular, with Sotheby as their epitome.

1. *"Ecrivain en poste".* 'Voyager en poste' means to travel post. Hence B probably intends this phrase to be taken as 'a travelling writer', or possibly as some such equivalent to our modern 'from our own Correspondent'.

2. *peace . . . "all understanding".* For Castlereagh, see n. 2 to 'A Letter on the State of French Affairs' above. The biblical allusion here is to *Philippians* 4: 7.

3. *Amundeville and Clutterbuck.* Prothero has 'Amandeville'. Amundeville is the name of the politician and owner of Norman Abbey, who hosts Don Juan in the English Cantos of *DJ* (XIII–XVII; *CPW* v. 525 ff.). Clutterbuck is the pseudonym under which B chose to write his letter 'To the Editor of the *British Review*' (1819, above). While Clutterbuck and Amundeville may have been intended to recall Lord Nevil and le Comte d'Erfeuil in *Corinne*, they are possibly fictional projections of B himself and Hobhouse. See following n. 4.

4. *Album of Arqua.* Arqua is the site of Petrarch's house and tomb. (Cf. *CHP* IV. 30–4; *CPW* ii. 134–5, 230–1, 322–3). John Cam Hobhouse recorded in his diary that he and B visited Arqua on 10 Sept. 1817: 'We put our names in a book which is only shown to polite gente [people]' (Broughton Papers, BL Add. MS 47234, f. 21v). See also *BLJ* v. 264. B later visited Arqua with Teresa Guiccioli, who recalled: 'We left Bologna on the fifteenth of September [1819]; we visited the Euganean Hills and Arquà, and wrote our names in the book which is presented to those who make this pilgrimage' (Moore, ii. 246 and n.; cf. *BLJ* vi. 223).

5. *barouche.* A horse-drawn, four-wheeled carriage with a collapsible half-hood, seating two couples facing each other.

6. *patience . . . Job.* For the proverbial (biblical) patience of Job, see the book of Job.

7. *Vetturino.* Italian for a 'driver' or 'coachman'.

8. *Bashkirs . . . it.* In Prothero 'Bashkirs' reads 'Bashkins'. The Bashkirs were a Turkic people, who lived a nomadic life in an area around the Urals. They were colonized by Russia in 1552, and revolted vainly against her on several subsequent occasions. There is no evidence to suggest that the French were ever interested in them or in their territory. However the context here suggests that B may have had in mind the following anecdote of Grimm's. In a review of *Memoirs of the History, Sciences, Arts, Manners, Usages, &c. of the Chinese; by the Missionaries of Pekin*, vol. x, Grimm wrote:

> Louis XV, who, as M. Schomberg used to say, was the greatest philosopher in his kingdom, was perfectly sensible at times that all did not go on well in France. In a conversation one day with M. Bertin, on the necessity of reforming so many abuses, he concluded by saying that it was impossible to succeed without entirely new moulding the mind of the nation, and entreated him to consider how that could with certainty be effected. M. Bertin promised to give the subject some consideration, and at the end of a few days he told the King that he believed he had at last found the secret of satisfying the paternal wishes of his Majesty.—'And what is that secret?'—'*Sire, it is to inoculate the*

French with the Chinese character.'—The King thought this idea so luminous, that he approved all that his minister had suggested for its execution. At a great expense certain young literati were imported from China; they were carefully instructed in our language and sciences; they were afterwards sent back again to Pekin; and the collection of which we have the honour to announce to you the tenth volume, is taken from the memoirs of these new missionaries. The national mind does not, in fact appear to have undergone the happy revolution which this ingenious decree of M. Bertin was intended to produce; but we can yet remember the time when all our chimney-pieces were covered with Chinese porcelain, and when the greater part of our furniture was in the Chinese taste. (Baron de Grimm, *Historical and Literary Memoirs and Anecdotes*, 2 vols. (1814), ii. 278–9)

This originally appeared in *Correspondance Littéraire, Philosophique et Critique, Adressée à un Souverain d'Allemagne, pendant une partie des années 1775–1776, et pendant les années 1782 à 1790 inclusivement, Par le Baron de Grimm et par Diderot*, 5 vols. (1813), iii. 394–5, which is where B almost certainly would have read it.

9. *Solemnboy ... day.* Sotheby published no such 'Ode'. No doubt B alludes ironically to *A Song of Triumph* (1814), in which Sotheby celebrates, in two hundred and twenty-two lines of rhyming couplets, the fall of Napoleon and the successes of the English against him. Cf. *BLJ* iv. 118.

10. *Galignani ... pirated.* Jean Antoine Galignani (1796–1873) and his brother William Galignani (1798–1882) published *Galignani's Messenger* (founded in 1814 by their father, Giovanni Antonio Galignani (d. 1821)), and reprints of many English works in Paris. B gave them the exclusive rights to publish his works in France. See *BLJ* vi. 33; vii. 216. Galignani's travel-books were mostly compiled from the writings of English travellers: for example, *Galignani's Traveller's Guide through France* (1819) and *Galignani's Traveller's Guide through Italy* (1819).

11. *Coxe's Guide-book.* William Coxe (1747–1828), Archdeacon of Wiltshire, travelled extensively and published such works as *Travels in Switzerland* (1789) and *Travels into Poland, Russia, Sweden, and Denmark* (1784, 1790).

SOME OBSERVATIONS UPON AN ARTICLE IN BLACKWOOD'S EDINBURGH MAGAZINE (1820)

Text: MS Yale University Library, MS Murray and MS Van Pelt Library, University of Pennsylvania. Collated with B's revised galley proof (Murray) (GP), and his revised proof (Van Pelt Library, University of Pennsylvania) (Proof). Excerpts from a copy made from Proof first published in Moore ii. 360–74. First published in full (except for the additional note on Keats; see below) from the copy made from Proof, in *Works* xv (1833), 55–98 and xvii (1833), 247–8 (*Works* (1833)). Thereafter published from *Works* (1833) in Prothero iv. 474–95.

Although B began 'Some Observations' on 15 Mar. 1820, he was still 'foaming an answer (in prose) to the Blackwood Article of last August' on 23 Mar. (*BLJ*

vii. 59). Five days later, on 28 Mar., he sent it to John Murray with instructions that his friend John Cam Hobhouse should 'have the correction of it' (*BLJ* vii. 60). This is the MS in Yale University Library. The following day, 29 Mar., he wrote again to Murray enclosing a note on Pope (*BLJ* vii. 60–1). This is the MS in the Van Pelt Library, University of Pennsylvania (see n. 176 below). With this note he may also have enclosed the dedication (MS Van Pelt Library; see below), the note on Wordsworth (MS Van Pelt Library; see n. 106 below), and the additional note on Keats (MS Murray; see n. 174 below). However, as he also requested in this letter of 29 Mar. 'to see the *proofs* of mine Answer—because there will be something to omit or to alter' (*BLJ* vii. 61–2), he may have sent these last three items at a later date, perhaps when he returned GP; there is no reference to them otherwise in his correspondence. On 23 Apr. he cautioned Murray that he did not intend to publish the '*prose* observations in answer to Wilson' '*at present*', but told him to keep them by him 'as *documents*' (*BLJ* vii. 83). At some point in early May he received GP; for he returned it to Murray on 20 May, remarking: 'the prose (the Edin. Mag. answer) looks better than I thought it would—& *you may publish it*—there will be a row—but I'll fight it out—one way or another' (*BLJ* vii. 102). Nevertheless, he was clearly unsettled by some strictures Hobhouse subsequently passed upon it in a letter to B which is no longer extant. For on 8 June B replied to Hobhouse: 'You are right—the *prose* must not be published—at least the merely *personal part*;—and how the portion on Pope may be divided I do not know.—I wish you would ferret out at Whitton—the "Hints from Horace". I think it (the Pope part) might be appended to that Popean poem—for publication or no—as you decide' (*BLJ* vii. 114. See also 22 June to Hobhouse, and 23 Sept. to Murray (*BLJ* vii. 121, 179), and *CPW* i. 426). Plans for publication were therefore dropped (see, for example, *BLJ* vii. 201) until the following year when, in a note dated 'January 11? 1821' written at the end of the galley proof of *Hints from Horace*, he instructed Murray:

> Will you have the goodness also to put all that regards *Pope* (in the prose letter to B[lackwood's] Editor sent last Spring to you) as a *note* under the name of *Pope* [where it?] first occurs in this Essay (which it does [begin?]) as that part of the letter was in fact distinct from the rest of it, it will do as well here. (*BLJ* viii. 61)

Murray did not follow these instructions, and on 1 Mar. 1821 B was mortified to receive 'the *Hints without* the *Latin*—and *without* the *Note* upon *Pope* from the Letter to the E[dinburgh] B[lackwood's] M[agazine]' (*BLJ* viii. 88). However, plans for publication again lapsed until 4 Sept. 1821, when B abruptly requested a proof of 'Some Observations' with a view to printing it as 'a separate publication' (*BLJ* viii. 197). At some point prior to 7 Nov. he received Proof; for Edward Williams (Shelley's friend) recorded in his journal on that date that B 'lends me a small pamphlet now printing, called "Some Observations," but upon S's recommendation does not intend to publish it' (Richard Garnett (ed.), *The Journal of Edward Ellerker Williams* (1902), p. 24). B eventually returned the revised proof to Douglas Kinnaird on 15 Nov., asking for his opinion as to whether or not to publish it (*BLJ* ix. 61).

On the proof (p. 1), there is the following query by the printer (cf. *BLJ* vii. 114; viii. 61, both cited above, and *CPW* i. 426):

> The Printer begs to observe to L[d] Byron that in the Proof of 'Hints from Horace' he has requested ⟨all⟩ "Take *from* the Letter to Blackwood—all that relates to Pope—and insert it as a Note [at?] the first place where Pope is mentioned"—must this be accepted?

To which B has replied:

> Answer Let this pamphlet remain as it is—
>
> B.
>
> No:[vr] 18:[th] 1821.

(The date here—distinctly and unmistakably thus in B's MS—must have been an error. For not only did B send this proof to Kinnaird on 15 Nov., but he confirmed having done so the following day (*BLJ* ix. 61).)

There is no further reference to this article until 8 Aug. 1822, when B merely informed Moore that it had been written but 'never published' (*BLJ* ix. 190). The final mention of it occurred on 21 Oct. 1822, when B requested Murray to send him for his own satisfaction, 'the *correct* and *complete* copy of the letter to the B[lackwood's] M[agazine]' (*BLJ* x. 64).

GP is only partially extant: it breaks off at 'Amidst the ties that have been dashed to pieces,' (see n. 54 below). It did *not* provide the basis for Proof, and none of B's revisions in it were adopted. Proof returned directly to B's MS, and incorporated his dedication and additional notes on Wordsworth and on Pope, but excluded the additional note on Keats (see n. 174 below). A printed copy (no longer extant) made from Proof provided the text for *Works* (1833); Prothero followed *Works* (1833). B's revisions in GP and Proof are noted at the foot of the present text: many of these, together with variant readings in *Works* (1833) and Prothero, are further detailed in the notes below. However, unless otherwise specified, *Works* (1833) and Prothero follow Proof as revised by B.

'Some Observations' is best regarded as a precursor to the 'Bowles/Pope Controversy'. For, once B is over the 'merely *personal part*', although the target of his attack is not Bowles, the cause he here champions is that of Pope against his then-current detractors (such as Wordsworth and Keats), and his arguments and criticisms anticipate those he deploys in the later controversy. The occasion of its writing was as follows. *DJ* I and II were published anonymously on 15 July 1819. In *Blackwood's Edinburgh Magazine*, vol. v, no. xxix (Aug. 1819), pp. 512–18, there appeared an article entitled 'Remarks on Don Juan' which is given in full below. It was not, as B supposed, written by John Wilson, 'Christopher North' (see n. 202 below), but by John Gibson Lockhart (1794–1854). See Alan Lang Strout, *A Bibliography of Articles in Blackwood's Magazine 1817–1825*, Library Bulletin no. 5 (Library, Texas, 1959), pp. 55–6.

REMARKS ON DON JUAN.

It has not been without much reflection and overcoming many reluctancies, that we have at last resolved to say a few words more to our readers concerning this very extraordinary poem. The nature and causes of our difficulties will be easily understood by those of them who have read any part of Don Juan—but we despair of standing justified as to the conclusion at which we have arrived, in the opinion of any but those who have read and understood the whole of a work, in the composition of which there is unquestionably a more thorough and intense infusion of genius and vice—power and profligacy—than in any poem which had ever before been written in the English, or indeed in any other modern language. Had the wickedness been less inextricably mingled with the beauty and the grace, and the strength of a most inimitable and incomprehensible muse, our task would have been easy: But SILENCE would be a very poor and a very useless chastisement to be inflicted by us, or by any one, on a production, whose corruptions have been so effectually embalmed—which, in spite of all that critics can do or refrain from doing, nothing can possibly prevent from taking a high place in the literature of our country, and remaining to all ages a perpetual monument of the exalted intellect, and the depraved heart, of one of the most remarkable men to whom that country has had the honour and the disgrace of giving birth.

That Lord Byron has never written any thing more decisively and triumphantly expressive of the greatness of his genius, will be allowed by all who have read this poem. That (laying all its manifold and grievous offences for a moment out of our view) it is by far the most admirable specimen of the mixture of ease, strength, gayety, and seriousness extant in the whole body of English poetry, is a proposition to which, we are almost as well persuaded, very few of them will refuse their assent. With sorrow and humiliation do we speak it—the poet has devoted his powers to the worst of purposes and passions; and it increases his guilt and our sorrow, that he has devoted them entire. What the immediate effect of the poem may be on contemporary literature, we cannot pretend to guess—too happy could we hope that its lessons of boldness and vigour in language, and versification, and conception, might be attended to, as they deserve to be—without any stain being suffered to fall on the purity of those who minister to the general shape and culture of the public mind, from the mischievous insults against all good principle and all good feeling, which have been unworthily embodied in so many elements of fascination.

The moral strain of the whole poem is pitched in the lowest key—and if the genius of the author lifts him now and then out of his pollution, it seems as if he regretted the elevation, and made all haste to descend again. To particularize the offences committed in its pages would be worse than vain—because the great genius of the man seems to have been throughout exerted to its utmost strength, in devising every possible method of pouring scorn upon every element of good or noble nature in the hearts of his readers. Love—honour—patriotism—religion, are mentioned only to be scoffed at and derided, as if their sole resting-place were, or ought to be, in the bosoms of fools. It appears, in short, as if this miserable man, having exhausted every species of sensual gratification—having drained the cup of sin even to its bitterest dregs, were resolved to shew us that he is no longer a human being, even in his frailties;—but a cool unconcerned fiend, laughing with a detestable glee over the whole of the better and worse elements of which human life is composed—treating well nigh with equal derision the most pure of virtues, and the most odious of vices—dead alike to the beauty of the one, and the deformity of the other—a mere heartless despiser of that frail but noble humanity, whose type was never exhibited in a shape of more deplorable degradation than in his own contemptuously distinct delineation of himself. To confess in secret to his Maker, and weep over in secret agonies the wildest and most phantastic transgressions of heart and mind, is the part of a conscious sinner, in whom sin has not become the sole principle of life and action—of a soul for which there is yet hope. But to lay bare to the eye of man and of *woman* all the hidden convulsions of a wicked spirit—thoughts too abominable, we would hope, to have been imagined by any but him that has expressed them—and to do all this without one symptom of pain, contrition, remorse, or hesitation, with a calm careless ferociousness of contented and satisfied depravity—this was an insult which no wicked man of genius had ever before dared to put upon his Creator or his Species. This highest of all possible exhibitions of self-abandonment has been set forth in mirth and gladness, by one whose name was once pronounced with pride and veneration by every English voice. This atrocious consummation was reserved for Byron.

It has long been sufficiently manifest, tht this man is devoid of religion. At times, indeed, the power and presence of the Deity, as speaking in the sterner workings of the elements, seems to force some momentary consciousness of their existence into his labouring breast;—a spirit in which there breathes so much of the divine, cannot always resist the majesty of its Maker. But of true religion terror is a small part—and of all religion, that founded on mere terror, is the least worthy of such a man as Byron. We may look in vain through all his works for the slightest evidence that his soul has ever listened to the *gentle voice* of the oracles. His understanding has been subdued into conviction by some passing cloud; but his heart has never been touched. He has never written one line that savours of the spirit of meekness. His faith is but for a moment—'he believes and trembles,' and relapses again into his gloom of unbelief—a gloom in which he is at least as devoid of HOPE and CHARITY as he is of FAITH.—The same proud hardness of heart which makes the author of Don Juan a despiser of the Faith for which his fathers bled, has rendered him a scorner of the better part of woman; and therefore it is that his love poetry is a continual insult to the beauty that inspires it. The earthy part of the passion is all that has found a resting place within his breast—His idol is all of clay—and he dashes her to pieces almost in the moment of his worship. Impiously railing against his God—madly and meanly disloyal to his Sovereign and his country,—and brutally outraging all the best feelings of female honour, affection, and confidence—How small a part of chivalry is that which remains to the descendant of the Byrons—a gloomy vizor, and a deadly weapon!

Of these offences, however, or of such as these, Lord Byron had been guilty abundantly before, and for such he has before been rebuked in our own, and in other more authoritative pages. There are other and newer sins with which the author of Don Juan has stained himself—sins of a class, if possible, even more despicable than any he had before committed; and in regard to which it is matter of regret to us, that as yet our periodical critics have not appeared to express themselves with any seemly measure of manly and candid indignation.

Those who are acquainted, (as who is not?) with the main incidents in the private life of Lord Byron;—and who have not seen this production, (and we are aware, that very few of our Northern readers have seen it)—will scarcely believe, that the odious malignity of this man's bosom should have carried him so far, as to make him commence a filthy and impious poem, with an elaborate satire on the character and manners of his wife—from whom, even by his own confession, he has been separated only in consequence of his own cruel and heartless misconduct. It is in vain for Lord Byron to attempt in any way to justify his own behaviour in that affair; and, now that he has so openly and audaciously invited inquiry and reproach, we do not see any good reason why he should not be plainly told so by the general voice of his countrymen. It would not be an easy matter to persuade any Man who has any knowledge of the nature of Woman, that a female such as Lord Byron has himself described his wife to be, would rashly, or hastily, or lightly separate herself, from the love which she had once been inspired for such a man as he is, or was. Had he not heaped insult upon insult, and scorn upon scorn—had he not forced the iron of his contempt into her very soul—there is no woman of delicacy and virtue, as he *admitted* Lady Byron to be, who would not have hoped all things and suffered all things from one, her love of whom must have been inwoven with so many exalting elements of delicious pride, and more delicious humility. To offend the love of such a woman was wrong—but it might be forgiven; to desert her was unmanly—but he might have returned and wiped for ever from her eyes the tears of her desertion;—but to injure, and to desert, and then to turn back and wound her widowed privacy with unhallowed strains of cold-blooded mockery—was brutally, fiendishly, inexpiably mean. For impurities there might be some possibility of pardon, were they supposed to spring only from the reckless buoyancy of young blood and fiery passions,—for impiety there might at least be pity, were it visible that the misery of the impious soul were as great as its darkness;—but for offences such as this, which cannot proceed either from the madness of sudden impulse, or the bewildered agonies of self-perplexing and self-despairing doubt—but which speak the wilful and determined spite of an unrepenting, unsoftened, smiling, sarcastic, joyous sinner—for such diabolical, such slavish vice, there can be neither pity nor pardon. Our knowledge that it is committed by one of the most powerful intellects our island ever has produced, lends intensity a thousand fold to the bitterness of our indignation. Every high thought that was ever kindled in our breasts by the muse of Byron—every pure and lofty feeling that ever responded from within us to the sweep of his majestic inspirations—every remembered moment of admiration and enthusiasm is up in arms against him. We look back with a mixture of wrath and scorn to the delight with which we suffered ourselves to be filled by one who, all the while he was furnishing us with delight, must, we cannot doubt it, have been mocking us with a cruel mockery—less cruel only, because less peculiar, than that with which he has now turned him from the lurking-place of his selfish and polluted exile, to pour the pitiful chalice of his contumely on the surrendered devotion of a virgin-bosom, and the holy hopes of the mother of his child. The consciousness of the insulting deceit which has been practised upon us, mingles with the nobler pain arising from the contemplation of perverted and degraded genius—to make us wish that no such being as Byron ever had existed. It is indeed a sad and an humiliating thing to know, that in the same year there proceeded from the same pen two productions, in all things so different, as the Fourth Canto of Childe Harold and this loathsome Don Juan. [*CHP* IV had been highly favourably reviewed by John Wilson in *Blackwood's Edinburgh Magazine*, vol. iii, no. xiv (May 1818), pp. 216ff.]

Lady Byron, however, has one consolation still remaining, and yet we fear she will think it but a poor one. She shares the scornful satire of her husband, not only with all that is good, and pure, and high, in human nature,—its principles and its feelings; but with every individual also, in whose character the predominance of these blessed elements has been sufficient to excite the envy, or exacerbate the despair of this guilty man. We shall not needlessly widen the wound by detailing its cruelty; we have mentioned one, and, all will admit, the worst instance of the private malignity which has been embodied in so many passages of Don Juan; and we are quite sure, the lofty-minded and virtuous men whom Lord Byron has debased himself by insulting, will close the volume which contains their own injuries, with no feelings save those of pity for Him that has inflicted them, and for Her who partakes so largely in the same injuries; and whose hard destiny has deprived her for ever of that proud and pure privilege, which enables themselves to despise them. As to the rest of the world, we know not that Lord Byron could have invented any more certain means of bringing down contempt inexpiable on his own head, than by turning the weapons of his spleen against men whose virtues few indeed can equal, but still fewer are so lost and unworthy as not to love and admire.

The mode in which we have now expressed ourselves, might be a sufficient apology for making no extracts from this poem itself. But our indignation, in regard to the morality of the poem, has not blinded us to its manifold beauties; and we are the more willing to quote a few of the passages which can be read without a blush, because the comparative rarity of such passages will, in all probability, operate to the complete exclusion of the work itself, from the libraries of the greater part of our readers. As it is out of the question for us to think of analyzing the story, we must quote at the hazard of some of our quotations being very imperfectly understood.

[quotes Canto i. 2–4, 54–61, 72–4 (first 4 lines only)]

Speaking of moonlight, he says:

[quotes Canto i. 114, 122–7]

The conclusion of the history of *this* passion is, that Don Juan is detected in the lady's chamber at midnight by her husband. Thinking her lover effectually concealed, Donna Julia rates her Lord in a style of volubility in which, it must be granted, there is abdundance of the true *vis comica.*—The detection which follows almost immediately after the conclusion of the speech, gives much additional absurdity to the amazing confidence of the lady.

[quotes Canto i. 145–58]

In consequence of this intrigue, Don Juan is sent on his travels; and the lady, who is shut up in a convent, takes leave of him in a beautiful letter, of which this is a part.

[quotes Canto i. 194–8]

Perhaps there are not a few women who may profit from seeing in what a style of contemptuous coldness the sufferings to which licentious love exposes them are talked of by such people as the author of Don Juan. The many fine eyes that have wept dangerous tears over his descriptions of the Gulnares and Medoras cannot be the worse for seeing the true side of *his* picture.

[quotes Canto ii. 199–201 (italicizing the final line)]

The amour with this Spanish lady is succeeded by a shipwreck, in which Juan alone escapes. He is dashed on the shore of the Cyclades, where he is found by a beautiful and innocent girl, the daughter of an old Greek pirate,—with whom, as might be supposed, the same game of guilt and abandonment is played over again. There is, however, a very superior kind of poetry in the conception of this amour—the desolate isle—the utter loneliness of the maiden, who is as ignorant as she is innocent—the helpless condition of the youth—every thing conspires to render it a true romance. How easy for Lord Byron to have kept it free from any stain of pollution! What cruel barbarity, in creating so much of beauty only to mar and ruin it! This is really the very suicide of genius.

[quotes Canto ii. 114–21, 182–6 (first 4 lines only), 188, 202, 204]

But the best and the worst part of the whole is without doubt the description of the shipwreck. As a piece of terrible painting, it is as much superior as can be to every description of the kind—not even excepting that in the Æneid—that ever was created. In comparison with the fearful and intense reality of its horrors, every thing that any former poet had thrown together to depict the agonies of that awful scene, appears chill and tame.

[quotes Canto ii. 52–3]

But even here the demon of his depravity does not desert him. We dare not stain our pages with quoting any specimens of the disgusting merriment with which he has interspersed his picture of human suffering. He paints it well, only to shew that he scorns it the more effectually; and of all the fearful sounds which ring in the ears of the dying, the most horrible is the demoniacal laugh with which this unpitying brother exults over the contemplation of their despair. Will our readers believe that the most innocent of all his odious sarcasms is contained in these two lines?

> 'They grieved for those that perished in the cutter,
> And also for the biscuit, casks, and butter.'
> [Canto ii. 61]

Dedication

Text: MS Van Pelt Library, University of Pennsylvania (bound in with Proof). Printed in Proof. First published in *Works* (1833). Thereafter published in Prothero.

The dedication is to Isaac D'Israeli (1766–1848), voluminous author and compiler of literary anecdotes, contributor to the *Quarterly Review*, and father of Benjamin Disraeli (1804–81), the future prime minister, author and first Earl of Beaconsfield. He published *Curiosities of Literature* (1791), *An Essay on the Manners and Genius of the Literary Character* (1795) (which went through various subsequent editions under the title of *The Literary Character*), *Miscellanies; or, Literary Recreations* (1796), *Calamities of Authors* (2 vols., 1812) and *Quarrels of Authors* (3 vols., 1814). In his preface to the fourth edition of *The Literary Character* (2 vols., 1828), which he dedicated to Southey, D'Israeli discussed B's character at length and with great sympathy; and he noted the irony that such an 'imperfect attempt to do justice to the character of LORD BYRON should be dedicated to MR. SOUTHEY', adding: 'Lord Byron once composed in prose, and printed, an attack on Mr. Southey, and in my character as the author of "The Calamities" and "The Quarrels of Authors," I received the honour of its dedication. This work was happily suppressed' (vol. i, pp. xxxvi, xxxvii). B himself had profound respect for 'that most entertaining and researching writer, Israeli' (*BLJ* iii. 251). See also in particular *BLJ* vi. 83–4; viii. 237; ix. 171–3.

1. —— *Israeli Esqre.* In *Works* (1833) this reads, 'J. D'Israeli, Esq.'; Prothero reads 'J.D. Israeli, Esq.'

2. Macbeth. *Macbeth*, III. v. 1: 'Why, how now, Hecate! you look angerly.'

Some Observations upon an Article in *Blackwood's Edinburgh Magazine* (1820)

1. *"The Life . . . earth"*. In the preface to his *Works* (1717), Pope wrote: 'I believe, if any one, early in his life, should contemplate the dangerous fate of authors, he would scarce be of their number on any consideration. The life of a Wit is

a warfare upon earth.' Pope himself echoes the Vulgate Job, 7: 1: 'Militia est vita hominis super terram' (the life of man is a war on earth—differently translated in the Authorized Version). Cf. also Captain Henrie Bell's first English translation of Martin Luther's *Tischreden* (1566, p. 421: 'Job saget, Des Menschen Leben ist ein Ritterschafft auff Erden'): '*Job* saith, *The life of an humane creature is a Warfare upon earth*' (*Colloquia Mensalia* (1652), p. 438).

2. *To this . . . too far.* B refers to such spurious attributions to him as: *Poems on his Domestic Circumstances* (1816), which includes, amongst some poems actually by B (e.g. 'Fare Thee Well'), 'Madame Lavalette' and an 'Ode' ('Oh, shame to thee, Land of the Gaul'); *Lord Byron's Farewell to England: with Three Other Poems, viz. Ode to St. Helena, To my Daughter, on the Morning of her Birth, and To the Lily of France* (1816); *Lord Byron's Pilgrimage to the Holy Land. A Poem. In Two Cantos. To which is added The Tempest. A Fragment* (1817); and *Childe Harold's Pilgrimage to the Dead Sea; Death on the Pale Horse; and Other Poems* (1818). For B's 'one' disavowal, see his letter to the Editor of Galignani's *Messenger* of 27 Apr. 1819 (*BLJ* vi. 118–19). See also n. 33 to B's letter 'To the Editor of the *British Review*', and the general note to 'Augustus Darvell: A Fragment of a Ghost Story' above; and *BLJ* v. 84–5, 138–9.

3. *"Childe Harold . . . person".* *Blackwood's Edinburgh Magazine*, vol. iii, no. xv (June 1818), pp. 323–9, contained a letter 'To the Author of Beppo'. After a somewhat vicious attack on B, the writer concluded: 'In evil hour did you step from your vantage-ground, and teach us Harold, Byron, and the Count of Beppo are the same' (p. 329). The writer signed himself 'PRESBYTER ANGLICANUS'. Of whom this was the pseudonym it is difficult to determine. Theodore Redpath suggests that it may have been that of John Gibson Lockhart or, more probably, that of the Revd Dr George Croly (*The Young Romantics and Critical Opinion 1807–1824* (1973), p. 43 and n.). However, in *Blackwood's Edinburgh Magazine*, vol. ii, no. viii (Nov. 1817), pp. 131–40, there appeared an article entitled 'On the Pulpit Eloquence of Scotland', which devoted itself entirely to the abilities of the Revd Dr Thomas Chalmers (1780–1847); and certainly B seems to have imagined (erroneously) that Chalmers was the 'celebrated Northern Preacher' who wrote the letter. In *Works* (1833), xv. 98 n., there is the following note: 'his Lordship was not less mistaken in attributing the "Remarks on Don Juan" in the Edinburgh Magazine to Professor Wilson, than in supposing Dr. Chalmers to have been the "Presbyter Anglicanus" who criticized his "Beppo" in the same journal'. See also Alan Lang Strout, *A Bibliography of Articles in Blackwood's Magazine 1817–1825*, Library Bulletin no. 5 (Library, Texas, 1959), p. 42.

4. *"like . . . once."* Sheridan, *The Rivals* IV. ii. (Mrs Malaprop speaking to Captain Jack Absolute).

5. *Moore . . . Guebre.* In GP, 'Guebre' reads 'Gueber' (uncorrected by B). The third tale of Moore's *Lalla Rookh* (1817) is entitled 'The Fire-Worshippers', the hero of which is Hafid, the Gheber.

6. *Scott . . . Burleigh.* In GP, Proof, *Works* (1833), and Prothero, 'Burleigh' reads 'Burley'. John Balfour of Burley is the rugged chief of the Cameronians in Scott's *Old Mortality* (1816); Roderick Dhu is the hero-chief of his poem *The Lady of the Lake* (1811).

7. *Magicians . . . Conjuror.* See also B's corrections in Proof; neither *Works* (1833) nor Prothero adopts B's three sets of substituted asterisks in this and the following sentence. Thalaba is the hero of Southey's poem *Thalaba* (1801) who eventually destroys the Magicians' seminary in Domdaniel at the expense of his own life.

8. *"Met . . . him".* Article iv of the *Quarterly Review*, vol. xxi, no. xlii (Apr. 1819), consisted of a review by Southey of three French works. In the course of this article Southey, describing the beauty of the scenery in the Valley of Lungern and the range of mountains rising over it, referred to 'the Wetterhorn, the Schreckhorn, the Eigir, and the Jungfrau, where Lord Byron's Manfred met the Devil and bullied him' (p. 366). See also n. 62 below.

9. *"Resist . . . you."* James 4: 7.

10. *M*[r] See B's correction in Proof. Both *Works* (1833) and Prothero read 'his most humble servant Mr. Southey'.

11. *"By my . . . words!" Henry IV, Part II*, II. iv. 183.

12. *Louis 15*[th] In GP, Proof, *Works* (1833), and Prothero this reads 'Louis XV'.

13. *and utterly.* In *Works* (1833) and Prothero this reads 'and to be utterly'.

14. *Sardanapalus . . . Individual.* For Sardanapalus, see B's drama *Sardanapalus* (1821); for Tiberius, see Suetonius, *The Twelve Caesars* (Bk. iii), and Tacitus, *The Annals of Imperial Rome*. See also *BLJ* iii. 256; viii. 37, for B's contemplating writing a drama on Tiberius. B refers to the 'Regency' (1715–23) of Philippe II, duc d'Orleans (1674–1723), the nephew of Louis XIV (1638–1715), and Regent during the minority of Louis XV (1710–74). The period was characterized by its reaction to the moral and political austerity of the latter part of Louis XIV's reign, Philippe himself being renowned for his dissoluteness. It is well documented in Voltaire's *Siècles de Louis XIV et de Louis XV* (5 vols., Paris, 1803). See also, for example, Antoine Hamilton, *Memoires de la Vie du Comte de Grammont* (Cologne, 1713).

15. *How far . . . decide.* By the Treaty of Campo Formio (1797) between France and Austria, Napoleon ceded Venice herself and a considerable portion of her territories to Austria, in return for Belgium, Lombardy, and Austrian acknowledgement of the Cisalpine Republic. See also B's 'Venice: An Ode' (*CPW* iv. 201–6, 495).

16. *pannel.* In *Works* (1833) and Prothero this reads 'panel'. In Scottish law, a 'pannel' is a person or persons indicted before a jury.

17. *this.* in GP, Proof, *Works* (1833), and Prothero this reads 'the'.

18. *If to the extent . . . asserted.* The Consul General at Venice was Richard Belgrave Hoppner (1786–1872) (for further details of whom see *BLJ* v. 294–5). Of B's generosity in Venice, Hoppner later furnished Moore with the following account:

He was also ever ready to assist the distressed, and he was most unostentatious in his charities: for besides considerable sums which he gave away to applicants at his own house, he contributed largely by weekly and monthly allowances to persons whom he had never seen, and who, as the money reached them by other hands, did not even know who was their benefactor. One or two instances might be adduced where his charity certainly bore an appearance of ostentation; one particularly when he sent fifty louis d'or to a poor printer whose house had been burnt to the ground, and all his property destroyed; but even this was not unattended with advantage; for it in a manner compelled the Austrian authorities to do something for the poor sufferer, which I have no hesitation in saying they would not have done otherwise; and I attribute it entirely to the publicity of his donation, that they allowed the man the use of an unoccupied house belonging to the government until he could rebuild his own, or re-establish his business elsewhere. (Moore ii. 265–6)

19. *waits.* In GP, Proof, *Works* (1833), and Prothero this reads 'wants'.

20. *I neither make . . . conduct.* For the numerous instances of B's selfless gifts and charities both in England and abroad, see e.g. those to Coleridge (*BLJ* v. 16n., 17; ix. 206–7, 208), to William Godwin (*BLJ* v. 16 and n., 17; x. 18), to Francis Hodgson (*BLJ* i. 196n., 198, 276; ii. 27n.; iii. 130n., 187 and n., 210n., 228 and n.), to Leigh Hunt (*BLJ* x. 13, 60, 105, 138), and to Harriette Wilson (*BLJ* vii. 64–5, 100). For his assistance to Hobhouse, see *BLJ* ii. 47 and n., 48, 161 and n. See also *Byron's Bulldog*, pp. 61–2, 101 and n. One of his earliest acts of generosity, that towards Lady Falkland, led him into a particularly tiresome and embarrassing situation (*BLJ* i. 195 and n.; iii. 17 and n., 24 and n.; see also Marchand i. 346–7; *BAP*, pp. 59, 126; and Leslie A. Marchand, 'Byron's Ordeal with Lady Falkland', *Byron Journal*, xvi (1988), 21–8. See also Doris Langley Moore, *Lord Byron: Accounts Rendered* (1974), pp. 264–396 *passim.*

21. *have sunk a Gulph.* In GP this reads 'have swoln a gulf'; B has deleted 'swoln a gulf' and substituted 'placed Eternity'. Proof does not adopt B's substitution and reads as GP. B has added in Proof 'sunk &'; hence *Works* (1833) and Prothero read 'have sunk and swoln a gulf'. (All this stems from a misreading of B's original MS 'sunk' as 'swoln'.) For the phrase itself, see Luke 16: 26. See also B's letter to his wife Annabella of 15 Feb. 1816 (*BLJ* v. 26). The implication of the whole of this sentence is that had B been 'a *prudent* man' he would never have married ('taken the step which was the first that led to the events') in the first place.

22. *Durandarte.* In GP this reads 'Durandante'; in correcting, B has merely stroked out the 'n', so as to read 'Durandate'. Proof reads as in MS; *Works* (1833) reads 'Durandearte', and Prothero reads 'Durande'. The correct spelling is 'Durandarte', as in MS and Proof. In Spanish romance literature, Durandarte and Montesinos are legendary heroes and friends, both present at

the Battle of Roncesvalles where the former is killed. Having carried his friend's heart to Durandarte's mistress, Balerma, Montesinos retires to a cave in La Mancha. In Cervantes' *Don Quixote*, Don Quixote visits the cave and has himself lowered into it. Here he experiences a beautiful vision of the enchanted Durandarte, Montesinos, Balerma, and his mistress, Dulcinea del Toboso, which he later recounts to Sancho Panza and the scholar. See Smollet's translation, *The History and Adventures of the Renowned Don Quixote*, 4 vols. (1782), vol. iii, pt. ii, bk. ii, chs. 5 and 6, pp. 191–207.

23. *"Patience ... Cards."* ('Digo, paciencia y barajar.') See foregoing n. 22 (Durandarte speaking, in ch. 6, p. 200; the phrase is repeated by Sancho Panza in ch. 7, p. 209).

24. *egoistical.* In GP and Proof this reads 'egotistical'; GP remains uncorrected, but in Proof B has stroked out the 't', so as to read 'egoistical' as in MS. Nevertheless, *Works* (1833) and Prothero read 'egotistical'.

25. *It is . . . full.* Cf. B's *Marino Faliero* (1820), V. i. 244–6: 'A spark creates the flame; 'tis the last drop / Which makes the cup run o'er, and mine was full / Already' (*CPW* iv. 422). See also Psalms 23: 5. The 'incident' was B's separation from his wife.

26. *But to return ... any body.* See *DJ* I. 10–23, 26–30 (*CPW* v. 12–18, 675). Despite B's repeated claims to the contrary, few of his friends (and fewer of his critics) were convinced that Donna Inez was not a veiled characterization of Lady B. (See, e.g. *BLJ* vi. 95 and n.; see also general note). For instance, Moore recalled in his journal for 31. Jan. 1819:

Went to breakfast with Hobhouse, in order to read Lord Byron's Poem—a strange production,—full of talent & singularity, as every thing he writes must be—some highly beautiful passages & some highly humourous ones—but, as a whole not publishable—Don Juan's mother is Lady Byron—and not only her learning, but various other points about her ridiculed—he talks of her favourite dress being *dimity* (which is the case)—dimity rhyming very comically to sublimity—& the conclusion of one stanza is 'I hate a dumpy woman'—meaning Lady B. again—This would disgust the Public beyond endurance— (*The Journal of Thomas Moore*, edited by Wilfred S. Dowden, i (1983), 141–2)

27. *But here . . . upon me.* Echoes Exodus 20: 5.

28. *landscape is.* In *Works* (1833) and Prothero this reads 'landscapes are'.

29. *"most sweet voices".* *Coriolanus* II. iii. 119.

30. *Ostracism . . . anonymous.* The allusion here is to Aristides, whose story is to be found in *Plutarch's Lives*, as is the system of 'ostracism':

It was performed, to be short, in this manner. Every one taking an *ostracon*, a sherd, that is, or piece of earthenware, wrote upon it the citizen's name he would have banished, and carried it to a certain part of the market-place surrounded with wooden rails. First, the magistrates numbered all the sherds in gross (for if there were less than six thousand, the ostracism was imperfect); then, laying every name by itself, they pronounced him whose name was written by the larger number banished for ten years, with the enjoyment of his estate. As, therefore, they were writing the names on the sherds, it is reported that an illiterate clownish fellow, giving Aristides his sherd, supposing him a common citizen, begged him to write *Aristides* upon it; and he being surprised and asking if Aristides had ever done him any injury, 'None at all,' said he, 'neither know I the man; but I am tired of hearing him everywhere called the Just.' Aristides, hearing this, is said to have made no reply, but returned the sherd with his own name inscribed. (*Plutarch's Lives: The 'Dryden Plutarch'*, revised by Arthur Hugh Clough, 3 vols. (1910), i, 'Aristides', pp. 496–7).

31. *by.* In GP, Proof, *Works* (1833), and Prothero this 'by' is omitted.

32. *The Man ... alleviation.* For this, and the ensuing four paragraphs, cf. Moore, i. 653–4:

Not content with such ordinary and tangible charges, the tongue of rumour was imboldened to proceed still further; and, presuming upon the mysterious silence maintained by one of the parties, ventured to throw out dark hints and vague insinuations, of which the fancy of every hearer was left to fill up the outline as he pleased. In consequence of all this exaggeration, such an outcry was now raised against Lord Byron as, in no case of private life, perhaps, was ever before witnessed; nor had the whole amount of fame which he had gathered, in the course of the last four years, much exceeded in proportion the reproach and obloquy that were now, within the space of a few weeks, showered upon him. In addition to the many who conscientiously believed and reprobated what they had but too much right to consider credible excesses, whether viewing him as a poet or man of fashion, there were also actively on the alert that large class of persons who seem to hold violence against the vices of others to be equivalent to virtue in themselves, together with all those natural haters of success who, having long sickened under the splendour of the *poet*, were now able, in the guise of champions for innocence, to wreak their spite on the *man.* In every various form of paragraph, pamphlet, and caricature, both his character and person were held up to odium;—hardly a voice was raised, or at least listened to, in his behalf; and though a few faithful friends remained unshaken by his side, the utter hopelessness of stemming the torrent was felt as well by them as by himself, and, after an effort or two to gain a fair hearing, they submitted in silence.

For the full details of B's separation from his wife and its immediate aftermath, see Marchand ii, ch. xv; *BAP*, ch. xv; *Recollections* ii. 191–355; Malcolm Elwin, *Lord Byron's Wife* (1962); id., *Lord Byron's Family* (1975). See also n. 38 below.

33. *been involved.* In GP and Proof 'been' is omitted; GP remains uncorrected, but in Proof B has added 'was'. *Works* (1833) and Prothero read 'was involved'.

34. *state their grievance.* In GP, Proof, *Works* (1833), and Prothero this reads 'state their grievances'.

35. *verses . . . treason.* The 'verses' in question were 'Fare Thee Well' (1816) and 'A Sketch from Private Life' (1816), the latter being far from 'complimentary' to its subject (*CPW* iii. 380–2, 382–6, 493–5).

36. *so . . . farther.* In GP, Proof, *Works* (1833), and Prothero this reads 'so I went a little farther'.

37. *like . . . waters.* Cf. *As You Like It* II. i. 29–40. See also Pope's 'To Mr. Gay', ll. 11–14, and Cowper's *The Task* III. 108–11.

38. *I was . . . Carriage.* B's 'most intimate friend' who had these apprehensions was Hobhouse, who together with Scrope Davies accompanied B to Dover and saw him embark for Ostend on 25 Apr. 1816. In his diary for 23 Apr., Hobhouse recorded their leaving London: 'Polidori and I went in Scrope Davies's chaise; Byron and Davies in Byron's new Napoleonic carriage built by Baxter for £500. There was a crowd about the door. When we got some way I looked back and, not seeing Byron's carriage, conjured up all sorts of accidents in my fancy' (*Recollections* i. 334). Moreover, on Tuesday 21 Apr. he recorded in his diary that 'Hanson repeated to me to day in L[d] B's presence that he was afraid Lady B. intended some violence to Lord B's person' (Broughton Papers, BL Add. MS 47232, ff. 109–8v). Also, in a letter to Scrope Davies from Venice on 7 Dec. 1818, B reminded him of the circumstances under which he had left England, saying that 'even Hobhouse thought the tide so strong against me—that he imagined I should be "assassinated"' (*BLJ* xi. 169). Scrope Davies and Hobhouse joined B at Diodati on 26 Aug. 1816; and Hobhouse and B toured the Bernese Oberland together between 17 and 29 Sept., before moving on to Italy. (Marchand ii. 645, 651–4; *BAP*, pp. 249, 151–4; *Recollections* ii. 6–65. See also *BLJ* v. 96–107.) It was probably during this tour that Hobhouse communicated these earlier fears to B.

39. *However . . . characters.* Edmund Kean (1789–1833), the great tragic actor who first made his mark on London audiences at the Drury Lane Theatre in 1814 (*BLJ* iv. 67). For B's appreciation of his abilities, see for instance *BLJ* iii. 244; iv. 67, 212, 216, 286; ix. 31.) Hobhouse recorded that on 4 and 9 Mar. 1816 he and B had seen 'wonderful' performances by Kean in the characters of, respectively, Sir Giles Overreach (in Massinger's *A New Way to Pay Old Debts*), and Prospero (*Recollections* i. 332–3; cf. also *BLJ* vi. 206).

40. *voting . . . principles.* B attended the House of Lords twice in 1816: on 19 Feb. and on 2 Apr. (See general note to 'Speeches' above.)

41. *I did not . . . had.* Jean-Jacques Rousseau (1712–78), the great French philosopher, suffered from an acute persecution mania throughout his life (see *Les Confessions*, and more particularly, *Rousseau jugé de Jean Jacques: Dialogues*, and *Les Rêveries du Promeneur solitaire*). B may also be covertly alluding here to John Wilson's laudatory review of *CHP* IV in the *Edinburgh Review*, vol. xxx, no. lix (June 1818), art. iii, pp. 87–120, in the first seven pages of which B is compared with Rousseau as being the most influential writer of his age (cf. *BLJ* ix. 11, 12).

42. *"being prejudged".* This reads 'being prejudiced' in Prothero.

43. *which last . . . difficulty.* This may very well refer to Sheridan, who 'got drunk very thoroughly and very soon', and whom B had to convey home on several occasions, which was 'no sinecure' (*BLJ* ix. 15; cf. also *BLJ* iv. 327; ix. 12–17,

32–3, 48). Otherwise, B may merely be referring again to his kindnesses noted above (see n. 20; and also Marchand ii. 567–8; *BAP*, p. 217).

44. *"You should . . . do."* B saw much of Madame de Staël at Coppet in the summer of 1816. For fuller details, see 'Some Recollections of my Acquaintance with Madame de Stael', *post.* See also n. 60 below.

45. *"Then . . . borne.* Closing quotation marks omitted by B. Thomas Campbell, 'Lines on Leaving a Scene in Bavaria', stanza 17, ll. 5–7. B had seen this poem in print before it was published, and greatly admired it (*BLJ* iv. 164).

46. *alledging.* In GP, Proof, *Works* (1833), and Prothero this reads 'alleging'.

47. *roof-tree.* Strictly speaking the 'roof-tree' is the ridge piece, or main beam of a roof. B uses it here as a metonymy for his household—his domestic security and family life. The phrase occurs frequently in Walter Scott's novels with a similar application: see for example *Guy Mannering*, ch. 8 (*Novels and Tales* (1825), iii. 87).

48. *I recollect . . . him.* Sir Samuel Romilly (1757–1818) was a lawyer of great repute, and had been Solicitor-General in 1806–7. After the death of his wife he committed suicide. During the proceedings leading to B's separation from his wife, he had been 'retained' (i.e. his professional services had been secured) by John Hanson, B's solicitor, to act on B's behalf. However, by an oversight it seems, he gave advice to Lady Noel, B's mother-in-law, in the last week of Jan. 1816, and to Lady Byron on 28 Feb. 1816 (Marchand ii. 568, 571; *BAP*, pp. 217, 218; Malcolm Elwin, *Lord Byron's Family* (1975), pp. 17, 21; see also *BLJ* v. 26, 34). He thus disqualified himself from advising B. On 15 Mar. 1816 B wrote a letter to Romilly which was delivered to him personally by Hobhouse (*BLJ* v. 50–1). On receiving this 'Sir Samuel Romilly declared to Mr. Hobhouse that he was not aware he had been retained by Lord Byron; and when his clerk showed him the retainer, remarked "that he had done a very incorrect thing in being consulted by Lady Byron, but that in the multiplicity of retainers, it was sometimes the case that names were overlooked"' (*Recollections* ii. 308). B never forgave Romilly, as is attested here. But see also, in particular, *BLJ* vi. 80–1, 82, 84, 90; *DJ* I. 15 (*CPW* v. 13, 675).

49. *go.* This reads 'get' in *Works* (1833) and Prothero.

50. *"perfervidum ingenium Scotorum."* 'The hot-blooded temperament of the Scots' (cf. Walter Scott's *The Heart of Mid-Lothian*, ch. 1 (*Novels and Tales* (1825), xi. 280)). The phrase is italicized in GP, Proof, *Works* (1833), and Prothero.

51. *Walter Scott . . . treated.* See B's additional note in GP. This is written in the margin of GP beside 'Walter Scott' to whose name B has added an asterisk (not adopted in Proof, *Works* (1833), or Prothero). The poet in question was Samuel Rogers, and the poem was *Human Life, A Poem* (1819). B's informant was Moore (*BLJ* viii. 132). In his journal for 28 Jan. 1819, Moore recorded:

Went to breakfast with Rogers—who is in the very agonies of parturition—and agonies they are indeed—showed me the work ready printed & in boards—but he is still making alterations—told me that Lord Byron's Don Juan is pronounced by Hobhouse & others unfit for publication . . . Rogers a good deal frightened, lest his praise of Byron—'Young B—n in the groves of academe' should bring him into disgrace among the righteous. (*The Journal of Thomas Moore*, edited by Wilfred S. Dowden, i (1983), 136)

And on 31 Jan. he noted:

Rogers going to cancel another leaf in order to soften down his praise of Lord B.—instead of 'Those that in youth a grace, a *glory* shed' it is to be 'a grace, a *lustre* shed'—as if this made a pin's-worth difference. (ibid., p. 142)

And sure enough the relevant lines in the first edition cited above read (p. 25):

They, that on Youth a grace, a lustre shed,
Of every age—the living and the dead! . . .
Young B—n in the groves of Academe.

52. *The article . . . England.*" Scott's review of *CHP* III appeared in the *Quarterly Review*, vol. xvi, no. xxxi (Oct. 1816), art. ix, pp. 172–208. It is an immensely generous and warm-hearted article, surveying very favourably B's poetical career up to the time and pronouncing him unquestionably 'the Champion of the English Parnassus' (p. 186). Scott also touches with the utmost tact and delicacy on B's personal affairs; but nowhere does he expressly state the desire here attributed to him by B. However he does seem to imply such a hope when he suggests that stanzas 8–16 of *CHP* III reveal 'the cause why Childe Harold has resumed his pilgrim's staff when it was hoped he had sat down for life a denizen of his native country' (p. 187). And again, perhaps more strongly, when comparing B with Churchill he adds: 'In the flower of his age Churchill died in a foreign land,—here we trust the parallel will cease, and that the subject of our criticism will long survive to honour his own' (pp. 203–4).

53. *Welbeck Street . . . hour.* Welbeck Street and Devonshire Place were fashionable areas in the West End of London. B may well have been informed of this reaction by Hobhouse, who had left Venice for Rome on 5 Dec. 1816, and who greeted B when he arrived there on 29 Apr. 1817. See Marchand ii. 691–2; *BAP*, pp. 265–6.

54. *pieces.* GP ends here.

55. *an enemy.* This was Henry Brougham, whom B intended to call out at the first opportunity if ever he returned to England. See B's challenge to him: *BLJ* vii. 95–6. See also *BLJ* vi. 86, 242 and n.; *CPW* v. 685–7. Brougham had spread malicious rumours about B on his departure from England, and had interfered with Madame de Staël's efforts to effect a reconciliation between B and Annabella in 1816. See Marchand ii. 613–14, 650; *BAP*, p. 317. Moore recorded in his journal on 25 Nov. 1820 that Lord John Russell had told him that 'Brougham returned his [B's] hate with interest & that there could not be found any where two more determined haters' (Wilfred S. Dowden (ed.), *The Journal of Thomas Moore*, i (1983), 364). See also n. 62 below.

56. *after my departure.* See B's correction in Proof. *Works* (1833) aqnd Prothero follow B's correction and read 'after it'.

57. *however . . . lost.* Echoes Proverbs 13: 12.

58. *"voluntary exile."* This aspersion is made neither in Scott's review nor in *Blackwood's Edinburgh Magazine*; B may merely be glossing his own 'Self-exiled Harold' (*CHP* III. 16), which Scott quotes approvingly (p. 189). See n. 52 above.

59. *Cologny . . . Geneva. Works* (1833) and Prothero read 'Coligny'. Be took up residence at the Villa Diodati, in the village of Cologny (its correct spelling), on 10 June 1816 (Marchand ii. 625; *BAP*, p. 241).

60. *The sole . . . Madame de Stael.* B's 'sole companion' was his doctor, Dr John Polidori—for whose social rounds in Geneva see *The Diary of Dr. John William Polidori*, edited by William Michael Rossetti (1911), pp. 99–152. Hobhouse recorded that B dined at Coppet (without Hobhouse) on 7 Sept. 1816; again (with Hobhouse and Polidori) on 12 Sept.; and again (with Hobhouse) on 1 and 3 Oct. (*Recollections* ii. 12, 14–16, 25–6, 26–8; see also Marchand ii. 635–6, 659; *BAP*, pp. 245–6; for further details, see B's 'Some Recollections of my Acquaintance with Madame de Stael', *post*). B's deletion in Proof of 'that of' is followed by *Works* (1833) and Prothero: both read 'with the exception of one English family'. The family in question was Percy Bysshe Shelley, his wife Mary and their son William, and Claire Clairmont, who had arrived in Geneva on 13 May 1816—twelve days before B. B and Shelley met for the first time at Sécheron on 27 May, and spent much time in each other's company from then until 29 Aug., when the Shelley party returned to England (Marchand ii. 620–46; *BAP*, pp. 240–50; see also 'Augustus Darvell: A Fragment of a Ghost Story', above).

61. *I quote . . . to me.* Echoing Scott's *The Lay of the Last Minstrel* II. xxii. 16. B's informant was almost certainly Shelley himself, when he visited B at Venice over 24–9 Sept. 1818 (Marchand ii. 752–3; *BAP*, p. 288).

62. *One of . . . Sorrow.* This story drew forth venom from B (see, e.g. *BLJ* vi. 76, 82–3; vii. 102). However, Southey was not responsible for its concoction nor for its circulation; neither did Coleridge ('*another* of that poetical fraternity') go about repeating it. B first made this accusation publicly, in rather general terms, in a note to *The Two Foscari*: 'I am not ignorant of Mr. Southey's calumnies on a different occasion, knowing them to be such, which he scattered abroad on his return from Switzerland against me and others' (*Sardanapalus, The Two Foscari, and Cain* (1821), p. 328). In reply to this, Southey wrote to the editor of the *Courier* on 5 Jan. 1822:

> I come at once to his lordship's charge against me, blowing away the abuse with which it is frothed, and evaporating a strong acid in which it is suspended. The residuum then appears to be, that 'Mr. Southey, on his return from Switzerland (in 1817), scattered abroad calumnies, knowing them to be such, against Lord Byron and others.' To this I

> reply with *a direct and positive denial.* . . . Once, and only once, in connexion with Switzerland, I have alluded to his lordship; and, as the passage was curtailed in the press, I take this opportunity of restoring it. In the 'Quarterly Review,' speaking incidentally of the Jungfrau, I said, 'it was the scene where Lord Byron's *Manfred* met the Devil and bullied him . . . though the Devil must have won his cause before any tribunal in this world, or the next, if he had not pleaded more feebly for himself than his advocate, in a cause of canonization, ever pleaded for him. (Robert Southey, *Essays, Moral and Political*, 2 vols. (1832), ii. 191–2)

(For the latter part of this passage, see also n. 8 above.) B in turn replied to this with his letter to the editor of the *Courier*, which in the event he never sent (*BLJ* ix. 95–100). Instead, he amply repaid Southey with *The Vision of Judgment* (1822).

The real culprit for spreading this story, and other malicious gossip about B, was Henry Brougham, who was in Switzerland during July and August 1816. Lady Frances Shelley, to whose party Brougham attached himself for a while, recorded in her diary on 20 July 1816, soon after arriving at Sécheron: 'Lord Byron is living near here with Percy Shelley, or rather, with his wife's sister, as the *chronique scandaleuse* says.' The *chronique scandaleuse* was Brougham (Richard Edgcumbe (ed.), *The Diary of Frances Lady Shelley 1787–1817* (1912), p. 231 and n.; see also Ethel Colburn Mayne, *Byron* (1924), p. 279 and n.). Moreover, Lady Anne Romilly, the wife of Sir Samuel, writing from Cheltenham to Maria Edgeworth on 26 Aug. 1816, said of B: 'I think I told you that his society at Coligny was such as precluded him from being much sought after.' And again, in a letter to the same recipient (undated, but Apr. 1817), she wrote with reference to Shelley: 'He then goes abroad with Mary and her sister, who are *daughters* of *Godwin*, and joins Lord Byron and his equally delectable party on the Banks of the Lake of Geneva, where you may have heard they all lived together in a way to shock common decency' (Samuel Henry Romilly (ed.), *Romilly–Edgeworth Letters 1813–1818* (1936), pp. 153, 165).

63. *The tale . . . old.* Mary Shelley was born in 1797, Claire Clairmont in 1798. The former was the daughter of William Godwin and Mary Wollstonecraft, who died in childbirth. Godwin subsequently married Mrs Clairmont, whose daughter Claire was the offspring of her former marriage.

64. *Pantisocracy . . . none.* 'Pantisocracy' was an ideal community conceived by Southey and Coleridge during their university days and intended to be realized on the banks of the Susquehanna in Pennsylvania. In essence it was an early form of communism: each would work the land to provide for all, and property would be owned in common. As Southey himself put it in *A Letter to William Smith, Esq. M.P. from Robert Southey, Esq.* (1817): 'My purpose was to retire with a few friends into the wilds of America, and there lay the foundations of a community, upon what we believed to be the political system of Christianity' (p. 20). The project came to nothing. See Malcolm Elwin, *The First Romantics* (1947), iv. 111–57.

65. *How far . . . Epitaph." Wat Tyler*, a highly revolutionary poem by Southey, 'was written, in the course of three mornings, in 1794' (preface, 1837). A pirated edition was first published in 1817, four years after he had become Poet Laureate. This was a great embarrassment to Southey, who attempted to take out an injunction against its publication. However, the Lord Chancellor (Lord Eldon) refused to grant an injunction on the grounds that 'a person cannot recover in damages for a work which is in its nature calculated to do an injury to the public' (*The Life and Correspondence of Robert Southey*, edited by his son the Revd Charles Cuthbert Southey, 6 vols. (1849, 1850), iv. 251). In a speech in a debate in the House of Commons on the Seditious Meetings Bill on 14 Mar. 1817, William Smith, MP for Norwich, fuelled Southey's embarrassment:

> He was far from supposing, that a man who set out in life with the profession of certain sentiments, was bound to conclude life with them. He thought there might be many occasions in which a change of opinion, when that change was unattended by any personal advantages, when it appeared entirely disinterested, might be the result of sincere conviction. But what he most detested, what most filled him with disgust, was the settled, determined malignity of a renegado. He had read in a publication (the Quarterly Review), certainly entitled to much respect from its general excellences, though he differed from it in its principles, a passage alluding to the recent disturbances, which passage was as follows:
>
> > 'When a man of free opinions commences professor of moral and political philosophy for the benefit of the public—the fables of old credulity are then verified—his very breath becomes venomous, and every page which he sends abroad carries with it poison to the unsuspicious reader. We have shown, on a former occasion, how men of this description are acting upon the public, and have explained in what manner a large part of the people have been prepared for the virus with which they innoculate them. The dangers arising from such a state of things are now fully apparent, and the designs of the incendaries, which have for some years been proclaimed so plainly, that they ought, long ere this, to have been prevented, are now manifested by overt acts.' [citing from Southey's review of various publications under the running title 'Parliamentary Reform' in *Quarterly Review*, vol. xvi, no. xxxi (Oct. 1816), art. xi, p. 227]
>
> With the permission of the House, he would read an extract from a poem recently published, to which, he supposed the above writer alluded (or at least to productions of a similar kind), as constituting a part of the virus with which the public mind had been infected:
>
> 'My brethren, these are truths and weighty ones:
> Ye are all equal; nature made ye so.
> Equality is your birthright;—when I gaze
> On the proud palace, and behold one man,
> In the blood-purpled robes of royalty,
> Feasting at ease, and lording over millions;
> Then turn me to the hut of poverty,
> And see the wretched labourer, worn with toil,
> Divide his scanty morsel with his infants,
> I sicken, and indignant at the sight,
> "Blush for the patience of humanity."'
> [citing from *Wat Tyler* I. i (John Ball speaking)]

He could read many other passages from these works equally strong on both sides; but, if they were written by the same person, he should like to know from the hon. and learned gentleman opposite, why no proceedings had been instituted against the author. The poem 'Wat Tyler,' appeared to him to be the most seditious book that was ever written; its author did not stop short of exhorting to general anarchy; he vilified kings, priests, and nobles, and was for universal suffrage and perfect equality. (Hansard, *Parliamentary Debates* xxxv (1817), 1090–2)

To this Southey replied with *A Letter to William Smith, Esq. M.P. from Robert Southey, Esq.* (1817). This consists of 43 pages written in high dudgeon. Southey explained the circumstances of the publication of *Wat Tyler*, and defended his change in opinion, saying:

The piece was written under the influence of opinions which I have long since outgrown, and repeatedly disclaimed, but for which I have never affected to feel either shame or contrition; they were taken up conscientiously in early youth, they were acted upon in disregard of all worldly considerations, and they were left behind in the same straight-forward course, as I advanced in years. (pp. 6–7)

He echoed Smith's phrase 'malignity of a renegado', expanding it to 'the malignity and baseness of a Renegade' (p. 9), and continued:

Mr. William Smith is said to have insulted me with the appellation of Renegade; and if it be indeed true that the foul aspersion past his lips, I brand him for it on the forehead with the name of SLANDERER. Salve the mark as you will, Sir, it is ineffaceable! You must bear it with you to your Grave, and the remembrance will outlast your Epitaph. (p. 28)

(Nowhere do Smith or Southey use the phrase 'rancorous renegado'; nor is the expression '. . . Calumniator' used.)

66. *He has . . . reviewer.* Southey accepted the office of Poet Laureate in 1813, after the death of its previous holder, Henry James Pye (1745–1813). On his death in 1843 he was succeeded by Wordsworth. In his edition of *The Remains of Henry Kirke White* (2 vols. (1807), i. 23), Southey wrote: 'An author is proof against reviewing, when, like myself, he has been reviewed above seventy times; but the opinion of a reviewer upon his first publication, has more effect, both upon his feelings and his success, than it ought to have, or would have, if the mystery of the *ungentle craft* were more generally understood.' Southey became a reviewer in the *Quarterly Review* at its inception in 1808. (For its establishment and his initiation into it, see *Life and Correspondence of Robert Southey* iii. 181–9, 194). Between 1808 and 1839, when he relinquished reviewing, Southey contributed 95 articles.

67. *he denounced . . . Waterloo.* Southey mocked the Battle of Blenheim in his poem of that title written in 1798; he applauded Waterloo in his long, anti-Bonapartist, moral, and nationalistic, partly allegorical poem *The Poet's Pilgrimage to Waterloo* (1815).

68. *he loved . . . mentioned.* Southey never 'loved' Mary Shelley's mother, Mary Wollstonecraft. He did howver address a sonnet to her in 1795, which he

prefixed to his juvenile poem *The Triumph of Women* (written in 1793), and had great admiration for her (see *Life and Correspondence of Robert Southey* i. 310–11).

69. *the Butt... Review.* The *Anti-Jacobin* was a weekly paper edited by William Gifford, who together with George Canning, George Ellis, and John Hookham Frere parodied many of the productions of the authors of the day. For their parodies of Southey, see *Poetry of the Anti-Jacobin* (1799), pp. 1–11, 18–20, 21–3. See also n. 66 above.

70. *I was born... sing.* B claimed descent through his mother from James I. For a full account of his genealogy, see Marchand i, ch. 1; *BAP*, ch. 1.

71. *"that... creed".* Pope, *The First Epistle of the Second Book of Horace*, l. 74.

72. *sworn foe ... Ogilby's".* Johnson, 'The Young Author', l. 24 (Johnson is warning the young author against ambition for fame). Johnson both hypercriticized and hotly disputed the authenticity of the Ossian poems published by James Macpherson. See *Boswell's Life of Johnson* ii. 296–302.

73. *"Proud... forgot."* Johnson, 'The Young Author', l. 30. In *Works* (1833) and Prothero inverted commas enclosed 'forgot' only.

74. *the Edinburgh... purchasers.* The *Edinburgh Review*, vol. i, no. i (Oct. 1802), art. viii, pp. 63–83, carried a review of Southey's *Thalaba* (1801); *Edinburgh Review*, vol. vii, no. xiii (Oct. 1805), art. i, pp. 1–28, carried a review of his *Madoc* (1805). Both were written by Francis Jeffrey, who denounced Southey as the leader of the dissenting sect of poetry. Interestingly enough, Walter Scott approached Southey in Nov. 1807 and suggested his reviewing for the *Edinburgh Review.* Though tempted, Southey declined on account of his difference in moral, political, and critical outlook (*The Life and Correspondence of Robert Southey* iii. 122–5, 127). Southey's articles in the Tory *Quarterly Review* earned him and his views considerable influence and respect. According to William Gifford, its editor, 'Southey's prose is so good that every one detects him' (Samuel Smiles, *A Publisher and His Friends*, 2 vols. (1891), i. 260). See also n. 66 above.

75. *Did he... coveted?* B refers here again to Mary Shelley and her mother, Mary Wollstonecraft, echoing Exodus 20: 17. See nn. 63 and 68 above.

76. *In a conversation ... written"* See B's deletion in Proof. Both *Works* (1833) and Prothero read 'Mr. —'. This story was totally untrue and was the concoction of Samuel Rogers (see following n. 77). Wordsworth told Henry Crabb Robinson on 22 Mar. 1837 that 'as he felt a warm affection for Southey and an admiration for his genius he never could have said that he would not give five shillings for all Southey had ever written' (Edith J. Morley (ed.), *Henry Crabb Robinson on Books and their Writers*, 3 vols. (1938), ii. 516).

77. *Mr. Southey... genealogy. Works* (1833) and Prothero read 'Dr. Southey'. See also B's correction in Proof; adopted in *Works* (1833) and Prothero: both read 'This anecdote was told me by persons who, if quoted by name, would prove

that its genealogy is poetical as well as true.' This substituted anonymity involved Henry Crabb Robinson in some extensive literary detective work, when 'Some Observations' was first published in 1833 (see *Henry Crabb Robinson on Books and their Writers* i. 428–9; ii. 504, 508, 516). But, astutely, right from the start he suspected Samuel Rogers, who later confessed to him that the story was indeed his but that B had 'misrepresented what he said' (ibid., i. 428n.). The matter was further exacerbated by Landor in *A Satire on Satirists* (1836), where he addresses these lines to Wordsworth: 'Tho' Southey's poetry to thee should seem / Not worth five shillings (such thy phrase)', and appends the note: 'So long as this was oral, and merely oral, however widely disseminated and studiously repeated, it was discreet to leave it uncastigated; now it has found its way into print; a thing inevitable, sooner or later' (p. 29 and n.). See also R. H. Super, *Walter Savage Landor: A Biography* (1954), pp. 276, 565 n. 80).

78. *I give . . . mentioned.* See B's additions in Proof; both adopted in *Works* (1833) and Prothero, who read, 'I can give my authority for this; and am ready to adduce it also for Mr. Southey's circulation of the falsehood before mentioned.'

79. *Of Coleridge . . . divine.* B wrote to Murray on 24 Nov. 1818: 'I can understand Coleridge's abusing me', 'for I had done him what is called a favour' (*BLJ* vi. 83). In fact B had done Coleridge several services. He had persuaded Murray to publish *Kubla Khan* and *Christabel*; he had encouraged Coleridge to write a tragedy for the Drury Lane Theatre; and he had aided him financially. See, for example, *BLJ* iv. 285–6, 321–2, 324; v. 150, 267; ix. 206–7. See also n. 20 above.

80. *"Over . . . broods".* Wordsworth, 'Resolution and Independence', 1, l. 5. In the preface to his first collected edition of his *Poems* (1815), Wordsworth cited this line, and various lines from stanzas 9, 10, and 11 of the same poem, together with a passage from Milton's *Paradise Lost* (bk. ii, ll. 636–43), as examples of the operations of the Imagination.

81. *"What . . . hedge". Hamlet*, IV. v. 123.

82. *Are they . . . "a drunken song".* B makes this same aspersion in his long note to *DJ* V. 147. See *CPW* v. 712, 713. In n. 21 to *The Feast of the Poets* (1814), Leigh Hunt wrote with reference to the Lake poets generally:

> Yet the feebler and idler part of the poets here mentioned affect to speak of such men as Johnson and Dryden with contempt,—of Johnson, who with all his defects and his bigotries, could master his morbidities to some purpose,—and of Dryden, who though deficient in sentiment, studied his art as they never did, and has written as they never can. I have heard, on good authority, that one of them calls Alexander's Feast 'a drunken song.' It is much to be wished that the sobrieties of the present Laureat could produce such another. (pp. 109–10)

83. *See . . . him.* In his *Biographia Literaria*, 2 vols. (1817), i. 40n., Coleridge wrote:

> I had yet experienced the same sensations myself, and felt almost as if I had been newly couched, when by Mr. Wordsworth's conversation, I had been induced to re-examine with impartial strictness Gray's celebrated elegy. I had long before detected the defects in 'the Bard;' but 'the Elegy' I had considered as proof against all fair attacks; and to this day I cannot read either, without delight, and a portion of enthusiasm. At all events, whatever pleasure I may have lost by the clearer perception of the faults in certain passages, has been more than repaid to me, by the additional delight with which I read the remainder.

84. *and have . . . Wordsworth is.* B refers to Wordsworth's preface to the second edition of *Lyrical Ballads* (1800), his 'Appendix' (enlarging on 'Poetic Diction') to the preface in the third edition of *Lyrical Ballads* (1802), his preface to *The Excursion* (1814), and to his preface and 'Essay, Supplementary to the Preface' in *Poems* (1815). It is in this last that Wordsworth launched his major attack against Pope and his style. In particular, he criticized Pope's translation of the moonlight scene in the *Iliad* (viii. 687–92) as being 'throughout false and contradictory', which passage Coleridge also criticized in his *Biographia Literaria* i. 39n.–40n. See also *BLJ* iv. 324–6.

85. *these.* This reads 'those' in Proof, *Works* (1833), and Prothero.

86. *the.* This reads 'though' in Proof, *Works* (1833), and Prothero.

87. *even if . . . Secret Service.* See B's deletion in Proof; followed in *Works* (1833) and Prothero: both read 'even if the government subscribe for it, and set the money down to secret service'. Moore visited Dublin in June 1818 and met an extraordinarily warm reception. An account of his sojourn there is given in James Burke, *The Life of Thomas Moore* (1852), pp. 50–65. On 8 June, for instance, a dinner was held in his honour at Morrison's Hotel. Lord Charlemont, proposing Moore's health, said: 'His character may be expressed in three words—Patriotism, Independence, Consistency' (p. 52). Moore himself, in a letter to Samuel Rogers of 18 June 1818, gave a lively description of his being fêted:

> I have been in such a giddifying labyrinth of bustle, acclamation, hurrahs, &c. . . . Never, certainly, was there anything more enthusiastic than my reception in Dublin. It was even better than Voltaire's at Paris, because there was more *heart* in it, and the call for me at the Theatre, and the bursts of applause when I appeared with my best bows at the front of the box (which I was obliged to repeat several times in the course of the night) were really all most overwhelmingly gratifying, and scarcely more delightful to me on my own account than as a proof of the strong spirit of nationality in my countrymen. (*The Letters of Thomas Moore*, edited by Wilfred S. Dowden, 2 vols. (1964), i. 451)

88. *to . . . but.* See B's correction in Proof; adopted in *Works* (1833) and Prothero: both read 'to the not opulent but'.

89. *warm hearted.* See B's correction in Proof; followed in *Works* (1833) and Prothero: both read 'warm-hearted'.

90. *Hence . . . years.* See also nn. 66 and 74 above. B has in mind particularly here a review of Hunt's *Foliage* (1818), which appeared in the *Quarterly Review*,

vol. xviii, no. xxxvi (Jan. [pub. June] 1818), art. iii, pp. 324–35. This savaged not only Hunt—both personally, and as a poet and critic—but also Shelley. B mistakenly attributed it to Southey (see *BLJ* vi. 83; see also *Medwin's Conversations*, p. 151, and *Life and Correspondence of Robert Southey* v. 356). It was, however, written by John Taylor Coleridge. Hunt was a consistent admirer of Wordsworth, and, while not uncritical of him as a poet, ranked him very highly. See, for example, his extensive n. 20 to *The Feast of the Poets* (1814), pp. 87–109 (cf. *BLJ* iv. 324), and the preface to *Foliage* (1818), in p. 14 of which he states that Wordsworth 'is generally felt among his own profession to be at the head of it' (cf. *BLJ* vi. 47).

91. *"next . . . it."* In *Biographia Literaria* (i. 39n.), Coleridge, referring to a comparison he had made in one of his lectures (that of 27 Jan. 1812) between the style of Pope's original compositions and that of his translation of Homer—which Coleridge regarded as 'the main source of our pseudo-poetic diction'—continued: 'And this, by the bye, is an additional confirmation of a remark made, I believe, by Sir Joshua Reynolds, that next to the man who formed and elevated the taste of the public, he that corrupted it, is commonly the greatest genius.' (Neither James Engell and W. Jackson Bate, the editors of the most recent edition of *Biographia Literaria* (1983), nor I, have been able to trace Coleridge's ascription here. Moreover, in an article entitled 'Jeffrey and Hazlitt' in *Blackwood's Edinburgh Magazine*, its author writes that Jeffrey 'may console himself with *the old reflection*, that, "next to the merit of having improved a nation's taste, the greatest merit is that of having corrupted it"' (*Blackwood's Edinburgh Magazine*, vol. iii, no. xv (June 1818), p. 305, emphasis added).

92. *No one . . . Century.* See B's correction in Proof; not adopted in *Works* (1833) or Prothero. Giovanni Battista Marino (1569–1625), Neapolitan poet and author of the long and immensely popular poem *Adone* (1623), based on the story of Venus and Adonis and written in French. His euphuistic style, involving hyperbole, complicated word-play, and elaborate metphors and conceits, was imitated to excess by French and Italian poets of the seventeenth century, and gave rise to the derogatory term *Marinisme* (or *Marinismo*). It was against such artificial and inflated poetry that Boileau (Pope's 'model', in Warton's view) reacted. See n. 96 below.

93. *Warton . . . it.* Joseph Warton (1722–1800), literary critic and brother of Thomas Warton, the Poet Laureate (1785–90), severely criticized Pope in *An Essay on the Genius and Writings of Pope* (1756). See n. 96 below. Charles Churchill (1731–64), satirical poet and friend of the radical, John Wilkes, had a strong antipathy to Pope, criticizing him for, amongst other things, his correctness and lack of variety, and even his 'excellence'. See, e.g. 'The Apology', ll. 366–75 (*The Poetical Works of Charles Churchill*, 2 vols. (1804), i. 95–7).

94. *heroes.* See B's correction in Proof; followed in *Works* (1833) and Prothero.

95. *must.* See reading in Proof (uncorrected by B); followed in *Works* (1833) and Prothero.

96. *has had . . . Dryden.* In *An Essay on the Genius and Writings of Pope* (2 vols. (1806), i. vi–vii, Joseph Warton wrote:

And because I am, perhaps, unwilling to speak out in plain English, I will adopt the following passage of Voltaire, which, in my opinion, as exactly characterizes POPE as it does his model Boileau, for whom it was originally designed:

'INCAPABLE PEUT-ETRE DU SUBLIME QUI ELEVE L'AME, ET DU SENTIMENT QUI L'ATTENDRIT, MAIS FAIT POUR ECLAIRER CEUX A QUI LA NATURE ACCORDA L'UN ET L'AUTRE, LABORIEUX, SEVERE, PRECIS, PUR, HARMONIEUX, IL DEVINT, ENFIN, LE POETE DE LA RAISON.')

(The French might be translated as: 'Incapable, perhaps, of sublimity which elevates the soul, and of sentiment which softens it, he was formed to enlighten those whom Nature had endowed with both; painstaking, stern, exact, pure and harmonious, he became at length the Poet of Reason.')

He then went on to divide English poets into four classes: Spenser, Shakespeare, and Milton occupying the highest class as the only 'sublime and pathetic poets'; Dryden, Prior, and others occupying the second class as poets having 'talents for moral, ethical, and panegyrical poesy' (vol. i, p. vii). At the close of his *Essay*, questioning where Pope might be placed, he replied: 'Not, assuredly, in the same rank with *Spenser*, *Shakespeare*, and *Milton* . . . but, considering the correctness, elegance, and utility of his works, the weight of sentiment, and the knowledge of man they contain, we may venture to assign him a place, *next* to *Milton*, and *just* above *Dryden*.' And he added: 'Surely it is no narrow and niggardly encomium, to say he is the great Poet of Reason, the *First* of *Ethical* authors in verse. And this species of writing is, after all, the surest road to an extensive reputation. It lies more level to the general capacities of men, than the higher flights of more genuine poetry' (ii. 404, 403). For the first edition of this *Essay*, see n. 93 above.

97. *"that will . . . die".* Milton, *The Reason of Church-Government* (1642). See, for example, C. A. Patrides, *John Milton: Selected Prose* (1974), p. 54.

98. *Goldsmith . . . Master.* B refers successively to Oliver Goldsmith (1730–74), Samuel Rogers (1763–1855), Thomas Campbell (1777–1844), William Hayley (1745–1820), and George Crabbe (1754–1832). Rogers, Campbell, and Crabbe received B's poetic applause as early as 1809 (see *EBSR*, ll. 799–810, 855–8; *CPW* i. 254, 256, 414, 415); Hayley was recognized at the same time, but only for *The Triumphs of Temper* (1781) (see *EBSR*, ll. 309–18; *CPW* i. 238, 405).

99. *Then . . . Antijacobin.* Erasmus Darwin (1731–1802), botanist and physician, was author of the poem *The Botanic Garden* (1789, 1791), pt. ii of which, 'The Loves of the Plants', was ridiculed and parodied in the *Anti-Jacobin* under the title of 'Loves of the Triangles. A Mathematical and Philosophical Poem' (see *Poetry of the Anti-Jacobin* (1799), pp. 113–29, 134–41.). B himself had castigated Darwin in *EBSR*, ll. 891–902 (*CPW* i. 257, 415–16).

100. *the Cruscans . . . Satirists.* The 'Della Cruscans' were a group of English poets, popular in the latter part of the eighteenth century, the features of whose affected and inflated style included meaningless metaphor and excessive ornamentation. Their pioneer was Robert Merry (1755–98), who settled for some time in Florence and belonged to the Florentine Accademia della Crusca. On his return to England, he published his poem 'Adieu and Recall to Love' in the *World* (29 June 1787), under the pseudonym of 'Della Crusca', which gave rise to a poetical correspondence between him and 'Anna Matilda' (Hannah Cowley (1743–1809)) conducted in the *World* until 5 Dec. 1787. This was collected and published, with other contributions signed by such initiates as 'Arley', 'Benedict', 'Edwin', and 'The Bard', in *The Poetry of The World* (2 vols., 1788); which in turn was republished, with various additions, as *The British Album* (2 vols., 1790). This publication in particular became the butt of the satires the *Baviad* (1791) and *Mæviad* (1795) by William Gifford (1756–1826), whom B held in high respect as a satirist. See also, e.g., *EBSR*, ll. 819–30 (*CPW* i. 255, 414–15)). B also attacks the 'Della Cruscans' in *EBSR*, ll. 755–64 (*CPW* i. 253, 413–14). Edward Jerningham (1727–1812), another 'Della Cruscan' satirized by Gifford, is treated kindly by B in his 'Postscript' to *EBSR* (*CPW* i. 264).

101. *At the . . . M.S.S.* For Southey's *Wat Tyler*, see n. 65 above; his *Joan of Arc, An Epic Poem* was published in 1796. Wordsworth's *Peter Bell* was composed in 1798, but was not published until 1819. See n. 125 below.

102. *and it was . . . Chancery.* By tradition (beginning with Ben Jonson), the Poet Laureate received a butt of Canary wine as part of his stipend. The gibe here is twofold: Wordsworth is qualified to 'gauge' its (alcoholic) strength in the light of such (drunken) conceptions as *Peter Bell* and *The Excursion*, and to 'gauge' its material value in his governmental capacity of Distributor of Stamps (appointed 1813). 'Gauger' was a colloquial term for an Excise man. Cf. *DJ*, 'Dedication', stanza 6, l. 6, and B's note (*CPW* v. 5, 671).

103. *Wordsworth . . . postscript.* For Wordsworth's prefaces, see n. 84 above. B is also punning here on 'brooding' (see n. 80 above), and 'peddling'—possibly Peter Bell, the peddling Potter, but certainly the Pedlar in *The Excursion.* Cf. *DJ* III. 100 (*CPW* v. 196). See also n. 116 below.

104. *both.* See B's deletion in Proof; followed in *Works* (1833) and Prothero.

105. *Wordsworth . . . it".* See Molière, *Le Bourgeois Gentilhomme* III. iv (Monsieur Jourdain speaking to le Maître de Philosophie).

106. *other.* The MS of the note appended here is bound in with Proof (see general note above), and bears the following superscription by B: 'Note to the remarks on Wordsworth's trash in the "Observations on an Article &c"'.

107. *Turnuses . . . it.* Turnus is the king of the Rutuli at the time of Aeneas' arrival in Italy, whom Aeneas eventually slays. Dido, founder Queen of Carthage, falls in love with Aeneas when he visits Africa, and takes her own life when he leaves her. See *The Aeneid*, bks. vii–xii and iv respectively.

108. *an honour . . . Buonaparte.* William Thomas Fitzgerald (?1759–1829), poet and writer of numerous patriotic addresses (see his *Miscellaneous Poems* (1801)), was lampooned by James and Horace Smith in their *Rejected Addresses* (1812), with a poem entitled 'Loyal Effusion, By W.T.F.'. He was a staunch anti-Bonapartist, and, in the capacity of 'Vates' (i.e. prophet), B no doubt has in mind his poem *The Battle of Waterloo* (1815), the first 28 lines of which recite a poem he originally delivered at the anniversary of the Literary Fund on 4 May 1815, concluding with the following couplets:

> But come there will, or soon or late the hour,
> Shall hurl THE DESPOT headlong from his Power,
> Pluck from his brow the transient Plume of Fame,
> And give to deathless Infamy his name!
>
> (ll. 25–8)

These lines, he adds in a note, 'proved prophetic of the Tyrant's downfall'. See *The Battle of Waterloo* (2nd edn., 1825), p. 21, n. 1). Fitzgerald is probably best known for being the butt of the opening lines of B's *EBSR* (*CPW* i. 229, 399–400). See also *BLJ* vi. 47; vii. 205, 236.

109. *predicating.* See B's correction in Proof: followed in *Works* (1833) and Prothero.

110. *infernal.* See B's deletion and restoration in Proof, restored reading followed in *Works* (1833) and Prothero.

111. *Coleridge . . . Year."* In Nov. 1797 Coleridge was engaged to write verses or political essays for the *Morning Post* which he proceeded to do at irregular intervals until the autumn of 1803 when the paper closed down. In the 1790s, Coleridge had been an admirer of Napoleon; but in the *Morning Post* his attacks on and allusions to him became progressively more virulent. Although he did not coin the nickname 'Corsican', he first used it in the *Morning Post* of 9 Oct. 1802, and the terms 'upstart Corsican' and 'low-born Corsican' in the *Morning Post* of, respectively, 4 and 9 Nov. 1802. See David V. Erdman (ed.), *Essays on His own Times*, 3 vols. (1978), vol. i, pp. lix–lx, 355, 386, 399. His poem 'Fire, Famine, and Slaughter. A War Eclogue', was first published in the *Morning Post* of 8 Jan. 1798; his 'Ode to the Departing Year', in the *Cambridge Intelligencer* on 31 Dec. 1796. In his 'Argument' to the latter he stated: 'The second Epode prophesies, in anguish of spirit, the downfall of this country.'

112. *by the . . . Poets.* This is a rather curious and misleading assertion. Neither the *Edinburgh Review* nor *Blackwood's Edinburgh Magazine* expressed any antipathy to Pope. Indeed, quite the contrary. For instance, in a review of Bowles's *The Invariable Principles of Poetry* (1819) in *Blackwood's Edinburgh Magazine* (vol. v, no. xxviii (July 1819), p. 387), Pope's genius was referred to as that 'of a poet whom it has lately been the vulgar fashion to decry'. And in a review of Spence's *Anecdotes* (1820) in the *Edinburgh Review* (vol. xxxiii, no. lxvi (May 1820), p. 314), the reviewer wrote:

In reading any such account of Pope's opinions, it is scarcely necessary to remark, that nothing can shake our opinion of him as an author. He is certainly one of the fixed stars in the firmament of English literature; and what he has *written* is so complete, so decisive, and so unrivalled in itself, as to be proof against any report of what he might say or think in other respects. But, fortunately, there is little in the account here given to disturb our settled idea of him.

113. *I would ... too*). In Proof, *Works* (1833), and Prothero 'too' is silently corrected to 'to'. B was fond of exploiting this fate of poor publications (see, for instance, *BLJ* viii. 12, and *CPW* i. 441; v. 683). There is also a covert allusion here to Pope's *The First Epistle of the Second Book of Horace*, ll. 415–19. A 'tertian' is a fever occurring every other day.

114. *Hunt ... school.* Hunt depreciates Pope in n. 3 to *The Feast of the Poets* (1814), and in his prefaces to *The Story of Rimini* (1816), and *Foliage* (1818). He, and his 'school', were christened 'The Cockney School of Poetry' by John Gibson Lockhart, in an article in *Blackwood's Edinburgh Magazine*. See 'Letter to John Murray Esq[re.]', n. 224 below.

115. *"Gentlemen ... written.* B omitted closing quotation mark. Oliver Goldsmith, *The Citizen of the World*, 2 vols. (1765), Letter xxix (vol. i, p. 120).

116. *Would ... pedlar?* Wordsworth, *The Excursion* (1814), the ubiquitous hero of which is the Wanderer, an industrious, philosophical pedlar.

117. *had it ... English.* See B's deletion and addition in Proof; followed in *Works* (1833) and Prothero: both read 'had it not unfortunately been written in good English'.

118. *Moore ... School.* See n. 152 below.

119. *lecturers at Institutions.* William Hazlitt (1778–1830), whose *Lectures on the English Poets* (1818) were first delivered at the Surrey Institution, London, in the early part of 1818. B has in mind particularly Lecture iv, 'On Dryden and Pope' (pp. 135–67), in which Hazlitt discussed Pope as 'the poet, not of nature, but of art'.

120. *elderly Gentlemen ... imitate.* B refers to William Sotheby (1757–1833), who translated Wieland's *Oberon* (1798) and Virgil's *Georgics* (1800), and was the author of *Saul* (1807). See nn. 22 and 24 to 'Letter to the Editor of the *British Review*' above; and see 'Italy, or *not* Corinna', *post.* Cf. also *EBSR*, ll. 818 (*CPW* i. 255, 414–15); *Beppo*, 72–5 (*CPW* iv. 152–3, 489), and *DJ* I. 206 (*CPW* v. 75).

121. *Baronets ... poets.* Sir George Howland Beaumont (1753–1827), artist, patron of the arts, and friend of Wordsworth, to whom Wordsworth dedicated his *Poems* (1815). The frontispiece to the first edition of *Peter Bell* (1819) is engraved 'by J. C. Bromley, from a Picture by Sir George Beaumont Bar[t].'.

122. *noblemen ... Country.* Wordsworth's patron (who secured him his appointment as Distributor of Stamps), William Lowther, second Earl of Lonsdale

(1787–1872), to whom Wordsworth dedicated *The Excursion* (1814). B may also be making a quiet gibe here at Moore who frequented Bowood, the house of his patron Henry Petty-Fitzmaurice, third Marquis of Lansdowne (1780–1863).

123. *great body ... Blues.* The 'Blues' or 'Blue-stockings' were terms of contempt applied to ladies of learned or literary leanings. See, for instance, B's *Beppo*, 72, 74 (*CPW* iv. 151, 152), *DJ* I. 206 (*CPW* v. 75), and *The Blues* (1821).

124. *begun.* In Proof, *Works* (1833), and Prothero this reads 'began'.

125. *Epic poem ... enquire.* In his preface to *Joan of Arc, An Epic Poem* (1796), Southey claimed that he 'wrote the first three hundred lines' early in July 1793, and that the 'subject was resumed on the 13th of August, and the original poem in TWELVE books, finished in six weeks, from that time' (p. v). (The first and subsequent editions consist of ten books.) Wordsworth's *Peter Bell, A Tale in Verse* (1819) is dedicated to Southey as follows:

> The Tale of Peter Bell, which I now introduce to your notice, and to that of the public, has, in its Manuscript state, nearly survived its *minority*;—for it first saw the light in the summer of 1798. During this long interval, pains have been taken at different times to make the production less unworthy of a favourable reception; or, rather, to fit it for filling *permanently* a station, however humble, in the Literature of my Country. (p. iii)

126. *our very ... System.* See B's deletion of 'very' in Proof; followed in *Works* (1833) and Prothero. For B's sentiments here, cf. his letter to Murray of 11. Sept. 1820:

> There never was such a *Set* as your ragamuffins—(I mean *not* yours only but every body's) what with the Cockneys and the Lakers—and the *followers* of Scott and Moore and Byron—you are in the very uttermost decline and degradation of Literature.—I can't think of it without all the remorse of a murderer—I wish that Johnson were alive again to crush them. (*BLJ* vii. 175)

127. *Madoc ... language.* In his preface to *Madoc* (1805), Southey wrote: 'It assumes not the degraded title of Epic; and the question, therefore, is not whether the story is formed upon the rules of Aristotle, but whether it be adapted to the purposes of poetry' (p. ix). In his preface to *Thalaba the Destroyer* (2 vols., 1801), Southey said of the varied metre in which he chose to write the poem:

> Let me not be supposed to prefer the metre in which it is written, abstractedly considered, to the regular blank verse; the noblest measure, in my judgement, of which our admirable language is capable. For the following Poem I have preferred it, because it suits the varied subject; it is the *Arabesque* ornament of an Arabian tale.... One advantage this metre assuredly possesses; the dullest reader cannot distort it into discord: he may read it with a *prose mouth*, but its flow and fall will still be perceptible. Verse is not enough favoured by the English reader: perhaps this is owing to the obtrusiveness, the regular Jews-harp *twing-twang*, of what has been foolishly called heroic measure. (vol. i, pp. vii, viii–ix)

Southey's *The Curse of Kehama* was first published in 1810, and dedicated to Walter Savage Landor (1775–1864)p, whose *Gebir; A Poem, in Seven Books* was published in 1798.

128. *Hunt ... explain.* Echoing Wordsworth's notions of poetic language expressed in his preface to *Lyrical Ballads*, Leigh Hunt wrote in his preface to *The Story of Rimini* (1816):

With the endeavour to recur to a freer spirit of versification, I have joined one of still greater importance,—that of having a free and idiomatic cast of language. There is a cant of art as well as of nature, though the former is not so unpleasant as the latter, which affects non-affectation. But the proper language of poetry is in fact nothing different from that of real life, and depends for its dignity upon the strength and sentiment of what it speaks. It is only adding musical modulation to what a fine understanding might actually utter in the midst of its griefs or enjoyments. The poet therefore should do as Chaucer or Shakspeare did—not copy what is obsolete or peculiar in either, any more than they copied from their predecessors,—but use as much as possible an actual, existing language,—omitting of course *mere* vulgarisms and fugitive phrases, which are the cant of ordinary discourse, just as tragedy phrases, dead idioms, and exaggerations of dignity, are of the artificial style, and yeas, verilys, and exaggerations of simplicity, are of the natural. (pp. xv–xvi)

129. *Moore has ... lost.* See added emphasis in Proof uncorrected by B, and B's original MS reading. The added phrase was written by B over the dashes following the full stop after 'Ireland', and the compositor in Proof clearly mistook these dashes for emphases. *Works* (1833) and Prothero read as here. The elliptical 'Moore has' suggests that B might have gone on to refer in some way to their disagreement over the current state of poetry (see n. 152 below; see also n. 126 above; and cf. n. 87 above). For George Crabbe, Samuel Rogers, and Thomas Campbell, see n. 98 above.

130. *"It is ... England."* See the *Connoisseur* (no. 61, 27 Mar. 1755).

131. *Sir George Beaumont.* See B's deletion in Proof; not followed in *Works* (1833) or Prothero. See n. 121 above.

132. *nobler ... hostile.* In *Works* (1833) and Prothero 'nobler' reads 'noble'. The implication is that Southey is a dog.

133. *Nevertheless ... desirable.* Wordsworth discussed his notion of poetic fame in his 'Essay, Supplementary to the Preface' to *Poems* (1815).

134. *and after it.* See B's addition in Proof; adopted in *Works* (1833) and Prothero: both read 'and, not long after it'.

135. *Dante's ... Divina Commedia.* Dante Alighieri (1265–1321) was born in Florence from which he was banished in 1301. He eventually settled in Ravenna, where he died and was buried. The Florentines made every effort to secure his ashes, but in vain. See also in particular, *CHP* IV. 40, 56–9 (*CPW* ii. 137, 142–4, 238–9, 326–7), and *The Prophecy of Dante* (*CPW* iv. 211–39, 499–504).

136. *Petrarch ... Capitol.* Francesco Petrarca (1304–74) was crowned in the

Capitol at Rome on 8 Apr. 1341. See also in particular *CHP* IV. 30–2, 56–7 (*CPW* ii. 134–5, 142–3, 228–31, 241, 322–3).

137. *Ariosto ... Orlando Furioso.* Ludovico Ariosto (1474–1533), author of the great Italian epic *Orlando Furioso* (1516). The story went that as Ariosto was travelling from Ferrara to Garfagnani, he passed a band of outlaws led by the notorious 'public Robber', Filippo Pacchioni, resting by the roadside under a tree. Having enquired of Ariosto's servant who his master was, and finding him to be the great author of the *Furioso*, Pacchioni chased after him and begged his pardon for not saluting him with due honour and respect. The story is apocryphal, but see Girolamo Baruffaldi, *La Vita di M. Lodovico Ariosto* (Ferrara, 1807), pp. 187–8. See also J. Shield Nicholson, *The Life and Genius of Ariosto* (1914), p. 67. See also *CHP* IV. 40–1(*CPW* ii. 137–8, 233, 324).

138. *I would not... Smugglers.* Wordsworth's *The Waggoner: A Poem* (1819) was advertised in the poetry section of the *Quarterly Review*, vol. xxi, no. xlii (Apr. 1819), p. 564. Earlier in the same list, *The Smugglers, A Tale, descriptive of the Sea-Coast Manners of Scotland* (no name) was also advertised. B may well have taken this to be Wordsworth's production (the title has a Wordsworthian ring to it); or he may merely be poking fun at Wordsworth's usual selection of poetical personae.

139. *Tasso... death.* Torquato Tasso (1544–95), author of the great Italian epic *Gerusalemme Liberata* (1581), which was heavily criticized by the Accademia della Crusca (founded in Florence in 1582 as the custodian of linguistic propriety), and led to a literary feud between his supporters and the followers of Ariosto. Tasso died before his prospective coronation in the Capitol which had been planned at the request of Pope Clement VIII. See also *CHP* IV. 35–9 (*CPW* ii. 136–7, 231–3, 323–5) and *The Lament of Tasso* (*CPW* iv. 116–24, 478–80).

140. *language.* See B's addition in Proof; adopted in *Works* (1833) and Prothero: both read 'language, the Italian'.

141. *Jonson.* See the reading of 'Johnson' in Proof uncorrected by B; not followed in *Works* (1833) or Prothero.

142. *Gray's elegy... Elegy.* B reflects the standard reception of Gray's *Odes* and *Elegy*, which were discussed, for instance, very much along these lines by Samuel Johnson in his life of Gray. See *Lives of the English Poets* iii. 433–42.

143. *Milton's politics... cotemporaries.* After the execution of Charles I in 1649, Milton was appointed Latin Secretary to the Council of State under Cromwell, which post he held until the Restoration in 1660, when he was arrested and deprived of most of his fortune. He was a fervid republican, and wrote numerous pamphlets against episcopacy. Dryden's laudatory 'epigram' is entitled 'Under Mr. Milton's Picture, Before His Paradise Lost'. Of the sale of *Paradise Lost* (first published in 1667), Johnson, to whom B is covertly alluding here, wrote:

> The sale of thirteen hundred copies in two years, in opposition to so much recent enmity and to a style of versification new to all and disgusting to many, was an uncommon example of the prevalence of genius. The demand did not immediately increase; for many more readers than were supplied at first the nation did not afford. Only three thousand were sold in eleven years; for it forced its way without assistance: its admirers did not dare to publish their opinion, and the opportunities now given of attracting notice by advertisements were then very few. (*Lives of the English Poets* i. 144)

See also following n. 144.

144. *I will venture . . . Wordsworth.* In his 'Essay, Supplementary to the Preface' of *Poems* (1815), Wordsworth dismissed Johnson's argument concerning the sale of *Paradise Lost* (see foregoing n. 143), and claimed that the slow progress of Milton's fame was proof of the lack of immediate popularity which works of genius were fated to suffer.

145. *Darwin . . . ascension.* For Darwin, see n. 99 above. Anna Seward (1747–1809), savant and poet, author of *Louisa. A Poetical Novel, in Four Epistles* (1782) and *Original Sonnets* (1799), whose *Poetical Works* were edited with a Memoir by Walter Scott (3 vols., 1810). Barbara Hoole (afterwards Hofland) (1770–1844), poet and novelist, author of *Poems* (1805), and numerous novels such as *The History of an Officer's Widow and her Young Family* (1809) and *The Son of a Genius* (1812). Richard Hole (1746–1803), antiquary and poet, author of *Ode to Imagination* (1772), and *Arthur, or the Northern Enchantment* (1789). The Revd Charles Hoyle (1773–1848), author of *Moses Viewing the Promised Land* (1804), and *Paul and Barnabus at Lystra* (1806); see also *EBSR*, l. 966, and B's note thereto (*CPW* i. 259, 416–17). For William Hayley (see B's erasure in MS), see n. 98 above.

146. *and his . . . Bedlam.* B wittily parodies Wordsworth's quotation of Milton's 'still govern thou my Song, / *Urania*, and fit audience find, though few' (*Paradise Lost* vii. 30–1), which appears in the concluding passage of his unpublished poem *The Recluse*, appended to the preface to *The Excursion* (1814). The relevant lines run: '. . . the law supreme / Of that Intelligence which governs all— / I sing:—"fit audience let me find though few!"' (ll. 21–3). Interestingly enough, in an article on 'The Cockney School of Poetry' in *Blackwood's Edinburgh Magazine* (vol. v, no. xxv (Apr. 1819), p. 97), John Gibson Lockhart had also exploited Wordsworth's reference to Milton: 'Mr Wordsworth may perhaps look very long before he finds fit audience; but when he does find them, there is no question they must be "few".'

147. *me.* See B's deletion in Proof; followed in *Works* (1833) and Prothero.

148. *possessing too.* See B's addition in Proof; adopted in *Works* (1833) and Prothero: both read 'possessing, or having possessed too'.

149. *"of filling . . . Country."* See n. 125 above.

150. *But I lived.* See B's addition in Proof; adopted in *Works* (1833) and Prothero: both read, 'But I have lived'.

151. *passion it is true ... Nature.* An 'Irishism' is a seeming paradox, or an illogical statement. For some of B's numerous references to poetry as passion, see for instance *BLJ* iii. 179, 184; v. 157; vii. 132; viii. 146. See also *DJ* IV. 106 (*CPW* v. 237). For B's writing from 'experience', see, e.g. *BLJ* v. 14.

152. *"we are ... Campbell."* B must have said this to Moore during his visit to B of 7–11 Oct. 1819. Otherwise, see B's letter to Moore of 2 Feb. 1818 (*BLJ* vi. 10). In his life of B, Moore appended the following note to this passage:

> I certainly ventured to differ from the judgment of my noble friend, no less in his attempts to depreciate that peculiar walk of the art in which he himself so grandly trod, than in the inconsistency of which I thought him guilty, in condemning all those who stood up for particular 'schools' of poetry, and yet, at the same time, maintaining so exclusive a theory of the art himself. (Moore ii. 369n.–370n.)

And he then cited no. 66 of B's 'Detached Thoughts' (1821–1822):

> One of my notions different from those of my contemporaries, is, that the present is not a high age of English Poetry——there are *more* poets (soi-disant) than ever there were and proportionally *less* poetry.——This *thesis*—I have maintained for some years—but strange to say—it meeteth not with favour with my brethren of the Shell—even Moore shakes his head—& firmly believe[s] that it is the grand Era of British Poesy.—— (*BLJ* ix. 35)

B had in fact aired this view much earlier. In a letter to Murray of 15 Sept. 1817, he wrote:

> With regard to poetry in general I am convinced the more I think of it—that he [Moore] and *all* of us—Scott—Southey—Wordsworth—Moore—Campbell—I—are all in the wrong—one as much as another—that we are upon a wrong revolutionary poetical system—or systems—not worth a damn in itself—& from which none but Rogers and Crabbe are free—and that the present & next generations will finally be of this opinion.—I am the more confirmed in this—by having lately gone over some of our Classics—particularly *Pope*—whom I tried in this way—I took Moore's poems & my own & some others—& went over them side by side with Pope's—and I was really astonished (I ought not to have been so) and mortified—at the ineffable distance in point of sense—harmony—effect—and even *Imagination* Passion—& *Invention*—between the little Queen Anne's Man—& us of the lower Empire—depend upon it [it] is all Horace then, and Claudian now among us—and if I had to begin again—I would model myself accordingly— (*BLJ* v. 265)

See also n. 161 below.

153. *what was right.* See B's substitution in Proof; adopted in *Works* (1833) and Prothero: both read 'what I think right'.

154. *Epistle ... Abelard?* Prothero misreads this as 'epistle to Eloisa from Abelard'.

155. *I have not ... Humour.* See also reading in Proof, uncorrected by B; followed in *Works* (1833) and Prothero: both read 'nor the Fudge Family'. B's distinction here between 'Wit' and 'Humour' is Augustan; the former is the apt association of thought and expression, best expressed perhaps by Pope in *An Essay on Criticism*: 'True wit is Nature to advantage dress'd; / What oft was

thought, but ne'er so well express'd' (ll. 297–8). 'Thomas Brown the younger' was the pseudonym of Moore, who published *The Fudge Family in Paris, Edited by Thomas Brown, the Younger*, in 1818. 'Whistlecraft' was the pseudonym of John Hookham Frere (1769–1846) whose *Prospectus and Specimen of an Intended National Work*, by William and Robert Whistlecraft (1817) provided the model for B's *Beppo* and *Don Juan.* See *CPW* iv. 482–3, 485; v. 667.

156. *and Crabbe.* See B's substitution in Proof; adopted in *Works* (1833) and Prothero.

157. *a heroic.* See B's correction in Proof; followed in *Works* (1833) and Prothero.

158. *proper.* See B's substitution in Proof; adopted in *Works* (1833) and Prothero.

159. *excellencies.* See reading in Proof, and B's correction; Proof followed in *Works* (1833) and Prothero. (B's spelling here was in fact an acceptable variant at the time; see *OED.*)

160. *We are . . . no poet.* See n. 96 above.

161. *set down . . . find them?* The character of Sporus (Lord Hervey (1696–1743)) was attacked by Pope in his *Epistle to Dr. Arbuthnot*, ll. 305–33. In a letter to Murray of Mar. 1821, B goes through these very lines (just as he suggests others should do here), noting their '*imagery*', '*variety*', '*poetry*', and '*imagination*' (*BLJ* viii. 93–4).

162. *They were ... literary treason.* The rejection of formal language and 'artificial' taste, as exemplified by, for instance, Dryden and Pope, and the French critics Boileau, D'Aubignac, Dacier, and Rapin, and a return to what they regarded as the natural language and genuine English taste of Chaucer, Spenser, Sidney, and Shakespeare, are the driving principles behind the literary criticism of Warton, Wordsworth, Coleridge, and Hazlitt, pursued by such of the younger generation as Hunt and, most notably, Keats. See nn. 84, 96, 114, 119, 128 above.

163. *"prevail . . . rhymer".* Discussing the merits of rhyme in his life of Milton, Johnson concluded: 'But whatever be the advantage of rhyme I cannot prevail on myself to wish that Milton had been a rhymer, for I cannot wish his work to be other than it is; yet like other heroes he is to be admired rather than imitated. He that thinks himself capable of astonishing may write blank verse, but those that hope only to please must condescend to rhyme'(*Lives of the English Poets* i. 194).

164. *The Opinions . . . decry.* Johnson was one of Wordsworth's particular *bêtes noires* in his preface to *Lyrical Ballads* (1800 and 1802), and in his 'Essay, Supplementary to the Preface' to *Poems* (1815). (See n. 144 above.)

165. *I am not . . . language.* Cf. B's preface to *The Prophecy of Dante* (1819) (*CPW* iv. 214–15, 500).

166. *The Seasons . . . composition.* James Thomson (1700–48), author of *The Seasons* (1726–30), written in blank verse, and of *The Castle of Indolence* (1748), written in Spenserian stanzas. For Southey's prefatory remarks to *Joan of Arc, An Epic Poem* (1796), see n. 125 above; for his *Madoc* (1805) (see B's erasure in MS), see n. 127 above.

167. *I recommend . . . Southey.* Southey published a number of odes on great national events between 1814 and 1820 in his capacity of Poet Laureate; such as 'Ode, Written during the Negociations with Buonaparte, in January, 1814', 'Ode on the Death of Queen Charlotte' (1818), and 'Ode for St George's Day' (1820). He was, however, the first Poet Laureate to be excused from writing the obligatory birthday and New Year odes—a practice followed by subsequent Poet Laureates. Dryden's great ode, *Alexander's Feast; or, The Power of Music; An Ode in Honour of St. Cecilia's Day*, was first published in 1697. B recommends readers to read the odes of Southey *before* that of Dryden, because having read the latter's they will hardly desire, in his view, to return to the former's.

168. *To the . . . day.* Echoes *The Two Gentlemen of Verona* III. ii. 72.

169. *John Dryden . . . Twickenham.* Dryden was admitted to B's old College, Trinity College, Cambridge, on 18 May 1650, and matriculated less than two months later on 6 July. The 'little Nightingale' was the affectionate sobriquet of Pope. In his beautiful description of Pope, Owen Ruffhead wrote:

> As to his person, it is well known that he was low in stature; and of a diminutive and mishapen [*sic*] figure, which no one ridiculed more pleasantly than himself. Nevertheless, his countenance reflected the image of his mind. His eye in particular was remarkably fine, sharp and piercing: there was something in short in the air of his countenance altogether, which seemed to bespeak strong sense and acute penetration, tempered with benevolence and politeness. This prepossession in his favour grew stronger when he spoke. His voice, even in common discourse, was so naturally musical, that he was called the *Little Nightingale* and all who were acquainted with him, acknowledged that his appearance and address were perfectly engaging.

And, in a footnote to '*Little Nightingale*', Ruffhead added: 'Our author likewise had naturally a very fine ear; by the help of which, though he never learnt music, yet he generally judged right of the most celebrated compositions' (Owen Ruffhead, *The Life of Alexander Pope* (1769), pp. 475–6 and n.).

170. *page.* See reading in Proof, unaltered by B; followed in *Works* (1833) and Prothero.

171. *"It is . . . reflection.* B omits closing quotation marks. B cites verbatim (though adding his own emphases) the note in his friend Francis Hodgson's *The Friends: A Poem* (1818), pp. 181–2.

172. *young Person.* This MS note is written along the bottom margin of pp. 56–9 of Proof: it is set as a footnote to the text in *Works* (1833) and Prothero. The phrase 'fantastic fopperies' (in line 32) echoes Johnson's 'fantastick foppery' in his life of Gray (*Lives of the English Poets* iii. 433). Johnson defines 'foppery' as

'affectation of show or importance; showy folly' (ibid. 433n.). For B's comments in this note, cf. *BLJ* viii. 102–4, 162–3. John Keats died at Rome on 23 Feb. 1821. The devastating review of his *Endymion* (1818) was written by John Wilson Croker and appeared in the *Quarterly Review*, vol. xix, no. xxxvii (Apr. 1818), art. ix, pp. 204–8 (cf. *DJ* XI. 60 (*CPW* v. 483), and '[John Keats]'). His fragment of *Hyperion* (bks. i, ii, iii) was published in *Lamia, Isabella, The Eve of St Agnes, and other Poems* (1820). For B's other opinions of Keats and his poetry, see *BLJ* vii. 200–1, 202, 217, 225, 229. For a recent appraisal of B's criticisms of Keats, see Joel A. Dando, 'Byron's Epistolary Criticism of Keats', *Byron Journal*, xviii (1990), 61–9.

173. *"—But . . . land.* Closing quotation marks omitted by B who cites (adding his own emphases) *Sleep and Poetry* (1817), ll. 193–206, 181–3. The two remarks respecting '*School*' and '*Scism*' are written beside those two words in the MS. They are set as footnotes to the text in *Works* (1833) and Prothero. In the first, B is punning on 'grammar' as the denomination of a type of school (such as his old school, Aberdeen Grammar School), and 'grammar' in its linguistic sense which, he implies, Keats lacks. In the second, he draws attention to the misspelling of 'scism', which reads as such in the first edition of Keats's poem (though later editions read 'schism'). See also the readings in Proof of '*chip*' and '*decrepit*' unaltered by B; followed in *Works* (1833) and Prothero. However, B's MS readings ('*clip*' and '*decrepid*') correctly follow the orthography of Keats's first and subsequent editions.

174. *Further on we have.* The MS of the passage which follows here ('Further on we have . . . of example.——') is bound in with the MSS of 'The Bowles/Pope Controversy' (see general note above) and bears the following superscription by B: 'Additions to the passages from Keats.' It was first published in Prothero (v. 588n.–589n.), where it was erroneously appended as a note to a reference to Keats ('a M[r] John Ketch . . . author') in the 'Addenda' to the 'Letter to John Murray Esq[re.]' (see *post*). The present is its proper location.

175. *"The hearty grasp . . . him: &c.* Closing quotation marks omitted by B in all three verse quotations. B cites verbatim (adding his own emphases) *Sleep and Poetry*, ll. 319–27, 331–2, 337–8, 347–50.

176. *mutual.* The MS of the note appended here is bound in with Proof (see general note above), and bears the following superscription by B: 'Append these as Notes to the passage from *Keat's* [*sic*] poetry quoted in the ⟨"⟩last pages of "the Observations["] sent by last post.——B'. It is appended as a note to B's quotation of *Sleep and Poetry*, ll. 181–3 in Proof, *Works* (1833), and Prothero. See n. 173 above.

177. *"Envy . . . vain.* B omits closing quotation marks. *Windsor Forest* (partly written, 1704; pub. 1713), ll. 419–22.

178. *Ah! . . . gold. Windsor Forest*, ll. 115–18.

179. *Round . . . quires. Windsor Forest*, ll. 69–72.

180. *Hail . . . days. Essay on Criticism* (written 1709; pub. 1711), l. 189. To this line B appends the following direction: 'Dear Murray, I am fearful of *misquoting*; ⟨add⟩ but do you add *the rest* of the passage it is ⟨fr⟩ in the "Essay on Criticism"—I have not the Book by me'. Accordingly this example runs as follows in Proof (so also in *Works* (1833) and Prothero):

Hail, bards triumphant! born in happier days;
Immortal heirs of universal praise!
Whose honours with increase of ages grow,
As streams roll down, enlarging as they flow;
Nations unborn your mighty names shall sound,
And worlds applaud that must not yet be found!
O may some spark of your celestial fire,
The last, the meanest, of your sons inspire,
(That, on weak wings, from far pursues your flights;
Glow while he reads, but trembles as he writes,)
To teach vain wits a science little known,
T'admire superior sense, and doubt their own!
(*Essay on Criticism*, ll. 189–200)

181. *Amphion . . . wall. The Temple of Fame* (written 1711; pub. 1715), ll. 85–8.

182. *So . . . years. The Temple of Fame*, ll. 53–60.

183. *Thus . . . regular. Essay on Criticism*, ll. 247–52.

184. *But like . . . Poetry.* Luke Milbourne (1649–1720), poet, critic, and clergyman, criticized Dryden's translation of Virgil in his *Notes on Dryden's Virgil* (1698). In his own note to *The Dunciad* ii. 325, Pope wrote: '*Luke Milbourn* a Clergyman, the fairest of Criticks; who when he wrote against Mr. *Dryden's Virgil*, did him justice, in printing at the same time his own translations of him, which were intolerable' (*The Poems of Alexander Pope*, vol. v, *The Dunciad*, ed. James Sutherland (1963), p. 141 n.).

185. *let those . . . Absurdity.* The principal target of B's attack here is Hunt. (See, for example, B's erasure in MS between 'a' and 'a tadpole' in l. 24.) For Moloch, see Leviticus 18: 21, and II Kings 23: 10, and also *Paradise Lost* i. 392–405. The name of Moloch is synonymous with the idea of bloodthirsty sacrifice.

186. *"Art . . . Poetry".* B alludes to Pope's *Peri Bathous: Of the Art of Sinking in Poetry*, which was first published in *Miscellanies in Prose and Verse*, 4 vols. (1727), iv. 5–92.

187. *Vida . . . example.* Here the inserted 'Additions to the passages from Keats' end (see n. 174 above). Marco Girolamo Vida (*c.*1485–1566), Italian scholar, Latin poet, member of the papal court and Bishop of Alba, was author of *De Arte Poetica* (1527) and of *Christias* (1535), an epic poem in Virgilian style on the life of Christ. He was praised by Pope in the *Essay on Criticism*, ll. 704–8.

188. *"If Pope . . . found?"* In his life of Pope, Johnson dismissed the question,

'Whether Pope was a poet?', by asking in return, 'If Pope be not a poet, where is poetry to be found?' (*Lives of the English Poets* iii. 251).

189. *Mr K. . . . twenty two. Works* (1833) and Prothero read 'Mr. Keats'. In the preface to his *Works* (1717), Pope wrote: 'there are very few things in this collection which were not written under the age of five and twenty'. (See also nn. 177, 180, 181, above.)

190. *Matthias . . . Merivale.* Thomas James Mathias (?1754–1835), satirist and Italian scholar and author of *The Pursuits of Literature* (1794–7). (See also n. 25 to B's review of Spenser's *Poems* (1812) above.) For Hayley, see n. 98 above. Thomas Brown (1778–1820), metaphysician and Professor of Moral Philosophy at Edinburgh University, was the author of *The Paradise of Coquettes, A Poem. In Nine Parts* (1814). The Revd George Richards (1767–1837), poet and author of *The Aboriginal Britons: A Poem* (1791) which B praises in *EBSR*, ll. 985–90 (*CPW* i. 260, 417). The Revd Reginald Heber (1783–1826), poet, contributor to the *Quarterly Review*, and later (1822) Bishop of Calcutta, author of the popular poem *Palestine* (1807) and of such well-known hymns as 'From Greenland's icy mountains' and 'Holy, Holy, Holy, Lord God Almighty' published in *Hymns* (1812). The Revd Francis Wrangham (1769–1842), poet and classical scholar, author of *The Death of Saul and Jonathan* (1813), editor of the John and William Langhorne translation of *Plutarch's Lives* (1808) and translator of *A Few Sonnets from Petrarch* (1817) (see *BLJ* iv. 128–9). For Hodgson, see n. 171 above. The Revd Robert Bland (?1779–1825), poet, classical scholar, and assistant master at Harrow, author of *Translations, Chiefly from the Greek Anthology, with Tales and Miscellaneous Poems* (1806), and of *The Four Slaves of Cythera* (1809). John Herman Merivale (1779–1844), scholar, poet, and contributor to the *Quarterly Review*, author of *Orlando in Roncesvalles* (1814). Bland and Merivale collaborated in *A Collection of the most Beautiful Poems of the Minor Poets of Greece* (1813) and in *Collections from the Greek Anthology and from the Pastoral, Elegiac and Dramatic Poets of Greece* (1813), and both were friends of Hodgson and B. See, for example, *BLJ* ii. 112, 129–30, 132; iii. 7; iv. 12, 293, 301. See also *EBSR*, ll. 881–90 (*CPW* i. 257, 415).

191. *"the race . . . Strong".* Ecclesiastes 9: 11.

192. *"like . . . many".* Mark 5: 9.

193. *Sotheby . . . models.* See also B's substitution in Proof, adopted in *Works* (1833) and Prothero. For Sotheby, see n. 120 above.

194. *Scott . . . Francis.* Margaret Holford (1778–1852), poet and author of *Wallace, or the Fight of Falkirk* (1809), *Poems* (1811), *Margaret of Anjou* (1816), and *Warbeck of Wolfstein* (1820). Mary Russell Mitford (1787–1855), author, contributed a series of essays entitled 'Our Village, Sketches of Rural Life, Character, and Scenery' to the *Lady's Magazine* from 1819 onwards, which were hugely successful and were later collected and published in five volumes (1824–32). She also published *Poems* (1810), *Christina, the Maid of the South Seas*

(1811), *Watlington Hill* (1812), and *Narrative Poems on the Female Character, in the Various Relations of Human Life* (1813). Eliza Francis (dates unknown), poet, author of *The Rival Roses* (1813) and *Sir Wilibert de Waverley: or, the Bridal Eve* (1815).

195. *none . . . Shepherd.* See also B's addition in Proof; adopted in *Works* (1833) and Prothero. James Hogg (1770–1835), 'the Ettrick Shepherd', poet, began life as a shepherd in Ettrick, Scotland. His poetical talents were discovered by Scott, for whom he furnished much material for Scott's *Border Minstrelsy* (3 vols., 1802–3). His own works include *The Forest Minstrel* (1810), *The Queen's Wake* (1813), and *Pilgrims of the Sun* (1815). He is perhaps best known for *The Confessions of a Justified Sinner* (1824). See also nn. 203 and 208 below.

196. *until . . . composition.* See also reading in Proof, unaltered by B; followed in *Works* (1833) and Prothero. Scott's *The Bridal of Triermain, or The Vale of St John*, was published anonymously in Mar. 1813; his *Harold the Dauntless; A Poem, in Six Cantos. By the Author of "The Bridal of Triermain"*, was published in 1817. Scott later explained that he had written the former at the request of his friend, William Erskine, 'on the condition that he should make no serious effort to disown the composition, if report should lay it at his door'. The 'train easily caught, and two large editions were sold', before Scott owned to being its author. See J. Logie Robertson (ed.), *The Poetical Works of Sir Walter Scott* (1909), p. 585.

197. *t'other fellow.* i.e. Wordsworth.

198. *"City . . . Plague."* See n. 202 below.

199. *"because . . . Just".* See n. 30 above.

200. *"Will . . . foes."* Pope, *Essay on Man* iv. 388.

201. *humbly.* See reading in Proof, uncorrected by B; followed in *Works* (1833) and Prothero.

202. *John Wilson . . . productions.* John Wilson (1785–1854), 'Christopher North', poet, editor of *Blackwood's Edinburgh Magazine*, elected Professor of Moral Philosophy at Edinburgh University in 1820, was author of *The Isle of Palms* (1812) and of *The City of the Plague* (1816). See also nn. 205 and 208 below. However, B was mistaken in attributing the *Blackwood's* article to him (see general note above). In a note to the sentence 'I like & admire Wilson—and *he* should not have indulged himself in such outrageous license' in B's letter to Murray of 10 Dec. 1819 (*BLJ* vi. 257), Moore wrote:

> This is one of the many mistakes into which his distance from the scene of literary operations led him. The gentleman to whom the hostile article in the Magazine is here attributed, has never, either then or since, written upon the subject of the noble poet's character or genius, without giving vent to a feeling of admiration as enthusiastic as it is always eloquently and powerfully expressed. (Moore ii. 292 n.)

203. *M^r. J. Wilson . . . it."* 'M^r. J. Wilson' reads 'Mr. John Wilson' in *Works* (1833)

and Prothero. See B's correction of '1815' to '1814' in Proof; followed in *Works* (1833) and Prothero. See reading of 'he'd' in Proof, unaltered by B; followed in *Works* (1833) and Prothero. In Prothero 'd—d' reads 'damned'; Proof and *Works* (1833) follow MS. Hogg's unpublished letter to B is in the Bodleian Library (Dep. Lovelace Byron 155, ff. 51–2). It is dated 13 Sept. 1814 from Westmorland, to where he had just travelled from Edinburgh (accompanied by Wordsworth): 'your letter was so perfectly true and accorded so exactly with what I had always been saying to them [the 'pond' poets: Wordsworth, Southey, Coleridge] d—n me if I could resist the fun of showing them it—they were in a terrible rage Wilson who is one of the most noble fellows in existence swore terribly about the *fishing* and challenges you fairly to a trial but after a previous perusal of *Wordsworth's Excursion* together and no little laughter and some parodying he has with your assistance fairly confessed to me yesterday that he now holds the *school* in utter contempt.' And he added the postscript: 'I have only showed the letter to Wilson who is honour itself.' This last statement cannot be wholly true. For Henry Crabb Robinson recorded in his diary on 1 Dec. 1816: 'Cargill was telling me the other day that in a letter written by Lord Byron to Hogg the Ettrick Shepherd, in his rattling way he wrote: "Wordsworth—stupendous genius! damned fool! These poets run about their ponds though they cannot fish. I am told there is not one who can angle—damned fools!"' (*Henry Crabb Robinson on Books and their Writers*, ed. Edith J. Morley, 3 vols. (1938), i. 199; see also *Diary, Reminiscences, and Correspondence of Henry Crabb Robinson*, ed. Thomas Saddler, 2 vols. (3rd edn. 1872), i. 286). The fragment of B's letter quoted here (which is all that remains of it) is printed from the first source cited above in *BLJ* v. 13 where it is incorrectly dated 1816. It should be dated Aug.–Sept. 1814, which is when the letter itself must have been written. See B's letters to Murray of 27 Aug. and 2 Sept. 1814 (*BLJ* iv. 162, 164). For earlier outspoken remarks to Hogg about Wordsworth, Southey, and Coleridge (though without the angling imagery), see B's letter to him of 24 Mar. 1814 (*BLJ* iv. 85).

204. *S. W. and C.* These read 'Southey, Wordsworth, and Coleridge' in *Works* (1833) and Prothero.

205. *And in return . . . Edinburgh?* In *Works* (1833) there is a note to this passage: 'The allusion here is to some now forgotten calumnies which had been circulated by the radical press, at the time when Mr. Wilson was a candidate for the Chair of Moral Philosophy in the University of Edinburgh' (*Works* (1833), xvii. 247 n.).

206. *If it were . . . nature.* See also reading in Proof, unaltered by B; followed in *Works* (1833) and Prothero. Although there were many such parodies in circulation at the time, William Hone and Richard Carlile were responsible for publishing numerous political squibs and satires couched in mock liturgical or biblical language (e.g. *A Political Litany* [Richard Carlile] (1817)). But B may have had in mind in particular here *The Order for the Administration*

of the Loaves and Fishes; or, The Communion of Corruption's Host [Richard Carlile] (1817), which contains a long parody of the Ten Commandments, and also 'The Creed for the use of Corruption's Host' which runs as follows (p. 8):

> I believe in Lord Castlereagh, the supreme director of all our affairs, maker of treaties for all nations, for the benefit of none; and in the excellence of his features, fundamental and unfundamental.
>
> And in one George Canning, of doubtful origin, the tool and puppet of Lord Castlereagh, who, together with Lord Castlereagh, falling out about their share of the public plunder, went into a certain field to fight with swords and pistols, unfortunately without any intent to kill, who came out again without injury, to the great grief of all the People; who went on an embassy to the Court of Portugal, where there was no King, for the sole purpose of recovering the health of his son, at the expence of many thousands of pounds to the People: he rose again to the Cabinet, from whence he judgeth the Reformers; and his impudence shall have no end.
>
> And I believe in the Prince Regent, Lord and Giver of Places, who, together with the Ministers, we should worship and glorify, who speaketh by Proclamations, Commissioners, and Green Bags; I believe in the stability of the funds, I look not for a remission of taxes, no, not till the Resurrection of the Dead. And I look not for a better Government in the world to come. Amen.

Benjamin Franklin (1706–90), American politician and diplomat, wrote 'A Parable against Persecution, in Imitation of Scripture Language' (see *The Works of the late Dr. Benjamin Franklin*, 2 vols. (1812), ii. 226–8. On p. 228 of this edition there is a note to the following effect: 'Dr Franklin, it is said, has often imposed this parable upon his friends and acquaintance, as part of a chapter of Genesis.')

207. *very . . . Don Juan?* See also reading in Proof, uncorrected by B; followed in *Works* (1833) and Prothero. B alludes in particular to the parody of the Ten Commandments in *DJ* I. 205–6 (*CPW* v. 74–5, 681), and his definition of a 'parody' in this passage is clearly an implicit defence of his own in those stanzas.

208. *Did . . . Magazine?* The phrase 'parody profane' no doubt echoes intentionally the phrase 'jests profane', which occurs in stanza 2 of 'Don Juan Unread', published in *Blackwood's Edinburgh Magazine* (vol. vi, no. xxxii (Nov. 1819), pp. 194–5). However, in an otherwise favourable review of *DJ* I and II in the *London Literary Gazette* (no. 130, 17 July 1819), the reviewer complained: 'But the most indefensible of these lapses is a profane parody, in which some of our modern bards are *roasted*' (p. 450). Moreover, in *The Radical Triumvirate* (1820), B was accused of 'exciting jest by profane parodies' of biblical expressions (p. 37). The first number of *Blackwood's Edinburgh Magazine* (vol. i, no. i (Oct. 1817), pp. 89–96) printed a 'Translation from an Ancient Chaldee Manuscript', a brilliant parody of scriptural writing along the lines of Revelation, in which certain well-known figures of Edinburgh were satirized. The jest was further compounded by a prefatory note in which the MS was said to be 'preserved in the great Library of Paris (Salle 2d, No 53, B.A.M.M.), by a

gentleman whose attainments in Oriental Learning are well known to the Public' (p. 89: a 'bam' was slang for a hoax). It was the combined production of James Hogg, John Wilson, and John Gibson Lockhart.

209. *"crying... defections"*. B has taken a slight liberty here with the dying words of 'douce' David Deans in Walter Scott's *The Heart of Mid-Lothian*: 'He was heard, indeed, to mutter something about national defections, right-hand extremes, and left-hand fallings off' (*Novels and Tales* (1825), xiv. 26). (These phrases are Deans's 'signatures' throughout the novel.)

210. *M^r. J^no Wilson... done.* See reading in Proof, unaltered by B; followed in *Works* (1833) and Prothero. See also addition in Proof, unaltered by B; adopted in *Works* (1833) and Prothero.

THE BOWLES/POPE CONTROVERSY

Letter to John Murray Esqre. (1821)

Text: MS Murray, *Letter to **** ******, on the Rev. W. L. Bowles' Strictures on the Life and Writings of Pope.* By the Right Hon. Lord Byron (1821, 3rd edn.), and *BLJ* viii. First published, entitled as in the aforementioned 3rd edn., in 1821 (three editions, the first consisting of two issues). Thereafter, published from the 3rd edn. in *Works* (1832), vi. 346–81, 408–16. Thereafter published from *Works* (1832) collated with MS in Prothero v. 536–66.

B first intimated his intention to take part in this controversy after receiving the *Quarterly Review* (see below) from Murray on 4 Nov. 1820. Writing to Murray on that date he stated (*BLJ* vii. 217):

> I have read part of the Quarterly just arrived.—Mr. Bowles shall be answered—he is not *quite* correct in his statement about E[nglish] B[ards] & S[cotch] R[eviewers].——They Support Pope I see in the Quarterly—Let them Continue to do so—it is a Sin & a Shame and a *damnation*—to think that Pope!! should require it—but he does.——Those miserable mountebanks of the day—the poets—disgrace themselves—and deny God—in running down Pope—the most *faultless* of Poets, and almost of men.

He reiterated this intention to Murray again on 18 Nov., to Moore on 9 Dec., and to Hodgson on 22 Dec. 1820 (*BLJ* vii. 299, 245, 253 respectively). However, the impulse lapsed; and not until 5 Feb. 1821, while he was writing *Sardanapalus* and deeply involved with the Carbonari, did it revive. He recorded in his Ravenna Journal on that date (*BLJ* viii. 43): 'Read some of Bowles's dispute about Pope, with all the replies and rejoinders. Perceive that my name has been lugged into the controversy, but have not time to state what I know of the subject. On some "piping day of peace" it is probable that I may resume it.' Two days later, on 7 Feb., he commenced writing the letter, completing it on 10 Feb. and sending it to Murray on 12 Feb. (*BLJ* viii. 44, 76). On 12 and 16 Feb. he directed Murray to make two minor additions to the letter, one of which Murray adopted (*BLJ* viii. 77, 79; see nn. 13, 118 below). Again, on

26 Feb. he recorded in his Ravenna Journal that he had written 'two notes on the "Bowles and Pope" controversy and sent them off to Murray by the post' (*BLJ* viii. 50). These notes are those concerning 'A Seedsman's Catalogue' (which was adopted), and Lady Mary Wortley Montagu (see nn. 27, 162 below). In his letter to Murray of 26 Feb. enclosing these, he wrote (*BLJ* viii. 85):

> Over the *second Note* viz—the one on Lady M. Montague—I leave you a complete discretionary power of *omission altogether* or curtailment, as you please—since it may be scarcely chaste enough for the Canting prudery of the day.—The *first* note on a different subject you had better append to the letters. ——Let me know what your Utican Senate say, and acknowledge all the packets.

To this Murray replied on 20 Mar. 1821 (Samuel Smiles, *A Publisher and His Friends*, 2 vols. (1891), i. 420: 'The pamphlet on Bowles is deemed excellent, and is to be published on Saturday; the note on Lady M. W. Montagu, though also very good, Mr. Gifford recommends to be suppressed.' This then is how the 1st edn. (first issue) of this letter appeared when it was first published on Saturday 31 Mar. 1821, on which date John Cam Hobhouse recorded in his diary: 'Byron's letter about Bowles & the Pope controversy published—it is very good I think—' (Broughton Papers, BL Add. MS 56542, f. 13v; see also *Recollections* ii. 143).

On 9 Mar. B sent Murray a further addition to the letter, which was appended at the end of the second issue of the 1st edn. (*BLJ* viii. 90; see n. 94 below). Three days later, on 12 Mar., he sent Murray yet another '*addenda*' (first published in *Works* (1832)), and the following day or so requested him to make some alterations and additions to that '*addenda*' and to the letter, none of which was adopted (*BLJ* viii. 92–4; see nn. 113, 217, 254 and 255 below). At the same time he may also have sent the additional notes (of which no MS is extant), which were first published at the end of the 3rd edn. (see nn. 131, 191 below). Finally, on 8 May he sent Murray more 'additional notes', which were first published in Prothero (*BLJ* viii. 109; see n. 103 below).

The Bowles/Pope controversy created quite a stir in literary circles, and several leading poets and critics published letters and pamphlets contributing to the debate. A chronological list of publications is given at the end of the general note.

The origin of this controversy lay as far back as 1806 when William Lisle Bowles (for whom see below) published his somewhat unsympathetic ten-volume edition of *The Works of Alexander Pope.* In particular, Bowles censured Pope's moral character (vol. i, pp. xv–cxxxi) and depreciated Pope's poetical character (vol. x, pp. 363–80). The pertinent opening portion of his 'Concluding Observations' is given here (x. 363–65):

> I presume it will readily be granted, that 'all images drawn from what is beautiful or sublime in the works of NATURE, are more beautiful and sublime than any images drawn from ART;' and that they are therefore, *per se*, more poetical.

In like manner, those *Passions* of the human heart, which belong to Nature in general, are, *per se*, more adapted to the *higher species* of Poetry, than those which are derived from *incidental* and *transient* MANNERS. A description of a Forest is more *poetical*, than a description of a cultivated Garden: and the *Passions* which are pourtrayed in the Epistle of an Eloisa, render such a Poem more *poetical* (whatever might be the difference of merit in point of execution), *intrinsically* more *poetical*, than a Poem founded on the characters, incidents, and modes of *artificial life*; for instance, the Rape of the Lock.

If this be admitted, the rule by which we would estimate Pope's general poetical character would be obvious.

Let me not, however, be considered as thinking that the *subject alone* constitutes poetical excellency.—The *execution** is to be taken into consideration at the same time; for, with Lord Harvey, we might fall asleep over the '*Creation*' of Blackmore, but be alive to the touches of animation and satire in Boileau.

The *subject*, and the *execution*, therefore, are equally to be considered;—the one respecting the *Poetry*,—the other, the *art* and *powers* of the *Poet*. The *poetical subject*, and the *art* and *talents* of the Poet, should always be kept in mind; and I imagine it is for want of observing this rule, that so much has been said, and so little understood, of the real ground of Pope's character as a Poet.

If you say he is not one of the first Poets that England, and the polished literature of a polished æra can boast,

> Recte necne crocos floresque perambulat Atti
> Fabula si dubitem, clamant periisse pudorem
> Cuncti pene patres.

[Horace, *Epistles* II. i. 79–81: 'If I express any doubt as to whether Atta's play treads the stage successfully among the flowers and saffron, our elders exclaim almost in unison that modesty has vanished from amongst us.']

If you say, that he stands *poetically* pre-eminent, in the highest sense, you must deny the principles of Criticism, which I imagine will be acknowledged by all.

In speaking of the *poetical subject*, and the *powers of execution*; with regard to the *first*, Pope cannot be classed among the highest orders of Poets; with regard to the *second*, none ever was his *superior*.

* By *execution*, I mean not only the colours of expression, but the design, the contrast of light and shade, the masterly management, the judicious disposition, and, in short, every thing that gives to a great subject relief, interest, and animation.

Some little time after its publication Bowles's edition was very favourable reviewed in the *British Critic* (vol. xxxiv (Nov. 1809), art. i, pp. 433–42), which, with reference to the above passage, wrote of Bowles's ranking of Pope: 'He allows him to be at the very head of the class to which he belongs, but does not place him in the highest class. In this opinion we think the most judicious readers will agree with him' (p. 442). However, the edition was most unfavourably reviewed in the *Edinburgh Review* (vol. xi, no. xxii (Jan. 1808), art. ix, pp. 399–413), which, again with reference to the above passage, conceived that Bowles had failed in his judgement upon the merits of Pope, attributing the cause of this failure to 'principles of criticism by no means peculiar to himself, but which have obtained too great an influence over the public taste of our age' (p. 407). It then proceeded to state (p. 408):

Now, it appears to us, we confess, that Pope's, or any other man's character as a poet, must depend upon 'his art and powers' solely, and in no degree upon the subject he has selected, however judicious or otherwise that choice may be, as to the end of displaying his talents to advantage. We submit to Mr Bowles, whether he has not fallen into a puzzle of ideas, not uncommon, of confounding the pleasure which a poem produces in us, with the degree of genius required for its composition.

Elsewhere it criticized Bowles for having been 'studious in bringing forward and dwelling upon the blemishes of his author's disposition' (pp. 400–1). B himself, of course, savaged Bowles in *EBSR*, ll. 327–84 (*CPW* i. 239–41, 405–6).

However, it was not until 1819, when Thomas Campbell, the poet, published his seven-volume edition of *Specimens of the British Poets* that the controversy really took off. In his introductory 'Essay on English Poetry', again with reference to the above passage, Campbell wrote (i. 262–4):

I would beg leave to observe, in the first place, that the faculty by which a poet luminously describes objects of art, is essentially the same faculty, which enables him to be a faithful describer of simple nature; in the second place, that nature and art are to a greater degree relative terms in poetical description than is generally recollected; and, thirdly, that artificial objects and manners are of so much importance in fiction, as to make the exquisite description of them no less characteristic of genius than the description of simple physical appearances. The poet is 'creation's heir.' He deepens our social interest in existence. It is surely by the liveliness of the interest which he excites in existence, and not by the class of subjects which he chooses, that we most fairly appreciate the genius or the life of life which is in him. It is no irreverence to the external charms of nature to say, that they are not more important to a poet's study, than the manners and affections of his species. . . . Nature, in the wide and proper sense of the word, means life in all its circumstances—nature moral as well as external. As the subject of inspired fiction, nature includes artificial forms and manners.

And in the brief biography of Pope prefixed to the selection from his work, Campbell stated (v. 110):

The faults of Pope's private character have been industriously exposed by his latest editor and biographer, a gentleman whose talents and virtuous indignation were worthy of a better employment. In the moral portrait of Pope which he has drawn, all the agreeable traits of tender and faithful attachment in his nature have been thrown into the shade, while his deformities are brought out in the strongest, and sometimes exaggerated colours.

To this Bowles responded with *The Invariable Principles of Poetry* (1819). As may be seen from B's extensive quotations, and from the notes below, this work rehearses and expands Bowles's argument in the passage given above. The pamphlet was reviewed in the *Quarterly Review* by Isaac D'Israeli, who wrote (p. 407):

It is with pain we have so long witnessed the attacks on the moral and poetical character of this great poet by the last two of his editors. Warton, who first entered the list, though not unwilling to wound, exhibits occasionally some of the courtesy of the ancient chivalry; but his successor, the Rev. Mr. Bowles, possesses the contest *à l'outrance*, with the appearance, though assuredly not with the reality, of personal hostility. It had been more honourable in this gentleman, with his known prejudices against the class of poetry in which Pope will always remain unrivalled, to have declined the office of editor, than to attempt to spread among new generations of readers the most unfavourable and the most unjust impressions of the POET, and of the MAN.

And with reference to the above passage again, as requoted by Bowles in *The Invariable Principles*, D'Israeli went on to say (p. 410):

It is clear to us that a theory, which frequently admitting every thing the votary of Pope could desire to substantiate the high genius of his master, yet terminates in excluding the poet from 'the highest order of poets,' must involve some fallacy; and this we presume we have discovered in the absurd attempt to raise 'a criterion of poetical talents.'...

It has frequently been attempted to raise up such arbitrary standards and such narrowing theories of art; and these 'criterions' and 'invariable principles' have usually been drawn from the habitual practices and individual tastes of the framers; they are a sort of concealed egotism, a stratagem of self-love.

Bowles mistakenly understood this review to have been written by Octavius Gilchrist (for whom see below), and (despite Southey's warning in a letter to him of 16 Oct. 1820: 'Do not be hasty in your reply . . . you should be *certain* that Gilchrist is the writer, before you make the remotest allusion to him. I never heard him mentioned as having contributed any thing to the Quarterly Review' (Garland Greever, *A Wiltshire Parson and his Friends: The Correspondence of William Lisle Bowles* (1926), p. 120), replied, citing Gilchrist as his antagonist, with 'A Reply' and the hastily written *Second Reply*. This latter, which was privately printed and made its appearance before that of the former, Bowles sent to Murray on 22 Oct. with a letter apprizing him of his intentions:

I shall answer the whole [of the review in the *Quarterly Review*], with my own name, and do not fear to twist the author round my little finger, and make those interested in the success of the Review ashamed they admitted such paltry arguments and such disgraceful personal spite to a man who never offended them....

The same author wrote in the London Review, and attacked me with the same flippancy, ignorance, affectation, and stupidity.... That such a writer (for Nature never made two such in one age) should have been permitted [to] disgrace the Quarterly is a matter, not of exultation to me, but regret. (Greever, *Wiltshire Parson*, pp. 122–3)

Now Gilchrist had indeed alluded to Bowles in an unsigned review of Spence's *Anecdotes* (1820) in the *London Magazine* of Feb. 1820 as follows (pp. 193–4):

Pope's last editor says, 'he trembles for every character, when he hears any thing of Spence's Anecdotes.—Neither friend nor foe is spared.' [*The Works* ii. 417n.–418n.] This, if it were true, would prove the candour of the compiler; but it is a gross misrepresentation of a volume which the writer had not examined; and it would have been but kind if Mr. Bowles had reserved some of these amiable tremblings, for the reputation of an author, of whose works he had undertaken the revision, but whose character and writings he seizes every opportunity to degrade, by gross insinuations and flippant sarcasm. How different was the conduct of Spence, a man of refined taste, and very considerable literary attainments; who, admiring the writings of Pope, became desirous of personal acquaintance with that eminent man. Upon a more intimate knowledge, he found, like Thomson,

> Although not sweeter his own Homer sung,
> Still was his life the more delightful theme:
> [Thomson, *The Seasons*, 'Winter', ll. 553–4]

and the joint impression induced him to keep a daily record of whatever was remarkable in the poet's conversation, and that of his associates; as well as minutes of his manners and habits. These represent Pope in private life, as uniformly gentle, amiable, and warm in his friendships, and of moral habits unimpeached, and (as we believe) unimpeachable. These testimonies to the worth and virtue of the poet, not consorting with the purpose of Mr. Bowles, he has preferred the representations of Pope's enemies; and having, with an obliquity unexampled in an editor, resolved to asperse the moral reputation of his author, it was necessary that he should affect to sneer at the friendly representations of a chronicler, actuated by feelings so unlike his own. The general defamation of Pope's character, Mr. Bowles only shares with Curl, and Gildon, and Welstead, and Weston; but the inquisition which he has instituted into the poet's attachment to Martha Blount, is eminently his own; and though the pruriency with which his nose is laid to the ground, to scent some taint in their connexion, and the anatomical minuteness with which he examines and determines on the physical constitution of Pope, might, in charity, be deemed only unseemly or unbecoming in a layman, and occasional critic,—in an editor and a clergyman such conduct appears to us indecent and insufferably disgusting.

This prompted Bowles to write a letter, signed 'L.S.C.', to the editor of the *London Magazine* (July 1820), defending himself in the third person against these charges. Gilchrist retorted with a *signed* letter to the editor of the *London Magazine* (Aug. 1820), in which he acknowledged being the writer of the above; and the following month Bowles made a brief repartee. It was Gilchrist's acknowledgement in his signed letter which, as Bowles revealed in his *Second Reply*, induced him '*to believe him the Author of the Criticism in the Quarterly Review*' (p. 35). However, in his response to this *Second Reply*, Gilchrist confessed with some relish and irony (*A Letter to* ... *Bowles* ... (1820), pp. 38–9):

After all Mr. Bowles's good-humoured criticism, half delivered 'with his beaver up' and half in 'a visor undismayed,' it grieves me sorely to acknowledge unequivocally, that I am *not* the author of the article on Spence in the Quarterly Review,—that I was not privy to its composition, and that I do not even now know the Nisus to whom I have thus played Euryalus. I say this not out of any sense of shame or shrinking, but because I would not seem to appropriate to myself what another has written so much better than I could have effected.

On account of this, in his next publication, the 'Observations', Bowles directed his attack on two fronts against both Gilchrist and the *Quarterly Review*. By this time the controversy had become thoroughly acrimonious, and the argument over the *poetical* had become smothered under the squabble over the *personal* character of Pope. It was at this juncture that B entered the fray with his letter, and its effect was immediate and decisive: it instantly defused the issue, and restored to the controversy its principal poetical focus. Bowles's initial reaction to it is evident in two letters he wrote to Murray, on 6 and 15 Apr. 1821 respectively, both of which Murray sent on to B. In the first, he wrote:

> I write once more to say I have just got Lord Byron's pamphlet, and I could not omit requesting you to return him my best thanks for the kind terms in which he introduces my name, and also for the pleasure I have receiv'd from a work as much mark'd by good sense, liberal principles, and just thinking as by its peculiar tone of good-humour and urbanity, to which I have been of late so little accustom'd. . . .
>
> Lord Byron is the first liberal, manly, and kind-hearted opponent I have ever met, and I feel even gratitude towards him, as much as I respect him, for the manly vindication, without asperity or unkindness, of Pope's moral character. It has weigh'd with me more than any thing I have ever read, particularly with regard to Pope's connection with Martha Blount.
>
> In the principles of poetical criticism I shall think myself invulnerable, even from the polish'd lance of such an opponent. . . .
>
> I shall probably have to discuss these points further with him. He has set me an example of urbanity which I am sure will never be infring'd by me, and if I enter into further explanation and discussion with him on this subject, it will be for the sake of truth, not victory.

And in the second:

> As to Lord Byron, whether for or against the question on which we are not agreed, it is a most delightful publication, and I hope my answer will appear, not as a solemn discussion, but as a conversation,—with a scholar, and gentleman, and high poet,—upon an interesting poetical topic. (Greever, *Wiltshire Parson*, pp. 124–6, 128)

And at the commencement of his 'answer' to B itself, the *Two Letters to the Right Honourable Lord Byron* (1821), Bowles reiterated these sentiments (pp. 1–2):

> I have just read your Remarks (addressed to a friend) on my Life of POPE, on the *first part* of my Vindication in the Pamphleteer, and on my PRINCIPLES of Poetical Criticism, which I had called (*foolishly*, in your Lordship's opinion) INVARIABLE.
>
> I thank you, cordially, for this opportunity of explaining my sentiments, which I know you would not intentionally pervert; for the flattering terms in which you have spoken of me personally; and, most of all, for the honourable and open manner in which you have met the questions on which we are at issue.
>
> The late contest in which I have been involved, with those of a character so opposite, has tended to make this contrast of urbanity and honourable opposition more gratifying. From you, my Lord, I was certain I should not meet coarse and insulting abuse, the foul ribaldry of opprobrious contumely, nor the petty chicanery that purposely keeps out of sight one part of an argument, and wilfully misrepresents another.
>
> Your opposition, as might become a person of so high a station, and of such distinguished genius, exhibits none of those little arts of literary warfare. Your letter is at once argumentative, manly, good-humoured, and eloquent.

All this somewhat disarmed B. On receiving Bowles's two private letters to Murray referred to above, from Murray himself on 10 May 1821, he replied immediately with instructions to suppress the publication of 'Observations upon Observations', which he had dispatched to Murray some three weeks earlier (see the general note to 'Observations upon Observations' below). And having read Bowles's *Two Letters to the Right Honourable Lord Byron*, he wrote again to Murray on 14 June 1821: 'I have read Bowles's answer—I could easily reply—but it would lead to a long discussion—in the course of which I should perhaps lose my temper—which I would rather not do with so civil & forbearing an antagonist.—I suppose he will mistake being *silent* for *silenced*' (*BLJ* viii. 136). B reiterated these sentiments in a letter to Moore of 22 June, and again in a letter to Kinnaird of 20 Nov. 1821 (*BLJ* viii. 141; ix. 66–7). Effectively B's participation in the controversy ends here, but the controversy itself continued in a desultory way until 1826.

The Revd William Lisle Bowles (1762–1850) was educated at Winchester under Dr Joseph Warton, and at Trinity College, Oxford. He took Holy Orders in 1792, and was Vicar of Bremhill, Wiltshire, from 1804 to his death. He was Prebendary of Salisbury Cathedral and Chaplain to the Prince Regent. As a poet, he was best known for his *Sonnets*, which went through nine editions between 1789 and 1805. In 1804 he published his first long poem, *The Spirit of Discovery; or, The Conquest of Ocean*; and in 1813, *The Missionary; A Poem*. This last, which was regarded as the best of his long poems, went through two further editions under the same title, during B's lifetime: the 'Second Edition, corrected and enlarged', 1815, and the 'Third Edition', 1816. (See n. 152 below, and 'Observations upon Observations', n. 115). As may be seen from many of the citations in B's texts (especially in 'Observations upon Observations'), and from the notes below, Bowles was a thoroughly tiresome and querulous old man. His Replies and Observations are excessively verbose, and are full of rancour, exaggeration, self-exoneration, and misquotation (even of himself, and even of Pope—let alone of others). It is truly remarkable that B should have managed to restrain his evident exasperation with him so effectively in his own writings. Bowles was, however, a diligent clergyman, popular with his parishioners, generous in his charities, and an intimate friend of Southey and Coleridge. For further details, see Garland Greever, *A Wiltshire Parson and his Friends: The Correspondence of William Lisle Bowles* (1926).

Octavius Graham Gilchrist, FSA (1779–1823), antiquary, was educated at Magdalen College, Oxford, but left before taking his degree, in order to help a relative in the grocery business (see n. 13 to 'Observations upon Observations'). He was a friend of William Gifford, whom he assisted with his editions of the dramatic works of Jonson and Ford, and he did much to advance the poetical career of John Clare (see n. 104 to 'Observations upon Observations'). In his preface to *The Dramatic Works of John Ford* (2 vols., 1827), Gifford wrote of him:

> This gentleman, whom . . . I lament to call 'the *late* ingenious Mr. Gilchrist,' had not reached the meridian of life when he fell a sacrifice to some consumptive complaint, which had long oppressed him. His last labour of love was an attempt to rescue Pope

> from the rancorous persecution of his editor, the Rev. Mr. Bowles. I know not why this doughty personage gives himself such airs of superiority over Mr. Gilchrist; nor why, unless from pure taste, he clothes them in a diction not often heard out of the purlieus of St. Giles. Mr. Gilchrist was a man of strict integrity; and in the extent and accuracy of his critical knowledge, and the patient industry of his researches, as much superior to the Rev. Mr. Bowles, as in good manners. (vol. i, pp. lii n.–liii n.)

(See also B's important letter to Gilchrist of 5 Sept. 1821 (*BLJ* viii. 199–201; also viii. 203).)

At the time of its publication, B's letter was reviewed in three of the major periodicals: by Henry Matthews in *Blackwood's Edinburgh Magazine*, vol. ix, no. l (May 1821), pp. 227–33, by the *British Critic*, xv (May 1821), 463–70, and by William Hazlitt in the *London Magazine*, vol. iii, no. xviii (June 1821), pp. 593–607. It also received a favourable notice in the *Gentleman's Magazine* (vol. xci (Jan. to June 1821), pt. i, pp. 291–4, 533–4), which remarked without irony: 'We are seriously inclined to think that the Publick are as much indebted to Lord Byron for this elegant Epistle in Prose, as for any of his lofty Poems' (p. 534). (Both the *Edinburgh Review* and the *Monthly Review* were silent on the topic altogether.) In varying degrees of wit, mirth, and deprecation, *Blackwood's* and the *British Critic* censured B for the illogicality of his argument and for the weight he gave to the 'execution' of an artist. But by far the most serious and attentive review was that written by Hazlitt in the *London Magazine*. Although he appreciated B's 'dry rubs' at Bowles, and 'good hits' at Southey, and allowed that the letter contained 'some good *hating*, and some good writing', he poured scorn on B's argument, challenged its dogmatic assertions, criticized its inconsistencies and self-contradictions, and questioned why B wrote prose at all. He added, however (p. 598):

> Yet, in spite of all this trash, there is one passage for which we forgive him, and here it is.
>
> 'The truth is, that in these days the grand *primum mobile* of England is *cant*; cant political, cant poetical, cant religious, cant moral; but always cant, multiplied through all the varieties of life. It is the fashion, and while it lasts, will be too powerful for those who can only exist by taking the tone of the times. I say *cant*, because it is a thing of words, without the smallest influence upon human actions; the English being no wiser, no better, and much poorer, and more divided among themselves, as well as far less moral, than they were before the prevalence of this verbal decorum.' These words should be written in letters of gold, as the testimony of a lofty poet to a great moral truth, and we can hardly have a quarrel with the writer of them.

Shelley also, writing to Mary from Ravenna on 11 Aug. 1821, remarked somewhat bluntly: 'I have read Albè's letter to Bowles—some good things—but he ought not to write prose criticism' (Frederick L. Jones (ed.), *The Letters of Percy Bysshe Shelley*, 2 vols. (1964), ii. 332). Moore, on the other hand, noted in his Journal on 3 May 1821 (*Memoirs* iii. 227): 'Looked again over his letter on Bowles. It is amusing to see through his design in thus depreciating all the present school of poetry. Being quite sure of his own hold upon fame, he contrives to loosen that of all his contemporaries, in order that they may fall away entirely from his side, and leave him unencumbered, even by their floundering.' While this betrays considerable lack of perception, and a distinct misunderstanding of B's aims, it does serve to demonstrate the singular status the letter holds in Romantic literature. For, however tenuous its argument may have appeared to the contemporary reader, and however eccentric or unorthodox its convictions, it documents a long-held and firm belief in the sovereignty of the classical tradition of literature, and is perhaps the more persuasive by virtue of its forcefulness and sincerity than by any strict observance of formal reasoning. As such, it may fairly be regarded (together with 'Some Observations' and 'Observations upon Observations') as a manifesto aimed directly at the poetical (and political) taste and tenets of the day, principally upheld by such poets as Southey, Wordsworth, Hunt, and Keats.

B's contribution to the Bowles/Pope controversy has received scanter critical attention than it deserves. See, however: Henry A. Beers, *A History of English Romanticism in the Nineteenth Century* (1902), pp. 63–73; George Saintsbury, *A History of Criticism*, 3 vols. (1904), iii. 281–2; Clement Tyson Goode, *Byron As Critic* (1923), ch. 4; J. J. Van Rennes, *Bowles, Byron and the Pope-Controversy* (1927); and René Wellek, *A History of Modern Criticism: 1750–1850*, vol. ii, *The Romantic Age* (1955), pp. 123–4. See also Alan Lang Strout, *John Bull's Letter to Lord Byron* (1947).

Chronological list of publications in the controversy

Abbreviations are given for those titles referred to in the notes.

[*The Works*] *The Works of Alexander Pope, Esq. in Verse and Prose*, by Revd William Lisle Bowles. 10 vols. 1806.

[*Specimens*] *Specimens of the British Poets: with Biographical and Critical Notices, and an Essay on English Poetry*, by Thomas Campbell. 7 vols. 1819. (NB The abbreviation *Specimens* applies to vol. I only; other volumes are referred to by number.)

[*The Invariable Principles*] *The Invariable Principles of Poetry: In a Letter addressed to Thomas Campbell, Esq; Occasioned by some Critical Observations in his Specimens of British Poets, Particularly relating to the Poetical Character of* POPE, by the Revd W. L. Bowles. 1819.

[*Anecdotes*] *Anecdotes, Observations, and Characters, of Books and Men. Collected from the Conversation of Mr. Pope, and Other Eminent Persons of his Time. By the Rev. Joseph Spence*, by Samuel Weller Singer. 1820.

Observations, Anecdotes, and Characters, of Books and Men: By the Rev. Joseph Spence, arranged with notes by Edmund Malone. 1820.

['Review'] A review by Gilchrist of the two immediately preceding publications above (i.e. *Anecdotes*, and Malone's edition of Spence) in the *London Magazine*, vol. i, no. ii (Feb. 1820), art. ii, pp. 191–4.

['L.S.C.'] A letter in response to Gilchrist's *Review*, entitled 'Mr. Bowles—As Editor of Pope', addressed 'To the Editor of the London Magazine', and signed 'L.S.C.' (Bowles himself), in the *London Magazine*, vol. ii, no. vii (July 1820), pp. 33–4.

[*Quarterly Review*] A review by D'Israeli of *The Invariable Principles*, *Anecdotes*, and Malone's edition of Spence, in the *Quarterly Review*, vol. xxiii, no. xlvi (July 1820), art. v, pp. 400–34.

['The Character of Pope'] An article in reply to 'L.S.C.' entitled 'The Character of Pope', addressed 'To the Editor of the London Magazine', and signed 'Octavius Gilchrist', in the *London Magazine*, vol. ii, no. viii (Aug. 1820), pp. 180–1.

A letter from Bowles (in his own name) in response to 'The Character of Pope' (above), entitled 'The Character of Pope', in the *London Magazine*, vol. ii, no. ix (Sept. 1820), p. 249.

[*Second Reply*] *A Reply to an "Unsentimental Sort of Critic," the Reviewer of "Spence's Anecdotes" in the Quarterly Review for October* [*sic*] *1820; Otherwise to the Longinus of "In-Door" Nature. By "One of the Family of the BOWLESES!!"* Bath, 1820. (Dated 28 Oct. 1820.)

['A Reply'] *A Reply to the Charges brought by the Reviewer of Spence's Anecdotes, in the Quarterly Review, for October* [*sic*] *1820, Against the Last Editor of Pope's Works; and Author of "A Letter to Mr. Campbell," on "The Invariable Principles of Poetry."*, by the Revd W. L. Bowles. (Dated 25 Oct. 1820.) *Pamphleteer*, vol. xvii, no. xxxiii (1820), pp. 73–96.*

[Gilchrist] *A Letter to the Rev. William Lisle Bowles, in Answer to a Pamphlet recently published, under the title of "A Reply to an Unsentimental Sort of Critic, the Reviewer of Spence's Anecdotes in the Quarterly Review for October, 1820."*, by Octavius Gilchrist. Stamford, 1820. (Dated 2 Dec. 1820.)

*Letter to **** ******, on the Rev. W. L. Bowles' Strictures on the Life and Writings of Pope*, by Lord Byron. 1821.

['Observations'] *Observations on the Poetical Character of Pope; further elucidating the "Invariable Principles of Poetry," &c. With a Sequel, in Reply to Octavius Gilchrist* (no name, no date). *Pamphleteer*, vol. xvii, no. xxxiv, pp. 369–84.*

['Observations' (2)] *Observations on the Poetical Character of Pope; further elucidating the "Invariable Principles of Poetry," &c. With a Sequel, in Reply to Octavius Gilchrist*, by the Revd W. L. Bowles. (Dated 17 Feb. 1821.) *Pamphleteer*, vol. xviii, no. xxxv (1821), pp. 213–58.*

* In the *Pamphleteer*, these three publications have two sets of pagination: the one in the inside margin is numbered according to the pamphlet (e.g. 1–18), the one in the outside margin according to the pamphlet's location within the relevant volume. As B refers to the former, and as the latter is unreliable, I have followed B in the notes below.

(B's 'Observations upon Observations', written but not published.)

[*A Vindication*] *A Vindication of the Late Editor of Pope's Works, from some Charges brought against him, by a Writer in the Quarterly Review, for October* [*sic*], *1820: with Further Observations on "The Invariable Principles of Poetry;" and a full exposure of the mode of criticising adopted by Octavius Gilchrist, Esq. F.A.S.* [*sic*], by the Revd W. L. Bowles. 2nd edn. 1821. (Dated 17. Feb. 1821.) (This comprises 'A Reply', 'Observations' and 'Observations (2)', published as one pamphlet.)

*Two Letters to the Right Honourable Lord Byron, in Answer to his Lordship's Letter to **** ******, on the Rev. WM.L. Bowles's Strictures on the Life and Writings of Pope: more particularly on the question, Whether* POETRY *be more immediately indebted to what is* SUBLIME *or* BEAUTIFUL *in the Works of* NATURE, *or the Works of* ART*?*, by the Revd WM. L. Bowles. 1821. (Dated 14 Apr. 1821; published 30 Apr. 1821.)

A Letter to the Rev. W.L. Bowles, in reply to his Letter to Thomas Campbell, Esq. and to his Two Letters to The Right Hon. Lord Byron; containing A Vindication of their Defence of the Poetical Character of Pope, and An Inquiry into the nature of poetical images, and of the characteristic qualities that distinguish poetry from all other species of writing, by M. M'Dermot. *Pamphleteer*, vol. xx, nos. xxxix and xl (1822), pp. 119–44, 386–410.

Letters to Mr. T. Campbell, as far as regards poetical criticism, &c. &c. and the Answer to the Writer in the Quarterly Review, as far as they relate to the same subjects. Second Editions. Together with An Answer to Some Objections; and Further Illustrations, by the Revd WM. L. Bowles. (Dated 14 Mar. 1822.) *Pamphleteer*, vol. xx, no. xl (1822), pp. 529–84.

The Works of Alexander Pope, by William Roscoe. 10 vols. 1824. (See n. 216 below.)

A Final Appeal to the Literary Public, relative to Pope, in Reply to certain Observations of Mr. Roscoe, in his Edition of that Poet's Works, by the Revd WM. L. Bowles. 1825. (Dated 1 Jan. 1825.)

A Letter to the Reverend William Lisle Bowles, A.M. . . . In Reply to His "Final Appeal to the Literary Public, Relative to Pope.", by William Roscoe. 1825.

A review written by George Taylor of the whole controversy to date, in the *Quarterly Review*, vol. xxxii, no. lxiv (Oct. 1825), art. i, pp. 271–311.

Lessons in Criticism to William Roscoe, Esq.; . . . In Answer to his Letter to the Reverend W.L. Bowles on the Character and Poetry of Pope. With Further Lessons in Criticism to a Quarterly Reviewer, by the Revd William Lisle Bowles. 1826. (Dated 7 Jan. 1826.)

Reference is also made in the notes below to Joseph Warton, *The Works of Alexander Pope*, 9 vols. (Basil, 1803) [abbreviated to Warton]. This was the edition that B possessed (see Sale Catalogue (1827), Lot 153, *post*).

1. *Letter... Esq*[re.] In the first three editions the title reads '*Letter to* **** ******, *on the Rev. W.L. Bowles' Strictures on the Life and Writings of Pope.*' In *Works* (1832) it reads, '*Letter to John Murray, Esq. on the Rev. W.L. Bowles's Strictures on the Life and Writings of Pope.*' In Prothero it reads '*Letter to* **** ****** [*John Murray*], *Esqre, on the Rev. W.L. Bowles's Strictures on the Life and Writings of Pope.*'

2. *Old Song.* B adapts a line from the final stanza of Song cclxi ('I'll sail upon the Dog-star'), which appears in *The Vocal Miscellany*, 2 vols. (3rd edn., 1738), i. 231:

> While I mount yon blue Cœlum,
> To shun the tempting Gispies;
> Play at Foot-ball with Sun and Moon,
> And fright ye with Eclipses.

As it happens, he could not have chosen a more unexpectedly appropriate epigraph. For, on the title-page of his *Two Letters to the Right Honourable Lord Byron*, Bowles parried it with another epigraph, '"He that plays at BOWLS, must expect RUBBERS." Old Proverb', and explained in his prefatory 'Advertisement':

> *I Trust Lord* BYRON *will excuse me for having made somewhat freee with the singular Motto to his book. It is, 'I will play at* BOWLS *with the* SUN *and the* MOON.'—Old Song.
>
> *A* 'certain Family' *had been spoken of, in the Quarterly Review, as* 'ringing changes on Nature for two thousand years.' [*Quarterly Review*, p. 409: '"Nature" is a critical term, which the Bowleses have been explaining for more than two thousand years.']
>
> *By a somewhat ludicrous coincidence, it happens that the 'arms' of this 'family' are, literally, a 'sun and moon,' a* Sun, OR, *and a* Moon, ARGENT, secundùm ARTEM.
>
> *It is, therefore, with this* SUN *and* MOON, *that Lord* BYRON, *I have no doubt, plays at* 'BOWLS!' *Not with the* SUN *and* MOON *in* NATURE.

3. *"My mither's... 169.* In *Works* (1832) and Prothero 'Stir' reads 'Sir'. In *Works* (1832) 'naebody' reads 'nobody'. In all editions 'page 169' reads 'page 163'. See Scott's *Tales of My Landlord*, 4 vols. (2nd edn., 1817), ii (*Old Mortality*), 163 (Cuddie speaking): 'My mother's [*sic*] auld, stir, and she has rather forgotten hersel in speaking to my leddy, that canna weel bide to be contradickit, (as I ken naebody likes it if they could help themsels,)'.

4. *Letter to ... vol 2*[d] The title and the two epigraphs are written on the final page of the MS, immediately following the paragraph on Grainger's 'Ode on Solitude' directed by B for insertion in the body of his text (see n. 73 below).

5. *M*[r] *Bowles... Quarterly.* As an example of forming a critical opinion 'at *second hand*', which he suspected Campbell of doing, Bowles introduced B into his argument by saying, 'let me mention one remarkable circumstance':

> Soon after Lord BYRON had published his vigorous satire, called 'English Bards and Scotch Reviewers,' in which, alas! *pars magna fui*, I met his Lordship at our common friend's house, the author of the 'Pleasures of Memory,' and the still more beautiful poem, 'Human Life.' As the rest of the company were going into another room, I said I wished to speak one word to his Lordship. He came back, with much apparent courtesy. I then said to him, in a tone of seriousness, but that of perfectly good humour, 'My Lord,

I should not have thought of making any observations on whatever you might be pleased to give to the world as your opinion of any part of my writings which were before the public; but I think, if I can shew that you have done me a palpable and public wrong, by charging me as having written what I *never wrote*, or thought of, your own principles of justice will not allow the impression to remain.' I then spoke of a particular couplet,* which he had introduced into his satire; and taking down the poem, which was at hand, I pointed out the passage to which his lines alluded, and said, 'If by any possible construction he could shew that my expressions could convey such idea as he had ludicrously held out, I fully deserved all he had said, and much more. If no construction of the words could possibly imply such a meaning as he had given, then he would acknowledge the injustice.' He examined the passage in my poem on the Spirit of Discovery; and then with a frank ingenuousness, acknowledged he had been entirely misled, saying that he took his opinion, not from the book itself, but from the representation of that very Review, which was one of the objects of his satire. He then said he had given orders that the poem should be entirely suppressed, and we shook hands, and parted.

* 'Thy woods, Madeira trembled to a kiss'—*Byron's Satire.*

If I had written this, or half what is attributed to me in criticism, I might well take to myself

'Some have at first for wits, then poets, pass'd;
Turn'd *critics* next, and prov'd *plain fools* at last.'
[Pope, *Essay on Criticism*, ll. 36–7]

(*The Invariable Principles*, pp. 33–5, 34n.)

Bowles referred again to this 'circumstance' in 'A Reply' (see n. 15 below). In bk. iv of Bowles's *The Spirit of Discovery* (1804), the following lines occur (pp. 153–4):

A kiss
Stole on the list'ning silence; never yet
Here heard: they trembl'd, e'en as if the Pow'r
That made the world, that planted the first pair
In Paradise, amid the garden walk'd,—

B alluded to these lines in *EBSR*, ll. 358–60: 'The Bard . . . gravely tells . . . When first Madeira trembled to a kiss'; and again in a note to l. 351 ('Awake a louder and a loftier strain'):

'Awake a louder, etc. etc' is the first line in Bowles's 'Spirit of Discovery'; a very spirited and pretty dwarf Epic. Among other exquisite lines we have the following:—

'A kiss
Stole on the list'ning silence, never yet
Here heard; they trembled even as if the power, etc. etc.'

That is, the woods of Madeira trembled to a kiss, very much astonished, as well they might be, at such a phenomenon.

However, annotating this note in his own copy of *EBSR* in 1816, he wrote: 'Misquoted—and misunderstood by me—but not intentionally.—It was not the "Woods" but the people in them who trembled—*why*—Heaven only knows—unless they were overheard making this prodigious smack.' (See *CPW* i. 240, 405–6, and nn. 11, 12 below.)

6. *The Quarterly . . . quotation. Quarterly Review* (p. 425) cited part of Bowles's anecdote given in n. 5 above (from 'Soon after' to 'I pointed out the passage'), and then quoted *EBSR*, ll. 365–78 (omitting ll. 369–72, from 'each fault' to 'CURLL'). Gilchrist (pp. 37–8) cited in full *EBSR*, ll. 361–84.

7. *"Lord B. . . . present.*) Bowles wrote: 'Whether I was, on this occasion, or on any other, where criticism is concerned, perfectly good-humoured, those who were present, and Lord Byron himself, if he remembers the circumstance, will *witness*' ('A Reply', p. 23n.; B has added his own emphasis to 'if he remembers'). B's parenthetical pun on '*witness in Italics*' refers very cleverly to the not very credible *Italian* witnesses at the trial of Queen Caroline, during Aug.–Nov. 1820. (See following n. 8.)

8. *"Non mi ricordo".* B pursues his punning allusion noted in n. 7 above. At the trial of Queen Caroline, the answer 'non mi ricordo' ('I don't remember') was repeated so frequently by the principal Italian witnesses, such as Majocchi, that it became the cant phrase of the day. William Hone, for example, amongst his numerous other squibs at the trial, published one entitled "*Non Mi Ricordo*" (1820). See also, Henry Brougham's brilliant exploitation of the phrase, and of Majocchi's lack of recollection, in his speech summing up for the defence at the trial on 3 Oct. 1820 (*Speeches of Mr. Brougham, Mr. Denman, and Dr. Lushington* (1820), p. 22).

9. *"Eng. B. and S.R." EBSR* was first published in 1809. The fifth edition was suppressed by B in Jan. 1812. (See *CPW* i. 397, and n. 12 below.)

10. *I had . . . poets.* This was Samuel Rogers (1763–1855), author of amongst other works *Human Life, A Poem* (1819). B first dined with him on 4 Nov. 1811, and thereafter was frequently in his company. (See Marchand i. 303–4, *BAP*, p. 109, and *BLJ* ii. 127, 286–7.) B refers to him here as 'the last Argonaut of Classic English poetry—and the Nestor of our inferior race of living poets', because of his consistently high regard for Rogers as a poet in the tradition of Pope. (See, e.g., *BLJ* iii. 220, and B's references to him in 'Some Observations' above.) (Nestor, King of Pylos, survived the slaughter of his eleven brothers by Hercules, and returned safely home from the voyage of the Argonauts and from the expedition to Troy. He ruled over three generations of men and was famed for his justice, wisdom, and skill in war.) Rogers objected to the epithet 'venerable'. B wrote to Hobhouse on 26. Apr. 1821: 'I hear "Rogers cuts *you*"—because I called him "Venerable"—the next time I will state his age without the respectable epithet annexed to it—which in fact he does not deserve' (*BLJ* viii. 100).

11. *The fact. . . review.* Bowles's *The Spirit of Discovery* (1804) was reviewed in the *Edinburgh Review*, vol. vi, no. xii (July 1805), art. v, pp. 313–21. Quoting the lines B had misunderstood (see n. 5 above), the reviewer commented: 'The reader will not fail to remark the poet's accuracy in fixing the date when the woods of Madeira first re-echoed to the sound of a human kiss' (p. 321).

12. *Mr. Rgs. . . . pleasure."* The 'one family' here was the Hollands, whose set B had ridiculed in *EBSR*, ll. 540–59. It was through Rogers that B became acquainted with Lord Holland in Feb. 1812, and it was at his suggestion that the fifth edition of *EBSR* was suppressed. (See *CPW* i. 246, 397, 410; Marchand i. 324; *BAP*, pp. 115–16; and, for instance, *BLJ* iv. 320.) These circumstances, together with those noted in nn. 5, 9, and 10 above, are also related by B in a postscript at present appended to his letter to Murray of 17 June 1817. This postscript should belong to a later letter: probably to his letter to Murray of 4. Nov. 1820, when he first acknowledged receiving the *Quarterly Review* (see general note above), or to his letter to Murray of 18 Nov. 1820 (*BLJ* vii. 216–18, 228–9). Its present location makes little sense chronologically, as can be seen (*BLJ* v. 240–1):

P.S.—Bowles's Story of the interview at the '*common* friend's[']' ('common' enough the Gods know) is not correct.—It did not occur '*soon* after the publication' &c. but in 1812—three good years after—I recollect nothing of 'seriousness' now as the company were going into another room—he said to me that all his friends had bothered him crying out 'Eh Bowles how come you to make the *woods* of Madeira tremble to a kiss' whereas it was not the woods but the lovers who trembled—though I see no great reason why they should either.——I have had no opportunity of restoring the 'trembling' to it's right owners—as I had previously suppressed the Satire at Rogers's particular suggestion 'that it would gratify Ld. Holland' and I beg leave to observe that this was some time after I was acquainted with Ld. Holland and *a consequence not a cause* of that connection.—Bowles was courteous and civilized enough & so was I too I hope.—

13. *of which . . . Ireland.* The phrase '*in Ireland*' is not in MS, which reads merely '(of which several had been made)'. But in his letter of 16 Feb. 1821, B instructed Murray: 'In the letter on Bowles—(which I sent by Tuesday's post) after the words "*attempts had been made*" (alluding to the republication of "English Bards")—add the words "*in Ireland*" for I believe that Cawthorn did not begin his attempts till after I had left England the second time.—Pray attend to this' (*BLJ* viii. 79). See also *BLJ* iv. 98 and *CPW* i. 397, 398, and 'Endorsement on a Power of Attorney' below. Murray followed these instructions; and accordingly the first and subsequent editions, and *Works* (1832) read '(of which several had been made in Ireland)'. Prothero reads as in MS.

14. *It is proper . . . person.* The one exception here may have been Walter Scott, whom B had ridiculed in *EBSR*, ll. 165–88 (*CPW* i. 234–5). Although Scott was the first to open their correspondence, he was prompted to do so in consequence of a letter from Murray containing information supplied by B concerning the Prince Regent's admiration for him (Samuel Smiles, *A Publisher and His Friends*, 2 vols. (1891), i. 213–14. See also *BLJ* ii. 182–3). However, Scott and B did subsequently meet; and of their meeting, Murray made the following memorandum: '1815. *Friday, April* 7.—This day Lord Byron and Walter Scott met for the first time and were introduced by me to each other. They conversed together for nearly two hours' (ibid., i. 267).

15. *"noble mind . . . suppressed."* In 'A Reply' (p. 23), Bowles referred again to the 'circumstance' noted in n. 5 above, as follows:

> Lord Byron had published, in his animated satire on 'English Bards and Scotch Reviewers,' a laughable passage, and ascribed this passage to me!
>
> No construction of my language could possibly bear him out, in such a representation. However, it was read, and believed, and laughed at! Lord Byron was of too noble a mind to misrepresent me deliberately; and on showing him the misstatement, he frankly acknowledged he had unintentionally done me wrong, and he had the generous magnanimity to say he would explain the circumstance, had he not given orders that the book should be suppressed!

16. *I hate . . . fools.* B hated the word 'magnanimity' because in his mind it was associated with the 'magnanimous' conduct of his wife Anabella, during and after their separation: i.e. her accusatory silence or 'mischief-making', as he calls it in a letter to Augusta (*BLJ* vii. 208). See also *BLJ* v. 232 and viii. 60; and *DJ* I. 12, 29, 30 (*CPW* v. 12, 17, 18).

17. *"Well . . . it."* In Scott's *Rob Roy*, Galbraith mistakes Bailie Nicol Jarvie for his father, the Deacon Nicol Jarvie (deceased). On being apprized of this, Galbraith exclaims, 'Well, the devil take the mistake and all that occasioned it!' (*Novels and Tales* (1825), vol. viii, ch. 6, p. 132).

18. *I have . . . them.* For some of the numerous poetical works ascribed to B, see for example n. 2 to 'Some Observations', above.

19. *I must . . . B.E.M.* B here refers to 'Some Observations' (1820) (above). Alluding to this sentence in the preface to *Blackwood's Edinburgh Magazine*, vol. xi (Jan.–June 1822), John Wilson ('Christopher North') wrote (p. viii):

> Lord Byron, too, has written something about us—but whether a satire or an eulogy seems doubtful. The Noble Lord—great wits having short memories, and sometimes not very long judgments—has told the public and Mr Murray that he has forgotten whether his letter is *on* or *to* the Editor of Blackwood's Magazine. From this we fear his Lordship was in a state of civilation when he penned it; and if ever he publishes it, as we scorn to take advantage of any man, we now give his Lordship and the public a solemn pledge, to drink one glass of Sherry, three of Champagne, two of Hock, ditto of Madeira, six of Old Port, and four-and-twenty of Claret, before we put pen to paper in reply.

20. *Whilst I was . . . Edition.* In the first edition of *EBSR* (1809), Hobhouse's lines on Bowles ran as follows (ll. 247–62, pp. 21–2):

> [Stick to thy Sonnets, man! at least they sell:]
> Or take the only path that open lies
> For modern worthies who would hope to rise:
> Fix on some well known name, and bit by bit,
> Pare off the merits of his worth and wit;
> On each alike employ the critic's knife,
> And where a comment fails prefix a life;
> Hint certain failings, faults before unknown,
> Review forgotten lies, and add your own;
> Let no disease, let no misfortune 'scape,
> And print, if luckily deformed, his shape:

Thus shall the world, quite undeceiv'd at last,
Cleave to their present wits and quit their past;
Bards once rever'd no more with favour view,
But give their modern sonneteers their due;
Thus with the dead may living merit cope,
Thus BOWLES may triumph o'er the shade of POPE.

In the second edition, B substituted his own lines (*EBSR*, ll. 363–84) and explained his reasons for so doing in his preface (p. vi). (See *CPW* i. 228, 240–1, 406.)

21. *"L[d] B. . . . character".* In 'A Reply' (p. 24), having quoted *EBSR*, ll. 367–78 (with some omissions), Bowles wrote: 'Lord Byron knows I do not deserve this character: he knows I never "affected a *candour* I did not feel;" and he is too generous to apply to me that character which I DO NOT DESERVE.'

22. *one of . . . Ali Pacha.* For B's meeting with Ali Pacha (1741–1822), the unprincipled, despotic ruler whose capital was at Ioannina, see *BLJ* i. 226–8. For other references to him, see *CHP* II. 47, 62; and *DJ* III. 13 ff., but particularly 41, 47–8, 53–6. (*CPW* ii. 59, 63, 288; v. 165–78.) See also Marchand i. 208–12; *BAP*, pp. 69–73.

23. *"And . . . antithesis".* Pope, *Epistle to Dr. Arbuthnot*, ll. 325.

24. *but . . . pleases.* B echoes Pope himself here. In a note to Johnson's life of Pope, there is an anecdote related by the Revd Dr Ridley concerning the couplet 'Slander or poison dread from Delia's rage; / Hard words, or hanging if your judge be ****' (*The First Satire of the Second Book of Horace*, ll. 81–2), which runs as follows:

Sir Francis Page, a judge well known in his time, conceiving that his name was meant to fill up the blank, sent his clerk to Mr. Pope, to complain of the insult. Pope told the young man, that the blank might be supplied by many monosyllables, other than the judge's name:—'but, sir,' said the clerk, 'the judge says that no other word will make sense of the passage.'—'So then it seems,' says Pope, 'your master is not only a judge, but a poet: as that is the case, the odds are against me. Give my respects to the judge, and tell him, I will not contend with one that has the advantage of me, and he may fill up the blank as he pleases.' (Samuel Johnson, *The Lives of the Most Eminent English Poets*, 4 vols. (1794), iv. 193 n.)

25. *"Why . . . prisoners". Henry IV, Part I*, I. iii. 77 (B's emphases).

26. *"he has . . . licentiousness." Quarterly Review* (p. 412) charged Bowles with having aspersed Pope for, amongst other things, 'the grossest licentiousness'. Bowles replied ('A Reply', p. 7):

But I have charged Pope with the 'GROSSEST LICENTIOUSNESS!' I have said that he had a libertine sort of love, which was in a great degree suppressed by his sense of moral duty [*The Works*, vol. i, p. cxxx]. I might say, that I have seen passages in his Letters to Martha Blount, which never were published by me, and I hope never will be by others; which are so gross as indeed to imply the 'grossest licentiousness:' but, not to speak of 'licentiousness' on account of letters which were never published, can any one acquit him of 'licentiousness,' as far as we may judge from language and ideas[?]

27. *works.* The note appended here was sent by B to Murray on 26 Feb. 1821. It was suppressed by Gifford, and was first published in part in *Works* (1832), and in full in Prothero (see general note above). The MS bears the following superscription by B: 'Note second—on the lines on Lady M.W. Montague.—'.

28. *In my opinion.* The passage from here to 'the refined . . . pernicious.' was omitted in *Works* (1832) and was first published in Prothero.

29. *It is . . . experiment.* B refers to Pope's *The First Satire of the Second Book of Horace*, ll. 83–4: 'From furious Sappho scarce a milder fate, / Pox'd by her love, or libell'd by her hate.' ('Sappho' here is Pope's literary cognomen for Lady Mary Wortley Montagu.)

30. *The coarseness . . . Balbus.* B refers to Johnson's *London: A Poem*, ll. 115–16, 150–1 respectively: 'All Sciences a fasting Monsieur knows, / And bid him go to Hell, to Hell he goes'; and 'Can *Balbo's* Eloquence applaud, and swear / He gropes his Breeches with a Monarch's Air.'

31. *"curst undiliket."* This may well have been the same 'Entremetteuse' with whom B had dealings, and to whom he ascribes the admonition, *Remember—Milor!—that delicaci ensure every Success* (*BLJ* vi. 90; see also *BLJ* vii. 115). B rehearses the story in full in 'Observations upon Observations' at n. 43. Although Trumpington is a village near Cambridge, and the 'young lady' may indeed have come from there, B may also be glancing here at the obliging wife and daughter of the Miller of Trumpington in 'The Reeve's Tale', in Chaucer's *Canterbury Tales.*

32. *Lady Mary . . . exasperating.* For instance, Spence recorded Lady Mary saying to him of the many letters she had received from Pope: 'You shall see what a goddess he made of me in some of them, though he makes such a devil of me in his writings afterwards, without any reason that I know of.' And again, in response to Spence's saying he thought Pope wrote verses well: 'Yes, he writes verses so well, that he is in danger of bringing even good verse into disrepute! from all his tune and no meaning' (*Anecdotes*, pp. 234, 237). In his edition of *The Works of the Right Honourable Lady Mary Wortley Montagu* (5 vols. (1803), i. 73–4), James Dallaway wrote:

> Irritated by Pope's ceaseless petulance, and disgusted by his subterfuge, Lady Mary now retired totally from his society, and certainly did not abstain from sarcastic observations, which were always repeated to him. One told him of an epigram,
>
> 'Sure Pope and Orpheus were alike inspired,
> The blocks and beasts flock'd round them and admired.'
>
> and another, how Lady Mary had observed, that 'some called Pope, little nightingale—all sound, and no sense.'

33. *"miserable body".* Spence wrote of Pope's 'wretched body' (*Anecdotes*, p. 236 n.), which *Quarterly Review* quotes (p. 418), and which Bowles repeats in 'A Reply' (p. 11). However Pope himself nowhere uses any of these phrases; but in a letter to Lady Mary he does refer to 'this body of mine (which is as ill matched to my mind as any wife to her husband)' (Warton, viii. 328). See also following n. 34.

34. *When he . . . be.* For this awareness of being crooked and short see, for example, *Epistle to Dr. Arbuthnot*, ll. 115–24. Also, in a letter to Lady Mary, Pope wrote: 'I am capable myself of following one I loved, not only to Constantinople, but to those parts of India, where, they tell us, the women best love the ugliest fellows, as the most admirable productions of nature, and look upon deformities as the signatures of divine favour' (Warton, viii. 321). In two papers in the *Guardian*, however (nos. 91, 92, 25 and 26 June 1713), signing himself 'Bob Short, *Secretary*', Pope took a jocular attitude towards his stature: 'I question not but it will be pleasing to you to hear, that a set of us have formed a society, who are sworn to dare to be short, and boldly bear out the dignity of littleness under the noses of those enormous engrossers of manhood, those hyperbolical monsters of the Species, the tall fellows that overlook us' (Warton, ix. 350; but see pp. 350–9). B's sympathy for Pope here cannot be wholly separated from his own sensitivity to his lameness.

35. *Montaigne . . . decent.* Montaigne's essay is entitled 'Of Cripples'. In this he wrote: 'It is a common proverb in Italy, "That he knows not all the pleasures of Venus to perfection, who has never lain with a cripple"' (*The Essays of Michael de Montaigne*, 3 vols. (1811), iii. 317).

36. *At least . . . Grammont.* Philibert de Gramont (1621–1707), successively l'abbé, le chevalier and le comte de Gramont, was a diplomat and notorious libertine who lived first at the court of Louis XIV and then at that of Charles II. His uninhibited memoirs were written by his brother-in-law. See Count Antony Hamilton, *Mémoires de la vie du Comte de Grammont* (1713).

37. *"the refined . . . pernicious."* This exact phrase is not Buffon's, though the sentiment is very much his. B is probably condensing Buffon's definition of love to which he refers in 'Observations upon Observations'. (See n. 28 thereto). Georges-Louis Leclerc, Comte de Buffon (1707–88), was an eminent French naturalist, and Keeper of the Jardin du Roi in Paris. His *Histoire Naturelle, générale et particulière* (which influenced the theories of both Jean-Baptiste de Lamarck (1744–1829), and Charles Darwin (1809–82)), was published in 44 volumes between 1749 and 1804. He was elected to the Académie Française in 1753, on which occasion he delivered his celebrated 'Discours sur le style'.

38. *quarrel.* Prothero reads 'ground'.

39. *"for . . . him".* This is not a quotation; B has merely put his own statement within inverted commas. Lady Mary had indeed encouraged Pope. For example, writing to him from Vienna on 14 Sept. 1716, she said:

> Perhaps you'll laugh at me for thanking you very gravely for all the obliging concern you express for me. 'Tis certain that I may, if I please, take the fine things you say to me for wit and raillery; and, it may be, it would be taking them right. But I never, in my life, was half so well disposed to believe you in earnest as I am at present; and that distance, which makes the continuation of your friendship improbable, has very much increased my faith in it. (Dallaway, *Works of Lady Mary* ii. 39–40)

40. *"he comes . . . denied."* The final line of Lady Mary's 'The Lady's Resolve, written on a window, soon after her marriage, 1713' (Dallaway, *Works of Lady Mary* v. 104).

41. *"if you . . . him".* Shortly before his death, Johnson told Boswell of his friendship for Henry Hervey which had cheered the 'cold obscurity' of his early life: 'He was a vicious man, but very kind to me. If you call a dog HERVEY, I shall love him' (*Boswell's Life of Johnson* i. 106).

42. "so . . . appellation. B's attachment to the name Mary arose from his love for Mary Duff and Mary Chaworth. (See e.g. *DJ* V. 4; *BLJ* iii. 221–2; ix. 24, 34.)

43. *She . . . Aristippus.* Lady Mary translated the *Enchiridion* of Epictetus, which greatly impressed Bishop Burnet and which 'received his emendations' (Dallaway, *Works of Lady Mary* i. 10–11, 265–309). Aristippus (*fl.* 370 BC) was a disciple and friend of Socrates, and founder of the Cyrenaic school of philosophy. He regarded pleasure as the only good in life (see *BLJ* i. 148).

44. *"And when . . . forgive.* These are the lines 'worthy of Aristippus' (see preceding n.). With very minor discrepancies, B here cites Lady Mary's 'The Lover: A Ballad. To Mr. Congreve', stanza 4 (Dallaway, *Works of Lady Mary* v. 206–7).

45. *Is not . . . two?* B alludes jocularly to the woods of Madeira (see n. 5 above).

46. *I mean . . . man.* Epicurus (341–270 BC), founder of the Epicurean school of philosophy, taught that the highest good to be attained was happiness (peace of mind) through virtue. However, his professed followers practised mere sensual enjoyment, which brought his system into disrepute.

47. *I have . . . saved."* The poet was Robert Burns, whose letters were lent to B in 1813 by John Allen, MD (1771–1843), one of the Holland House set. In his journal for 13 Dec. 1813 B wrote: 'Allen . . . has lent me a quantity of Burns's unpublished, and never-to-be-published, Letters. They are full of oaths and obscene songs. What an antithetical mind!—tenderness, roughness—delicacy, coarseness—sentiment, sensuality—soaring and grovelling, dirt and deity—all mixed up in that one compound of inspired clay!' (*BLJ* iii. 239; see also iii. 202). In a letter to Robert Cleghorn of 25 Oct. [?1793] Burns wrote: 'There is, there must be, some truth in original sin.—My violent propensity to B—dy convinces me of it.—Lack a day! if that species of Composition be the Sin against "the Haly Ghaist," "I am the most offending soul alive"' (J. De Lancey Ferguson (ed.), *The Letters of Robert Burns*, 2 vols. (1931), ii. 213).

48. *"D[r] Young . . . &c. &c."* In his *Conjectures on Original Composition* (1759), Edward Young enthusiastically applauded what he regarded as Addison's exemplary manner of dying:

> After a long, and manly, but vain struggle with his distemper, he dismissed his physicians, and with them all hopes of life: But with his hopes of life he dismissed not his concern for the living, but sent for a youth nearly related, and finely accomplished, but not above being the better for good impressions from a dying friend: He came; but

life now glimmering in the socket, the dying friend was silent: After a decent, and proper pause, the youth said, 'Dear Sir! you sent for me: I believe, and I hope, that you have some commands; I shall hold them most sacred:' May distant ages not only hear, but feel, the reply! Forcibly grasping the youth's hand, he softly said, 'See in what peace a Christian can die.' He spoke with difficulty, and soon expired. Thro' Grace divine, how great is man? Thro' divine Mercy, how stingless death? Who would not thus expire? (pp. 101–2).

In a letter to George Montagu of 16 May 1759, Horace Walpole wrote:

Dr Young has published a new book, on purpose as he says himself to have an opportunity of telling a story that he has known these forty years—Mr Addison sent for the young Lord Warwick, as he was dying, to show him in what peace a Christian could die—unluckily he died of brandy—nothing makes a Christian die in peace like being maudlin!—but don't say this in Gath, where you are! (W. S. Lewis and Ralph S. Brown (eds.), *Horace Walpole's Correspondence with George Montagu*, 2 vols. (1941), i. 236 and n. The final phrase here alludes to II Samuel 1: 20, 'Tell it not in Gath, publish it not in the streets of Askelon.')

Young's story is of dubious authority. Apparently he got it from Tickell; but even in Samuel Johnson's time it was current knowledge that Addison's life had been shortened by excessive drinking.

49. *Suppose . . . peacemaker.* Defending himself against the imputation in *Quarterly Review* that he had aspersed Pope for, amongst other things, 'taking bribes to suppress satires' (p. 412), Bowles (quoting himself) had written:

'One circumstance is mentioned by Horace Walpole, which, if true, was indeed flagitious: Walpole informs Gray, that the character of ATOSSA was shown to the Duchess of Buckingham and the Duchess of Marlborough; that Pope received a thousand pounds from the Duchess of Marlborough, promising, on these terms to suppress it; that he took the money and then published it!'

I had already expressed warmly what I felt at the baseness of such transaction, IF TRUE; not at all implying that I believed it true. My 'Life' contains the following remarks on it, and these remarks are republished in the letter to Campbell [*The Invariable Principles*, pp. 36–7]; and here is a man, who has read those remarks, and having first perverted my obvious meaning, tells me I charge Pope with 'taking a bribe to suppress a satire, and then publishing it.'

Here then, again, I must quote my own words:

'A story *so base* ought not for a moment to be admitted, solely on the testimony of Walpole; till there is other proof, besides the assertion of Walpole, the same candour which made us REJECT what, upon no better foundation, was said of Addison, ought to make us *reject*, with equal readiness, the belief of a circumstance so DEROGATORY to the character of Pope!

Whatever can be proved ought not to be rejected; whatever (charge) has no other foundation than the "*ipse dixit*" *of an adversary* is entitled to NO REGARD.' ('A Reply', pp. 9–10 (quoting *The Works*, vol. i, pp. ci–cii).)

Pope's 'character of ATOSSA' is delineated in his *Moral Essays*, Epistle ii, 'To A Lady' ('Of the Characters of Women'), ll. 115–50). See also *As You Like It* V. iv (Touchstone on the merits of an 'if'), especially: 'Your "if" is the only peacemaker; much virtue in "if."'

50. *Why talk . . . recreation.* In *A Letter from Mr. Cibber to Mr. Pope* (1742), Colley

Cibber (1671–1757), Poet Laureate and the hero of *The Dunciad*, told the following malicious anecdote about Pope:

He may remember, then (or if he won't I will) when *Button's* Coffee-house was in vogue, and so long ago, as when he had not translated above two or three Books of *Homer*; there was a late young Nobleman (as much his *Lord* as mine) who had a good deal of wicked Humour, and who, though he was fond of having Wits in his Company, was not so restrained by his Conscience, but that he lov'd to laugh at any merry Mischief he could do them: This noble Wag, I say, in his usual *Gayetè de Coeur*, with another Gentleman still in Being, one Evening slily seduced the celebrated Mr. *Pope* as a Wit, and myself as a Laugher, to a certain House of Carnal Recreation, near the *Hay-Market*; where his Lordship's Frolick propos'd was to slip his little *Homer*, as he called him, at a Girl of the Game, that he might see what sort of Figure a Man of his Size, Sobriety, and Vigour (in Verse) would make, when the frail Fit of Love had got into him; in which he so far succeeded, that the smirking Damsel, who serv'd us with Tea, happen'd to have Charms sufficient to tempt the little-tiny Manhood of Mr. *Pope* into the next Room with her: at which you may imagine, his Lordship was in as much Joy, at what might happen within, as our small Friend could probably be in Possession of it: But I . . . observing he had staid as long as without hazard of his Health he might, I,

Prick'd to it by foolish Honesty and Love,

As *Shakespear* says [*Othello*, III. iii. 413 (Iago speaking)], without Ceremony, threw open the Door upon him, where I found this little hasty Hero, like a terrible Tom Tit, pertly perching upon the Mount of Love! But such was my surprize, that I fairly laid hold of his Heels, and actually drew him down safe and sound from his Danger. (pp. 47–8)

This story was refuted by Pope himself and his friend Mr. Cheselden. Spence recorded Pope saying:

The story invented by Cibber was an absolute lie, as to the main point. He was invited by Lord W. to pass an evening with him; and was carried by him, with Cibber and another, to a bagnio [brothel]; but nothing happened of the kind that Cibber mentions, to the best of my memory, and I had so few things of that kind ever on my hands, that I should have scarce forgot so material a circumstance.

And Mr Cheselden: 'I could give a more particular account of Mr. Pope's health than perhaps any man. Cibber's slander (of a carnosity), is false. He had been gay, but left that way of life upon his acquaintance with Mrs. B.' (*Anecdotes*, pp. 338–9).

51. *Mr. Bowles . . . might be.* B related this story in full in his letter to Murray of 10 May 1821. 'The anecdote of Mr. B. is as follows—& of course *not* for the public':

After dinner at Ld. Lansdowne's they were talking one evening as Sir Robert Walpole used to talk always [i.e. bawdy].—Bowles said that after all *love* was the only thing worthy the risk of damnation.—'When I was a very young man (said he) a friend of mine would take me to Paris.—I was not very eager to go till he said that Paris contained the *finest women in the world—and the kindest.*—We then set off.—It was deep winter—I was dying of all kinds of cold and inconvenience—but still thought no more of it—when I heard perpetually that there were the finest women in the world to be had at Paris.—When we got to Paris—I sallied forth the first evening—and thinking that it was only to ask and have—I accosted several with the tenderest politeness—but whether my French or my figure displeased them—I know not—I had short answers or none at all.—I returned—disconsolate—but having dined—my love revived—whatever my hope might.—At last wound up to a pitch of amatory desperation, I rushed forth determined to bring the question to a point with the first fair one of whatever quality I met with.——I had not gone far before I met with a lady-like modest-looking female—whom I accosted as follows: "Madame—voulez vous *foutre*?" she replied "*Si vous plaît Monsieur*" in the softest accents—I did so, caught a rousing p[ox]—was laid up for two months—& returned perfectly persuaded that there were the finest women in the world at Paris.' (*BLJ* viii. 111–12)

The 'third person' and B's informant was Moore, who was not at all pleased at B's exploiting this story. In his journal for 13 Apr. 1821, Moore wrote:

Found, on my return home at night, Lord Byron's letter about Bowles and Popery, which Fielding had sent me to look over. The whole thing is unworthy of him; a leviathan among small fry. He had had the bad taste to allude to an anecdote which I told him about Bowles's early life; which is even worse than Bowles in his pamphlet quoting me as entirely agreeing with him in the system he is combating for. (*Memoirs* iii. 222)

52. *is.* This has been silently corrected to 'it' in all editions.

53. *"second . . . Negus."* Having transcribed John Clare's sonnet 'Anxiety' (for which see J. W. Tibble (ed.), *Poems of John Clare*, 2 vols. (1935), i. 126), Gilchrist commented: 'This . . . may it please your reverence, is somewhat more poetical and rational than "sighing to the chime of *glad* bells," over the second tumbler of hot white-wine negus!' (Gilchrist, p. 13; referring to Bowles's Sonnet xxvii, 'On Revisiting Oxford', ll. 1–3: 'I never hear the sound of thy glad bells, / OXFORD! and chime harmonious, but I say, / (Sighing to think how time has worn away)'. See *Sonnets and Other Poems* (1798), p. 34). 'Negus' was a concoction of hot sweetened wine and water. Gilchrist is not aspersing Bowles's drinking habits here, but is drawing a contrast between the maudlin nature of his poetry, and 'compositions superior to his own' (p. 12), as well as insinuating Bowles's comfortable life in comparison with John Clare's genuine poverty.

54. *"he . . . Scripture."* Henry Fielding, *Jonathan Wild*, bk. iv, ch. 13.

55. *Judge . . . dose.* Sir William Blackstone (1723–80), Professor of Law at Oxford and author of the famous *Commentaries on the Laws of England* (1765–9). He was made a judge in 1770. Joseph Addison (1672–1719), poet and classical scholar, whom Pope ridiculed in the lines on 'Atticus' in his *Epistle to Dr. Arbuthnot* (ll. 193–214). (See also n. 48 above.) Boswell recorded that on Easter Day, 15 Apr. 1781, he called on Johnson and during his visit:

Dr. Scott, of the Commons, came in. He talked of its having been said, that Addison wrote some of his best papers in 'The Spectator,' when warm with wine. Dr. Johnson did not seem willing to admit this. Dr. Scott, as a confirmation of it, related, that Blackstone, a sober man, composed his 'Commentaries' with a bottle of port before him; and found his mind invigorated and supported in the fatigue of his great Work, by a temperate use of it. (*Boswell's Life of Johnson* iv. 91)

56. *Perhaps . . . operation.* This is Wordsworth, at whose expense B is making

some humorous capital. In fact, in his preface to *Poems* (1815), Wordsworth actually admitted to being a 'water-drinker'.

57. *These . . . title.* In 'A Reply' (p. 28), Bowles wrote that the editor of the *London Magazine* (John Scott) had sent him a letter, 'in which he informed me how much his own opinions differed from those of the contributor to the Magazine [i.e. Gilchrist]; and he has since as frankly declared his sentiments with Mr. Southey, Mr. Moore, &c. &c., that the arguments in the letter to Campbell [*The Invariable Principles*] were unanswerable'. In his *Second Reply* (p. 41), Bowles again cited his supporters:

> 'I thank you for your Letter to CAMPBELL. I had seen in a newspaper the passage which provoked it, but I had no suspicion that it was founded on so gross a mis-statement as that which you have proved. It is needless to add, I agree with you entirely on the "Invariable Principles of Poetry."[']—Mr. SOUTHEY, *one of the very ablest and most eloquent writers in the Quarterly Review.*
>
> Mr. SCOTT, the author of 'Paris Revisited,' and Editor of the London Magazine says, in that very Magazine, 'Mr. BOWLES has convicted Mr. CAMPBELL of ignorance.'
>
> Speaking of what is said, in the Letter, of works of nature and art, the Editor of BLACKWOOD'S Magazine says, 'All this is so very judicious, rational, and true, that neither Mr. CAMPBELL, *nor any other person, can* have a single word to say against it.'

On receiving his copy of *The Invariable Principles* from Bowles, Southey thanked him for it in a letter of 1819, adding: 'It is needless to add that I agree with you entirely upon the invariable principles of poetry: we learned them in the same school, and I was confirmed in them in my youth by seeing them exemplified in your writings.' And on 16 Oct. 1820, he wrote to Bowles saying: 'You are quite at liberty to make use of any thing in my letter which may suit your purpose' (Greever, *Wiltshire Parson*, pp. 115–16, 120). Moore, in a postscript to a letter to Bowles of Apr. 1819, had written: 'Your pamphlet is unanswerable, but I fear the public *will not* read' (*The Letters of Thomas Moore*, edited by Wilfred S. Dowden, 2 vols. (1964), ii. 475). Moore was not pleased at Bowles quoting him (see n. 51 above). In an editorial note in the *London Magazine* (vol. ii, no. vii (July 1820), pp. 5–6), John Scott wrote of Bowles:

> Having received much pleasure from the perusal of this gentleman's poetry, we are happy to be afforded an opportunity of stating so—and of adding that, in our view of the dispute between him and Mr. Campbell, he has completely convicted the latter gentleman of ignorance, in regard to what he took as the subject matter of accusation against Mr. Bowles,—and has entirely justified all that he ever advanced on 'the principles of poetry,' with reference to the writings of Pope.

In a very favourable review of *The Invariable Principles* in *Blackwood's Edinburgh Magazine* (vol. v, no. xxviii (July 1819), pp. 387–93), the reviewer cited a passage from that pamphlet concerning what Bowles says about works of nature and art, and commented: 'We think that all this is so very rational, judicious, and true, that neither Mr Campbell nor any other person can have a single word to say against it' (p. 388). Campbell did not indeed make any further response to Bowles, but not because he was 'astounded by the title'. In fact, on 18 Apr. 1819, a very civil exchange of letters took place between Bowles and Campbell, in which they both expressed a high regard for each other and the wish to become better acquainted. (See Greever, *Wiltshire Parson*, pp. 117–18.)

58. *The Sultan . . . League".* See also B's erasure in MS: 'La Fronde' was the name of two revolts against the absolute monarchy of Louis XIV (1638–1715), King of France (1643–1715), which took place in 1648–9, and 1651–2 respectively. B's anecdote here is slightly inaccurate. He refers to the alliance between Francis I (1494–1547), King of France (1515–47), and Suleiman I, 'The Magnificent' (1494/5–1566), Sultan of the Ottoman Empire (1520–66). In 1526 they exchanged embassies, and in 1536 signed a treaty of amity, which was essentially a trade agreement. In 1542, however, when Francis appealed to Suleiman for aid in his struggle against Charles V (1500–58), Holy Roman Emperor (1519–56), Suleiman agreed to 'joine further courtesies' to those he had already extended to Francis, but refused to 'joine in league with him, or in his quarrell to take up armes'. The reason for his refusal being that 'leagues are confirmed by like profit, by making even the charge and mutuall dangers'; but whereas he had always come promptly to the assistance of Francis, Francis had made him no 'requitall' 'in deeds and certaine aid, but onely in bare letters and embassages'. (Richard Knolles, *The Generall Historie of the Turkes* (1603), pp. 726–7.)

59. P*adishaw* (*not Pacha*). In all editions, excepting Prothero, 'Pa*di*shaw' reads 'Padishan', and the parenthesis '(*not Pacha*)' is omitted; Prothero follows MS. 'Padishaw' or 'Padishah' was the title of the Sultan of Turkey ('Pati', Lord; 'shah', King (Persian)); 'Pacha' or 'Pasha' (or 'Bashaw') is the title of a Turkish commander or a governor of a province ('Pacha' (from 'baş'), Chief, leader or head (Turkish)).

60. *struck to . . . skip.* No doubt B meant to write 'struck with'. Closing quotation marks omitted by B, who quotes stanza 4 of Coleridge's *The Rime of the Ancient Mariner*, as the text appears in the editions of *Lyrical Ballads* 1798–1805. (See, e.g. R. L. Brett and A. R. Jones (eds.), *Lyrical Ballads* (1965), pp. 10, 273.)

61. *I am . . . Customer."* This was doubtless a Liston quip (see n. 11 to 'To the Editor of the *British Review*' above).

62. *M*r *B. . . . poles."* This is where B's engagement with Bowles's aesthetic argument commences. In *Specimens* (pp. 265–6), Campbell had written.

Those who have ever witnessed the spectacle of the launching of a ship of the line, will perhaps forgive me for adding this to the examples of the sublime objects of artificial life. Of that spectacle I can never forget the impression, and of having witnessed it reflected from the faces of ten thousand spectators. They seem yet before me—I sympathise with their deep and silent expectation, and with their final burst of enthusiasm. It was not a vulgar joy, but an affecting rational solemnity. When the vast bulwark sprang from her cradle, the calm water on which she swung majestically round gave the imagination a contrast of the stormy element on which she was soon to ride. All the days of battle and the nights of danger which she had to encounter, all the ends of the earth she had to visit, and all that she had to do and to suffer for her country, rose in awful presentiment before the mind; and when the heart gave her a benediction, it was like one pronounced on a living being.

To which Bowles replied (*The Invariable Principles*, p. 11):

Let us examine the ship which you have described so beautifully. On what does the poetical beauty depend? not on *art*, but NATURE. Take away the *waves*, the *winds*, the *sun*, that, in association with the streamer and sails, make them look so beautiful! take all poetical associations away, ONE will become a strip of blue bunting, and the *other* a piece of coarse canvass on three tall poles!!

63. *Man is . . . poesy.* For the various echoes here, see Genesis 2: 7, Isaiah 40: 6, and (see B's erasure in MS), Lucretius, *De Rerum Natura* i. 155–6 ('nil posse creari / de nilo': nothing can be created of nothing); Persius, *Satire* iii. 84 ('de nihilo nihilum, in nihilum nil posse reverti': from nothing nothing can come, and to nothing nothing can return), and *King Lear* I. i. 92 (Lear to Cordelia): 'Nothing will come of nothing.'

64. *poem . . . Shipwreck.* For William Falconer's poem *The Shipwreck*, see n. 74 below.

65. *I recollect . . . without them.* For B's and Hobhouse's long anchorage off the Dardanelles on board the *Salsette* frigate during Apr.–May 1810, see Marchand i. 236–8; *BAP*, p. 82; and *BLJ* i. 236–43. See also *CHP* II. 77–81, and 'Written after swimming from Sestos to Abydos' (*CPW* ii. 69–71, 290; i. 281–2, 422–3). In his letter to Henry Drury of 3 May 1810, B wrote that he was on board 'a 36 gun frigate' (*BLJ* i. 239); but on the reverse side of an announcement of a performance of *All the World's a Stage* on 27 Apr. 1810, he noted that the *Salsette* was a frigate of '44 guns (rated 36)'. (See 'Fragmentary Writings', *post*.)

66. *The Euxine . . . upon.* Cf. *CHP* IV. 175–6, *DJ* V. 5 (*CPW* ii. 183; v. 242). The Euxine (the Black Sea) was no doubt 'a noble Sea to look upon' in B's mind because of its association with the famous cry of the Ten Thousand when they first saw it from the top of Mount Thechia (θήχης), after their wanderings in Asia Minor: 'θάλαττα, θάλαττα' (the Sea, the Sea). See Xenophon, *Anabasis* IV. vii. 24. (See also following n. 67.)

67. *As for . . . Argo?* In his letter to Henry Drury from Constantinople of 17 June 1810, B wrote:

I am just come from an expedition through the Bosphorus to the Black Sea and the Cyanean Symplegades, up which last I scrambled at as great a risk as ever the Argonauts escaped in their hoy. You remember the beginning of the nurse's dole in the Medea, of which I beg you to take the following translation, done on the summit:

'Oh how I wish that an embargo
Had kept in port the good ship Argo!
Who, still unlaunch'd from Grecian docks,
Had never pass'd the Azure rocks;

But now I fear her trip will be a
Damn'd business for my Miss Medea, &c. &c.[']

as it very nearly was to me,—for, had not this sublime passage been in my head, I should never have dreamed of ascending the said rocks, and bruising my carcass in honour of the ancients. (*BLJ* i. 245–6)

B translates the opening lines of the *Medea* of Euripides: the 'Symplegades' were the Clashing Rocks which the Argonauts had to negotiate on their way to Colchis over the Euxine to obtain the Golden Fleece.

68. *"Why bring . . . Stocks"?* See n. 62 above. Bowles continued his response to Campbell's description of the launching of the ship as follows (*The Invariable Principles*, p. 20):

Now let me ask you, when you so beautifully described this ship, why was it necessary to describe its LAUNCHING at all? If images derived from art are as beautiful and sublime as those derived from nature, why was it necessary to bring your ship *off the stocks*? It was complete, as far as art was concerned, before; it had the same sails, the same streamers, and the same tackle. But . . . to make the object of art so poetically interesting, you are obliged to have recourse to NATURE!

69. *Wordsworth . . . I.* In Wordsworth's *Poems, in Two Volumes* (1807), which B reviewed (see above), stanza 23 of 'The Blind Highland Boy' runs as follows (ii. 72):

But say, what was it? Thought of fear!
Well may ye tremble when ye hear!
—A Household Tub, like one of those
Which women use to wash their clothes,
This carried the blind Boy.

On Coleridge's advice, however, this stanza was dropped from Wordsworth's edition of *Poems* (1815), and a 'Shell of a green Turtle' conveyed the blind boy over Loch Leven. In his review of *Poems, in Two Volumes*, in the *Edinburgh Review* (vol. xi, no. xxi (Oct. 1807), art. xiv, pp. 214–31), Francis Jeffrey also ridiculed this stanza (p. 225):

'But say, what was it?' a poetical interlocutor is made to exclaim most naturally; and here followeth the answer, upon which all the pathos and interest of the story depend.

'A HOUSEHOLD TUB, like one of those
Which women use to wash their clothes!!'

This, it will be admitted, is carrying the matter as far as it will well go.

70. *"What . . . Poetry".* This phrase is not in inverted commas in any edition. B is parodying the persistent questions of Bowles.

71. *in.* In all editions, this reads 'or'.

72. *Grainger's . . . Johnson?* In his *Life of Johnson*, Boswell recorded:

He praised Grainger's 'Ode on Solitude,' in Dodsley's collection, and repeated, with great energy, the exordium:

'O Solitude, romantick maid,
Whether by nodding towers you tread;
Or haunt the desart's trackless gloom,
Or hover o'er the yawning tomb;
Or climb the Andes' clifted side,
Or by the Nile's coy source abide;
Or, starting from your half-year's sleep,
From Hecla view the thawing deep;
Or, at the purple dawn of day,
Tadnor's marble wastes survey';

observing, 'This, Sir, is very noble.' (*Boswell's Life of Johnson* iii. 197)

Johnson recites ll. 1–10 of James Grainger's 'Solitude. An Ode'. 'Tadnor' should read 'Tadmor'; its spelling here is explained by Hill: 'In the first three editions of Boswell we find *Tadnor* for *Tadmor*' (p. 197n.). 'Tadmor' is the Hebraic name for the ancient city in Syria more commonly known in modern tymes as 'Palmyra' (hence B's reference to it under that name in l. 32).

73. *"What . . . place.* This paragraph is written at the end of the MS of this letter immediately after B's 'Post Scriptum'. It bears the following direction by B: '⟨Add⟩ present this somewhere in the body of the letter *appropriately*'. Accordingly, in the first and all subsequent editions the passage is located here.

74. *Ask . . . them?* William Falconer's *The Shipwreck* was first published in 1762. The following lines describe the shipwreck itself:

It comes! the dire Catastrophe draws near,
Lashed furious on by destiny severe:
The ship hangs hovering on the verge of death,
Hell yawns, rocks rise, and breakers roar beneath! . . .

In vain the cords and axes were prepar'd,
For every wave now smites the quivering yard;
High o'er the ship they throw a dreadful shade,
Then on her burst in terrible cascade;
Across the foundered deck o'erwhelming roar,
And foaming, swelling, bound upon the shore.
Swift up the mounting billow now she flies,
Her shattered top half buried in the skies;
Borne o'er a latent reef the hull impends,
Then thundering on the marble crags descends:
Her ponderous bulk the dire concussion feels,
And o'er upheaving surges wounded reels—
Again she plunges! hark! a second shock
Bilges the splitting vessel on the rock.—
Down on the vale of death, with dismal cries,
The fated victims shuddering cast their eyes
In wild despair; while yet another stroke,
With strong convulsion rends the solid oak:
Ah Heaven!—behold her crashing ribs divide!
She loosens, parts, and spreads in ruin o'er the tide.

(*The Shipwreck* (1819), III, pp. 129–30)

75. *buried . . . confusion.* Although exploration of the sites of both Babylon and Nineveh had begun during B's lifetime, neither was excavated until much later in the nineteenth century.

76. (*who . . . skating*). This parenthesis is omitted in all editions except Prothero.

77. *I opposed . . . them.* For B's opposition to Lord Elgin's transportation of Grecian marbles to England, see especially *The Curse of Minerva*, and *CHP* II. 11–15 (*CPW* i. 320–30, 444–52; ii. 47–9, 189–92, 284).

78. *Mr. B. . . . fields".* With reference to the 'Pyramids of Egypt' and 'the Chinese Wall', Bowles wrote (*The Invariable Principles*, p. 10):

> I supposed that any reflecting person would see that these were poetical, *not essentially as works of art*, but from associations both with the highest feelings of nature, and some of her sublimest external works. The generations swept away round the ancient base of the Pyramids, the ages that are past since their erection, the mysterious obscurity of their origin, and many other complex ideas, enter into the imagination at the thought of these wonderful structures, besides the association with boundless deserts; as the Wall of China is associated with unknown rocks, mountains, and rivers. Build a pyramid of *new* brick, of the same dimensions as the pyramids of Egypt, in Lincoln's Inn fields, and then say how much of the poetical sublimity of the immense and immortal piles in the deserts of Egypt is derived, *not from art*, but from the association with GENERAL NATURE!

79. *Michel Agnolo.* Despite B's alteration here (see his erasure in MS), the first, second, and third editions of this letter read 'Michel Angelo'; *Works* (1832) reads 'Michael Angelo'; Prothero follows MS. The correct spelling is 'Michelangelo' (Michelangelo de Lodovico Buonarroti Simoni (1475–1564), the great Italian sculptor, painter, architect, and poet).

80. *It appears . . . Canova.* For B's visit to Florence and Rome in Apr.–May 1817 and his appreciation of their various works of art, see Marchand ii. 690–1, *BAP*, pp. 265–6; *CHP* IV. 48–55, 128–9, 140–62 (*CPW* ii. 140–2, 166–7, 171–9), and *BLJ* v. 218, 221, 227. Antonio Canova (1757–1822), the Italian sculptor greatly admired by B (see *BLJ* v. 218; *CHP* IV. 55 (*CPW* ii. 142)). After seeing Canova's bust of Helen at the house of the Countess d'Albrizzi in 1816, B wrote to Murray (25 Nov. 1816): 'The *Helen* of Canova . . . is without exception to my mind the most perfectly beautiful of human conceptions—and far beyond my ideas of human execution' (*BLJ* v. 133; see also 'On the Bust of Helen by Canova' (*CPW* iv. 46, 461)). In 1822 B subscribed to a memorial to Canova (*BLJ* x. 21, 76).

81. *the System . . . deity.* Baruch de Spinoza (1632–77), moral and political philosopher, and author of *Tractatus Theologico-Politicus* (1670) and *Ethics* (1677), rejected the Cartesian dualism of spirit and matter. He maintained that all things material were merely aspects or manifestations of an immanent and infinite creative force in nature that was 'the deity'.

82. *"The dirt . . . rose".* Pope, *Essay on Man* iv. 292.

83. *and whoever . . . Nymphs.* Pope, *The Dunciad* ii. 323–52. B's allusion is peculiarly apt, since Pope here satirizes two clergymen, 'The plunging Prelate, and his pond'rous Grace' (l. 323; respectively, Bishop Sherlock and John Potter, the Archbishop of Canterbury). See also B's erasure in MS. In naval language a 'lubber' is a clumsy sailor or an unseamanlike person; in its less specific usage it is a lazy, stupid, clumsy lout (which is not what B would wish to imply of Bowles here).

84. *The very . . . domain.* The 'Cloaca' ('sewer' (Latin)), was the underground drainage system built by Tarquin in the seventh and sixth centuries BC. For the site of future Rome, see *Aeneid*, bk. viii. (Evander was a mythical Arcadian king who settled with his followers some sixty years before the Trojan War on the banks of the Tiber at the foot of the Palatine Hill, and there built the town of Pallantium which later became part of Rome.)

85. *M! B. . . . it.*" Bowles wrote:

> To proceed; you say, 'HOMER himself is a minute describer of works of art!' [Campbell, *Specimens*, p. 264 (without the upper case or exclamation)] But are his descriptions of works of art more poetical than his descriptions of the great feelings of nature? Nay, that great part of the Odyssey derives its peculiar charm from the scenes of NATURE; as the Iliad does from its loftier passions. The most remarkable of the works of *art* mentioned by HOMER, are the ships in the catalogue and the shield of Achilles. The first is solely rendered *poetical* by the brief interspersions of natural landscape. The shield of Achilles derives its poetical interest from the subjects described on it, far more than from its workmanship, and these subjects are the creation of the heaven and earth, scenes of Pastoral and Military life, the rural dance, &c. Besides, was the age of HOMER an æra of refinement or *artificial* life? by whom not even such a *poetical work* of *art* as a *bridge* is mentioned! (*The Invariable Principles*, p. 15)

For the catalogue of ships, see the *Iliad*, bk. ii; for the shield of Achilles, see following n. 86.

86. *And from . . . Greeks?* For the helmet and mail of Patroclus and the armour of Achilles made by Hephæstus, see the *Iliad*, bks. xvi and xviii respectively.

87. *In that case . . . weapons.* For the combat between Hector and Achilles see the *Iliad*, bk. xxii. See also B's erasure in MS. Tom Cribb (1781–1848), Bob Gregson (1778–1824), and John Gulley (1783–1863) were famous prize-fighters in B's time. (See for example *BLJ* i. 182, iii. 221; but see *post*, 'Observations upon Observations'.) B may also have had in mind here John Wilson's highly entertaining article in *Blackwood's Edinburgh Magazine* (vol. iv, no. xxiv (Mar. 1819), pp. 722–8), entitled 'On the Connexion between Pugilism, Statuary, Painting, Poetry and Politics', in which Wilson observed facetiously that 'the chief advantage which the ancient sculptor possessed over the modern, was that of beholding the naked body in contention as well as in repose' (p. 722).

88. *Is there . . . unsophisticated?* For Odysseus striking the horses of Rhesus with his bow, see the *Iliad*, bk. x.

89. *'shapeless sculpture"?* Gray's 'Elegy Written in a Country Churchyard', stanza 20.

90. *Of Sculpture . . . opinion.* Cf. *DJ* II. 118–19; IV. 61; and 'A Note on Sculpture', *post.*

91. *But . . . ideal.* B has omitted closing parenthesis after 'ago'. B refers to the Venus di Medici by Cleomenes (*fl.* during 2nd century BC), which he saw at Florence on 23 Apr. 1817 (*BLJ* v. 216, 218). Lady Charlemont, the wife of the second Earl of Charlemont, was a famous Irish belle. B first met her in Nov. 1813, and although she was a 'Blue' (bluestocking) he was struck by her beauty. In his journal for 22 Nov. 1813, for instance, he recorded his impression of her: 'but I say nothing of *her*—"look in her face and you forget them all," and every thing else. Oh that face!—by "te Diva potens Cypri" I would, to be beloved by that woman, build and burn another Troy' (*BLJ* iii. 214–15; see also iii. 171, 228; viii. 54).

92. *I recollect . . . mountains.* In his Ravenna Journal (1821), B recalled having seen women 'mending the roads in Epirus with good success' (*BLJ* viii. 15). And in his note to *CHP* II. 38 he remarked: 'the most beautiful women I ever beheld, in stature and in features, we saw *levelling* the *road* broken down by the torrents between Delvinachi and Libochabo' (*CPW* ii. 195).

93. *neither.* In all editions this has been silently changed to 'never'.

94. *Let us . . . fields".* *Henry V* II. iii. 17–18. The MS of the passage here (from 'Let us examine' to '"Tis distance . . . hue?'), was sent by B to Murray on 9 Mar. 1821, with the request that it should 'be inoculated into the body of the letter' (*BLJ* viii. 90). Evidently it failed to reach Murray in time for inclusion in the first edition (first issue), and was first published at the end of the second issue of the first edition as an Addenda, with the direction to the reader that it should be inserted at this point. Accordingly, in the second and all subsequent editions, the passage is located here. In B's MS it is superscribed merely 'Additions & insertions, &c.' (See also n. 117 below.)

95. *I have . . . spoken.* This reads 'I have just spoken' in all editions, except Prothero, which follows MS.

96. *the Greek . . . Venus.* B has in mind here the painter Zeuxis (*c.*400 BC), who embodied his picture of Helen (*not* Venus) from the beauties of five different women. (See n. 27 to 'Comments in Hobhouse's *Imitations*', *post.*)

97. *"Oh fons . . . vitro".* B quotes from Horace, *Carminum* III. xiii. 1: 'O fons Bandusiae splendidior vitro' (O spring of Bandusia, clearer than glass).

98. *"You . . . through.* *Julius Caesar* III. ii. 175, 179 respectively. (B adds his own italics.)

99. *"Who . . . Bozrah?* Isaiah 63: 1 (B's emphasis).

100. *The mother . . . Chariot."* Judges 5: 28.

101. *Solomon . . . exaggeration.* Song of Solomon 7: 4.

102. *"The . . . sex—".* Addison, *Cato* I. iv (B's emphasis; Juba, Prince of Numidia, is speaking of Marcia, the daughter of Cato).

103. *purposes.* The note appended here was sent by B to Murray on 8 May 1821, with the direction to 'print it on a separate page and distribute it to the purchasers of the former copies' (*BLJ* viii. 109). There is no evidence to suggest that Murray did this. It was first published in Prothero. The MS bears the superscription by B: '*Additional note to Letter 1st to J.M. Esqre.*'

104. *this.* Prothero reads 'the'.

105. *Johnson's . . . &c.* Samuel Johnson's life of Congreve (*Lives of the English Poets* ii. 229–30). Johnson quotes Congreve's *The Mourning Bride* II. i. 1–18. B omits the first two exchanges between Leonora and Almeria (ll. 1–6) which Johnson quotes.

106. *Garrick . . . effect.* David Garrick (1717–79), the great actor and manager of the Drury Lane Theatre, where he produced many of Shakespeare's plays. On 16 Oct. 1769 Boswell gave a dinner party at which, amongst others, Garrick, Goldsmith, Johnson, and Sir Joshua Reynolds were guests. Boswell recorded:

> Johnson said, that the description of the temple, in 'The Mourning Bride,' was the finest poetical passage he had ever read; he recollected none in Shakspeare equal to it.—'But, (said Garrick, all alarmed for the "god of his idolatry,") we know not the extent and variety of his powers. We are to suppose there are such passages in his works. Shakspeare must not suffer from the badness of our memories.' Johnson, diverted by this enthusiastick jealousy, went on with greater ardour: 'No, Sir; Congreve has *nature*;' (smiling on the tragick eagerness of Garrick;) but composing himself, he added, 'Sir, this is not comparing Congreve on the whole, with Shakspeare on the whole; but only maintaining that Congreve has one finer passage than any that can be found in Shakspeare. . . . What I mean is, that you can shew me no passage where there is simply a description of material objects, without any intermixture of moral notions, which produces such an effect.' . . .
> Some one mentioned the description of Dover Cliff.
> JOHNSON. 'No, Sir; it should be all precipice,—all vacuum. The crows impede your fall. The diminished appearance of the boats, and other circumstances, are all very good description; but do not impress the mind at once with the horrible idea of immense height. The impression is divided; you pass on by computation, from one stage of the tremendous space to another. . . .' (*Boswell's Life of Johnson* ii. 85–7)

For the description of Dover Cliff, see *King Lear* IV. vi. 12–25, of which B quotes ll. 15–16 here: 'half way down / Hangs one that gathers samphire, dreadful trade!'

107. *"idiot . . . glory."* Wordsworth, 'The Idiot Boy' (closing couplet of the final stanza): 'Thus answered Johnny in his glory, / And that was all his travel's story.' B mocked this couplet in *EBSR*, ll. 253–4: 'all who view the "idiot in his glory", / Conceive the Bard the hero of the story' (*CPW* i. 236).

108. *"mast . . . Ammiral".* With reference to Milton's *Paradise Lost* i. 284–94,

Campbell had written (*Specimens*, pp. 264–5): 'Homer himself is a minute describer of works of art; and Milton is full of imagery derived from it. Satan's spear is compared to the pine that makes "the mast of some great ammiral," and his shield is like the moon, but like the moon artificially seen through the glass of the Tuscan artist.' To which Bowles had answered (*The Invariable Principles*, pp. 15–17):

> it is remarked, as if the argument was at once *decisive*, that MILTON is full of imagery derived from art; 'Satan's spear,' for example, is compared to the 'MAST OF SOME GREAT AMMIRAL!' Supposing it is, do you really think that such a comparison makes the description of Satan's spear a whit *more poetical*; I think *much less* so. But MILTON was not so unpoetical as you imagine, though I think his simile does not greatly add to our poetical ideas of Satan's spear! The 'mast of the great admiral' [*sic*] might have been left out; but remark, in this image MILTON DOES NOT compare Satan's spear '*with the mast of some great admiral* [*sic*],' as you assert. The passage is,
>
> 'His spear, to equal which the TALLEST PINE
> Hewn on NORWEGIAN HILLS, TO BE the mast
> Of some great admiral, were but a wand!!'
> [*Paradise Lost* i. 292–4; 'admiral' should read 'ammiral', and the upper case and exclamations are Bowles's.]
>
> You leave out the chief, I might say the only, circumstance, which reconciles the 'mast' to us; and having detruncated MILTON'S image, triumphantly say, 'MILTON is full of imagery derived from art!!' You come on, '*detrâque sinistrâque* [left and right],' and say, not only Satan's spear is compared to an '*admiral's mast*,' but '*his shield to the moon seen through a telescope*!'
>
> My dear Sir, consider a little.... I beseech you recollect MILTON'S image.
>
> 'His pond'rous shield,
> Hung on his shoulders like the moon, whose orb
> Through optic glass the Tuscan artist views
> At EVENING, FROM THE TOP OF FESOLE,
> Or in VALDARNO, TO DESCRY NEW LANDS,
> RIVERS, OR MOUNTAINS, IN HER SPOTTY GLOBE.'
> [*Paradise Lost* i. 284, 287–91 (Bowles's upper case).]
>
> Who does not perceive the art of the poet in introducing, besides the telescope, as if conscious how unpoetical it was in itself, all the circumtances from NATURE, *external nature.* The evening—the top of Fesole—the scenes of Valdarno,—and the LANDS, MOUNTAINS, and RIVERS, in the moon's orb? It is these which make the passage poetical, and not the '*telescope*!!'

109. *In what ... learning."* In all editions 'Shipwrecks'' reads 'shipwrecks' Canto III, para. iii of William Falconer's *The Shipwreck* (1819, pp. 109–19), contains a long digression on the philosophers and heroes of ancient Greece, such as Plato, Xerxes, Solon, Hero, and Leander, which disrupts both the narrative and the pace of the poem. (See also n. 74 above.) For B's quotation see Sheridan, *The Rivals* I. ii (Mrs Malaprop speaking to Sir Anthony Absolute).

110. *"Sed ... &c.* Lucretius, *De Rerum Natura* I. 936–8 (emphasizing 'pocula', cup; 'tetra' should read 'taetra', and 'dulci mellis', 'mellis dulci'). These lines

might be translated: 'but as with children, when doctors wish to administer a bitter medicine to them, they first smear the rim of the cup with sweet yellow liquid honey'. This image (which recurs in IV. 11–13) is employed by Lucretius as a metaphor for the manner in which he conveys harsh truths in the sweetness of verse.

111. *"Cosi. . . &c.* Tasso, *Gerusalemme Liberata*, I. iii, which lines might translate: 'So we give a sick child a cup [of unpleasant medicine] the rim of which is smeared with a sweet liquid.' (Cf. the foregoing n. 110; Tasso is also referring to his revelation of truth in the beauty of verse.)

112. *In Cowper. . . Shrubbery.* See also n. 161 below. In the opening lines of *The Task*, bk. iv ('The Winter Evening'), Cowper announces the arrival of the Postman thus:

Hark! 'tis the twanging horn o'er yonder bridge,
That with its wearisome but needful length
Bestrides the wintry flood, in which the moon
Sees her unwrinkled face reflected bright;—
He comes, the herald of a noisy world,
With spatter'd boots, strapp'd waist, and frozen locks;
News from all nations lumbering at his back.

There is no 'Toby "banging the door"' in Cowper's works. But see his 'Epistle to Joseph Hill, Esq.' (ll. 20–3):

Horatio's servant once, with bow and cringe,
Swinging the parlour-door upon its hinge,
Dreading a negative, and overaw'd
Lest he should trespass, begg'd to go abroad.

113. *In Dyer's . . . image.* The three passages of verse that follow here (the quatrain, the couplet, and the sextuplet) B cites from John Dyer's *Grongar Hill* (ll. 99–102, 121–2, 123–8 respectively (B's italics)). The note appended here is taken from B's letter to Murray of (?13–16) Mar. 1821, in which he instructed Murray as follows (*BLJ* viii. 94): 'In the letter to you upon Bowles &c.—insert *these* which follow (*under* the place as a Note—where I am speaking of Dyer's Gronger [*sic*] Hill—and the use of *artificial* imagery in illustrating *Nature*)—'. There then follows this note. Murray did not pursue B's instruction; nor does this note appear in Prothero. For B's quotation in the note see Corneille, *Polyeucte* IV. ii. 6–10 (Polyeucte soliloquizing):

Toute votre félicité,
Sujette à l'instabilité,
En moins de rien tombe par terre;
Et comme elle a l'éclat du verre,
Elle en a la fragilité.

('All your happiness, being subject to instability, in less than no time can crumble to earth; and just as she has the brilliance of glass, so has she also its fragility.')

114. *And here . . . Campbell.* See n. 108 above.

115. *By the way.* In all editions 'And here' has been substituted for 'By the way'.

116. *Is it not this.* In all editions this reads 'Is not this'.

117. *"Tis . . . hue?* See also n. 94 above; the inserted passage ends here. B cites ll. 7–8 of Thomas Campbell's *The Pleasures of Hope*, pt. i.

118. *"i Murazzi".* This phrase is taken from B's letter to Murray of 12 Feb. 1821, in which he instructed Murray (*BLJ* viii. 77): 'In the letter on Bowles—after the words "the long walls of Palestrina and Malamocco" [*sic*] add "*i Murazzi*" which is their Venetian title.' Murray did not follow this direction; nor does this addition appear in Prothero. B refers to the gigantic sea-wall which stretches for some two and a half miles along the shore of the island of Pellestrina, and which took 38 years to complete (1744–82). Malamocco is a town below the Lido. While B was living in Venice, he used to take 'a spanking gallop of some miles daily along a firm and solitary beach, from the fortress to Malamocco, the which contributes considerably to my health and spirits' (*BLJ* vi. 10).

119. *"thus . . . further".* Job 38: 11.

120. *Hog . . . wind?* In Walter Scott's *Old Mortality*, the Laird of Langcale presents himself before the gates of the castle and uplifts, 'with a Stentorian voice, a verse of the twenty-fourth Psalm'; at which Major Bellenden demands 'to know for what purpose or intent he made that doleful noise, like a hog in a high wind, beneath the gates of the castle' (*Novels and Tales* (1825), x. 299. The Laird would have been singing verse 7 of Psalm 24: 'Lift up your heads, O ye gates; and be ye lift up, ye everlasting doors.' See also verse 9.)

121. *"what . . . scenery".* Bowles inquired rhetorically (*The Invariable Principles*, p. 27): 'I would ask you, what makes the venerable towers of Westminster Abbey, on the side of the Thames, more poetical, as objects, than the tower for the manufactory of *patent shot*, surrounded by the same scenery, and *towering* amidst the smoke *of the city*?'

122. *the Parthenon . . . consequence.* Francesco Morosini (1618–94), elected Doge of Venice in 1688, besieged Athens under the Turks in 1687. In *A History of Venice* (1982, p. 566), John Julius Norwich writes that on

> Monday, 26 September 1687, at about seven o'clock in the evening, a mortar placed by Morosini on the Mouseion Hill opposite the Acropolis was fired by a German lieutenant at the Parthenon—which, by a further curse of fate, the Turks were using as a powder magazine. He scored a direct hit. The consequent explosion almost completely demolished the *cella* and its frieze, eight columns on the north side and six on the south, with their entablatures.

(See also *CHP* II. 1, and B's n. (*CPW* ii. 44, 189–90, 282); and see George Finlay, *A History of Greece*, ed. Revd H. F. Tozer, 7 vols. (1970), v. 185.)

123. *Cromwell's . . . Cathedral.* Although Cromwell's troops did indeed plunder both the town and the cathedral of Worcester after the Siege (1642) and Battle (1651) of Worcester, it was the Royalists who used the cathedral as a depot during the former, and Charles as his headquarters during the latter.

124. *Waterloo . . . inferior.* By an Act of Parliament in 1816, the bridge which spans the Thames from the Strand to Lambeth and whose foundation stone had been laid on 11 Oct. 1811 was named 'Waterloo'. It was opened by the Prince Regent and the Duke of Wellington on 18 June 1817, the second anniversary of the Battle of Waterloo (18 June 1815). Although a monument to commemorate Nelson and the Battle of Trafalgar (21 Oct. 1805) was discussed in parliament in 1818, the matter was not pursued until after B's death.

125. *"whether . . . forest?* Bowles wrote (*The Invariable Principles*, p. 29):

> Now I would put to you a few plain questions . . . Whether you think the description of a game of cards be as *poetical*, supposing the execution in the artists equal, as a description of a WALK in a FOREST? Whether an age of refinement be as conducive to pictures of poetry, as a period less refined? Whether passions, affections, &c. of the human heart be not a higher source of what is pathetic or sublime in poetry, than habits or manners, that apply only to artificial life?

Bowles alludes to the game of cards in Pope's *The Rape of Lock*, canto iii, and to Cowper's description of a wood in *The Task*, bk. i, 'The Sofa' (see n. 161 below).

126. *But . . . art.* Bowles's '"ordering" of poets' may already be apparent; however, he summarized his argument as follows (*The Invariable Principles*, p. 22):

> The plain course of my argument was simply this:—1st. *Works of nature*, speaking of those *more* beautiful and sublime, are *more* sublime and beautiful than works of art; therefore more poetical.—2d. The passions of the human heart, which are the same in all ages, and which are the causes of the sublime and pathetic in sentiment, are more *poetical* than *artificial manners*.—3d. The great poet of human passions is the most consummate master of his art; and the heroic, the lofty, and the pathetic, as belonging to this class, are distinguished.—4th. If these premises be true, the descriptive poet, who paints from an intimate knowledge of external nature, is more poetical, supposing the fidelity and execution equal, *not* than the painter of human passions, but the painter of external circumstances in *artificial life*; as COWPER paints a morning walk, and POPE a game of cards!!

127. *is . . . highest.* In all editions this reads 'is one of the highest'. This notion goes back at least as far as Aristotle (the *Poetics*). However, B may also have in mind here Dante's ranking the tragic the highest style (see n. 134 below), and the discussion of tragedy as one of the highest species of art (with particular reference to Addison, Otway, Rowe, and Young (see n. 129 below)) by Hugh Blair, in his *Lectures on Rhetoric and Belles Lettres* (2 vols. (1783), ii. 477–527). (See also n. 130 below.)

128. *Hughes . . . none.* John Hughes (1677–1720), dramatist and poet, author of

the highly successful tragedy *The Siege of Damascus* (1720). Elijah Fenton (1683–1730), dramatist and poet, author of *Mariamne: A Tragedy* (1723).

129. *Was even . . . since?* Addison's tragedy *Cato* was first produced, with huge and immediate success, in 1713. Nicholas Rowe (1674–1718), dramatist, most renowned for his tragedies *The Fair Penitent* (1703) and *Jane Shore* (1714). Edward Young (1683–1765), poet and dramatist, author of the immensely popular poem *The Complaint, or Night Thoughts* (1742–5), and the successful tragedies *Busiris* (1719) and *The Revenge* (1721). Thomas Otway (1652–85), dramatist, author of amongst many other works one of B's favourite tragedies, *Venice Preserv'd* (1682). Thomas Southerne (1659–1746), poet and dramatist, best known for his tragedies *The Fatal Marriage* (1694) and *Oroonoko* (1703).

130. *let him . . . poem.* No doubt B has in mind here Hugh Blair's observations on 'descriptive poetry':

> By Descriptive Poetry, I do not mean any one particular species or form of Composition. There are few Compositions of any length, that can be called purely descriptive, or wherein the Poet proposes to himself no other object, but merely to describe, without employing narration, action or moral sentiment, as the ground-work of his Piece. Description is generally introduced as an embellishment, rather than made the subject, of a regular work. (Blair, *Lectures on Rhetoric and Belles Lettres* ii. 371)

Cf. also Pope's view of descriptive poetry:

> It is a great fault, in descriptive poetry, to describe every thing. The good antients, (but when I named them, I meant Virgil) have no long descriptions: commonly not above ten lines, and scarce ever thirty. One of the longest in Virgil is when Æneas is with Evander; and that is frequently broke by what Evander says. (*Anecdotes*, pp. 139–40)

Pope refers to the *Aeneid*, bk. viii. (See also n. 84 above.)

131. *Alfieri.* The note appended here, of which there is no MS extant, was first published as a supplementary note at the end of the third edition of this letter, referring the reader to this location. Accordingly, in *Works* (1832) and Prothero it is printed as a footnote to this passage. The present text is taken from the third edition.

132. *who ever . . . Africa?* Petrarch's *Africa*, written in Latin on the subject of the second Punic war (Rome v. Carthage, 218–201 BC), was begun *c.*1338, and published posthumously in 1396.

133. *Of these . . . at all.* For Dante, Petrarch, Ariosto, and Tasso, see respectively nn. 135, 136, 137, and 139 to 'Some Observations' above. Vittorio Alfieri (1749–1803), poet and dramatist, author of a number of plays on classical subjects, of which B mentions in particular *Filippo* (1775–6) and *Mirra* (1784). On 11 Aug. 1819 B saw a performance of the latter that threw him into 'convulsions' from which he took some time to recover. (See *BLJ* vi. 206, 217; viii. 12, 15, 210; see also Hobhouse's note to *CHP* IV. 54 (*CPW* ii. 142, 236–7).)

134. *He himself . . . explain.* In his *Storia della Letteratura Italiana* (11 vols. (1772–95), v. (1775), 393), Girolamo Tiraboschi (1731–94), one of the foremost of

'commentators' on Dante at the time, maintained that Dante, having pronounced the high style Tragedy, the middle style Comedy and the low style Elegaic, entitled his great work *La Divina Commedia* because he felt that he had written it in the middle style. Tiraboschi himself, however, regarded the poem as belonging neither to Tragedy, Comedy, Epic, nor to any other regular genre.

135. *It is . . . century.* B refers to the famous 'Querelle des Anciens et des Modernes', which took place during the latter half of the seventeenth century between the advocates of *classicisme* (with its strictness of 'taste') and the champions of *les Modernes* (with their *relativité du goût*). The cause of *les Anciens* was represented by such writers as Boileau (*L'Art Poétique* (1674), *Discours sur l'ode* (1693), *Lettre à M. Pérrault* (1701)) and La Bruyère (*Caractères* (1688)); that of *les Modernes* by such writers as Charles Pérrault (*Poème sur le siècle de Louis le Grand* (1687); *Parallèles des anciens et des modernes* (1688–97)) and Fontenelle (*Réflexions sur le poétique et sur la poésie en général* (1678); *Discours sur l'eglogue* (1683); *Digression sur les anciens et les modernes* (1688)). Pierre Corneille (1606–84), dramatist, commonly regarded as the father of French tragedy; Jean Racine (1639–1699), dramatist, Corneille's successor and rival. In his *Britannicus* (1669) and *Bérénice* (1670), and in their respective prefaces, Racine attacked Corneille for his complexity of plot and argued for greater simplicity of action in drama. Prosper Jolyot, Sieur de Crebillon (1674–1762), dramatist, author of many melodramatic tragedies such as *Électre* (1708), *Zénobie* (1711), and *Sémiramis* (1717). In his *Mémoires*, Marmontel recorded how the enemies of Voltaire exploited Madame de Pompadour's patronage of Crebillon to oust Voltaire from favour at the court of Louis XV. (See *Mémoires d'un père*, 4 vols. (1804), i. 367–74.)

136. *Bettinelli . . . "that barbarian".* Saverio Bettinelli (1718–1808), poet and critic, author of the famous *Lettere Virgiliane* (1757), in which he depreciated Dante and other poets of his age. In his *Dissertazione Accademica sopra Dante*, he accused Dante of extravagance and obscurity. (See Saverio Bettinelli, *Opere*, 24 vols. (1801), xxii. 151–230.) Vincenzo Monti (1754–1828), poet and translator of the *Iliad* into Italian, first achieved critical notice with *La Vizione d'Ezechiello* (1776). His output was prolific and its style earned him the sobriquet 'Dante ingentilito' (the 'refined Dante'). He supported Dante against Bettinelli in his *Lezioni d'Eloquenza* (1803; *Lezione Nona*, 'Dante') and in *Lettera all'abate Saverio Bettinelli* (1807). (See *Prose e Poesie di Vincenzo Monti*, 5 vols. (1847), iv. 169–181, 189–252 respectively.) Hobhouse and B met him in Milan in Oct. 1816 and it may well have been then that Monti told them of his reproval by Bettinelli for reading 'that barbarian'. (See Marchand ii. 662–7; *BAP*, pp. 255–6; *BLJ* v. 119; see also Hobhouse's note to *CHP* IV. 57: 'Bettinelli one day rebuked his pupil Monti, for poring over the harsh, and obsolete extravagances of the *Commedia*' (*CPW* ii. 239).) B admired Monti's poetry but not his politics: 'that

Judas of Parnassus', he called him (*BLJ* vii. 152—Monti having praised first Napoleon, and then the Austrians).

137. *Schlegel . . . romantic.* In *De la littérature* (1800) and *De l'Allemagne* (1810), Madame de Staël interpreted foreign literature to her fellow countrymen in the light of the distinction between 'classical and romantic' writers. Her views were greatly influenced by August Wilhelm von Schlegel, who formulated the same distinction in the lectures he originally gave in Berlin and Vienna. See general note to 'Some recollections of my acquaintance with Madame de Stael' (1821), *post.*

138. *Had Gray . . . fame.* B echoes the common opinion exemplified by Samuel Johnson. (See n. 142 to 'Some Observations' above.)

139. *ingenuous.* This reads 'ingenious' in Prothero.

140. *"That . . . Song.* Pope, *Epistle to Dr. Arbuthnot*, ll. 340–1.

141. *am.* See also B's erasure in MS. Although B altered the pronoun here from 'I' to 'we', he forgot to alter the verb. In all editions 'am' has been silently emended to 'are'.

142. *The Georgics . . . burnt.* The story runs that Virgil's dying wish was that the *Aeneid* should be burnt, but that this was countermanded by Augustus, and he was persuaded instead to allow his two poet friends Tucca and Varius Rufus to edit and publish it.

143. *"The . . . Man".* Pope, *Essay on Man* ii. 2.

144. *It is . . . qualities.* B covertly attacks here the theories of poetry propounded by Wordsworth, Coleridge, Hazlitt, Hunt, and Keats.

145. *If Lucretius . . . ethics.* Lucretius (99–55 BC), author of *De Rerum Natura*, which follows the system of Epicurus (see n. 46 above). For Lucretius' praise of Epicurus as his master, see *De Rerum Natura* i. 62–79; iii. 1–13; v. 1–23, 49–56; vi. 1–34. B no doubt feels that the poem is ruined by its ethics because, as with Epicurus, Lucretius maintained an atomic theory of nature (creation of the universe and all existing things by a concourse of atoms), and denies the immortality of the soul (mind and body exist only in union; the soul permeates the body, and like the body is mortal). (See in particular *De Rerum Natura*, bk. iii.) Lucretius' object was to liberate man from both his dependence on and fear of the gods. (Cf. also *DJ* I. 43.)

146. *has.* Omitted in all editions.

147. *Milton . . . therewithal.* Bowles wrote ('Observations' (2), p. 20—referring to *Paradise Lost* vi. 482–91): 'Who does not draw back with peculiar distaste, from those passages, where the Satanic army bring their great guns charged with the gunpowder! Why is this? Because an image from art is brought too close, and too immediately and distinctly to our view!'

148. *"villainous salpetre". Henry IV, Part I*, I. iii. 60. In all editions 'salpetre' has been silently corrected to 'saltpetre'. See also B's erasure in MS. For 'the Lake with liquid fire' and the 'Plain . . . That underneath had veins of liquid fire / Sluc't from the Lake', see *Paradise Lost* i. 229, 701 respectively.

149. *&.* In all editions this is included within the following parenthesis: '(and in fact, *blasphemous*)'.

150. *It would . . . Jehovah.* See also n. 147 above. The thunderbolt is the attribute of Jove (Zeus), who is almost invariably depicted with it. Jehovah (or Yahweh), the God of the Old Testament, has no such material attribute.

151. *In a portion . . . subject.* In 'A Reply' (p. 7), Bowles wrote of Pope:

That he could have no invidious feelings I deny. He envied Phillips, for the success of his Pastoral [*sic*]; and he surely showed the gratification of a contracted mind, when Gay so successfully ridiculed them, in his Shepherd's Week; and his paper in the Guardian, is a lasting proof of *invidious* feelings, in this respect, as it is of the insidious mode he took to gratify them.

The allusion is to the *Guardian*, no. 40 (27 Apr. 1713), in which Pope anonymously compares his own pastorals with those of Ambrose Philips (?1675–1749), ironically showing how much the latter's are superior to his own. The following is a fair specimen of 'that most admirable model of irony':

Having now shown some parts, in which these two writers may be compared, it is a justice I owe to Mr. Philips to discover those in which no man can compare with him. First, That beautiful rusticity, of which I shall only produce two instances out of a hundred not yet quoted:

'O woeful day! O day of woe! quoth he,
And woeful I, who live the day to see!'

The simplicity of diction, the melancholy flowing of the numbers, the solemnity of the sound, and the easy turn of the words in this Dirge (to make use of our author's expression) are extremely elegant.

In another of his pastorals, a shepherd utters a Dirge not much inferior to the former, in the following lines:

'Ah me the while! a me! the luckless day,
Ah luckless lad! the rather might I say;
Ah silly I! more silly than my sheep,
Which on the flow'ry plains I once did keep.'

How he still charms the ear with these artful repetitions of the epithets; and how significant is the last verse! I defy the most common reader to repeat them, without feeling some motions of compassion. (Warton ix. 338–9)

152. *If Mr . . . "envy?"* For William Thomas Fitzgerald, see n. 108 to 'Some Observations' above. For Bowles's *The Spirit of Discovery*, see n. 5 above; his *The Missionary; A Poem* was first published in 1813. (See for example *BLJ* v. 187, 193, 197, and *CPW* iv. 114, 'Versicles'.) B is here playfully drawing a parallel between Philips and Fitzgerald, and Pope and Bowles (and is incidentally complimenting the latter).

153. *The Authors . . . them?* In their *Rejected Addresses* (1812), James and Horace Smith parodied twenty-one eminent authors of the day whose Addresses, for the opening of the Drury Lane Theatre, they pretended had been submitted to and rejected by the Committee. Their parody of B (specifically *CHP* I and II) is written in twelve Spenserean stanzas and is entitled 'Cui Bono?' ('What's the good?'). B thought it excellent fun. (See *BLJ* ii. 221, 235; iii. 7.) See also n. 167 below.

154. *Welsted . . . Dunciad.* In Prothero 'Theobalds' reads 'Theobald'. Smedley, Theobald, and Welsted are ridiculed by Pope in *The Dunciad* ii. 291–4, i. 133, 286; and ii. 207–10 and iii. 169–72 respectively.

155. *Did . . . ridicule.* In Prothero, 'Ings' reads 'Inge'. In his life of Ambrose Philips, Samuel Johnson wrote:

> He had great sensibility of censure, if judgement may be made by a single story which I heard long ago from Mr. Ing, a gentleman of great eminence in Staffordshire. 'Philips,' said he, 'was once at table when I asked him, How came thy king of Epirus to drive oxen, and to say "I'm goaded on by love"? After which question he never spoke again.' (*Lives of the English Poets* iii. 323–4)

The reference is to Philips's adaptation of Racine's *Andromaque, The Distrest Mother* (1712) I. i, in which Orestes (not King Pyrrhus) says 'Goaded on by love / I canvass'd all the suffrages of Greece'; but he does not 'drive oxen' here or elsewhere in the play.

156. *Did he . . . "Beggar's Opera"?* In all editions, 'Bollingbroke' has been silently emended to 'Bolingbroke' (Henry St John, Viscount Bolingbroke (1678–1751), statesman, philosopher and man of letters, and close friend of Swift and Pope). B repeats the interrogative 'did he envy' in turning over the page; the repetition has been silently eliminated in all editions. John Gay's musical *The Beggar's Opera* was first produced with enormous success at Lincoln's Inn Fields Theatre in 1728. In his life of Gay, Johnson wrote of its 'unexampled success': 'This play, written in ridicule of the musical Italian Drama, was first offered to Cibber and his brethren at Drury-Lane, and rejected; it being then carried to Rich [manager of Lincoln's Inn Fields Theatre] had the effect, as was ludicrously said, of making Gay *rich*, and Rich *gay*' (*Lives of the English Poets*, ii. 275).

157. *the most . . . one.* This is Rogers, who was noted for his back-biting and malicious gossip, and of whom B wrote for instance 'he is malignant too—& envious—and—he be damned!' (*BLJ* ix. 20; and see ix. 27, 53, 152).

158. *Goldsmith . . . did.* In his life of Johnson, Boswell wrote of Goldsmith:

> Those who were in any way distinguished, excited envy in him to so ridiculous an excess, that the instances of it are hardly credible. When accompanying two beautiful young ladies with their mother on a tour in France, he was seriously angry that more attention was paid to them than to him; and once at the exhibition of the *Fantoccini* in London, when those who sat next him observed with what dexterity a puppet was made

to toss a pike, he could not bear that it should have such praise, and exclaimed with some warmth, 'Pshaw! I can do it better myself.'

In his footnote to this Boswell added: 'He went home with Mr. Burke to supper; and broke his shin by attempting to exhibit to the company how much better he could jump over a stick than the puppets' (*Boswell's Life of Johnson* i. 413–14 and n.).

159. *In that . . . Mac'Flecknoe.* Dryden's *Mac Flecknoe* (1682) satirizes Thomas Shadwell (?1642–92), who superseded him as Poet Laureate and historiographer at the Revolution.

160. (*the same . . . page*). In a letter to Pope of 29 Sept. 1725, Swift wrote: 'Oh if the world had but a dozen of Arbuthnots in it, I would burn my Travels!' To which Bowles in his edition appended the following note:

Had Swift looked farther, and with a more liberal eye, he might perhaps have found in the world *more* than *a dozen* Arbuthnots!! This is something like poor Cowper's idea, who being disgusted with the world, fell in love with the first venerable gentlewoman he saw at Huntingdon, and wondered all the world was not like her; when probably he would have met with a being just as good in the first respectable old Lady he saw on a Sunday going to church at Brentford! What heart, however, can blame Cowper, when we consider his general philanthropy and kindness, his sensibilities and energies, perverted like Swift's, but always amiable; and even in their greatest weaknesses commanding respect, veneration, and sympathy: and who but must speak with tenderness of a mind that produced the pathetic and affecting Stanzas 'to Mary.' (*The Works* ix. 60, 60n.–61n.)

161. *in particular . . . wood.* See also B's erasure in MS. A 'hortus siccus' (a dry garden (Latin)) is a herbarium, or an arrangement of dried plants; figuratively, it may be applied to the detailing of dry, uninteresting facts. By 'Dutch delineation' B means in the manner of the Dutch style of painting, with its close attention to detail. In *The Works*, Bowles wrote thus of Pope's deficiency as a poet (ix. 370–1):

no one can stand pre-eminent as a great Poet, unless he has not only a heart susceptible of the most pathetic or most exalted feelings of Nature, but *an eye attentive to*, and *familiar with*, every external appearance that she may exhibit, in every change of season, every variation of light and shade, every rock, every tree, every leaf, in her solitary places. He who has not an eye to observe these, and who cannot with a glance distinguish every diversity of every hue in her variety of beauties, must so far be deficient in one of the essential qualities of a Poet.

Upon which Campbell, quoting this passage rather freely, commented (*Specimens*, p. 269): 'Every rock, every leaf, every diversity of hue in nature's variety! Assuredly this botanizing might be essential to a Dutch flower painter; but Sophocles displays no such skill, and yet he is a genuine, a great, and affecting poet.' To which Bowles, having asked rhetorically 'Why is COWPER so eminent as a descriptive poet? . . . Because he is the most accurate describer of the works of *external nature*, and for that reason is superior, as a *descriptive poet*, to POPE' (*The Invariable Principles*, pp. 12–13), in turn replied:

The quotation introduced by yourself from COWPER's Poems [Campbell, *Specimens* vii. 366–7], is here inserted to exemplify the accurate knowledge of external nature which a true painter of our [her] beauties must possess.

> Nor less attractive is the woodland scene,
> Diversified with *trees* of *ev'ry growth*,
> Alike, *yet various.* Here the *gray smooth* trunks
> Of ash, or lime, or beech, *distinctly shine*,
> Within the *twilight of their distant shades*;
> There, lost behind the rising ground, the *wood*
> *Seems* sunk, and *shorten'd to its topmost boughs.*
> *No tree* in all the grove but has its charms,
> Though each *its hue peculiar*; *paler* some,
> And of a *wannish* gray; the *willow* such,
> And *poplar*, that with *silver lines his leaf*,
> And ash far stretching his *umbrageous arm*;
> Of *deeper green* the *elm*; and *deeper still*,
> Lord of the woods, the long-surviving oak.
> Some *glossy-leav'd*, and *shining in the sun*,
> The *maple*, and the *beech* of oily nuts
> Prolific, and the lime at dewy eve
> Diffusing odours: nor unnoted pass
> The sycamore, capricious in attire,
> Now *green*, now *tawny*, and, ere autumn yet
> Have chang'd the woods, in *scarlet honours bright*.
> O'er these, but far beyond (a spacious map
> Of hill and valley interspersed between)
> The Ouse, dividing the well-water'd land,
> Now glitters in the sun, and now retires, &c.

It is this knowledge that gives such original interest to the scenes painted by SOUTHEY and WORDSWORTH, and may I not conclude that the quotation, which you have selected (of which this description is only a part,) was selected on account of its beauty, though perhaps you may consider it too much in the Dutch style of painting? At all events, it is beautiful in its place, as relieved by other and more distant views of the same landscape. (*The Invariable Principles*, pp. 44–5)

Bowles quotes Cowper's *The Task*, bk. i, 'The Sofa', ll. 300–24, adding his own emphases.

162. *a Seedsman's Catalogue.* The note given here was sent by B to Murray on 26 Feb. 1821 with instructions to 'append' it to this letter (*BLJ* viii. 85; see general note). Accordingly it was published in the first issue of the first edition of this letter, and in all subsequent editions, as a footnote to this passage. The MS bears the following superscription by B:

Note to that passage (in my letter to J. Murray Esq[re] on Bowles's Pamphlets) which compares Cowper's description of a Wood—quoted by Campbell and requoted by Bowles—to—

"A Seedsman's Catalogue"
Note.

163. *"Splendid Shilling. The Splendid Shilling*, a burlesque play written by John Philips (1676–1709) was published in 1705. Written in Miltonic verse with much display of classical learning, it contrasts the penurious lot of the poet with the possessor of the 'Splendid Shilling'.

164. *Sylvan Sampler.* A 'sampler' is a piece of embroidery on which a young lady would work to show her proficiency in that occupation. B has emphasized the 'r' in order to distinguish the word from 'sample', and to draw attention to the effeminate and embroidered style of Cowper's description. (See n. 161 above.)

165. *"Thy . . . (My Mary).* B cites stanza 3 of Cowper's 'To Mary' (adding his own emphasis). B originally quoted the first line only, but on second thoughts completed the stanza without erasing the second quotation mark or the '&[c]': in all editions these have been silently eliminated. B chose to cite this particular stanza partly because it complements and continues the notion of embroidering ('Sample*r*', '*Needles*'; see the foregoing note).

166. *"indoor". . . image.* Although the distinction between 'indoor' and 'outdoor' or 'external' images of nature was frequently deployed by all parties in the controversy, the first to make use of it was D'Israeli: 'It happened, however, that Pope preferred *in-door* to *out-door* nature; but did this require inferior skill or less of the creative faculty than Mr. Bowles's *Nature*?' (*Quarterly Review*, p. 410; see also the full title of Bowles's *Second Reply* in the general note above).

167. *"L[d] B. . . . feather."* See also n. 153 above. Samuel Whitbread (1758–1815), brewer, politician, and manager of the Drury Lane Theatre, under whose aegis the theatre was rebuilt in 1811–12, after the fire of 1809. Lord Holland recalled:

> When first Lord Byron agreed to write this address, he said to me, 'I will try, but how shall I avoid that d—d Phœnix? We must not for the world have a feather of that rare bird, which is become as commonplace as a turtledove.' Mr. Whitbread, in doubt whether Lord Byron would comply, composed an address himself of more than fifty lines, in which the burning and rebuilding of the theatre were very elaborately compared to the death and revival of the Phœnix, whose plumage, appearance, and natural history were very minutely described. I mentioned this circumstance to Mr. Sheridan, with the obvious remark that Byron felt about his task like a poet, and Whitbread like a schoolboy. 'Like a schoolboy!' exclaimed Sheridan, who had seen the copy. 'No, rather like a poulterer.' (Henry Richard Vassall, Third Lord Holland, *Further Memoirs of the Whig Party 1807–1821, With Some Miscellaneous Reminiscences*, ed. Lord Stavordale (1905), pp. 163–4)

For B's Address, written at the request of Lord Holland and not as part of the competition, see *CPW* iii. 17–21, 393–395.

Of the memorable dinner party given by Rogers to which B refers here, Moore recorded:

> The company consisted but of Mr. Rogers himself, Lord Byron, Mr. Sheridan, and the writer of this Memoir. Sheridan knew the admiration his audience felt for him; the presence of the young poet, in particular, seemed to bring back his own youth and wit; and the details he gave of his early life were not less interesting and animating to himself than delightful to us. It was in the course of this evening that, describing to us the poem which Mr. Whitbread had written and sent in, among the other Addresses for the opening of Drury-Lane, and which, like the rest, turned chiefly on allusions to the Phenix, he said,—'But Whitbread made more of this bird than any of them:—he entered into particulars, and described its wings, beak, tail, &c.; in short, it was a *Poulterer's* description of a Phenix.' (Thomas Moore, *Memoirs of the Life of the Right Honourable Richard Brinsley Sheridan* (1825), p. 683)

See also B's letter to Moore (?June 1813): 'Was not Sheridan good upon the whole? The "Poulterer" was the first and best' (*BLJ* iii. 54).

168. *The Bust . . . Adrian?* For B's visits to Florence and Rome, and his appreciation of the Venus see nn. 80 and 91 above. Antinous, a youth of great beauty born in Bithynia, was the 'Male Minion' of the Roman Emperor Hadrian (AD 76–138), accompanying the latter on all his travels. He drowned in the Nile in 130, and was deified by Hadrian.

169. *much?* The question-mark here has been silently eliminated in all editions.

170. *And sometimes . . . tools.* B refers to two English proverbs dating from the seventeenth century.

171. *These two . . . Homer.* For B's opinion of Cowper, cf. *BLJ* iii. 179. Cowper's *The Iliad and Odyssey of Homer* was published in 1791. His aim was that his translation should supersede that of Pope's *The Iliad of Homer* (1715–20) and *The Odyssey of Homer* (1725–6).

172. *"not . . . Spondanus".* In *An Essay on the Genius and Writings of Pope* (2 vols., 1806), Joseph Warton remarked (ii. 228): 'ATTERBURY, being in company with [Dr] Bentley and POPE, insisted upon knowing the Doctor's opinion of the English Homer; and that, being earnestly pressed to declare his sentiments freely, he said, "These verses are good verses; but the work is not Homer, it is *Spondanus*."' Jean de Sponde (1557–95) was a French scholar who, besides editions of Hesiod and Aristotle, published under his Latinized name *Homeri poematum versio latina ac notae perpetuae* (Bâle, 1583). For a full discussion of Pope's translation, see Maynard Mack, *Translations of Homer: The Poems of Alexander Pope*, vol. vii (1967), pp. xxxv–ccxlix. In 1823, B told Lady Blessington: 'Translations almost always disappoint me; I must, however, except Pope's "Homer," which has more of the spirit of Homer than all the other translations put together' (*Lady Blessington's Conversations*, p. 141).

173. *Cowper.* This reads 'Cowper's' in all editions.

174. *came.* This reads 'come' in all editions.

175. *He attempted . . . sinecure.* In 1763 the office of Clerk of the Journals of the House of Lords, which was in the gift of his cousin Major Cowper, became vacant and Cowper sought the appointment. However, it required his being examined for fitness for the office at the bar of the House of Lords. As the time for the examination drew near, he became increasingly unnerved and made three suicide attempts (laudanum, drowning, and hanging). The application was abandoned and his first fit of madness ensued shortly afterwards.

176. *Cowper . . . warrant.* All editions read 'Mrs. Throgmorton'. In fact Cowper was the almoner of John Thornton, a liberal benefactor at Olney. He became intimate with John Courtenay Throckmorton when he moved from Olney to Weston Underwood in 1791. Throckmorton is characterized as 'Benevolus' in *The Task*, bk. i, 'The Sofa', ll. 262–5, 330–3. Pope's numerous beneficences, especially to the poets John Dennis (1657–1734) and Richard Savage (d. 1743), are recorded by Spence (*Anecdotes*, pp. 212–13, 356), and by Owen Ruffhead (*The Life of Alexander Pope* (1769), pp. 502–3, 507). See also n. 200 below.

177. *M^r. B. . . . Poetry."* See n. 57 above.

178. *I should . . . "Amen".* See *Macbeth* II. ii. 32–4. B alludes to Southey's somewhat *variable* politics (see, for example, n. 65 to 'Some Observations' above).

179. (*Et tu Brute!*) *Julius Caesar* III. i. 77. See also nn. 51, 57 above, and n. 181 below. In fact Moore did not altogether approve. In his letter to Moore of 3 May 1821, B wrote (*BLJ* viii. 109):

> So, you have got the Letter on Bowles? I do not recollect to have said any thing of *you* that could offend,—certainly, nothing intentionally. . . . What have I said of you? I am sure I forget. It must be something of regret for your approbation of Bowles. And did you *not* approve, as he says? Would I had known that before! I would have given him some more gruel.

Moore's letter to B is no longer extant; but when Moore first published B's letter he appended the following note to the above passage (Moore ii. 463 n.):

> It may be sufficient to say of the use to which both Lord Byron and Mr. Bowles thought it worth their while to apply my name in this controversy, that, as far as my own knowledge of the subject extended, I was disposed to agree with *neither* of the extreme opinions into which, as it appeared to me, my distinguished friends had diverged;—neither with Lord Byron in that spirit of partisanship which led him to place Pope *above* Shakspeare and Milton, nor with Mr. Bowles in such an application of the 'principles' of poetry as could tend to sink Pope, on the scale of his art, to any rank below the very first. Such being the middle state of my opinion on the question, it will not be difficult to understand how one of my controversial friends should be as mistaken in supposing me to differ altogether from his views, as the other was in taking for granted that I had ranged myself wholly on his side.

180. *and . . . Scott.* In all editions except Prothero, this reads 'and a Mr. J. Scott'; Prothero reads 'and Mr. I. Scott'. B wrote to Murray on 14 June 1821:

'In the 1st. pamphlet it is printed "*a* Mr. J.S." it should be "Mr. J.S." and not "*a*" which is contemptuous—it is a printer's Error & was not thus written' (*BLJ* viii. 136). John Scott (1784–1821) was the editor of the *London Magazine* 1819–21, see n. 57 above). B refers to him again at more length in 'Observations upon Observations', *post.*

181. "*You . . . him remain.* In the third edition of this letter and in *Works* (1832), 'four *Asterisks*' reads 'Five *Asterisks*' (to suggest Moore, presumably (see below)). In his *Second Reply*, Bowles wrote (p. 19):

I am tempted on this occasion to produce one testimony from a Poet of the very highest rank in his art, and also a friend of Mr. CAMPBELL's, which has been shewn to me. The note is short, but characteristic; and I leave it for you to make such comments as you have done with the plain fact about Lord BYRON.

'You have *hit the nail* in the head, and **** on the head also.
I remain your's affectionately, ****.'

In his letter to Moore of 4 June 1821, B wrote (*BLJ* viii. 134):

I learn from some private letters of Bowles's, that *you* were 'the gentleman in asterisks.' Who would have dreamed it? you see what mischief that clergyman has done by printing notes without names. How the deuce was I to suppose that the first four asterisks meant 'Campbell' and *not* '*Pope*', and that the blank signature meant Thomas Moore. You see what comes of being familiar with parsons.

When Moore first published this letter he appended the following note to this passage (Moore ii. 492n.):

In their eagerness, like true controversialists, to avail themselves of every passing advantage, and convert even straws into weapons on an emergency, my two friends, during their short warfare, contrived to place me in that sort of embarrassing position, the most provoking feature of which is, that it excites more amusement than sympathy. On the one side, Mr. Bowles chose to cite, as a support to his argument, a short fragment of a note, addressed to him, as he stated, by 'a gentleman of the highest literary, &c. &c.,' and saying, in reference to Mr. Bowles's former pamphlet [i.e. *The Invariable Principles*], 'You have hit the right nail on the head, and **** too.' This short scrap was signed with four asterisks; and when, on the appearance of Mr. Bowles's Letter, I met with it in his pages, not the slightest suspicion ever crossed my mind that I had been myself the writer of it;—my communications with my reverend friend and neighbour having been (for years, I am proud to say) sufficiently frequent to allow of such a hasty compliment to his disputative powers passing from my memory. When Lord Byron took the field against Mr. Bowles's Letter, this unlucky scrap, so authoritatively brought forward, was, of course, too tempting a mark for his facetiousness to be resisted; more especially as the person mentioned in it, as having suffered from the reverend critic's vigour, appeared, from the number of asterisks employed in designating him, to have been Pope himself, though, in reality, the name was that of Mr. Bowles's former antagonist, Mr. Campbell. The noble assailant, it is needless to say, made the most of this vulnerable point; and few readers could have been more diverted than I was with his happy ridicule of 'the gentleman of asterisks,' little thinking that I was myself, all the while, this veiled victim,—nor was it till about the time of the receipt of the above letter, that, by some communication on the subject from a friend in England, I was startled into the recollection of my own share in the transaction.

While by one friend I was thus unconsciously, if not innocently, drawn into the scrape, the other was not slow in rendering me the same friendly service;—for, on the appearance of Lord Byron's answer to Mr. Bowles, I had the mortification of finding that, with a far less pardonable want of reserve, he had all but named me as his authority for an anecdote of his reverend opponent's early days, which I had, in the course of an after-dinner conversation, told him at Venice, and which,—pleasant in itself, and, whether true or false, harmless,—derived its sole sting from the manner in which the noble disputant triumphantly applied it. Such are the consequences of one's near and dear friends taking to controversy.

(For the 'anecdote' to which Moore alludes here, see n. 51 above.) Bowles himself, in a letter to Murray on 15 Apr. 1821, confirmed that Moore 'was "the Midas," I tell you confidentially, who wrote, You have hit the nail on the head! and I now tell you, more confidentially, it was Campbell who was hit in the head, not Pope' (Greever, *Wiltshire Parson*, p. 129).

182. *Whoever... enough.* Midas, King of Phrygia, whose touch turned all things to gold, was once chosen to judge a musical contest between Apollo and Pan. He decided in favour of Pan, whereupon Apollo changed his ears into those of an ass. Midas concealed them under his cap, but his barber discovered them and told the secret to a hole in the earth out of which reeds eventually grew which whispered 'King Midas has ass's ears'. 'Long-eared' is a term for a dupe or a gullible person.

183. *The attempt... "the Just."* See n. 30 to 'Some Observations' above.

184. *They have... ever.* Cf. B's letter to Moore of 3 May 1821 (*BLJ* viii. 109):

As to Pope, I have always regarded him as the greatest name in our poetry. Depend upon it, the rest are barbarians. He is a Greek Temple, with a Gothic Cathedral on one hand, and a Turkish Mosque and all sorts of fantastic pagodas and conventicles about him. You may call Shakespeare and Milton pyramids, if you please, but I prefer the Temple of Theseus or the Parthenon to a mountain of burnt brickwork.

185. *Babel... tongues.* See Genesis 11: 1–9.

186. *"Line... Soho.* Pope, *The First Epistle of the Second Book of Horace*, ll. 418–19.

187. *You... same.* B refers to 'Some Observations' above, and to many of his private letters to Murray, in which he expressed his high regard for Pope. See, e.g., *BLJ* vii. 61, and n. 161 to 'Some Observations' above.

188. *It would... Milton.* In his chapter on the potato in *A Year's Residence in the United States of America* (1818, 1819), William Cobbett (1763–1835) expressed strong and somewhat eccentric views on Milton and Shakespeare, both of whose works he regarded as 'barbarous trash' which it was '*the fashion* to extol'.

189. *as Plato... done.* See *The Republic* iii. 398, and also the following n. 190.

190. *he who... "tale teller"?* B here juxtaposes the Platonic notion of the poet as a maker of 'fictions'/'lies' ('pseudos'—the pun inheres in the original Greek), and the Aristotelian concept of the poet as an original 'creator' ('poietes'). See

n. 189 above, and also *The Republic* ii. 377 and Aristotle, *Poetics* i (B sides with Aristotle rather than with Plato.)

191. *I shall not . . . them.* For Joseph Warton's ranking of Pope, see n. 96 to 'Some Observations' above. The note appended here, of which there is no MS extant, was first published as a supplementary note at the end of the third edition of this letter, directing the reader to this location. Accordingly, in *Works* (1832) and Prothero it is printed as a footnote to the present passage. The present text is taken from the third edition.

192. (*once . . . Sophia's*). B refers to the great Greek Orthodox Cathedral of St Sophia at Constantinople (Istamboul), then the main mosque of the Turks. See *CHP* II. 79: 'turbans now pollute Sophia's shrine' (*CPW* ii. 70); and cf. B's letter to his mother of 28 June 1810 (*BLJ* i. 250–1).

193. *"To rival . . . below."* B alludes to Campbell's *The Pleasures of Hope* i. 472, but there is no indication that Campbell had Burns in particular in mind.

194. *There are . . . songs. Tam O'Shanter* (1790), which Burns regarded as his best poem; 'The Cotter's Saturday Night' (1796), which is descriptive of Scottish peasant life at the time. As B says, Burns is best known for his songs.

195. *Of Pope . . . literature.* B refers again to 'Some Observations' above.

196. *If the . . . laurel.* In his life of Pope, Johnson adversely criticized Pope's poetry in several minor particulars on various occasions. He was critical of Pope's *Pastorals*, for instance, and more especially of his *Epitaphs.* (See *Lives of the English Poets* iii. 224–5, 254–72 respectively.) In his edition of *The Works*, Bowles frequently rehearsed Johnson's criticisms, but often expressed his own dissent from them. The laurel is the emblem of the poet. Johnson is indeed a severe critic of the poets generally of whom he treats in his *Lives.* Moreover, in his Life of Milton, he states that 'it is the business of impartial criticism to discover' the 'faults and defects every work of man must have' (*Lives of the English Poets* i. 180).

197. *instruction and delight.* B echoes the great *dictum* of Horace (*Ars Poetica*, ll. 342–3): 'omne tulit punctum qui miscuit utile dulci, / lectorem delectando pariterque monendo' ('He gains all who mixes profit with pleasure, both delighting and instructing the reader'). Cf. *Hints from Horace*, ll. 529–30 (*CPW* i. 308).

198. *the only . . . reproach.* In his *Curiosities of Literature* (New edition, Enlarged, 1817), D'Israeli wrote (p. 101): 'The imitative powers of Pope, who possessed more industry than genius—though his genius was *nearly* equal to that of the greatest poets—has contrived to render every line faultless: yet it may be said of Pope, that his greatest fault consists in having none.'

199. *"a sordid . . . so." Quarterly Review* accused Bowles of aspersing Pope with, amongst other things, 'a sordid money-getting passion . . .' (p. 412). Quoting this in 'A Reply', Bowles retorted (p. 6): 'Of a "*sordid money-getting passion*" I

have never accused him; and if I had ever done so, I should be glad to find any testimony that might show he was *not* so.'

200. *"Probably . . . legatee."* Martha Blount told Spence: 'Mr. Pope's not being richer may be easily accounted for.—He never had any love for money: and though he was not extravagant in any thing, he always delighted, when he had any sum to spare, to make use of it in giving, lending, building, and gardening; for those were the ways in which he disposed of all the overplus of his income.—If he was extravagant in any thing it was in his grotto, for that, from first to last, cost him above a thousand pounds' (*Anecdotes*, pp. 212–13). Quoting this in 'A Reply' (pp. 5–6), Bowles remarked (p. 6n.): 'Probably she thought he did not save enough for her as legatee.'

201. *Then . . . Addison.* Spence recorded the following four anecdotes, the first of which he had from '*Mr. Warburton, who had it from Mr. Pope*,' the remaining three of which he had from Pope himself. Alderman Barber:

Mr. Pope never flattered any body for money, in the whole course of his writing. Alderman Barber had a great inclination to have a stroke in his commendation inserted in some part of Mr. Pope's writings. He did not want money, and he wanted fame. He would probably have given four or five thousand pounds, to have been graqtified in this desire: and gave Mr. Pope to understand as much, but Mr. Pope would never comply with such a baseness. And when the Alderman died, he left him a legacy only of a hundred pounds; which might have been some thousands, if he had obliged him only with a couplet.

Lord Hallifax:

In the beginning of George the First's reign, Lord Hallifax sent for me of his own accord. He said he had often been concerned that I had never been rewarded as I deserved; that he was very glad it was now in his power to be of service to me, that a pension should be settled on me, if I cared to accept it; and that nothing should be demanded of me for it.—I thanked his lordship, in general terms, and seemed to want time to consider of it.—I heard nothing further for some time; and about three months after I wrote to Lord Hallifax, to thank him for his most obliging offer; saying, that I had considered the matter over fully, and that all the difference I could find in having or not having a pension, was, that if I had one, I might live more at large in town, and that if I had not, I might live happily enough in the country.—There was something said too, of the love of being quite free, and without any thing that might even look like a bias laid on me.—So the thing dropped, and I had my liberty without a coach.

Craggs:

Craggs, afterwards, went farther than this [i.e. farther than Lord Hallifax].—He told me, as a real friend, that a pension of three hundred pounds a year was at my service; and that, as he had the management of the secret-service money in his hands, he could pay me such a pension yearly without any one's knowing that I had it.—I declined even this: but thanked Mr. Craggs for the heartiness and sincerity of his friendship . . .

And Addison. The circumstances here are somewhat different from the above. Addison encouraged Pope to translate Homer, yet promoted Tickell's translation; he was jealous of Pope's increasing fame, and caused scandals to be spread about him. On learning this, Pope told Spence:

> The next day, while I was heated with what I had heard, I wrote a letter to Mr. Addison, to let him know, 'that I was not unacquainted with this behaviour of his; that if I was to speak severely of him in return for it, it should not be in such a dirty way; that I should rather tell him himself fairly of his faults, and allow his good qualities; and that it should be something in the following manner.' I then subjoined the first sketch of what has been since called my satire on Addison.—He used me very civilly ever after; and never did me any injustice, that I know of, from that time to his death, which was about three years after.

The above four quotations are from *Anecdotes*, pp. 308, 305–6, 307, 149 respectively. Fuller details of the final anecdote here are given by Owen Ruffhead in *The Life of Alexander Pope* (1769), pp. 184–93. For Pope's 'satire on Addison', see *Epistle to Dr. Arbuthnot*, ll. 193–214.

202. *line.* This reads 'lines' in all editions.

203. *"And . . . alive.* Pope, *The Second Epistle of the Second Book of Horace*, ll. 68–9.

204. *the whole . . . Dunces.* Echoes the 'Te Deum': 'The noble army of martyrs' (*Book of Common Prayer*).

205. *"would . . . wrote.* In 'A Reply' (p. 8), Bowles wrote rather lamely of Pope: 'Whether he was, as to money, saving or profuse, his noble generosity to the outcast, Richard Savage, and other instances of a compassionate and generous heart, are undoubted. I should have spoken of them [in *The Works*] as cheerfully as I now admit them, had they occurred to my recollection when I wrote.' See also n. 176 above.

206. *"covered . . . Sins"?* See I Peter 4: 8.

207. *There . . . Quarterly.* In his dedication 'To William Gifford, Esq.', prefixed to 'A Reply' (pp. 2–3), Bowles made Gifford responsible not only for the admission of all articles to the *Review*, but also for the opinions expressed in them.

208. *Mr. Southey . . . publication.* In a footnote to his dedication (see foregoing n. 207), Bowles stated that 'Mr. Southey, the most able and eloquent writer in this very Review, wrote to me the warmest and kindest letter on the occasion' ('A Reply, p. 2n.; see also n. 57 above).

209. *the great . . . Quarterly.* In the third edition of this letter, and in *Works* (1832) and Prothero, this phrase appears within inverted commas. The reference is to Southey; see foregoing n. 208.

210. *In the . . . Devil.* In the *Quarterly Review* (vol. xxiii, no. xlv (May 1820), art. x, pp. 198–225), there appeared a review by Bishop Heber of the Revd Henry Hart Milman's *The Fall of Jerusalem, a Dramatic Poem* (1820) which ends as follows (p. 225):

> Remarkably as Britain is now distinguished by its living poetical talent, our time has room for him [Milman]; and has need of him. For sacred poetry, (a walk which Milton

alone has hitherto successfully trodden,) his taste, his peculiar talents, his education, and his profession appear alike to designate him; and, while, by a strange predilection for the worser half of manicheism, one of the mightiest spirits of the age has, apparently, devoted himself and his genius to the adornment and extension of evil, we may be well exhilarated by the accession of a new and potent ally to the cause of human virtue and happiness, whose example may furnish an additional evidence that purity and weakness are not synonymous, and that the torch of genius never burns so bright as when duly kindled at the Altar.

211. *I believe . . . publication.* In the third edition of this letter, and in *Works* (1832) and Prothero, this sentence concludes with a question-mark. See also foregoing n. 210. On 17 July 1820 B wrote somewhat stiffly to Murray (*BLJ* vii. 132; see also xi. 232 for correction):

I should be glad to know why your Quarter*ing* Reviewers—at the Close of 'the Fall of Jerusalem' accuse me of Manicheism?—a compliment to which the sweetener of 'one of the mightiest Spirits' by no means reconciles me.——The poem they review is very noble—but could they not do justice to the writer—without converting him into my religious Antidote?—I am not a Manichean—nor an *Any*-chean.

There is no reference, here or elsewhere in B's letters, to a 'Note in the book of travels' and B's not wishing to have 'a single line cancelled' on his account.

212. *Conductors.* In all editions this reads 'conductor'.

213. *"by his Style."* Pope, *Epistle to Dr. Arbuthnot*, l. 282. Also, Spence recorded that Pope frequently expressed the opinion: 'There is nothing more foolish than to pretend to be sure of knowing a great writer by his style' (*Anecdotes*, p. 168).

214. *M^r. B. . . . denounces.* See general note above. Bowles incorrectly denounced Gilchrist as the writer of the review in the *Quarterly Review*, whereas in truth its author was Isaac D'Israeli—a fact at which B had correctly guessed on the receipt of that periodical. Writing to Murray on 9 Nov. 1820, B remarked: 'D'Israeli wrote the article on Spence—I know him by the mark in his mouth—I'm glad that the Quarterly has had so much Classical honesty and honour as to insert it—it is good & true' (*BLJ* vii. 223).

215. *The Surgeon . . . it.* This was undoubtedly Mr Bates, the surgeon on board the *Salsette* with B and Hobhouse while they were lying at anchor off the Dardanelles in April and early May 1810. On 19 Apr. 1810 Hobhouse recorded in his diary: 'play'd 3 games of chess with Mr Bates the surgeon who wears a wig—and who let the pilot die with a stricture in his throat' (Broughton Papers, BL Add. MS 56529, f. 41v).

216. *You say . . . degeneracy.* Although there is no reference to this in Murray's extant correspondence with B, the new edition of Pope's works being prepared at the time and eventually published by Murray was William Roscoe's *The Works of Alexander Pope*, 10 vols. (1824). See general note. In a postscript to his letter to Octavius Gilchrist of 5 Sept. 1821, B commented (*BLJ* viii. 201):

I saw Mr. Mawman the other day;—he tells me that the Booksellers have engaged Roscoe to edite Pope—and I think the choice is a very judicious one.—Roscoe has all the elegance and classical turn of mind requisite to do Pope justice.—Hitherto he has only been edited by his enemies or by Warburton who was a polemical parson and as fit to edite Poetry as Pope to preach in Gloucester Cathedral.—The Attorney-bishop did him no good—& Warton & Bowles have done him harm. Mr. Mawman tells me that Roscoe is requested (by the publishers) to keep the Controversy with Mr. Bowles &c. quite out of sight—& not to allude to it at all.—This is the *quietest* way—but whether it is the best I know not.—I suppose it it.

In fact Roscoe did not keep the Controversy 'quite out of sight'; he both alluded to it at some length and criticized Bowles for his rough treatment of Pope, in his preface (vol. i, pp. xvi–xix). This of course set Bowles going again.

217. *Addenda.* B sent these to Murray on 12 Mar. 1821 with the following instructions (*BLJ* viii. 92): 'Insert where they may seem apt—the *inclosed addenda* to the *Letter on Bowles* &c.; they will come into the body of the letter if you consult any of your Utica where to place them.—If there is too much—or too harsh—or not intelligible &c. let me know—and I will alter or omit the portion pointed out.' See also general note above, and n. 255 below. Murray followed none of these instructions. They were first published in *Works* (1832) as 'Further Addenda' immediately following 'Observations upon Observations'. Thereafter they were published in Prothero, who similarly placed them immediately after 'Observations upon Observations'. As insertion within 'the body of the letter' does not altogether 'seem apt', the present is the next best location. The MS is superscribed by B: 'Further Addenda for insertion in the Letter to J.M. Esq.[re] on "Bowles's Pope &c."'.

218. *'indoor . . . images".* See n. 166 above.

219. *"It hence . . . Pope.* B quotes (adding his own emphases) Joseph Warton, *An Essay on the Genius and Writings of Pope*, 2 vols. (1782), ii. 243. (This was the first publication of vol. ii, and its pagination tallies with that given later on in this addendum by B.)

220. *Walpole . . . acres."* In his *Anecdotes of Painting in England*, 4 vols. (1762–71), vol. iv (1771), ch. 7, '*On Modern Gardening*', Horace Walpole, fourth Earl of Orford (1717–97), wrote (pp. 140–1):

But just as the encomiums are that I have bestowed on Kent's discoveries, he was neither without assistance or faults. Mr. Pope undoubtedly contributed to form his taste. The design of the prince of Wales's garden at Carlton-house was evidently borrowed from the poet's at Twickenham. There was a little of affected modesty in the latter, when he said of all his works he was most proud of his garden. And yet it was a singular effort of art and taste to impress so much variety and scenery on a spot of five acres. The passing through the gloom from the grotto to the opening day, the retiring and again assembling shades, the dusky groves, the larger lawn, and the solemnity of the termination at the cypresses that lead up to his mother's tomb, are managed with exquisite judgment; and though lord Peterborough assisted him

To form his quincunx and to rank his vines,
[*The First Satire of the Second Book of Horace*, l. 130]

those were not the most pleasing ingredients of his little perspective.

I do not know whether the disposition of the garden at Rousham, laid out for general Dormer, and in my opinion the most engaging of all Kent's works, was not planned on the model of Mr. Pope's, at least in the opening and retiring shades of Venus's vale.

However, this was not B's immediate source of reference. In *An Essay*, Joseph Warton wrote (ii. 238–9):

MR. WALPOLE, in his elegant and entertaining History of *Modern Gardening*, has clearly proved that *Kent* was the artist to whom the English nation was chiefly indebted for diffusing a taste in laying out grounds, of which the French and Italians have no idea. But he adds, much to the credit of our author, that POPE undoubtedly contributed to form Kent's taste.

Warton then continued in the words of Walpole (cited above), but without any acknowledgement to him by way of quotation marks. Hence B's ascribing to Warton *Walpole's* applauding Pope's 'singular effort of art and taste . . .' See also n. 226 below. William Kent (1686–1748), painter, interior designer, architect, and landscape-gardener, was an intimate friend of Pope and Burlington. His conception of landscape-gardening (the mixing of natural with formal scenery, the garden and the wild) was greatly influenced by Pope; and his laying out of the grounds at Rousham House, Oxfordshire, exemplify Pope's instructions in *Moral Essays*, Epistle iv, 'To Burlington' ('Of the Use of Riches').

221. *Pope . . . "the Guardian."* In *An Essay*, Joseph Warton wrote (ii. 240–1):

Pope seems to have been the very first person that censured and ridiculed the formal, French, Dutch, false and unnatural, mode in gardening, by a paper in the Guardian, Number 173, levelled against capricious operations of art, and every species of *verdant* sculpture, and *inverted* nature; which paper abounds with *wit* as well as *taste*, and ends with a ridiculous catalogue of various figures cut in ever-greens.

Warton was referring to Pope's article in the *Guardian*, no. 173 (29 Sept. 1713), in which he wrote:

We seem to make it our study to recede from Nature, not only in the various tonsure of greens into the most regular and formal shapes, but even in monstrous attempts beyond the reach of the art itself: we run into sculpture, and are yet better pleased to have our Trees in the most aukward figures of men and animals, than in the most regular of their own. . . . A Citizen is no sooner proprietor of a couple of Yews, but he entertains the thought of erecting them into Giants, like those of Guildhall. I know an eminent Cook, who beautified his country-seat with a Coronation-dinner in greens, where you see the champion flourishing on horseback at one end of the table, and the Queen in perpetual youth at the other. (*The Works*, ix. 467–9)

222. *"Pope . . . Gardening."* B quotes Warton, *An Essay* ii. 236–7 (the emphases are Warton's).

223. *"Kendal Green". Henry IV, Part I*, II. iv. 249–52 (Falstaff speaking): 'But, as the devil would have it, three misbegotten knaves in Kendal-green came at my back and let drive at me; for it was so dark, Hal, that thou couldst not see thy hand.' B's allusion is peculiarly apt, since the *three* 'Lakers' to whom he refers (Southey, Wordsworth, and Coleridge) also lived near Kendal in Westmorland.

224. *Bucolical Cockneys.* B has in mind in particular here Hunt and Keats. The Cockney School, which included Hunt, Keats, Hazlitt, and Cornelius Webb, was so christened by John Gibson Lockhart in an article entitled 'On the Cockney School of Poetry', in *Blackwood's Edinburgh Magazine*, vol. ii, no. vii (Oct. 1817), pp. 38–41.

225. *Bathurst . . . Stow.* Pope was on familiar terms with and stayed at the country seats of Allen Bathurst, first Earl Bathurst (1684–1775), whose seats were at Cirencester and Slough; Sir Richard Temple, Viscount Cobham (?1669–1749), whose seat was Stowe, Buckinghamshire; Richard Boyle, third Earl of Burlington (1695–1753), whose seats were Burlington House, Piccadilly, and Chiswick House; Charles Mordaunt, third Earl of Peterborough (1658–1735), whose seat was Bevis Mount, near Southampton; the Hon. Robert Digby (d. 1726) whose father, William Digby, fifth Baron Digby (1661–1752), had his seat at Sherbourne Castle; and Henry St John, Viscount Bolingbroke (1678–1751), whose seat was Dawley, near Uxbridge. The grounds at Stowe were laid out by William Kent. See n. 220 above.

226. *"That . . . Vale."* This was Walpole's opinion, quoted by Warton. See n. 220 above. 'Venus's Vale' is in the grounds of Rousham House.

227. *It is true . . . eye.* See n. 169 to 'Some Observations' above.

228. *"here . . . sang."* Bowles wrote (*The Works*, vol. i, p. xxv):

> There was a particular beech-tree, under which Pope used to sit; and it is the tradition of the place, that under that tree he composed the Windsor Forest. The original tree being decayed, Lady Gower of Bill-hill had a memorial carved upon the bark of another immediately adjoining: 'Here Pope sang.'—The marks are visible to this day, but are *fast wearing* out. During Lady Gower's life, the letters were new cut every three or four years.

229. *Bolingbroke . . . field.* In a letter to Swift dated 28 June 1728, written from Dawley (Bolingbroke's seat), Pope wrote (*The Works* ix. 123): 'I now hold the pen for my Lord Bolingbroke, who is reading your letter between two Haycocks; but his attention is somewhat diverted by casting his eyes on the clouds, not in admiration of what you say, but for fear of a shower.'

230. *"I understand . . . poetical."* In a letter to Richard Bentley dated 19 Dec. 1753, Walpole commented (with reference to a letter to him from Bentley no longer extant): 'you write with more wit, and paint with more *melancholy*, than ever anybody did: your woody mountains hang down *somewhat so poetical*, as Mr. Ashe said, that your own poet Gray will scarce keep tune with you. All this refers to your cascade scene and your letter.' And in his own note to 'Mr. Ashe', Walpole wrote: 'A nurseryman at Twickenham. He had served Pope. Mr Walpole telling him he would have his trees planted irregularly, he said, "Yes, Sir, I understand: you would have them hang down somewhat poetical"' (W. S. Lewis (ed.), *The Yale Edition of Horace Walpole's Correspondence* xxxv (1973), 157 and n.).

231. *whom . . . unjust.* See nn. 90, 172 to 'Some Observations' above; and see n. 224 above and n. 236 below. B no doubt also has in mind here, for example, such damning reviews in the *Quarterly Review* (none of which was written by Southey) as those of the following: Hazlitt's *Characters of Shakespear's Plays* (1817) (vol. xviii, no. xxxvi (Jan. 1818), art. ix, pp. 458–66); Hazlitt's *Lectures on the English Poets* (1818) (vol. xix, no. xxxviii (July 1818), art. ix, pp. 424–34); Shelley's *Laon and Cythna* (1818) and *The Revolt of Islam* (1818) (vol. xxi, no. xlii (Apr. 1819), art. vii, pp. 460–71); and Hazlitt's *Political Essays, with Sketches of Public Characters* (1819) (vol. xxii, no. xliii (July 1819), art. viii, pp. 158–63).

232. *"entusymusy".* John Braham (?1774–1856), the celebrated tenor, who collaborated with the composer Isaac Nathan (?1791–1864) in setting B's *Hebrew Melodies* to music in 1815. (*BLJ* iv. 274.) B often referred 'to what Mr Braham terms "*entusymusy*"' (see for example, *BLJ* iii. 209, iv. 263, and v. 218), and Nathan gives the following explanation for the expression. When rehearsing the part of Prince Orlando in Thomas Dibdin's *The Cabinet* (first produced at Covent Garden Theatre in 1802), in which the line 'They followed me to the field with enthusiasm' occurred (*The Cabinet* (1805), II. ii), Braham, being unfamiliar with the word 'enthusiasm', 'could not recall the *jaw-breaker* to his memory, and vexed at his own seeming dullness, he vociforated [*sic*] with "towzy mowzy." This anecdote was communicated to us by Edmund Kean in the presence of Lord Byron, Thomas Moore, Cam Hobhouse, and the honourable Douglas Kinniard [*sic*], which afforded us so much mirth that thenceforth *towzy mowzy* became the cant term in our circle for *enthusiasm*' (Isaac Nathan, *The Southern Euphrosyne* (1848), pp. 150–1).

233. *"high argument"?* In *Works* (1832) and Prothero the question mark here has been silently eliminated. B quotes from Wordsworth's *The Recluse* (as appended to his preface to *The Excursion* (1814)), l. 71: 'this is our high argument'. The phrase echoes Milton's 'the highth of this great argument' (*Paradise Lost*, i. 24).

234. *While they . . . Brick?* B is exploiting a good pun here. 'Windsor brick' was a well-known fire-resistant red brick, made from 'Windsor loam', the local earth mined at Hedgerley, near Windsor.

235. *would.* In *Works* (1832) and Prothero this reads 'could'.

236. *The most . . . Capo d'Opera.* For Leigh Hunt's *The Story of Rimini* see n. 244 below. B's manner of alluding to Hunt here and hereafter suggests that he is implicitly supporting Hunt against his reviewers (see, e.g. p. 380, n. 90 above); and, in particular, defending him (though not his 'proselytes') against Lockhart's annihilating remarks in the article 'On the Cockney School of Poetry' (pp. 39–40; see n. 224 above), e.g.:

> Mr. Hunt cannot utter a dedication, or even a note, without betraying the *Shibboleth* of low birth and low habits. He is the ideal of a Cockney Poet. . . . [He] is altogether unacquainted with the face of nature in her magnificent scenes; he has never seen any

mountain higher than Highgate-hill, nor reclined by any stream more pastoral than the Serpentine River. ... The poetry of Mr. Hunt is such as might be expected from the personal character and habits of its author. As a vulgar man is perpetually labouring to be genteel—in like manner, the poetry of this man is always on the stretch to be grand.

237. *Like ... Criticism.*" B refers to David Garrick's *Ode Upon Dedicating the Town Hall and Erecting a Statue to Shakspeare during the Jubilee at Stratford-upon-Avon* (1769), which was noted for the variety of measures in which it was written. B's '*they defy Criticism*' does not appear to be a quotation of any comment referring to the *Ode*, but echoes *Hamlet* V. ii. 232: 'we defy augury'.

238. *One ... author.* This is Keats, whom B enjoyed miscalling 'Ketch'. See, e.g. *BLJ* vii. 217; 'Jack Ketch' was the name for the common hangman. See also 'Some Observations' above, and nn. 172–6 thereto. It should perhaps be borne in mind that soon after hearing of Keats's death (23 Feb. 1821) B wrote to Murray (*BLJ* viii. 163): 'You know very well that I did not approve of Keats's poetry or principles of poetry—or of his abuse of Pope—but as he is dead—omit *all* that is said *about him* in any *M.S.S.* of mine—or publication.—His Hyperion is a fine monument & will keep his name—'.

239. *"march ... flat". Henry IV, Part I*, IV. ii. 42–3.

240. *"led ... peppered." Henry IV, Part I*, V. iii. 36–7.

241. *the Alps ... River.* Cf. n. 236 above. The New River, completed in 1613, was cut by Hugh Myddleton to supply London with water. It runs from Amwell in Hertfordshire to Islington.

242. *would.* In *Works* (1832) and Prothero this reads 'could'.

243. *when he ... renown.* For Pope's lines immortalizing 'the Man of Ross', see *Moral Essays*, Epistle iii, 'To Bathurst' ('Of the Use of Riches'), ll. 250–90. John Kyrle (1637–1724) of Ross in Herefordshire was renowned for his public spirit and beneficence. B would have seen a portrait of Kyrle either at *The King's Head Inn* at Ross, or at *The Swan Inn*, Tewkesbury, *en route* to Eywood, the Oxfords' country house near Presteign, during his liaison with Lady Oxford (Oct. 1812–Apr. 1813).

244. *I would ... System.*" B had read the MS of *The Story of Rimini* in 1815 and had pencilled some comments upon it (see 'Fragmentary Writings', *post*, and n. 128 to 'Some Observations' above). B wrote to Hunt at the time: 'I have not time nor paper to *attack* your *system*—which ought to be done—were it only because it is a *system*' (*BLJ* iv. 332). Writing to Moore on 1 June 1818, B remarked (*BLJ* vi. 46):

When I saw 'Rimini' in *MSS.*, I told him [Hunt] that I deemed it good poetry at bottom, disfigured only by a strange style. His answer was, that his style was a system, or *upon system*, or some such cant; and, when a man talks of system, his case is hopeless: so I said no more to him, and very little to any one else.

The poem itself opens with the couplet: 'The sun is up, and 'tis a morn of May / Round old Ravenna's clear-shewn towers and bay.' Writing to Annabella from Ravenna on 20 July 1819, B commented: 'He (Hunt) has made a sad mistake—about "old Ravenna's *clear-shewn towers* and *bay*" the city Lies so low that you must be close upon it before it is "shewn" at all—and the Sea had retired *four miles* at least, long before Francesca was born—and as far back as the Exarchs and Emperors' (*BLJ* vi. 181–2). See also *BLJ* vi. 189.

245. *"alone . . . glory"*. B quotes the final line of 'The Burial of Sir John Moore at Corunna' (1817), by Charles Wolfe (1791–1823): 'But we left him alone with his glory.' B greatly admired this poem, and Medwin thought that B had written it himself (*Medwin's Conversations*, pp. 114–16).

246. *I should said.* In *Works* (1832) and Prothero this has been silently emended to 'I should have said'.

247. *But . . . Twickenham.* See n. 169 to 'Some Observations' above.

248. *His poetry . . . story.* For the phrase 'the Book of Life', see Revelation 3: 5; 13: 8; 20: 12, 15; 21: 27. Sir William Temple (1628–99), author and statesman. B cites from his essay 'Of Poetry' (*The Works of Sir William Temple*, 4 vols. (1814), iii. 416–17).

249. *"D^r. Clarke . . . kind.* B's repetition of 'out' here, which occurs at the end of one line and at the beginning of the next in the MS, has been silently eliminated in *Works* (1832) and Prothero. See also n. 172 above. Continuing his comments on Pope's *Homer*, and alluding to the classical scholar and divine Dr Samuel Clarke (1675–1729), whose *Homeri Ilias Græce et Latine* was published in 1729, Warton wrote (*An Essay* (1806), ii. 228):

> It may, however, be observed, in favour of POPE that Dr. CLARKE, whose critical exactness is well known, has not been able to point out above three or four mistakes in the sense through the whole Iliad. The real faults of that translation are of a different kind. They are such as remind us of Nero's gilding a brazen statue of Alexander the Great, cast by Lysippus.

250. *By this . . . termed.* 'Shabby genteel' denotes trying to appear genteel, or keeping up the appearances of gentility despite shabbiness—*OED*.

251. *"a Sunday Blood"*. A 'blood' was a 'fast' or fashionable man; a 'Sunday Blood' was one who affected to be such but was not the genuine article. (Cf. a 'Sunday man', who was one who only walked abroad on Sundays, because on any other day of the week he might have been arrested, most commonly, for instance, for debt.) The term was one of contempt for pretentiousness.

252. *They . . . "Evelina."* In *Works* (1832) and Prothero 'Branghtons' reads 'Broughtons'. In Fanny Burney's *Evelina, or The History of a Young Lady's Entrance into the World* (3 vols., 1778), the pretentious and affected Mr Smith imposes upon Miss Evelina Belmont to accompany him to the Hampstead Assembly Ball. Among those of the party are Thomas and Biddy Branghton.

In her subsequent letter to the Revd Mr. Villars (no. xix), Evelina writes of Mr. Smith (ii. 168):

In the afternoon, when he returned, it was evident that he purposed to both charm and astonish me by his appearance; he was dressed in a very showy manner, but without any taste, and the inelegant smartness of his air and deportment, his visible struggle, against education, to put on the fine gentleman, added to his frequent conscious glances at a dress to which he was but little accustomed, very effectually destroyed his aim of *figuring*, and rendered all his efforts useless.

During tea, entered Miss Branghton and her brother. I was sorry to observe the consternation of the former, when she perceived Mr. Smith.

253. *"the . . . Swell"*. In 'Flash' language (i.e. slang), 'the Flash' was the underworld (of boxers, sportsmen, thieves, and so forth), 'the Swell' were persons of good social position or fashionable society. See also *DJ* XI. 17, 19 (*CPW* v. 470, 747–8).

254. *I do not . . . Euphuism.* These words do not appear in the original MS. They are taken from B's letter to Murray of ?13–16 Mar. 1821, in which he instructed Murray: 'After the words "that there ever was or can be an Aristocracy of poets"—add—& insert—these words' (*BLJ* viii. 92). See also following n. 255. B's allusion is to 'Song. By a Person of Quality' (for which, see his 'Review of Spencer's *Poems*' (1812) above, n. 17). To *parle Euphuism* is to speak, or write, in an affected or artificial style (after John Lyly (?1554–1606), the author of *Euphues* (1578–80)).

255. *Hunt . . . chorus.* In *Works* (1832) and Prothero, 'Hunt little chorus' has been silently emended to 'Hunt's little chorus'. See also n. 217 and the foregoing n. 254. Concerning the remainder of these Addenda, B wrote to Murray on ?13–16 Mar. 1821 (*BLJ* viii. 92–3):

In my packet of the 12th Instant . . . *omit* the sentence which (defining or attempting to define what and who are gentlemanly) begins—'I should say at least in life—that most military men have it & few naval—that several men of rank have it—& few lawyers &c. &c.'——I say— omit the whole of that Sentence—because like the 'Cosmogony or Creation of the World' in 'the Vicar of Wakefield'—it is not much to the purpose.—In the Sentence above too—almost at the top of the same page—After the words 'that there ever was or can be an Aristocracy of poets'—add—& insert—these words——'I do not mean that they should write in the Style of the Song by a person of Quality—or *parle Euphuism*—but there is a *Nobility* of thought and expression to be found no less in Shakespeare—Pope—and Burns—than in Dante and Alfieri—&c. &c.' & so on.——Or if you please—perhaps you had better omit the whole of the latter digression on the *vulgar* poets—and insert only as far as the end of the Sentence upon Pope's Homer—where I prefer it to Cowper's—and quote Dr. Clarke in favour of it's accuracy.——Upon all these points—take an opinion—take the Sense (or nonsense) of your learned visitants—and act thereby—I am very tractable—in PROSE.

256. *An Irishism.* A paradoxical or illogical statement.

257. *"signifying nothing."* *Macbeth* V. v. 28 (Macbeth speaking).

258. *"this . . . flies."* In *Works* (1832) and Prothero, 'Pidcocks' reads 'Pidcock's'. B refers to the menagerie well-known at the time, housed at the Exeter Exchange in the Strand and run by Mr Pidcock. B visited it on several occasions. See, e.g., *BLJ* iii. 206; iv. 278.

259. *life?* In *Works* (1832) and Prothero the question mark here has been silently eliminated.

Observations upon Observations (1821)

Text: MS Murray. First published as *Observations Upon "Observations." A Second Letter to John Murray, Esq. on The Rev. W. L. Bowles's Strictures on the Life and Writings of Pope*, in *Works* (1832), vi. 382–407 (*Works* (1832)). Thereafter published from *Works* (1832) collated with MS in Prothero v. 567–86.

There is no external evidence to indicate that B was engaged in writing this letter; but from the start he had doubts about its publication. Sending it to Murray on 21 Apr. 1821, he stated, 'I enclose you another letter on "*Bowles*".—But I premise that it is not like the former—and I am not at all [sure] how *much*—if *any* of it—should be published. Upon this point you can consult with Mr. Gifford—and think *twice* before you publish it at all' (*BLJ* viii. 99; see also viii. 102). Whether or not Murray did consult with William Gifford, his literary adviser, or whether he had any intention of publishing the letter at all, there is no means of knowing. At all events, by 10 May 1821 B himself had decided against its publication. Having received a package from Murray on that date, in which Murray enclosed Bowles's letters to him of 6 and 15 Apr. (see general note to 'Letter to John Murray Esq[re.]' above), B replied (*BLJ* viii. 111):

> I have just got your packet.—I am obliged to Mr. Bowles—& Mr. B. is obliged to me—for having restored him to good humour.—He is to write—& you to publish what you please—*motto* and subject—I desire nothing but fair play for all parties.—Of course, after the new tone of Mr. B.—you will *not* publish my *defence of Gilchrist*—it would be brutal to do so—after his urbanity—for it is rather too rough like his own attack upon G.—You may tell him what I say there of *his Missionary* (it is praised as it deserves) however—and if there are any passages *not personal* to Bowles—& yet bearing upon the question—you may add them to the reprint (if it is reprinted) of my 1st. letter to you.—Upon this consult Gifford—& above all don't let anything be added which can *personally* affect Mr. B.

No passage from this letter was extracted and added to B's first letter, and the text was first published posthumously, as detailed above, in 1832. Prothero noted that it was 'First published in 1835' (Prothero v. 567n.), but this is wrong. In 1835 Murray issued a reprint of the 1832 edition of B's *Works*, with an additional title-page tipped into the first volume only, bearing the date 1835. But the original title-page bearing the date 1832 remains in that and successive volumes. The texts of vol. vi of the 1832 edition and of the 1835 reprint are identical—even to the extent of the latter's unfortunately repeating '*Now first published*.' No doubt this led to Prothero's mistake.

While it is a shame that B should have suppressed such a finely balanced, temperate, and again good-humoured response to Bowles's pitiable and extremely tedious 'Observations', his decision to do so was tactful and judicious. For, as noted in the general note to 'Letter to John Murray Esq[re.]', his first letter had already had the immediate result of deflecting the controversy away from *personal* rancour and hostilities, and of returning it to its literary focus. This second letter is rather more explicitly a '*defence of Gilchrist*', as B aptly terms it, relating specifically to Bowles's vindication of himself, than it is a literary manifesto or defence of Pope. Its publication at the time would doubtless have merely provoked a further tirade from Bowles in his own defence.

For further details, see general note to 'Letter to John Murray Esq[re.]' above. In the following notes, references to 'general note' refer to both that one and this, and the abbreviations used are those explained in the earlier general note.

1. *Observations* . . . *&c.* B wrote this title below his signature on the final page of the MS. See n. 130 below.

2. *M.r B.* . . . *opponents.*" Bowles wrote ('Observations', pp. 3–4):

> I shall here make one general observation; that, IF ANY CIRCUMSTANCE MORE THAN ANOTHER, COULD WEIGH WITH ME IN CONFIRMING THE CONVICTION, that what I said of the moral part of Pope's character, was (generally speaking,) true; and that the principles of poetical criticism, which I had laid down, were 'invariable' and invulnerable, it would be THE FACT, that the opponent of my statements and principles, is obliged scandalously to exaggerate, in the first instance, and wilfully to confuse the plainest reasonings in the other.

3. *After* . . . *forth.* Here, and in the subsequent paragraphs, B refers to the following passage ('Observations', pp. 4–5):

> As the greatest personal abuse is heaped upon me, in the peculiar *slang* of this gentleman, it will be necessary to go back to some circumstances materially connected with this discussion.
>
> I shall not enter into a particular examination of the pamphlet, which, by a *mis-nomer*, is called 'GILCHRIST'S ANSWER TO BOWLES,' when it should have been called 'GILCHRIST'S ABUSE OF BOWLES;'—but as he derides my peculiar 'sensitiveness to criticism;' before I show how destitute of truth is this representation, I will here explicitly declare the only grounds upon which I have thought it at all necessary to reply to any criticism, and the only grounds upon which I think any writer has a right to reply to public criticisms, on public works. The grounds, then, are these, and by these I am willing to abide the decision of the literary world, whether I am not justified in replying to the criticism in the Quarterly Review.
>
> An author is justified in appealing to every UPRIGHT AND HONOURABLE MIND in the kingdom when his sentiments are artfully misrepresented, when base motives are assigned, and when exaggerations are deliberately advanced, the tendency of which must be to excite injurious impressions of his honorable [*sic*] conduct or moral character.
>
> These are the grounds on which I thought it necessary to reply to the article in question, and I shall now plainly set before the literary public, all the circumstances that

have led to my name and Mr. Gilchrist's being brought together on this occasion; and what I have to say on this point, I would particularly address to the consideration of those most respectable characters, who have the direction and management of the Periodical Critical Press.

I concluded my observations in the last Pamphleteer, with feelings not unkind towards Mr. Gilchrist, or to the author of the Review of Spence, be he whom he might. I was in hopes, as I have been always ready to admit any errors I might have been led into, or prejudices I might have entertained, that even Mr. Gilchrist might be disposed to a more amicable mode of discussing what I had advanced in regard to Pope's moral character.

But I have since read a publication by him, containing such vulgar slander, affecting my private life and character, (which are beyond *his malice* to injure) that I am obliged to set before the public the mode of *Christian* criticism, of which I believe he has set the first example, in Europe. I trust, therefore, some severer tone of castigation will be pardoned, in regard to such an infamous mode of literary discussion, and such infamous 'arguing from perversions.'

As ever, Bowles is somewhat free with his quotations (see the second paragraph here). Nowhere did Gilchrist refer to his 'sensitiveness to criticism'. He merely exclaimed, 'Can there remain any hope of contenting so sensitive a plant!' (Gilchrist, p. 5). The *Quarterly* also merely said, 'Mr. Bowles, we suspect, does not love criticism' (p. 424). The 'publication' to which Bowles refers in the final paragraph here is Gilchrist (see general note to 'Letter to John Murray Esq[re.]' above).

4. *M^r. Gilchrist . . . written it.* For the various publications by Gilchrist to which B refers here, see general note.

5. *Pope . . . further".* *Macbeth* III. ii. 23–6.

6. *"Ego . . . meus".* *Henry VIII* III. ii. 315. B was fond of this phrase; see, for example, *BLJ* iii. 157–8; vi. 76.

7. *in page 16. . . . phrases.* The lines and phrases B quotes here are from Bowles's *ad hoc* poem, the 'Gilchrisiad', which actually appears in pp. 17–18 of 'Observations'. B refers to it later at greater length; and it is given in full in n. 120 below.

8. *"I concluded . . . might."* See n. 3 above. In fact, B's parenthetical quibble here as to Bowles's grammar is misleading. Bowles was not distinguishing between two different writers (as in, *neither* X *nor* Y), but between substitutes for the same writer (as in, X, *or* whoever he may be).

9. *prejudices.* This reads 'prejudice' in *Works* (1832) and Prothero. MS correctly follows Bowles's text: see n. 3 above.

10. *"there . . . Colonel."* Samuel Foote, *The Mayor of Garratt* I. i:

MAJOR STURGEON. . . . I must do the regiment the justice to say, there never was a set of more amiable officers.
SIR JACOB. Quiet and peaceable.
MAJOR STURGEON. As lambs, Sir Jacob. Excepting one boxing-bout, at the Three

Compasses in Acton, between Captain Sheers and the Colonel, concerning a game at All-fours, I don't remember a single dispute.

B was fond of this passage: see, e.g., *BLJ* vi. 187; xi. 108.

11. *an.* This reads 'the' in *Works* (1832) and Prothero.

12. "Friendly *Society*" ... *paces.* Friendly societies were mutual aid organizations (of sixteenth-century origin), whose members voluntarily combined to protect themselves against debt or hardship arising from death, illness, old age, fire, and other such accidents. I have been unable to trace the particular institution to which B alludes here.

13. *Mr Gilchrist* ... *page.* B refers to the title-page of Bowles's *Second Reply* (see general note), in which work Bowles wrote (pp. 7–8):

But I trust this language, and even the name of 'grocer,' (which I have used without the least disrespect to any honest man in that line of business,) will not be thought applied *impertinently*; forasmuch as a '*shop*,' that beautiful specimen of 'in-door nature,' is an object more pleasant to contemplate than a *mad-house*!!

In his '*shop*,' then, let this Reviewer, this lover of the 'sublime and beautiful' of in-door nature, indulge his own poetical and romantic reveries, till the pipe in his own mouth becomes, in his glowing imagination, that of THEOCRITUS; the old ledger-book, the Georgicks of VIRGIL; a grove of *green canisters*, a grove of green trees; the dingy shop-boy, a shepherd of Arcadia; and a lake of brown treacle, in half-a-hogshead by the window, more enchanting to the view than the lakes of Cumberland, with their mountains and woods shining to the glorious sun-set!

Gilchrist himself had parried this imaginative thrust by saying:

But you have made the marvellous discovery that I am a GROCER!—As Mistress Malaprop has it,—'I own the soft impeachment.' I could, too, if it affected the point in dispute, explain how I escaped being a parson: a circumstance I might have regretted, if I had not learned from your example, how little the assumption of a profession has to do with the inward man. (Gilchrist, p. 35)

The reference is to Sheridan's *The Rivals* V. iii.

14. "*Sir* ... *short-sighted.*" Boswell recorded that on 12 Apr. 1778, during a dispute between Johnson and Dr Percy over the descriptive talents of the painter Pennant, the following exchange took place:

PERCY. 'But, my good friend, you are short-sighted, and do not see so well as I do.' I wondered at Dr. Percy's venturing thus. Dr. Johnson said nothing at the time; but inflammable particles were collecting for a cloud to burst. In a little while Dr. Percy said something more in disparagement of Pennant. JOHNSON. (pointedly) 'This is the resentment of a narrow mind, because he did not find every thing in Northumberland.' PERCY. (feeling the stroke) 'Sir, you may be as rude as you please.' JOHNSON. 'Hold, Sir! Don't talk of rudeness; remember, Sir, you told me (puffing hard with passion struggling for a vent) I was short-sighted. We have done with civility. We are to be as rude as we please.' (*Boswell's Life of Johnson* iii. 273)

They soon made it up.

15. *Glover* ... *peers.* Richard Glover (1712–85), son of a merchant, was the

author of *Leonidas* (1737), an epic poem in blank verse and nine books, which was widely acclaimed and went through several editions. Robert Bloomfield (1766–1823), son of a tailor, was the author of such poems as *The Farmer's Boy* (1800), *Rural Tales* (1802), and *The Banks of the Wye* (1811). See also *EBSR*, ll. 775–86 (*CPW* i. 253–4, 414). B's point here is that these poets, together with Burns (the son of a Cottar) and Chatterton (the son of an impoverished schoolmaster), were all men of accomplishments, yet of humble origin and reduced means.

16. *What... Quintilian.* Zoilus (*fl.* 359–336 BC) was a misanthropic grammarian of Amphipolis, whose name became a by-word for a captious, carping critic. He was nicknamed 'The Rhetorical Dog'. He censured the works of Aristotle, Plato, Xenophon, Demosthenes (to name but a few), and was so envious of the reputation of Homer that he devoted his life to denigrating him. He was eventually burnt at the stake at Smyrna, after disparaging Homer during festivities in his honour—his own critical works forming his pyre. See 'The Life of Zoilus', in Thomas Parnell's *Poems on Several Occasions* (1737). Aristarchus Grammaticus of Samothrace (*c.*217–145 BC), the greatest critic of antiquity, produced editions of, and wrote critical works on, Homer and other Greek writers. He was greatly respected by Cicero and Horace. Of the surviving works of Aristotle, B presumably has particularly in mind here the *Poetics*; of Longinus, *On the Sublime*; and of Quintilian, *Institutio Oratoria.*

17. *But... "the Monthly."* Philelphus, the Latinized name of Francesco Filelfo (1398–1481), Italian scholar, poet, and critic, who translated Aristotle, Xenophon, and other Greek writers into Latin. Poggius, the Latinized name of Giovanni Francesco Poggio Bracciolini (1380–1459), Italian scholar, who rediscovered during his researches in various libraries many lost works of classical authors, such as Cicero, Diodorus Siculus, and Lucretius. He and Filelfo were bitter enemies. Julius Caesar Scaliger (the elder Scaliger) (1484–1558), French-Italian grammarian, classical scholar, and poet, whose enormously influential *Poetices Libri Septem* (1561) laid the foundations of literary criticism and theory. Salmasius, the Latinized name of Claude Saumaise (1588–1653), French classical scholar, whose *Defensio regia pro Carolo I* (1649) prompted Milton's rejoinder *Pro Populo Anglicano Defensio* (1651). The Accademia della Crusca was established in Florence in 1582 to monitor the Tuscan dialect (the literary language of the Italian Renaissance), and to purify it of its 'chaff' (*crusca*). It drew up a 'Vocabolario degli Accademici della Crusca' in 1612, and criticized Tasso's *Gerusalemme Liberata* (1581) on moral and literary grounds, which caused him to revise it. (See also 'Some Observations', n. 139 above.) Pierre Corneille's *Le Cid*, the most significant drama in the history of French literature, was first produced in 1637. It was immensely popular, but provoked Corneille's rival dramatist, Georges de Scudéry, to indict it before the newly founded Académie Française. The Académie published its judgement in *Les Sentimens de l'Académie Françoise sur la*

Tragicomédie du Cid (1638), which was drafted by Chapelain under the watchful eye of Cardinal Richelieu, criticizing its subject, 'denoûment', some 'épisodes inutiles', and 'beaucoup de vers bas'. This discouraged Corneille, who wrote nothing for three years. Voltaire's *Lettres Philosophiques* (1734) caused such a scandal that he was induced to seek exile; and his outspoken views led to his falling into disfavour with both Louis XV of France and Frederick II of Prussia. (See also 'Letter to John Murray Esq[re.]', n. 135.) Of the 'antagonists' of Pope, B presumably has specifically in mind Churchill and Warton (see 'Some Observations', nn. 93, 96 above). B's final reference here to the *Monthly Review*, which began in 1749 and was to close in 1845.

18. *It is . . . panegyrist.* B may well have himself in mind here and the imminent production of *Marino Faliero* at the Drury Lane Theatre, against which he protested vehemently, and which precipitated much discussion in the Italian papers. For example, in a letter to Teresa Guiccioli of 18 Jan. 1821 B wrote:

> The tragedy they are talking about—is not (and never was) either written for or adapted to the theatre. . . . I hear from your Gazette that a 'cabala' has been formed—a party—and a devil of a *row* and without my having taken the slightest part in it.—They say that *the author read it aloud*!!!—*here perhaps*—in *Ravenna*! and to whom? perhaps to Fletcher!!! that illustrious man of letters! (*BLJ* viii. 64; see also viii. 67, 69, 116–120)

Fletcher was B's valet. See also B's letter to the editor of a Venice newspaper, dated ?Apr. 1817, denying that Napoleon was the protagonist of *CHP* III (*BLJ* v. 201–2).

19. *"the pruriency . . . omitted.* In *Works* (1832) and Prothero the final phrase here reads 'might have been omitted'. B quotes Bowles ('Observations', p. 5) quoting, with much italicization and capitalization, Gilchrist's 'Review' (p. 194). See general note.

20. *"Many . . . truth."* 'Observations', p. 6 (quoting *The Works*, vol. i, pp. cxxviii–cxxix). Bowles refers to Owen Ruffhead's comment on Pope's feelings for Martha Blount: 'though he had the strongest friendship and affection for Mrs. Blount, yet it was of a kind the most innocent and pure, notwithstanding what malignant or mirthful people might suggest to the contrary, either in jest or earnest' (*The Life of Alexander Pope* (1769), p. 548 n.). Elsewhere Ruffhead wrote: 'Mr. POPE appears to have had a very sincere and tender friendship for this Lady, which malice was forward to misconstrue' (ibid., p. 404 n.).

21. *She appears . . . rusts.* Martha Blount (1690–1763), to whom Pope became increasingly attached from 1718 onwards, seems to have been much as B characterizes her here. Ruffhead wrote: 'no excuse can be made for Mrs. Blount's abuse of the influence she had over him; or for the indifference and neglect she shewed to him throughout his whole last illness' (*The Life of Alexander Pope*, p. 548 n.). See also, e.g., F. W. Bateson (ed.), *Epistles to Several Persons* (*Moral Essays*) (1961), p. 47 n. B's touching and evocative image of the 'Needle' may have been inspired by a recent notice, entitled 'North-west

Passage, Magnetic Attraction, &c.', in *Blackwood's Edinburgh Magazine*, vol. viii, no. xliii (Oct. 1820), p. 106:

> the compasses on board both ships were found, whenever they approached within 5 or 6 miles to the north shore [of Lancaster Sound], which was high, rugged, and mountainous, to have lost entirely their magnetic virtue, standing in any direction to which they were placed, without indicating the least appearance of being attracted either the one way or the other; but as soon as the ships had reached beyond this distance (5 or 6 miles) from the land, towards the middle of the straits, the compass needles again acquired their usual power, and exercised it without apparent obstruction. This phenomenon, of which the navigators were entirely ignorant, had nearly led the ships into serious and alarming consequences.

22. *But . . . something.* Cf. B to Lady Melbourne, 9 Nov. 1812: 'I cannot exist without some object of love' (*BLJ* ii. 243; see also iii. 142, 178; iv. 111).

23. *his head . . . eyes.* The description of Pope which B has in mind here is given in full in n. 169 to 'Some Observations' above.

24. *Wycherley . . . "cankered Bolingbroke."* William Wycherley (?1640–1716), dramatist; Jonathan Swift (1667–1745), poet and satirist and Dean of St Patrick's; Francis Atterbury (1662–1732), Bishop of Rochester; Joseph Spence (1699–1768), Regius Professor of Modern History at Oxford and author of the *Anecdotes*; William Warburton (1698–1779), theologian and Bishop of Gloucester and the first editor of Pope (*The Works of Alexander Pope*, 1751); George Berkeley (1685–1753), philosopher, theologian, and Bishop of Cloyne. The term 'cankered Bolingbroke' was Addison's nickname for Henry St John, first Viscount Bolingbroke (1678–1751), statesman, philosopher, and intimate friend of Pope. Pope reported to Spence: 'On Parnell's having been introduced into Lord Bolingbroke's company, and speaking afterward of the great pleasure he had in his conversation: Mr. Addison came out with his usual expression, "If he had but as good a heart as he has a head!" and applied to him, "that canker'd Bolingbroke!" from Shakspeare' (*Anecdotes*, p. 146; the reference is to *Henry IV, Part I*, I. iii. 176.

25. *Bolingbroke . . . Addison.* Of Bolingbroke and Pope's last hours Spence related:

> When I was telling his Lordship, that Mr. Pope, on every catching and recovery of his mind, was always saying something kindly either of his present or his absent friends: and that this was so surprising, that it seemed to me as if his humanity had outlasted his understanding.—Lord B. said;—'It has so!'—and then added, 'I never in my life knew a man that had so tender a heart for his particular friends, or a more general friendship for mankind!'—'I have known him these thirty years: and value myself more for that man's love, than —.' (Sinking his head, and losing his voice in tears.—*Spence.*) (*Anecdotes*, p. 321)

For the 'more ostentatious account of the death-bed of Addison', see n. 48 to 'Letter to John Murray Esq[re.]' above.

26. *The soldier . . . intimates.* Charles Mordaunt, third Earl of Peterborough (1658–1735), Admiral, General, diplomatist and politician (see also n. 5 to B's

'Roman Catholic Claims Speech' above); John Gay (1685–1732), dramatist and poet; William Congreve (1670–1729), dramatist; Nicholas Rowe (1674–1718), dramatist and Poet Laureate; Henry Cromwell (?1658–1728), critic, man about town, and correspondent with Pope (1708–11); Allen Bathurst, first Earl Bathurst (1684–1775), statesman.

27. *Pope . . . "Masterpiece."* Referring to Pope's *Moral Essays*, Epistle ii, 'Of the Characters of Women', Joseph Warton wrote (*An Essay on the Genius and Writings of Pope* (1806), ii. 138): 'Bolingbroke, a judge of the subject, thought it the master-piece of POPE.'

28. *And even . . . Buffon.* See also n. 37 to 'Letter to John Murray Esq[re.]' above. Buffon's 'definition of Love' runs thus, in William Smellie's translation *Natural History, General and Particular, by the Count de Buffon*, 9 vols. (1780), iii. 274–5 (the same *translation*, but not the edition that B possessed):

love is common to all animals. Love is an innate desire, the soul of nature, the inexhaustible fountain of existence, the germ of perpetuity infused by the Almighty into every being that breathes the breath of life. It softens the most ferocious and obdurate hearts, and penetrates them with a genial warmth. It is the source of all good; by its attractions it unites the most savage and brutal tempers, and gives birth to every pleasure. Love! Thou divine flame! Why dost thou constitute the happiness of every other being, and bring misery to man alone? Because this passion is only a physical good. Notwithstanding all the pretences of lovers, morality is no ingredient in the composition of love. Wherein does the morality of love consist? In vanity; the vanity arising from the pleasure of conquest, an error which proceeds from our attempts to exalt the importance of love beyond its natural limits; the vanity of exclusive possession, which is always accompanied with jealousy, a passion so low, that we uniformly wish to conceal it; the vanity proceeding from the mode of enjoyment, which only multiplies efforts, without increasing our pleasures. There is even a vanity in relinquishing the object of our attachment, if we first wish to break it off. But, if we are slighted, the humiliation is dreadful, and turns into despair, after discovering that we have been long duped and deceived.

Brute animals suffer none of these miseries. They search not after pleasure where it is not to be found. Guided by sentiment alone, they are never deceived in their choice. Their desires are always proportioned to the power of gratification. They relish all their enjoyments, and attempt not to anticipate or diversify them. But man, by endeavouring to invent pleasures, destroys those which correspond to his nature; by attempting to force sentiment, he abuses his being, and creates a void in his heart which nothing can afterwards fill up.

29. *Madame Cottin . . . "France."*) Madame Sophie Cottin (1773–1807), author of such highly acclaimed novels as *Claire d'Albe* (1798), *Malvina* (1800), and *Amélie Mansfield* (1802), married at seventeen and was widowed at twenty. Lady Morgan wrote (*France*, 2 vols. (1818), ii. 270n.):

Madame Cottin was one of the most popular writers in France. She united all suffrages in her favour; and the modest simplicity and blameless excellence of her life have contributed greatly to her popularity. Without beauty, almost without those graces which supply its place, Madame de Cottin inspired two ardent and fatal passions, which ceased only with the lives of her lovers. Her young kinsman, Monsieur D * * *, shot himself in her garden; his unsuccessful and sexagenary rival, Monsieur * * * *, poisoned himself, ashamed, it is said, of a passion equally hopeless and unbecoming his years.

30. *Voltaire . . . attachments.* In *Works* (1832) and Prothero 'tell' has been silently emended to 'tells'. François-Henri de Montmorency-Bouteville, Duc de Luxembourg (1628–1695), was instructed in the military arts by the Prince de Condé and became one of Louis XIV's most distinguished generals. He was a hunch-back. In *Siècle de Louis XIV*, 2 vols. (1816) Voltaire wrote (i. 222):

Le maréchal duc de Luxembourg avait dans le caractère des traits du grand Condé, dont il etait l'élève; un génie ardent, une exécution prompte, un coup d'œil juste, un esprit avide de connaissances, mais vaste et peu réglé: plongé dans les intrigues des femmes; toujours amoureux, et même souvent aimé, quoique contrefait et d'un visage peu agréable, ayant plus de qualités d'un héros que d'un sage.
(The Marshal Duke of Luxembourg had several traits in his character in common with those of the great Condé whose pupil he had been: a keen spirit, an alacrity in action, a discerning eye, and a mind eager for knowledge, but broad and undisciplined; continually intriguing with women, always in love and often even loved in return—despite being deformed and far from handsome,—he had more the qualities of a hero than of a philosopher.)

31. *La Valiere . . . defect.* Louise-Françoise de la Baume le Blanc, Duchesse de la Vallière (1644–1710), was the mistress of Louis XIV during the 1660s. She was supplanted by Madame de Montespan, and retired to a Carmelite convent in 1674, assuming the name of 'Soeur Louise de la Miséricorde'. According to Voltaire (*Siècle de Louis XIV* i. 403), Louis 'goûta avec elle le bonheur rare d'être aimé uniquement pour lui-même' ('enjoyed with her the rare delight of being loved solely for himself'). In *Mélanges Historiques, Anecdotiques et Critiques, sur la Fin du Règne de Louis XIV et le Commencement de Celui de Louis XV*, by Madame La Princesse Elisabeth-Charlotte de Bavière (Paris, 1807), there is the following description of la Vallière (p. 77):

La duchesse de la Vallière étoit très-bien; elle avoit la plus belle taille du monde et le regard le plus enchanteur et le plus touchant qu'il soit possible de voir, surtout le maintien le plus modeste. Elle boitoit un peu; mais il sembloit qu'au lieu d'y nuire, ce défaut ajoutoit à ses graces.
(The Duchess of Vallière was perfectly delightful; she had the most beautiful figure in the world, the most enchanting and striking looks imaginable, and, above all, the most modest deportment. She limped a little—but this seemed only to add to her charms, rather than to detract from them.)

32. *The Princess . . . Goldsmith.* In *Works* (1832) and Prothero 'Maguiron' has been silently emended to 'Maugiron'. Anne de Mendoza, Princess of Eboli, a woman of great beauty, became the mistress of Philip II of Spain in 1570; Louis de Maugiron, Baron d'Ampus, a very handsome man, was the mignon of Henry III of France. The 'famous Latin epigram' which B quotes here was

cited with the following comment by Warton (*An Essay on the Genius and Writings of Pope* (1806), i. 286):

They were made on Louis de Maguiron [*sic*], the most beautiful man of his time, and the great favourite of Henry III. of France, who lost an eye at the siege of Issoire; and on the Princess of Eboli, a great beauty, but who was deprived of the sight of one of her eyes, and who was at the same time mistress of Philip II. King of Spain.

[The lines translate roughly thus:

Acon has lost his right eye, Leonilla her left,
And both in beauty could become as Gods;
Give your sighted eye to your sister, boy,
So you will be Cupid, and she Venus.]

Although Warton was almost certainly B's source (the spelling of 'Maguiron' tends to confirm this), the epigram, with certain variants, is also given by Voltaire in n. 4 to 'Chant Premier' of *La Henriade* (see *Oeuvres Complètes de Voltaire* (1785), x. 204). Goldsmith is not known to have 'translated or imitated' these lines.

33. *Wilkes . . . circumstances.* John Wilkes (1727–97), writer, wit, and celebrated radical politician, was MP for Aylesbury, and later for Middlesex. Often prosecuted (for libel or obscenity), and often expelled from the House of Commons, he became Lord Mayor of London in 1774. He was a member of the 'Hell Fire Club', and a notorious profligate. In a letter to the Duke of Richmond of Nov. 1772, Edmund Burke wrote (Thomas W. Copeland (ed.), *The Correspondence of Edmund Burke*, 10 vols. (1958–1978), ii (ed. Lucy S. Sutherland, 1960), 374):

Your Grace is very sensible that you have not made your Court to the world by forming yourself to a flattering exterior but you put me in mind of Mr Wilkes's observation when he makes love, that he will engage in such a pursuit against the handsomest fellow in England, and only desires a month start of his Rival on account of his face.

Wilkes desired a considerably shorter advantage according to E. H. Barker (*Literary Anecdotes and Contemporary Reminiscences*, 2 vols. (1852), i. 203): 'Wilkes, who was one of the ugliest men of his time, had the tact of making himself eminently agreeable, conscious of which he used to say that it took him just half an hour to talk away his face.'

34. *Swift . . . servants.* B quotes Swift's 'Cadenus and Vanessa', ll. 524–5: 'Vanessa, not in Years a Score, / Dreams of a Gown of forty-four'. 'Vanessa' was Swift's literary cognomen for Esther Vanhomrigh, whom he met in 1708. She became his pupil, fell in love with him, and died of shock after his rebuttal of her in 1723. 'Stella' was his literary cognomen for Esther Johnson (1681–1728), with whom he was on intimate terms, and whom he may have secretly married. She is the subject of such poems as 'Stella's Birthday', and 'On the Death of Mrs. Johnson'. She died of ill health. (See also Harold Williams (ed.), *Jonathan Swift, Journal to Stella*, 2 vols. (1974), vol. i, pp. ix–xlvii.) Swift's decline set in around 1736, and in 1742 the Court of Chancery appointed

guardians to look after him. His last years were recorded by the Earl of Orrery: 'from an outragious [*sic*] lunatic, he sunk afterwards into a quiet, speechless idiot; and dragged out the remainder of his life in that helpless situation. He died towards the latter end of *October* 1745' (The Earl of Orrery, *Remarks on the Life and Writings of Dr. Jonathan Swift* (1752), p. 265; see also pp. 139–44, 263–82).

35. *"They . . . Translation."* In *Works* (1832) 'reverence' reads 'renounce', and 'subscribe' 'submit'. In *Works* (1832) and Prothero 'Ægira' reads 'Ægina'; B correctly follows Taylor's text. B cites verbatim from Thomas Taylor, *The Description of Greece by Pausanias*, 3 vols. (1794), ii. 246. With regard to B's opinion here, cf. *DJ* VII. 33: 'There's Fortune even in fame, we must allow' (*CPW* v. 237), and 'Detached Thoughts', no. 83 (*BLJ* ix. 41): 'Like Sylla—I have always believed that all things depend upon Fortune & nothing upon ourselves.'

36. *Grimm . . . ago.* The following passage, alluding in the first instance to Crébillon *fils* and in the second to Rousseau, appeared in *Correspondance Littéraire, Philosophique et Critique, Adressée à un Souverain d'Allemagne, depuis 1770 jusqu'en 1782*, by the Baron Grimm and Diderot, 5 vols. (1812), i. 449:

On sait même qu'une jeune Anglaise d'une naissance distinguée*, fut tellement éprise et de l'ouvrage, et de l'idée qu'elle s'était faite de l'auteur, que, pour le voir, elle fit exprès le voyage de Paris; et après s'être assurée qu'elle pouvait faire le bonheur de son héros, l'épousa secrètement, et voulut bien renoncer pour lui à son nom, à sa famille et à sa patrie. M. de Crébillon a vécu plusieurs années avec elle à Paris dans une grande retraite, mais dans l'union la plus fortunée. Ce n'est qu'après la mort de cette tendre héroïne, qu'on a su les circonstances d'un mariage si romanesque: voilà comme tout dans le monde n'est qu'heur et malheur. L'auteur d'un conte libertin inspire une belle passion à une grande dame qui veut bien franchir les mers pour venir le chercher; et l'amant *de la Nouvelle Héloïse*, de tous les amans [*sic*] le plus passioné, le plus fidèle, est réduit à épouser sa servante!

* Mademoiselle de Strafford.

This work was reviewed by Francis Jeffrey in the *Edinburgh Review*, vol. xxi, no. xlii (July 1813), article i, pp. 263–99, in which the above passage was referred to and roughly paraphrased as follows (p. 285):

It is a little more difficult, however, to account for the fact, that the perusal of his [Crébillon's] works inspired a young lady of good family in this country with such a passion for the author, that she ran away from her friends, came to Paris, married him, and nursed and attended him with exemplary tenderness and affection to his dying day. But there is nothing but luck, good or bad—as M. Grimm sagely observes—in this world. The author of a licentious novel inspires a romantic passion in a lady of rank and fortune, who crosses seas, and abandons her family and her native country for his sake;—while the author [Rousseau] of the *Nouvelle Heloise*, the most delicate and passionate of all lovers that ever existed, is obliged to clap up a match with his chamber-maid!

Rousseau lived happily for 25 years with Thérèse Le Vasseur, the chamber-maid in his lodgings, whom he describes meeting in his *Confessions*, bk. viii.

37. *a few . . . letters.* George Farquhar's entertaining and candid letters might have been found by B in *The Works Of the late Ingenious Mr. George Farquhar*, 2 vols. (1718–1736), i. 38–74. See also Charles Stonehill (ed.), *The Complete Works of George Farquhar*, 2 vols. (1930), ii, pp. 221 ff.

38. *The Comedies . . . Addison's.* B refers to William Congreve (1670–1729), author of *The Double Dealer* (1693) and *The Way of the World* (1700); Sir John Vanbrugh (1664–1726), dramatist and architect, author of *The Relapse* (1697) and *The Provok'd Wife* (1698); George Farquhar (1678–1707), author of *The Recruiting Officer* (1706) and *The Beaux' Stratagem* (1707); Colley Cibber (1671–1757), dramatist, actor, and butt of Pope's wit, author of *The Careless Husband* (1705), *The Double Gallant* (1707), and English adaptations of Molière; Sir Richard Steele (1672–1729), essayist, dramatist, and politician, founder of the *Tatler* (1709–11) and the *Spectator* (1711–12), and the creator of the character Sir Roger de Coverley; and to the Right Honourable Joseph Addison (1672–1719), essayist, statesman, and poet, author of *Cato* (1713), friend of Steele and contributor to the *Spectator*.

39. *We . . . topics."* Sir Robert Walpole, first Earl of Orford (1676–1745), the great Whig statesman and first Prime Minister, who held office from 1721 to 1742. Boswell recorded the following exchange between himself and Johnson (*Boswell's Life of Johnson* iii. 57):

> When I complained of having dined at a splendid table without hearing one sentence of conversation worthy of being remembered, he said, 'Sir, there seldom is any such conversation.' BOSWELL. 'Why then meet at table?' JOHNSON. 'Why to eat and drink together, and to promote kindness; and, Sir, this is better done when there is no solid conversation; for when there is, people differ in opinion, and get into bad humour, or some of the company who are not capable of such conversation, are left out, and feel themselves uneasy. It was for this reason, Sir Robert Walpole said, he always talked bawdy at his table, because in that all could join.'

40. *Even . . . allusions.* For the passages in Johnson's *London* which B has in mind here, see 'Letter to John Murray Esq$^{re.}$', n. 30. Addison's unsuccessful bawdy comedy *The Drummer* was first produced in 1715.

41. *Several . . . high.* In Prothero 'B–ll–gh–t' reads 'B–ll–gh–m'. There is no record of any person whose name might fill up these blanks in the pugilistic and sporting annals of the time. Robert Barclay Allardice (1779–1854), generally known as Captain Barclay, was celebrated for his prodigious pedestrian performances; most notably, the occasion on which he walked a thousand miles in a thousand successive hours at Newmarket, between 1 June and 12 July 1809. He could life half a ton, and could lift a man of eighteen stone from the floor to the table on his right hand alone. For a full account of him and his achievements, see W. Thom, *Pedestrianism* (1813), pp. 101–219. Henry Angelo (1760–1839) became head of his father's school of fencing in about 1785, and retired in 1817. He was B's instructor from his Harrow days onwards, and remembered him affectionately in *Reminiscences of Henry Angelo*,

2 vols. (1828–30), ii. 37–44, 123–33, and in *Angelo's Pic Nic* (1834), pp. 16–18. John 'Gentleman' Jackson (1769–1845), pugilist and champion of England from 1795 to 1803, instructed B at his rooms at no. 13, Bond Street. In a not very sympathetic notice of B's residence at Cambridge, J. W. Clark reported the following anecdote (*Cambridge*: *Brief Historical and Descriptive Notes* (1881), p. 40):

He was fond of boxing, and affected the society of Jackson, the celebrated pugilist, with whom he often walked and drove in public. When his tutor, Mr. Tavel, remonstrated with him on being seen in company so much beneath his rank, he replied, 'Really, sir, I cannot understand you. With the single exception of yourself, I can assure you that Mr. Jackson's manners are infinitely superior to those of the Fellows of the College whom I meet at the high table.'

For B's letters and other references to Angelo and Jackson, see, e.g., Marchand i. 110; *BAP*, p. 39; *BLJ* i. 92, 162, 169, 170–1; iii. 221, 251, 253, 255, 257. See also *Hints from Horace*, l. 598, and B's note to *DJ* XI. 19 (*CPW* i. 311, 439; v. 747).

42. *It would . . . divorce.* In *Works* (1832) and Prothero 'trials for divorce' reads 'trials of divorce'. B presumably has in mind here such 'expurgated editions' as those compiled by Thomas Bowdler (1754–1825), whose *The Family Shakespeare* was first published in 1807. See also, however, *DJ* I. 44 and B's note thereto (*CPW* v. 22–3, 676). B also refers here to the trial of Queen Caroline, which took place during Aug. to Nov. 1820, and to which he alludes in 'Letter to John Murray Esq[re.]' (see nn. 7, 8 thereto).

43. *"Remember . . . Succès."* Cf. *BLJ* vi. 90; vii. 115. See also 'Letter to John Murray Esq[re.]', and n. 31 thereto.

44. *To return . . . it.* Immediately after the passage noted in n. 20 above, Bowles continued ('Observations', p. 6):

If what is here extracted does, or can excite in the mind, (I will not say of any 'Layman,' of any Christian, but) of any *human being*, such disgusting images as have sprung up under Mr. Gilchrist's 'nose,' and which he has drawn with 'minuteness' truly anatomical, and with congenial 'pruriency;' then I confess, with sorrow, my conduct deserves the severest animadversions.

But, on the contrary, if, as I verily believe, the passage in my Life of Pope, that speaks of his connection with Martha Blount, &c. does not, and cannot excite these filthy ideas and images (here 'minutely' specified), except in the brain of Mr. Gilchrist, I ask, whether, in attributing an article, full of exaggerations, on the same subject, in the Quarterly Review, to this critic, or, in introducing his name, I had any reason for distinguishing him with that courtesy which I had hitherto always endeavoured to show, from principle as well as disposition, in literary controversy?

45. *'peremptorily . . . Magazine.'* The circumstances leading up to the sentence which B quotes here were as follows. In both 'A Reply' (p. 28) and *Second Reply* (p. 13), Bowles had mentioned having received a letter from John Scott, the editor of the *London Magazine* (see following n.), in which, Bowles claimed,

Scott had dissociated himself from the views expressed by Gilchrist in his 'Review'. Gilchrist challenged the veracity of this (Gilchrist, p. 16):

I defy you to justify this assertion. That you might write to the editor of the London, to complain of your castigation, is more than most likely; but that Mr. Scott disingenuously and secretly 'wrote a most obliging letter to you, lest it should be thought such a piece of criticism came from his more forcible and elegant pen,' [Bowles's *Second Reply*, p. 13] is so totally at variance with his sentiments, personally expressed to myself, and so utterly unbecoming a man of honour, that I will not, even on Mr. Bowles's positive declaration, believe it.

To this Bowles now replied in the following manner:

I am now peremptorily called upon to speak of a circumstance which gives me the greatest pain; the mention of a letter I received from the Editor of the London Magazine.

It is now too late for me to recede, however I may lament that the name of the editor was introduced on the occasion; but the *fact* has been, by Mr. Gilchrist, positively denied. I am defied to prove this circumstance, and I must consider my own veracity as now called in question. I therefore assert, in my own name, and I dare Mr. Gilchrist to contradict me, that the editor of the Magazine, which contained Mr. Gilchrist's filthy caricature, did write to me, to say that in the case of Spence's Anecdotes, *as the correspondent spoke in the style of editor*, the article CERTAINLY SHOULD NOT HAVE BEEN *admitted*, had not the editor, at the time, been dangerously ill, and incapable of attending to the Magazine! ('Observations', pp. 6–7)

Bowles had told Murray much the same story in his letter to him of 22 Oct. 1820: 'the editor wrote me a manly and generous letter totally disclaiming any participation in the sentiments and accounting for the admission by illness' (Greever, *Wiltshire Parson*, p. 123). See also p. 423, n. 57 above.

46. *Poor . . . New Aberdeen.* John Scott (1784–1821) was educated at Aberdeen Grammar School and became editor of the *Champion* in 1814. Between 1814 and 1819 he spent much time abroad, and recorded his travels in two highly acclaimed books: *A Visit to Paris in 1814* (1815), and *Paris Revisited in 1815* (1816). His final work, *Sketches of Manners, Scenery, &c. in the French Provinces, Switzerland, and Italy*, was posthumously published in 1821. In 1819 he returned to England to take up the appointment of editor of Baldwin's newly established *London Magazine*, which post he held until his death. Thomas Noon Talfourd recorded (*Final Memorials of Charles Lamb*, 2 vols. (1848), ii. 1–2): 'Never was a periodical work commenced with happier auspices, numbering a list of contributors more original in thought, more fresh in spirit, more sportive in fancy, or directed by an editor better qualified by nature and study to preside, than this "London."' The contributors included Hazlitt, Lamb, Barry Cornwall, and John Hamilton Reynolds. Between May 1820 and Jan. 1821, Scott, in his capacity as editor of the *London Magazine*, sharply attacked *Blackwood's Edinburgh Magazine*, his principal target being John Gibson Lockhart. This eventually led to a duel between Scott and a friend of Lockhart's, John Henry Christie, which took place by moonlight at 9 o'clock

in the evening of 16 Feb. 1821 at Chalk Farm, just outside London. At the second fire, Scott was hit; and, though he was expected to recover, he died a lingering death on 27 Feb. 1821. See also the *Gentleman's Magazine*, vol. xci, pt. i (Jan. to June 1821), pp. 271–2, 369–70. His family was left destitute, and a subscription was raised by a committee which included Sir James Mackintosh and Murray. Murray asked B to contribute £10; to which request B replied with his usual generosity on 21 Apr. 1821:

> You may make my subscription to Mr. Scott's widow &c. *thirty* instead of the proposed *ten* pounds—but do not put down *my name*—put down N.B. only—The reason is, that I have mentioned him in the enclosed pamphlet—it would look indelicate.—I would give more——but my disappointments of last year—about Rochdale—and the transfer from the funds—render me more economical for the present. (*BLJ* viii. 99)

The 'enclosed' pamphlet was 'Observations upon Observations'.

For a biography of Scott, see Patrick O'Leary, *Regency Editor: Life of John Scott, 1784–1821* (1983).

47. (*save one*). Augusta Leigh, B's half-sister. See also, e.g., 'To [Augusta]' (*CPW* iii. 386–8), and *BLJ* v. 67–8, 89.

48. *With . . . vituperative.* B's 'Lines to a Lady Weeping' were first published anonymously in the *Morning Chronicle* on 7 Mar. 1812. When he republished them with *The Corsair* in 1814 (thus publicly acknowledging himself their author for the first time), they caused an outcry, and the *Courier* was particularly virulent in its attack. See *CPW* iii. 10, 391–2; Marchand i. 318–19, 323; *BAP*, p. 115; and also B's letter to the *Courier* (*BLJ* vi. 41–3). At the time of B's separation from his wife Annabella in 1816, however, the *Courier* refrained from joining in the general newspaper assaults on B. On the other hand, John Scott (see n. 46 above) attacked B viciously in three issues of the *Champion*. Having been furnished with copies of B's 'Fare Thee Well!' and 'A Sketch from Private Life' by Henry Brougham, Scott printed them in the *Champion*, no. 171 (14 Apr. 1816), with the following comments:

> His Lordship, then, is determined that nothing shall stand between him and public animadversion.—He will compel that notice which an honorable [*sic*] sense of delicacy would have withheld, if he had been content to offend in silence. . . . Lord Byron will not pretend that these poems were not designed as an appeal to the public, to throw the blame of his early separation from Lady Byron on the weak and defenceless party. (pp. 117–18)

See also *CPW* iii. 380–6, 493–5.

In his diary for 15 Apr. 1816 John Cam Hobhouse recorded: 'On arriving at Piccadilly to day I found Sam Rogers & Leigh Hunt up in arms at the publication of Fare thee well and the Sketch in Scott's Champion of Yesterday with violent abuse of Lord Byron—' (Broughton Papers, BL Add. MS 47232, f. 112v). This prompted Hunt to write a kind and sympathetic defence of B, and a scathing rebuttal of Scott, entitled 'Distressing Circumstance in High Life', in the *Examiner*, 21 Apr. 1816. See Lawrence Huston Houtchens and

Carolyn Washburn Houtchens (eds.), *Leigh Hunt's Literary Criticism* (1956), pp. 95–102. On the same day, in the *Champion*, no. 172, Scott reviewed at length and with a certain malicious relish the general reaction of the press to the two poems. Hobhouse recorded tersely in his diary on that date: 'violent attack in the Champion which I did not read—' (Broughton Papers, BL Add. MS 47232, f. 108). Finally, Scott attacked both B and Hunt in the *Champion*, no. 173 (28 Apr. 1816)—by which time of course B was beyond the Channel.

49. *Two years . . . dialogue.* John Scott's son, Paul, died at Paris on 8 Nov. 1816, aged 8½, which event Scott painfully recorded in his elegy *The House of Mourning* (1817). Although there is no further mention in either Scott's writings or B's correspondence of their meeting, it clearly occurred in Jan.–Feb. 1819, when Scott was in Venice. Patmore relates the following anecdote which he had from Scott himself soon after his return from Italy, where he had spent a 'week' with B in Venice (P. G. Patmore, *My Friends and Acquaintance*, 3 vols. (1854), ii. 285–6):

> Until their meeting at Venice, there had been an estrangement between Byron and Scott, in consequence of the part the latter had taken in the 'Champion,' relative to the publication of the celebrated 'Farewell;' but they were now reconciled, and were on the water together in Byron's gondola, under circumstances which led Scott to express a strong sense of danger as to their position. 'Oh!' said Byron, in a tone of perfect seriousness, 'you need not be afraid of anything happening to you while you are with me, *for we are friends now*.' And Scott explained that Byron had the most intimate persuasion, that any of his friends who had quarrelled with him were never safe from some strange accident, until they had 'made it up.'

And, as a measure of his reconciliation to B, in speaking of Ferrara and the story of Parisina and Ugo connected with it, *after* he had left Venice, Scott wrote:

> Another interest is added to the story for us Englishmen, by the muse of Lord Byron. This distinguishes him from all our other poets, that he has connected the tribute of English poetry and prose with the most celebrated places of the earth, and the finest names, and the most touching stories, more than any other we have ever had, or than any other nation has ever had. He has thus united the name of England, and an Englishman, with the most celebrated points of the world's history, in a more intimate manner than any other country can boast of. (John Scott, *Sketches of Manners, Scenery, &c. in the French Provinces, Switzerland, and Italy* (1821), pp. 307–8)

Scott refers to B's *Parisina* (1816), for which see *CPW* iii. 358–75, 488–9.

50. *Poor . . . Italy.* In *Works* (1832) 'Sir J.[as] Mackintosh' reads 'Sir James Mackintosh'. Sir James Mackintosh (1765–1832), philosopher, historian, and politician, secured John Scott's appointment as editor of the *London Magazine.*

51. *I pass . . . M.[r] S.* See n. 45 above.

52. *We now . . . outrage.* B refers *en passant* to Edmund Kean (1789–1833), the actor, whose performances—particularly of Richard III—he greatly admired.

See, e.g., *BLJ* iii. 244. More directly, B refers to the following criticism by Bowles of Gilchrist:

I shall therefore set before the reader another specimen of this gentleman's *ars maledicendi* in criticism, from the pamphlet, which he calls 'An Answer to Bowles.' This sentence there appears:

'With the exception of the passage in which, with the MOST UNBLUSHING EFFRONTERY, you suggest that Pope MADE AN ATTEMPT on Lady Mary's person, and was REPULSED, you have not urged one reason for our believing that Pope was the aggressor, &c.; and yet, without any argument besides YOUR OWN GROSS INVENTION of ATTEMPT at RAPE! you persist in repeating, *terque quaterque*, Pope was the aggressor.' ('Observations', p. 8)

Bowles quotes, with omissions, minor variants and his own capitalization, Gilchrist, pp. 23–4. The phrase *ars maledicendi* (the art of abuse), is Scaliger's, and was first introduced in this controversy by Gilchrist (Gilchrist, p. 20).

53. *"Ranald . . . victuals."* In *Works* (1832) 'Ranald's' reads 'Ranold's'. B correctly follows Walter Scott's orthography. In *A Legend of Montrose*, Dugald Dalgetty says to Ranald, the performer of the prank: 'It was a merry jest that, of cramming the bread into the dead man's mouth, but something too wild and salvage, besides wasting the good victuals' (*Novels and Tales* (1825), xvi. 140).

54. *The first . . . compliance.* In Henry Fielding's *Jonathan Wild*, bk. iii, ch. 7, Wild sends Fireblood with a letter to his beloved, the 'chaste Lætitia', who is very taken with the courier's good looks: 'Fireblood, who was no backward youth, began to take her by the hand, and proceeded so warmly, that, to imitate his actions with the rapidity of our narration, he in a few minutes ravished this fair creature, or at least would have ravished her, if she had not, by a timely compliance, prevented him' (*Jonathan Wild* (1982 edn.), p. 141).

55. *The second . . . punishment.* For the lines by Pope that B has in mind here, see n. 29 to 'Letter to John Murray Esq[re.]' above.

56. *The passage . . . more.* In his edition of *The Works of the Right Honourable Lady Mary Wortley Montagu*, 5 vols. (1803), ii. 30–8, James Dallaway first published, from the original MS, a letter from Pope to Lady Mary dated 'Twick'nam, Aug. 18, 1716', in which Pope wrote (p. 35):

The unhappy distance at which we correspond, removes a great many of those punctillious restrictions and decorums that oftentimes in nearer conversation prejudice truth to save good breeding. I may now hear of my faults, and you of your good qualities, without a blush on either side. We converse upon such unfortunate generous terms as exclude the regards of fear, shame, or design in either of us. And methinks it would be as ungenerous a part to impose even in a single thought upon each other, in this state of separation, as for spirits of a different sphere, who have so little intercourse with us, to employ that little (as some would make us think they do), in putting tricks and delusions upon poor mortals.

To this passage, included in full but with certain discrepancies in his edition of Pope's *The Works*, Bowles added a note (vii. 218n.). Alluding to this note, and to Gilchrist's accusation that he had aspersed Pope with an 'attempt at rape' (see n. 52 above), Bowles wrote in 'Observations':

> The only passage I can find, to which I suppose he [Gilchrist] must allude, is the following:—
>
> 'Lady Montague was at this time at Constantinople. Pope has here suppressed part of the letter, which may be seen in Dalloway's [*sic*] edition. The grossness of it will sufficiently explain Pope's meaning; and I have little doubt, but that the lady, disdaining the stiff and *formal* mode of *female* manners at that time prevalent, made the lover believe he might proceed a *step* farther than *decorum* would allow.'...
>
> Christian reader! such are the 'beauties' of Gilchristian criticism. This is a specimen of a Gilchrist's heart. I am certain, no words of mine will be necessary to excite disdain and abhorrence of such unblushing effrontery. 'A STEP BEYOND DECORUM,' in this man's repertory of pure conceptions, is 'AN ATTEMPT TO COMMIT A RAPE!' (Observations, p. 9)

Lady Mary's reply to Pope's letter appears in vol. ii, pp. 39–44 of Dallaway's edition, cited above. For a portion of it see p. 418, n. 39 above.

57. *"I am ... also."* In a footnote in his *Life of Johnson* Boswell recorded (iv. 398n.): 'Dr. Johnson related, with very earnest approbation, a story of a gentleman, who, in an impulse of passion, overcame the virtue of a young woman. When she said to him, "I am afraid we have done wrong!" he answered, "Yes, we have done wrong;—for I would not *debauch her mind*."'

58. *"kill... Soul." Othello* V. ii. 32.

59. *"Ce ... coûte."* Alluding to the superstition that the decapitated 'Catholic martyr' Pope Sylvester II 'had carried his head in his hands a considerable way', Gibbon continued: 'yet, on a similar tale, a lady of my acquaintance once observed, "La distance n'y fait rien; il n'y a que le premier pas qui coûte"' (The distance is nothing; it's only the first step that counts). See J. B. Bury (ed.), *The History of the Decline and Fall of the Roman Empire By Edward Gibbon*, 7 vols. (1898–1900), iv. 202n.). The 'lady' in question was the Marquise du Deffand (1697–1780), who was famed for her wit, and whose *salon* was one of the most celebrated of the eighteenth century. Grimm has another version of her *bon mot* (*Correspondance Littéraire, Philosophique et Critique, Adressée à un Souverain d'Allemagne, Depuis 1753 jusqu'en 1769*, by the Baron Grimm and Diderot, 6 vols. (1813), iv. 113–14).

60. *Has... crime?* See Matthew 5: 28.

61. *M.r B.... irresistible.* See n. 56 above.

62. *"a hasty ... appear."* Bowles wrote: 'Under the immediate impression that Mr. Bowles was indebted for the criticism in the Quarterly, to the same hand which wrote the criticism in the London, a hasty pamphlet was suffered to appear, in which some personalities respecting Mr. Gilchrist were admitted' ('Observations', p. 9). The 'hasty pamphlet' was Bowles's *Second Reply*, in the Advertisement to which he admits its having been 'hastily written' (p. 3). For the 'personalities respecting Mr. Gilchrist', see n. 13 above.

63. *The grand . . . Quarterly.* Bowles took exception to 'The coarse and illiberal remarks of the Quarterly Review, in which a clergyman, residing chiefly in the country, is described as a distempered hypochondriac' ('Observations', p. 9). He alludes to the *Quarterly Review* in which the following passage appeared (pp. 411–12):

Provincial authors too are liable to a sort of literary hypochondriasm, where they see nothing but the creation of a morbid fancy, a phantom in a dark room. . . . It is only on this principle that we can account for the injury inflicted on Pope by the strange proceedings of his last editor [i.e. Bowles], who, having probably possessed himself of all the ravings of all the dunces on their arch-enemy, dwelt on them till their sinister influence operated on his imagination, and prompted him to hesitate, and suggest, and surmise away every amiable characteristic of the poet; and, incredible as it may appear, to accuse him of the contrary dispositions! Solitary attention strangely magnifies by its intensity. Had he rather, in these distempered moments, opened the window—fresh air and 'rural sights' might have thrown over every object the hue of truth and nature.

64. *"I will . . . Physician."* Laurence Sterne, *A Sentimental Journey through France and Italy* (1768), 'In the Street, Calais'. (See, e.g., the Harmondsworth edn. (1967), p. 52.)

65. *Regnard . . . saturnine.* Atrabilarious is a variant spelling of atrabilious and means melancholic; saturnine means gloomy, melancholic. Molière (Jean-Baptiste Poquelin) (1622–73), the great French comic dramatist and actor, was known in private to be of a melancholy disposition. Jean-François Regnard (1655–1709), the greatest French comic dramatist after Molière and author of such comedies as *Le Joueur* (1696), *Le Distrait* (1697), and *Les Folies Amoureuses* (1704). B learnt of his condition from Grimm, who observed that:

Regnard, et la plupart des poëtes comiques étaient gens bilieux et mélancholiques; et que M. de Voltaire, qui est très-gai, n'a jamais fait que des tragédies, et que la comédie gaie, est le seul genre où il n'ait point réussi. C'est que celui qui rit et celui qui fait rire, sont deux hommes fort différens.
(Regnard, and most of the comic poets were bilious and melancholic; and that Voltaire, who is very cheerful, has only written tragedies—comedy being the only genre in which he has not succeeded. Thus it is that he who laughs, and he who makes others laugh, are two very different sorts of men.) (*Correspondance Littéraire, Philosophique et Critique*, by Grimm and Diderot, vi. 54)

See also *BLJ* viii. 31, where B quoted this very passage. However, he there mentioned that Regnard 'is supposed to have committed suicide'. This is not so. He has unfortunately confused Regnard with the subject of an anecdote related by Grimm in the same paragraph just preceding the above passage (pp. 53–4). This tells of a young Englishman whose doctors prescribe a trip to France to cure him of his depression. Arriving in Paris on the first night of Regnard's *Le Joueur* at the *Comédie Française*, he attends the performance in the hope of cheering himself up. But it only aggravates his condition, and he returns to his inn and hangs himself in despair ('il s'était pendu de désespoir').

66. *D^r. Johnson . . . Smart.* For similar observations on the indispositions of poets in general, and those mentioned here in particular, see *BLJ* iv. 332; vi. 85. The 'more awful malady' shared by the poets William Collins (1721–59), Cowper, Christopher Smart (1722–71), and Swift was insanity.

67. (*Penrose.*) B quotes the final two lines of stanza 2 of Penrose's poem 'Madness' (*Poems by the Revd Thomas Penrose* (1781), p. 31).

68. *Mendehlson . . . themselves.* 'Mendehlson' is so spelt by B in MS, and appears as such in *Works* (1832) and Prothero. B refers to Moses Mendelssohn (1729–86), Jewish philosopher, friend of Lessing, and hero of his *Nathan the Wise* (1779). He was the grandfather of the composer Felix Mendelssohn. Pierre Bayle (1647–1706), the French philosopher and compiler of the *Dictionnaire Historique et Critique* (1697–1702). In his *Curiosities of Literature* (2 vols. (1807), ii. 158), D'Israeli wrote:

> There are heavy hours in which the mind of a man of letters is unhinged; when the intellectual faculties lose all their elasticity, and when nothing but the simplest actions are adapted to their enfeebled state. At such hours it is recorded of the Jewish Socrates, Moses Mendelsohn, that he would stand at his window, and count the tiles of his neighbour's house. An anonymous writer has told of Bayle, that he would frequently wrap himself in his cloak, and hasten to places where mountebanks resorted; and that this was one of his chief amusements.

A slightly different version of Mendelssohn's distraction is given by D'Israeli in *The Literary Character* (1818), p. 143.

69. *"would . . . Spirits."* Of Johnson's disposition in the spring of 1764 Boswell wrote (*Boswell's Life of Johnson* i. 483):

> About this time he was afflicted with a very severe return of the hypochondriack disorder, which was ever lurking about him. He was so ill, as, notwithstanding his remarkable love of company, to be entirely averse to society, the most fatal symptom of that malady. Dr. Adams told me, that, as an old friend, he was admitted to visit him, and that he found him in a deplorable state, sighing, groaning, talking to himself, and restlessly walking from room to room. He then used this emphatical expression of the misery which he felt: 'I would consent to have a limb amputated to recover my spirits.'

70. *"Go . . . me."* Pope, *Epistle to Dr. Arbuthnot*, ll. 119–20.

71. *"But . . . &c.* Bowles wrote ('Observations', p. 10):

> But, in extenuation, not only the great provocation should be remembered, but it ought to be said, that orders were sent to the London booksellers, that the most direct personal passages [about Gilchrist in his *Second Reply*] should be *omitted entirely*; nor did I know that any copy of that publication, except with the leaves cancelled, had been sent out for general sale. This I think it right to declare publicly. For the rest, Mr. Gilchrist has no right to object, as the reader will see, by what has been fairly set before him.

72. *"breaking . . . plaister".* In *Works* (1832) 'plaister' (both here and at his reiteration six words later in this sentence) reads 'plaster'. The proverb is of fifteenth-century origin and means to redress one's mistake, or to right one's wrong. See also, for example, Walter Scott's *Rob Roy*, where Bailie Jarvie,

having singed the plaid of the Gallant Galbraith while fighting him with a red-hot poker (for want of his claymore), promises: 'Gin I hae broken the head, . . . I sall find the plaister. A new plaid sall ye hae, and o' the best . . .' (*Novels and Tales* (1825), viii. 127).

73. *rust . . . Surgery."* See *Henry IV, Part I*, V. i. 135, and *Henry VI, Part II*, V. i. 99–101. B probably also has in mind the original legend of Achilles' spear possessing the power of both wounding and curing, in Ovid, *Metamorphoses*, xii. 112; xiii. 171.

74. *L.M. . . . Q.R.* In *Works* (1832) 'L.M.' and 'Q.R.' read 'London Magazine' and 'Quarterly Review'. In Prothero they read 'L[ondon Magazine]' and 'Qterly. Rev.'.

75. *"Mr. G. . . . &c.—".* Exaggerating various accusations made by Gilchrist (Gilchrist, pp. 4, 5, 11, 12, 34), Bowles wrote ('Observations', p. 10):

> Mr. Gilchrist has had ample revenge; for, in his 'answer,' (as he calls it) I am represented as wrapped up in self-love, and paying attention only to the rich and great—sneering on the obscure and humble possessor of talents [John Clare], only because he *is* poor—sensitive, in a peculiar manner, to all criticism, and complaining unless it 'chants my praise'—having the affectation of 'gentylness,' a super-stratum to 'innate vulgarity,' being a 'priest in drink,' &c. &c. And this abuse is heaped on me, and these personal, and these foul and false representations of my *private life* and character are called 'an answer.'

76. *Mr. B. . . . "Scavenger."* Gilchrist having called Bowles's *Second Reply* a 'mud-cart' (Gilchrist, p. 34), Bowles appropriated the term and applied it to Gilchrist ('Observations', p. 10):

> This pamphlet is indeed a 'mud-cart!' and even, whilst the scavenger is emptying it, I am recommended by him to learn, in controversy, the language of Hooker and Lowth! [and others for their 'moderation', Gilchrist, p. 6] . . . Is he to come with a 'mud-cart,' and never expect a 'splash' in return? Shall he be *licensed* to outrage feelings and character, and demand himself to be treated as a *gentleman*? Shall he insult with the foulest ribaldry of critical slang, and expect smiles and courtesies in return? Shall he fling dirt, and receive rose-water?

77. *Champfort . . . Rose-Water?"* In *Works* (1832) and Prothero 'Champfort' reads 'Chamfort'. During a discussion with the fanatical supporter of the Revolution Nicolas-Sébastien Roch de Chamfort (1741–94), Jean-François Marmontel (1723–99) recorded Chamfort saying to him: 'Mais, . . . je vois que mes espérances vous attristent: vous ne voulez pas d'une liberté qui coûtera beaucoup d'or et de sang. Voulez-vous qu'on vous fasse des révolutions à l'eau rose?' (But, . . . I see that my hopes upset you: you don't want a liberty which costs so much blood and money. Would you have revolutions made for you with rose water?) (*Œuvres Posthumes de Marmontel, Mémoires d'un Père*, 4 vols. (1804), iv. 84). B was fond of citing this: see, e.g. *BLJ* vi. 226; vii. 63, 77.

78. *"Consule Planco".* Horace, *Odes* III. xiv. 7: 'non ego hoc ferrem calidus iuventa / consule Planco' (I shouldn't have put up with this in my hot youth

when Plancus was Consul). For B's brilliant version, see *DJ* I. 212: 'And would not brook at all this sort of thing / In my hot youth—when George the Third was King' (*CPW* v. 77).

79. *I remember . . . man.* Bob Gregson (1778–1824), John Gulley, or Gully (1783–1863), and Tom Cribb (1781–1848) were all prize-fighters of great renown, the latter two being champions. Gulley and Gregson fought twice, and both were famous occasions. The first took place on 14 Oct. 1807. Gulley won after 36 rounds. Their second fight, and the one to which B refers here, took place on 10 May 1808. Gulley won again after 24 rounds. For accounts of both fights and their background see Pierce Egan, *Boxiana*, 4 vols. (1818–24), i. 179, 181–2, 184–5, 353.

As for the fight between Tom Cribb and Horton (whose only claim to fame was this fight), Egan wrote in his *Sporting Anecdotes* (1825) that 'in this little spree, . . . the Champion sewed him up in great style, in double quick time' (p. 541; see also *Boxiana*, i. 396). For B's dining at Cribb's, and for his further comments on Tom, see *BLJ* iii. 221.

80. *Salmoneus.* Salmoneus, the mythological king of Elis, had pretensions to being the equal of Zeus. He imitated Zeus's thunder and lightning by driving his chariot noisily and throwing torches. Zeus soon dispatched him to Hades with a real thunderbolt. See the *Aeneid*, vi. 585ff. B was fond of the phrase 'brazen thunders'. See, e.g., *DJ* XI. 67: 'Then roll the brazen thunders of the door' (*CPW* v. 485). Cf. also *Paradise Lost* xi. 713: 'The brazen Throat of Warr had ceas't to roar.'

81. *My.* In *Works* (1832) and Prothero this reads 'Why'.

82. *"Coals of Fire."* See Proverbs 25: 21–2.

83. *Arcadians.* In *Works* (1832) and Prothero this reads 'avocations'. B correctly follows Bowles's text. See following n. 84.

84. *I pass . . . like.* Having written that Gilchrist's 'ardent "genius" is resolved to "SIN UP TO MY SONG!"' (Pope, *Epilogue to the Satires* ii. 9), Bowles continued ('Observations', p. 11 and n.):

> Though he did not write the article in the Quarterly, he seems scarce able to restrain his delight in contemplating its triumph. With applauding sympathy he seems to exclaim,
>
> 'Oh! let MY little bark attendant sail,
> Pursue the triumph, and partake the gale.'[a]
>
> And no wonder; for it is impossible that any article could be so perfectly in unison with his feelings and taste, and mode of reasoning.
>
> Without applying the quotation which he has applied with so much adroitness, 'Arcades Ambo!'* we may consider the writer in the Quarterly Review and himself 'both Arcadians,' 'in-door' Arcadians indeed![b]
>
> Or we might rather figure the two critics as the 'two Kings of Brentford' in the Rehearsal, and as these two kings are introduced, 'smelling to ONE NOSEGAY;'[c] and moreover, as Pope was known to visit his female friends frequently with such a personal decoration, it would make the comparison more complete, by imagining these two

critics, like the aforesaid two kings, entering on the stage, and withdrawing, smelling to 'ONE NOSEGAY,' and that the perennial nosegay of their favorite [*sic*] and injured bard.

* This quotation, with the addition of 'Oh! Juvenes!' in his flippant tirade, in the London Magazine, is applied, with IRONICAL derision, to the deprivations of old age, with equal manliness, humanity, and taste![d]

[a] Pope, *Essay on Man* iv. 385–6.

[b] For Bowles's reference to '"in-door" Arcadians' here, see 'Letter to John Murray Esq[re.]', n. 166.

[c] The 'two Kings of Brentford' are characters in George Villiers's comedy *The Rehearsal* (1672), who first make their appearance in Act II, sc. ii, 'hand in hand'. Although the 'nosegay' does not appear in the stage directions, it used to be added to further the absurdity. (These characters are proverbial for two rivals who become reconciled.)

[d] Nowhere did Gilchrist use the phrase 'Arcades Ambo!' (Virgil, *Eclogue* vii. 4: Arcadians both); but he closed his third-to-last paragraph of *The Character of Pope* with the phrase '*Agite, o juvenes*!' (p. 181), from Juvenal, *Satire* vii. 20: 'hoc agite, o iuvenes' (to it, young men).

85. *Page 12. ... Catch.* Referring to various accusations, admissions and assertions in the *Quarterly Review*, Bowles wrote:

I can produce more reasons, than I have yet given, to show why I attributed the critique in the Quarterly, to Octavius Gilchrist. I did not suppose there could exist a man in the kingdom, *so impudent* as to pretend he did not know the meaning of 'subject and execution' of a poem; except Octavius Gilchrist, Esq., F.S.A.

I did not think there was one man in the kingdom, who would pretend ignorance of the meaning of 'disposition,' 'relief,' &c. except Octavius Gilchrist. I did not conceive that one man in the kingdom would utter such stupid flippancy, about 'squaring the circle,' except a man of the identical taste and sense of Octavius Gilchrist. I did not think there was one man in the kingdom, who, if he did not understand the common terms of 'external nature,' 'moral nature,' &c. would so entirely show his ignorance, combined with conceit, in confessing it, except Octavius Gilchrist.

I did not believe there was a man in the kingdom so perfect in Mr. Gilchrist's 'Old Lunes,' as daringly to assert, I had been prompted to surmise away EVERY AMIABLE CHARACTERISTIC of the poet (Pope) except Octavius Gilchrist; I did not believe any one would or could be so unfeelingly pert as to talk, as he has done, of the hypochondriasm of 'provincial authors,' except Octavius Gilchrist; I did not think the mean mind of any one in the kingdom could be gratified by a quotation from a professed satire, seriously imputing 'Gall' and Hate, to the editor of Pope's Works, except the mean mind of Octavius Gilchrist. ('Observations', p. 12)

For 'Old Lunes', see *The Merry Wives of Windsor* IV. ii. 21: 'Why, woman, your husband is in his old lunes again.' ('Lunes' are fits, rages.) The 'satire' to which Bowles refers finally here is *EBSR*.

86. *"It . . . yesterday."* In Walter Scott's *A Legend of Montrose*, Dugald Dalgetty, having been made a prisoner by the Marquis of Argyle, is thrust unceremoniously into an unlit cell. As he gropes his way down the stairway he stumbles over a body. 'When Dalgetty had recovered, his first demand was to know over whom he had stumbled. "He was a man a month since," answered a hollow and broken voice' (*Novels and Tales* (1825), xvi. 134).

87. *One ... F.S.A.* Besides the single instance cited in n. 85 above, Bowles

referred to 'Octavius Gilchrist, Esq., F.S.A.' on two further occasions ('Observations', pp. 12, 13). The abbreviation stands for Fellow of the Society of Antiquaries.

88. *I am . . . Service.* B was elected a Fellow of the Royal Society on 11 Jan. 1816. This illustrious body, whose full title was and is The Royal Society of London for the Improvement of Natural Knowledge, was founded in 1660 and had included such Fellows as Dryden, John Evelyn, and Robert Boyle (1627–91).

89. *"There . . . unknown".* Bowles wrote ('Observations', p. 12):

> There are some more reasons, that justified me in supposing the author of the offensive ribaldry in the London, was the author also of the notable criticism in the Quarterly. Whoever the author is, (and he is now not unknown) in some respects, though not in 'provincial' conceit and insolence, he might claim kindred with the gentleman who has been so often mentioned.

90. *"deterré."* Boswell recorded the following anecdote of Pope's reaction to Johnson's poem *London*, when it appeared in May 1738:

> POPE, who then filled the poetical throne without a rival, it may reasonably be presumed, must have been particularly struck by the sudden appearance of such a poet; and, to his credit, let it be remembered, that his feelings and conduct on the occasion were candid and liberal. He requested Mr. Richardson, son of the painter, to endeavour to find out who this new authour was. Mr. Richardson, after some inquiry, having informed him that he had discovered only that his name was Johnson, and that he was some obscure man, Pope said, 'He will soon be *déterré*.'

And he recorded of Johnson: 'He told us, with high satisfaction, the anecdote of Pope's inquiring who was the authour of his "London," and saying, he will soon be *déterré*' (*Boswell's Life of Johnson* i. 128–9; ii. 84–5). 'Déterré' means discovered.

91. *The . . . letters."* Alluding to a charge made by Bowles in his *Second Reply* (p. 17), Gilchrist wrote (Gilchrist, pp. 28–9):

> There is one point on which you delight to dwell: the following passage in 'the Reply' will illustrate it—it is Pope's DUPLICITY. 'The letters,' you say, 'printed by Curll, compared with the originals, prove that he was, where *self-love* was concerned, never free from a mixture of duplicity and art.' It is not in the shape of a threat, but of counsel, that I entreat you to repress this imputation in what you propose to offer concerning Pope in the Pamphleteer, and to consider if *your own conduct* relative to Pope's letters be free from *duplicity*. I think, sir, you will understand to what I allude.

Clearly Bowles didn't; for he retorted ('Observations', p. 13): 'I am as ignorant as the dead, of what your meaning is, when you speak of my being conscious of some "duplicity" myself, in regard to the publication of Pope's Letters. I am conscious of no "duplicity"—I have not the most distant idea of what you mean.'

92. *"Pope's . . . Pope".* Bowles wrote: 'Pope's duplicity, not Pope, were the objects of my dislike, and I firmly believed, and do believe him, guilty of it; and that *facts*—clear, positive facts—justified this belief' ('Observations', p. 13).

93. *"Eloisa . . . licentiousness".* Of Pope's 'Eloisa to Abelard' Bowles wrote: 'The "Eloisa," alone, is sufficient to convict him of licentiousness, *gross licentiousness*' ('Observations', pp. 13–14).

94. *mingled . . . licentious?* In *Works* (1832) and Prothero the 'with' immediately after 'mingled' has been silently eliminated. See Catullus, *Carmina* lxiii. The poem tells of Attis, a Greek youth, who sails to Phrygia to become a devotee of the Mother-Goddess Cybele, and who ritually castrates himself. Throughout the poem Catullus plays brilliantly on the androgynous state of Attis, who is alluded to as both masculine and feminine, and who soon regrets his action. Abelard, as B goes on to intimate, was castrated by the henchmen of Fulbert, Heloise's uncle (see n. 93 above).

95. *"I fear . . . passion."* In *Works* (1832) and Prothero 'draught' reads 'draft'. Campbell wrote of Dryden: 'This great High Priest of all the Nine was not a confessor to the finer secrets of the human breast. Had the subject of Eloisa fallen into his hands, he would have left but a coarse draught of her passion' (*Specimens*, p. 258).

96. *Ovid . . . women?* B refers to Ovid's *Amores*, *Ars Amatoria*, and *Remedia Amoris*, to Anacreon's *Odes* (translated, for instance, by Moore: *Odes of Anacreon*, 1800), and to Sappho's *Ode.* The translation of this last by Ambrose Philips is fortunately adopted in the following translation of Longinus' *On the Sublime*, x, to which section B is alluding here:

> Let us consider next, whether we cannot find out some other means to infuse *Sublimity* into our writings. Now, as there are no subjects which are not attended by some adherent *Circumstances*, an accurate and judicious choice of the most suitable of these *Circumstances*, and an ingenious and skilful connexion of them into one body, must necessarily produce the Sublime. For what by the judicious choice, and what by the skilful connexion, they cannot but very much affect the imagination.
>
> *Sappho* is an instance of this, who having observed the anxieties and tortures inseparable to jealous love, has collected and displayed them all with the most lively exactness. But in what particular has she shewn her excellence? In selecting those *circumstances* which suit best with her subject, and afterwards connecting them together with so much art.
>
> Blest as th'immortal gods is he,
> The youth who fondly sits by thee,
> And hears, and sees thee all the while
> Softly speak, and sweetly smile.
>
> 'Twas this depriv'd my soul of rest,
> And rais'd such tumults in my breast;
> For while I gaz'd, in transport tost,
> My breath was gone, my voice was lost.
>
> My bosom glow'd; the subtle flame
> Ran quick thro' all my vital frame;
> O'er my dim eyes a darkness hung;
> My ears with hollow murmurs rung.

In dewy damps my limbs were chill'd;
My blood with gentle horrors thrill'd;
My feeble pulse forgot to play,
I fainted, sunk, and dy'd away.

PHILIPS.

Are you not amazed, my friend, to find how in the same moment she is at a loss for her soul, her body, her ears, her tongue, her eyes, her colour, all of them as much absent from her, as if they had never belonged to her? And what contrary effects does she feel together? She *glows*, she *chills*, she *raves*, she *reasons*; now she is in *tumults*, and now she is *dying away*. In a word, she seems not to be attacked by one alone, but by a combination of the most violent passions.

All the symptoms of this kind are true effects of jealous love; but the excellence of this Ode, as I observed before, consists in the judicious choice and connection of the most notable *circumstances*. (William Smith, D.D. (trans.), *Dionysius Longinus on the Sublime* (1800), pp. 84–9)

97. *Moravian . . . Comedy.* The Moravians were a Lutheran sect who fled from Moravia and settled at Herrnhut in Saxony in 1722. During the 1730s they had strong ties with Methodism in England, and Wesley's hymns were written under their influence. Such hymns, and hymn-singing itself, were still controversial at the time of B's writing, on account of their use of popular, secularized tunes, their aim of emotional arousal of religious fervour, and their congregational orientation. Moreover, as Thomas Cotterill informs us, 'the languge and matter' of hymns, such as their 'Familiarity in addresses to God, vulgarity of expression, and coarseness of allusion . . . excited great and reasonable disgust' (the Revd T. Cotterill, *A Selection of Psalms and Hymns* (8th edn., 1819), p. xiii. This edition for the first time included nearly sixty hymns supplied by the Moravian, James Montgomery.) See, e.g., *The New Grove Dictionary of Music*, ed. Stanley Sadie, 20 vols. (1980), viii. 849. With regard to 'German Comedy', B has in mind particularly the comedies and sentimental dramas of the German playwright August von Kotzebue (1761–1819), for whom he entertained little respect (see, e.g., *BLJ* vi. 104; viii. 184). Moreover, he reflects a common distaste of the day. In a letter to Thomas Harris, prefaced to his adaptation of Kotzebue's comedy *The Birth-Day* (1800), Thomas Dibdin wrote: 'As it was last year the rage to applaud, it has now become the fashion to decry, the introduction of the German drama to our theatres' (p. vi). See also Wordsworth's outburst against 'sickly and stupid German Tragedies', in his preface to *Lyrical Ballads* (1800); and Jane Austen's *Mansfield Park* (1814), for a celebrated (fictional) amateur production of Kotzebue's *Lovers' Vows*, and Edmund's agonizing over the propriety of performing the piece (chs. 13–18).

98. *The Sentimental . . . systematize.* B has particularly in mind here Rousseau's *Les Confessions* and *La Nouvelle Héloïse*, and Madame de Staël's *De l'influence des passions sur le bonheur des individus et des nations* (1796) and *Corinne* (1807). Cf. also *DJ* IV. 106 (*CPW* v. 237, 705), and *BLJ* viii. 146.

99. *"to point . . . believes."* Bowles wrote (laboriously, as B intimates):

Let me now point out to you the difference between a traducer, and him who sincerely states what he sincerely believes.

The 'traducer' writes that deliberately, which he knows is NOT TRUE; the traducer draws pictures from his own imagination, and affirms that, which *he is conscious* he cannot justify. On this account, I have received from *you*, *at least*, not one *twentieth* part of the *candor* [*sic*] I have shown! I have set before the public the passage which you wickedly twist into 'attempt at a rape.' My 'pruriency' and the '*anatomical*' process, on Pope's '*physical* infirmities,' '*so indecent* and disgusting in a clergyman,' you have brought no passage to prove; and you did right, for it would *confound* you! The *traducer*, then, '*falsifies*,' exaggerates, and invents. ('Observations', p. 14)

See also general note and nn. 52, 56 above.

100. *in a falsehood.* In *Works* (1832) and Prothero this reads 'in falsehood'.

101. *"Would . . . lie."* Swift, 'Verses on the Death of Dr. Swift', ll. 131–2.

102. *character.* See B's erasure in MS, and cf. Juvenal, *Satire* xi. 27: 'e caelo descendit *γνῶθι σεαυτόν*' (it came from heaven, Know thyself). By substituting 'character', B makes considerably less explicit the suggestion that Bowles is himself a 'traducer' (of Pope).

103. *we are . . . Servant."* 'Observations', p. 14; and see Sheridan, *The Critic* I. i (Sir Fretful Plagiary speaking).

104. *"One thing . . . received."* Gilchrist had reviewed *Poems, descriptive of Rural Life and Scenery*, by John Clare, a Northamptonshire Peasant, 2nd edn. (1820), in the *Quarterly Review*, vol. xxiii, no. xlv (May 1820), art. viii, pp. 166–74. In his *Second Reply*, Bowles referred to this as follows (p. 11):

I must now beg the reader's attention, whilst I give some reasons which induce me to believe that this critic in the Quarterly Review is no less a personage than a certain Mr. OCTAVIUS GILCHRIST; who, if I am not mistaken, is the same critic who figured, also, in the same Review last month upon certain productions of a 'Poet of nature.' If so, his praise or blame may be held in equal contempt.

Gilchrist responded to this by saying (Gilchrist, p. 11):

Mr. Bowles's 'contempt' I shall endeavour to merit,—but, poor John Clare, what is his offence? . . . Is it Clare's only crime that Mr. Bowles believes *me* to be the lad's reviewer in the Quarterly; or is it that the Northamptonshire poet has burned no incense under the nose of his brother sonneteer; or, which is yet more likely, being neither rich, nor 'high and honourable in the literary world,' his celebrity could not confer that sort of distinction which Mr. Lisle Bowles so sedulously covets.

To this Bowles now replied ('Observations', pp. 14–15):

One thing has given me concern. I take this opportunity of explanation.—

In the small pamphlet to which your's [*sic*] is called an answer, there occurs a passage which might seem to reflect on the patronage a young man has received.

Nothing could be farther from the writer's thoughts, than any thing that might look like a wish to throw coldness on the patronage, which a poet in poverty and obscurity, has obtained.

The observation related, not to the poet, but the critic, whose pompous and pedantic criticism rather injured than promoted the cause of him it was intended to serve.

Gilchrist's sympathetic review of Clare is far from 'pompous and pedantic', as Bowles here claimed it to be; rather it is, as B goes on to say, 'able and amiable', 'judicious and honest'.

105. *"Willing . . . strike.* Pope, *Epistle to Dr. Arbuthnot*, l. 203.

106. *With . . . concur.* In the 'next two paragraphs' following those cited in n. 104 above, Bowles wrote:

> I only wish that the hand of patronage could be further extended. There are many men of genius and talents, whose daily bread is steep'd in tears. Let me here mention the name of Pennie, who has written a sublime poem, on a sacred subject. The name of the poem is the 'Royal Minstrel.'
>
> I might here also mention a poor Somersetshire weaver, with a wife and three children, who has written many far from indifferent poems, and whose affecting music is heard in half the parish churches, and half the dissenting places of worship, in England. His name is Shoel, and I was enabled some years ago to get a large subscription for him. ('Observations', p. 15)

Bowles refers to John Fitzgerald Pennie (1782–1848), author of *The Royal Minstrel; or, The Witcheries of Endor, An Epic Poem, in Eleven Books* (1817), and to Thomas Shoel (n.d.), poet and musician, author of *Mileshill, A Poem* (1803) and *The Harmonic Preceptor; or, Young Composer's Guide* (*c.* 1810).

107. *M.r B. . . . men."* 'Observations', p. 15; and see Goldsmith, *The Good Natur'd Man*, Act II (Mr Lofty speaking).

108. *"The . . . Bowles!!!"* Referring to Bowles, Gilchrist had written (Gilchrist, pp. 4–5):

> The difficulty of pleasing the gentleman,—for so, he assures us, he is,—a trifling literary anecdote will suffice to prove. No very long time has elapsed since, in one of our periodical miscellanies, an ingenious writer fancied a pilgrimage of the living poets to the fountain of Aganippe, and in proportion as each was imbued with poetical inspiration, the pilgrim was supposed to quaff at the sacred spring. I write altogether from memory,—but, as I recollect, Byron was represented as drinking out of an ample goblet; Southey, Scott, and Wordsworth in, I know not what, proportion: at length came the sonneteer, Mr. W. Lisle Bowles, who was described as repeatedly dipping his little cockle-shell into the *fons sacra*, and retreating therefrom self-satisfied and smiling. Ingenious and unoffending as was this apologue, scarcely had the printer's devil washed his inky fingers, before Mr. Lisle Bowles presented a remonstrance against the writer and his cockle-shell, and triumphantly referred to the sixth or eighth edition of his sonnets for his well-earned and unbought popularity.

To this Bowles replied ('Observations', p. 15):

> The letter I wrote to the editor of the newspaper, was not on account of the *criticism* you allude to. It was indifferent to me, whether I was represented as going to the fountain of Aganippe, or mistaking any other stream for it, as long as it was not the muddy pool at Stamford. . . .
>
> I wrote to the editor of the paper where the criticism appeared, because the newspaper which contained it, with ingenious refinement, lest I or my friends should be ignorant of the contempt in which I was held, was sent down by a frank, *directed to Mrs. Bowles!!!*

As it happens, Bowles's memory was conveniently defective. In the 'Miscellanea' page of the *Champion*, no. 170, 7 Apr. 1816, there appeared an article signed 'J.H.R.' (John Hamilton Reynolds), entitled 'The Pilgrimage of Living Poets to the Stream of Castaly'. This imagines (as Gilchrist rightly recalls) the manner in which the various poets of the day quaff from the Castalian Spring. B comes first:

> And first, methought, a lonely and melancholy figure slowly moved forth and silently filled a Grecian urn:—I knew by the look of nobility, and the hurried and turbulent plunge with which the vessel was dashed into the stream, that the owner was Lord BYRON. He shed some tears while gazing on the water, and they seemed to make it purer and fairer:—he declared that he would keep the urn by him, untouched 'for some years;'—but he had scarcely spoken, ere he had sprinkled forth some careless drops on the earth. He suddenly retreated.

After B, Scott, Southey, Wordsworth, and others have taken their respective measures, the writer continues to watch expectantly for further pilgrims to appear at the spring:

> On a sudden I heard a confusion of tongues behind me;—on turning round, I found that it arose from a mistaken set of gentlemen who were chattering and bustling and dipping at a little brook, which they deemed was the true Castalian;—their splashing and vociferation and bustle, can only be imagined by those who have seen a flock of geese wash themselves in a pond with gabbling importance.

Amongst these, there was 'BOWLES laboriously engaged in filling fourteen nutshells' (i.e. sonnets). Bowles retorted to this with an undated letter which appeared in the *Champion*, no. 175, 12 May 1816, in which he confessed: 'I have no right to complain, and it is a matter of indifference to me, whether I am introduced among the geese or the swans.' Evidently piqued, however, he continued:

> I think, Sir, I could venture to appeal to your own judgment and candour, after you had given a quiet and dispassionate review of these small poems, (which are so contemptuously spoken of) because I am convinced that those writings cannot be quite so *contemptible*, of which there have been published eleven editions, of nearly one thousand to fifteen hundred copies each; and which have been indebted to no particle of their success, either from romantic narratives or detraction of the fair fame of others. The writer in your paper is one of the readers of those poems which he condemns,—one of upwards of ten thousand!
>
> This, Sir, you may call self-applause. No—it is not;—it is a plain fact.

And he added the PS: 'May I take the liberty of requesting your acceptance of my first small volume, which contains the "*nut-shells*."' There is no mention of any incorrect franking, nor of 'Mrs. Bowles'.

109. *The Adder . . . extend.* For the 'deaf adder' see Psalms 58: 4. In *Works* (1832) and Prothero, 'does not yet extend' has been changed to 'has not yet extended'.

110. *To keep . . . convinced.* In *Works* (1832) 'Cardinal Legate of R.' reads 'Cardinal Legate of Romagna'. Cardinal Antonio Rusconi, Bishop of Imola,

was Cardinal Legate of the Romagna in Ravenna from 1819 to 1824. (For B's cordial relations with him, see, e.g., Marchand ii. 848–9, 878–9, 888–9; *BAP*, pp. 333, 336, 339, 343, 345, and *BLJ* vii. 47, 73). In his letter to Murray of 21 Apr. 1821, enclosing these 'Observations upon Observations', B promised: 'by next post I will send you the threatening Italian trash alluded to in the enclosed letter'; but on 26 Apr. 1821 he retracted this, explaining: 'I put off also for a week or two sending the Italian Scrawl which will form a Note to it.—The reason is that letters being opened I wish to "bide a wee"' (*BLJ* viii. 99, 102). At the time B was deeply involved with the Carbonari (the Italian insurgents), and was under police surveillance. For another apparently threatening letter, see B's entry dated 23 Feb. 1821 in his Ravenna Journal (*BLJ* viii. 49).

111. *"Promise to pay"*. B puns on the phrase 'promise to pay' which appears on a promissory note, and on an English bank note.

112. (*See Waverley*). In Walter Scott's *Waverley*, the Baron of Bradwardine tells Waverley: 'when my kinsman came to the village with the new factor, Mr James Howie, to lift the rents, some wanchancy person—I suspect John Heatherblutter, the auld game-keeper, that was out wi' me in the year fifteen—fired a shot at him in the gloaming' (*Novels and Tales* (1825), ii. 293).

113. *"my . . . afternoon"*. *Hamlet* I. v. 60.

114. *Mr B. . . . better.* Bowles wrote: 'In the mean time I must succumb; for, with Lord Byron turned against me, I have no chance.' Only 'five lines afterwards', however, he promises defiantly: 'I therefore hereby promise, that, for every twenty-four lines, quoted by you or your friend [D'Israeli in the *Quarterly Review*], from Lord Byron, I will greet you with as many from my unpublished poem of the "Gilchrisiad"' ('Observations', p. 16). See also n. 120 below. B's 'Letter to John Murray Esqre.' had not yet been published (see general note). But Bowles may have heard from Murray that B was preparing an attack against him.

115. *As a poet . . . praise.* Bowles's *The Missionary; A Poem* was first published in 1813. For further references to it, see, e.g., *BLJ* v. 187, 193, 197, and *CPW* iv. 114; see also 'Letter to John Murray Esqre.', n. 152 above. For B's 'previous opinions' of Bowles's poetry, see *EBSR*, ll. 327–84 (*CPW* i. 241–3, 405–6), and 'Letter to John Murray Esqre.', nn. 5, 11, 20 above.

116. *"to be . . . Next."* 'Observations' closes with the notice: 'TO BE CONCLUDED IN OUR NEXT.' (p. 18). This does not appear in the second edition, *A Vindication* (see general note above). For the 'lines' to which B refers here, see n. 120 below.

117. *"He . . . song"*. Pope, *Epistle to Dr. Arbuthnot*, l. 34.

118. *let us . . . Pope's.* 'Coryphæus' was the name given to the leader of the Chorus in Greek drama. B is suggesting that Bowles is the leader of the chorus of antagonists of Pope.

119. *"sinning . . . down".* Pope, *Epilogue to the Satires* ii. 9. See also n. 84 above.

120. *And now . . . all.* The lines which B quotes here are taken from Bowles's *ad hoc* poem, the 'Gilchrisiad', to which reference has been made earlier (see nn. 7, 114, 116 above). The whole appalling piece runs as follows ('Observations', pp. 17–18):

What! shall the dark reviler cry, 'oh shame,'
If *one* vile slanderer is held up by name!
Shall the rank, loathsome miscreant of the age,
Sit, like a night-mare, grinning on a page,
Turn round his murky orbs, that roll in spite,
And clench his fiendish claws, in grim delight;
And shall not an *indignant* flash of day
Scare the voracious vampire from his prey?

Ye dark inquisitors, a monk-like band,
Who, o'er some shrinking victim-author stand,
A solemn, secret, and vindictive brood,
Only terrific in your cowl and hood;
Yes! BYRON once more sternly shall arise,
Snatch from your grasp the panting sacrifice,
Dash in your face the code of bloody law,
And lash you with your own red scourges raw!

But chiefly THEE, whose MANLY, GENEROUS mind,
So *nobly-valiant*, against *woman-kind*,
Thinks that the man of satire, unreprov'd,
Might stab the heart of Her he fondly lov'd,
And thus, malignantly as mean, apply,
The ASSASSIN'S vengeance, and the COWARD'S lye;

THEE, whose coarse fustian, strip'd with tinsel phrase,
Is ek'd with tawdry scraps, and tags of PLAYS;
Whose pye-bald character so aptly suit
The two extremes of BANTAM and of BRUTE;
Compound grotesque of sullenness and show,
The *chattering magpie*, and the *croaking crow*;

Who, with sagacious nose, and leering eye,
Dost '*scent* the TAINT' of distant '*pruriency*,'
Turn every object to *one loathsome* shape,
Hear but 'a laugh,' and cry, 'a RAPE, a RAPE!'
Whose heart contends with thy Saturnian head,
A *root of hemlock*, and a *lump of lead*;
Swelling vain Folly's self-applauding horn,
Shall the indignant muse hold forth to scorn.

GILCHRIST, proceed, to other hearts impute,
The feelings that thy own foul spirit suit:
Round thy cold brain, let loathsome demons swarm,
Its native dulness into life to warm,
Then with a visage half-grimace, half-spite,
Run howling, 'Pope, Pope, Pope,'—howling, bite.

Reckless, thy hideous rancor I defy,
All which thy brain can brood, thy rage apply,
And thus stand forth spite of thy venom'd foam,
To give thee BITE for BITE, or lash thee limping home.

121. *"Ormskirk Medicine"*. B refers to a preparation invented by William Hill (d. ?1778) of Ormskirk, Lancashire for the cure of hydrophobia (rabies), which was known throughout England at the time as 'the Ormskirk Medicine', or more simply, as 'the Ormskirk'. Its efficacy was extremely dubious. See W. R. Hunter, 'William Hill and the Ormskirk Medicine', *Medical History* xii (1968), 294–7.

122. *German professor . . . cured.* Under the heading of 'Hydrophobia', the following report appeared in the *London Literary Gazette*, no. 197, 28 Oct. 1820 (pp. 700–1):

In consequence of a petition from Mr. Francis William Sieber . . . respecting the discovery of a cure for the hydrophobia, his Majesty the Emperor of Austria, has signified to him that he has been pleased to grant him for life an annual pension of 500 florins . . . This pension is to commence as soon as the efficacy of the means proposed shall be shewn to be proved by experiments made in his Majesty's dominions.

Franz Wilhelm Sieber (1789–1844), botanical traveller and explorer, funded his researches by subscription. The 'Memoir' in question here was entitled *Über die Begründung der Radicalcur ausgebrochener Wasserchеu* [Concerning the Proof of a Cure against the Outbreak of Hydrophobia] (Munich, 1820), which was reviewed in the *Allgemeine Medizinische Annalen* in Apr. 1820 (pp. 640–2).

123. *B.* In *Works* (1832) and Prothero this reads 'BYRON.'; in the MS it is merely a flourishing scrawl resembling a 'B'. Immediately following the signature, both *Works* (1832) and Prothero conclude with '*To John Murray, Esq.*'; not in MS.

124. *"The . . . lie."* See n. 120 above, l. 22 of Bowles's 'Gilchrisiad'.

125. *In my . . . benevolence.* See B's 'Post Scriptum' to his 'Letter to John Murray Esq[re.]' above.

126. *"with sorrow"*. Bowles wrote ('Observations' (2), p. 2): 'I would not attempt to defend what justice should think *indefensible.* "I would retrace my steps;" with sorrow, that I had written one word that might be thought derogatory of the fair fame of a man of talents and virtues.'

127. *his tears . . . Clergyman.* In *Tristram Shandy*, Tristram records Uncle Toby exclaiming of the sick lieutenant Le Fever: 'He shall not die, By G—, cried my uncle Toby.—The ACCUSING SPIRIT, which flew up to heaven's chancery with the oath, blushed as he gave it in;—and the RECORDING ANGEL, as he wrote it down, dropped a tear upon the word, and blotted it out for ever' (Laurence Sterne, *The Life and Opinions of Tristram Shandy* (1967 edn.), p. 411).

128. *He . . . victim.* B echoes Pope, *The First Epistle of the Second Book of Horace*, l. 74: 'The life to come, in every poet's creed'.

129. *"Mingere . . . cineres".* Horace, *Ars Poetica*, l. 471: 'minxerit in patrios cineres' (he descrates the ashes of his fathers). See also *Hints from Horace*, l. 795, and B's own note thereto (*CPW* i. 318, 443).

130. *B.* There is no closing signature here whatever in *Works* (1832) and Prothero. In the MS it is merely a flourishing scrawl resembling a 'B', exactly the same as that noted in n. 123 above. Immediately following this in the MS B has written the title (see n. 1 above). See also n. 217 to 'Letter to John Murray Esq[re.]' above. In *Works* (1832) and Prothero, B's 'Further Addenda' is incorrectly placed immediately after the end of the text here.

WRITINGS (1821–1824)

Some Recollections of my Acquaintance with Madame de Staël (1821)

Text: MS Harry Ransom Humanities Research Centre, University of Texas. First published in *Murray's Magazine* i. (Jan.–June 1887), 4–6. (Not published in Coleridge or Prothero.)

On 4 Aug. 1821 (the same date as the writing of this piece), B wrote to Murray:

> They write from Paris that Schlegel is making a fierce book against *me*—what can I have done to the literary Col-captain of late Madame?—*I* who am neither of his country nor his horde?—Does this Hundsfot's intention appal you? if it does—say so.—It don't *me*—for if he is insolent—I will go to Paris and thank him;—there is a distinction between *native* Criticism—because it belongs to the Nation to judge and pronounce on natives,—but what have *I* to do with Germany or Germans neither my subjects nor my language having anything in common with that Country?—He took a dislike to me—because I refused to flatter him in Switzerland—though Madame de Broglie begged me to do so—'because he is so fond of it.[']——'Voila les hommes!'— (*BLJ* viii. 166–7)

See also *BLJ* viii. 172–3.

B's informant was Thomas Moore, then at Paris, who had noted in his journal for 21 May 1821:

> Had much talk with Schlegel in the evening, who appears to me full of literary coxcombry . . . Is evidently not well inclined towards Lord Byron; thinks he will outlive himself, and get out of date long before he dies. Asked me if I thought a regular critique of all Lord B.'s works, and the system on which they are written, would succeed in England, and seems inclined to undertake it. (*Memoirs* iii. 235)

Although Moore wrote to B the following day, 22 May, it seems more likely that he told him of Schlegel's intentions when he wrote to him again on 27 July (*Memoirs* iii. 260), for B, in his reply to that letter of 12 Aug., says 'I know S[chlegel] well—that is to say, I have met him occasionally at Copet' (*BLJ* viii. 164).

The 'meditated abuse' was never pursued by Schlegel, and after B's letter to Murray of 7 Aug. 1821 (*BLJ* viii. 172–3), there is no further reference to the matter.

August Wilhelm von Schlegel (1767–1845) was a scholar, critic, poet, orientalist, and translator of Shakespeare. He was appointed Professor at the University of Jena in 1798, and between 1797 and 1810 he translated into German seventeen of Shakespeare's plays. He met Madame de Staël in 1804, became tutor to her children, and remained her constant companion, adviser, and fellow traveller. He travelled with her through Germany, Italy, France, and Sweden—in which last country he was appointed Press Secretary to Crown Prince Bernadotte for a year (1813–14). He was later made Professor of Literature at the University of Bonn, a post which he held till his death. His most important and influential work of the period was translated into English by John Black, and published in two volumes under the title of *A Course of Lectures on Dramatic Art and Literature* in 1815. This consists of lectures originally delivered in Berlin and Vienna (some as early as 1801), in which Schlegel expounded his views on the distinction between the 'Classical' and the 'Romantic' in literature. In Lecture xii (vol. ii, pp. 91–259) he dealt almost exclusively with Shakespeare (though references to him abound elsewhere). B had almost certainly read this work: it was very probably the book which Madame de Staël lent him in Aug. 1816 (*BLJ* v. 88).

B met Schlegel at Coppet in July 1816, where he found him 'in high force' (*BLJ* v. 86). Later he recalled that, while finding him irksome and ridiculous on account of his vanity, egoism, and other 'peculiarities', he had none the less 'uniformly treated him with respect' (*BLJ* viii. 172). In his 'Detached Thoughts' (1821–22), he dubbed him 'the Dousterswivel of Madame de Stael' (*BLJ* ix. 26). (Dousterswivel is the pseudo-antiquarian and satellite of Sir Arthur Wardour in Walter Scott's *The Antiquary*.) See also Marchand ii. 636; *BAP*, pp. 245–6.

Madame de Staël-Holstein (1766–1817), *née* Anne Louise Germaine Necker, was the daughter of Jacques Necker, Finance Minister to Louis XVI. In 1786 she married (*de convenance*) the Swedish Ambassador to Paris, Baron Erik de Staël-Holstein (d. 1802), from whom she separated in 1797. During the Revolution she favoured the Girondins, but when the 'Terror' broke out in 1793 she left Paris and established her salon at the family residence, Coppet, near Geneva. In 1794 she returned to Paris where her liaison with Benjamin Constant began—lasting until 1806. (Cf. his *Adolphe* (1816).) Owing to her resistance to Napoleon, she was banished by him in 1803 to a distance of 40 miles from Paris. Thenceforth Coppet became her headquarters, though she continued to be harrassed by Napoleon's police. She travelled in Germany (1803–4) and Italy (1805). In May 1811 she secretly married 'John' Rocca, a young Swiss officer, whom B 'liked' and regarded as 'a gentleman and a clever man' (*Medwin's Conversations*, p. 185). Throughout 1812 and early 1813 she travelled in various countries including Austria, Russia, Finland, and Sweden, before arriving in London in June 1813 (where she lived in Argyle Street until 10 May 1814). When the Bourbons were restored in 1814 she removed to Paris, travelled through Italy again (1815), spent the summer of 1816 at Coppet, and returned in the autumn to Paris where she died the following year.

Her most important publications were: *De l'influence des passions sur le bonheur des individus et des nations* (1796), *De la Littérature* (1800), *Delphine* (1802), *Corinne* (1807), *De l'Allemagne* (1810) (proscribed by Napoleon), and *Considérations sur la Revolution française* (published posthumously, 1818), which B recommended to Murray to publish as 'her best work—& permanently historical', though he had not in fact read it himself (*BLJ* v. 205).

B's relations with Madame de Staël were cordial, and in 1816 intimate, though he was never uncritical of her. They met many times at the Jerseys', Hollands', and elsewhere in England in 1813 and 1814; and in 1816 B was a frequent guest of hers at Coppet. She offered to negotiate a reconciliation between him and his estranged wife Annabella but to no avail. Although he disliked her politics, 'at least, her *having changed* them' (*BLJ* iii. 227), and was exasperated by her prolix literary talk, he had a genuine regard for her and for her intellect. He gave a particularly handsome tribute to her memory in his note to l. 478 (stanza 54) of *CHP* IV (see *CPW* ii. 235–6).

For further references to her and to B's opinions of her, see Marchand i. 392–4; ii. 633–51; *BAP*, pp. 143–4, 245–6, 249; *BLJ* iii, *passim* (character sketch, 272–3); v. 85–8, 92, 109, 111, 114; *Lady Blessington's Conversations*, pp. 22 ff.; *Medwin's Conversations*, pp. 12, 181–5. See also Lady Blennerhassett, *Madame de Staël* (3 vols., 1889), particularly vol. iii, ch. 6, pp. 404–78); Robert Escarpit, *L'Angleterre dans l'oeuvre de Madame de Staël* (1954); Doris Gunnell, 'Madame de Staël en Angleterre', *Revue d'histoire littéraire de la France* (1913); J. C. Herold, *Mistress to an Age: A Life of Madame de Staël* (1958).

1. *"with her Glory"*. See n. 245 to 'Letter to John Murray Esq[re.]' above.

2. *Lady Jersey's.* Madame de Staël arrived in England on 20 June 1813, and B was invited to meet her at Lady Jersey's that evening (Marchand i. 392; *BAP*, p. 143).

3. *the most . . . men.* That is, Napoleon. Crabb Robinson, who dined with Madame de Staël on 18. Oct. 1813, noted in his diary:

> Our hostess spoke freely of Buonaparte. She was introduced to him when a victorious general in Italy; even then he affected princely airs, and spoke as if it mattered not what he said—he conferred honour by saying anything. He had a pleasure in being rude. He said to her, after her writings were known, that he did not think women ought to write books. She answered, 'It is not every woman who can gain distinction by an alliance with a General Buonaparte.' Buonaparte said to Madame de Condorcet, . . . 'I do not like women who meddle with politics.' Madame de Condorcet instantly replied, 'Ah, mon Général, as long as you men take a fancy to cut off our heads now and then, we are interested in knowing why you do it.' (Thomas Sadler (ed.), *Diary, Reminiscences, and Correspondence of Henry Crabb Robinson*, 2 vols. (3rd edn. 1872), i. 219–20)

4. *"with noble . . . bye." Henry IV, Part I*, V. v. 109–10.

5. *Sir Humphrey Davy's.* B dined at the Davys' in the company of Madame de Staël, with Sheridan, Whitbread, Grattan, and the Marquis of Lansdowne on 21 June 1813 (Marchand i. 392–3; *BLJ* iii. 66). Sir Humphry Davy (1778–1829) was a natural philosopher and Professor of Chemistry at the Royal

Institution. He greatly advanced the fields of chemistry, galvanism, and electricity, his most famous invention being the miners' Safety Lamp. His wife, Lady Jane Davy (1780–1855), *née* Kerr, had previously married the wealthy Shuckburgh Ashby Apreece in 1799, and been widowed in 1807. She retired to Edinburgh, where she held brilliant salons and was the admiration of society. She married Sir Humphry at the height of his fame in 1812, and thereafter held regular salons in London. B was fond of the Davys and saw much of them during his time in England. Sir Humphry later visited him when he was at Ravenna (*BLJ* vii. 78, 98, 105).

6. *"a legion of honour".* B is making a triple pun here, on the medal instituted by Napoleon and awarded for military and civilian service (the 'Legion d'honneur'), on the 'legion' assembled to 'honour' the advent of Madame de Staël, and the biblical 'My name is Legion: for we are many' (Mark 5: 9).

7. *Sheridan . . . Lansdowne.* Richard Brinsley Sheridan (1751–1816), the famous playwright, politician, and wit, in whose company B passed many a convivial evening; Samuel Whitbread (1758–1815), Whig politician and manager of the Drury Lane Theatre; Henry Grattan (1746–1820), the famous Irish MP and barrister who staunchly supported the cause of the Irish Roman Catholics at Westminster; and Henry Petty-Fitzmaurice, third Marquis of Lansdowne (1780–1863), Whig politician and Chancellor of the Exchequer in the Grenville administration of 1806. He was a friend and patron of Moore.

8. *youngest . . . poets.* That is, B himself. (B's repetition of 'and'.)

9. *Of these guests . . . aged.* For the deaths of Sheridan, Whitbread, and Grattan, see n. 7 above. Madame de Staël died on 14 July 1817, and the 'great cause of their meeting' (i.e. Napoleon) died on 5 May 1821 (b. 15 Aug. 1769).

10. *Lord L.* That is, the Marquis of Lansdowne (see n. 7 above). For Madame de Staël's prolixity, see, e.g., B's journal entry for 16 Nov. 1813: 'Today received Lord Jersey's invitation to Middleton—to travel sixty miles to meet Madame * * [De Staël]! I once travelled three thousand to get among silent people; and this same lady writes octavos, and *talks* folios' (*BLJ* iii. 207).

11. *"what . . . him?"* See n. 10 to 'Leake's *Researches in Greece*' above.

12. *"grand peutetre".* A great perhaps. One of the apocryphal sayings attributed to Rabelais on his death-bed: 'Je m'en vais chercher un grand peut-être' (I am going to look for a great perhaps). If Hobhouse's memory is correct, B thought the phrase was d'Alembert's: 'He often said to me, "It may be true. It is, as d'Alembert said, a 'grand peut-être'"' (*Recollections* iii. 39).

13. *Who will be . . . prevented.* George III reigned from 1760 to 1820, although his son had been Prince Regent from 1811 to 1820 on account of his insanity. George IV (1762–1830) was crowned on 19 July 1821 and reigned until 1830. He had a particularly difficult time both as prince and as Regent. Apart from political controversy, his mistresses caused public outcry, the trial of his wife Queen Caroline in 1820 was a national scandal, and the death of his only child

Princess Charlotte in childbirth on 6 Nov. 1817 deprived the country of a sure successor to the crown. See also *BLJ* v. 276. George IV was eventually succeeded by his younger brother William IV, whose two daughters had died in infancy in 1819 and 1821.

14. *"Hope ... sick"*. Proverbs 13: 12. The remainder of the sentence echoes Juvenal, *Satire* x. 356: 'mens sana in corpore sano' (a healthy mind in a healthy body).

Some Account of the Life and Writings of the late George Russell of A— by Henry Ferguson (1821)

Text: MS Murray. First published in Prothero v. 604–7.

There is nothing in B's correspondence nor in his 'Detached Thoughts' (1821–2) to suggest that B was engaged in writing this piece. When Prothero published it, he introduced it by saying: 'It is possible that this fragment may have been suggested by the death of John Scott, who had been Byron's school-fellow at Aberdeen. But no external evidence exists to support this conjecture' (p. 604). Unfortunately this is thoroughly misleading. The piece has nothing whatever to do with John Scott, the editor of the *Champion*, and of the *London Magazine*, who had died after a duel in Feb. 1821 and whose obituary B had already written in 'Observations upon Observations' (see above). Rather, it is an elaborate skit on the art of biography, or more probably autobiography, engaging once again with *Blackwood's Edinburgh Magazine*. It is perhaps needless to add that 'George Russell' and 'Henry Ferguson' are fictitious characters, though 'A—' undoubtedly stands for Aberdeen.

The date, which may also be part of the fiction, none the less indicates that B wrote this at the Casa Lanfranchi soon after his arrival in Pisa. He had recently been introduced to Thomas Medwin, who had immediately set about Boswellizing him, and he had recently received a letter from John Cam Hobhouse (no longer extant but dated 6 Nov. 1821), in which Hobhouse had accused him of 'buying a biographer' by permitting Moore to sell his memoirs to Murray. (See Hobhouse's letter to B of 3 Jan. 1821, and the notes thereto (*Byron's Bulldog*, pp. 320–3).) This had stung B to the quick, though on 23 Nov. he had replied to it with 'as temperate an answer as I believe ever human being did in the like circumstances' (*BLJ* ix. 70). (See also *BLJ* ix. 67–72, 82.) The vicissitudes of biographies and of biographers, therefore, preoccupied B at the time. However, of far greater significance here is B's reply on 12 Dec. to a letter of Moore's (also no longer extant), in which he wrote (*BLJ* ix. 79–80):

> What you say about Galignani's two biographies is very amusing: and, if I were not lazy, I would certainly do what you desire. But I doubt my present stock of facetiousness—that is, of good *serious* humour, so as not to let the cat out of the bag. I wish *you* would undertake it. I will forgive and *indulge* you (like a Pope) beforehand, for any thing ludicrous, that might keep those fools in their own dear belief that a man is a *loup garou*.

When Moore first published this letter he added the following explanatory note (Moore ii. 565 n.):

Mr. Galignani having expressed a wish to be furnished with a short Memoir of Lord Byron, for the purpose of prefixing it to the French edition of his works, I had said jestingly in a preceding letter to his lordship, that it would be but a fair satire on the disposition of the world to 'bemonster his features,' if he would write for the public, English as well as French, a sort of mock-heroic account of himself, outdoing, in horrors and wonders, all that had been yet related or believed of him, and leaving even Goëthe's story of the double murder at Florence far behind.

It seems highly likely, therefore, that this piece is the beginning of what B may have intended as just such 'a sort of mock-heroic account of himself'. It is written in B's Swiftian 'Wortley Clutterbuck' vein, along lines prompted by a series of articles in *Blackwood's Edinburgh Magazine*. In vol. ii, no. xi (Feb. 1818), pp. 562–7 of that periodical, there appeared an article entitled 'Some Account of the Life and Writings of Ensign and Adjutant Odoherty, late of the 99th Regiment'. This was a thinly veiled satire on Edinburgh society, and on contemporary poets, in which a supposed editor delineates the life, and edits the remains of his deceased friend, the fictitious Morgan Odoherty. The account continued through three subsequent issues, till at length, in vol. iv, no. xxiii (Feb. 1819), p. 567, a note from Odoherty himself announced that he was still alive, and would continue his editor's work for him *in propria persona.* This he proceeded to do, and in his succeeding articles included some splendid parodies of, amongst others, Wordsworth, Coleridge, Keats, Campbell, and B himself. He was the creation of Thomas Hamilton, though many of his later contributions were written by John Gibson Lockhart, John Herman Merivale, David Macbeth Moir, and John Wilson.

Simultaneously, B also appears to be having some fun here at the expense of the phrenologist Johann Christoph Spurzheim (1776–1832), whose notions concerning the conformation of the head enjoyed much popularity at the time, and were in great vogue. On 26 Sept. 1814 he had visited B himself, who gave an account of his examination to Annabella in a letter of the same date (*BLJ* iv. 182):

I have just been going through a curious scene[.] Sir W. Knighton brought Spurtzheim (I believe is the name) the *craniologist* to see me—a discoverer of faculties & dispositions from heads.—He passes his hand over the head & then tells you—curious things enough—for I own he has a little astonished me.—He says all mine are strongly marked—but very antithetical for every thing developed in & on this same skull of mine has its *opposite* in great force so that to believe him my good & evil are at perpetual war—pray heaven the last don't come off victorious.———

There are several indications to suggest that Spurzheim and phrenology were in B's mind at the time of writing the present skit. He informed Medwin, who had arrived in Pisa in Nov. 1821 (*Medwin's Conversations*, p. 58): 'The phrenologists tell me that other lines besides that of thought . . . are strongly developed in the hinder part of my cranium; particularly that called philoprogenitiveness. I suppose, too, the pugnacious bump might be found somewhere, because my uncle had it.' And a variant of ll. 15–16 of stanza 2 of *DJ* VI (which he had resumed in Jan.–Feb. 1822) runs: 'Man with his head reflects—(as Spurzheim tells) / But Woman with the heart—or something else' (*CPW* v. 299). B may also have seen a facetious article on Spurzheim, entitled 'On Heads', in the *New Monthly Magazine* (ii (1821), 593–6), in which he himself is represented as having unsuccessfully attempted to obtain the 'wrinkles of thought' (p. 595).

In his book *The Physiognomical System of Drs. Gall and Spurzheim* (1815), Spurzheim detailed his theory of the organization of the brain, localizing its functions, attributing a separate organ to each faculty, 'propensity', and sentiment, and claiming that their development could be determined by the size and shape of the head. To these organs, he gave his own specific names—such as the 'Organ of Philoprogenitiveness' (cf. *DJ* XII. 22 (*CPW* v. 501)), or (most relevant here) the 'Organ of Covetiveness', the construction of which words he explained as follows:

> Having established different propensities as peculiar faculties of the mind; in order to designate propensity, I have employed the termination IVE as indicating *the quality of producing*, and NESS as indicating *the abstract state*; I have therefore joined IVENESS to different roots or fundamental words. . . . I know that *Covetiveness* is a pléonasm; but this fault is observed in many other words which are employed without hesitation. Covet itself indicates propensity or wishing for; and I have added *iveness* solely for the sake of uniformity: otherwise I should have said covetingness.— (pp. ix, and xi; see nn. 10 and 14 below).

1. *The poems . . . men.* For 'Ensign Odoherty', see general note above. Thomas Moore's pseudonymous *The Poetical Works of the Late Thomas Little* was published in 1801. Henry Kirke White (1785–1806), poet and scholar, died of overwork during his sizarship at St John's College, Cambridge. His works were posthumously edited by Southey under the title of *The Remains of Henry Kirke White* (1807). B admired Kirke White's work (see *ESBR*, ll. 831–48, and his own note thereto (*CPW* i. 255, 415)). B also has in mind here such 'other young men' as Chatterton and Keats (d. 23 Feb. 1821).

2. *"Whose . . . prime".* Wordsworth, 'Resolution and Independence' vii. l. 2.

3. *"nothing . . . further". Macbeth* III. ii. 25–6.

4. (*or to dream*—). This reads '(or dream)' in Prothero.

5. *least harmless.* Prothero has silently altered this to 'most harmless'. This of course makes sense of the passage, but B may equally well have intended to write 'least harmful'.

6. *Fox . . . Grattan.* B refers to the great statesmen Charles James Fox (1749–1806), William Pitt (1759–1806), and Henry Grattan (1746–1820), all of whom are buried in Westminster Abbey. See also, e.g., *BLJ* ix. 13–14, 26–7.

7. *George Russell . . . England.* Enjoying the double-bluff here, B alludes to the

Dukes of Bedford whose family name was Russell. Lord John Russell (1792–1878), for instance, the third son of the sixth Duke of Bedford, and later first Earl Russell, was a friend of Moore's and first editor of his *Memoirs, Journal and Correspondence* (8 vols., 1853–6).

8. *"Southron"*. Scottish for a Southerner, i.e. an Englishman.

9. *Exercitator.* Usually, someone who writes an 'exercitation' or disquisition: here, the performer, practitioner, or operator. The 'taws' is exactly as B describes it.

10. *propensity.* This is a word of special connotation in the Spurzheim vocabulary (see general note and n. 14 below).

11. *Pope's Homer... Scottish Ballads.* Pope's *The Iliad of Homer* (1715–20) and *The Odyssey of Homer* (1725–6); Blind Harry or Henry the Minstrel (?1440–?1492), author of *The Wallace* (?1460), a long poem in heroic couplets which recounts the feats of the Scotsman Sir William Wallace, who was executed by the English in 1305; and the *Ballad of Chevy Chase* and the *Ballad of Gil Morrice*, both of which were collected in Percy's *Reliques* (1765).

12. *Caledonia.* The Roman name for Scotland. B uses the word jocularly.

13. *Amidst ... Orchards.* B alludes jocularly to the youthful pranks of Oliver Cromwell, the Lord Protector of England from 1653 to 1658. In *Flagellum: or The Life and Death, Birth and Burial of Oliver Cromwel* [*sic*] *The late Usurper* (1663), James Heath wrote:

> Among the rest of those ill qualities which *fructuated* in him at this age, He was very notorious for *robbing of Orchards*; a *puerile* crime and an ordinary trespasse, but grown so scandalous and injurious by the frequent spoyls and damage of Trees, breaking of Hedges and inclosures committed by this *Apple Dragon*, that many solemn Complaints were made both to his Father and Master for redresse thereof; which missed not their satisfaction and expiation out of his hide, on which so much pains were lost, that, that very offence ripened in him afterwards to the throwing down all boundaries of Law or Conscience, and the stealing and tasting the *forbidden fruit* of Soveraignty[.] (pp. 5–6. Cf. *DJ* III. 92 (*CPW* v. 194))

B may also have in mind Saint Augustine (see, for example, *The Confessions of St. Augustine*, trans. E. B. Pusey (1907), pp. 25–6), and more especially, *Roderick Random*, ch. ii:

> I have been found guilty of robbing orchards I never entered, of killing cats I never hurted, of stealing gingerbread I never touched, and of abusing old women I never saw. (Tobias Smollett, *Roderick Random* (1927), p. 14)

14. *Organ of Covetiveness.* See also general note above. The *New Monthly Magazine* (p. 596) made much humorous capital out of this particular organ. In *The Physiognomical System* (pp. 327–9), Spurzheim discussed the 'Organ of the Propensity to Covet, or of Covetiveness' as follows:

> According to all that I have observed, in comparing animals and man with respect to the functions of this faculty, it seems to me, that the special faculty of this organ is the

propensity to gather and acquire—to covet, without determining the object to be acquired or the manner of acquiring it. This faculty gives a desire for all that is desirable: money, property, animals, servants, land, cattle, or any thing upon the earth. The faculty produces egotism and selfishness; and persons endowed with it in a very high degree will never forget themselves; but the objects they desire, and their manner of acquiring them, whether by industry, commerce, gaming, or stealing, depend on the influence of all the other faculties. It is in consequence of this faculty also, that we ask 'what is this or that object good for?'

This faculty is essentially necessary to man and animals, because their subsistence depends on it. By means of this faculty also, in my opinion, man and animals make provision for the future. The activity of this propensity may indeed be more energetic than is necessary . . . animals and man not only gather what is useful and permitted, but sometimes take away what belongs to others, and that of which they cannot make any use. These latter actions then constitute abuses: and have different names, as usury, plagiarism, fraud, or theft. . . . This organ is situated at the upper part of the temples on the anterior inferior angle of the parietal bone.

15. *than his head.* This reads 'than in his head' in Prothero.

16. *"Gradus ad Parnassum".* (a step to Parnassus). This was a dictionary of prosody and poetic manual, such as Edward Bysshe's *The Art of English Poetry* (1702).

17. (*"the . . . call"*). *The Merry Wives of Windsor* I. iii. 30.

18. *a copy . . . Psalms.* George Buchanan (1506–82), author of *Psalmorum Dauidus paraphrasis poetica . . . auctore G. Buchanano* (1566). See also n. 43 to B's 'Reading List' above.

An Italian Carnival (1823)

Text: MS Olin Library, Cornell University. First published in Prothero vi. 439–41.

This is the last piece of prose B wrote before leaving Italy for Greece, and it is appropriate that he should have chosen a subject so characteristically Italian. It was written at Genoa, but there is no reference to it in B's correspondence, nor is there any external evidence to suggest that he was engaged in writing it. Prothero makes the sound suggestion that it may have been intended for the *Liberal* (Prothero vi. 439). There being no title in the MS, I have borrowed that supplied by Prothero, which seems a fair one provided that it does not obscure the evident political symbolism of the piece.

1. *City of T.* Prothero has 'City of I—,'.

2. *Starke . . . Manual.* B refers to the various popular travel books of the time: John Chetwode Eustace, *A Tour through Italy* (1813–19); Joseph Forsyth, *Remarks on Antiquities, Art, and Letters during an Excursion in Italy* (1813); John Cam Hobhouse, *Historical Illustrations to the Fourth Canto of Childe Harold: Containing Dissertations on the Ruins of Rome; and an Essay on Italian Literature* (1818; see also *CPW* ii. 218–64); Henry Matthews, *The Diary of an Invalid; being*

The Journal of a Tour in pursuit of health; in Portugal, Italy, Switzerland, and France, in the years 1817, 1818, and 1819 (1820); and Mariana Starke, *Letters from Italy* (1800) and *Travels on the Continent; Written for the Use and Particular Information of Travellers* (1820).

3. *Welbeck Street . . . precincts.* Welbeck Street was a fashionable residential area in the West End of London at the time.

4. *middle ton . . . possessed.* 'Middle ton' denotes the gentry; '*bon ton*' means polite or fashionable society.

5. *Holy Alliance . . . despotism.* The Holy Alliance was formed in 1815 between Russia, Prussia, and Austria. At the Congress of Vienna (1815) Italy was partitioned, Lombardy and Venetia coming under Austrian dominion.

6. *"Christian fools . . . faces".* *The Merchant of Venice* II. v. 33 (Shylock speaking to Jessica).

7. *"quantum sufficit".* Enough, a sufficient amount. B uses the Latinate version as a deliberate and ironic display of pedantry.

8. *"he . . . alone.* See Samuel Rogers, *Human Life, A Poem* (1819), p. 61, ll. 9–10: 'But there are moments which he calls his own. / Then, never less alone than when alone.' Actually, Rogers is paraphrasing Cicero, *De Officiis* III. i: 'nec minus solum quam cum solus esset' (nor less alone than with himself alone).

9. *Saturnalia.* Strictly speaking, the great Roman festival in honour of Saturn held in December; but generally, any period of unlicensed behaviour and unrestrained celebration.

10. *but they . . . latter.* Cf. B's Ravenna Journal: 'To-night at the theatre, there being a prince on his throne in the last scene of the comedy,—the audience laughed, and asked him for a *Constitution.* This shows the state of the public mind here, as well as the assassinations' (*BLJ* viii. 15).

11. *Life . . . themselves.* This passage might profitably be compared with B's references to parliament as a 'stage', to 'parliamentary mummeries', and to the 'hypocrisy' of the politician (*BLJ* iii. 32, 206; v. 168), and with *DJ* VII. 2, '*What* after *all*, are *all* things—but a *Show?*', and *DJ* XI. 37, 'And, after all, what is a lie? 'Tis but / The truth in masquerade' (*CPW* v. 337, 476). B's point here is that the Italian 'Masquerade' made no pretensions to being other than what it was—'a drama without the fiction' in which all could participate; whereas the English parliament did make such pretensions, by masquerading as the representative of the people when it was not.

The Present State of Greece (1824)

Text: Prothero vi. 441. First published by Prothero from the original MS (now no longer extant).

This is the last prose piece B wrote, and it was written at a particularly harassing time for him. He had left Cephalonia at the end of Dec. 1823, and had been at Missolonghi in Western Greece since 4 Jan. 1824—having finally committed himself personally and actively to the Greek Revolution, and more specifically to aiding the Commander-in-Chief, and Governor of Western Greece, Prince Alexander Mavrocordatos (1791–1865). He was still recovering from his first illness at Missolonghi (15–17 Feb.), and was already disillusioned with the corps of Suliote Greeks he had taken into his pay a month earlier (*BLJ* xi. 111–12). Moreover, the ten days preceding its composition were packed with vexations and disturbances: the projected expedition against the Turkish stronghold at Lepanto, on which B had placed so much hope, had had to be abandoned; Lieutenant Sass, a popular Swedish officer reputed for his mildness and courage, had been assassinated; the English mechanics, who had only recently come out with William Parry (the fire master) to work in the arsenal, had demanded their return home; mutinies had broken out amongst the German officers sent to Greece by the London Greek Committee, and the Suliotes (who also threatened to massacre the town)—and B, in utter frustration, had first disbanded, and then reluctantly reorganized his corps. He had, however, at his own expense, recently 'obtained from the Greeks the release of eight and twenty Turkish prisoners, men, women, and children, and sent them to Patras and Prevesa' (*BLJ* xi. 117) (Count Peter Gamba, *A Narrative of Lord Byron's Last Journey to Greece* (1825), pp. 186–97; William Parry, *The Last Days of Lord Byron* (1825), pp. 60–72; Colonel Leicester Stanhope, *Greece in 1823 and 1824* (1824; new edn. 1825), pp. 118–21. See also Marchand iii. 1185–91; *BAP*, pp. 441–5; *BLJ* xi. 111–27). It is therefore some testimony to B's equanimity that in such turbulent circumstances he should have composed so restrained and impartial an account of the situation of Greece as he saw it at the time.

Prothero makes no suggestion concerning this item, nor is there any evidence in B's correspondence or elsewhere to indicate what he might have intended to do with it (or, indeed, that he was writing it at all). However, since it has neither the tone nor the character of a journal entry, a memo or private letter, it was most probably intended *at first* for the projected *Greek Telegraph* (the *Telegrafo Greco*), to which B had reluctantly agreed to contribute on 15 Feb. 1824. Pietro Gamba (Teresa Guiccioli's brother who had come to Greece with B) records that on that date (just before B's convulsive fit), a conversation between B, Colonel Leicester Stanhope (the agent of the London Greek Committee), and himself had 'turned upon our newspaper' (the *Greek Chronicle* (*Hellenica Chronica*), founded by Stanhope in Jan. 1824, and edited by Dr Jean Jacques Meyer—see general note to 'Replies to Stanhope's Questionnaire' below): 'We agreed that it was not calculated to give foreigners the necessary intelligence of what was passing in Greece; because, being written in Romaic, it was not intelligible, except to a few strangers. We resolved to publish another, in several languages, and Lord Byron promised to furnish some articles himself' (Gamba, *A Narrative*, p. 174). This is corroborated by Stanhope, who wrote to John Bowring (the Secretary of the London Greek Committee) on the same date: 'Count Gamba is named as the editor [of the *Telegrafo Greco*]: the articles will be written in English, French, Italian, and German: . . . Lord Byron will contribute largely in both money and matter' (Stanhope, *Greece in 1823 and 1824*, p. 114). A 'Prospectus' of the *Telegrafo Greco* was issued on 6 Mar., and the first number was published on 20 Mar. 1824 (Gamba, *A Narrative*, pp. 305–7; Julius Millingen, *Memoirs of the Affairs of Greece* (1831), p. 113).

However, although B certainly 'subscribed' financially to the paper, 'to get rid of Stanhope's importunities, and it may be, keep Gamba out of mischief' (Parry, *The Last Days*, p. 191), it is almost as certain that he did not do so materially. For, in a letter to Dr James Kennedy of 10 Mar. 1824 concerning the *Telegrafo Greco*, he stated: 'I have not written, nor am inclined to write, for that or for any other paper'—a statement he reiterated the same day to Charles Hancock, and again to Samuel Barff on 19 Mar. (*BLJ* xi. 132, 134, 139). It seems most likely, therefore, that on second thoughts B withheld (or possibly withdrew) this piece from publication.

1. *revolution.* The Greek Revolution, or the Greek War of Independence from Turkish rule, had broken out in 1821. B did not live to see Greece free: that did not occur until the battle of Navarino in 1827, and even then her struggle had not ended.

2. *vileins.* B follows the Middle English or Old French spelling of 'villein', a feudal serf.

3. *tars.* A colloquial name for sailors or seamen.

FRAGMENTARY WRITINGS (1801–1824)

Inscriptions in a Schoolbook (1801)

Text: Moore i. 60n.

Moore gives us no information about the schoolbook in which these inscriptions are written; he merely appends them as a note to the following observation (Moore i. 60): 'From the memorandums scribbled by the young poet in his schoolbooks we might almost fancy that, even at so early an age, he had a sort of vague presentiment that every thing relating to him would one day be an object of curiosity and interest.'

B entered Harrow in Apr. 1801, and remained a pupil there (with the odd hiatus or two) until July 1805. Harrow School was founded in 1571 by John Lyon (1514–92). B's Latin inscription, entered in the book with such formality and sense of occasion, translates: 'Pupil for the first time at Lyon's School in the year of Our Lord 1801, Ellison Headboy.' For B's Harrow days, see Marchand i. 64–100; *BAP*, pp. 22–34; *BLJ* i. 41–70; for B's reflections on his Harrow days, see *BLJ* ix. 37, 42–4. The following information comes from M. G. Dauglish and P. K. Stephenson (eds.), *The Harrow School Register* (3rd edn., 1911). Cuthbert Ellison, son of H. Ellison of Hebburn Hall, Durham, entered Harrow 1796, Monitor 1800, Head of School 1801, left 1801–2, d. 1860. Philip, Viscount Royston, son of Philip, third Earl of Hardwicke, entered Harrow 1795, Monitor 1800, left 1800–2, drowned 1808. Henry Hinxman, son of H. Hinxman of Ivychurch, Wiltshire, entered Harrow 1795, Monitor 1800, Head of School 1802, left 1802, d. 1854. George Rashleigh, son of the Revd P. Rashleigh of Southfleet Rectory, Kent, entered Harrow 1797, left 1800–2, d. 1874. Langham Rokeby, son of the Revd L. Rokeby of Arthingworth Manor, Northamptonshire, entered Harrow 1797, Head of School 1802, left 1802–3, d. 1844. Little is known of Leigh; but he lived in Kent, entered Harrow 1792, and left 1800–2.

Inscriptions in *Homeri Ilias* (1804)

Text: MS Murray. First published (in part) in Moore i. 60n.

These inscriptions were written by B on the penultimate and ultimate flyleaves of vol. i of his copy of Samuel Clarke's edition of *Homeri Ilias Græce et Latine* (2 vols., 1760). The volumes were sold as Lot 131 at the sale of B's library in 1816, and were bought by Murray (see Sale Catalogue (1816) below). The following notes owe much of their information to M. G. Dauglish and P. K. Stephenson (eds.), *The Harrow School Register, 1800–1911* (3rd edn., 1911). See also the notes on 'Inscriptions in *Scriptores Græci*', and 'An Extract from a Journal' below.

1. This is written on the penultimate flyleaf of the volume. For further details of Dr Joseph Drury (then headmaster of Harrow), Henry Hoare, and Charles Gordon, see general note to 'An Extract from a Journal' below; for William Drury, Thomas Calvert, and Hoare again, see 'Inscriptions in *Scriptores Græci*', nn. 1, 6, below; and for George Sinclair, see 'Harrow Notebook', n. to folio 2 below. Henry Boldero, son of E. G. Boldero, entered Harrow 1798, left 1804–5, d. 1859. Charles Annesley Francis Annesley, son of A. Annesley of Bletchington Park, Oxford, entered Harrow 1799, left 1805, d. 1863. Thomas Linwood Strong, son of C. S. Strong of Limpsfield, Surrey, entered Harrow 1799, left 1803–4, d. 1865. Sir Thomas Dyke Acland, son of Sir T. D. Acland, entered Harrow 1799, Monitor 1804, left 1804, d. 1871. Charles Drummond, son of C. Drummond of London, entered Harrow 1798, left 1804–5, d. 1858.

2. This is written on the final flyleaf of the volume, and is here published for the first time. Under Dr Drury's headmastership, at 3 p.m. on Mondays and Wednesdays, the Upper and Lower Sixths translated about 35 lines of Homer.

See Percy M. Thornton, *Harrow School and its Surroundings* (1885), pp. 434, 435. That is what B should have been doing when he penned this little distraction.

Inscription in *Euripidis Hecuba* (1804)

Text: MS The Vaughan Library, Harrow School. First published in Moore's *Memoirs* v (1854), 190.

This inscription was written by B on the first flyleaf of Richard Porson's edition of *Euripidis Hecuba* (1802). In fact, B did not finally leave Harrow until July 1805. But writing from thence to his half-sister Augusta on 21 Nov. 1804, he remarked: 'I have some idea that I leave Harrow these holidays' (*BLJ* i. 59). He did indeed do so for a protracted period, on the advice of Drury, the Headmaster, but he returned in Feb. 1805. See Marchand i. 92–100, and *BAP*, pp. 32–4).

Richard Porson (1759–1808) was Fellow of Trinity College and Professor of Greek at Cambridge. When at Cambridge B had enormous respect for his 'powers of mind, and writings' (*CPW* i. 371), but later could never remember him 'except as drunk or brutal and generally both' (see *BLJ* vi. 12). The *Hecuba* was first published in 1797, and was severely criticized by Gilbert Wakefield (1756–1801) in his *In Euripidis Hecubam . . . diatribe extemporalis* (1797). This gave rise to the following well-known anecdote which, though also recorded elsewhere, was noted by Moore in his journal on 12 Sept. 1827 as follows: 'At some college dinner, where, in giving toasts, the name was spoken from one end of the table, and a quotation applicable to it was to be supplied from the other, on the name of Gilbert Wakefield being given out, Porson, who hated him, roared forth, "What's Hecuba to him or he to Hecuba?"' (*Memoirs* v. 204). This brilliant repartee is of course a 'quotation' from *Hamlet* II. ii. 593.

Inscriptions in *Scriptores Græci* (1804–1811)

Text: MS Cottrell Dormer, Rousham House, Oxford. First published (in part) in Moore i. 61. Thereafter published from Moore (with omissions) in Prothero iv. 187n.

These inscriptions were written by B in his copy of *Scriptores Græci*, a textbook comprising selections in Greek and Latin prose from various classical Greek authors, such as Xenophon and Plato, which he originally had at Harrow. The following notes owe much of their information to M. G. Dauglish and P. K. Stephenson (eds.), *The Harrow School Register, 1800–1911* (3rd edn., 1911).

1. This is written on the inside front cover. During Dr Drury's headmastership, at 3 p.m. on Wednesdays, Monitors and Upper and Lower Sixths translated about 35 lines of Homer (see Percy M. Thornton, *Harrow School and its Surroundings* (1885), pp. 434, 435). Thomas Calvert, son of T. Calvert of

London, entered Harrow 1801, Monitor 1805, left 1805, and died while dancing at a ball in London, 5 June 1808. Thomas Wildman, son of T. Wildman of Bacton Hall, Suffolk, entered Harrow 1797, Monitor 1804, left 1805, served in the Peninsular War and, as ADC to Lord Anglesey, at Waterloo. He purchased B's home, Newstead, in 1818, and died in 1859. Edward Noel Long, son of E. B. Long of Hampton Lodge, Farnham, entered Harrow 1801, Monitor 1805, left 1805, entered the Coldstream Guards in 1807, and was drowned in 1809 on his way to join the army in the Peninsular. See also general note to 'An Extract from a Journal' below. B himself was also a monitor at the time.

2. This is written in the outer margin of the inside front cover alongside the foregoing inscription (see n. 1 above). In Moore and Prothero 'four years' reads 'five years'. The 'one . . . dead' was Calvert; Long's death occurred some months later (see *BLJ* i. 200). Wildman was in the Peninsular. These melancholy thoughts may have been prompted by B's sense of loneliness at the time, and by the prospect of his coming of age (21) on 22 Jan. 1809. See Marchand i. 164; *BAP*, pp. 55.

3. This is written along the top margin of the inside front cover, in the same hand as the foregoing inscription (see n. 2 above). It was one of B's favourite tags from the classics (see for example, *BLJ* viii. 31), and translates: 'Alas, Postumus! how the fleeting years flee by' (Horace, *Carminum* ii. xiv. 1–2). Not published in Prothero.

4. This is written on the first flyleaf (recto). See also B's erasures in MS (which precede his inscription). William Assheton was the son of W. Assheton of Downham Hall, Clitheroe, Lancashire. He entered Harrow in 1802, played in B's cricket XI in 1805, left Harrow in 1805, and died in 1858. Why B should have written Assheton's name twice, with the date, and then crossed them out is difficult to conjecture: there is no reference to Assheton elsewhere in his writings, and the date does not appear to have any significance, unless perhaps Assheton gave B the book on this date, and B wished to record the fact.

5. This is written along the bottom margin of the first flyleaf (recto) below the preceding item (see n. 4 above). It was first published, with a misreading by myself ('about' for 'absent') in the *Byron Journal* viii (1980), 18. For the itinerary of B's Grand Tour, see Marchand i, chs. 7, 8; *BAP*, chs. 7, 8.

6. These are written on the last flyleaf (recto) of the book. Henry Charles Hoare, son of Sir H. H. Hoare of Stourhead, entered Harrow 1801, Monitor 1805, Head of School 1806, d. 1852. 'Pug' was his Harrow nickname. See *BLJ* i. 109, and 'An Extract from a Journal' below. William Franks, son of W. Franks of Beech Hill, Barnet, entered Harrow 1798, Monitor 1804, Head of School 1805, left 1805, d. 1860. Henry Capel Purling Bazett, son of Major H. Bazett of Richmond, Surrey, entered Harrow 1802, Monitor 1805, left 1805.

James Buller East, son of the Rt. Hon. Sir E. H. East, 1st Baronet, of Calcutta, entered Harrow 1802, Monitor 1805, Head of School 1805, left 1805–7, d. 1878. William James Joseph Drury, son of Mark Drury, the under-master of Harrow and brother of Dr Joseph Drury, entered Harrow 1795, Monitor 1805, Head of School 1807, left 1808, d. 1878. The latter part of this inscription refers to the 'Speakers' at the Harrow School Speech Day of 4 July 1805, when B delivered Lear's address to the storm (*King Lear* III. ii). See also Marchand i. 97; *BAP*, pp. 33, *BLJ* i. 69 and n.). First published in *Byron Journal* vii (1980), 18.

7. These are written at random all over the inside back cover of the book in B's school hand.

Harrow Notebook (1805)

Text: MS Bodleian (Dep. Lovelace Byron 156, ff. 1–111). Unpublished.

These entries were made by B in a small pocket diary ($4\frac{3}{4}'' \times 3''$), bound in red leather, and entitled *Peacock's Polite Repository, or Pocket Companion; Containing an Almanack, The Births, Marriages, &c. of the Sovereign Princes of Europe, Lists of both Houses of Parliament. Officers of State, Navy, and Army. The Baronets of England, And various other articles of Useful Information* (1805). B has written on both its blank and its printed pages, though not on every page. (The exact location of each entry, as foliated by the Bodleian, is given in the notes below.) In the side pocket of its front cover there is an advertisement, cut from a contemporary newspaper, announcing that the third edition of *EBSR* 'This day is published.' Since the third edition of *EBSR* was published in 1810, B obviously referred to the notebook on various occasions after 1805—as indeed is evinced by the variform handwriting of the entries, and as can be seen from certain of the entries themselves. It is not altogether clear, however, why B made these lists; I have offered tentative suggestions in the following notes only where they might be more helpful than silence. The notes to the later folios owe much of their information to the following: George Butler, *Harrow. A Selection of Lists of the School* (1849); Percy M. Thornton, *Harrow School and its Surroundings* (1885); M. G. Dauglish and P. K. Stephenson (eds.), *The Harrow School Register, 1800–1911* (3rd edn. 1911); J. G. Cotton Minchin, *Our Public Schools* (1901) and *Old Harrow Days* (1898); W. W. Rouse Ball and J. A. Venn (eds.), *Admissions to Trinity College*, vol. iv, *1801 to 1850* (1911); and Willis W. Pratt, *Byron at Southwell* (1948). Although reference is made to *BLJ* in the later folios, for the general background to them, see Marchand i, chs. 4–6, and *BAP*, chs. 4–6.

Folio 2. This is the first flyleaf verso of the notebook. There is no record of any 'Collins' contemporary with B at Harrow, and indeed B has deliberately and no doubt facetiously altered his original 'William' to 'Wolliams'; so the name may be a mere doodle. 'Lord Byron.' is written in pencil, and is the only item so written throughout the whole of the notebook. As B tells us, the notebook was the gift of George Sinclair ('Ex dono Georgii Sinclair'), who was the son of the Rt. Hon. Sir John Sinclair of London, and who entered Harrow 1802, left 1804–5, and died 1868. B later recalled in his 'Detached Thoughts' (1821–2) that Sinclair was the 'prodigy of our School days'; and that in return for doing some of B's exercises, B 'fought for him—or thrashed others for him—or thrashed himself to make him thrash others when it was necessary as a point of honour'. They also 'talked politics' together, 'and were very good friends'. See *BLJ* ix. 43–4.

Folio 4. This, and the following two entries (on ff. 5 and 6) which are written in the same hand, appear to be part of the same continuous list. This list comprises statesmen, orators, authors, and actors, and B has marked with a cross those who were in some way physically disabled. (For ease of identification I have marked these persons with an asterisk in the following brief notices.) *Agesilaus (444–360 BC), King of Sparta (399–360 BC) in whose reign Sparta lost forever its hegemony in Greece at the Battle of Leuctra (371 BC); he was lame. Thomas Wolsey (1475–1530), great cardinal and statesman during the reign of Henry VIII. *William Pitt, first Earl of Chatham (1708–78), Whig statesman and orator, who suffered from hereditary gout (see also 'To the Rev. J. T. Becher', stanza 5 (*CPW* i. 178, 384), and *BLJ* ix. 14). Charles Mordaunt, third Earl of Peterborough (1658–1735), distinguished Admiral, General, diplomatist, and politician (see also n. 5 to B's 'Roman Catholic Claims Speech' above). Quintus Roscius (d. 62 BC), the most celebrated comic actor of antiquity, and close friend of Cicero. Marcus Aemilius Scaurus (163–90 BC), Roman Consul and orator, the last great *princeps senatus*, warmly admired by Cicero. Socrates (469–399 BC), the great Athenian philosopher whose most renowned pupil was Plato. *Richard III, King of England (1483–5), a hunchback. William Barrymore (1759–1830), actor and singer at the Drury Lane Theatre. John Lowin (Lowine, Lowen, Lowyn, Lewen) (1576–1659), one of the foremost actors of his day, performing in works by Shakespeare, Massinger, Webster, and Beaumont and Fletcher. George Drummond (1687–1766), considered the greatest Lord Provost of Edinburgh, and six times elected to that office. *James Douglas, fourth Duke of Hamilton (1658–1712), Scottish politician, statesman, and diplomatist, who vigorously opposed the Act of Union (1708), but none the less sat as one of the sixteen Scottish representative peers in the united Houses of Parliament; he suffered from a wound in the thigh, received during a duel in early life with the Earl of Peterborough (see above). John Philpot Curran (1750–1817), Irish judge, orator, politician, and wit (see also *BLJ* ix. 20, 26–7). Richard Edgcumbe, first Baron Edgcumbe (1680–1758), statesman, Lord Lieutenant of Cornwall, Chancellor of the Duchy of Lancaster, and one of Sir Robert Walpole's most trusted colleagues. Anacreon (d. *c.*478 BC), great Greek lyric poet of antiquity (for B's translations, see *CPW* i. 8–11, 73–5, 357, 370). David Garrick (1717–79), the great Shakespearean actor and friend of Samuel Johnson. Publius Aelius Hadrianus (AD

76–138), Roman Emperor (AD 117–38) and patron of the arts. William Pitt (1759–1806), second son of the Earl of Chatham (see above), statesman and Prime Minister (1783–1801). Charles James Fox (1749–1806), orator and politician. (For further references to Pitt and Fox, see *CPW* i. 42–3, 366, and *BLJ* ix. 13–14.) Henry Grattan (1746–1820), statesman and orator (see also *BLJ* ix. 13, 26–7). *Georges Couthon (1755–94), colleague of Robespierre and St Just, and partly responsible for the measures which unleashed the French Reign of Terror; he was a paralytic. Honoré Gabriel Riquetti, Comte de Mirabeau (1749–91), French statesman and orator for whose moderation and intellect B entertained immense respect (see, e.g., *BLJ* iii. 218; vii. 80; ix. 14). Marcus Tullius Cicero (106–43 BC), the greatest of Roman orators. *Alexander Pope (1688–1744), poet and B's particular favourite, a hunch-back. Samuel Johnson (1709–84), lexicographer, author, and conversationalist. John Foster, Baron Oriel (1740–1828), last Speaker of the Irish House of Commons. John Wilkes (1727–97), celebrated radical politician. Robert Burns (1759–96), Scottish poet.

Folio 5. *Richman, unidentified. Gaius Julius Caesar (100–44 BC), Roman dictator, statesman, general, historian and orator. *Louise-Françoise de la Baume le Blanc, Duchesse de la Vallière (1644–1710), mistress of Louis XIV; she was lame (see also 'Observations upon Observations', n. 31 above). Grigory Aleksandrovich Potemkin (1739–91), Russian statesman and Field Marshal, and the paramour of Catherine II for two years (see also *DJ* VII. 36–40 (*CPW* v. 348–9, 724)). Edward Gibbon (1737–94), historian. Jem Belcher (1781–1811) and his brother Tom (1783–1854), both wrestlers (see also *BLJ* i. 162 and n.). *Parkyns: this may be one of the Parkyns family of Nottingham, with whom B was on familiar terms (see, e.g., *BLJ* i. 39 and n.); otherwise B may have in mind Sir Thomas Parkyns (1664–1741), of Bunny Park, Nottingham, an indefatigable, eccentric man whose chief passion was wrestling, and who founded a competition on his estate which continued until 1810 (he suffered from no disability, however). Frederick North, second Earl of Guilford, better known as Lord North (1732–92), leading Tory politician, First Lord of the Treasury, and Chancellor of the Exchequer (1770–82), and joint Secretary of State with Fox (see n. on f. 4 above) in the Fox–North coalition of 1783–4. John Dunning, first Baron Ashburton (1731–83), politician and statesman, who was generally considered the greatest orator of his day (see also 'Presentation of Major Cartwright's Petition', n. 1 above). *Charles-Maurice de Talleyrand-Périgord (1754–1838), Bishop of Autun, politician, diplomat, and Foreign Minister under the Directoire and Napoleon; he was lame (see also 'A Letter on the State of French Affairs' above). François-Henri de Montmorency-Bouteville, duc de Luxembourg (1628–95), Maréchal de France under Louis XIV, and one of his greatest generals. (Although B has not marked him with a cross, he was also a hunch-back.) Zanger (so spelt in, for instance, David Mallet's *Mustapha: A Tragedy*

(1739) and its prefatory essay *The History of the Life and Death of Sultan Solyman the Magnificent* (1739), pp. 20–7): son of Suleiman I, 'The Magnificent' (?1495–1566), fourth Emperor of the Turks (1520–1566), by his wife Roxolana. He was particularly attached to his half-brother Mustapha, son of Suleiman by a Circassian slave. When Roxolana successfully contrived Mustapha's murder, Zanger committed suicide. He was a hunchback: '*Tzihanger* surnamed *Crouchbacke*' (Richard Knolles, *The Generall Historie of the Turkes* (1603), p. 760; see also pp. 757–65). Gaspar de Guzmán y Pimental, Duque de Sanlúcar de Barrameda, Conde-Duque de Olivares (1587–1645), Court favourite and Prime Minister of Spain under Philip IV. Henry Flood (1732–91), eminent statesman and orator in the Irish House of Commons, but unsuccessful in the English House of Commons (see also *BLJ* ix. 12–13). *Tamerlane (Timur Lenc) (1336–1405), the great Mogul Emperor (1369–1405); he was lame (see also 'The Tale of Calil' above). *Topal Osman (d. 1733), the Grand Vizier of Mahmud I; he was lame. Of Robinson the cricketer, I have only been able to ascertain the following notice (*Cricketana* (1865), p. 63):

> Robinson was one of the best hitters of his day—left-handed, and a very hard off-hitter. He was a cricketer under difficulties, for he could only catch with his left hand, the fingers of his right hand having been burnt off when a child. He was called 'Long Robin,' being six feet one inch high, and by some 'Three-fingered Jack.'

William Mason (1724–97), poet, author of *Caractacus* (1759) and biographer of Gray. *Robert Kerr (1755–1813), surgeon, and translator of Lavoisier's *Elements of Chemistry* (1790), Linnaeus' *The Animal Kingdom* (1792), and Cuvier's *Essay on the Theory of the Earth* (1813); he was lame in both legs. *Sir John Carr (1772–1832), the popular travel-writer, who published such works as *The Stranger in France* (1803) and *A Northern Summer* (1805); he was obliged to travel on account of poor health (see also *BLJ* i. 217, 221; *EBSR*, l. 1026 (*CPW* i. 261, 418)). Sir Hew Whitefoord Dalrymple (1750–1830), general, negotiated the Convention of Cintra (1808) (see *CHP* I. 24–6 (*CPW* ii. 19–21, 276–7)). Colonel Isaac Barré (1726–1802), army officer and politician, who held various offices in Bute's, Pitt's and Shelburne's Ministries, and was an unrivalled orator in opposition. (Barré and Wilkes (see n. on f. 4 above) were the two men in England most disliked by George III.) Æsop: either the legendary fabulist, who was reputedly ugly and deformed, or Æsopus, the 1st-century BC tragic actor, and contemporary of Roscius (see n. on f. 4 above), who was much admired by Horace, and who taught Cicero elocution. Pedro de la Gasca (1485–1560), Spanish theologian and politician, and Viceroy of Peru (1546–50). William Gifford (1756–1826), author of *The Baviad* (1791) and *The Maeviad* (1795), and later first editor of the *Quarterly Review*, whom B regarded as his literary godfather. Matthew Gregory ('Monk') Lewis (1775–1818), author and politician, who was most renowned for his Gothic novel *The Monk* (1796) which earned him his sobriquet; B later wrote of him as 'a good man—a clever man—but a bore—a damned bore' (*BLJ* ix. 18).

Folio 6. Cornelius Mussus (Cornelio Musso) (1511–74), Venetian theologian and Franciscan, successively Bishop of Forlimpopoli and of Bitonto, famed throughout Italy for his oratory; his *Sermons* were posthumously published in 4 vols. (1582–90). Appius Claudius Caecus (*fl.* during 4th–3rd centuries BC), Roman statesman and lawyer, who carried out many liberal reforms, and during whose consulship the Via Appia and the Aqua Appia were built; he was blind in old age ('Caecus', blind). Muleasses (so spelt in, for instance, Richard Knolles, *The Generall Historie of the Turkes* (1603), pp. 643–69, 745–9): Muley Hassan, King of Tunis (1533–43), whose tyranny earned him the hatred of his subjects, and who was eventually dethroned by his son (who also put out his eyes). John Milton (1608–74), English poet; he was blind. Democritus (*c.*460–*c.*370 BC), Greek philosopher (known also as the 'laughing philosopher') who, according to one tradition, put out his eyes in order to apply himself the better to his philosophical speculations. Lucius Annaeus Seneca (*c.*4 BC–AD 65), the Roman philosopher, orator, and tragedian, who was ordered to take his own life by Nero. Quintus Horatius Flaccus (65–8 BC), Roman poet under Augustus. Władysław IV Vasa (1595–1648), King of Poland (1632–48), a popular monarch who restored stability to his nation. Epictetus (AD 60–140), Stoic philosopher and author of the *Enchiridion*; he was lame. Alexander the Great (356–323 BC), the greatest military commander of antiquity. Gaius Julius Caesar Octavianus Augustus (63 BC–AD 14), first Roman Emperor (27 BC–AD 14), and great patron of the arts. Homer, Greek epic poet, traditionally represented as blind. Thomas Blacklock (1721–91), blind poet and protégé of Hume. Philipp Melanchthon (1497–1560), German Protestant humanist and theologian, educator, and colleague of Luther. Servius Sulpicius Galba (3 BC–AD 69), governor of Spain, and Roman Emperor (AD 68–9) who was assassinated.

Folio 7. This appears to be a continuation of the foregoing, though the hand is of a different occasion. Bocchoris (8th century BC), the last King of Egypt of the 24th dynasty, and a liberal law-reformer. John Wolcot (alias Peter Pindar) (1738–1819), the satirist who over a period of twenty years wrote numerous satires, principally against royalty, which enjoyed considerable acclaim (not least amongst royalty); in later years he became progressively blind. Paul Scarron (1610–60), French burlesque poet, author of such works as *Recueil de quelques vers burlesques* (1643), *Typhon* (1644), and *Virgile travesti* (1648–52); he became paralysed at the age of 27. The mythological figure Tydeus, son of Oeneus, King of Calydon, was sent on an embassy from Argos to Thebes where he was mortally wounded by Melanippus whom he killed. Before his own death, he tore out the brains of Melanippus with his teeth and ate them. This so disgusted Athena that she withheld the gift of immortality she was about to bestow on him. Jonathan Swift (1667–1745), satirical writer and friend of Pope; he died insane. Lepaux: variant spelling of Louis-Marie de La Revellière-Lépeaux (1753–1824), member of the *Directoire* (1795–9), and supporter of the deistic cult of Theophilanthropy. He was a hunchback.

George Ellis and George Canning satirized him in the *Anti-Jacobin*, xxxvi (9 July 1798), 285–6. Erasmus Darwin (1731–1802), physician, botanist, and poet, author of *The Botanic Garden* (1789–92); he was crippled in the leg after a coach accident. Edmund Burke (1729–97), statesman and orator, author of *Reflections on the Revolution in France* (1790). Vincent Voiture (1598–1648), French poet, letter-writer, wit and court favourite under Louis XIII, whose works were posthumously published in 1650; he suffered from a delicate disposition and died of gout. Horace: see n. to f. 6 above. Publius Vergilius Maro (70–19 BC), epic poet under Augustus. Laurence Sterne (1713–68), the author of *Tristram Shandy* (1760–7) and *A Sentimental Journey* (1768), was of a frail disposition and suffered from acute sensitivity. *Sir Walter Scott (1771–1832), Scottish poet and novelist, knighted in 1820; he was lame.

Folios 9–11. This is written on a single page, though numbered folios 9–11. This and the following two entries (on folios 12 and 14) are all part of the same continuous list, written in the same hand, which is of a later date than the foregoing. The list comprises poets and public figures (the left-hand column) and their critics or antagonists (the right-hand column). Zoilus (*fl.* 359–336 BC), a grammarian of Amphipolis, devoted his life to disparaging Homer. See also n. 16 to 'Observations upon Observations' above. John Dennis (1657–1734), critic, wrote virulent attacks on Pope's poetry (particularly his *Homer* and *The Dunciad*), and severely criticized Addison's *Cato* (1713) (see Edward Niles Hooker (ed.), *The Critical Works of John Dennis*, 2 vols., (1939, 1943)). Elkanah Settle (1648–1724), dramatist and poet, was appointed City Poet in 1691. Dryden ridiculed his drama *The Empress of Morocco* (1673) with *Notes and Observations on the Empress of Morocco* (1674), to which Settle retorted with *Notes and Observations on the Empress of Morocco Revised* (1674). Dryden again ridiculed Settle as 'Doeg' in the lines he contributed to the second part of *Absalom and Achitophel* (1682), to which Settle replied with *Absalom Senior: or, Achitophel Transpros'd. A Poem* (1682). Settle also published *Reflections on Several of Mr. Dryden's Plays* (1687). William Cowper's *Poems* (1782) were favourably reviewed in the *Monthly Review* lxvii (Oct. 1782), 262–5, but were condemned as mediocre in the *Critical Review*, liii (Apr. 1782), 287–90. His *The Task* (1785) was favourably reviewed in the *Monthly Review* lxxiv (June 1786), 416–25, and was even more favourably reviewed in the *Critical Review* lx (Oct. 1785), 251–6. 'Jefferies' refers to Francis Jeffrey (1773–1850), editor of the *Edinburgh Review*. William Hayley's *The Triumph of Music: A Poem, in Six Cantos* (1804) was condemned by Jeffrey in the *Edinburgh Review*, vol. vi, no. xi (Apr. 1805), art. v, pp. 56–63. Lord Strangford's *Poems from the Portuguese of Luis de Camoens* (1803) were also condemned in the *Edinburgh Review*, vol. vi, no. xi (Apr. 1805), art. iii, pp. 43–50. Thomas Moore's *Odes of Anacreon* (3rd edn., 1803) were very unfavourably reviewed by Brougham in the *Edinburgh Review*, vol. ii, no. iv (July 1803), art. xvii, pp. 462–76; and his *Epistles, Odes, and other Poems* (1806) received even worse treatment from Jeffrey in the *Edinburgh Review*, vol. viii, no. xvi (July 1806), art. xviii, pp. 456–65. Cf. 'To the Earl of [Clare]', stanza 8 (*CPW* i. 96, 372, where the number of the *Edinburgh Review*, there dated July 1807, should be dated as here). William Lauder (d. 1771), forger, and author of *An Essay on Milton's Use and Imitation of the Moderns in his Paradise Lost* (1750), for which, unfortunately, Johnson provided a preface. The work pretends to trace the influence of various classical writers on passages in *Paradise Lost*; but, since Lauder fabricated his sources, it is a mere tissue of fictions. With regard to his own Life of Milton, which is severe, Johnson himself told Malone that: 'we have had too many honeysuckle lives of Milton, and that his should be in another strain'. (See *Lives of the English Poets* i. 84n.; and pp. 84–200 for the whole Life.) See also *DJ* III. 91 (*CPW* v. 193–4).

Folio 12. This is a continuation of the foregoing. William Mason (see n. on f. 5 above) and Thomas Gray (1716–71), the poet, were both satirized by George Colman the elder (1732–94), poet and dramatist, and Robert Lloyd (1733–64), poet, in their joint production *Two Odes* (1760). In his Life of Gray (*Lives of the English Poets* iii. 421–45), Johnson opened his censorious discussion of Gray's poetry with the words: 'Gray's poetry is now to be considered, and I hope not to be looked on as an enemy to his name if I confess that I contemplate it with less pleasure than his life' (p. 433). George Lyttelton, first Baron Lyttelton (1709–73), statesman, poet, historian, patron of the arts, and friend of Pope and Fielding, was the author of *Dialogues of the Dead* (1760) and *The History of the Life of King Henry the Second*, 4 vols. (1767–71). He is the subject of one of Johnson's Lives (*Lives of the English Poets* iii. 446–61), and was scoffed at by Smollett as Earl Sheerwit, in *The Adventures of Roderick Random*, 2 vols. (1748), vol. ii, ch. 63, pp. 286–302, and as Gosling Scrag, Esq., 'the best milch-cow that any author ever stroaked', in *The Adventures of Peregrine Pickle*, 4 vols. (1751), iv. 120–3 (this passage was eliminated in subsequent editions). John Hill, MD (?1716–75), an eccentric and prolific writer on herbs and herbal remedies, and scientific and literary topics, whose farce *The Rout* (1758) lived up to its name by being hissed off stage, was the author of an essay which attempted to prove that Garrick was an inferior actor to Barry, and of a pamphlet entitled *To David Garrick, Esq; The Petition of I. In behalf of herself and her Sisters* (1759), which criticized his pronunciation. Garrick avenged himself on Hill with a series of epigrams. See Arthur Murphy, *The Life of David Garrick*, 2 vols. (1801), ii. 209–10, 291–2). There are many instances of Voltaire's criticisms of Shakespeare. For the most comprehensive account, see Theodore Besterman (ed.), *Voltaire on Shakespeare*, in Theodore Besterman (ed.), *Studies on Voltaire and the Eighteenth Century* liv (1967). The next two pairs of persons whom B has listed here were all involved in the same political drama. John Wilkes (1727–97), radical politician, founder of the *North Briton*, and MP for Aylesbury and for Middlesex, was accused of seditious libel, convicted of outlawry, and twice expelled from the House of Commons. On the occasion of his second expulsion he found a staunch defender in the Earl of Chatham

(1708–78), who condemned the House of Commons for the manner in which it had proceeded against Wilkes, and unsuccessfully moved for his reinstatement (May 1770). Junius (Sir Philip Francis (1740–1818)) also advocated Wilkes's cause; and, in a series of letters written over the period 1768–72, attacked, amongst others, William Murray, first Earl of Mansfield (1705–93), Lord Chief Justice, and presiding judge at the various trials for seditious libel, accusing him of attempting to subvert the course of justice. See for example, *Junius*, 2 vols. (1805), and in particular, Letter xli, 'To the Right Honourable Lord Mansfield', Letter lxv, 'To Lord Chief Justice Mansfield', and Letter lxviii, 'To Lord Chief Justice Mansfield' (ii. 37–50, 198–9, 206–37 respectively). Charles Symmons (1749–1826), man of letters, Rector of Narberth and of Lampeter Velfrey in Pembrokeshire, and author of *Sermons* (1787) and of *Inez, A Tragedy* (1796), was the editor of *The Prose Works of John Milton; with A Life of the Author*, 7 vols. (1806). In the Life, which occupies the whole of vol. vii, Symmons criticized Johnson severely for his treatment of Milton in his own Life of the poet.

Folio 14. This completes the foregoing. Richard Glover (1712–85), poet, and author of the immensely successful epic poem *Leonidas* (1737), was highly acclaimed by Henry Pemberton in his *Observations On Poetry, Especially the Epic: Occasioned by The Late Poem upon Leonidas* (1738), in which Pemberton ranked Glover with Milton, Virgil, and even Homer himself. This gave rise to the following lines by Arthur Murphy, in his 'To Dr. Johnson, A Poetic Epistle' (*The Works of Arthur Murphy*, 7 vols. (1786), vii. 10–11):

> For freedom when LEONIDAS expires,
> Tho' PITT and COBHAM feel their Poet's fires,
> Unmov'd, lo! GLOVER hears the world commend,
> And thinks ev'n PEMBERTON too much his friend.

Charles Dibdin (1745–1814), dramatist and song-writer (father of Thomas John Dibdin (1771–1841), actor, dramatist, and song-writer, whom B later knew as the manager of the Drury Lane Theatre), was the author of *The Complete History of the Stage*, 5 vols. (1800). In vol. v of this (pp. 294–302), Dibdin criticized the playwright Richard Brinsley Sheridan (1751–1816) for his lack of originality as a dramatic writer, charging him with having written merely 'scenes, hints, and circumstances, most ingeniously wrought together indeed, but as far as any thing on the stage from originality' (p. 295). William Shenstone (1714–63), poet, perhaps best known for his burlesque poem *The School-Mistress* (1742), lived a retired life devoted to the laying out of his grounds at the Leasowes, near Halesowen in Worcestershire. He contributed a number of poems to an edition of Robert Dodsley's *Collection* (*A Collection of Poems in Six Volumes by Several Hands* (1758), v. 211–16; vi. 1–59). In a letter to Thomas Wharton of 8 Mar. 1758, Thomas Gray referred to these as follows:

> Then here is the Miscellany (Mr. Dodsley has sent me the whole set gilt and lettered, I thank him). Why, the two last volumes are worse than the four first; . . . there is Mr.

Shenstone, who trusts to nature and simple sentiment, why does he do no better? he goes hopping along his own gravel-walks, and never deviates from the beaten paths for fear of being lost.

And again, in a letter to his friend Nicholls of 24 June 1769, on the publication of *The Works, in Verse and Prose, of William Shenstone*, 3 vols. (1769), Gray wrote, referring specifically to vol. iii which contains the letters:

I have read too an octavo volume of Shenstone's Letters: Poor man! he was always wishing for money, for fame, and other distinctions; and his whole philosophy consisted in living against his will in retirement, and in a place which his taste had adorned; but which he only enjoyed when people of note came to see and commend it: his correspondence is about nothing else but this place and his own writings, with two or three neighbouring Clergymen who wrote verses too. (*The Poems of Mr. Gray. To which are prefixed Memoirs of his Life and Writings by W. Mason, M.A.* (1775), pp. 261, 347)

John Philip Kemble (1757–1823), actor, was manager of Drury Lane Theatre (1788–1802) and of Covent Garden Theatre (1803–17). Shortly after the conflagration of the latter on 20 Sept. 1808, the Earl of Carlisle, B's guardian, published a pamphlet entitled *Thoughts upon The Present Condition of The Stage, and upon The Construction of a New Theatre* (1808). Although Kemble is nowhere personally named in this, Carlisle severely criticized the proprietors of the theatre for the profligacy and moral depravity amongst audiences, and for the slovenly and undisciplined performances on stage; and he suggested various improvements in the design and management of the new theatre, by which theatrical standards might be raised again to the level of the days of Garrick and Barry. See also *EBSR*, n. to l. 732 (*CPW* i. 413). Dr Joseph Drury, the headmaster of Harrow, took a great interest in the stage, and was later instrumental in getting Edmund Kean (1787–1833) his appointment at Drury Lane Theatre. But there is no record of his opinion of Kemble.

Folio 26. This and the following entry (on f. 27) are in the same hand, which is of a different period from the foregoing, and together form part of the same list. The list comprises residents of Southwell in Nottinghamshire and one or two Harrovians, to whom B possibly intended sending copies of his poetry. But this is pure speculation. I am afraid I can offer no suggestion as to the significance of the *signum* 'K', in this and subsequent entries (on folios 27, 45, 48). Dr Barrow and Mrs Burland are unidentified. For Smith, the Revd John Becher, the Pigots, and Thomas Falkner, see *BLJ* i. 93–136, 157–8, 162–3. G. Wylde took part in the amateur dramatics at Southwell in Sept. 1806, and was one of the Southwell family of bankers (see *BLJ* i. 149n., 196n.). Hutchinson was possibly John Hely-Hutchinson, third Earl of Donoughmore (1787–1851), who entered the army in 1807 and served with the Grenadier Guards in the Peninsular war.

Folio 27. This completes the foregoing. S. Wright and Nickinson are unidentified. For Major Watson, Anne Houson, Dr Pearson and the Revd Robert Lowe, see *BLJ* i. 94 and n., 104, 126, 157–60, 172, 203. B addressed several poems to Anne Houson (see *CPW* i. 12–13, 187–8, 190–1, 358, 385–6). Mary Ann Bristoe was another Southwell belle, who performed in the amateur dramatics of Sept. 1806, and who spread rumours that B had proposed to her. She is also the subject of some of B's poems (see *CPW* i. 13–17, 191–3, 358, 386). George Lucy, son of the Revd J. Lucy of Charlecote Park, Warwick, entered Harrow 1804, left 1805, d. 1845. Thomas Calvert, son of T. Calvert of London, entered Harrow 1801, Monitor 1805, left 1805, d. 1808. Charles Pindar Shee, son of Sir G. Shee, entered Harrow 1803, left 1805, d. 1856.

Folio 34. This is of a different period from the foregoing. George John, fifth Earl Delawarr (1788–1869), entered Harrow 1801, left 1808–9, and was one of B's favourites. He is the addressee of 'To [George, Earl Delawarr]', and is the 'Euryalus' of 'Childish Recollections', ll. 301–24 (see *CPW* i. 119–21, 376, 168, 383; see also *BLJ* i. 53–5, 106, 109, 143). For Clare, De Bathe, Claridge, Dorset, Gordon, Wingfield, Tattersall, and Long, see nn. to 'An Extract from a Journal' below. James Bradshaw, son of J. Bradshaw of London, entered Harrow 1804, left 1807–8, d. 1847. 'G. D. R.' is Henry Edward, nineteenth Baron Grey de Ruthyn (?1780–1810), the lessee of B's home Newstead (1803–8), to whom B took a particular dislike (see *BLJ* i. 46–60, 168). Susan Pepper was another Southwell belle. Mary Duff was B's cousin and childhood sweetheart. She is the subject of 'Song', and of ll. 55–60 of 'The Adieu' (*CPW* i. 47–8, 366–7, 184, and Addenda; see also *BLJ* i. 116, 117n.; iii. 221–3). For George Sinclair, see n. to f. 2 above. John Edleston, the Cambridge choirboy to whom B became devotedly attached, and to whom he addressed a number of poems (see *CPW* i. 124, 376–7, 150–1, 381, 181–2, 384–5, 184 and Addenda, 354, 459; see also *BLJ* i. 122–5; ii. 114, 119–20). Joseph George Brett, son of J. G. Brett of Grove House, Old Brompton, London, entered Harrow 1804, left 1807, d. 1852. Richard Thomas Dawson, son of R. Dawson, MP of Ardee, Louth, in Ireland, entered Harrow 1801, left 1804–5, d. 1827.

Folio 36. This is of a different period from the foregoing. For Dr Drury, see nn. to 'An Extract from a Journal' below. Hargreaves Hanson, the son of B's solicitor, John Hanson of 6 Chancery Lane, London, entered Harrow with B 1801, left 1804, d. 1811. For Pigot, Pepper, Hutchinson, and Becher, see nn. to ff. 26 and 34 above. Captain John Leacroft and his sister Julia both performed in the Southwell amateur dramatics of Sept. 1806. B's poem 'To Lesbia' is addressed to Julia, whose parents hoped to entrap B into marriage with her (see *CPW* i. 143–4, 380; and *BLJ* i. 51, 94, 104–6). For Mrs Elizabeth Massingberd, with whom B lodged in London, and who stood surety for some of his loans, see *BLJ* i. 82 and n., 84–5, 93, 100. Mary Ann Chaworth of Annesley Hall, with whom B fell hopelessly in love in 1803, married John Musters in 1805. B addressed several poems to her (see *CPW* i. 48–50, 367, 129–30, 377–8, 135–6, 378, 221–3, 391, 266–8, 419; see also *BLJ* i. 43, 173–4; ix. 24, 34). William John Bankes of Kingston Lacy, Dorset, was a Cambridge friend of B's (see *BLJ* i. 110–12, 198). Frederick Howard, fifth Earl of Carlisle (1748–1825), B's guardian, to whom B dedicated *Poems Original and Translated* (1808) (see also *CPW* i. 364; *BLJ* i. 76 n., 137 and n.). For Sinclair, see n. to f. 2 above. Faulkner is almost certainly Dr Thomas Falkner, the landlord of Burgage Manor (see n. to f. 26 above). Henry Ellis, entered Harrow 1799, left 1803. James Arthur Murray, son of Lord W. Murray, entered Harrow 1801, left 1803–4, d. 1860. Brough, unidentified. Gervaise Anthony Eyre, son of Colonel A. H. Eyre of Grove, Nottinghamshire, entered Harrow 1804, left 1808–9, killed 1811. For Thomas Wildman, the future purchaser of B's home Newstead, see 'Inscriptions in *Scriptores Græci*' above.

Folio 37. This is of a different period from the foregoing. Here, we are back again to public figures celebrated for their oratory. For Chatham, Fox, Cicero, and Mirabeau, see n. to f. 4 above. Demosthenes (384–322 BC), the greatest Greek orator of antiquity. John Carteret, second Baron Carteret, first Earl Granville (1690–1763), statesman, and Secretary of State (1742–4) under George II (reigned 1727–60). From 1720 to 1744 he was the leading politician in opposition to Sir Robert Walpole, first Earl of Orford (1676–1745), the staunch Whig and first Prime Minister of England (1721–42). Henry St John, first Viscount Bolingbroke (1678–1751), statesman, philosopher, and friend of Pope and Swift, renowned for his eloquent opposition to Walpole. Armand-Jean du Plessis, Cardinal and Duke de Richelieu (1585–1642), French statesman, patron of the arts, and Louis XIII's chief minister from 1624 to 1642. David Garrick (1717–79) and Spranger Barry (1719–77) were the leading actors of their day. In *A Complete History of the Stage*, 5 vols. (1800), vol. v, Charles Dibdin wrote of their respective merits: 'That GARRICK reached perfection, as far as it is in the power of a human being to be perfect, nothing can controvert' (p. 326). 'Next to GARRICK it will be proper to mention BARRY, an actor of most extraordinary merit; which was confined, however, to tragedy, and serious parts in comedies. In some few respects it is questionable whether he did not excel every actor on the stage' (p. 331). The most famous occasion on which Garrick and Barry contested their acting abilities occurred in Oct. 1750, just after Barry had deserted Drury Lane for Covent Garden. Both houses put on *Romeo and Juliet*, repeating it for 28 consecutive nights (to the tedium of the public and the newspapers). Although the palm was eventually given to Garrick, both his and Barry's performances were highly acclaimed, and 'it was extremely difficult to say who should stand first; . . . Mr. GARRICK commanded most applause—Mr. BARRY most tears' (*The Dramatic Censor; or, Critical Companion*, 2 vols. (1770), i. 189–90. See also Arthur Murphy, *The Life of David Garrick*, 2 vols. (1801), i. 192–5).

Folio 39. This is of a different period from the foregoing. The presence here of Jackson, Angelo, and in particular Grimaldi suggests that this list may be of a sporting party, or of a party to a masquerade. Cf., e.g., B's letters to Henry Angelo of 16 May 1806, and to Edward Noel Long of 5 Feb. 1808 (*BLJ* i. 92, 152–3). However, there is no external evidence that might support such speculations. For Murray, Pigot, Becher, and Pearson, see nn. to ff. 26, 27, and 36; for Long, Tattersall, and De Bathe, see nn. to 'Inscriptions in *Scriptores Græci*' above, and nn. to 'An Extract from a Journal' below. Giles, Sir Busick H., and Chisholme are unidentified. Price is possibly [?] Price who entered Harrow 1803, left 1804–5 (see also *BLJ* vii. 230). Ferrall is Orson Farrell, a 'wild Irishman' whom B knew at Cambridge (*BLJ* vii. 230, 232). Wilson is possibly William Wilson, entered Harrow 1798, Monitor 1802, left 1802–3, d. 1857. Thomas Crawford, son of William Crawford of London, was educated at Harrow and Trinity. John 'Gentleman' Jackson (1769–1845), pugilist, and B's boxing instructor (see B's note to *DJ* XI. 19 (*CPW* v. 747); see also *BLJ* i. 92 n., 162, 169–71). The Revd George Frederick Tavell was B's tutor at Trinity College, on his return to Cambridge in Oct. 1807 (see also, *Hints from Horace*, ll. 226–8 (*CPW* i. 297, 435)). Thomas Tyringham Bernard, son of Sir S. Bernard, entered Harrow 1800, shared B's dormitory, left 1804–5, d. 1883. The Honourable Charles Fitzroy, son of George, Earl of Euston, entered Harrow 1802, left 1805–7, served in the Peninsular war, d. 1865. Lord John Saville Pollington, son of John, Earl of Mexborough, was educated at Eton and Trinity College, Cambridge. Henry Angelo (1760–1839), the fencing master at Harrow, from whom B took lessons, and who shared rooms with Jackson in London (see above). Charles Devon, son of W. Devon of Teddington, Middlesex, entered Harrow 1803, left 1804–5, d. 1869. John Cam Hobhouse, B's greatest friend, whom he first met at Cambridge, but who did not at first take kindly to B (see *BLJ* vii. 230). M. Bernard: presumably a relation of Thomas Bernard above. Joseph Grimaldi (1779–1837), actor and clown, who first made his name in 1806 in the pantomime *Mother Goose*. Moore wrote of B in 1808 (Moore i. 148): 'He also honoured with his notice, at this time, D'Egville, the ballet-master, and Grimaldi, to the latter of whom he sent, as I understand, on one of his benefit-nights, a present of five guineas.' See also *BLJ* i. 152, 159 and n.; iv. 153. There are one or two references to B in Grimaldi's *Memoirs*, an abridged version of which, edited and largely written by Charles Dickens, was first published in 1838 (see *Memoirs of Joseph Grimaldi*, Edited by 'BOZ.', 2 vols. (1838), ii. 94–9, 126–9). Caroline Cameron was B's 'blue eyed' mistress of sixteen, whom he kept at Brompton, London, for the first six months of 1808 (see *BLJ* i. 157, 167; *Byron's Bulldog*, p. 29; Marchand i. 147, 151, 156; *BAP*, pp. 51–2). Captain Wallace was one of 'a very sad set,' of which B formed a part in Apr. 1808 (*BLJ* i. 165; see also i. 184, 187; ix. 19). According to his own account, B first met 'Bold' Webster (James Wedderburn Webster) in '1806–7' (*BLJ* iii. 105). He later fell in love with Webster's wife, Lady Frances, but 'spared' her (*BLJ* iii. 146; see also *BLJ* i. 171 and n.; and 'Bramblebear and Lady Penelope' above).

Folio 40. This, and the following entry (on f. 41) are in the same hand, which is of a different period from the foregoing, and together form part of the same list. This list undoubtedly refers to the Harrow Speech Day of 6 June 1805, and may very well comprise the party B played host to on that day. The '3' after Dr Drury may signify the three Drurys: Dr Drury himself, and his two sons, Henry Joseph Drury and Benjamin Heath Drury, both assistant masters at Harrow. For Delawarr, see n. to f. 34 above. For Dr Drury, Dr Butler, Mark Drury, De Bathe and Tattersall, see nn. to 'Inscriptions in *Scriptores Græci*' above, and nn. to 'An Extract from a Journal' below. The Duchess of Dorset (*née* Arabella Diana Cope) was the widow of John, third Duke of Dorset (1745–99), whom she had married in 1790, and the mother of George John Frederick, the fourth Duke of Dorset, one of B's favourites at Harrow (see 'An Extract from a Journal', *post*). Matthew Montagu, MP (b. *c.*1763), politician and later Baron Rokeby, was educated at Harrow and Trinity College, Cambridge, and was a close friend of Spencer Perceval (1762–1812), the Prime Minister (1807–12). For Sir Thomas Dyke Acland, see nn. to 'Inscriptions in *Homeri Ilias*' above. 'Ed. M. P.ost.' is Nicholas Byrne (d. 1833), editor of the *Morning Post* from 1803 to 1833. Under the title 'Harrow Public Speeches', the *Morning Post*, no. 11,443 (8 June 1805), reported the Harrow Speech Day as follows:

> Thursday last, the 6th inst. was the first public speech day since the resignation of Dr. DRURY, and and [*sic*] the appointment of Dr. BUTLER. The company began to collect about eleven o'clock, and proved unusually numerous. The speeches commenced soon after one, and closed at three. They consisted of interesting selections from English and Latin authors; SALLUST appeared the favourite. No French or Greek was spoken. Lord BYRON and Mr. LLOYD, sen. were very successful in their respective parts. The latter Gentleman is *Captain* of Harrow. Mr. DRURY, also, (the Doctor's nephew,) gave great expression to his speech of MEMMIUS. When the speeches were ended, the visitors were elegantly entertained with hot and cold collations at the different boarding-houses, or by their friends in the vicinity. Many Cambridge Dignitaries honoured Harrow with their presence and approbation.

'Ed. B. P.ress.' covers George Lane, J. B. Capes, and Robert Heron (1764–1807), the editors of the *British Press*, which was begun in 1803. Under the title 'Harrow School', the *British Press*, no. 763 (7 June 1805), reported the Speech Day as follows:

> Yesterday was a grand day at Harrow School. Though this be the age of infant orators, expectations were fully gratified by the public speeches delivered by the Youths of this celebrated Seminary. They were as follows:—

DOVETON	*Canuleius*	Ex Livio.
FARRER, Sr.	*Medea*	Ex Ovidio.
LONG	*Caractacus*	Mason.
ROGERS	*Manlius*	Ex Sallustio.
MOLLOY	*Micipsa*	Ex Sallustio.
Lord BYRON	*Zanga*	Young.
DRURY, Sr.	*Memmius*	Ex Sallustio.
HOARE	*Ajax*	} Ex Ovidio.
EAST	*Ulysses*	
CALVERT, Sr.	*Galgacus*	Ex Tacito.
BAZETT	*Catilina ad Consp.*	Ex Sallustio.

FRANKS, Sr.	*Antony*	Shakespeare.
WILDMAN, Maj.	*Sat.* IX *Lib.* I	Ex Horatio.
LLOYD, Sr.	*The Bard, an Ode*	Gray.

Among the most distinguished performances were the speech of *Canuleius*, by Master DOVETON; of *Zanga*, by Lord BYRON; and *Caractacus*, by Master LONG. Master LEEKE was to have spoken *Collins's Ode on the Passions*, but he was taken ill. A great number of fashionable company attended this elegant and interesting performance.

(The second sentence here covertly alludes to the child prodigy actor, William Henry West Betty (1791–1874), the 'young Roscius', a debate on whose abilities was being conducted in the *Morning Post* and the *British Press* at the time (see also *BLJ* i. 67 and n.).) M. D. Wise, unidentified. 'G. De. R.' is Lord Grey de Ruthyn (see n. to f. 34 above). B visited Harrogate with John Pigot in Sept. 1806. Fisher may have been a Harrovian whom he met there: either [?] Fisher, entered Harrow 1801, left 1805–7; or [?] Fisher, entered Harrow 1804, left 1804–5.

Folio 41. This completes the foregoing. The words 'Incomparably Open' are written beside the list, but do not appear to relate to it. Sir Robert John Wilmot (1784–1841) (Sir Robert John Wilmot-Horton, from 1823 to his death), B's cousin, was educated at Eton and Oxford, and later acted as mediator during the proceedings leading to B's separation from his wife Annabella (see *BLJ* v. 47–50, 55). Henry Drummond, son of H. Drummond of London, entered Harrow 1794, Monitor 1803, left 1803–4, d. 1860. Edward Bowater, son of Admiral E. Bowater of Hampton Court, Middlesex, entered Harrow 1798, left 1804, d. 1861. For Mark Drury and Dr Butler, see nn. to 'An Extract from a Journal' below. Charles Egleton-Kent, son of Sir C. Egleton-Kent, entered Harrow 1795, Monitor 1802, left 1802–3, d. 1834. The Honourable John George Monson, son of John, third Baron Monson, entered Harrow 1797, left 1800–2, d. 1809. John Rushout, second Baron Northwick (1770–1859), was a governor of Harrow School (appointed 1801). Haybrooke, unidentified. For Bernard, see n. to f. 39 above. Lady Calthorpe (*née* Frances Carpenter) was the widow of Henry, first Baron Calthorpe (1749–98), and the mother of the Honourable George Gough Calthorpe (1787–1851), who entered Harrow 1800, left 1804, and whom B fought for calling him an 'Atheist' (Marchand i. 91; *BAP*, p. 32). Mr Birch is possibly J. Birch, the partner of John Hanson, B's solicitor (see *BLJ* i. 101–2, 174). Mrs Adolphus is possibly Martha Elizabeth (*née* Leycester), the wife of John Adolphus (1768–1845), for whom see n. 42 to 'Reading List' above. For the Earl of Clare, to whom B was particularly attached, see n. to 'Endorsement on a Letter from the Earl of Clare' below.

Folio 42. This is of a different period from the foregoing. The phrase 'Variety of Action' is written at the head of the page, but does not appear to relate to the list. For Long, Gordon, and De Bathe, see nn. to 'An Extract from a Journal' below. S. Webb is possibly Mr Webb, who taught singing and dancing at

Harrow. Elizabeth Bridget Pigot, B's close friend and confidante at Southwell. For B's letters to her, see especially, *BLJ* i. 122–7, 130–3, 135–6 (see also *BLJ* i. 277). For Mary Chaworth, see n. to f. 36 above. Simmons is possibly Samuel Simmons (?1777–1819), the actor. N. Bernard is probably another relation of Thomas Bernard (see n. to f. 39 above). Saunders, Emerson, Pownall, 'H. X. U.', Rogerson, and Vince, are unidentified. Hammersley may refer to the firm of international bankers, with whom B arranged letters of credit for his first trip abroad (see *BLJ* i. 202, 205, 214). For Edleston, see n. to f. 34 above. For Becher, see n. to f. 26 above. B. Maltby is possibly a relation of Harriet Maltby, a Southwell belle, to whom B addressed his poems 'To Marion' and '[To Harriet]' (*CPW* i. 52–3, 367–8, 187, 385; see also *BLJ* i. 127). Kent is probably *not* Charles Egleton-Kent (see n. to f. 41 above), but George Kent, son of Nathaniel Kent of Fulham, London, who was educated at Eton and Trinity College, Cambridge. John Cam Hobhouse, B's great friend (see n. to f. 39 above). John Macnamara, son of John Macnamara of London, educated at St Paul's and Trinity College, Cambridge (see also *BLJ* vii. 230). William Lort Mansel (1753–1820), Master of Trinity College and Bishop of Bristol (see *BLJ* vii. 234; for B's epigrams on Mansel, see *CPW* i. 226–7, 392–3). Philips is probably Thomas Melville Phillips (or Philips), who was at Trinity College with B.

Folio 43. This is of a different period from the foregoing. The phrases 'Modulation of Voice', 'Oratorical Talents' and 'Matter' are written above the list of actors which follows, but do not appear to bear any relation to it. The '2.' after 'Kemble' presumably signifies both the actors of that name, John Philip Kemble (1757–1823) and his brother Charles Kemble (1775–1854). Robert William Elliston (1774–1831), actor and manager of the Drury Lane Theatre. John Braham (?1774–1856), contemporary tenor singer. For William Henry West Betty, see n. to f. 40 above. Madame Josephine Grassini (1773–1850), a celebrated Italian singer of the day, who was brought to Paris by Napoleon after the Battle of Marengo (1800), and was engaged in London from 1802 to 1804.

Folio 44. This is of a different period from the foregoing. The list comprises B's cousins and Nottinghamshire friends. For his cousin Mary Duff, see n. to f. 34 above. Fanny Parkyns, who appears to have been in love with B, was one of the Parkyns family of Nottingham, with whom he lodged for a while (see *BLJ* i. 39 and n., 206 and n.; iii. 223). For Susan Pepper, to whom there is no further reference in B's works, see also n. to f. 34 above. The Parkers were B's cousins. Antoinetta Parker is not known, but perhaps she was a sister of Augusta and Margaret Parker, for whom see *BLJ* i. 39n., and for a perfectly beautiful description of the latter, who inspired B's 'first dash into poetry', see *BLJ* ix. 40. Alice Hill, Alice Ellis, and Alice Thomson are unidentified. For Mary Ann Chaworth and Julia Leacroft, see n. to f. 36 above. For Elizabeth Pigot, see n. to f. 42 above. Jesse Abercrombie was the malicious woman in

Edinburgh who wrote to B's mother to inform her (and B) of Mary Duff's marriage (see *BLJ* iii. 222, 223).

Folio 45. This is of a different period from the foregoing. As mentioned in the n. to f. 26 above, I regret that I can offer no suggestion as to the significance of B's *signum* 'K' here. For Dorset, John Wingfield, De Bathe, Claridge, Gordon, and Clare, see nn. to 'An Extract from a Journal' below. For Delawarr and James Bradshaw, see n. to f. 34 above. Brock is unidentified; but it may possibly be an abbreviation of William Brockman, son of J. D. Brockman of Beachborough, Hythe, who entered Harrow 1800, played in B's Cricket XI in August 1805, and left 1805–7. William Harness (1790–1868), son of J. Harness, MD, entered Harrow 1802, Monitor 1808, left 1808–9. B was initially attracted to him because he was lame. For B's letters to him, see *BLJ* i. 154, 155–6, 163–4, 166, 197–8; ii. 137–8, 142–3, 148–50; xi. 174–5, 176–7.

Folio 46. This is of a different period from the foregoing. The list comprises B's cousins, local people in Nottinghamshire, and one or two Harrovians. For Mary Duff, Susan Pepper, and the Parkyns family, see nn. to ff. 34, 44 above. Morgan is probably Charles Morgan Robinson Morgan, son of Sir C. Morgan, who entered Harrow 1801, left 1803–4, and d. 1875 (see also n. to 'An Extract from a Journal' below, and *BLJ* iv. 257). Stuart, Curtis Reid, Paul and Reid Senior are unidentified. Nicolson is possibly 'Nicholson the Carpenter' (see *BLJ* i. 170). Lowes is possibly the Revd Robert Lowe of Southwell (see n. to f. 27 above, and *BLJ* i. 203). Ellis is possibly Henry Ellis (see n. to f. 36 above), or Alice Ellis (see n. to f. 44 above). Lord Sidney Godolphin Osborne (1789–1861), a cousin of B's, was the son of the Duke of Leeds by his second marriage; for B's first mention of him, see *BLJ* i. 45. John Musters married Mary Chaworth, B's 'former flame', in Aug. 1805 (see *BLJ* i. 116, 183, and see n. to f. 36 above. For B's reaction to their marriage, see Marchand i. 99–100; *BAP*, pp. 33–4).

Folio 48. This, and the following entry (on folio 49) are in the same hand, which is of a different period from the foregoing, and together form part of the same list. This comprises friends and contemporaries of B at Harrow. Again, I regret that I can offer no explanation for the *signum* 'K' (see nn. to ff. 26, 45 above). For Delawarr, see n. to f. 34 above. For Dorset, De Bathe, Claridge, John Wingfield, Gordon, Tattersall, Clare, Hunter, Curzon, and Long, see nn. to 'An Extract from a Journal' below. The Hon. Richard Wingfield (brother of John) entered Harrow 1801, left 1808–9, d. 1823. For James Bradshaw, Joseph George Brett, and Richard Thomas Dawson, see n. to f. 34 above. Robert Peel, son of Sir R. Peel, entered Harrow 1800, Monitor 1804, left 1804, d. 1850 (see also *BLJ* ix. 14, 43). John Grey Porter, son of Dr J. Porter, Bishop of Clogher, entered Harrow 1802, Monitor 1807, left 1807, d. 1873. William Yates Peel (brother of Robert) entered Harrow 1802, left 1805–7, d. 1858. George Ackers, entered Harrow 1803, left 1805–7, d. 1836. For Thomas Wildman, the future purchaser of B's home, Newstead, see n. to

'Inscriptions in *Scriptores Græci*' above. Pitt (no forename), entered Harrow 1801, left 1804–5. For Price, see n. to f. 39 above. For Brock, see n. to f. 45 above. Blackburne (no forename) entered Harrow 1804, left 1805–7 (see also *BLJ* i. 160). Robert Cotton St John, Baron Clinton, son of Robert, seventeenth Baron Clinton, entered Harrow 1800, left 1800–2, d. 1832. Charles Drummond, son of C. Drummond of London, entered Harrow 1798, left 1804–5, d. 1858 (see also n. to 'Inscriptions in *Homeri Ilias*' above). John Drummond, son of J. Drummond of London, entered Harrow 1800, left 1805–7, d. 1861. For George Sinclair, see n. to f. 2 above. For Cuthbert Ellison, see 'Inscriptions in a Schoolbook' above.

Folio 49. This completes the foregoing. James Munro McNabb entered Harrow 1799, left 1805–7, d. *c.*1858. For William Harness, see n. to f. 45 above.

Folio 109. These, and the following entries (on folios 110 and 111), are in the same early hand, which is of a different period from the foregoing. For Sinclair, see n. to f. 2 above. For Delawarr, see n. to f. 34 above. For Clare, John Wingfield, and Tattersall, see 'An Extract from a Journal' below. For Charles Drummond, see n. to f. 48 above. The number, written beneath each name except Delawarr, may signify how many times B had written to, or received letters from that person; or how many visits he had paid or received from them. (The 'G' written beneath Tattersall remains, I am afraid, a mystery.)

Folio 110. B quotes *Henry VI, Part II*, III. ii. 353–6.

Folio 111. The first quotation is from *As You Like It* I. iii. 78–9; the second is from Ovid, *Metamorphoses* xv. 871–2 (B significantly omits the first three words): 'Iamque opus exegi, quod nec Iovis ira nec ignes / nec poterit ferrum nec edax abolere vetustas.' (And now I have finished the work, which neither the wrath of Jove, nor fire, nor the sword, nor devouring age, shall have power to destroy.) These three quotations (see also n. to f. 110 above) form a suitable commentary on B's attachment to his school-friends, indicating the strength and the nature of his affection for them (see *BLJ* ix. 44: 'My School friendships were with *me passions*').

Inscriptions in *Catullus, Tibullus et Propertius* (1806)

Text: MS Murray. Unpublished.

These inscriptions were written by B on the first flyleaf of vol. i of his copy of George Grævius's edition of *Catullus, Tibullus et Propertius*, 2 vols. (1680). At the time of the sale of his library in 1816, the volumes were apparently mislaid and there was some hitch in their discovery (*BLJ* v. 36). However, they were eventually sold as Lot 65, and were bought by Murray (see Sale Catalogue (1816) below). The poems, of Catullus only, 'translated or paraphrased' by B, are located in vol. i under the number and title of, respectively (I give their modern numeration in square brackets): LII [LI], *Ad Lesbiam*, 'Ille mi par esse deo videtur', pp. 74–5; III [III], *Luctus in morte Passeris*, 'Lugete, o Veneres, Cupidinesque', pp. 7–8; C [XCIX], *Ad Juventium*, 'Surripui tibi, dum ludis, mellite Juventi', pp. 176–7; and XLIX [XLVIII], *Ad Juventium*, 'Mellitos oculos tuos, Juventi', p. 72. No MS or printed version by B of the third item here (C [XCIX]) is known to exist; but for the remaining three items, see *CPW* i. 70–2, 369–70. (These inscriptions would seem to confirm beyond any doubt the conjectural dating of 1806 which McGann has given to the composition of B's pieces.)

Recipients of *Hours of Idleness* (1807)

Text: MS Harry Ransom Humanities Research Center, University of Texas. First published in Willis W. Pratt, *Byron at Southwell* (1948), p. 67.

This list of names is written by B on a small scrap of paper. Although the item is catalogued at Texas as being addressed to an 'unidentified recipient', Pratt's suggestion as to why and for whom B drew it up seems to me cannot be bettered: 'It is apparently a list, made out for Ridge, of the Harrow friends to whom he was considering sending copies' of *Hours of Idleness.* 'It is possible, of course, that this could be an order for copies of *Poems on Various Occasions*, but it would seem a little late in the day to be sending them copies of this book, when the new one was to be out in another month' (p. 67). *Poems on Various Occasions* was printed for private circulation and made its appearance in early Jan. 1807. In Mar. 1807, B set about preparing *Hours of Idleness* for public issue by John Ridge, the printer and bookseller in Newark, which took place eventually in late June 1807 (*CPW* i. 361). In a letter to William Bankes in Mar. 1807, B wrote: 'I am now preparing a volume for the Public at large, my amatory pieces will be expunged, & others substituted, in their place; the whole will be considerably enlarged, & appear the latter end of May' (*BLJ* i. 112). It would therefore seem plausible that this list does refer to the distribution of *Hours of Idleness*, rather than *Poems on Various Occasions.*

The Hon. John Wingfield, third son of Richard, 4th Viscount Powerscourt, entered Harrow 1801. The Revd Henry Joseph Drury (1778–1841), son of Dr Drury the former headmaster of Harrow, was the housemaster of Drury's from 1806 to 1841. James Wynne Butler De Bathe, son of Sir J. M. De Bathe, entered Harrow 1800, left 1808—in which year he succeeded his father as second Baronet. When he died in 1828, he was succeeded as third Baronet by his younger brother, William Plunkett De Bathe, who entered Harerow 1800, and left 1805–7. Mrs Leith's were boarding lodgings at The Old Vicarage, Harrow. Charles David Gordon, son of David Gordon of Abergeldie, entered Harrow 1803, d. 1826. He was the elder brother of Michael Francis Gordon, who entered Harrow 1806–7, Monitor 1811, left 1811–13, and d. 1860. John Fitzgibbon, 2nd Earl of Clare, son of John, 1st Earl of Clare, entered Harrow

1801, d. 1851. The Revd George Butler (1774–1853), headmaster of Harrow from 1805 to 1829, was housemaster of The Head Master's over the same period. For fuller details of all but 'Mother' Leith here, see nn. to 'An Extract from a Journal' and 'Endorsement on a Letter from the Earl of Clare' below.

Memo on Playbill (1810)

Text: MS Bodleian (Dep. Lovelace Byron 154, f. 195v). Unpublished.

This memo is written on the reverse side of a playbill for a performance of *All the World's a Stage*, dated 'HMS Salsette Friday April 27th 1810'.

B and Hobhouse were on board the *Salsette*, anchored off the Dardanelles between 14 Apr. and 11 May 1810. Hobhouse recorded in his diary on 27 Apr. 1810 that, after a visit to Rabbit Island where they dined, they 'return'd ½ p[ast] 7 to the ship—where saw a play again. "All the world's a stage"' (Broughton Papers, BL Add. MS 56529 f. 42). For further references to Isaac Jackman's farce *All the World's a Stage*, which was first published in 1777, see *BLJ* i. 192; vi. 207. Robert Adair was the English Ambassador at Constantinople from 1809 to 1810. For B's and Hobhouse's visit to Constantinople, see Marchand i. 236–49; *BAP*, pp. 82–6; *BLJ* i. 236–57. For B's swimming feat, see the following n. to 'A Note in Hobhouse's Diary'.

A Note in Hobhouse's Diary (1810)

Text: MS British Library (Broughton Papers, BL Add. MS 56529, f. 43). First published (very incorrectly) in *Recollections* i. 28. Thereafter published from MS in Marchand i. 238.

Given here is Hobhouse's diary entry for 3 May 1810, with B's added note in the outer margin of the diary dated 26 May 1810. B has also interpolated the word 'hour' in the penultimate sentence of Hobhouse's entry. In the second line 'm' and 'p' mean 'minutes' and 'past'.

B and Lieutenant William Ekenhead of the Marines swam the Hellespont on 3 May 1810, while the *Salsette* frigate was anchored off the Dardanelles (see the foregoing n. to 'Memo on Playbill'). B was enormously proud of this aquatic accomplishment, and informed many people of it—Dallas, Edward Ellice, Drury (twice), Hanson (twice), Hodgson (twice), and his mother (four times) (*BLJ* i. 237, 240, 242–4, 246–8, 250, 253, 255; ii. 34). For a full account of the feat see Marchand i. 238–9; *BAP*, pp. 82–3, and particularly B's own in *BLJ* viii. 80–3. See also 'Written after swimming from Sestos to Abydos', and *DJ* II. 105 (*CPW* i. 281–2, 422–3; and v. 121, 690, respectively). It was, of course, Leander who swam *to* Hero; but for Hobhouse's reference, see Ovid, *Epistolæ Heroïdum* xviii (Leander to Hero), and xix (Hero to Leander).

Endorsement on a Letter from Suleyman Aga (1811)

Text: MS Bodleian (Dep. Lovelace Byron 155, f. 158v). Unpublished.

This endorsement is written on the back of a letter (written in florid Ottoman Turkish) from Suleyman Aga, the Waywode (Turkish governor) of Thebes in Greece. For details of the letter see below. At the time of receiving it, B was on the point of leaving Athens for Malta on the first stage of his return journey to England from the East. However, his ship, the *Hydra*, due to depart on 11 Apr. 1811, did not in the event set sail until 22 Apr. (Marchand i. 271; *BAP*, p. 96).

When B and Hobhouse first arrived in Athens in Dec. 1809, Suleyman Aga was the Waywode of that town (as it then was). Hobhouse found him 'a well-mannered man, with more information than is usually possessed by those of his nation, and who, having served with our forces in the Egyptian wars, was somewhat partial to our countrymen' (J. C. Hobhouse, *A Journey through Albania* (1813), p. 291). In his 'Additional Note, On the Turks' in his notes to *CHP* II, B recorded of him (*CPW* ii. 209):

> Suleyman Aga, late Governor of Athens, and now of Thebes, was a *bon vivant*, and as social a being as ever sat cross-legged at a tray or a table. During the carnival, when our English party were masquerading, both himself and his successor were more happy to 'receive masks' than any dowager in Grosvenor-Square.
>
> On one occasion of his supping at the convent, his friend and visitor, the Cadi of Thebes, was carried from table perfectly qualified for any club in Christendom; while the worthy Waywode himself triumphed in his fall.

This last paragraph almost certainly refers to the dinner-party B gave at the Franciscan convent (his headquarters) in Athens on 12 Nov. 1810. He wrote to Francis Hodgson on 14 Nov. 1810: 'The day before yesterday, the Waywode (or Governor of Athens) with the Mufti of Thebes (a sort of Mussulman Bishop) supped here and made themselves beastly with raw Rum, and the Padrè of the convent being as drunk as *we*, my *Attic* feast went off with great eclât' (*BLJ* ii. 27; see also Marchand i. 263; *BAP*, p. 92). Suleyman and B were evidently on extremely good terms with each other, as can be seen from the material below. Moreover, writing to William Bankes (who was planning a trip to Greece) on 26 Dec. 1812, B told him: 'If you mention my name to Suleyman of Thebes I think it will not hurt you' (*BLJ* ii. 262).

For the following information concerning the contents of Suleyman's letter, and of other papers in the same deposit in the Bodleian referred to here, I am deeply grateful to Celia Kerslake of the Oriental Institute, Oxford.

Suleyman's letter (f. 158) is dated '25 Rebiülevvel 1226' (19 Apr. 1811), and is clearly a reply to a letter from B (which is no longer extant). Suleyman acknowledges the receipt of that letter, and of 1000 *kuruş* (Turkish piastres) from B, and some *kinakina* (Cinchona bark, or quinine) B has sent him. In his letter B had apparently offered to send Suleyman anything he required from England. Accordingly, Suleyman requests two items: a pair of ornamented pistols with gold trappings, and a gold watch—both of which must be of the highest quality (this is repeated three times in the letter), and together can amount to anything up to 5000 *kuruş*, for which he will reimburse B at whatever place he designates. In a postscript he adds that he is enclosing a letter of introduction for B to his friend Ibrahim Efendi, the *mühürdar* (private secretary) of the Governor of Egypt, and closes with another postscript (apparently in his own hand rather than that of his scribe) apologizing for troubling B with his requests. The envelope (f. 159) is addressed to: 'My loving friend, the honourable, respected, intelligent, sagacious, Milor Byron, an English nobleman currently resident in Athens'. In his letter of introduction to Ibrahim Efendi (ff. 161–2), Suleyman states that he has known B for over a year, and is on terms of sincere friendship with him. He requests that every honour and hospitality be shown to B during his visit to Cairo, and that arrangements be made for him to meet the Governor of Egypt.

In the event, B did not make this projected trip to Egypt; but for his intending to do so, see his letters to Hanson, Hobhouse, and his mother of 1, 2, and 28 Feb. 1811 (*BLJ* ii. 38–41: the 'firman' to which he refers in these letters is also in this deposit in the Bodleian, f. 157). The sum of 1000 *kuruş*, of which Suleyman acknowledges the receipt in his letter, appears to be the repayment of a loan. In an earlier letter from Suleyman to B (f. 163), dated '17 Rebiülevvel 1226' (11 Apr. 1811), and again clearly a reply to another letter from B (which is no longer extant), Suleyman agrees to B's request for 1000 *kuruş*, and informs him that he is sending the money by his emissary, Edhem Aga. Having also learnt from B's letter that his departure for England is imminent, Suleyman trusts that the friendship between them will never be forgotten.

Endorsement on a Copy of a Romaic Song (1811)

Text: MS Yale University Library. First published in facsimile by C. M. Dawson and A. E. Raubitschek, 'A Greek Folksong Copied for Lord Byron', *Hesperia*, vol. xiv, no. i (Jan.–Mar. 1945), plate xxxiv.

This endorsement is written on the back of a Romaic song, copied out for B by Dudu Roque just before his departure from Athens for England on 22 Apr. 1811 (see general note to 'Endorsement on a Letter from Suleyman Aga' above). From this copy, B later made his 'Translation of the Romaic Song' (*CPW* i. 336–7, 454).

Mariana ('Dudu') Roque was the daughter of Phokion Roque de Carcassone—a French merchant living in Athens, who had married the sister of Mrs Macri, the landlady of B and Hobhouse, and mother of Teresa, the 'Maid of Athens'. Dudu appears to have been the special attraction of B's multilingual servant, Andreas Zantachi: 'Andreas is fooling with Dudu as usual', B wrote to Hobhouse on 23 Aug. 1810 (*BLJ* ii. 13); and her name may also have suggested that of the voluptuous Dudu in *DJ* VI–VII. See also Marchand i. 222, 255, 269;

BAP, p. 79; *CPW* ii. 200–1; Dawson and Raubitschek, 'A Greek Folksong', pp. 33–7.

Memorandum (1811)

Text: MS Bodleian (Dep. Lovelace Byron 154, f. 196). Unpublished.

This memorandum, which I have divided into two items, is written by B on the recto (item 1) and verso (item 2) of a small slip of paper. 'Memorandum' is B's own title, written just beneath item 2 on verso. For the details of his Grand Tour, see Marchand i. 183–276; *BAP*, pp. 61–100, and *BLJ* i. 211–57; ii. 3–59. For his splendid and exuberant verse epistle to Francis Hodgson on the eve of his departure from England in 1809, see *BLJ* i. 211–13; *CPW* i. 268–70.

1. B sailed with Hobhouse from Falmouth on board the *Princess Elizabeth* on 2 July 1809. On 2 July 1811 he wrote to Hobhouse from the frigate *Volage*: 'We have been beating about with hazy weather this last Fortnight, and today is foggy as the Isle of Man' (*BLJ* ii. 55).

2. B landed at Sheerness on 14 July 1811, and was in London at Reddish's Hotel the same day.

Memo on a Letter Wrapper (1811)

Text: MS the editor. Unpublished.

This memo is written on a small piece of paper, and may refer either to Mrs Byron's personal letters, or to those she wrote to B (five of which, sent to him at Malta, Constantinople, and Patras during 1809–11, are in the Bodleian Library, Dep. Lovelace Byron 154, ff. 128–37).

Mrs Byron, B's mother, died at Newstead, the family home, after a short illness on 1 Aug. 1811. B, who had only recently returned from the East (14 July 1811) and was in London, 'heard *one* day of her illness, the *next* of her death' (*BLJ* ii. 67). He immediately set out for Newstead, where he arrived on 3 Aug. and began to settle her affairs. On 4 Aug. (the date of this memo), he wrote to John Hanson, his solicitor: 'The effects of the deceased are sealed & untouched, I have sent for her agent Mr. Bolton, to ascertain the proper steps, & nothing shall be done precipitately' (*BLJ* ii. 68). See also Marchand i. 204–6; *BAP*, pp. 102–3.

Comments in Hobhouse's *Imitations* (1811)

Text: MS Murray. Unpublished.

B wrote these comments at home at Newstead in Sept. or early Oct. 1811. They are written in pencil in his mother's copy of Hobhouse's *Imitations and Translations from the Ancient and Modern Classics, together with Original Poems never before published* (1809). This collection includes imitations, translations, and other poems by Hobhouse, George Lamb, Jeffrey Hart Bent, and others, as well as nine original poems by B (see *CPW* i. 214, 216–23, 224–6, 265–8, 390–2, and 419; see also *BLJ* ii. 45). The volume was more familiarly known amongst B's Cambridge friends as the 'Miscellany', and was facetiously referred to by Charles Skinner Matthews as 'the "*Miss-sell-any*"' (*BLJ* vii. 232), on account of its miserable sales. Indeed, in his letters to B during his return journey from the East, Hobhouse frequently deplored the lack of recognition the work had suffered. However, when he finally arrived in England, he found that it had at least been reviewed in the *Eclectic Review*—the only periodical that took any notice of it at all (*Byron's Bulldog*, pp. 38, 51, 53, 58–9). The reviewer was dismissive of the volume as a whole, and particularly critical of its moral tendency, though he regarded B's contributions as the best pieces in it (see *Eclectic Review*, vol. vi, pt. i (Jan. 1810), art. xii, pp. 174–8).

(For details concerning the presentation and typography of the text and comments here, see the Editorial Introduction.)

1. The preface runs from pp. v to xi; B's comment is written on p. xi. In these seven pages Hobhouse draws attention to the youth of the contributors to the volume, and somewhat laboriously defends its publication on the grounds of their natural desire to be seen in print. Charles Skinner Matthews, a Cambridge friend of Hobhouse and B, had drowned in the River Cam on 2 Aug. 1811. For B's references to him in connection with the preface and his Walshean observations, see *BLJ* ii. 45, 49, 55; vii. 230–4. William Walsh (1663–1708) was the poet and critic who befriended Pope (see, e.g., *Epistle to Dr. Arbuthnot*, l. 136).

2. These are the opening four lines of the first poem in the collection: Hobhouse's Imitation of Juvenal, *Satire* xi, 'Ad Persicum', which is addressed 'To the Right Honourable Lord ***********' (i.e. B himself), and dated 'Trin. Coll. Camb. 1806.' The lines, and B's comment, appear on p. 3. B particularly admired this production. He wrote to Hobhouse on 15 May 1811: 'I think . . . the "Imitations of Juvenal" are certainly as good in their kind as any in our language' (*BLJ* ii. 45). The following items 3 to 16, and their respective notes, refer to this poem.

3. This footnote (to l. 54 of the poem, which is also quoted in the note), and B's comment, appear on p. 9. The reference is to John Gale Jones (1769–1838), politician, and friend of Sir Francis Burdett and Sir Samuel Romilly, who was renowned for his outspoken advocacy of democratic doctrines. He was imprisoned for breach of privilege in 1810. See also *BLJ* ii. 22.

4. These lines (81–4), and B's comments, appear on p. 11. 'B---y', 'Britton', and 'Moore' are unidentified, but there are many references in B's letters to the money-lenders Thomas, King, and Howard: see in particular his memorandum on annuities and loans of 16 Jan. 1812 (*BLJ* ii. 154–5).

5. This line (89), and B's comment, appear on p. 13. The reference is to money-lenders again, and B's approval of 'synagogues' may be at the use of a corporate noun rather than a specific name.

6. These lines (104–5), and B's comment, appear on p. 15. Hobhouse does not appear to be alluding to any particular 'priest', but rather to the archetypal image of the self-indulgent clergyman.

7. This line (120), its note, and B's comments, appear on p. 15. Although eggs were certainly imported into England (see *The Duties, Drawbacks, and Bounties, of Customs and Excise, Payable in Great Britain, On Merchandize, Imported, Exported, or Carried Coastwise* (1809), pp. 16, 42), I have been unable to discover whether they came from Scotland or Ireland. Hobhouse was in Ireland with his regiment at the time of B's writing these comments. He first informed B of his being posted to Enniscorthy, County Wexford, in his letter to him of 25 Aug. 1811 (*Byron's Bulldog*, p. 77), which B acknowledged on 30 Aug. (*BLJ* ii. 83).

8. These lines (122–3), and B's comment, appear on p. 17. A 'flounder' is a flat-fish; a 'jowl' is the head and shoulders of a fish, particularly a salmon. B had obviously seen an earlier version of this poem; but it is more likely that there Hobhouse had written 'sole' (another species of fish) than 'Soul'.

9. This note (to l. 132), and B's comment, appear on p. 17. Sir William Temple (1628–99), author, statesman, and patron of Swift, served as embassy to The Hague in 1674, and negotiated the marriage between William of Orange and Princess Mary (the niece of Charles II). Swift became his secretary in 1689, and held the office until Sir William's death. A complete edition of *The Works of Sir William Temple* was published in 1720.

10. These lines (140–1), and B's comment, appear on p. 17. 'Cranch' is a variant of 'crunch'.

11. These lines (156–7), and B's comment, appear on p. 21. (B has also underscored the rhymes 'son'/'town' in lines 160–1 on the same page, but without comment.) B's exclamations refer to Edward Bysshe's *The Art of English Poetry*, first published in 1702, and particularly to ch. 2, 'Of Rhyme'.

12. These lines (190–1), and B's comment, appear on p. 25.

13. These lines (252–5), and B's comment, appear on p. 31. 'Ca––sh' and 'F–––r' are unidentified, though the former may very well stand for 'Cavendish'.

14. This note (to ll. 288–9: 'If cruel cholic, or as cruel cough / Should keep for once the youthful Douglas off'), and B's comment, appear on p. 37. William Henry West Betty (1791–1874), the child prodigy actor who first made his name in the role of Osman in an English version of Voltaire's *Zaire*, at The Theatre, Belfast, on 19 Aug. 1803. On 24 Aug. 1803 he performed the title role in Home's *Douglas*, which thereafter became a standard part of his repertoire. He performed throughout England and Scotland, and was idolized by the

public, who dubbed him the 'Young Roscius'. His final performance as a boy actor was in 1808. B saw him perform in 1805, and thought him 'tolerable in some characters, but by no means equal to the ridiculous praises showered upon him by *John Bull*' (*BLJ* i. 67).

15. These lines (300–1), their note, and B's comments, appear on p. 37. To what painful pantomime Hobhouse referred, I have been unable to gather. 'Catwife' is a word of B's own compounding, and is probably drawn from 'cat' (slang for a prostitute) and 'wife'. 'Sporco' means filthy (Italian).

16. This comment is written on p. 39 at the end of Hobhouse's first poem (see n. 2 above).

17. These are ll. 121–2 of the second poem in the volume: Hobhouse's Imitation of Horace, *Satire* III. i, dated merely 'Trin. Coll. Camb'. (The following items 18 to 20, and their respective notes, refer to this poem.) The couplet, and B's comments, appear on p. 53. Henry Gally Knight (1786–1846) was a Cambridge acquaintance, and poet, for whom B entertained little regard. He told Murray on 31 Aug. 1820: 'I despise the middling mountebank's mediocrity in every thing but his Income' (*BLJ* vii. 169). For the 'wild Irishman', Orson Farrell (another Cambridge acquaintance), see *BLJ* vii. 232.

18. These lines (147–8), and B's comment, appear on p. 55. William John Bankes (1787–1855), of Kingston Lacy, Dorset, was one of the Cambridge set to whom B later referred as having been his 'collegiate pastor, and master, and patron' (*BLJ* vii. 230). His father, Henry, represented Corfe Castle in Dorset—which was also the family seat (see also *Byron's Bulldog*, p. 30; *BLJ* ii. 84).

19. These lines (151–6), and B's comments, appear on p. 55. Sir Godfrey Webster (1788–1836) was one of Hobhouse's and B's 'pot-house cronies' (*BLJ* i. 165 and n.; see also *Byron's Bulldog*, p. 33). Precisely when he performed this theft is uncertain; but the Bedford Head Tavern and Coffee House was in Maiden Lane, Covent Garden, and we know that B was fond of 'lobster-salad, and champagne, and chat' (*DJ* I. 135 (*CPW* v. 52)). Hobhouse alludes to Andrew Fuller (1754–1815), a well-known theologian and missionary advocate in Northamptonshire, renowned for his vociferous rebukes.

20. This comment is written on p. 65 at the end of Hobhouse's second poem (see n. 17 above). The poem is in iambic tetrameters, rather than iambic pentameters—the measure of heroic couplets.

21. These are ll. 67–8 of the third poem in the volume: Hobhouse's Imitation of Horace, *Epistle* XIX, Bk. i, which is addressed 'To ********** A Water Drinker', and dated 'Trin. Coll. Camb. 1807'. (The following items 22 and 23, and their respective notes, refer to this poem.) This couplet, its note, and B's comments, appear on p. 75. Both Hobhouse and B refer to the *Edinburgh Review*, the very review in which Brougham had damned B's *Hours of Idleness* in 1808. The 'names like these' refer to Dryden, Pope, and Young. Hobhouse alludes to William Gifford (1756–1826) in his capacity as satirist, and author of

the *Baviad* (1791) and *Mæviad* (1795), *not* as the first editor of the *Quarterly Review*—which was founded in 1809.

22. The first four lines here (71–4) appear on p. 75; the remaining lines (75–86), their note, and B's comments, appear on p. 77. B's exclamations (which are written at spaced intervals down the margin of the page), echo Horace's advice against a poet reciting his poetry to a friend: 'clamabit enim "pulchre! bene! recte!"' (*Ars Poetica*, l. 428: 'for he will exclaim "beautiful! splendid! perfect!"'). To 'Hafiz' Hobhouse has appended the note: 'Hafiz, put for any admired writer in the Newspapers'. Samuel Jackson Pratt (1749–1814), priest, actor, poet, and prolific miscellaneous writer, wrote under the pseudonym of 'Courtney Melmoth', and patronized the cobbler-poet Joseph Blacket (1786–1810). See also *EBSR*, ll. 319–26 variant, and B's note (*CPW* i. 239, 405). For Strangford, see n. 28 to B's 'Review of Spencer's *Poems*' above. Frederick Howard, fifth Earl of Carlisle (1748–1825), was B's guardian, and the author of *Tragedies and Poems* (1801). See also *EBSR*, ll. 725–40, and B's notes (*CPW* i. 252, 413). Hobhouse's note is a little unfair. He refers to Carlisle's pamphlet *Thoughts upon the Present Condition of the Stage, and upon the Construction of a New Theatre* (1808), in which the word 'wretches' occurs only once throughout the whole of its 43 pages. Reflecting on the confusion that would arise on the outbreak of fire at a theatre, Carlisle observed: 'This was demonstrated not long ago at Saddler's Wells, when many perished by the same miserable deaths as was the lot of those wretches who were trampled upon and suffocated at an execution of some criminals near Newgate' (p. 33). Moreover, nowhere did Carlisle suggest the construction of a 'spiral' staircase. He merely proposed (pp. 38–9):

> An additional solid staircase to each tier should be flung open to facilitate the escape of the multitude, on the appearance or apprehension of danger. Under the conviction that the moment such places were reached, all peril would cease, a fair hope might be entertained, that these staircases would be descended with little dangerous precipitation, whereby some of the worst calamities might be avoided, the terrible accidents that happen from pressure, and one unfortunate being falling over the other.

23. This comment appears on p. 79 at the end of Hobhouse's third poem (see n. 21 above), and refers also to the poem cited in n. 2 above.

24. The first sentence here is written beneath Hobhouse's poem 'An Impromptu to a Lady Splendidly Dressed' (dated 'Trin. Coll. Camb. 1806') on p. 129. The second sentence appears at the foot of p. 128. John Mortlock (d. 1816) was Mayor of Cambridge for 16 years (1794–1810), and was regarded by B as an '*impertinent Bourgeois*', and an '*Upstart* Magistrate, who seems to be equally deficient in Justice, and common Civility' (*BLJ* i. 92). Hobhouse's poem to his daughter is in three quatrains, and consists of a plea by the poet to 'Louisa' to trust her conquest of him to her natural beauties rather than the ornaments of art. For B's objection to the preface, see item 1 above.

25. This comment appears on p. 135 at the end of Hobhouse's poem 'The

Loving Lady's Complaint. A Pastoral', dated 'Trin. Coll. Camb. 1808'. (B has also underlined the word 'friend' in l. 76 of the same poem on p. 134, but without comment.) The poem is 98 lines long, and consists of a bucolical 'Complaint' by Amoret for Alexis, which is overheard by the narrator and framed by his narrative.

26. These are the final four lines of Hobhouse's 'Epistle to a Young Nobleman in Love' (i.e. B), dated 'Trin. Coll. Camb. 1808'. The lines, and B's comment, appear on p. 141. The poem is 110 lines long, and celebrates the amenities of bachelorhood—with the proviso that if one must marry one might as well marry well.

27. This is l. 38 of Hobhouse's 'Verses Written in Lord Strangford's Translation of Camoens, and presented to a young lady who was going to Lisbon for her health', dated 'Trin. Coll. Camb. 1804'. The line, and B's comment, appear on p. 166. B plays marvellously on the pronunciation of Zeuxis ('Xeuxis') (*c.*400 BC), the painter from Heraclea in Southern Italy. In his *Classical Dictionary* (first published in 1788), Lemprière has the following story concerning Zeuxis' painting of Helen:

> This . . . piece he had painted at the request of the people of Crotona, and that he might not be without a model, they sent him the most beautiful of their virgins. Zeuxis examined their naked beauties, and retained five, from whose elegance and grace united, he conceived in his mind the form of the most perfect woman in the universe, which his pencil at last executed with wonderful success.

28. This is l. 49 of the same poem as 27, and appears with B's comment on p. 167. By the time of B's writing, of course, both he and Hobhouse had visited Lisbon (July 1809).

Memo on a Billet-Doux from Susan Vaughan (1812)

Text: MS Murray. First published in Prothero ii. 92n.–93n. Thereafter published from Prothero in Marchand i. 312.

This memo was written by B along the bottom of Susan's billet-doux—a transcription of which is given here.

Susan Vaughan, whose nickname was 'Taffy' on account of her being Welsh, and who was exactly three years younger than B (she was 21 on 22 Jan. 1812 when he became 24), was probably engaged by B as a maid at his home, Newstead, in Sept. 1811. Writing to Francis Hodgson on 25 Sept. 1811, B stated: 'I am plucking up my spirits, and have begun to gather my little sensual comforts together. Lucy is extracted from Warwickshire; some very bad faces have been warned off the premises, and more promising substituted in their stead' (*BLJ* ii. 105–6). No doubt Susan was one of these 'more promising' faces; but it is unlikely that any intimacy took place between them at that time. For, in a letter to Hobhouse from London on 17 Nov. 1811, B wrote, apropos his 'Establishment at Newstead': 'I have Lucy, Susan a very pretty Welsh Girl, & a third of the Nott's breed [Bessy], whom you never saw, all under age, and very ornamental. But my diet is so low that I can carry on nothing carnal' (*BLJ* ii. 131). Nevertheless, on 25 Dec. 1811, when he had been back at Newstead for under a week (with Hodgson and William Harness as guests), B was happy to inform Hobhouse again: 'I am at present principally occupied with a fresh face & a very pretty one too, as H[odgson] will tell you, a Welsh Girl whom I lately added to the bevy, and of whom I am tolerably enamoured for the present' (*BLJ* ii. 151).

Although Hodgson and Harness have no revelations to offer here (Harness merely records that the three of them sat up into the small hours discussing religion, rose late, but that 'nothing in the shape of riot or excess occurred when I was there' (A. G. L'Estrange, *The Literary Life of the Rev. William Harness* (1871), p. 12)), the affair clearly intensified during B's visit, and caused no little jealousy amongst others of his household. See, e.g., *BLJ* ii. 155, 157.

Susan probably slipped B this billet-doux at the very moment of his departure from Newstead for London on 11 Jan. 1812, before running up to the top of the house to watch his coach disappear into the distance. Over the next fortnight, she wrote him six letters, while he apparently wrote her five (three on his way to London; two from London itself)—none of which is extant. He also sent her a locket from Nottingham, which drew from her the following somewhat ludicrous response:

> I am extremely obliged to you for it; and, believe me, I prize it more than any thing because it will contain your hair. . . . The locket is beautiful indeed—far more handsome than I could expect. I am very angry with myself for being so stupid. I have spent hours over it but cannot open it; therefore, I must leave it untill my dear Lord Byron comes to compleat it . . . (George Paston and Peter Quennell, *"To Lord Byron"* (1939), p. 28; the spelling is Susan's)

That Susan was reasonably articulate and could express her ardour for B with some conviction (if a little dramatically), can be seen from the following passage in her letter to him of 20 Jan. 1812 (ibid., p. 33):

> I loved you most affectionately when you where in my sight; but, since you have been absent, my love still increases for you, while I often think and fear your regard for poor little *T.* will not be so lasting. Will you tell me, in your next letter, wether there is not a pretty girl you have seen since you left me that you will prefer to *me*? My dearest friend, I never knew untill now what a bitter thing jealousy was. I really am jealous of those I have never seen. I'm so much afraid you will see a handsome girl. Then good bye to ugly Taffy. You once told me it should bee so. Will you bee kind enough to Let me know when it happens that I may prepare myself for the other world, as I'm sure I shall not be an inhabitant to this long after.

Her final letter to him was written in the early hours of 23 Jan. 1812, after their mutual birthday, and describes at some length the party she had given to celebrate the occasion. However, by the time B received this letter he had been informed by Robert Rushton of Susan's infidelity, or 'some improper levities on the part of the girl'—as Moore euphemistically and unrevealingly puts it (Moore i. 332); and on 28 Jan. 1812, in his only letter to her that now survives, he wrote to dismiss her, 'with some regret, & without resentment' (*BLJ* ii. 159). That he was deeply affected by her betrayal is evident from the letters he wrote to Moore, Hodgson, and to Susan herself, as well as from the three (possibly four) poems he addressed to her on the occasion (see *BLJ* ii. 159–60, 163, and *CPW* iii. 1–3, 6–7, 389–90).

For the best account of the whole affair, see Doris Langley Moore, *Lord Byron: Accounts Rendered* (1974), pp. 165–76. See also George Paston and Peter Quennell, *"To Lord Byron"* (1939), ch. 3, 'Susan Vaughan', pp. 23–39, and Marchand i. 310–12; *BAP*, pp. 111–12.

Note on Lady Caroline Lamb's Forgery (1813)

Text: MS Murray. First published in facsimile in *Lord Byron's Correspondence*, 2 vols. (1922), i. 130–1.

This note was written by B on Lady Caroline Lamb's forgery of a letter from B to herself, which she executed in late Dec. 1812 or early Jan. 1813. She took it in person to Murray, and succeeded in procuring from him the much desired 'Newstead Miniature' of B. The forgery, of which a transcription is given here, is not a good one, and should not have deceived Murray. B was at Eywood near Presteign with Lady Oxford at the time, and heard of the theft from none other than Caroline herself. In his letter to Murray of 8 Jan. 1813, B wrote (*BLJ* iii. 10):

> You have been imposed upon by a letter forged in my name to obtain the picture left in your possession.—This I know by the confession of the culprit, & as she is a woman (& of rank) with whom I have unfortunately been too much connected you will for the present say little about it, but if you have the letter *retain* it—& write to me the particulars.

The portrait was eventually restored at B's request to Lady Melbourne, Caroline's mother-in-law and B's confidante, in Apr. 1813. See Marchand i. 381; *BAP*, p. 139. See also *BLJ* iii. 11–12, 15, 17, 37.

Memo on invitation card (1813)

Text: MS William Andrews Clark Memorial Library, University of California, Los Angeles. First published in Marchand i. notes, 36. Thereafter published in *BLJ* iii. 72n.

This memo was written by B along the bottom and right-hand margins of Lady Heathcote's invitation card, a transcript of which is given here.

B attended Lady Heathcote's ball, and stayed until 5 o'clock in the morning of Tuesday 6 July. The ball proved to be a memorable and famous one on account of this 'dagger Scene'. There are various versions of what occurred.

Writing to Medwin in (?) Nov. 1824, Lady Caroline herself told him (Prothero ii. 452–3):

> The scene at Lady Heathcote's is nearly true—he had made me swear I was never to Waltz. Lady Heathcote said, Come, Lady Caroline, you must begin, & I bitterly answered—oh yes! I am in a merry humour. I did so—but whispered to Lord Byron 'I conclude I may waltze *now*' and he answered sarcastically, 'with every body in turn—you always did it better than any one. I shall have a pleasure in seeing you.'—I did so you may judge with what feelings. After this, feeling ill, I went into a small inner room where supper was prepared; Lord Byron & Lady Rancliffe entered after; seeing me, he said, 'I have been admiring your dexterity.' I clasped a knife, not intending anything. 'Do, my dear,' he said. 'But if you mean to act a Roman's part, mind which way you strike with your knife—be it at your own heart, not mine—you have struck there already.' 'Byron,' I said, and ran away with the knife. I never stabbed myself. It is false. Lady Rancliffe & Tankerville screamed and said I would; people pulled to get it from me; I was terrified; my hand got cut, & the blood came over my gown. I know not what happened after—but this is the very truth.

John Galt, who heard of the event from Prince Peter Kozlovsky the following morning, recorded in *The Life of Lord Byron* (1830), p. 187:

> The immediate cause of this tragical flourish was never very well understood; but in the course of the evening she had made several attempts to fasten on his Lordship, and was shunned . . . seeing herself an object of scorn, she seized the first weapon she could find—some said a pair of scissors—others more scandalously, a broken jelly-glass, and attempted an incision of the jugular, to the consternation of all the dowagers, and the pathetic admiration of every Miss, who witnessed or heard of the rapture.
>
> Lord Byron at the time was in another room, talking with Prince K— [Kozlovsky], when Lord P— came, with a face full of consternation, and told them what had happened. The cruel poet, instead of being agitated by the tidings, or standing in the smallest degree in need of a smelling-bottle, knitted his scowl, and said, with a contemptuous indifference, 'It is only a trick.'

Cf. *The Autobiography of John Galt*, 2 vols. (1833), ii. 245–6.

B himself however was apparently unaware that anything untoward had taken place while he was at the ball. But the following day he wrote two letters to Lady Melbourne, his confidante and Caroline's mother-in-law, in the second of which he gave this explanation of the incident:

> Since I wrote ye. enclosed I have heard a strange story of C[aroline]'s scratching herself with glass—& I know not what besides—of all this I was ignorant till this Evening.—What I did or said to provoke her—I know not—I told her it was better to *waltze*—'because she danced well—& it would be imputed to *me*—if she did not'—but I see nothing in this to produce cutting & maiming—besides before supper I saw her—& though she said & did even then a foolish thing—I could not suppose her so frantic as to be in earnest.—She took hold of my hand as I passed & pressed it against some sharp instrument—& said—'I mean to use this'—I answered—[']against me I presume[']—& passed on with Ly. R[ancliffe] trembling lest Ld. Y. & Ly. R[ancliffe] should overhear her—though not believing it possible that this was more than one of her not uncommon *bravadoes*—for *real feeling* does not disclose its intentions—& always shuns display.—I thought little more of this—& leaving the table in search of her would have appeared more particular than proper—though of course had I guessed her to be serious or had I

been conscious of offending I should have done every thing to pacify or prevent her.—— I know not what to say or do—I am quite unaware of what I did to displease—& useless regret is all I can feel on the subject—Can she be in her senses?—yet—I would rather think myself to blame—than that she were so silly without cause.—I really remained at Ly. H[eathcote]'s till 5 totally ignorant of all that passed—nor do I now know where this cursed scarification took place—nor when—I mean the room—& the hour.—————(*BLJ* iii. 72)

See also Marchand i. 396–8; *BAP*, pp. 144–6; *BLJ* iii. 71.

The Couplet Club (1814)

Text: MS Murray. Unpublished.

This splendid *jeu d'esprit* is written in Hobhouse's hand, and signed by himself and B. In his diary for 12 Mar. 1814, Hobhouse recorded that, after seeing a performance by Kean in *Hamlet*, 'I came home and sat up until one with Byron, drawing up rules for a club of which he and I are to be the only members.' On 18 Mar., he wrote: 'Dined at the Cocoa-Tree with Byron on fish alone, this being the first day of our club' (*Recollections* i. 96, 97–8). The next week, B invited Scrope Davies to dine with them the following Monday (thereby infringing the first of the club's rules), saying: 'Hobhouse & I have a kind of a dual Club once a week at the Cocoa—to which we are allowed to ask one visitor—who must be a *Cocoan*—will you dine with us on Monday next? at 6.—We are restricted to fish all the year—except Lent when *flesh* is strictly enjoined—the season is luckily in your favour for greater variety of viands as a guest—pray come' (*BLJ* xi. 162–3). The dinner was eventually brought forward to Sunday, and Hobhouse being unable to join them, Scrope and B dined alone together (*BLJ* iii. 255; see also, iv. 86). Whether this exclusive club met thereafter, and whether or not its illustrious members ever resolved the issue of 'eggs' (surely a covert and jocular allusion to the squabble between the 'Big Endians' and 'Little Endians' in Lilliput, in *Gulliver's Travels*, pt. i, ch. iv), are matters for conjecture. There is no further reference to it in either of its members' writings. However, B kept up the Catholic habit of eating fish only on Fridays. For example, in his Ravenna Journal for Friday 26 Jan. 1821, he recorded, having returned from a ride: 'On dismounting, found Lieutenant E. just arrived from Faenza. Invited him to dine with me to-morrow. Did *not* invite him for to-day, because there was a small *turbot*, (Friday, fast regularly and religiously,) which I wanted to eat all myself. Ate it' (*BLJ* viii. 36).

Comments on Hunt's *Rimini* (1815)

Text: MS British Library (Ashley 906). With the exception of B's final comment (see item 18 below), unpublished.

These comments were written by B in pencil on Hunt's first clean draft MS of cantos ii and iii of *The Story of Rimini.* Unfortunately many pages of the draft are missing, and B clearly made considerably more comments on these cantos than those extant. The 31 folios of the MS which do exist are numbered 1–31 consecutively by the BL, and this numbering has been followed in the references below. There is no precise indication as to when B wrote his comments on canto ii, although he almost certainly did so at some point during the autumn of 1815; the comments on canto iii however, were made between 18 and 22 Oct. 1815. Having read this canto, B wrote Hunt the following important letter on 22 Oct. (*BLJ* iv. 319–20):

> You have excelled yourself—if not all your Contemporaries in the Canto which I have just finished—I think it above the former books—but that is as it should be—it rises with the subject—the conception appears to me perfect—and the execution perhaps as nearly so—as verse will admit.——There is more originality than I recollect to have seen elsewhere within the same compass—and frequent & great happiness of expression—in short—I must turn to the faults—or what appear such to me—there are not many—nor such as may not be easily altered being almost all *verbal*:—and of the same kind as those I pretended to point out in the former cantos—viz—occasional quaintness—& obscurity—& a kind of harsh & yet colloquial compounding of epithets—as if to avoid saying common things in the common way—'difficile est proprié communia dicere' seems at times to have met with in you a literal translator.—I have made a few & but a few pencil marks in the M.S.—which you can follow or not as you please.——The poem as a whole will give you a very high station—but where is the Conclusion?

And writing to him again on 30 Oct., he added: 'Pray let me have the rest of "Rimini["] [i.e. canto iv] you have 2 excellent points in that poem—originality—& Italianism' (*BLJ* iv. 326).

As can be seen, B repeats many of these criticisms in his comments on the MS; in particular, his objections to Hunt's various '*verbal*' infelicities, awkward cadences, and colloquialisms on the one hand (e.g. items 1, 5–8, 10), and on the other, his approbation of those passages or images he found striking or decorous (e.g. items 2, 9, 11–17). There is no doubt that he regarded the poem very highly 'as a whole' (see also, e.g. *BLJ* iv. 330; v. 35), and his comments are especially valuable and interesting in so far as, together with those on Keats in 'Some Observations' above, they afford a rare and revealing insight into his detailed criticism of a contemporary writer's work.

In his depreciatory *Lord Byron and Some of His Contemporaries* (1828), Hunt gave B the following acknowledgement: 'While I was writing the "Story of Rimini," Lord Byron saw the manuscript from time to time, and made his remarks upon it. He spoke also to Murray respecting the publication' (p. 29). However, neither here nor elsewhere does he mention that in some instances he adopted B's suggestions (see notes 1, 5, 8 below). B was indeed instrumental in the publication of the poem. At some point in late Oct. or early Nov. 1815 he recommended it to Murray, and on 4 Nov. wrote to him (*BLJ* iv. 331):

> I have written to Mr. L[eig]h Hunt stating your willingness to treat with him—which when I saw you—I understood you to be——terms & time I leave to his pleasure & your

discernment—but this I will say—that I think it the *safest* thing you ever engaged in—I speak to you—as a man of business—were I to talk as a reader or a Critic—I should say it was a very wonderful & beautiful performance—with just enough of fault to make its beauties more remarked & remarkable.

On 18 Dec. Hunt followed this up by sending Murray the first three cantos (with B's remarks in cantos ii and iii carefully sealed over), and asking £450–£500 for the poem when complete. Murray replied on 27 Dec.: 'I have now read the MS. poem, which you confided to me, with particular attention, and find that it differs so much from any that I have published that I am fearful of venturing upon the extensive speculation to which your estimate would carry it.' He then made various suggestions concerning other publishers, failing which he undertook to print an edition of a limited number of copies on a profit-sharing basis, with Hunt retaining the copyright. This letter he sent through B with the following covering note:

I wish your lordship to do me the favour to look at and to consider with your usual kindness the accompanying note to Mr. Leigh Hunt respecting his poem, for which he requests £450. This would presuppose a sale of, at least, 10,000 copies. Now, if I may trust to my own experience in these matters, I am by no means certain that the sale would do more than repay the expenses of paper and print. But the poem is peculiar, and may be more successful than I imagine, in which event the proposition which I have made to the author will secure to him all the advantages of such a result. (Samuel Smiles, *A Publisher and His Friends*, 2 vols. (1891), i. 308–9)

Hunt found this arrangement most satisfactory; and the poem, in four cantos and dedicated to B, was published by Murray in Feb. 1816. As B had foretold it was a success and assured Hunt his reputation as a poet. But the dedication caused an outcry amongst the reviewers on account of its familiarity. It is given in full here (*The Story of Rimini* (1816), pp. v–vi):

To the Right Honourable LORD BYRON.

MY DEAR BYRON,

You see what you have brought yourself to by liking my verses. It is taking you unawares, I allow; but you yourself have set example now-a-days of poet's dedicating to poet; and it is under that nobler title, as well as the still nobler one of friend, that I now address you.

I shall be thought indeed by some to write a very singular dedication, when I say that I should not have written it you at all, had I not thought the poem capable of standing on its own ground. I am far from insensible of your approbation of it, as you well know, and as your readers will easily imagine; but I have an ambition, at the same time, to have credit given me for a proper spirit; and in fact, as I should be dissatisfied with my poetry without the one, I should never have thought my friendship worth your acceptance without the other.

Having thus,—with sufficient care, I am afraid,—vindicated my fellow-dignity, and put on my laurel in meeting you publicly, I take it off again with a still greater regard for those unceremonious and unpretending humanities of private intercourse, of which you know so handsomely how to set the example; and professing to be nothing more, in that sphere, than a hearty admirer of what is generous, and enjoyer of what is frank and social, am, with great truth,

My dear BYRON,
affectionately yours,
LEIGH HUNT.

B's own response to this, however, was exceptionally generous. In the midst of marital difficulties, he wrote to Hunt on 26 Feb. 1816 (*BLJ* v. 32):

Your prefatory letter to 'Rimini' I accepted as it was meant as a public compliment & a private kindness—I am only sorry that it may perhaps operate against you—as an inducement & with some a pretext—for attack—on the part of the political & personal enemies of both:—not that this can be of much consequence—for in the end the work must be judged by it's merits—& in that respect you are well armed.

Recalling this episode in *Lord Byron and Some of His Contemporaries* (1828), Hunt wrote (pp. 32–3):

I dedicated the 'Story of Rimini' to Lord Byron, and the dedication was a foolish one. I addressed him, as at the beginning of a letter, and as custom allows in private between friends, without his title; and I proceeded to show how much I thought of his rank, by pretending to think nothing about it. My critics were right so far; but they were wrong in thinking that I would have done it to every lord, and that very romantic feelings were not mixed up with this very childish mistake. . . . But talents, poetry, similarity of political opinion, the flattery of early sympathy with my boyish writings, more flattering offers of friendship, and the last climax of flattery, an earnest waiving of his rank, were too much for me in the person of Lord Byron; and I took out, with my new friend as I thought him, hearty payment for my philosophical abstinence. Now was the time, I thought, to show, that friendship, and talents, and poetry, were reckoned superior to rank, even by rank itself; my friend appeared not only to allow me to think so, but to encourage me to do it. I took him at his word; and I believe he was as much astonished at it (though nobody could have expressed himself more kindly to me on the subject), as at this present writing I am mortified to record it.

The Story of Rimini is based on the episode of Francesca and Paolo in Dante's *Inferno* (v. 97–142). As can be seen from the quotations here, it is written in rather loose heroic couplets, with many feminine endings, and much description of natural scenery. In his *Autobiography* (3 vols., 1850), Hunt discussed the poem in the light of these and other aspects, and made two very sweeping and questionable claims for himself (ii. 169–71):

It was written in what, perhaps, at my time of life, and after the degree of poetical reputation which has been conceded me, I may be allowed, after the fashion of painters, to call my 'first manner;' not the worst manner conceivable, though far from the best; as far from it (or at whatever greater distance modesty may require it to be put) as Dryden's *Flower and the Leaf*, from the story in Chaucer which Dryden imitated. I must take leave, however, to regard it as a true picture, painted after a certain mode; and I can never forget the comfort I enjoyed in painting it, though I think I have since executed some things with a more inward perception of poetical requirement.

This poem, the greater part of which was written in prison, had been commenced a year or two before, while I was visiting the sea-coast at Hastings, with my wife and our first child. I was very happy; and looking among my books for some melancholy theme of verse, by which I could steady my felicity, I unfortunately chose the subject of Dante's famous episode. I did not consider, indeed at that time was not critically aware, that to enlarge upon a subject which had been treated with exquisite sufficiency, and to his immortal renown, by a great master, was not likely, by any merit of detail, to save a tyro in the art from the charge of presumption, especially one who had not yet even studied mastery itself, except in a subordinate shape. Dryden, at that time, in spite of my sense of Milton's superiority, and my early love of Spenser, was the most delightful name to me in English poetry. I had found in him more vigour, and music too, than in Pope, who had been my closest poetical acquaintance; and I could not rest till I had played on his instrument. I brought, however, to my task a sympathy with the tender and the pathetic, which I did not find in my master; and there was also an impulsive difference now and then in the style, and a greater tendency to simplicity of words. My versification was not so vigorous as his. There were many weak lines in it. It succeeded best in catching the variety of his cadences; at least so far as they broke up the monotony of Pope. But I had a greater love for the beauties of external nature; I think also I partook of a more southern insight into the beauties of colour, of which I made abundant use in the procession which is described in the first canto; and if I invested my story with too many circumstances of description, especially on points not essential to its progress, and thus took leave *in toto* of the brevity, as well as the force of Dante, still the enjoyment which led me into the superfluity was manifest, and so far became its warrant. I had the pleasure of supplying my friendly critic, Lord Byron, with a point for his *Parisina* (the incident of the heroine talking in her sleep); of seeing all the reigning poets, without exception, break up their own heroic couplets into freer modulation (which they never afterwards abandoned); and of being paid for the resentment of the Tory critics in one single sentence from the lips of Mr. Rogers, who told me, when I met him for the first time at Lord Byron's house, that he had 'just left a beautiful woman sitting over my poem in tears.'

With regard to Hunt's claim to have influenced B's *Parisina* (the reference is to ll. 65–106 (*CPW* iii. 360–2)), his own 'incident of the heroine talking in her sleep' occurs in canto iv, ll. 169–76:

> Next night, as sullenly awake he lay,
> Considering what to do the approaching day,
> He heard his wife say something in her sleep:—
> He shook and listened;—she began to weep,
> And moaning loudlier, seemed to shake her head,
> Till all at once articulate, she said,
> 'He loves his brother yet—dear heaven, 'twas I—'
> Then lower voiced—'only—*do* let me die.'

But there is no evidence to suggest that B ever saw canto iv of *The Story of Rimini* before its publication, by which time *Parisina* had already been published (13 Feb. 1816). Moreover, B asserted both in his notes to the poem and to the same effect in his letter to Hunt of 26 Feb. 1816 that *Parisina* 'was composed prior to "Lara" and other compositions since published' (see *CPW* iii. 488–9, 491; and *BLJ* v. 32). Besides, B hardly needed Hunt to prompt him towards the use of such a poetical contrivance: sleep and its concommitants, whether tumultuous or serene, already formed part of the psychological machinery of his earliest Eastern tales.

As to Hunt's claim to have witnessed, on account of his poem, 'all the reigning poets, without exception, break up their own heroic couplets into freer modulation', George Saintsbury, for example, writes: 'In verse, he had, beyond doubt, the credit of being the first deliberately to desert the stopped decasyllabic couplet which had reigned over the whole eighteenth century and the latter part of the seventeenth, reviving the overrun of the Jacobeans and first Carolines' (*The Cambridge History of English Literature* xii (1953), 221). And elsewhere he states: 'There is no doubt that his versification in "Rimini" . . . had a very strong influence both on Keats and on Shelley, and that it drew from them music much better than itself' (*Essays in English Literature 1780–1860* (1890), p. 220). See also Albert C. Baugh, *A Literary History of England* (1976), p. 1173, and esp. Barnette Miller, *Leigh Hunt's Relations with Byron, Shelley and Keats* (1910).

The Story of Rimini was reviewed in the *Eclectic Review*, new series, vol. v (Apr. 1816), art. ix, pp. 380–5; by Francis Jeffrey in the *Edinburgh Review*, vol. xxvi, no. lii (June 1816), art. xi, pp. 476–91; in the *Monthly Review*, vol. lxxx (June 1816), art. iii, pp. 138–47; and by John Wilson Croker in the *Quarterly Review*, vol. xiv, no. xxviii (Jan. [pub. May] 1816), art. ix, pp. 473–81. It also received notice by John Gibson Lockhart in his first general attack 'On the Cockney School of Poetry', and on Hunt personally in particular, in *Blackwood's Edinburgh Magazine* ii (Oct. 1817), pp. 38–41. While Croker and Lockhart were the most condemnatory (both also taking outraged exception to the dedication), the reviewers generally agreed that the poem was not without its merits (principally in point of versification), but deplored its vulgarisms, colloquialisms, and quaintnesses.

The following notes include the folio number of the MS on which Hunt's lines appear, the location of B's comments in the MS, the location of the lines in the first edition of *The Story of Rimini* (1816), and whether or not B's recommendations were adopted. On two folios B has marked words or passages for which his own comments (if he made any) are no longer extant—because the pages of Hunt's MS on which they would have been written are themselves no longer extant. These are f. 1, where he has underscored the words 'We'll pass' and 'got' (which appear in canto ii, ll. 1 and 7 respectively in the first edition), and f. 30, where he has marked the whole passage relating to Francesca's reading the tale of 'Launcelot of the Lake' (which appears in canto iii, ll. 539–60 in the first edition). Neither of these has been reproduced here. For details concerning the presentation and typography of the text and comments, see the Editorial Introduction.

1. Folio 3. B's comment appears on f. 2v. Canto ii, ll. 170–1 ('as you go by' changed to 'as they go by').

2. Folio 3. B's comment appears on f. 2v. Canto ii, ll. 176–87.

3. No MS extant; clearly it held canto ii, ll. 188–95 (here supplied in square brackets from the first edition). B's comment appears on f. 2v.

4. Folio 4 (the words in square brackets have been torn off with a seal, and are here supplied from the first edition). B's comment appears on the same folio. He may also have commented on 'caged', 'leafy', and 'tear-dipp'd', on the verso of the preceding leaf of the MS which is no longer extant. Canto iii, ll. 3–10.

5. Folio 5. B's first and third comments appear on f. 4v; his final comment appears at the foot of f. 5. The second and fourth items are written above the words in Hunt's text to which they refer. Canto iii, ll. 14–29 (l. 27 adopts B's recommendation, and reads 'Was more robust, the other finelier spun').

6. Folio 6. B's comment appears on f. 5v. Canto iii, ll. 30–1 (unchanged).

7. Folio 6. B's comment (alluding to the infernal deities in Milton's *Paradise Lost*, and Tasso's *Gerusalemme Liberata*), appears on f. 5v. Canto iii, ll. 38–9 (unchanged).

8. Folio 6. B's comment appears on f. 5v. Canto iii, l. 46 (which follows B's recommendation, and reads 'A graceful nose was his').

9. Folio 7. B's comment appears on f. 6v. Canto iii, ll. 50–4 (unchanged).

10. Folio 8 (B's interpolation of a comma after 'chose'). B's comments appear on f. 7v. Canto iii, ll. 67–86 (unchanged).

11. Folio 9. B's comment appears on f. 8v. Canto iii, ll. 87–98.

12. Folio 12. The first item is written above 'trembling' in Hunt's text; the second item appears on f. 11v. Canto iii, ll. 157-60 (unchanged).

13. Folio 15. The first item is written above 'taste' in Hunt's text; the second item appears on f. 14v. Canto iii, ll. 205–12 (unchanged).

14. Folio 17 (except for the first couplet which is taken from f. 16). B's comment appears on f. 16v. Canto iii, ll. 243–58.

15. Folio 20. B's comment appears on f. 19v (a 'concetto' is a conceit, a far-fetched comparison or fanciful idea). Canto iii, ll. 309–13 (unchanged).

16. Folio 21 (except for the lines in square brackets which are taken from f. 20). B's comment appears on folio 20v. Canto iii, ll. 314–27.

17. Folio 24. B's comment appears on f. 23v. Canto iii, ll. 388–93.

18. No MS extant; clearly it held the close of Canto iii, ll. 602–8 (here supplied in square brackets from the first edition). Hunt's question, B's answer, and his comment on the poem as a whole, appear on f. 31v. The 'couplet' to which Hunt refers is almost certainly the final one. (This item was first published in *BLJ* iv. 295, with some differences in reading and dating.)

A Note in Boswell's *Life of Johnson* (1815)

Text: MS Bodleian (Dep. Lovelace Byron 154, f. 208). Unpublished.

B wrote this at a particularly distressing time during the last months of his wife Annabella's pregnancy, when he was in great financial difficulties and was being hounded by creditors. In Nov. 1815 a bailiff encamped in the house, and in the same month B resolved to part with his library (see Marchand ii. 548; *BAP*, p. 206; *BLJ* iv. 333). In the same deposit at the Bodleian as the above, there is the following note by Annabella concerning this fragment (f. 209): 'This slip of paper I cut off from Boswell's Life of Johnson, when Lord Byron's books were sent away—thinking it improper to be seen—On opening the book for that purpose—I found the concluding words "unless I go quite mad" blotted out—the ink not dry—'. Fortunately, the page number also appears on this slip of paper, and indicates that B wrote this note in the outer margin of p. 363 of vol. iii of the fifth edition of James Boswell's *The Life of Samuel Johnson* (4 vols., 1807). This copy was sold as Lot 39 at the sale of B's library on 5 Apr. 1816, and was bought by Murray for £2. See Sale Catalogue (1816) below. Given here is the passage in this edition to which B's note refers.

Endorsement on a Power of Attorney (1816)

Text: MS The Lord Byron. First published (with some discrepancies) in the *Byron Journal* xvi (1988), 86.

This endorsement was written by B at the end of a Power of Attorney, dated 29 Mar. 1816 and signed by him, which deputes to Murray the power, in B's absence, to prevent or suppress the publication or sale of *EBSR* and *Hints from Horace* by any other publisher. It does not however empower Murray to publish the poems himself. The text in full, in all its legal jargon and lack of punctuation, is as follows (the words between solidi and numbered by me in the margin being the interpolations referred to at the end of the document):

TO ALL TO WHOM THESE PRESENTS shall come The Right honorable [*sic*] Lord Byron sends
Greeting Whereas the said Lord Byron is the Author and Composer of the Poem a work
intitled English Bards and Scotch Reviewers /and also of Poems and works which he 6
has intitled 'Hints from Horace' & which consist of translations Imitations and Original
poems/ and has now the sole and exclusive Copyright thereof and being about to travel
on the Continent is desirous that no one during his absence shall publish the said
poems /or either of them/ or sell any Copies thereof to the infringement of that 10
Copyright and has therefore resolved to empower and authorize John Murray of Albemarle Street Piccadilly in the County of Middlesex Bookseller to take every legal and proper measure for restraining the publication and sale of the said works without the permission of the said Lord Byron Now Know Ye that the said Lord Byron Hath for divers good and sufficient reasons him thereunto moving Made authorized constituted and appointed and by these presents Doth make authorize constitute and appoint and in his place and stead put and depute the said John Murray his true and lawful Attorney

for him the said Lord Byron and at his Expence and in his name to institute commence and prosecute all and every such proceedings both at law and in Equity by Action Suit Bill Information Indictment or otherwise howsoever as shall be proper and necessary and to the said John Murray shall seem most expedient to restrain prevent or repress the publication of the said Poems or Works /or of either of them/ or the sale of any Copies thereof or of any part thereof by any person or persons whomsoever & an Attorney or Solicitor for the purposes aforesaid to make and at the pleasure of him the said John Murray to revoke and to do all such other things in the premises as shall be necessary and proper to be done for the purposes aforesaid And the said Lord Byron agrees to ratify confirm and approve of All and whatsoever the said John Murray shall lawfully do in the premises aforesaid /And to pay and indemnify him against all the Costs and Expences that he shall incur in so doing/ In witness whereof he has hereunto set his hand and seal this Twenty ninth day of March in the Year of our Lord One thousand Eight hundred and sixteen

Signed Sealed and Delivered in the presence of—
the words "and also of Poems and Works which he has intitled "Hints from Horace" & which consists [*sic*] of translations imitations and original poems" being first interlined in the sixth line—the words "or either of them"—in the tenth line "or of either of them" in the thirtieth line and the words "to pay and indemnify him against all the Costs and Expences that he shall incur in so doing" in the fortieth line—being interlined before the Execution

Byron

James Holmes N° 9
Cirencester Place Fitzroy Square

At the time of drawing up this Power of Attorney, B was not only embroiled in all the turmoil of the proceedings leading to separation from his wife, but was settling his literary affairs with Murray; and he may well have sent this document to him on 29 Mar. 1816 with 'the papers concerning the copyrights' (*BLJ* v. 57). At all events, he later recalled that signing it was 'almost my last act' before leaving England. See 'Letter to John Murray Esq$^{re.}$' above, and n. 13 thereto. B's witness was James Holmes (1777–1860), the painter and engraver, esteemed mostly for his miniatures, of which he made several of B. (See, e.g., Marchand i. 423; ii. 689; iii. 1067; *BAP*, p. 156; *BLJ* v. 190.)

'M^{r} J^{y}' is Francis Jeffrey (1773–1850), editor of the *Edinburgh Review*. When B's *Hours of Idleness* (1807) was harshly reviewed by Henry Brougham in the *Edinburgh Review* (vol. xi, no. xxii (January 1808), art. ii, pp. 285–9), B erroneously imagined that Jeffrey himself was the writer, and accordingly savaged him in *EBSR*, ll. 438–539 (see *CPW* i. 242–6, 407–10), and again in *Hints from Horace* (see below). When, however, *CHP* I and II (1812) were fairly and favourably reviewed by Jeffrey in the *Edinburgh Review* (vol. xix, no. xxxviii (Feb. 1812), art. x, pp. 466–77), B reacted with his customary good nature and clemency: 'The Edin[burgh] is very polite—& I of course very grateful', he told Murray; and to Edward Clarke he wrote: 'Jeffrey has behaved most handsomely' (*BLJ* ii. 174, 178). Thereafter he was reconciled to Jeffrey, and wrote him two friendly letters, only one of which survives (see *BLJ* xi. 188; see also Marchand i. 346; *BAP*, p. 126).

In 1812, at the prompting of Samuel Rogers, B suppressed the fifth edition of *EBSR*, of which a few copies had already been run off by James Cawthorn. This did not however prevent Cawthorn (who had printed the first four authorized editions) from continuing to issue many further editions of *EBSR* under a false imprint. (For instance, he issued 'third' editions, dated 1810, printed on paper watermarked 1818.) Although *Hints from Horace* (written in Athens in Mar. 1811) reached proof stage with Cawthorn in late 1811, B delayed the publication of the poem until after the appearance of *CHP* I and II, by which time he had no further intention of publishing it; nor did Cawthorn, in the event, ever publish it himself (see *BLJ* ii. 80, 81, 90, 104, 107, 109). In Mar. 1820, however, in consequence of the upsurge in the Bowles/Pope controversy, B's intention to publish *Hints* revived, and he called for proofs from Murray (*BLJ* vii. 60, 179; see also *Byron's Bulldog*, p. 302, and 'Some Observations' above). On receiving these, he was indignant to find the Jeffrey passage included (*BLJ* viii. 88):

> I have received the remainder of the *Hints without* the *Latin*—and *without* the *Note* upon *Pope* from the Letter to the E[dinburgh] B[lackwood's] M[agazine].——Instead of this you send the *lines* on *Jeffrey*—though you knew so positively that they were to be omitted—that I *left the direction that they should be cancelled appended to my power of Attorney* to you previously to leaving England—and in case of my demise before the publication of the 'Hints'.—Of course they must be omitted—and I feel vexed that they were sent.

Hereafter B's interest in publishing the poem lapsed, and it was first published posthumously in *The Works of Lord Byron*, 6 vols. (1831), v. 273–327 (in which the lines on Jeffrey were incorporated in pp. 309–11). See, however, *CPW*, where McGann has respected B's wishes and has printed the 'Jeffrey passage' separately as 'Lines Associated with *Hints from Horace*' (*CPW* i. 318–19, 443–4). For the full details of the publishing histories of *EBSR* and *Hints from Horace*, see *CPW* i. 397–8 and 425–6 respectively. See also 'Letter to John Murray Esq[re.]' above, and nn. 12 and 13 thereto.

Detail of Domestic and Intended Itinerary (1816)

Text: MS Murray. First published in Moore i. 670.

This detail is jotted down on a sheet of paper, at the head of which appears the date 14 Apr. 1816 (not in B's hand), and at the foot of which is written '*Austend*' (also not in B's hand).

B left England for the last time on 25 Apr. 1816, sailing from Dover in the morning and arriving at Ostend at midnight. He was accompanied by Dr John William Polidori, whom he had engaged as his personal physician on 28 Mar., Berger, a Swiss guide, William Fletcher, his valet, and Robert Rushton, his page, whom he sent back to England from Geneva with Scrope Davies on 5 Sept. 1816.

This detail was probably a notification to the Customs officials at Ostend of the members of his party and his intended itinerary on the Continent. In fact, B was refused permission to enter France and never set foot in that country. See also Marchand ii. 602, 606 n., 607, 647; *BAP*, pp. 232, 233, 250; *BLJ* v. 71.

Marginalia in D'Israeli's *The Literary Character* (1818)

Text: MS Van Pelt Library, University of Pennsylvania. First published by D'Israeli in the third and fourth editions of *The Literary Character*, as specified below.

With the exception of the first item here (see n. 1 below), all these marginalia were written by B in ink in his copy of the second edition of Isaac D'Israeli's *The Literary Character, Illustrated by the History of Men of Genius, Drawn from their own Feelings and Confessions* (1818). This work was first published in 1795 under the title of *An Essay on the Manners and Genius of the Literary Character*. As D'Israeli tells us, B possessed a copy of that edition, and had read and annotated it on two separate occasions during his first visit to Greece (see items 1 and 2, and nn. 1 and 2 below). This came into the hands of Murray—probably in Nov. 1815 when he bought B's library (see *BLJ* v. 42 and n.; it is not among the books listed in the catalogue of the sale of B's library on 5–6 Apr. 1816), who subsequently showed it to D'Israeli, who was thereby prompted to rewrite it and to publish it as a second edition under the new title. In his letter to Murray of 24 Nov. 1818, B wrote (*BLJ* vi. 83–4):

> I got some books a few weeks ago—many thanks; amongst them is *Israeli's* new edition. It was not fair in you to show him my copy of his former one, with all the marginal notes and nonsense made in Greece when I was not two-and-twenty, and which certainly were not meant for his perusal, or for that of his readers. I have a great respect for *Israeli* and his talents, and have read his works over and over and over repeatedly, and have been amused by them greatly, and instructed often. Besides, I hate giving pain unless provoked; and he is an author, and must feel like his brethren; and although his liberality repaid my marginal flippancies with a compliment—the highest compliment—that don't reconcile me to myself, nor to *you*—it was a breach of confidence to do this without my leave. I don't know a living man's books I take up so often, or lay down more reluctantly, as *Israeli's* . . .

B's annotated copy of the first edition (1795) has since disappeared, and I have been unable to trace it. From the above passage, however, it is evident that his marginal comments were more extensive than D'Israeli leads us to believe.

B possessed two copies of *The Literary Character* (1818). One copy was later sold as Lot 56 in the sale of his books on 6 July 1827, and was bought by a Mr Badeley (see Sale Catalogue (1827) below). The present copy he gave to Captain Fyler as a gift during the latter's visit to Italy in 1818. On his return to England, Fyler gave the volume to D'Israeli, who then set about a third edition. This was published in two volumes in 1822, and incorporated items 3 (with one omission), 4, 5, and 6 of the present marginalia (see nn. 3, 4, 5, and 6 below). B received a copy of this edition from D'Israeli himself in Apr. 1822 (*BLJ* ix. 136), and observed to Murray on 16 May 1822: 'Israeli has quoted my remarks frequently in his notes—but I would have furnished him with better remarks than those of mine—which he has printed—if I had thought that he reckoned them worth the copying—or that the book was to fall into his hands.——I gave it to Capt. Tyler [*sic*]' (*BLJ* ix. 156). On its title-page D'Israeli has written the following note: 'This book belonged to Lord Byron & was given by him to Mr Fyler when he parted from him at Athens [*sic*].' The name is quite clearly 'Fyler', *not* 'Tyler', and the initials 'J.B.F' are inscribed on the inside front cover of the book. 'Athens' should of course read 'Venice'.

In his letter to D'Israeli of 10 June 1822, thanking him for the volume, Byron reiterated these observations (*BLJ* ix. 172): 'I wish to say that had I known that the book was to fall into your hands, or that the M.S.S. notes you have thought worthy of publication would have attracted your attention, I would have made them more copious and perhaps not so careless.' In the fourth edition of *The Literary Character* (2 vols., 1828), D'Israeli included those items of B's which he had omitted from the second and third editions (see nn. 1, 2, and 3 below).

For further details concerning D'Israeli, see B's dedication to 'Some Observations' above.

For details concerning the presentation and typography of the text and marginalia here, see the Editorial Introduction. In the following notes all editions of *The Literary Character* are referred to by their dates only: 1795, 1818, 1822, and 1828.

1. No MS extant (see general note). This sentence appears on page 113 of 1795. In a note to his preface to 1828 (vol. i, p. xxix n.), D'Israeli wrote: 'In the copy of the Literary Character which Lord Byron had with him at Athens, this sentence is deeply scored under. He could not have marked his approbation with greater energy, had he been aware of the present consolation of the dunces of to-day.'

2. This passage appears on pp. iv–v of the preface to 1818 (the 'copy' to which D'Israeli refers is that of 1795); B's comment is written on p. iv. First

published in a footnote to the preface to 1828 (vol. i, p. xxn.), with the following explanation (vol. i, pp. xix–xx):

In 1822 I published a new edition of this work, greatly enlarged, and in two volumes. I took this opportunity of inserting the Manuscript Notes of Lord Byron, with the exception of one, which, however characteristic of the amiable feelings of the noble poet, and however gratifying to my own, I had no wish to obtrude on the notice of the public.

3. This passage, and B's comments, appear on p. 51 of 1818. The first two items were first published in 1822, with the following introduction (vol. i, p. 102n.):

I find in a copy of the second edition of this work [i.e. 1818], with a sight of which I have been favoured by the gentleman who possesses it [i.e. Captain Fyler], a manuscript note by Lord BYRON on this passage. It cannot fail to interest the lovers of poetry, as well as the inquirers into the history of the human mind. His lordship's recollections of his first readings will not alter the tendency of my conjecture; it only proves that he had read much more of Eastern history and manners than Rycaut's folio, which probably led to this class of books.

The third item was first published in 1828, with the remark (vol. i, p. 110n.): 'I omitted the following note in the last Edition, but I shall now preserve it, as it may enter into the history of his Lordship's character.'

For B's references here to Knolles, Cantemir, and Rycaut, see nn. 35, 36, and 37 to his 'Reading List' above. He also refers to *Mémoires du baron de Tott sur les Turcs et les Tartares* (1784), to *Letters of the Right Hon. Lady M[ar]y W[ortle]y M[ontagu]e, Written, During her Travels in Europe, Asia and Africa to Persons of Distinction* (1763), and to Vincent Mignot's *Histoire de l'Empire Ottoman, depuis son origine jusqu'à la paix de Belgrade en 1740* (1771), which was translated into English by A. Hawkins as *The History of the Turkish or Ottoman Empire, From its Foundation in 1300 to the Peace of Belgrade in 1740* (1787).

4. This passage appears on pp. 99–100 of 1818. B's first comment is written just below 'brothers' at the foot of p. 99; his second comment is spread over pp. 100–1. (He has also erased the word 'on' after 'contemplate' in D'Israeli's text.) First published in 1822 (vol. i, pp. 173n.–174n.), in which edition, after the word 'contemn', D'Israeli changed the remainder of the passage to run thus: 'Does he accept with ingratitude the fame he loves more than life? I foresee the columns which would be raised to his awful genius struck down by his own hands, and his name in our poetry to be a fixed and dark cloud hanging over posterity.'

For B's quotation, see *Coriolanus* III. iii. 133 (Coriolanus speaking). For his determination to write his 'best work' in Italian, see his letter to Murray of 6 Apr. 1819 (*BLJ* vi. 105): 'I mean to write my best work in *Italian*—& it will take me nine years more thoroughly to master the language—& then if my fancy exists & I exist too—I will try what I *can* do *really*.'

5. This passage, and B's comments, appear on p. 109 of 1818. First published in 1822 (vol. i, pp. 192n.–193n.). D'Israeli refers to the Italian dramatist and poet, Conte Vittorio Alfieri (1749–1803).

6. This passage, and B's comment, appear on p. 342 of 1818. First published (with the omission of the phrase 'short of Venus') in 1822 (vol. ii, p. 272n.). Francesco Petrarca was born in Arezzo in 1304. He was crowned on the Capitol at Rome on 8 Apr. 1341, and he died at Arqua in 1375.

Anecdote of an Amatory Affair in Spain (1818–1820)

Text: Moore i. 198.

Having partially quoted B's letter to his mother of 11 Aug. 1809 (for the full text of which see *BLJ* i. 218–22), Moore continued (Moore i. 198):

> To these adventures, or rather glimpses of adventures, which he met with in his hasty passage through Spain, he adverted, I recollect, briefly, in the early part of his 'Memoranda;' and it was the younger, I think, of his fair hostesses at Seville, whom he there described himself as having made earnest love to, with the help of a dictionary.

He then gave this anecdote. (For his reference to B's 'Memoranda', see general note to 'Four Memoranda from B's Memoirs', below. If Moore's recollection is correct, then the hostess in question would have been the younger sister of Donna Josepha Beltram, at one of whose six houses in Seville Hobhouse and B lodged for three nights (25–7 July 1809). However, B appears to have gained the particular attention of Donna Josepha herself; for, in the letter to his mother mentioned above, he wrote (*BLJ* i. 219):

> we lodged in the house of two Spanish unmarried ladies, who possess *six* houses in Seville, and gave me a curious specimen of Spanish manners.—They are women of character, and the eldest a fine woman, the youngest pretty but not so good a figure as Donna Josepha ... The eldest honoured your *unworthy* son with very particular attention, embracing him with great tenderness at parting (I was there but 3 days) after cutting off a lock of his hair, & presenting him with one of her own about three feet in length, which I send, and beg you will retain till my return.—Her last words were 'Adio tu hermoso! me gusto mucho' 'Adieu, you pretty fellow you please me much.'—She offered a share of her apartment which my *virtue* induced me to decline ...

Hobhouse merely recorded that he and B left Seville on 28 July 'after kissing our hostess & sister (one of whom asked L[d] B why he had not come to bed to her at 2 o clock according to invitation)' (Broughton Papers, BL Add. MS 56527, ff. 14v–15). See also Marchand i. 189–90; *BAP*, p. 63.

B eventually lost both his 'heart and ring' to Mrs Constance Spencer Smith at Malta in Sept. 1809. John Galt recorded, not very charitably, that B 'affected a passion for her; but it was only Platonic. She, however, beguiled him of his valuable yellow diamond-ring' (*The Life of Lord Byron* (1830), p. 68). For B's affair with her, see Marchand i. 199–201; *BAP*, pp. 67–8; *BLJ* i. 224, 239. For his poems addressed to or connected with her, see *CPW* i. 273–80, 420–3; see also *CHP* II. 30–5 (*CPW* ii. 53–5, 287).

1. *away.* Immediately after this word Moore has continued with his own paraphrase of B's story: 'The young Spaniard grew angry as the contention

went on, and it was not long before the lover became angry also; till, at length, the affair ended by their separating unsuccessful on both sides.' He then resumes with B's words ('Soon . . . ring.')

Four Memoranda from B's Memoirs (1818–1820)

Text: Moore i. 667n.; ii. 34n.

Moore introduced each of these items as follows. In a footnote to B's exclamation in his 'Detached Thoughts' (1821–2), 'Curran!—Curran's the Man who struck me most' (see *BLJ* ix. 20), he wrote: 'In his Memoranda there were equally enthusiastic praises of Curran.' He then gave item 1 here, and immediately continued: 'In another part, however, he was somewhat more fair to Madame de Staël's personal appearance.' He then gave item 2 here (Moore i. 667n.). Again, in a footnote to his mentioning B's visit to Coppet in 1816, he wrote: 'In the account of this visit to Copet [*sic*] in his Memoranda, he spoke in high terms of the daughter of his hostess, the present Duchess de Broglie, and, in noticing how much she appeared to be attached to her husband, remarked that'. He then gave item 3 here, and immediately continued: 'Of Madame de Staël, in that Memoir, he spoke thus'; and he then gave item 4 here (Moore ii. 34n.).

The 'Memoir' or 'Memoranda', as Moore randomly refers to them, were the famous memoirs of his own life up to 1816 which B had begun between 10 and 17 July 1818, and which he gave to Moore on 11 Oct. 1819, and additions to which he sent him in Dec. 1820. (See *BLJ* vi. 59, 61, 232; vii. 244; and Wilfred S. Dowden (ed.), *The Journal of Thomas Moore* i (1983), 227, 371–2.) I have therefore dated these memoranda accordingly. (For a full account of the disastrous destruction of the memoirs, see Doris Langley Moore, *The Late Lord Byron* (1961), pp. 12–53.)

For details of Madame de Staël, and B's relationship with her, see 'Some Recollections of my Acquaintance with Madame de Staël' above. For B's other references to her daughter, Albertine, Duchesse de Broglie, see, e.g., *BLJ* vi. 127; viii. 167; ix. 47.

John Philpot Curran (1750–1817), formerly Master of the Rolls in Ireland, was renowned in Whig circles for his sparkling wit and brilliant conversation. B first met him at Holland House in 1813, and was immediately 'electrified . . . with his imagination' (*BLJ* iii. 128). Writing to Moore in Oct. 1813, he reported:

> I have met Curran at Holland-house—he beats every body;—his imagination is beyond human, and his humour (it is difficult to define what is wit) perfect. Then he has fifty faces, and twice as many voices, when he mimics;—I never met his equal. . . . He is quite fascinating. . . . I almost fear to meet him again, lest the impression should be lowered. . . . What a variety of expression he conjures into that naturally not very fine countenance of his! He absolutely changes it entirely. (*BLJ* iii. 130–1)

See also *BLJ* viii. 230, 245, 246; ix. 20, 26–7.

Two Notes in Foscolo's *Jacopo Ortis* (1819)

Text: *Lord Byron jugé par les témoins de sa vie*, [Countess Guiccioli] 2 vols. (Paris, 1868), ii. 86, 87n.

Teresa Guiccioli, B's mistress, informs us that both these notes were written by B one day at Ravenna on the opening page of Foscolo's *Jacopo Ortis* (see below). She is no more specific than this as to their dating, nor does she say whether the volume (which is apparently no longer extant) was her own. However, in introducing the second note here, she says that B had prefaced it by remarking the curious coincidence by which the work had come a *second* time to his notice when, just as on the former occasion, he was feeling depressed ('Après avoir observé par quelle étrange coïncidence ce volume lui était tombé une seconde fois sous la main, lorsqu'il se trouvait comme la première fois dans une extrême agitation de coeur, il continua ainsi: . . .'). Precisely when B first read the book is uncertain; his first reference to it appears to be in his letter to Murray of 6 Apr. 1819 (*BLJ* vi. 105). But in the light of his marginalia and letter to Teresa written in her copy of Madame de Staël's *Corinne* on 23 Aug. 1819 (see below), it seems most likely that the volume belonged to her and that B wrote these notes in it during his first visit to Ravenna (10 June–9 Aug. 1819), when he was indeed in a very melancholy state of mind about Teresa's health and their liaison. See, in particular, Marchand ii. 792–806; *BAP*, pp. 304–9; *BLJ* vi. 167, 168–70, 178–80, 190–1, 199–200, 202–3; see also general note to 'Marginalia in de Staël's *Corinne*' below).

With respect to the text, I have corrected what I am certain are either three misreadings by Teresa of B's script, or three typographical errors. In the first note, 'animum' reads 'animam' in her text, and in the second (given in B's original English on p. 87n.), 'fruition' reads 'fruiction' and 'Most' 'Must'. (I have let 'Cœlum' stand, though its usual orthography is 'Caelum'.) The Latin tag is from Horace, *Epistles* I. xi. 27: 'Caelum, non animum, mutant, qui trans mare currunt' ('Those who cross the sea change their skies but not their souls').

Niccolò Ugo Foscolo (1778–1827), patriot, poet, and dramatist, was a keen Bonapartist until the Treaty of Campo Formio (1797), when Napoleon ceded Venice to the Austrians. His *Ultime Lettere di Jacopo Ortis* (1798–1802) was written in reaction to this event. This novel, which is indeed very similar to Goethe's *The Sorrows of Young Werther* (1774, 1787), traces in a series of letters a tragic love story against the background of the fall of Italy. Jacopo, a disillusioned liberal and patriot deploring the state of his country, is in love with Teresa, who reciprocates his feelings but is obliged by her father to marry *de convenance* Odoardo, whom she does not love. In despair Jacopo eventually commits suicide with a small dagger.

Marginalia in De Staël's *Corinne* (1819)

Text: MS Biblioteca Classense, Ravenna. With the exception of item 11 (see below), unpublished.

B wrote these marginalia in Teresa Guiccioli's copy of an Italian translation of Madame de Staël's *Corinne* (first published in French in 1807), which was published as *Corinna* by Guglielmo Piatti in 1808. They are written in ink over pp. 84–93 of bk. xviii, ch. v, '*Frammenti dei Pensieri di Corinna*' ('Fragments of Corinna's Thoughts'). In bk. xx of this same work, and on the same date as these marginalia (23 Aug. 1819), B wrote the letter to Teresa which is published in *BLJ* vi. 215–16. The preceding evening he had begun his witty letter 'To the Editor of the *British Review*' (see its general note above); yet, as these marginalia show, he was in a melancholy and reflective state of mind. At the time, he was alone at Bologna and missing his mistress Teresa, who had been obliged to accompany her husband Count Guiccioli on a round of his properties for a few days. See Marchand ii. 810–11; *BAP*, pp. 310–11; see also *BLJ* vi. 214–17, and Iris Origo, *The Last Attachment* (1949), pp. 111–13).

For details concerning the presentation and typography of the text and marginalia here, see the Editorial Introduction. I have transcribed the Italian *verbatim et literatim* from Teresa's copy. The following notes refer to the marginalia as numbered by me; the translations are my own.

1. *Il mio . . . perduto.* This translates: 'My genius no longer exists; I lament its loss.'

2. *Fa egli . . . core.* This translates: 'Should we submit to the force of love or combat it? Ah! what storms rage in the recesses of the heart.'

3. *Il talento . . . tutto.* This translates: 'Genius should be a resource. When Domenichino was confined in a convent, he painted superb frescoes on the walls of his prison, and left masterpieces to mark his sojourn there. But he suffered from external circumstances only, his misery was not in the soul; when it is there, nothing is possible, the source of all is dried up.' Iris Origo (*The Last Attachment*, p. 113), was the first to mention B's reference to this passage, and to translate the clause '*ma egli . . . di tutto*'. (B has erased the word 'non', so that the phrase as applied to himself reads 'his misery was in the soul'.) There is no record that the painter Domenichino (Domenico Zampieri (1581–1641)) was ever actually imprisoned, though on account of the jealousy his work inspired in such rival artists as Ribera, Lanfranco, and Corenzio, he did lead a secluded life, and was indeed tormented by his enemies. Besides other works, he painted a series of frescoes on the lives of St Nilus and St Bartholomew in the Basilian Abbey of Grotta Ferrata, near Rome; and, for the last ten years of his life, was similarly occupied on the life of St Januarius in the Cappello de Tesoro in Naples. Perhaps Corinna has one of these periods in

mind. B saw Domenichino's paintings at Bologna in June 1819, and thought them 'superlative' (*BLJ* vi. 148).

4. *Qualche . . . male?* This translates: 'I sometimes examine myself as a stranger to me might do, and I pity myself. I was witty, sincere, kind, generous, tender-hearted—why should all this turn out so badly?'

5. *E'propriamente . . . respirare.* This translates: 'It is truly pitiable: I was born to be a person of distinction, but I shall die without anyone having the least idea of me—despite my celebrity. Had I been happy, had the fever at the heart not consumed me—I should have contemplated human destiny from a greater height, and should then have discovered the mysterious relationship between nature and heaven. But the grip of misfortune holds me fast; how can I think freely when it makes itself felt every time I try to breath.' B has initialled this passage three times vertically in the margin.

6. *vi . . . cangiare.* This translates: 'there is something barren in reality which we try in vain to change'. No comment by B. Iris Origo was the first to give this in translation (*The Last Attachment*, p. 113). Unfortunately she also gives the first part of the sentence ('Io avea imparato a vivere nei poeti; ma non è la vita in quel modo'), translated as 'I had learned to love [*sic*] . . . from the poets, but real life is not like that' ('love' should read 'live'), which B has very clearly *not* marked.

7. *Quando . . . amata?* This translates: 'When I recall my good fortunes, I feel angry. Why was I to be told that I was charming, if I was not to be beloved?' No comment by B.

8. *Quanto . . . rischio!* This translates: 'How many men find their happiness in going to war, in exposing their lives to danger, and in submitting to their enthusiasm for risk and glory?' B's marginalia here are remarkable. The remainder of the paragraph, which he has *not* marked, runs: 'Ma non vi è nulla esteriormente, che sollevi le donne; la loro esistenza, immobile in faccia alla sventura, è un supplizio assai lungo' ('But there is nothing in external life to console women; their existence, motionless in the face of misery, is one long torment.') Cf. Julia's letter to Juan in *DJ* I, and especially stanza 194 (*CPW* v. 71). B's double negative to this passage, and his avoiding marking the remainder of the paragraph, suggest very strongly that while Julia's letter, and that stanza in particular, may indeed be what McGann has phrased 'an eloquent statement of a deeply traditional set of ideas' (*CPW* v. 680), B himself dissociates himself from them.

9. *Qualche . . . Oimè!* This translates: 'Sometimes, when I hear music, I am reminded of the talents I once had for singing, dancing, and poetry; I then feel inclined to shrug off my misery, Alas!' (cf. *BLJ* viii. 43: 'Music is a strange thing').

10. *Fermossi . . . tanto.* This translates: 'At length this heart which beat so fast has stopped.' No comment by B. Corinna slightly misquotes Ippolito

Pindemonte's 'Clizia', l. 55: 'Fermasi alfin quel cor, che balzò tanto' (*Poesie di Ippolito Pindemonte* (1800), ii. 36).

11. This item was first published (with some discrepancies) in Moore ii. 241 n. The two 'of's in the final sentence ('of but of') are B's. For B's friendship with Madame de Staël, see 'Some Recollections of my Acquaintance with Madame de Staël' above; for some amusing usages to which B put her *Corinne* in his relationship with Teresa, see *BLJ* vi. 248; vii. 18, 38; viii. 170, 213.

A Note on Apostasy (1821)

Text: Moore ii. 788.

Referring to B's 'mobility', and citing *DJ* XVI. 97, Moore wrote:

> That he was fully aware not only of the abundance of this quality in his own nature, but of the danger in which it placed consistency and singleness of character, did not require the note on this passage, where he calls it 'an unhappy attribute,' to assure us. The consciousness, indeed, of his own natural tendency to yield thus to every chance impression, and change with every passing impulse, was not only for ever present in his mind, but,—aware as he was of the suspicion of weakness attached by the world to any retractation or abandonment of long professed opinions,—had the effect of keeping him in that general line of consistency, on certain great subjects, which, notwithstanding occasional fluctuations and contradictions as to the details of these very subjects, he continued to preserve throughout life. A passage from one of his manuscripts will show how sagaciously he saw the necessity of guarding himself against his own instability in this respect. (Moore ii. 787–8)

(See also *CPW* v. 649, 769.) Moore then gave this note. It is undated; but I suggest the date 1821 as the thought has a quality of reflection about it which belongs more to the period of B's Ravenna Journal (1821) or his 'Detached Thoughts' (1821–2), than to that of his journal of 1813–14. However, cf. his entry for 16 Jan. 1814 (*BLJ* iii. 242):

> I shall adhere to my party, because it would not be honourable to act otherwise; but, as to *opinions*, I don't think politics *worth* an *opinion. Conduct* is another thing:—if you begin with a party, go on with them. I have no consistency, except in politics; and *that* probably arises from my indifference on the subject altogether.

(See also B's long comment on Southey's apostasy in his letter to Murray of 9 May 1817 (*BLJ* v. 220–1).

A Note on Sculpture (1821)

Text: MS Fales Collection, New York University Library. First published (with some discrepancies) in *BLJ* viii. 53.

Although this note is undated, B almost certainly wrote it while he was drafting his 'Letter to John Murray Esq$^{re.}$', above, and may well have intended it as a gloss to his discussion of sculpture therein (see n. 90 thereto). His allusions here are to Genesis 1: 27, and to Exodus 20: 3–5.

An Extract from a Journal (1821)

Text: Moore i. 42–3.

Having quoted 'Detached Thoughts', no. 91 (see *BLJ* ix. 42), Moore continued (Moore i. 42): 'The following extract is from another of his manuscript journals.' He then gives this passage. It is undated; but I suggest the date 1821, as B was reflecting on his Harrow days and friendships particularly at this period, and the style in which it is written is the same as that of his 'Detached Thoughts' (1821–2; see especially nos. 71, 72, 87–91, 113 (*BLJ* ix. 37, 42–4, 49)).

Of the various people B mentions here, I give the following brief account with reference to M. G. Dauglish and P. K. Stephenson (eds.), *The Harrow School Register, 1800–1911* (3rd edn., 1911). H—— is probably Henry Charles Hoare, for whom see 'Inscriptions in *Scriptores Græci*', above. Charles Morgan Robinson Morgan, son of Sir C. Morgan, entered Harrow 1801, left 1803–4, d. 1875, witnessed B's bet with Hay and others at Brighton in the summer of 1808 that he would never marry (see *BLJ* iv. 257). Rice: there was no such named pupil at Harrow during B's time there; Moore almost certainly misread the name Rich. There were four Rich brothers, sons of the Revd Sir Charles Rich, three of whom entered Harrow in 1799. B probably refers to the fourth brother, Edward Ludlow Rich, who entered Harrow 1802, and d. 1869. Edward James Raynsford, son of N. Raynsford of Brixworth, Northamptonshire, entered Harrow 1801, d. 1842. Robert, Viscount Jocelyn, son of Robert, 2nd Earl of Roden, entered Harrow 1801, d. 1870. B later met him in Cadiz on 30 July 1809 (Marchand i. 191; see also *BLJ* iii. 106). Dr Drury and Dr Butler are described below. P. Hunter, entered Harrow 1802 (see also *BLJ* ii. 126; ix. 42). The Hon. George Augustus William Curzon, son of the Hon. P. A. Curzon and Sophia, 2nd Baroness Howe, entered Harrow 1801, d. 1805 (see *BLJ* ix. 42). Edward Noel Long, son of E. B. Long, entered Harrow 1801 and went with B to Trinity College, Cambridge. He entered the Coldstream Guards in 1807, and was drowned in 1809 on his way to join the army in the Peninsular, when his ship was run foul of in the night by another of the convoy. He is the 'Cleon' of 'Childish Recollections', ll. 325–40, and the addressee of 'To E[dward] N[oel] L[ong] Esq.' (see *CPW* i. 116–19, 375–6, and 168–9, 384). For B's letters to him, see *BLJ* i. 95, 109–10, 114–15, 117–19, 121–2, 139, 150, 152–3. For B's lengthy reminiscence of him in his Ravenna Journal (1821), see *BLJ* viii. 23–5; see also B's letter to Long's father on hearing of his death (*BLJ* i. 200 and n.). John Cecil Tattersall ('Tatersall' so spelt by Moore), son of the Revd J. Tattersall of Otterden, Kent, entered Harrow 1801, d. 1812. He is the 'Davus' of 'Childish Recollections', ll. 265–86 (*CPW* i. 166–7, 383), to whom B affectionately refers elsewhere as 'That

Madcap' (*BLJ* i. 109). John Fitzgibbon, 2nd Earl of Clare, son of John, 1st Earl of Clare, entered Harrow 1801, d. 1851. He was B's dearest friend, and the 'Lycus' of 'Childish Recollections', ll. 287–300, and the addressee of 'To the Earl of [Clare]' (*CPW* i. 167–8, 383, and 94–8, 371–2). For further details, see B's 'Endorsement on a Letter from the Earl of Clare', *post.* George John Frederick, 4th Duke of Dorset, son of John, 3rd Duke of Dorset, entered Harrow 1802, and was killed by a fall from his horse while out hunting near Dublin, on 22 Feb. 1815. For B's poems addressed to him, see 'To the Duke of D[orset]', and the two 'Stanzas' (*CPW* i. 66–9, 369; iii. 284–7, 462–4). B was enormously fond of Dorset, who was one of his fags at Harrow, and was 'very much shocked' by his death (see *BLJ* iv. 274–5, 279). Charles David Gordon, son of David Gordon of Abergeldie, entered Harrow 1803, d. 1826. For B's letters to him, see *BLJ* i. 70–2, 74–5. James Wynne Butler De Bathe ('Bath' so spelt by Moore), son of Sir J. M. De Bathe, entered Harrow 1800, d. 1828. At one point B said he was the 'Lycus' of 'Childish Recollections', ll. 287–300 (see *BLJ* i. 109 and n., and *CPW* i. 383). For B's letter to him, see *BLJ* i. 151–2. John Thomas Claridge, son of J. F. Claridge of Sevenoaks, Kent, entered Harrow 1805, d. 1868. He later stayed at B's home, Newstead, during Sept. and Oct. 1811, and bored B stiff for three weeks (see *BLJ* ii. 102–3, 115, 126–7). The Hon. John Wingfield, third son of Richard, 4th Viscount Powerscourt, entered Harrow 1801, and was one of B's fags (*BLJ* i. 176). He later joined the Coldstream Guards and served in the Peninsular War, dying of fever at Coimbra, Portugal, on 14 May 1811. He is the 'Alonso' of 'Childish Recollections', ll. 243–64, and is affectionately remembered in *CHP* I. 91–2 and B's note thereto (*CPW* i. 166, 383; ii. 43, 189, 282). B was shattered on hearing of his death (see, e.g., *BLJ* ii. 69, 77, 81, 84, 118).

The Revd Dr. Joseph Drury, DD (1750–1834), was educated at Westminster and Trinity College, Cambridge. He was headmaster of Harrow from 1785 to 1805, and the father of Henry Joseph Drury (1778–1841), the assistant master at Harrow and B's first tutor. The Revd George Butler (1774–1853) was educated at his father's school in Chelsea and at Sidney Sussex College, Cambridge. He was elected successor to Joseph Drury on 11 Apr. 1805, and remained headmaster until 1829. He later became Dean of Peterborough. B rebelled against his election, supporting Mark Drury (?1763–1835), the under-master and brother to Joseph, out of loyalty to Dr Drury himself. (See 'On a Change of Masters, at a Great Public School', 'Childish Recollections', ll. 89–120, '[Portrait of Pomposus]' and '[A Dialogue on Pomposus]' (*CPW* i. 132, 378, and 161–2, 383, and 172–3, 384). See also, e.g., *BLJ* i. 53–4, 64). B was later reconciled to Butler, who gave him some helpful advice for his first tour and a gold pen (see *BLJ* i. 145 and n., 153–4, 239).

Although B's relations with Dr Drury appear to have been somewhat fractious at first, B soon became utterly devoted to him (see, for instance, *BLJ* i. 43, 49, 53, 56). Much later, in a note to *CHP* IV. 75, he gave Drury the most unmitigated praise (*CPW* ii. 248–9):

I believe no one could, or can be more attached to Harrow than I have always been, and with reason;—a part of the time passed there was the happiest of my life; and my preceptor, (the Rev. Dr. Joseph Drury), was the best and worthiest friend I ever possessed, whose warnings I have remembered but too well, though too late—when I have erred, and whose counsels I have but followed when I have done well or wisely. If ever this imperfect record of my feelings towards him should reach his eyes, let it remind him of one who never thinks of him but with gratitude and veneration—of one who would more gladly boast of having been his pupil, if, by more closely following his injunctions, he could reflect any honour upon his instructor.

Whether or not Drury ever saw this eulogy of himself is uncertain; but he later furnished Moore with the following account of B:

Mr. Hanson, Lord Byron's solicitor, consigned him to my care at the age of 13½, with remarks, that his education had been neglected; that he was ill prepared for a public school, but that he thought there was a *cleverness* about him. After his departure I took my young disciple into my study, and endeavoured to bring him forward by inquiries as to his former amusements, employments, and associates, but with little or no effect;—and I soon found that a wild mountain colt had been submitted to my management. But there was mind in his eye. In the first place, it was necessary to attach him to an elder boy, in order to familiarize him with the objects before him, and with some parts of the system in which he was to move. But the information he received from his conductor gave him no pleasure, when he heard of the advances of some in the school, much younger than himself, and conceived by his own deficiency that he should be degraded, and humbled, by being placed below them. This I discovered, and having committed him to the care of one of the masters, as his tutor, I assured him he should not be placed till, by diligence, he might rank with those of his own age. He was pleased with this assurance, and felt himself on easier terms with his associates;—for a degree of shyness hung about him for some time. His manner and temper soon convinced me, that he might be led by a silken string to a point, rather than by a cable;—on that principle I acted. . . .

After my retreat from Harrow, I received from him two very affectionate letters. In my occasional visits subsequently to London, when he had fascinated the public with his productions, I demanded of him, why, as in *duty bound*, he had sent none to me? 'Because,' said he, 'you are the only man I never wish to read them:'—but, in a few moments, he added—'What do you think of the Corsair?' (Moore i. 38–40)

See also *BLJ* ix. 16, 43. For further details of the persons and circumstances alluded to here, see Marchand i, ch. iv; *BAP*, ch. iv; and Percy M. Thornton, *Harrow School and its Surroundings* (1885), pp. 191–247.

Endorsement on a Letter from the Earl of Clare (1821–1822)

Text: Moore i. 50.

This endorsement is written on a letter to B from the Earl of Clare, dated 'Harrow on the Hill, July 28th, 1805', in which Clare complains of B's cutting him, calling him names and undervaluing his friendship. (It is given in full in Moore i. 49.) The endorsement itself is undated; but I suggest the date 1821–2 as Clare was much in B's mind at that period, and B may have intended showing him the letter while Clare was in Italy. They had met briefly on the road between Imola and Bologna in Oct. 1821, and had agreed to meet again the following spring (see 'Detached Thoughts', nos. 91, 113, and B's letter to Murray of ?Nov. 1821 (*BLJ* ix. 44, 49, 53)). Medwin recorded B saying (*Medwin's Conversations*, p. 63): 'Of all my schoolfellows I know no one for whom I have retained so much friendship as for Lord Clare. I have been constantly corresponding with him ever since I knew he was in Italy; and look forward to seeing him, and talking over with him our old Harrow stories, with infinite delight.' B and Clare did meet again, for one day between 5 and 8 June 1822, and B gave him the MS of his 'Detached Thoughts' to convey to Murray. (See *BLJ* ix. 167–8.) Writing to Moore on 8 June, B told him (*BLJ* ix. 170):

> A few days ago, my earliest and dearest friend, Lord Clare, came over from Geneva [Genoa?] on purpose to see me before he returned to England. As I have always loved him (since I was thirteen, at Harrow) better than any (*male*) thing in the world, I need hardly say what a melancholy pleasure it was to see him for a *day* only; for he was obliged to resume his journey immediately.

Teresa Guiccioli, B's mistress, later informed Moore (Moore ii. 614):

> Lord Clare's visit also occasioned him extreme delight. He had a great affection for Lord Clare, and was very happy during the short visit that he paid him at Leghorn. The day on which they separated was a melancholy one for Byron. 'I have a presentiment that I shall never see him more,' he said, and his eyes filled with tears. The same melancholy came over him during the first weeks that succeeded to Lord Clare's departure, whenever his conversation happened to fall upon this friend.'

John Fitzgibbon, second Earl of Clare (1792–1851), was educated at Harrow and Christ Church, Oxford (BA 1812), and later became Governor of Bombay (1830–4). He was B's dearest friend, though they hardly met at all after B had left Harrow. For B's early letters to him, see *BLJ* i. 101–2, 106–7, 129, 133–4. He is the 'Lycus' of 'Childish Recollections' (ll. 287–300); and see also, 'To the Earl of [Clare]' (*CPW* i. 167–8, 383, and 94–8, 371–2). See also Marchand i. 90–1, 97; *BAP*, p. 31.

Notes on Crawford's Deposition (1822)

Text: MS Murray. First published (with minor discrepancies) in C. L. Cline, *Byron, Shelley and their Pisan Circle* (1952), p. 237.

These notes were written by B on Dr James Crawford's deposition concerning the 'Pisan Affray'. The deposition is brief, written in Italian and dated Pisa, 27 Mar. 1822. Extracted here is the passage to which B has alluded with asterisks. Since the 'Original' was sent to the Governor of Pisa, the Marquis Viviani (father of Emilia, the addressee of Shelley's *Epipsychidion* (1821)) (*BLJ* xi. 195–6), and the 'other English Copy' to the English Chargé d'Affaires, Edward Dawkins, in Florence (*BLJ* ix. 129), this is undoubtedly the copy which B sent with other papers to Douglas Kinnaird on 28 Mar. 1822, explaining (*BLJ* ix. 130):

To prevent misstatements I send you authentic copies of some circumstances which occurred on Sunday last.——You can use them according to the circumstances related by others; if there is anything stated incorrectly in the papers these will serve to rectify them by.—You must get them translated by a very careful hand.——They are the same papers directed to the Government here & our Ambassador at Florence.

The 'Pisan Affray', or 'Masi Affray', has been thoroughly documented by C. L. Cline in *Byron, Shelley and their Pisan Circle*, chs. 6 and 7, and is covered in Marchand iii. 980–90; *BAP*, pp. 370–1, Doris Langley Moore, *Lord Byron: Accounts Rendered* (1974), ch. 9, and in Iris Origo, *The Last Attachment* (1949), pp. 301–11 (see also *BLJ* ix. 128–61, *passim*). Very briefly, the incident was as follows. On the evening of Sunday 24 Mar. 1822, Shelley, Pietro Gamba, Edward Trelawny, Captain John Hay, and B were returning home from pistol-shooting outside Pisa when they were joined by John Taaffe. Shortly afterwards they were overtaken at great speed by an Italian Sergeant-Major, Stefani Masi, who brushed past Taaffe between him and the ditch beside the road. Taaffe's horse started and reared out of control, and Taaffe exclaimed to B, 'Have you ever seen the like of that?'. All, excepting Taaffe, set off in hot pursuit of Masi and accosted him at the gates of the city. Much argument and violence ensued, during which Shelley and Hay were severely wounded, while B rode on to the Casa Lanfranchi to send for the police. Returning with his swordstick to the gates, he encounterd Masi riding up the Lung' Arno; and it is at this point that Dr Crawford's testimony becomes effective. Crawford was a Scottish physician who happened to be looking out of his window at the time. B considered his 'evidence ... essential' (*BLJ* ix. 132). Enclosing the 'other English Copy' of Crawford's deposition to Dawkins on 27 Mar. 1822, B wrote (*BLJ* ix. 129):

The testimony of an impartial eye-witness, Dr. Crawford, with whom I had not the honour of a personal acquaintance, will inform you as much as I know myself.

It is proper to add that I conceived the man to have been an officer, as he was well dressed, with scaled epaulettes, and not ill-mounted, and *not* a serjeant-major (the son of a washerwoman, it is said) as he turns out to be.

When I accosted him a second time, on the Lung' Arno, he called out to me with a menacing gesture, 'Are you content?' I (still ignorant of what had passed under the gateway, having ridden through the guard to order my steward to go to the police) answered. 'No; I want your name and address.' He then held out his hand, which I took, not understanding whether he intended it as a pledge of his hostility or of his repentance, at the same time stating his name.

1. *Lord Byron ... Suo.* These lines translate: 'Lord Byron had a Cane in his hand. The Dragoon threatened to draw his Sword. Meeting together beneath my Window Lord Byron Extended his Hand to the Dragoon, and demanded his Name, and His address.'

Notes on Taaffe's Deposition (1822)

Text: MS Murray. First published (with the exception of item 1) in C. L. Cline, *Byron, Shelley and their Pisan Circle* (1952), pp. 115–16.

For the background to this, see n. to 'Notes on Crawford's Deposition' above. B added these notes at, respectively, the head (item 1) and the end (item 2) of a copy of John Taaffe's deposition, written in Italian and dated Pisa, 28 Mar. 1822, before enclosing it with his letter to Edward Dawkins of 31. Mar., in which he observed: 'I add a testimony of Mr. Taaffe's—upon which you will form your judgement also.—There is a note of mine appended to it' (*BLJ* ix. 133). By 4 Apr. 1822 Dawkins had returned the deposition to B, which B then forwarded to Douglas Kinnaird on the same day (*BLJ* ix. 135, 137).

A transcript and translation of the deposition which Taaffe himself had sent earlier to Dawkins (which differs only in minor verbal points from the copy that B sent him) are given by Cline, in pp. 208–12. It is a most cowardly affair: Taaffe was reluctant to make any deposition at all, and it had to be wrung out of him. In his deposition he merely admits that the dragoon rushed past him, without touching him though startling his horse, and that he had exclaimed to B 'Have you ever seen the like of that?' (which he claims was a common expression of his). He denies that he had been, or felt that he had been, insulted, and dwells much on his preoccupation with trying to restrain his horse while the rest of the party was pursuing Masi. His attempt to exculpate himself caused a rift between him and the rest of the Pisan party, by whom he was soon dubbed 'Falstaaffe' (see *BLJ* ix. 131).

Memo on Shelley's Cremation (1822)

Text: MS British Library (Add. MS 39168, f. 179r and v). Unpublished.

This memo was written by B on the last page of a draft MS account of the cremations of Edward Ellerker Williams and Shelley, composed by Edward Trelawny and emended by Leigh Hunt, entitled 'Loss of the Don Juan' and dated '⟨Aug⟩ July 8. 1822'. The particular passage under which B has written is dated 16 Aug. 1822; and the relevant portion to which he alludes, and which relates specifically to the cremation of Shelley, runs thus (ff. 178r and v–179r):

> Although we made a most tremendous fire the body burnt very slow; three hours elapsed before it separated and then fell open across the breast. It is a curious circumstance that the heart, which was unusually large, together with some other vessels in that quarter, seemed almost proof against fire, for it was still entire in figure and apparently in substance, though the intensity of heat was so great that harder substances were reduced to a white dust. The same rites were performed with the frankincense &c. as on the preceding day. After cooling the reliques together with the furnace in the Sea, we then placed the remains in the box & shipped it on board the schooner. There had been,

during the whole of the ceremony a solitary sea bird crossing and recrossing the funeral pile which was the only intruder that baffled the vigilance of our guards to keep off. Lord Byron and M.r Hunt M.r Shenley and myself with the officers in attendance now slowly retraced our steps to the town; the two former starting for Pisa, and we on board the Bolivar for Leghorn.

I thus fulfilled the last melancholy offices to the dead in compliance with the earnest entreaties of their families, and in further compliance have made out a Narrative of those melancholy facts, in which all their happiness has been lost—with the wreck of those they loved.

Trelawny later recorded that 'Byron could not face this scene, he withdrew to the beach and swam off to the "Bolivar"' (see Edward John Trelawny, *Records of Shelley, Byron, and the Author* (1973 edn.), pp. 172, 314–15). B himself wrote to Moore on 27 Aug. 1822:

The other day at Viareggio, I thought proper to swim off to my schooner (the Bolivar) in the offing, and thence to shore again—about three miles, or better, in all. As it was at mid-day, under a broiling sun, the consequence has been a feverish attack, and my whole skin's coming off, after going through the process of one large continuous blister, raised by the sun and sea together. I have suffered much pain; not being able to lie on my back, or even side; for my shoulders and arms were equally St. Bartholomewed. But it is over,—and I have got a new skin, and am as glossy as a snake in its new suit.

We have been burning the bodies of Shelley and Williams on the sea-shore, to render them fit for removal and regular interment. You can have no idea what an extraordinary effect such a funeral pile has, on a desolate shore, with mountains in the back-ground and the sea before, and the singular appearance the salt and frankincense gave to the flame. All of Shelley was consumed, except his *heart*, which would not take the flame, and is now preserved in spirits of wine. (*BLJ* ix. 197; see also ix. 194)

Hunt later gave the following account of B's and his own reaction in the aftermath of Shelley's cremation:

But we dined and drank after it,—dined little, and drank much. Lord Byron had not shone that day, even in his cups. For myself, I had bordered upon emotions which I have never suffered myself to indulge, and which foolishly as well as impatiently render calamity, as somebody termed it, 'an affront, and not a misfortune.' The barouche drove rapidly through the forest of Pisa. We sang, we laughed, we shouted. I even felt a gaiety the more shocking, because it was real and a relief. What the coachman thought of us, God knows; but he helped to make up a ghastly trio. . . . I wish to have no such waking dream again. It was worthy of a German ballad. (Leigh Hunt, *Lord Byron and Some of His Contemporaries* (1828), p. 69)

(A slightly expanded version of this appears in *The Autobiography of Leigh Hunt*, 3 vols. (1850), iii. 17–18.) For fuller details, see Edward Trelawny's *Recollections of the Last Days of Shelley and Byron* (1858), pp. 126–35, and *Records of Shelley, Byron, and the Author*, 2 vols. (1878), i. 204–14; H. Buxton Forman (ed.), *Letters of Edward John Trelawny* (1910), pp. 13–14, 269–70; Marchand iii. 1018–25; *BAP*, pp. 382–4; William St Clair, *Trelawny* (1977), pp. 80–2; and in particular, see Leslie A. Marchand, 'Trelawny on the Death of Shelley', *Keats–Shelley Memorial Bulletin* iv (1952), 9–34.

Queries concerning the Greeks (1823)

Text: E. S. De Beer and Walter Seton, *Byroniana: The Archives of the London Greek Committee* (1926), p. 13.

Of these queries, De Beer and Seton write: 'The following document is apparently Byron's set of queries, roughly scribbled in pencil' (*Byroniana*, p. 12). They tentatively date the document *c.* Sept. 1823. This is accurate. At the time B was in Cephalonia, cautiously awaiting the most favourable circumstances before proceeding to mainland Greece. Edward Trelawny and James Hamilton Browne however, were anxious to leave for Tripolitza, the seat of government in the Morea, at the earliest opportunity. They set sail from Cephalonia on 6 Sept. 1823, and B almost certainly sketched these queries for them prior to their departure. In his letter to Hobhouse of 11 Sept., B wrote: 'Mr. Browne and Mr. Trelawny are since then gone over in a boat to a part of the Coast out of the blockade with letters from me to the Greek Government at Tripolitza—and to collect information' (*BLJ* xi. 23). And in his Journal in Cephalonia (1823), he recorded on 30 Sept. (*BLJ* xi. 33):

> After remaining here some time in expectation of hearing from the G[ree]k G[overnmen]t I availed myself of the opportunity of Messrs B[rowne] and T[relawny] proceeding to Tripolitza—subsequently to the departure of the Turkish fleet to write to the acting part of the Legislature. My object was not only to obtain some accurate information so as to enable me to proceed to the Spot where I might be if not most safe at least more serviceable but to have an opportunity of forming a judgement on the real state of their affairs.

These queries forcefully endorse the conviction that, far from 'shilly-shallying' in Cephalonia, B was approaching his onerous commitment to the Greek cause with the utmost circumspection. See the general notes to 'The Present State of Greece' above, and 'A Note in Count Teotoky's Letter' below. (See also Marchand iii. 1117–18; *BAP*, pp. 418–19; and William St Clair, *Trelawny* (1977), pp. 94–5.) For B's reference to 'Good men and true' (query 7), see *Much Ado about Nothing* III. iii. 1.

A Note in Count Teotoky's Letter (1823)

Text: MS Murray. Unpublished.

This note was written by B at the end of a copy of a letter written in Italian, dated 'Tripolitza—17/27 Settembre—1823', and signed 'Il Patriota Gian Battista Teotoky'. At the head of the first sheet B has written: 'Copy of a letter dated 27. 7.bre 1823. and addressed to Count Delladecima a nobleman of Cephalonia.—'; and on the verso of the final sheet: 'Copy of a Letter from Tripolizza (copied 8.bre 16.º 1823.—) but dated 7.bre 27.th 1823.———'. B enclosed this with his letter to Hobhouse of 16 Oct. 1823, saying (*BLJ* xi. 50):

Enclosed is a further report from the Morea—it is full and supposed to be authentic on the state of parties there. You and Mr. Bowring can form your own judgements and use yr. discretion in laying it before the Committee. The enclosed is a Copy—only altered into *better* Italian—the original not being very pure—but the sense and the tenor of the expressions are still retained as nearly as possible.

The letter draws attention to the divisive factions in the Peloponnese, to the misappropriation and squandering of public revenue, and to the inertia of the Greek fleet. It describes the squabbling that had broken out between the factions on their hearing of B's arrival in Cephalonia, 'with sufficient funds for the whole Nation' ('con sufficiente somma di denaro per la Nazione'), and seeks to dissuade B from coming to the Morea. Rather, it urges him to go to Western Greece, the area in the greatest danger and in the most need, where his funds would encourage the troops, relieve their distresses, and provide Missolonghi with food and munitions. It further states that his funds could secure eight or ten armed Greek ships to raise the blockade of Missolonghi and to free the communication of the sea, and rally three thousand troops in the Morea thus assured of food and pay.

(E. S. De Beer and Walter Seton (*Byroniana: The Archives of the London Greek Committee* (1926), pp. 13–14) print a summary in English of a French translation of this letter.)

B was in Cephalonia at the time, awaiting an opportune moment before embarking for the mainland. He had recently given instructions to James Hamilton Browne and Edward Trelawny on their departure for Tripolitza, and had received their initial reports (see William St Clair, *Trelawny* (1977), p. 99, and 'Queries concerning the Greeks', above). This letter did much to influence B against setting out for the seat of the provisional government of Greece at Tripolitza, in accordance with the invitation which he had already accepted. As Marchand observes, it 'neutralized the favorable reports of Browne and of Anarghiros, the emissary of the Provisional Government in the Morea' (Marchand iii. 1129; *BAP*, p. 421).

Count Giambattista Marin Teotoky, or Teotochi (b. 1778), was the eldest son of Carlo Antonio, a Venetian nobleman, and Isabella Teotochi, of an old and noble Corfiote family. Having divorced Carlo Antonio in 1795, Isabella married Count Giuseppe Albrizzi in 1796. This is the Countess Albrizzi whom B first met in 1816, and whose brilliant *conversazioni* he attended frequently in Venice. (It is unlikely that B was aware of the connection between Teotoky and the Countess; but for a brief biographical sketch of the latter, see *BLJ* v. 293.) Count Teotoky was a supporter of Prince Alexander Mavrocordatos, a founding member of the Philanthropic Society of Greece, and the Minister of Justice in the provisional government. (See Edward Blaquiere, *Narrative of a Second Visit to Greece* (1825), ii. 147, 153, 167.)

Count Demetrius Delladecima (the addressee of the original letter) was B's principal adviser on Greek affairs in Cephalonia. Julius Millingen (*Memoirs of the Affairs of Greece* (1831), p. 18), wrote of him as 'a Cephaloniot nobleman, of considerable shrewdness, sound judgment, and deep acquaintance with the Greek character' (see also *BLJ* xi. 54, 89, 109). Of B, Delladecima said: 'Of all the men . . . whom I have had an opportunity of conversing with, on the means of establishing the independence of Greece, and regenerating the character of the natives, Lord Byron appears to entertain the most enlightened and correct views' (Moore ii. 701 n.).

Replies to Stanhope's Questionnaire (1824)

Text: Colonel Leicester Stanhope, *Greece in 1823 and 1824* (1824), p. 91.

Writing to John Bowring, the Secretary of the London Greek Committee, on 24 Jan. 1824, Stanhope told him: 'I am in the habit of putting written questions to Lord Byron for his decision. The following have received his Lordship's answers, and I am desirous of submitting them to the Committee' (p. 91). He then subjoined this questionnaire. However, he must have presented it to B almost immediately upon B's arrival in Missolonghi (4 Jan. 1824). For, in a letter to Bowring dated 6 Jan. Stanhope informed him: 'His Lordship has given £100 towards the support of the artillery corps, and £50 in aid of the press. His Lordship, however, thinks the press will not succeed. I think it will' (p. 73: see questions 2 and 4). Moreover, in a letter dated 7 Jan. to the General Government of Greece in Cranidi ('where the legislative body were assembled', Count Peter Gamba, *A Narrative of Lord Byron's Last Journey to Greece* (1825), p. 132), Stanhope announced:

The English Committee has sent hither several presses, for the purpose of spreading the light of the nineteenth century, and causing it to act on the destinies of the Greek nation . . . I am desirous of lending one of the said presses to the most excellent General Government of Greece, seeing that it has both the will and the means of putting it into a state of useful activity.

I have written to Signor Psylas, at Athens, to know if he is disposed to conduct the said press on perfectly liberal and impartial principles, at the seat of government. As I am in hopes of setting out as soon as possible for the Peloponnesus, I beg of you to give me an early answer to this communication. (pp. 74 n.–75 n.: see question 3)

(On 21 Feb. Stanhope was to depart for Athens, where he set up the press under the auspices of Odysseus. See 'Two Notes in Stanhope's Letter', *post*, and its general headnote below.)

The editor of the Greek Chronicle (the *Hellenica Chronica*) was Dr Jean Jacques Meyer, a doctrinaire Swiss, who caused B a considerable amount of trouble on account of his paper. 'Of all petty tyrants he is one of the pettiest', B wrote of him to Samuel Barff on 19 Mar. (*BLJ* xi. 139; see also xi. 132 and n., and 138–9 and n.). Stanhope's opinion of Meyer was radically different from B's. Writing to Bowring on 7 (?17) Jan. he reported:

The press which you sent out has been made over to Dr. J. J. Meyer, of Missolonghi. He had previously only the use of a press, but this being but an indifferent one, and belonging to the printer who refused to publish Mr. Bentham's remarks in the prospectus, I thought it desirable to secure the freedom of writing and publishing by placing our press in the hands of a bold, honest, and intelligent Swiss. (p. 84: see questions 1 and 7)

In question 7, perhaps Stanhope intended to write 'belonging to the printer' (as in this letter), rather than 'belonging to the editor'.

Captain Henry Hesketh (see question 6) was one of B's aides-de-camp. Stanhope mentioned that he was sent to Cephalonia 'to concert measures for Parry's safe embarkation' (p. 90). He was later ordered by B to arrest a Prussian officer for rioting in his lodgings (*BLJ* xi. 149–50).

Colonel Leicester Stanhope (1784–1862) was sent out by the London Greek Committee to act with B as their agent in Greece. He was a fervid Benthamite, and thought the Greek Revolution could best be served by setting up schools and printing presses (which earned him the nickname of 'the Typographical Colonel'). He established the *Hellenica Chronica* in Jan. 1824, and the *Telegrafo Greco* in Feb. 1824. See the general note to 'The Present State of Greece' above; see also Marchand iii. 1156–7; *BAP*, pp. 432–3.

Directives to Lega Zambelli (1824)

Text: MS British Library (Zambelli Papers, vol. viii, BL Add. MS 46878 f. 22). Unpublished. An English translation was first published in Doris Langley Moore, *Lord Byron: Accounts Rendered* (1974), pp. 403–5.

These directives, dated 2 Feb. ('F°', Febbraio) 1824, were given by B to Lega Zambelli, formerly Count Guiccioli's, but since 1820 B's, secretary and scrupulous steward (see Marchand ii. 858; *BAP*, p. 326; D. L. Moore, *Lord Byron: Accounts Rendered*, ch. 7). Lukas Chalandritsanos was B's protégé and page, adopted by B in Cephalonia in 1823 (see Marchand iii. 1146ff.; *BAP*, pp. 427ff. and, for a brief biographical sketch, *BLJ* xi. 213–14). As Doris Langley Moore has shown, by 2 Feb. 1824 Lukas, taking advantage of B's patronage, had become increasingly presumptuous, demanding privileges above his station (*Lord Byron: Accounts Rendered*, p. 403). The first two directives here were intended to put him squarely in his place. Draco (George Drake) was a Suliote chief whom B most trusted and the leader of B's bodyguard (Marchand iii. 1192; *BAP*, p. 446). Who his 'lieutenant' was remains unknown. The following translation is my own; and I have not tampered with B's Italian, though normally 'Thè' would read 'tè', 'veece' 'vece', and 'chio' 'ciò'.

1. Tea is not a Greek drink—therefore Master Lukas can drink Coffee instead—or water—or nothing.—

2. The pay of the said Lukas will be five dollars per month paid like the others of the household.—He will eat with the Suliotes—or where he wishes.———

3. Draco's lieutenant may eat with those of my house——others may not—without at least my knowing of it first.—

Two Notes in Stanhope's Letter (1824)

Text: Stanhope, *Greece in 1823 and 1824* (1824), pp. 124n., 126n.

Stanhope tells us that these comments were added by B to Stanhope's letter to him of 6 Mar. 1824 written from Athens, before B sent it on to the Committee on 19 Mar. 1824. On the back of this letter B wrote a note to John Bowring (see *BLJ* xi. 139). Given here are the two passages in Stanhope's letter to which B's comments refer.

Stanhope left Missolonghi for Athens on 21 Feb. 1824. Once in Athens he became greatly involved with Odysseus (the 'He' of the second passage). For B's vexatious relations with the Suliotes, his anxieties over the press, and for the Lepanto expedition, see Marchand iii, chs. 28, 29; and *BAP*, chs. 28, 29. See also general notes to B's 'Replies to Stanhope's Questionnaire', and 'The Present State of Greece' above.

APPENDIX

Sale Catalogues (1816 and 1827)

Sale Catalogue (1816)

Text: British Library, Sale Catalogues (S.C. Evans 5).

To meet the demands of his creditors, B was obliged to sell his library prior to his departure from England in April 1816. Transcribed here are the books, together with the names written in MS of their purchasers (on the right), listed in the sale catalogue which is entitled *A Catalogue of a Collection of Books, Late the Property of a Nobleman About to leave England on a Tour.* The sale took place by auction on 5 and 6 Apr. 1816, at the house of Mr R. H. Evans at 26, Pall Mall, London, and fetched the total of £723 12*s.* 6*d.* For further details see, e.g., *BLJ* v. 42–3, 62; see also Marchand ii. 598; *BAP*, p. 230 (though in both of these the date of the sale is incorrectly given as 8 Apr.).

It may be helpful to explain the following terms in this list: russia and morocco (e.g. lots 3, 23) are types of leather binding; half-bound (e.g. lot 190) means bound in board covers with leather corners and spine; in boards (e.g. lot 258) means bound in board covers; Large paper (e.g. lot 47) is a size of paper used for special editions, and having wider margins than ordinary editions; Fine paper (e.g. lot 88) means good quality paper; Elephant paper (e.g. lot 164) is very large and strong paper; India paper (e.g. lots 174–8, 363–8) means a soft, absorbent paper, imported from the East, and used for proofs in engraving; uncut (e.g. lot 190) means the pages have not been cut; passed (lot 133) means withdrawn from sale.

Apparently lot 383 was not sold; no purchaser is recorded, nor is any figure given in the margin.

Sale Catalogue (1827)

Text: British Library, Sale Catalogues (S.C. Evans 30).

B died on 19 Apr. 1824, but the library he had accumulated since 1816 was not finally disposed of until 1827. Transcribed here are the books, together with the names written in MS of their purchasers (on the right), listed in the sale catalogue which is entitled *Catalogue of the Library of The Late Lord Byron.* The sale took place by auction on 6 July 1827, at the house of Mr R. H. Evans at 93, Pall Mall, London, and fetched the total of £159 9*s.* 6*d.* For a further account see Doris Langley Moore, *The Late Lord Byron* (1961), pp. 216–17.

For an explanation of some of the terms in this list, see the general note to Sale Catalogue (1816). In addition, cuts (lots 188, 232) means woodcuts: illustrations of views in lot 188; the Aldine device of a sea-serpent-entwined anchor on the first page only of lot 232.

INDEX

The index refers exclusively to B's text (pp. 1–230). It should be used in conjunction with the note cues given in the text wherever access to the further information provided in the notes is required.